THE NEW
BACH READER

The earliest engraved portrait of Bach, by Samuel Gottlob Kütner, 1774
(see No. 393)

The New
BACH READER

A LIFE OF
Johann Sebastian Bach
IN LETTERS AND DOCUMENTS

Edited by

HANS T. DAVID *and* ARTHUR MENDEL

Revised and enlarged by

CHRISTOPH WOLFF

W·W·NORTON & COMPANY

New York   London

The text of this book is composed in Garamond #3
with the display set in Garamond Italic
Composition by Binghamton Valley Composition
Manufacturing by The Maple-Vail Book Manufacturing Group
Book design by Jacques Chazaud

Library of Congress Cataloging-in-Publication Data

The new Bach reader : a life of Johann Sebastian Bach in letters and
documents / edited by Hans T. David and Arthur Mendel ; revised and
enlarged by Christoph Wolff.
p.   cm.
Rev. and enl. ed. of: The Bach reader. Rev. ed. 1966.
Includes bibliographical references and index.

ISBN 0-393-04558-7
ISBN 0-393-31956-3 pbk.

1. Bach, Johann Sebastian, 1685–1750.   2. Composers—Germany—
Biography.   I. David, Hans T. (Hans Theodore), 1902–1967.
II. Mendel, Arthur, 1905–   .   III. Wolff, Christoph.   IV. Bach reader.
ML410.B1D24   1998
780'.92—dc21
[B]   97-41850
CIP
MN

W. W. Norton & Company, Inc., 500 Fifth Avenue, New York, N.Y. 10110
www.wwnorton.com

W. W. Norton & Company Ltd., 10 Coptic Street, London WC1A 1PU

2 3 4 5 6 7 8 9 0

Contents

Acknowledgments

Illustrations are reproduced by permission of: Bach-Archiv Leipzig (Nos. 133, 151, 155, 161, 166, 171, 174, 178, 200, 206, 220, 225, 237–38, 242–44, 251, 260, 293, 302, 373; p. 386); Bachhaus Eisenach (Nos. 283b, 310); British Library (No. 296); The Houghton Library, Harvard University (Nos. 45, 301); Staatsbibliothek zu Berlin, Preußischer Kulturbesitz (Nos. 27, 69, 83, 88, 90, 92, 227, 259, 283a, 286–92, 294–95, 297–300); Music Library, Yale University (No. 79).

PREFACE TO
The New Bach Reader

The Bach Reader, first published in 1945, has long since become a classic in its field. Conceived and edited by Hans T. David and Arthur Mendel, the book represented, at its original appearance, a completely new approach to musical biography in which primary and secondary documents, manuscript and printed sources, short and lengthy records, bureaucratic prose and poetic rhetoric, and contemporaneous and posthumous materials were all combined to offer—in eminently readable form—an accurate and lively picture of Johann Sebastian Bach's small yet colorful world and to give an informative impression of his remarkably wide and profound influence from the early eighteenth century through the mid-nineteenth. Twenty-one years after the first edition of *The Bach Reader,* David and Mendel published an enlarged and revised version in which they sought to reflect the achievements of two decades of rapidly progressing Bach scholarship. For the most part, this 1966 edition achieved its goal of providing an up-to-date account. However, in order to avoid a thorough overhauling and resetting of the text, the additions and revisions were largely confined to a forty-page supplement.

Of course, Bach scholarship did not enter a period of stagnation after 1966, so further additions and more substantial revisions were soon called for, but by then the book had become such an indispensable reference work as well as an impressive monument to its own history that it could easily survive in an unrevised state for several more decades without losing much of its usefulness or appeal. However, fifty years after the date of its original publication and thirty years after the appearance of the revised edition, a complete remaking of the serviceable and venerable *Bach Reader* needs little justification. It is worth emphasizing, however, that *The New Bach Reader* preserves all the essential features and materials of its predecessor and, most definitely, its original purpose: to present "a collection of the most significant early material on Johann Sebastian Bach" where the historical figure of Bach is "revealed in his own words, in the testimony of his contemporaries, and in the judgments of the generations immediately following his own."

The past three decades have seen considerable advances and important discoveries pertaining not only to the documentation of Bach's life but also to the reception history of his music. It seems remarkable that in 1945 and even in 1966 *The Bach Reader* had, as a comprehensive collection of historical sources, absolutely no counterpart in any language. Only in 1963 did the Leipzig Bach-Archiv launch the first volume of a four-volume series called *Bach-Dokumente (BD)*, edited by Werner Neumann and Hans-Joachim Schulze. The series was designed to incorporate all archival and iconographical material on Bach and to serve as a supplement to the new critical edition of Bach's music in the *Neue Bach-Ausgabe (NBA,* in progress since 1954). Volume 1 of the *Bach-Dokumente* (1963) comprises the written material originating with Bach himself—that is, all autograph letters, reports, testimonials, receipts, and the like. Volume 2 (1969) contains all documents dating from 1685 to 1750 that are related to Bach's life and work but that did not originate with the composer himself. Volume 3 (1973) includes all documents from the time of Bach's death in 1750 until 1800. Volume 4 (1974) is an iconographical documentation. *The New Bach Reader* draws heavily on materials presented for the first time in the *BD,* but it also goes beyond the *BD* series, for it includes materials that were excluded from the *BD* series or that came to light after *BD III,* as well as documents that exceed the scope of the *BD* series, which has an 1800 cutoff date.

Like its predecessor (see the 1945 preface, reprinted below), *The New Bach Reader* presents a selective rather than a complete documentary, although Part II contains all the known significant writings of Bach himself in the form of letters, testimonials, and other records. The goal for Part II to be as up-to-date as possible in assembling all available primary biographical material was facilitated by the publication in late 1996 of Nos. 35 and 38 and the discovery of Nos. 262 and 263 by a former student of mine virtually as this book went into production. I am grateful to Peter Wollny for having immediately shared with me his important find of what are the two latest samples of signed documents from the end of Bach's life. Another important goal was for Parts V and VII to make a more specific contribution to a broader and deeper understanding of the early Bach reception, ranging from the earliest discussion of a Bach cantata movement (No. 357b) and a diagram placing Bach among the German composers of the late 18th century (No. 373) to Hans Georg Nägeli's famous subscription announcement for the B-minor Mass (No. 410) and Lowell Mason's report on visiting Leipzig (No. 412)— the latter being a genuinely American document that has absolutely no historical equivalent anywhere, for only a foreign observer would take note of things that to local residents may have mattered very little.

Besides containing more than one hundred additional documents,* *The New Bach Reader* differs from its predecessor in a number of ways:

- *Organization.* Parts I ("A Portrait in Outline") and VI (Forkel's biography of Bach) remain essentially the same. Some restructuring has taken place in the other five parts: the Leipzig period in Part II (which presents documents from Bach's lifetime) has been divided into three phases in order to create smaller units; Part III now accommodates the three earliest biographical sources; the former Section Five ("Bach as Viewed by His Contemporaries") is now Part IV; Part V, comprising writings about Bach between 1750 and 1800, has been separated from Part IV (they originally formed one large section); and Part VII (retitled "Bach in the Romantic Era") has been reshaped.

- *Additions.* A chronology details events in Bach's life and includes references to the pertinent document numbers. A new section in Part II includes sixteen music manuscript facsimiles, most in the composer's hand and the others written by his chief copyists. Entirely new sections of Parts IV and V deal with Bach the teacher and record the transmission and dissemination of his music. A new appendix provides substantial information regarding money and living costs in Bach's time.

- *Revisions.* The essays in Parts I and VII, as well as some commentaries and notes, have been revised in the light of recent Bach scholarship. The English translations of the documents, however, needed little change. The few exceptions occurred primarily where the wording was based on an inaccurate German text and where the terminology had to be adapted to modern usage. Also, the names of churches and institutions have been anglicized to a greater extent (Church of Our Lady, the St. Thomas School, etc.).

- *Presentation and description of entries.* Headings (in large and small capitals) are used to characterize the content of each item or group of items. Then each document is provided with a number, for ease of identification and reference; a title (in boldface) that reproduces the original title, if any, or details the source of the item; and a modern source (*BD, BJ,* etc.). Editorial comments appear in square brackets in the body of the documents, in italic notes following the documents, and in thirteen introductory notes to important items or groups of items. Because information is now concentrated in the titles and editorial comments, most editorial footnotes to documents have been eliminated.

- *Illustrations.* Almost all the illustrations have been replaced by new ones, and those of merely ornamental function have been omitted. Numerous plates have been added, both to replace the English transcriptions typeset to resemble original title pages and to provide illustrative materials for the new section in Part II on Bach's music manuscripts.

*Documents not contained in *The Bach Reader* (1945; rev. 1966): 1, 6, 9, 10, 12–14, 17, 19, 28, 29, 35–38, 40, 41, 44, 46, 47, 52, 54–56, 61, 63–66, 70, 73, 75–78, 85, 87, 95, 102, 105, 108–11, 114, 116–18, 121, 136, 140, 141, 147, 159–161, 165, 168–70, 191, 207, 220, 228, 234, 246–48, 255, 256, 261–64, 267, 269, 280–82, 286–302, 305, 310, 312, 313, 320–23, 334, 337, 339, 341, 342, 349, 357, 365–67, 373, 377, 383, 385–88, 390–92, 406, 409, 410, and 412.

- *References.* Nearly all the documents include direct references in the main text to the (mostly) German originals. In the few instances where such references would be cumbersome, the original sources can be easily identified through the bibliography (pp. 531–32).
- *Deletions.* A very few documents of questionable value have been dropped, as has *The Precepts and Principles . . . for Playing a Thorough Bass* (which is available in an annotated facsimile edition, prepared by Pamela Poulin, 1994) and the canon resolutions (which appear with critical commentary in *NBA* VIII / 1, edited by Christoph Wolff, 1974).

For most of the documents that are newly included, new English translations had to be prepared. About a third of these were expertly and expediently executed by Alfred Mann, professor emeritus at the Eastman School of Music (the others were done by the undersigned). I am glad to express my profound gratitude to Professor Mann for his invaluable assistance. Ruth Libbey, my resourceful assistant in the Dean's office of the Graduate School, lent a most helpful hand, for which I am particularly grateful. My deep thanks also to Michael Ochs, music editor at W. W. Norton, for his unfailing advice and careful guidance from the inception of this project through the editorial work and production process.

Original sources and historical documents can speak for themselves. The editors of *The Bach Reader,* Hans T. David and Arthur Mendel, were not only aware of this; they provided much more than a documentary, presenting us with a volume that spoke eloquently, powerfully, and objectively of and about Johann Sebastian Bach and his music. The editor of *The New Bach Reader* very much hopes that this book will serve the same end and therefore cannot think of a more meaningful gesture than dedicating his work on this volume gratefully and respectfully to the memory of Professors David and Mendel.

Harvard University   Christoph Wolff
Cambridge, Massachusetts
November 1997

PREFACE TO
THE FIRST EDITION OF

The Bach Reader
1945

The Bach Reader is a collection of the most significant early material on Johann Sebastian Bach. The figure of Bach is here revealed in his own words, in the testimony of his contemporaries, and in the judgments of the generations immediately following his own. The material has been gathered together in one volume for the first time; much of it has never appeared in English before. The items, which in general are presented in chronological order, are coordinated by the essays "Johann Sebastian Bach, a Portrait in Outline," and "The Story of His Fame." Where explanations were necessary they have been inserted in brackets or given as footnotes. But in general it has been our aim to let the original sources speak for themselves.

This book contains all the surviving sources of any importance from which our knowledge of Bach's life and reputation has been drawn. As the reader becomes familiar with layer after layer of evidence, he builds up his own biography of Bach, along the paths that any biographer must necessarily follow. In doing so he is in a position to determine where independent sources confirm each other and where, on the other hand, an early source contains a legend or an inference that has been magnified beyond its true importance by later writers. Forkel's *On Bach's Life, Genius, and Works,* which appears, unabridged, as Section VI of this volume, illustrates both ends of the biographer's procedure. Forkel was personally acquainted with Bach's sons, and to the extent that he reports what they told him, his book is itself a primary source. But he also had access to some of the documents given in Sections II to V. What he learned from them he repeated—sometimes precisely and sometimes less so, although in jumping to conclusions and letting the imagination expand on the significance of meager data he was one of the least offenders among Bach biographers. The reader, with all the evidence before him, can estimate the proportions of fact and of guesswork in Forkel's writing—or, for that matter, in almost any statement about the facts of Bach's life.

The few contemporary translations available—chiefly for Sections VI and VII—have been used. Each has been carefully compared with the original, and revised wherever the meaning had been incorrectly or incompletely rendered. Most of the translations, however, are new. They seek to convey not only the meaning but as far as possible the character of the original German. Where the original reads smoothly and easily we have tried to make the translation smooth and easy; and where the original was rough we have kept the English rough. In this way, we hope, the pictures of the varying personalities contained in their writings have survived the process of translation.

Bach himself—who in music created structures as elaborate and at the same time graceful as any ever conceived—sometimes wrote a German that is not even grammatical, let alone reasonably clear. It is interesting to compare, for instance, in Bach's dispute with Ernesti, the relatively free-flowing language of the Rector with the involved mazes of Bach's own style. To revise his thinking and put his words into fine, literate English would conceal an illuminative paradox of personality. To prettify his writing would, in addition, obscure the stubborn intractability with which he fought for his rights, or the awkward bowings and scrapings with which he sought to show the respect for authority or noble birth required by the custom of the times. It would substitute an urbane and facile expression for his own style of writing, which was often that of a provincial choirmaster—now ineptly wordy, now sputteringly inarticulate.

The original spellings of names and German words, however inconsistent, have been preserved. Since for most of the old handwritten documents we have had access only to printed copies, some inconsistencies may be due to nothing more than different readings of the not too legible originals. But German spelling was as little standardized in Bach's time as English spelling in the Elizabethan period, and even Mozart, to an amazing degree, spelled phonetically rather than correctly. Particularly inconsistent was the use of *k* in place of *c* in words of Latin origin. The *c* was then still more common, but we find, for instance, that words like *Musikus* and *Musikant* were spelled with a *k* in Scheibe's *Critischer Musikus* and with a *c* in Mizler's *Musikalische Bibliothek.* In the older English sources, too—Stephenson's translation of Forkel and the quotations from Wesley—we have preserved some of the freedom of the originals in their treatment of spelling, capitalization, and punctuation.

Of the editors, Hans T. David had been responsible, in general, for the plan of the book, the assembling of the material, and the comments given in the essays and notes, while the translation has been provided by Arthur Mendel. But there has been active partnership in every phase of the work: every word has been scrutinized and agreed upon by both editors. . . . For helpful suggestions we thank Dr. Alfred Einstein, Dr. Albert Riemenschneider, Mr. Kurt Stone, and Mr. Carl Weinrich.

HANS T. DAVID

ARTHUR MENDEL

Hans T. David (1902–1967) grew up in Germany and studied at the Universities of Tübingen, Göttingen, and Berlin; he came to the United States in 1936 and was professor of music at the University of Michigan from 1950 to 1967. Arthur Mendel (1905–1979) was educated at Harvard University and the École Normale de Musique in Paris; he was professor of music at Princeton University from 1952 until his retirement in 1973.

Bibliographical Abbreviations

BD   *Bach-Dokumente.* Leipzig and Kassel, 1963–72.
- Complete critical edition of the source material on Bach, with extensive commentaries, edited under the auspices of the Bach-Archiv Leipzig as a supplement to the *Neue Bach-Ausgabe.*

BD I   Werner Neumann and Hans-Joachim Schulze, eds. *Schriftstücke von der Hand Johann Sebastian Bachs: Kritische Gesamtausgabe.* Bach-Dokumente, I. 1963.
- Complete critical edition of Bach's own writings.

BD II   Werner Neumann and Hans-Joachim Schulze, eds. *Fremdschriftliche und gedruckte Dokumente zur Lebensgeschichte Johann Sebastian Bachs, 1685–1750: Kritische Gesamtausgabe.* Bach-Dokumente, II. 1969.
- Complete critical edition of other documents relating to Bach's life, from the period 1685–1750.

BD III   Hans-Joachim Schulze, ed. *Dokumente zum Nachwirken Johann Sebastian Bachs, 1750–1800.* Bach-Dokumente, III. 1972.
- Documents relating to Bach from the period 1750–1800.

BJ   *Bach-Jahrbuch.* Leipzig and Berlin, 1904– . Edited by Arnold Schering (1904–39), Max Schneider (1940–52), Alfred Dürr and Werner Neumann (1953–74), Hans-Joachim Schulze and Christoph Wolff (1975–).
- The principal organ documenting Bach research, issued annually. It periodically includes a bibliography of the most recent writings on Bach.

BWV   Wolfgang Schmieder, ed. *Thematisch-systematisches Verzeichnis der musikalischen Werke Johann Sebastian Bachs.* Leipzig, 1950; rev. and enl. ed., Wiesbaden, 1990. [*Bach-Werke-Verzeichnis*]
- A thematic catalogue of Bach's musical works.

NBA   Johann Sebastian Bach. *Neue Ausgabe sämtlicher Werke.* Edited under the auspices of the Johann-Sebastian-Bach-Institut Göttingen and the Bach-Archiv Leipzig. Kassel, Leipzig, 1954– . [*Neue Bach-Ausgabe.*]
- Complete critical edition of Bach's musical works.

Other books are referred to in this volume by author; full citations appear in the bibliography (pp. 531–32). For monetary abbreviations, see p. 527.

Conspectus

OF PARTS I–VII

NOTE: Entries shown in **boldface** include a facsimile of the original source. The year of a document's origin is shown for the first item in a new year, in parentheses following the heading.

PART V. BACH IN THE SECOND HALF OF THE EIGHTEENTH CENTURY

PART VI. FORKEL'S BIOGRAPHY OF BACH

PART VII. BACH IN THE ROMANTIC ERA

Chronology

←Mar. 21 = prior to Mar. 21
Mar. 21→ = after Mar. 21

EISENACH AND OHRDRUF (1685–1700)

1685 Mar. 21	Birth of Johann Sebastian, seventh and youngest child of Johann Ambrosius Bach and Maria Elisabeth Bach, née Lämmerhirt **Nos. 303–4**
Mar. 23	Baptized at St. George's, Eisenach's main church **No. 2**
1690–93	Attends a German school in Eisenach
1693–95	Attends the Latin School in Eisenach **No. 6**
1694 May 3	Burial of mother Elisabeth Bach (age 50) **No. 3**
Oct. 23	Wedding of brother Johann Christoph in Ohrdruf; Johann Ambrosius Bach, Johann Pachelbel, and others perform
Nov. 27	Johann Ambrosius Bach marries Barbara Margaretha Bartholomaei, née Keul **No. 4**
1695 Feb. 20	Death of father Johann Ambrosius Bach (age 50), buried Feb. 24 **No. 5** Johann Sebastian, orphaned at age 10, and his brother Johann Jacob (age 13) join the household of their oldest brother, Johann Christoph Bach, in Ohrdruf
1695–1700	Attends the Lyceum in Ohrdruf **No. 8**

LÜNEBURG AND WEIMAR (1700–1703)

1700 Mar. 15	Leaves for Lüneburg **No. 8**

1700–1702   Choral scholar at St. Michael's School in
                 Lüneburg   No. 11
                 Contact with Georg Böhm in Lüneburg and frequent
                 visits to Johann Adam Reinken in Hamburg

1702 Jul. 9 →   Applies for the organist position at St. Jacobi Church,
                 Sangerhausen   No. 189

1703 Jan.–Jun.   Lackey and court musician in the private capelle of
                 Duke Johann Ernst of Saxe-Weimar   No. 13

    c. Jul. 3   Examines the new organ at the New Church (also called
                 St. Boniface's or St. Sophia's) in Arnstadt No. 15

ARNSTADT (1703–1707)

1703 Aug. 9   Appointed organist at Arnstadt's New Church No. 16

1705 Aug.   Dispute with Johann Heinrich Geyersbach   No. 19
     Nov. →   Visit with Dietrich Buxtehude in Lübeck for
                 3–4 months   No. 20
     Dec. 2–3   Buxtehude's oratorios *Castrum doloris* and *Templum honoris*
                 performed in Lübeck

1706 Feb. 21   Disciplinary problems discussed with Arnstadt
                 consistory   Nos. 20–21
     Nov. 28   Organ examination in Langewiesen, near Gehren

1707 Apr. 24   Easter Sunday: Audition for the organist position at St.
                 Blasius's Church in Mühlhausen: Performance of a
                 cantata (BWV 4?)   No. 22a
     Jun. 14–15 Negotiations with the Mühlhausen town
                 council   Nos. 22–23
     Jun. 29   Returns organ keys to Arnstadt authorities Nos. 24–25

MÜHLHAUSEN (1707–1708)

1707 Jul. 1   Begins as organist at St. Blasius's in Mühlhausen
     Oct. 17   Marriage with Maria Barbara, daughter of Johann
                 Michael Bach (1648–1694) of Gehren, in
                 Dornheim   No. 26

1708 Feb. 4   Mühlhausen town council election: Performance of
                 BWV 71   Nos. 27–28

c. Feb. 25	Cantata BWV 71 published	No. 28c
Feb.	Submits plans for organ renovation at St. Blasius's	No. 31
Jun. 25	Appointed organist and chamber musician at the court of the co-reigning Dukes Wilhelm Ernst and Ernst August of Saxe-Weimar; requests and receives dismissal from Mühlhausen	No. 33

WEIMAR (1708–1717)

1708	Jul.	Moves to Weimar	No. 36
	Dec. 29	Daughter Catharina Dorothea baptized (d. 1774)	
1709	Feb. 4	Mühlhausen town council election: Guest performance of a (lost) cantata	No. 28b
	Feb. 7→	Cantata published (no extant copies)	No. 28e
	Mar.	Visit of the violinist Johann Georg Pisendel in Weimar	
1710	Feb. 4	Mühlhausen town council election: Guest performance of a (lost) cantata	No. 28c
	Oct. 26	Organ examination and dedication in Traubach, near Weimar	
	Nov. 22	Son Wilhelm Friedemann born	No. 41
1713	Feb. 21–22	In Weissenfels: Performance of the hunting cantata BWV 208 in conjunction with the birthday of Duke Christian of Saxe-Weissenfels	No. 44
	Feb. 23	Twins, Maria Sophia and Johann Christoph, born; Johann Christoph dies shortly after birth	
	Mar. 15	Burial of Maria Sophia	
	Jul. 8	Prince Johann Ernst returns from study trip, bringing with him new musical repertoires	No. 312c
	Sep. 7	In Ohrdruf: Baptism of Johann Sebastian, son of brother Johann Christoph Bach	
	Nov. 6	Participates in festive dedication of the newly built St. Jacobi Church in Weimar	
	Nov. 28–Dec. 15	In Halle, invited to audition for organist post at Our Lady's (Market) Church (successor to F. W. Zachow); Bach elected Dec. 13	Nos. 46–49
1714	Feb.	Withdraws candidacy for Halle post	No. 50
	Mar. 2	Appointed concertmaster at the Weimar court	No. 51

1714 (continued)

| Mar. 8 | Son Carl Philipp Emanuel born | No. 55 |
| Mar. 25 | Palm Sunday / Visitation: Performance of BWV 182, first cantata after concertmaster appointment | |

1715 May 11 Son Johann Gottfried Bernhard born No. 56

Aug. 1– / Nov. 3 Official mourning period after the death of Prince Wilhelm Ernst

1716 Apr. 28– / May 2 Organ examination and dedication in Halle, Our Lady's (Market) Church Nos. 58–61

Jul. 31 Organ examination in Erfurt, St. Augustine's Church No. 62

Dec. 1 Death of court capellmeister Johann Samuel Drese

1717 Mar. 26 Good Friday: Guest performance of a (lost) Passion at the court of Gotha Nos. 63–65

Aug. 5 Signs contractual agreement to accept capellmeistership in Cöthen No. 70

fall Travels to Dresden for keyboard contest with Louis Marchand at the electoral court No. 67

Nov. 6– / Dec. 2 Detention in conjunction with his dismissal from court service No. 68

CÖTHEN (1717–1723)

1717 Dec. 2→ Moves to Cöthen No. 70

Dec. 16–18 Organ examination in Leipzig, St. Paul's (University) Church Nos. 71–73

1718 c. May 9– / Jul. 15 With Prince Leopold in Carlsbad No. 70h

Nov. 15 Son Leopold Augustus born; baptized Nov. 17 No. 78

Dec. 10 Birthday of Prince Leopold: Performance of BWV 66a, Anh. 5

1719 ←Mar. 1 Trip to Berlin; purchase of a harpsichord for the court No. 77

May 14– / Jul. 27 Failed attempt at meeting Handel in Halle No. 396

Sep. 28 Son Leopold Augustus dies

1720 Jan. 22 Title page of *Clavier-Büchlein* for Wilhelm Friedemann Bach No. 79

late May– Jul. 7→	With Prince Leopold in Carlsbad	
Jul. 7	Burial of Bach's wife, Maria Barbara Bach	No. 80
←Nov. 21	Audition for organist post at St. Jacobi Church in Hamburg	Nos. 81–82
1721 Feb. 22	Death of brother Johann Christoph (age 49), organist in Ohrdruf	
Mar. 25	Dedication of Brandenburg Concertos	Nos. 83–84
←Aug. 7	Guest performance in Schleiz at the court of Count Reuss	No. 85
Dec. 3	Marriage to Anna Magdalena Wilcke, princely court singer at Cöthen	No. 86
Dec. 11	Marriage of Prince Leopold to Princess Henrietta of Anhalt-Bernburg	
1722 Apr. 16	Death of brother Johann Jacob (age 40), court musician in Stockholm	
Aug. 9	Guest performance in Zerbst: Birthday of Prince Johann August of Anhalt-Zerbst	
←Dec. 15	Inheritance of 224 thaler from the Lämmerhirt estate, Erfurt	No. 89
←Dec. 21	Application for the cantorate at St. Thomas's in Leipzig	No. 94a
1723 Feb. 7	Audition for the cantorate at St. Thomas's in Leipzig; performance of cantatas BWV 22 and 23	Nos. 93, 95
spring	Daughter Christiana Sophia Henrietta born	
Apr. 13	Requests dismissal from Cöthen, which he receives; is permitted to keep title of princely Anhalt-Cöthen capellmeister	No. 96

LEIPZIG (1723–1730)

1723 Apr. 19	Signs provisional contract with the Leipzig town council	No. 97
Apr. 22	Elected cantor and music director at St. Thomas's by the Leipzig town council	No. 98
May 5	Signs final contract with the Leipzig town council	No. 100
May 8	Theological examination by theology professors Schmid and Deyling	No. 101
May 13	Signs visitation article	

1723 (continued)

May 15	First Leipzig salary payment	No. 108
May 16	Whitsunday: First performance at St. Paul's (University) Church	No. 119
May 22	Bach's family relocates to Leipzig and moves into a spacious apartment in the St. Thomas School	No. 102
May 30	1st Sunday after Trinity: First performance of BWV 75 and beginning of first annual cantata cycle (Jahrgang I)	No. 105
Jun. 1	Formal installation at the St. Thomas School	
Jun. 14	Sons Wilhelm Friedemann and Carl Philipp Emanuel enroll in the St. Thomas School	No. 111
c. Nov. 2	Organ examination and dedication in Störmthal, near Leipzig: Performance of BWV 194	
Dec. 25	Christmas vespers: Performance of Magnificat, BWV 243a	

1724 Feb. 26	Son Gottfried Heinrich born; baptized Feb. 27	
Apr. 7	Good Friday: Performance of the *St. John Passion,* BWV 245 (1st version)	Nos. 114–16
Jun. 11	Beginning of second (chorale) contata cycle (Jahrgang II), with BWV 20	
Jun. 25	Organ examination and dedication in Gera, Salvator Church	
←Jul. 18	Guest performance in Cöthen, with Anna Magdalena	No. 117a

1725 Feb. 23	Guest performance in Weissenfels (birthday of Duke Christian): BWV 249a	
Mar. 30	Good Friday: Performance of the *St. John Passion,* BWV 245 (2nd version)	No. 114
Apr. 14	Son Christian Gottlieb baptized	
Sep. 14	Petition to the Elector of Saxony, Friedrich August I, re university service	No. 119a
Sep. 19–20	Organ recitals at St. Sophia's in Dresden	No. 118
Nov. 3	Petition to the Elector of Saxony, Friedrich August I	No. 119b
Nov. 30–Dec. 15	Guest performances in Cöthen, with Anna Magdalena (birthdays of Princess Charlotte Friederike Wilhelmine and Prince Leopold)	No. 117a
Dec. 31	Petition to the Elector of Saxony, Friedrich August I	No. 119c

1726	Apr. 5	Daughter Elisabeth Juliana Friederica baptized	
	Apr. 19	Good Friday: Performance of Reinhard Keiser's *St. Mark Passion,* with additions by Bach	No. 114
	Jun. 29	Daughter Christiana Sophia Henrietta (age 3) dies; buried Jul. 1	
	Nov. 1	Announcement of the *Clavier-Übung* series (BWV 825)	No. 127
	Fall	Michaelmas fair: separate edition of BWV 825 published (BWV 226–230 published 1727–30)	No. 127
1727	Mar.–Apr.	Renovations of Bach's apartment in the St. Thomas School completed	
	Apr. 11	Good Friday: *St. Matthew Passion,* BWV 244 (1st version)	No. 114
	Sep. 7– Jan. 6, 1728	Official state mourning period after death of Electoress Christiane Eberhardine of Saxony	
	Oct. 17	Academic Memorial Service for the Electoress of Saxony (BWV 198)	No. 136
	Oct. 30	Son Ernestus Andreas baptized; dies Nov. 1, buried Nov. 2	
1728	←Jan. 5	Guest performance in Cöthen (for New Year's Day festivities)	No. 116c
	Sep. 21	Son Christian Gottlieb dies (age 3); buried Sep. 22	
	Oct. 10	Daughter Regina Johanna baptized	
	Nov. 19	Death of Prince Leopold of Anhalt-Cöthen	
1729	Jan. 12	Visit in Leipzig of Duke Christian of Weissenfels: Performance of BWV 210a	
	c. Feb. 23	Several days: Guest performances in Weissenfels (birthday of Duke Christian); appointment as titular capellmeister of the Saxon-Weissenfels court	
	Mar. 5	Matriculation of son Wilhelm Friedemann at the University of Leipzig	
	←Mar. 20	Bach absent from Leipzig for 3 weeks (no details known)	No. 130
	spring	Assumes directorship of Collegium Musicum	No. 130
	Mar. 23–24	Funeral services for Prince Leopold in Cöthen (BWV 244a)	No. 139
	Apr. 15	Good Friday: Performance of the *St. Matthew Passion,* BWV 244	No. 114

1729 (continued)

Jun. 29   Vain invitation for George Frideric Handel (visiting
                 with his mother in Halle) to come to Leipzig; Bach
                 himself ill, sends son Wilhelm Friedemann to Halle
                                                                No. 396

Jul 30   Friedelena Margaretha Bach, sister of Bach's first wife,
                 Maria Barbara (age 53), buried; had lived in Bach's
                 household since c. 1709

Oct. 20   Funeral of Johann August Ernesti, rector of St. Thomas's
                 (BWV 229)

←Dec. 24   Auditions organists for post at St. Nicholas's (Bach's
                 student Johann Schneider appointed)

1730 Jan. 1   Daughter Christiana Benedicta baptized; dies Jan. 4,
                 buried Jan. 5

Apr. 7   Good Friday: Performance, with additions by Bach, of
                 anonymous *St. Luke's Passion,* BWV 246   **No. 114**

Aug. 23   Memorandum of a Well-Appointed Church
                 Music   **No. 151**

LEIPZIG (1731–1740)

1731 spring(?)   Publication of Opus 1, Part I of the *Clavier-*
                 Übung   **No. 155**

Mar. 18   Daughter Christiana Dorothea baptized

Mar. 23   Good Friday: Performance of *St. Mark Passion,*
                 BWV 247   **No. 114**

May→   Major renovations of the St. Thomas School building;
                 the Bach family moves into temporary quarters

c. Sep. 14   In Dresden for several days: Organ recital at St. Sophia's
                 (Sep. 14) and other performances at the court; attends
                 premiere of Johann Adolf Hasse's opera *Cleofide*
                 (Sep. 13)   **No. 307**

Oct. 1   Son Carl Philipp Emanuel matriculates at the
                 University of Leipzig

Nov. 12   Organ examination in Stöntzsch

1732 Feb. 4   Reexamination of organ in Stöntzsch

Apr. 24   St. Thomas School building renovations nearly
                 completed; Bach and his family return to their residence

Jun. 5   Dedication of the renovated St. Thomas School (BWV
                 Anh. 18)

Jun. 21	Son Johann Christoph Friedrich born; baptized Jun. 23	
Aug. 31	Daughter Christiana Dorothea dies (age 1); buried the same day	
Sep. 21→	Trip to Kassel, with Anna Magdalena; organ examination at St. Martin's Church and dedication recital on Sep. 28	**Nos. 157–58, 338**
1733 Feb. 15– Jul. 2	Official state mourning period after death on Feb. 1 of Elector Friedrich August I of Saxony	**No. 160**
Apr. 21	St. Nicholas's Church: Fealty ceremony for August II, Elector of Saxony	
Apr. 25	Daughter Regina Johanna (age 4) dies; buried Apr. 26	
Jun. 7	Son Wilhelm Friedemann applies for organist post at St. Sophia's in Dresden; is appointed on Jun. 23	
c. Jul. 27	In Dresden for several days: Dedication of the *Missa* (Kyrie & Gloria), BWV 232, to the new Elector of Saxony (Jul. 27)	**No. 162**
Nov. 5	Son Johann August Abraham baptized; dies Nov. 6, buried Nov. 7	
1734 Jan. 17–19	Celebration in Leipzig of the coronation of Friedrich August II of Saxony as King of Poland (BWV 214a)	
←Mar. 13	Visit of Franz Benda in Leipzig	
Sep. 9	Matriculation of son Carl Philipp Emanuel at the University of Frankfort-on-the-Oder, where he directs the Collegium Musicum	
Oct. 4	St. Thomas School bids farewell to Rector Johann Matthias Gesner, who becomes founding dean of the arts and sciences faculty of the newly established University of Göttingen	
Nov. 21	Installation of Dr. Johann August Ernesti as rector of the St. Thomas School (BWV Anh. 19)	
Dec. 25	Christmas Day: Performance of first part of *Christmas Oratorio*, BWV 248^I (subsequent parts performed on Dec. 26, Dec. 27, Jan. 1, 1735, Jan. 2, and Jan. 6)	
1735 spring	Publication of Part II of the *Clavier-Übung*	**No. 174**
Jun.	Tip to Mühlhausen for more than a week: Audition of son Johann Gottfried Bernhard for organist post at St. Mary's (←Jun. 9), organ examination at St. Mary's (←Jun. 16)	**Nos. 175–76**
Sep. 5	Son Johann Christian born; baptized Sep. 7	

1736 Mar. 30	Good Friday, at St. Thomas's: *St. Matthew Passion,* BWV 244 (revised version, using "swallows nest" organ for first and last movements of Part I)	No. 114
Jul.	Beginning of the dispute regarding appointment of prefects	Nos. 180–86
Jul. 17→	Plans to be absent from Leipzig for two weeks (no details known)	
Nov. 19	Appointed Royal Polish and Electoral Saxon Court Composer	No. 190
c. Dec. 1	In Dresden for several days: Organ recital at Our Lady's (Dec. 1)	No. 191
1737 Jan. 14	Son Johann Gottfried Bernhard appointed organist at St. Jacobi Church in Sangerhausen	
Mar. 4	Resigns temporarily as director of the Collegium Musicum	
Apr. 10	Town council decision regarding appointment of prefects	No. 192
c. May	Trip to Sangerhausen (no details known)	No. 204
May 14	Learns of Johann Adolph Scheibe's critique	No. 343
Sep. 28	In Wiederau: Performance of BWV 30a	
←Oct. 18	Cousin Johann Elias Bach begins service as private secretary to Bach and tutor of his children	No. 202
Oct. 20	Daughter Johanna Carolina baptized	
Dec. 12	The king's decree in the dipute between Bach and Ernesti	No. 196
1738 Jan 8	Publication of Johann Abraham Birnbaum's defense against Scheibe's attack	No. 344
spring	C. P. E. Bach appointed harpsichordist of the crown prince, later King Friedrich II of Prussia	
←May 22	In Dresden for several days	No. 203
1739 Jan. 28	Son Johann Gottfried Bernhard matriculates at the University of Jena	No. 305
May 27	Death of son Johann Gottfried Bernhard (age 24) in Jena	No. 305
←Aug. 11	Son Wilhelm Friedemann back home for 4 weeks; concerts with lutenists Sylvius Leopold Weiss and Johann Kropffgans of Dresden	No. 209
← Sep. 7	In Altenburg: Dedication of organ at the Castle Church	
Sep.	Michaelmas Fair: Publication of Part III of the *Clavier-Übung*	No. 206

1739 (continued)
    Oct. 2   Resumes directorship of the Collegium Musicum
                                                     No. 210
    Nov. 7–14   Trip to Weissenfels, with Anna Magdalena (no details
                    known)   **No. 212**

1740 Apr. 17   Trip to Halle (no details known)   **No. 217**

LEIPZIG (1741–1750)

1741 ←Aug. 5   Trip to Berlin, for at least one week (no details known)
                                                     No. 222
    Sep.   Michaelmas Fair(?): Publication of Part IV of the
                    Clavier-Übung   **No. 225**
    ←Nov. 17   Extended trip to Dresden (return on Nov. 17); visit with
                    Count Keyserlingk

1742 Feb. 22   Daughter Regina Susanna baptized
    c. May 13–   Official state mourning period after the death of
        20   Empress Maria Amalia
    Aug. 30   In Kleinzschocher: Performance of BWV 212
    Oct. 31   Johann Elias Bach leaves Leipzig and his post as private
                    secretary to Bach and tutor of his children   **No. 226**

1743 ←Dec. 13   Organ examination at St. John's in Leipzig

1745 Nov. 30   Occupation of Leipzig by Prussian troups (ends Dec. 25)

1746 Apr. 16   Son Wilhelm Friedemann appointed organist and music
                    director of Our Lady's (Market) Church in Halle
    Aug. 7   Organ examination in Zschortau, near Leipzig **No. 235**
    Sep. 24–28 Organ examination in Naumburg, St. Wenceslas's
                    Church   **No. 236**

1747 c. May 8   Trip to Potsdam and Berlin: Visit with King Friedrich
                    II of Prussia in Potsdam (May 7); organ recital in the
                    Church of the Holy Spirit (May 8); visits new opera
                    house in Berlin   **No. 239**
    Jun.   Accepts membership in the Society of Musical Sciences
                    (Lorenz Christoph Mizler, secretary, present in Leipzig);
                    contributes publication of *Canonic Variations,* BWV 769
                                                      Nos. 241–42
    Jul. 7   Dedication of the *Musical Offering,* BWV 1079 **No. 245**
    Jun. 28   Start of major organ repairs at St. Thomas's

1747 (continued)		
Sep.	Michaelmas Fair: Publication of the *Musical Offering,* BWV 1079	Nos. 244, 248
Nov.	Examination of renovated organ at St. Thomas's	
1748 Sep. 26	Grandson Johann Sebastian Bach jun., son of Carl Philipp Emanuel, baptized in Berlin (Bach not present)	
←Dec. 21	Audition of town musicians	
1749 Jan. 20	Daughter Elisabeth Juliana Friederica marries Bach's student Johann Christoph Altnickol	
Apr. 2	Corresponds with Count Questenberg of Moravia	No. 261
Apr.	Conference with organ builder Heinrich Andreas Cuntzius	
May 6	Sale of a fortepiano to Count Branitzky of Poland	No. 262
Jun. 8	Premature audition of Gottlob Harrer, capellmeister of Count Brühl in Dresden, for the cantorate at St. Thomas's, at the special request of his patron, the Saxon prime minister, takes place in the concert hall "Three Swans," not in the church	Nos. 265–66
Oct. 6	Grandson Johann Sebastian Altnickol baptized in Naumburg (Bach not present); buried Dec. 21	
Nov. 30	First Sunday in Advent: W. F. Bach performs his cantata Fk 80 in Leipzig(?)	
←Dec. 11	Unspecified absence(s) of Bach	No. 263
1750 Jan.	Appointment of son Johann Christoph Friedrich as court musician of Count Wilhelm of Schaumburg-Lippe in Bückeburg	No. 266
Feb. 2	Purification (or Mar. 25, Visitation): C. P. E. Bach performs his Magnificat Wq 215 in Leipzig	
Mar. 28–31	First operation by the London eye surgeon Dr. John Taylor	No. 269a
Apr. 5–8	Second operation by Dr. Taylor	Nos. 269b–70
May 4	Arrival of Bach's last pupil, Johann Gottfried Müthel, in Leipzig	
Jul. 22	After a stroke, receives last communion at home	
Jul. 28	Death (age 65) at "a little after" 8:15 P.M.	Nos. 271–73, 306
Jul. 30 or 31	Burial at St. John's cemetery	No. 272

POSTHUMOUS YEARS (1750–1809)

1750 fall	Johann Christian Bach (age 15) joins the household of his stepbrother Carl Philipp Emanuel Bach in Berlin; Gottfried Heinrich (26) joins the household of his brother-in-law J. C. Altnickol in Naumburg
Aug. 7	Election of Johann Gottlob Harrer as cantor of St. Thomas's (other applicants for the position were C. P. E. Bach, Johann Gottlieb Görner, A. F. Graun, Johann Ludwig Krebs, and J. Trier) No. 274
Aug. 29→	The Leipzig town council acquires performing parts of chorale cantata cycle from Anna Magdalena Bach for the use of the St. Thomas cantor
Oct. 2	Installation of J. G. Harrer as cantor of St. Thomas's No. 275
1750–51 winter	C. P. E. Bach and Johann Friedrich Agricola write obituary (published 1754) No. 306
1751 May	*Jubilate* (Spring) Fair: Publication of *The Art of Fugue,* BWV 1080
Jun. 1	Subscription announcement for *The Art of Fugue* Nos. 281–82
1752 May	2nd edition of *The Art of Fugue* No. 375
1755 Jul. 9	Death of the St. Thomas cantor J. G. Harrer
Sep. 29	Special services to commemorate the 200th anniversary of the Augsburg Religious Peace at both St. Thomas's and St. Nicholas's: Performance of BWV 126, conducted by the prefect (probably C. F. Penzel)
Oct. 8	Appointment of Johann Friedrich Doles, cantor at the Cathedral in Freiberg (a pupil of Bach's from 1739 to 1743) as cantor of St. Thomas's; he held the position until 1789
1760 Feb. 27	Death of Anna Magdalena Bach (age 59); buried Feb. 29
1765, 1769	Publication of four-part chorales (2 vols.) by Birnstiel, Berlin Nos. 378–79
1763 Feb. 12	Death of son Gottfried Heinrich (age 39) in Naumburg
1774 Jan. 14	Death of daughter Catharina Dorothea (age 65) in Leipzig

1781 Aug. 18	Death of daughter Johanna Carolina (age 43) in Leipzig
Aug. 24	Death of daughter Elisabeth Juliane Friederica Altnickol (age 55) in Leipzig
1782 Jan. 1	Death of son Johann Christian (age 46) in London
1784 Jul. 1	Death of son Wilhelm Friedemann (age 73) in Berlin
1784–87	Publication of four-part chorales (4 vols.) by Breitkopf, Leipzig **Nos. 381–84**
1786	Performance of the Symbolum Nicenum from the B Minor Mass by Carl Philipp Emanuel Bach **No. 367**
1788 Dec. 14	Death of son Carl Philipp Emanuel (age 74) in Hamburg
1795 Jan. 26	Death of son Johann Christoph Friedrich (age 63) in Bückeburg
1800	The music publisher Hoffmeister & Kühnel of Leipzig undertakes the first collected edition: *Oeuvres complettes de Jean Sebastien Bach*
1801	Three firms (Hoffmeister & Kühnel, Simrock of Bonn, and Nägeli of Zurich) simultaneously and independent of each other publish editions of *The Well-Tempered Clavier,* with wide European distribution
1809 Dec. 14	Death of daughter Regina Susanna (age 67) in Leipzig

PART I

*Johann
Sebastian
Bach:
A Portrait
in
Outline*

Johann Sebastian Bach: A Portrait in Outline

For well over two centuries, the Bachs were a family of successful musicians, constituting an example that was exceptional even among their contemporaries and has seemed increasingly spectacular to each succeeding age.

We are accustomed to the passing on of trades and crafts from parent to child. But we look upon artistic talent as too individual a gift to be handed down and shared, like a landed estate, by a whole family. The line we draw between art and craft is, however, largely artificial, and to earlier centuries would have seemed entirely so. Printing is certainly a craft. But as practiced by the Elzevirs of Leiden, for example, it was just as certainly an art. Even as a family of musicians, the Bachs were not unique: in Elizabethan times the Italian name of Ferrabosco belonged to several prominent contributors to Italian and English musical life, and contemporary with the Bachs were the Couperins, who held the post of organist at St. Gervais in Paris through four generations, and of whom François, "the Great," was merely the greatest.

In such families, and in the Bachs above all, heredity and early training combined to form solid musical craftsmen. Each generation seemed to carry on from where the last left off, until the increase in knowledge and ability culminated in one transcendent figure. But if Johann Sebastian Bach realized that he was the peak of the development up to his time, which is not sure, he certainly did not intend that the ascent should end with him. His first wife, Maria Barbara, seems to have been musical, and his second, Anna Magdalena, was a professional musician.[1] Johann Sebastian himself gave Anna Magdalena instruction and trained his sons as they came of age, particularly

---

1. In order not to encumber these pages, no references are given to the many bits of evidence—contained within the covers of this book—upon which the Portrait in Outline is based. The specific passages alluded to may be located through the index.

Wilhelm Friedemann and Carl Philipp Emanuel. Carl Philipp Emanuel, in turn, taught Johann Sebastian's youngest son, Johann Christian, who belonged to an age that took life and work less seriously. Johann Christian stated frankly that he composed "to live"—a significant admission, for the line of the great Bachs ended with him.

The Bach family originated, as far as we know, in Wechmar, a little town between Gotha and Arnstadt in Thuringia, the land that had also produced Martin Luther. The first known ancestor of the family was Veit, or Vitus, a baker from Pressburg (Bratislava), then the capital of the kingdom of Hungary. But when during the period of the Counter Reformation the country became hostile to Protestantism, "simple old Veit," as Emanuel calls him, journeyed to Thuringia rather than change his faith. He settled in Wechmar, where he apparently had some family connections.

It is again symbolic of Johann Christian's role as the last of the great Bachs that he was apparently the first Bach to become a Roman Catholic. His conversion was required if he expected to be offered the post of organist at the Cathedral of Milan. But perhaps he was motivated as strongly by the splendor of the Roman ritual and the sensuousness and vivacity of its music as by any considerations of advancement in his career.

Johann Christian, who eventually settled in England, Johann Jacob, who journeyed in the suite of Charles XII from Sweden to Russia and Turkey, and the Johann Christoph who "found his greatest *plaisir* in traveling" were notable exceptions in a family most of whose members stayed close to their native Thuringia. But any German chauvinism, such as that found even at this early date in the critical writings of Mattheson, Mizler, Scheibe, and others, seems to have been foreign to the Bachs. Johann Sebastian knew that his ancestor Veit had come from Hungary. So this man, boasted of by writers of his time (and by how many since!) as an ornament of German art not to be equaled by other nations, believed that he was descended from Hungarian stock.

Up to and including Bach's time, most German musicians earned their living by entering the regular service of a noble or princely patron as court or chamber musician; of a town council as town piper; or of a municipal or ecclesiastical authority as church organist, music director, or cantor—the latter function including the teaching of music in a school. Most of the Bachs were town or church musicians, and so many of them were members of certain Thuringian musical "companies" that at Eisenach, for instance, the town musicians were called *"die Baache"*[2] long after the last Bach had ceased to serve in such a capacity.

---

2. The fact that the name was frequently spelled with two *a*'s shows that the vowel was pronounced long, approximately as in "father," and not short as in the modern German pronunciation of the word for brook *(Bach)*.

The outward life of Johann Sebastian was as matter-of-fact as the careers of most members of his family. His father was a musician in the service of the town council of Eisenach. After his death, which came when the boy was only ten years old, Johann Sebastian was taken into the home of his elder brother Johann Christoph, in Ohrdruf, south of Gotha. In the school of that town he advanced rapidly, and later he received a scholarship in a well-known secondary school in Lüneburg, then still one of Germany's more important towns. At the age of seventeen, he was ready to start out on a career that, though in no way meteoric, was marked by steady progress. After an unsuccessful application to become organist at Sangerhausen—the same post that his son was to hold thirty years later with distressing consequences—Johann Sebastian obtained a minor musical position at the court of Weimar. Then, in rapid succession, he became organist in the small town of Arnstadt, in the considerably larger Imperial Free City of Mühlhausen, and at the court of Weimar, where he soon was promoted to the rank of concertmaster, with the salary of a capellmeister. But his first actual title as capellmeister was at the court of Cöthen.

The first few years at Cöthen must have been the happiest of Bach's life, for Prince Leopold was truly musical and was Bach's good friend and patron. But when the prince married a princess who was unmusical, his interest in music lagged. At this juncture of Bach's life, the post of cantor in Leipzig became vacant.

The position of cantor at the St. Thomas School and director of music at the principal churches in Leipzig was one of the most prominent in the Lutheran realm, corresponding in many ways, though on a smaller scale, to that of *Maestro di Cappella* at St. Mark's in Venice. It had been filled by some of the ablest German musicians of the seventeenth century: Johann Hermann Schein, Tobias Michael, Sebastian Knüpfer, Johann Schelle, and the learned and progressive Johann Kuhnau, who wrote a satirical novel as well as the first sonatas on record for a keyboard instrument alone. Nevertheless, Bach hesitated to give up his position of capellmeister for that of cantor. And the members of the Leipzig council did not decide to give him the appointment until they had concluded that they could not get Telemann or Graupner. Clearly the relations between Bach and the Leipzig authorities were not based on love at first sight, on either side; and although they were never to develop into anything like complete mutual confidence and respect Bach served the city for twenty-seven years.

The St. Thomas School was mainly a school for foundationers in residence. Scholarships were awarded partly on the basis of proficiency in the classical languages and partly in consideration of musical ability, since the boys made up the choirs for the churches under the council's jurisdiction. It was the rector's duty to strike a proper balance between the demands of music and those of other studies. Bach seems to have been satisfied with the balance achieved by Johann Heinrich Ernesti, who was rector during his first years in the school. His relations with Ernesti's successor, Johann Matthias Gesner, were apparently even better: Gesner was a warm admirer of Bach's musicianship, as we see from his description of Bach as organist and conductor contained in a note to an edition of Quintilian. But things took a sharp turn for the worse when Gesner was succeeded by Johann August Ernesti (who, as far as can be learned, was not related to Gesner's predecessor). A long series of documents marks the struggle between Bach and Ernesti. However the reader may adjudicate the controversy, and whoever was originally at fault, it is clear that Ernesti ended by weighting the scales as heavily as he could against music. The documents reveal the tenacity with which Bach fought to defend the rights of his position and the place of music in general in the life of the school.[3]

But Bach was dissatisfied even before the feud with Ernesti had embittered his relations with the school authorities, and he wrote to his old Ohrdruf and Lüneburg classmate Erdmann in Danzig to ask whether a suitable position could be found for him there. His income in Leipzig was nearly ten times what it had been in his first position, in Arnstadt, but the high cost of living in the city and the lack of musical understanding on the part of the authorities combined to prevent him from enjoying what should have been a fine post.

Danzig was farther from home than Bach had ever been and farther than he was ever to get again. His whole life was spent within one small area of Germany, bounded on the north by Lübeck and Hamburg, on the west by Kassel, on the south by Carlsbad, and on the east by Dresden.

The journeys he undertook to hear celebrated organists are famous. He paid his visit to Carlsbad as a member of the Prince of Cöthen's suite. The rest of his travels, except for occasional trips from Leipzig to Dresden, were undertaken mostly for the purpose of examining and rendering reports on new or newly rebuilt organs. The first organ he inspected, in Arnstadt, soon became the first officially entrusted to him as organist. In Halle he joined Kuhnau in a 1716 report on the great new organ there. He also examined organs in Erfurt (1716), Leipzig (St. Paul's, 1717, and St. John's, 1744), Kassel (1732), Zschortau (1746), and finally Naumburg (1746), where he made a joint examination with Silbermann, the greatest German organ builder of the time. (Apparently Bach was never called upon to judge any of

3. Everything conspires to make the dispute between Bach and Ernesti more intricate: not only were there two rectors named Ernesti during Bach's cantorate, though his difficulties were only with the second, but the dispute itself hinged on two young men both named Krause.

the organs built by Silbermann although he did play on some of them, as well as on some of Silbermann's pianofortes.) His last journey was to Potsdam and Berlin to visit Frederick the Great, King of Prussia—the most colorful episode in his rather uneventful career.

Bach's salient personal characteristics, like those of his entire family, were typical of the solid citizen. As soon as he achieved an adequate position, he married. His first wife, a distant cousin, died after bearing seven children. He soon married again, and seems to have been as thoroughly happy in his second marriage as he is reported to have been in his first. Altogether he had twenty children, of whom nine survived him. Both marriages produced sons of exceptional musical talent. Wilhelm Friedemann and Carl Philipp Emanuel were children of Maria Barbara, and Johann Christoph Friedrich and Johann Christian of Anna Magdalena. One of the children was mentally deficient, and Wilhelm Friedemann and Johann Gottfried Bernhard lacked the solid, purposeful character of their father. But at least three were successful enough: Johann Christoph Friedrich held the post of capellmeister at the court of Bückeburg for almost forty years, and both Philipp Emanuel and Johann Christian became more famous in their own lifetimes and more prosperous than their father had ever been.

If Bach in his youth sometimes exhibited an artist's disregard for the prosaic requirements of his post, he later showed himself to be a thoroughly reliable church and school official, except when he was provoked by the opposition of Ernesti or the Leipzig council. He was hospitable, but he knew the value of a thaler. He could dryly point out that a healthy year had deprived him of many of the funeral fees he might normally have expected, and he had no hesitation in asking a cousin to pay the full price for a copy of the *Musical Offering* or in pointing out to the same cousin that high import duties and transportation costs made his gift of a cask of wine hardly worth receiving.

As the servant of a prince, a parish, or a town council, he was expected to show due respect to his superiors, and he seems at times almost to have relished the accumulation of fulsome terms with which it was customary to address them. But beneath all the formalities he was not in the least afraid of the authorities. When a Worshipful University of Leipzig did not satisfy him in the matter of fees, he appealed to the king. When the *Herr Rector* of the St. Thomas School encroached upon his rights, he protested to a Noble and Most Wise Council; when the council did not act, he complained to the Magnificences and Most Reverend Sirs of the Consistory; and when the consistory failed to right matters, he again appealed to the king himself.

Our knowledge of Bach's personality in action, apart from music making, is sparse indeed. He seems to have thoroughly enjoyed a good battle of words when he felt that someone was trying to take advantage of him. He was apt to be impatient and quick-tempered with incompetents. His sense of humor was apparently more vigorous than subtle and, in keeping with the temper of the time, somewhat on the coarse side. Few purely personal letters survive, and presumably he was too busy to write many: on one occasion he could not even find time to write a personal acknowledgment of a christening gift. Most of his correspondence was official: reports on organs, letters about possible appointments for himself or his pupils, memorials and protests to one authority or another. The small body of his literary expressions includes a poem or two and the dedications and elaborate titles of a number of his works. The few occasional canons for friends and acquaintances are of personal as well as musical interest.

For the expression of emotion, however, Bach hardly needed to resort to words. The focus of his emotional life was undoubtedly on religion, and on the service of religion through music. This emphasis would be clear from his work alone, of which music written for church services makes up by far the greater portion—music that constitutes his greatest effort and achievement. But there is external evidence, too, of his deep interest in religious matters in the extensive list of theological books included in the appraisal of his estate. In the religious controversies of the time, Bach quite naturally ranged himself, although passively, on the side of orthodoxy and against Pietism— a movement that, on the one hand, sought an intensification of individual religious experience and, on the other, was tinged with a certain hostility toward elaborate church music. He was a pious but not fanatical Lutheran who considered the performance of every duty to be in the service of God, whether it was that of organist, court musician (capellmeister), or cantor.

Bach did not feel any urge to contribute to the literature of music theory. It was expected that an accomplished musician of his time could realize a figured bass at sight, that is, improvise a complete accompaniment, usually in four voices. Bach wrote down or dictated the meaning of the figures while teaching Anna Magdalena, but after a few pages he remarked, characteristically, that the rest had better be taught by word of mouth. He also dictated the fundamentals of figured-bass realization to his pupils, for the most part following a good textbook by Friedrich Erhardt Niedt, though Bach added a few interesting ideas of his own. These two sets of thorough-bass rules constitute the whole of Bach's theoretical writing. In his later years he was persuaded to become a member of the Society of Musical Sciences, which had been founded by one of his lesser pupils, but his contributions consisted exclusively of music, and Carl Philipp Emanuel expressly stated—referring to the discussions of proportions and temperament of which certain contemporaries were particularly fond—that "he was never a friend of dry, mathematical stuff."

What Bach looked like is hard to tell, for we have only one definitely authentic portrait of the composer, from the time when he was in his sixties. This picture was painted by Elias Gottlob Haussmann, official portraitist of the Leipzig town council, and has survived in two copies, one from 1746 (today in the City Museum of Leipzig, formerly in the possession of the St. Thomas School, and in relatively poor condition) and one—an exact replica—from 1748 (presumably later owned by Carl Philipp Emanuel Bach, today in the possession of William H. Scheide of Princeton, New Jersey, and in fine condition—see the dust jacket of this volume).[4]

Haussmann's portraits were copied several times at various periods. The first engraved portrait of Bach, executed in 1774 by Samuel Gottlieb Kütner, acknowledges a painting by Haussmann as its model. Kütner had studied in Leipzig together with Carl Philipp Emanuel's son Johann Sebastian, a gifted artist who died in Rome, not quite thirty years old, in 1778. Carl Philipp Emanuel, who may have had a personal influence on Kütner's portrait, called it "clearly done and a fair likeness."

The fact that in all the portraits Bach is wearing the wig customary in his period is doubtless partly responsible for a certain neutral, official, impersonal air they display. Yet by the Romantic standards we might apply he seems to have looked more like a magistrate than an artist.

HERITAGE AND ACHIEVEMENT

Bach's musical education was begun by members of his family, presumably his father, and certainly his brother, the Ohrdruf organist Johann Christoph. While he was at Lüneburg, Bach may have studied with the able organist and composer Georg Böhm. But by far the greater part of his musical knowledge he had to acquire for himself.

Throughout his life Bach showed an insatiable interest in all kinds of music, old and new, and of all nations. In his youth he traveled to hear the great musicians who were within what he considered walking distance—a radius of well over two hundred miles. So he heard Johann Adam Reinken, pupil of Jan Pieterszon Sweelinck, the great Netherlander who had made important contributions to the development of fugue composition and had passed along, to a host of organists, his knowledge of musical practice and

4. For a discussion of Bach iconography see *BD* IV, pp. 11–40 and 353–64, and Wolff, *Bach Essays*, pp. 20 and 400.

theory—the latter based partly on Gioseffo Zarlino's. For weeks Bach listened to the greatest northern musician of an older generation, Dietrich Buxtehude, who gave to organ playing an unheard-of majesty, splendor, and intensity, and who also excelled in the composition of church and chamber music. In his early years, too, he heard the court capelle of Celle and its cultivation of French music in an attempt to imitate the court of the kings at Versailles.

A great asset in Bach's development must have been his friendship with Johann Gottfried Walther, a distant relative who was town organist at Weimar when Bach was court organist there. The individual who, in Forkel's story, convinced Bach that music could be written that was too hard for him to play at sight was presumably Walther. Like Bach, he developed great interest in the newest Italian instrumental music, and the two vied with each other in transcribing violin concertos so that they could be played on an organ or harpsichord alone. Walther was an outstanding scholar as well as musician; his *Musicalisches Lexicon,* the first dictionary of music to include biographical articles, contained the first published biographical note on Bach.

Bach assimilated all the achievements to which his time was heir as completely as if he had consciously set out to do so. He knew some of the music of the sixteenth century, and on occasion he arranged a Mass by Palestrina for performance with wind instruments, double bass, and organ accompaniment. His treatment of a *cantus firmus,* in such movements as the Credo and Confiteor of the B Minor Mass, recalls procedures antedating even Palestrina. And he had a comprehensive knowledge of what had gone on in seventeenth-century Italy. He possessed a volume of music by Girolamo Frescobaldi, published in 1635, and as late as 1747 he wrote old-fashioned fugues that constituted, both in their structure and in his use for them of the name *ricercari,* an homage to Frescobaldi. Bach used themes by Girolamo Legrenzi, employed compositions by various other seventeenth-century Italian composers for thorough-bass exercises, knew the music of Arcangelo Corelli, and was familiar with works of Tomaso Albinoni, Francesco Antonio Bonporti (from whom he borrowed the title *invention*), and Antonio Vivaldi. Italy, too, had been the birthplace of the concerto, in which one or several solo instruments were set against a larger body of *ripieno* (filling in) instruments. Bach's Brandenburg Concertos make use of various concerto ideas as if in systematic review.

But it was not only to Italy that Bach's attention turned. In France musical development had been given a significant impetus by Jean-Baptiste Lully, the Florentine who became the founder of French opera. A dancer himself, Lully stylized a whole galaxy of dances for the use of the opera and the court. His pointed rhythms and his new technique of orchestral performance fascinated the English and the Germans as well as the French artists for whom they were devised. He greatly influenced a succession of French harpsichordists—who cultivated a brilliant and variegated style of writing for the organ as well as for the clavier—the greatest of whom was François Couperin. That Bach was entirely at home in the French style is illustrated both by the story of a contest he was ready to engage in with Louis Marchand and by his own writing. His early keyboard style owes much to Jean-Henri d'Anglebert, Nicolas de Grigny, and Couperin.

The so-called Andreas Bach Book and the Möller Manuscript, two hand-written anthologies compiled after 1700 by Johann Christoph Bach of Ohr-druf, Johann Sebastian's principal keyboard teacher, shed some welcome light on the technically demanding, musically attractive, stylistically diversified, "international" body of materials that the young virtuoso and composer was exposed to early on. The multifaceted repertoire included north, middle, and south German works as well as Italian and French pieces in various genres and formats.[5]

It need hardly be stated that Bach was well versed in the music of the German-speaking countries. Carl Philipp Emanuel's hastily written letters to Forkel mention three Austrians whose music Bach studied and esteemed: Johann Jacob Froberger, who united the fruits of his studies under Fre-scobaldi with what he learned from French composers; Johann Caspar Kerll, an outstanding composer of Masses; and Johann Joseph Fux, who codified the teaching of counterpoint in a form still in use today. Strangely enough, Carl Philipp Emanuel does not mention the greatest German musician of the seventeenth century, Heinrich Schütz—a musician of the first rank who, as a pupil of Giovanni Gabrieli and capellmeister at Dresden and Copenhagen, was also an important link between the North and the South. Doubtless the concise and vigorous vocal language of the man whose music follows the inflections of German speech more eloquently than that of any other com-poser, and who first gave lyric and dramatic intensity to the musical setting of the Passion, meant little to Carl Philipp Emanuel.[6] But the library of the school Johann Sebastian attended in Lüneburg and, especially, the music collection of the Leipzig St. Thomas School contained several works by Schütz, and it is not likely that, with his insatiable curiosity, he neglected to examine them. One other name, at least, is missing from Carl Philipp Ema-nuel's brief list: Johann Theile, pupil of Schütz and teacher of both Buxte-hude and Friedrich Wilhelm Zachow, the teacher of Handel. Theile, a scholarly musician, was the author of a *Musicalisches Kunstbuch,* a book of

5. Cf. the detailed inventory in *Keyboard Music from the Andreas Bach Book and the Möller Manuscript,* ed. Robert Hill, Harvard Publications in Music, vol. 16 (Cambridge, Mass., 1991), pp. xxix–xlvi.

6. He owned, however, a rare copy of Schütz's obituary, which may have come from his father's library (cf. *BJ* 1991, p. 121).

applied music theory of which Walther made a copy and which might have supplied Bach with the idea of the construction of *The Art of Fugue.* Closer to Bach's time were Johann Pachelbel, master of the organ chorale and teacher of Bach's Ohrdruf brother, Johann Christoph; the greatly gifted Johann Kuhnau, Bach's immediate predecessor in Leipzig; and finally Johann Caspar Ferdinand Fischer, who may have studied with Lully and whose *Ariadne Musicae* furnished Bach with themes for his Inventions and the idea for *The Well-Tempered Clavier.*

Among the composers of his own generation there were fewer to whom he was deeply indebted. But they included Vivaldi, whose concertos Bach transcribed, and Domenico Scarlatti, born in the same year as Bach, whose sparklingly original compositions for the harpsichord left their mark on Bach's own keyboard style.

The musicians of the late seventeenth and early eighteenth centuries were much concerned with the differences in national styles, and these differences formed a favorite topic of contemporary comment. But whereas Couperin aimed at *les goûts réunis,* the French and Italian styles united, and Henry Purcell deliberately introduced Italian elements into English music in order to counteract French domination, Bach, who assimilated any style, form, or pattern within reach, took care to treat separately the material he drew from different sources. This is strikingly illustrated in Part II of the *Clavier-Übung,* which contains two compositions for harpsichord: the *Italian Concerto* and the *French Overture.* Similarly, he opened Part III with a *Praeludium* that was really a full-fledged toccata, including fugued sections, in the manner of the north German organists; and he concluded the book with a great *Fuga* in three sections, a modernized version of the *ricercar* cultivated by the seventeenth-century Italians. The two pieces are in the same key and have become popular together, the fugue being known as the St. Anne's.

Bach's gift of differentiation was not confined to keeping apart elements derived from different sources. Even more strikingly, it seized on what to casual inspection would have seemed minor differences, and it evolved out of these differences clearly distinguished types. By imparting to each piece the most consistent development of a particular technique and character, Bach gave to his work as a whole an inexhaustible variety. Even the straightforward four-part chorale harmonizations illustrate this; frequently in them a particular melodic turn or rhythmic pattern is introduced at the beginning and by the most perfect dovetailing is carried right through to the end. The more elaborate chorales and chorale preludes show the same procedure. Many an individual one has a spectacular uniformity, while seen together they exhibit the most astonishing diversity. An instance in which Bach explicitly calls attention to this favorite principle of his is in Part I of the *Clavier-Übung*, which contains six suites called partitas, a name used by his German predecessors. Each partita opens with an introductory movement of a different type, and each bears a different name: *praeludium, sinfonia, fantasia, ouverture, praeambulum, toccata.*

The ability corollary to that of differentiation was that of bringing any potentiality to its fullest possible realization. It will be worthwhile to consider briefly three of the many aspects in which that ability was supreme.

In the matter of pure size—the maximum extension of the material consistent with its perfect coherence and inner tension—Bach realized one of the goals toward which music had been tending since 1600. His preludes and fugues, sonatas, concertos, and suites, as well as the individual movements of which they are made up, are in general conceived on a larger scale than any earlier ones. This is equally true of his choral works. The B Minor Mass, to take the most extreme example, is subdivided into more sections than any other composition of its kind, and, as unprecedented intensity is poured into each section, the work leaves all its models far behind in greatness of execution as well as conception. The oratorios and Passions likewise show this new monumentality, achieved through the realization of Bach's ideal of unity in diversity. Whereas the texts of the Passions of Schütz had been exclusively biblical, except for the opening and closing movements, and those set by Telemann, for example, had consisted exclusively of verses by contemporary writers, Bach's oratorios and Passions characteristically included not only both these elements but chorales as well. In them, too, the various classes of participants—the narrative evangelist, the individual characters, the groups and crowds participating in the action, and finally the individual and collective commentators on the story—were each distinguished and developed to an unexampled degree, giving these works dimensions far greater than those of their predecessors.

Or take the matter of contrapuntal intricacy. Not the least part of Bach's genius was his gift of inventing entirely independent and contrasting themes that would go well together, and themes that would combine well with their own precise imitations. The application of this talent made his music more complex and exciting than that of any of his contemporaries. Undoubtedly he was the greatest master of fugue who ever lived. And fugue was not just a type of piece but a whole technique that permeated the entire body of early eighteenth-century music—a technique of which *a fugue* represents only the most comprehensive and consistent application. The opening movement of a cantata, the allegro of an overture, and the second and perhaps the last movement of a sonata were likely to be fugues. Even the *ritornello* of an aria or concerto movement was often cast in the mold of a short fugue. And where the treatment of a piece was freer, its texture was usually shot through with canonic or fugal imitation. Assayed for its contrapuntal content, Bach's music is richer than any other music based on functional harmony, and thus in this respect, too, it marks the climax of a long ascent.

The third aspect particularly worth considering here is Bach's treatment of rhythmic motion. Any piece of his music has a sort of atomic rhythmic basis—a smallest note value beyond which there is no further significant subdivision. In many of the four-part chorales, for example, the atomic unit is the eighth note, and the four parts taken together produce an almost uninterrupted perpetual motion in eighths. In countless other, more complex compositions (like, say, the Allemande of the G Major French Suite) the unit is the sixteenth; and the continuous sixteenth-note motion, never interrupted from the beginning to the end except for cadences of primary importance, is shared and divided up among the parts with a subtlety and variety that seem infinite. The superimposing of varying rhythmic relations on this continuous flow represents another triumphant realization of the ideal of many things in one. This rhythmic treatment was not Bach's invention. Examples of it are to be found in Corelli, Vivaldi, and, above all, Buxtehude. But in their hands it had been no more than an effective device, whereas in his it became an infinitely fruitful artistic principle.

What is true of the monumental proportions, the contrapuntal intensity, the rhythmic consistency of Bach's works is just as true of the cogency of his themes, the expressiveness of his melodies, the force and richness of his harmony, the diversity and logic of his orchestration. In all of them he brought seeds well germinated by his predecessors to fruition on a scale undreamed of before him. And thus without any break with the past—in fact, as the great conservator of its legacies—Bach took what had been handed down to him and treated it with a boldness that often seemed almost revolutionary.

He took the cantata of Buxtehude and Kuhnau, for example, which had been a comparatively small genre, and amplified it in some instances almost beyond recognition by the introduction of patterns and forms that had grown up in the Italian opera: the recitative with figured-bass accompaniment or with obbligato instruments, and the *da capo* aria. He also evolved a scheme for his cantatas that was largely new, though composed of old elements. In this scheme the text of the cantata was based on one of the fine old Lutheran hymns. One of the stanzas was presented complete and unchanged in the first movement, in the form of a great and elaborate chorale setting; another was sung in a straight four-part setting at the end. In between, there came other stanzas, some perhaps unchanged, some paraphrased by the libretto writer, some using the chorale melody either in the vocal parts or in the orchestra, some made into recitatives and arias on completely original material.

The unaccompanied sonatas and partitas for violin and for violoncello represent another instance of Bach's taking hints from the past and basing on them structures of the utmost complexity. Once the figured bass had been introduced, chamber music without it was a rarity. By the end of the seventeenth century the technique of polyphonic playing on a stringed instrument had been fully developed, particularly on the violin and the viol, by such musicians as Thomas Baltzer, Niccola Matteis, J. H. Schmelzer, Biber, J. J. Walther, and J. P. Westhoff. But none of them had written unaccompanied music for a stringed instrument on any such scale as even one of the Bach works, let alone such series of them as his two sets of six each.

In ensemble music Bach changed the role of the harpsichord in instrumental combinations from that of mere accompanying instrument to that of full partner. Before him, it had been used either alone or merely to supply the harmonies indicated by the figured bass. Chamber music with a fully written-out, contrapuntal part for the harpsichord had been a rarity; with Bach it became almost the rule, so far as works for one other independent instrument and harpsichord were concerned. The harpsichord, furthermore, had never been made the soloist in a concerto. Bach wrote and arranged concertos not only for one harpsichord but also for two, three, and four harpsichords with accompanying instruments.

And although in many of the achievements mentioned, Bach represented the climactic end of long lines of development (lines abandoned after him, partly, as his sons confessed, because he had carried them to heights his successors felt unable to surpass), his use of the harpsichord as a primary instrument in chamber music and the concerto was one of the ways in which he pointed directly forward. Chamber music with obbligato clavier (but no clavier concerto) was written in France, too, during the last decade of Bach's life, independently of his influence, by J. J. Cassanéa de Mondonville, Jean-Philippe Rameau, and others. Carl Philipp Emanuel acted upon the stimuli he had received from his father's work as well as from France. Through him, then, and through his brother and pupil Johann Christian, the idea spread and became fashionable in the last third of the eighteenth century. This marked the beginning not only of the sonata for pianoforte and another solo instrument but also of the piano trio, quartet, and so on. And the concerto for one or more keyboard instruments and orchestra, which Bach originated, never ceased to inspire Mozart and has remained, through many metamorphoses, a standard type of composition to this day.

ATTITUDE TOWARD THE ART OF MUSIC

Bach did not care to write about himself. Although publicly invited by Johann Mattheson to contribute biographical notes to Mattheson's *Ehren-pforte*, the "Triumphal Arch" that was to contain a collection of biographies of various outstanding musicians, Bach remained silent. As far as we know, he never wrote a word concerning the aesthetic speculations or controversies of the time, although he was directly involved in the Scheibe-Birnbaum controversy of the late 1730s and he did help bring to print the rebuttal of a rector's attack on music in the late 1740s. He was a practical musician and evidently had no desire to appear to be anything else. Yet he possessed a definite artistic creed. It shows in certain casual remarks (about which we are informed chiefly through Johann Nikolaus Forkel's book), in the titles he gave to certain works, and in his music itself. So the task of piecing together Bach's philosophy of music is not as hopeless as it might at first seem.

When Johannes Tinctoris, the musical cyclopedist of the fifteenth century, wrote his book on the effects of music, he began with the words *Deum dele-ctare, Dei laudes decorare* ("To please God, to embellish the praise of God"). This description of the function of art reflects a conception prevalent throughout the Middle Ages. Tinctoris added a commentary that is worth remembering: "For it is proper to any artist that he be most satisfied with his work if it be perfect. Wherefore it must be held that God, who has not known a work of imperfection, must be most pleased with the most perfect art since he has created most perfect work himself." Such thoughts were still deeply rooted in Bach's mind, as they had been in the minds of his predecessors. That his church music was designed to deepen the worship of God and to embellish His service need not be emphasized. Bach expressed his attitude clearly enough by regularly inscribing his scores of sacred music with the letters J. J. (*Jesu, Juva:* "Jesus, help") at the beginning, and S. D. G. (*Soli Deo Gloria:* "to God alone the glory") at the end. Even in an unpretentious little volume of pieces for the musical instruction of his firstborn son, the *Clavier-Büchlein* for Wilhelm Friedemann Bach, he opened the first page of music with the letters I. N. J. (*In Nomine Jesu:* "in the Name of Jesus"). He did not shed his religion when he composed for instruction or other secular purposes.

The feeling that all music was in the service of God went even further. When Bach dictated to his pupils excerpts from Niedt's book on thorough bass, he reworded thoughts expressed by Niedt as follows: "The thorough bass is the most perfect foundation of music, being played with both hands in such manner that the left hand plays the notes written down while the right adds consonances and dissonances, in order to make a well-sounding harmony to the Glory of God and the permissible delectation of the spirit; and the aim and final reason, as of all music, so of the thorough bass should be none else but the Glory of God and the recreation of the mind. Where this is not observed, there will be no real music but only a devilish hubbub."

These sentences reveal that for both musicians even the realization of a figured bass—the most rudimentary element of musical craft, used in instrumental as well as vocal performance and in secular as well as sacred music—was considered an act of homage to God. Quite clearly, it had to be proper if it was to be useful at all; and if it was perfect, it necessarily—as Tinctoris's words imply—pleased God as well as the player or composer himself. In his secular work Bach without doubt strove for perfection as earnestly as in his compositions for divine service. Secular and sacred music were used with different texts and in different surroundings, but evidently Bach did not recognize a difference in principle between the two. For this reason he did not hesitate to make double use of originally secular works by adapting them to sacred texts, or to include movements from concertos and other instrumental compositions in his cantatas. The Osanna in the B Minor Mass was originally a movement in a *dramma per musica,* a secular choral cantata performed as a serenade during a visit the king and queen made to the city of Leipzig, but in its later position within the Mass it forms as glorious a piece of religious praise as any music written specifically for the purpose could have been. The fact is that we, though we may well live in an irreligious age, have come back to the realization that there is no essential difference between religious and secular music, since, as we would put it, any fine music can serve to intensify the emotional content of any text that is at all similar in mood. And often the music Bach wrote for secular festivities rose so far above its text and the occasion for which it was composed that it fairly cried out to be refitted to words more appropriate to its sublime qualities.

In the opinion of Bach's time, one of the foremost aims of music, sacred or secular, was the *Ausdrückung der Affecten,* the expression of the *affetti.* The somewhat elusive word *affetto* means mood, emotion, or passion. Literature had striven since the sixteenth century to represent human passions in their most arresting forms. The same striving in music had first crystallized in the madrigal, a splendid vehicle for the new self-assertion of the individual that was typical of the Renaissance. When the classicist attitude of the early Renaissance was superseded by the Baroque urge to create more and more grandiose effects, the artistic expression of emotions became increasingly exaggerated and exalted in tone. Bach's contemporaries trusted the expressive power of music implicitly; they believed, for instance, that music could voice

love, jealousy, and hate, as well as joy and sorrow. Bach himself strove sedu-
lously to vest his texts with the most intense, appropriate music—exactly as
Handel did, using different means. He carefully suited his music to the mood
and meaning of the text even in his organ chorales, where the text itself was
not presented with the music, though it was familiar to the congregation.
He expected his pupils to do the same; one of them made a special point, in
a letter of application for an organist's post, of the fact that he had been
instructed by Capellmeister Bach to present chorales "not just offhand but
in accordance with the *Affect* of the words."

It is obvious that fast, high, diatonic, lightly harmonized music will tend
to sound animated or joyful; slow, low, chromatic, elaborately harmonized
music, reflective or sad. Bach, while utilizing to the fullest extent such natural affinities between musical means and the emotions, developed a musical
language that was at once expressive and flexible. Attempts have been made
to describe this language as a kind of formula technique: a set of symbolic
patterns to which Bach would recur whenever the textual situation required.
But to ascribe to Bach a predominantly intellectual routine of this sort is to
overestimate the importance of certain elements apparent in his music. He
was neither so poorly endowed with imagination that he had to establish
for himself a whole reservoir of ready-made patterns, to draw on whenever
inspiration failed, nor so theoretically minded that he would heed the pedantic attempts of his contemporaries to establish music as a branch of rhetoric.

It is true, however, that Bach frequently used descriptive musical patterns.
The word "ascend" he would usually set to a series of ascending notes; the
word "fall," to a large skip downward; and instances such as the scale runs
picturing the rending of the veil in the temple in both Passions are famous.
The idea of following is often made evident by parts following one another
in canon at a close distance. Wonderful examples of musical description are
in the *St. Matthew Passion* the slow tremoli of the strings reflecting the tremor
of the tortured heart, or the accompaniment in waving lines alluding to the
soul that "swims in tears"; in the *St. John* the tortured climactic line of the
Evangelist as he tells how Peter "wept bitterly," or the whiplike rhythm of
the passage that tells about the scourging of Jesus; in the *Actus Tragicus*, the
duet with its sudden hush of the accompaniment at the words *sanft und stille*
(soft and still). In introducing such patterns, Bach followed a tradition that
had originated in the French chanson of the sixteenth century, grown in the
madrigal, and found noble application to sacred music in the work of Schütz
and others. Bach's own pictorial devices are occasionally somewhat naïve, but
usually they form a close bond between the text and the music, and often
they not only illustrate the words but add great depth to the expression of
their *Affect*.

Not the least asset in Bach's musical setting of his texts was his contrapuntal ingenuity. This statement may seem surprising. We are accustomed to considering the consistent application of technical devices in music as an impediment to the free flow of imagination. We are inclined to say that a fugue is expressive *in spite* of being a fugue. But there is, as Goethe remarked, "no form without content." Bach was the last of a great line of composers for whom the contrapuntal was a normal mode of thinking and in whose music contrapuntal devices were a natural and idiomatic element, not an archaic one to be revived for special purposes.

When Bach combines two subjects, they are almost invariably of different type and motion. One, perhaps, proceeds in skips, the other in steps; one in long notes, the other in short ones. Each has its definite character (disjunct and slow, conjunct and fast) and, undoubtedly, its individual affective connotations—definite in that they are unlike those of any other melodic configuration, but not in the sense that their "emotional character" can be defined in words. When two such differentiated subjects are played or sung together, we experience the mutual penetration of two more or less related, more or less contrasted elements, and perhaps the complementing of one group of affective connotations by another. Inversion of a subject, on the other hand, establishes a new thematic character without relinquishing the original material. And the use of canon creates a feeling of compact and vigorous logic that could not be achieved by any other means. Bach never lost sight of this basic truth. Like many a great contrapuntist before him, he employed specific contrapuntal devices to emphasize in a specific way the musical expression of his text; and we feel the same expressive values when we encounter the corresponding contrapuntal devices in instrumental music. In the *Symbolum Nicenum* of the B Minor Mass, the opening movement, the Credo, climaxes the elaboration of the initial theme by introducing an augmentation. And the Confiteor, the concluding movement of the Creed, introduces, against the background of a subject whose development seemed fully sufficient to carry the entire movement, a slower-moving intonation in canon and then crowns it with an appearance of the subject in augmentation. At such moments, Bach seems to use a hierarchy of speeds to symbolize the hierarchy of worlds.

In 1747 Bach obliged Johann Gottfried Fulde, a student of theology, by writing a puzzle canon in the latter's autograph book.[7] It was a double canon—that is, two different melodies, each with its own canonic imitation

---

7. See No. 242. This canon belongs to the Fourteen Canons, BWV 1087, written on the ground of the aria from the so-called Goldberg Variations; cf. Wolff, *Bach Essays*, pp. 162–77.

(the English composers of the period would have called it "four parts in two")—moving above the bass Bach had used in the canon for the Musical Society, which appears on the 1746 portrait. Bach did not indicate the solution in musical terms, but he added the inscription *Christus Coronabit Crucigeros* ("Christ will Crown the Crossbearers"). This *symbolum* contains a contrast of moods, with its promise that the sad (the top begins with a mournful chromatic descent) shall be happy. Such a contrast of moods, the reader was supposed to conclude, could be expressed in the canon only by contrary motion, and Bach, in his *symbolum,* not only hinted in this manner at the principle of solution but also indicated by the three capital *C*'s that the "pivot tone" of the original lines and their inversion was C. The canon is an occasional and unpretentious composition, without text, but it reveals to us how strongly Bach felt the change of *Affect* accomplished solely by inversion, trusting the mere indication of a similar contrast in words to tell any able musician the puzzle's solution.

   "*Le génie n'est autre chose qu'une grande aptitude à la patience*" (Genius is nothing but a great aptitude for patience). Thus did Buffon in his inaugural speech at the French Academy in 1753 express an idea that was a favorite with Bach, too, who used to say, in homelier fashion, "I have had to work hard; anyone who works just as hard will get just as far." In these words he harked back to the heritage of his family. Music was a craft. It could be taught, and it could be learned. Assiduity must lead to perfection. To have talent was a matter of course: had not everybody, for instance, five healthy fingers on each hand, just like Bach?

   How far the view of music as a craft went can be seen from the fact that Carl Philipp Emanuel Bach ended his "Essay on the True Art of Playing the Clavier" (1753) with instructions on how to create a "free fantasy." The rules he offered—and definite rules they were—had been applied by Johann Sebastian in parts of his *Chromatic Fantasy* and certain preludes, and Bach himself could have derived them from examples by d'Anglebert and Froberger. Not even the free fantasy, then, was a form in which the composer could simply abandon himself to the vagaries of romantic dreaming. It was Carl Philipp Emanuel, too, who reported to Forkel that when Father Bach had heard the beginning of a fugue he would at once state "what contrapuntal devices it would be possible to apply, and which of them the composer by rights ought to apply." The fugue had definite principles, and a given opening would raise certain expectations; anyone who knew the craft would derive satisfaction from the very fulfillment of those expectations.

   Bach not only believed that music could be taught; he was himself the most successful teacher of organists and composers since the days of Giovanni Gabrieli and Sweelinck. In teaching composition, he saw to it that his pupils did not compose at the instrument. They were to learn a spiritual craft and a mental discipline, not just a manual technique. What they had to say should be completely thought out in their minds, and their imagination should be reliable enough not to need a clavier. Bach himself, it appears from his manuscripts, wrote down his compositions with remarkably little hesitation, on the whole, and the greatest exceptions to this statement are indeed among the pieces that had to be written in a hurry. He did not write great numbers of drafts and work over them repeatedly, as Beethoven did. But he did make sketches, and he not infrequently changed what he had written, not only during the first writing down of a composition but sometimes long after that.[8] Particularly when he had occasion to copy a work he had written some time earlier, he usually did not resist the urge to revise it as he went along.[9] Unless he was in great haste, as he was occasionally when he had to get a new cantata ready for the coming Sunday, his writing was exceptionally clear, and his holographs radiate the calm assurance of a man who was never in doubt about what he wanted and how to achieve it.

One of Bach's chief concerns was the purity of polyphony, the logic of part writing. It is the essence of polyphony that a definite number of voices is maintained throughout a section, movement, or entire composition. On the title pages of his cantatas, Bach used to indicate the number of parts, reckoning all the sopranos as one, all the first violins as one, a solo oboe as one. He saw to it that each part strictly preserved its independence and individuality. He required the same strictness of his pupils, reminding them that the parts were to behave like "persons who conversed together as if in a select company." "Knights of the Keyboard" was his ridiculing term for those who intermixed their parts or failed to give each of them a consistent continuity. Any of Bach's polyphonic compositions for a keyboard instrument could easily be set out in open score and played by an ensemble of instruments, exactly as some of Frescobaldi's works had been and a few of Bach's own last compositions were.

When the first pupils assembled around Bach, he undertook, in his thorough manner, to teach them composition through practical examples. While at Weimar, he composed a set of organ chorales that would cover the needs of the entire church year—the *Little Organ Book,* which he never quite completed. The music was evidently designed for use in divine service, but at the same time it was meant to show how pieces of this kind should be contrived, as appears from the characteristic antithesis with which he inscribed the work:

---

8. For an extensive and exemplary discussion of the subject see Robert L. Marshall, *The Compositional Process of J. S. Bach: A Study of the Autograph Scores of the Vocal Works,* 2 vols. (Princeton, N.J., 1972).

9. Cf. Forkel's account, "Bach the Reviser of His Own Works," below, pp. 474–76.

Dem Höchsten Gott allein zu Ehren,   In praise of the Almighty's will,
Dem Nächsten, draus sich zu belehren.   And for my neighbor's greater skill.

It was during Bach's years at Cöthen, however, that he most clearly expressed pedagogical intentions. For the instruction of Wilhelm Friedemann he wrote fifteen two-part *praeambula* (preludes) and fifteen three-part *fantasiae.* When he collected these pieces into a separate work, calling the two-part compositions *inventiones* and the three-part ones *sinfoniae,* he provided the new manuscript with a title page on which he promised the "lovers of the clavier, and especially those desirous of learning, upright instruction" that he would teach them to play well in two and three parts and, in addition, "not alone to have good *inventiones* [ideas, particularly thematic ones] but to develop them well." These were not idle words. The first six Inventions Bach composed (in C major, D minor, E minor, F major, G major, and A minor) were all built up on short motifs and thus strikingly illustrated the technique of elaboration of such motifs. The initial motifs of the first three were all based on stepwise progressions including only isolated skips; the other three, on broken chords. Of the latter, the first outlined a tonic; the second, tonic and dominant; the third, tonic, dominant, and tonic. This was as systematic a demonstration as any student of composition might ask for, and it showed how inspiration could be summoned and channeled at the bidding of the mind.

Bach did not believe in teaching isolated elements or fragments of music. He avoided using "species" in teaching counterpoint. He never wrote an exercise in composition or velocity that was not a fully rounded composition. Even where he set out to demonstrate a specific technical feature, he was never only a teacher. More than a third of the preludes of *The Well-Tempered Clavier* (Part I) were conceived as studies for Wilhelm Friedemann, but the very consistency with which a definite point was carried through in them is one of the secrets not only of their greatness but of their attractiveness as well. And this, clearly enough, was the aim of Bach himself, who stated that the work was intended "for the use and profit of the musical youth desirous of learning as well as for the pastime of those already skilled"—words that might be taken as a motto for the whole of his work, vocal as well as instrumental.

Neither the Inventions and the Sinfonias nor the two books of *The Well-Tempered Clavier,* though ready and probably meant for publication, were printed during Bach's lifetime. The list of his works that actually achieved such distinction was extraordinarily small. Of the vocal works, only one was printed, in part books, a cantata—it will be noticed that Bach used the term *motetto,* since he still applied the term "cantata" in general only to works for solo voice—written at Mühlhausen when Bach was twenty-two years old, to celebrate the inauguration of new town councilors. The texts of a number of other cantatas were printed for special occasions; and the Organ Chorales published by Johann Georg Schübler in the last years of Bach's life were actually arrangements of cantata movements. But with these exceptions the works published in Bach's lifetime were exclusively instrumental. There were altogether seven items: four bearing the *Clavier-Übung* ("Keyboard Practice"); the Canonic Variations on the Christmas Song *Vom Himmel hoch da komm ich her;* the *Musical Offering;* and *The Art of Fugue*—the last not actually issued until after the composer's death.

Part I of the *Clavier-Übung* contained six partitas, published singly at first; when the series of six was completed, Bach called it his *opus primum,* disregarding, in accordance with the custom of the time, the vocal work that had preceded it. Part II of the *Clavier-Übung* presented orchestral genres in the garb of harpsichord music. Part III contained music for the organ—in particular, a selection of organ chorales in generous variety. The last part of the *Clavier-Übung* consisted of the *Aria with 30 Variations,* which became known as the Goldberg Variations. The *Musical Offering,* finally, represented chamber music, in the form of a sonata, fugues, and canons. These five works together constitute a complete survey of contemporary instrumental music.

With his talent for differentiation and his striving for perfection, Bach succeeded in giving to every form included in these works what appears its ultimate and perfect shape. Accordingly they, too, offer ideal models for the study of composition. But Bach did not emphasize this point on the title pages of the *Clavier-Übung,* which simply promise the "lovers of music" and, in one case, the "connoisseurs of such work" a "spiritual enjoyment" or "refreshment of the mind" *(Gemüths-Ergötzung).*

The Canonic Variations (really a chorale partita) were written as a candidate's exercise upon joining the Musical Society. This was the most "learned" work Bach had ever composed, a true showpiece of art and artifice, but it was also a thoroughly enjoyable piece of music. It shows the tendency of Bach in his later years to concern himself with the greatest intricacies of his art. As he grew older, he reduced what he said more and more to its essentials. Less than ever concerned with worldly success, he sought perfection increasingly in the utmost consistency of logic and construction. This last phase of his inner development led to the composition of *The Art of Fugue*—one of the loftiest accomplishments of the human mind.

The Art of Fugue professed to be a work of instruction, just as the Inventions had been. It was not a textbook but, like Theile's *Kunstbuch,* a collection of compositions, demonstrating progressively the vast possibilities of fugue writing in all its complexity. Centering on one tonality and based on a single chief subject, it led from the simple beauty of archaic one-theme fugues to heights of contrapuntal accumulation and emotional intensity never before reached. Bach finished a first version of the work around 1742, but the original plan grew in his mind over the next several years, and he died before he could finish the dome with which he had intended to crown the structure.

Bach was intensely interested in the problems of form. When he wrote the Inventions, he evidently intended to give as systematic a demonstration of formal construction as he actually offered of thematic invention, but he let himself be carried away by his interest in asymmetrical formations. Years later, in Part III of the *Clavier-Übung,* he fulfilled the unredeemed promise. Here he included four *duetti* (inventions, we might call them, had not Bach himself abandoned the name) that demonstrate not only four different patterns of form but four different principles of construction as well. These pieces prove how conscious Bach himself was of constructive technique. His form was in general based on relations between separate sections. These relations ranged from complete identity of passages, on the one hand, to the return of a single principle of elaboration or a mere thematic allusion, on the other. The resulting patterns were often symmetrical, but by no means necessarily so. Sometimes the relations between the various sections make up a maze of interwoven threads that only detailed analysis can unravel. Usually, however, a few dominant features afford proper orientation at first sight or hearing, and while in the course of study one may discover unending subtleties, one is never at a loss to grasp the unity that holds together every single creation by Bach.

He was not satisfied with the accomplishment of unity in single movements. While he acquiesced in the use of the four-movement Baroque sonata (slow-fast-slow-fast), which had become a traditional scheme, chiefly through Corelli, he strove in most of his other works, and even in certain sonatas, to create stronger connections between the movements. He would tie separate parts to each other, just as within individual movements, by twofold use of the same material or principle. Such connections often involved symmetry. A characteristic example is in the concluding movement of the first Brandenburg Concerto, where there is a minuet with three interludes: a trio for wind instruments, a polacca in contrasting meter, for strings, and a second trio for winds. Equally striking symmetry may be found in one of the sonatas for harpsichord and violin (G major, first version) and in the motet *Jesu, meine Freude.* More or less strictly applied, the same kind of construction appears in the vast majority of his vocal works. The *St. John Passion* contains a huge centerpiece of symmetrically arranged matching choruses, surrounding the recitative in which Pilate questions Jesus, the crisis in the narrative. The Credo of the B Minor Mass was conceived as a perfectly symmetrical structure (Bach later refocused the symmetry by adding the *Et incarnatus est*), and the last movements of the entire Mass point back to the first with increasing definiteness until one of the early movements *(Gratias agimus tibi)* can return without change (to the words *Dona nobis pacem*), concluding and rounding out the gigantic structure.

He went even further. It was the custom of his time to create and publish series of works, not individual compositions. Every single work Bach intended for publication was a collection of compositions that might be performed singly. His indomitable desire to create unity in whatever he produced found ways to tie together even the separate and independent parts of a collection. Here, too, he followed a century-old tradition. There had been many publications that deliberately presented all of the acknowledged church modes. Then, when musical practice and theory began to recognize major and minor modes and their transpositions, the tonics used in certain series of works were arranged in rational order. Among the masters concerned with this problem were Couperin, Purcell, Buxtehude, Kuhnau, and Fischer. The influence of the last two can be traced in Bach's work. The most conspicuous of his tonal plans was, of course, that of *The Well-Tempered Clavier,* which offered a prelude and fugue in every major and minor key. The most interesting similar plans were those of the Inventions (originally written in the order *C, d, e, F, G, a, b, Bb, A, g, f, E, Eb, D, c*-major tonalities being indicated by capitals, minor by small letters); the English Suites *(A, a, g, F, e, d);* and the first two books of the *Clavier-Übung (Bb, c, a, D, G, e; F, b).* The last work making use of such a scheme was Part III of the *Clavier-Übung;* it was, at the same time, the first in which Bach created material relations between separate compositions exactly corresponding to those he employed to connect movements or sections. There followed works each based on one theme and centering on one tonality: the Goldberg Variations, the Canonic Variations, the *Musical Offering,* and *The Art of Fugue.* Each of these has a ground plan as logical as any single movement by Bach; and particularly the last two display unique greatness of formal conception.

Bach's delight in complicated ground plans, asymmetrical designs, and centralized structures reflects the spirit of his period as strongly as his craving for intensity. The word *baroque,* it will be recalled, originally indicated something oblique or not quite rounded, such as an imperfect pearl, and expressive irrationality of design was one of the foremost characteristics of Baroque art in contrast to the quiet balance of proportions previously sought. But the Baroque artist aimed at monumentality as well as passionate expression. If Bach's desire to portray the emotions found its counterpart chiefly in the literature of his time, his concept of form corresponds more closely to concepts realized in contemporary architecture. The first half of the eighteenth century witnessed a flowering of architecture in Germany that, though based on Italian and, to a lesser extent, French models, was highly original. Bach worked largely in Gothic churches, such as St. Thomas's in Leipzig. But in his own time he saw rise some of the finest structures ever erected in Germany. Augustus the Strong (1670–1733)—who was Frederick Augustus I in Saxony and Augustus II in Poland—had ambitious plans for the embellishment of Dresden. The most important of those carried out was that of the Zwinger, a decorative array of structures surrounding a wide courtyard, intended for all kinds of festivities. When the work was finished (1722), the town council of Dresden, evidently to compete with the king, decided to erect the Church of Our Lady as a landmark worthy of the capital. It was an effectively centralized structure, surmounted by a high stone dome, dominating a large section of the town. The picture of Bach giving a concert on the Silbermann organ in this church, before the nobles and musicians of the court, is one in which all the elements are manifestations of the same spirit: the most eminent organist of his time, playing a representative instrument by the outstanding contemporary organ builder, in a magnificent church erected in his own day.

Bach's reputation was based largely on events such as his organ concerts in Hamburg, Dresden, or Kassel and his appearance before the Prussian court—most of which were acknowledged by the daily press. As an organ virtuoso he was fully recognized in his time. In fact, nobody was deemed his equal in playing or improvising except perhaps Handel, whose playing may have been more enrapturing than Bach's, though it was certainly less profound.

As a composer of fugues and a learned composer in general, Bach was also held in high esteem, at least by connoisseurs. His publications were duly noted in the few musical periodicals of the time, and many of his compositions circulated in manuscript copies. Outside of Leipzig, however, his reputation as a composer rested primarily on his keyboard music. He could not complain of any lack of high patrons: in addition to the offices he actually held, he enjoyed the honorary titles of Royal Polish and Electoral Saxon Court Composer, and capellmeister to one or two minor middle-German courts.

The composer of Bach's time was hardly more concerned with posthumous fame than the medieval artist had been. On the other hand, Bach clearly saw himself, for example, within the tradition of his own extended musical family. He collected the works of the older family members—thereby establishing what Carl Philipp Emanuel Bach later called the "Old-Bach Archive" (*Alt-Bachisches Archiv*)—paying close attention to the modern compositions of his own offspring. Indeed, he began in the late 1730s and 1740s to take precautions in order to preserve his musical estate. Thus, he made—or arranged for—fair copies and duplicate copies of major works. At the same time, Bach had good reason to assume that his successors would not perform the works he wrote any more frequently than he performed compositions written by his predecessors; and indeed most of his vocal works were as promptly laid aside when he died as theirs had been. Among the more notable exceptions, however, were the motets, which have been in the repertoire of the St. Thomas choir in Leipzig since 1750. On a much broader scale and well beyond the Leipzig boundaries, some major keyboard repertories such as the organ works, *The Well-Tempered Clavier,* and *The Art of Fugue* have never ceased to serve as exemplary compositions in strict style. Moreover, Bach had published a sufficient number of works to prove to the musical world that he was a many-sided and able composer. But his success during his own lifetime was never as spectacular as that of Hasse, Telemann, or Handel, and there is little indication either in his own writings or in contemporary comments that his works were considered timeless.

In this respect, as in so many others, Bach was a thoroughly unromantic figure. He carried out any resolve of his—as he proudly pointed out in the dedication of the *Musical Offering*—"as well as possible" and never shrank, as Johann Philipp Kirnberger relates, from the "impossible." But every bit of evidence that comes down to us from his own time makes it clear that he looked upon himself primarily as a capable worker, conscientiously attending to his duties. Surely his unpretentious absorption in his tasks helped give his works the qualities that have made them transcend his time and station.

PART II

Bach's Life in His Own Writings and Other Documents

Eisenach

1685–1695

1. **Report from the Eisenach town chronicle** (*BJ* 1927, p. 142)

    In 1672 at Easter the new Town Musician made music with organ, violins, voices, trumpets, and military drums, as had never before been done by any cantor or town musician [*Haussmann*] as long as Eisenach stood, nor did anything like it happen when Duke Wilhelm visited or at the installation of Duke Johann Georg with his wife.

    J. A. Bach was director of town music in Eisenach and court musician beginning in October 1671, having previously been town musician in Erfurt. In 1684 he was offered an important position as director of the town band in Erfurt but had to decline because the Duke of Eisenach refused to grant him permission to leave.

EISENACH CHURCH RECORDS ON BACH
AND HIS PARENTS

2. **Bach's baptism** (*BD* II, no. 1)

    Monday, March 23, 1685. To Mr. Johann Ambrosius Baach, Town Musician, a son, g[odfathers] Sebastian Nagel, Town Musician at Gotha, and Johann Georg Koch, Ducal Forester of this place. Name: Joh. Sebastian.

    The officiating minister was M. Johann Christoph Zerbst (1643–1719). The actual birthday, Saturday, March 21, is indicated by Walther (No. 304) and the Genealogy (No. 303).

3. **Burial of Bach's mother, Maria Elisabeth Bach, née Lämmerhirt** (Freyse, p. 20)

May 3, 1694. Buried, Johann Ambrosius Baach's wife—without fee.

4. **Remarriage of Bach's father, to Barbara Margaretha, née Keul**
    (Freyse, p. 20)

    November 27, 1694. Johann Ambrosius Baach, Town Musician here,
    and Mrs. Barbara Margaretha, widow of the late Jacob Bartholomaei,
    Deacon at Arnstadt. Married at home.

    *B. M. Bach, daughter of the burgomaster of Arnstadt, was first married to
    Johann Günther Bach (1653–1683), musician and instrument builder in
    Arnstadt.*

5. **Burial of Bach's father** (Freyse, p. 21)

    February 24, 1695. Buried, Mr. Johann Ambrosius Baach, Town Musi-
    cian—without fee.

BACH ATTENDS THE LATIN SCHOOL
IN EISENACH

6. **Excerpts from the student registers for 1693–1695** (*BD* II, no. 2)

    a. *Of the 81 students in the fifth class (quinta), 1693:*
        47. Johannes Sebastianus Bach. 96 [half-days] absent.

    b. *Of the 74 students in the fifth class, 1694:*
        14. Joh. Sebastian Bach. 59 [half-days] absent.

    c. *Of the 45 students in the fourth class (quarta), 1695:*
        23. Joh. Sebastian Bach of Eisenach. 103 [half-days] absent.

    *Students generally stayed in one class for two years; on entering and leaving
    each class, they were listed in ranked order. There were morning and afternoon
    periods of instruction.*

BACH'S STEPMOTHER WORRIES ABOUT WANING
MUSICAL TALENT IN THE FAMILY

7. **Excerpt from a petition for a bounty by Barbara Margaretha
    Bach, widow of Johann Ambrosius, 1695** (*BD* II, no. 3)

    . . . and in Arnstadt, too, it happened that after the death of Mr. Johann
    Christoph Bach, town musician here, and brother of our husband and

father, who died a year and a half ago, the Noble Count and Lord of that place most graciously inquired of the widow in these words: whether there was not another Bach available who would like to apply for the post, for he should and must have a Bach again. But this was not to be, for the dear God has caused the springs of musical talent in the Bach family to run dry within the last few years.

While this letter—composed by the Eisenach cantor Andreas Christian Dedekind and addressed to the burgomaster and council of Eisenach on behalf of the "sorrowing widow and poor fatherless orphans"—was being written, the young Sebastian was no doubt giving some evidence in an adjoining room that the reports claiming the exhaustion of the Bach family's musical talent were greatly exaggerated.

Ohrdruf
1695–1700

8. **Excerpts from the student registers for 1696–1700** (*BD* II, no. 4)

a. *Of the students in the third class (tertia) after final examinations, July 20, 1696:*
4. Jo. Sebast. Bach, of Eisenach [*Isennacensis*]. Age 10 [*recte:* 11].

b. *Of the 21 students in the third class after final examinations, July 19, 1697:*
1. Jo. Sebast Bach, of Eisenach. Age 11 [*recte:* 12].
Transfered to the second class.

c. *Of the students in the second class (secunda) after final examinations, July 18, 1698:*
5. Jo. Sebast. Bach, of Eisenach. Age 14 [*recte:* 13].

d. *Of the 11 students in the second class after final examinations, July 24, 1699:*
2. Jo. Sebast. Bach, of Eisenach. Age 15 [*recte:* 14].
Transfered to the first class.

e. *Later addition:*
Left for Lüneburg, in the absence of free board [*ob defectum hospitiorum*], on March 15, 1700.

f. *Later postscript by the Rector, J. C. Kiesewetter:*
Appointed organist [*musicus organicus*] at St. Sophia's Church in Arnstadt, thereafter in Mühlhausen.

Bach was promoted to the first class when only 14 years and 4 months old (the oldest student in this class was 21, the average age 17.7). Also enrolled in the same class at the Ohrdruf Lyceum were Bach's brother Johann Jacob, who left the school in July 1696, at age 14, halfway through the third class, to become apprenticed in Eisenach to Johann Heinrich Halle, their father's successor;

Bach's cousin Johann Ernst Bach (ranked 7th in the second class), who left in July 1699 and later succeeded Bach in Arnstadt; and Georg Erdmann (ranked 11th in the second class), who departed on January 19, 1700, for St. Michael's School in Lüneburg, just two months before Bach did so.

BACH'S BROTHER JOHANN CHRISTOPH WRITES
ABOUT HIMSELF

9.   J. C. Bach's autobiographical note (*BJ* 1985, p. 60)

I, the undersigned, was born honorably in Erfurt on June 16th of the year 1671. At the time my father, Joh. Ambrosius Bach, was town musician there, my mother was Elisabetha, née Lemmerhirt; both of them now deceased. These, my dear parents, readily had holy baptism given to me. My godfather was Mr. Christoph Herthumb, kitchen manager for the Schwarzburg court as well as court and town organist at Arnstadt.

Since my late father was called to Eisenach by the Honored and Most Wise Town Council in the year stated above, I was schooled and educated there in the Christian belief. After I attended school until my 15th year, my father, seeing that I was more inclined toward music than toward the studies, sent me to Erfurt, to Mr. Johann Pachelbel, then organist at the Predigerkirche, in order to master the keyboard, and I remained under his guidance for three years. In the last year of my tutelage I was called to be organist at St. Thomas's; but since I found both the remuneration and the structure of the organ—the latter being my principal concern—to be poor, I followed the wish of my cousin and went to Arnstadt. As the old organist there, he could no longer easily attend to his duties, because of age, and I took them over until God led me here in the year 1690. Having been admitted to the examination, I was accepted by the Count's Consistory, and since I did not tend toward school instruction, this was ordered to be entrusted to Mr. Joh. Günther Schneider. I was assigned to work only at the organ.

In the year 1696 there came a call to the vacant organist position from the Honored and Most Highly Esteemed Magistrate of Gotha, but since during my stay here I always experienced good will, from both high and low, and having beseeched God's wisdom, I resolved to remain here and be content with the smaller pay and benefits.

When in the year 1700 my colleague of the Sexta class was called to be verger, I applied in turn for his post, since my predecessor had also held it along with his organist's duties, and it was assigned to me by the Count's Consistory. But after I had worked in the Sexta for a quarter of a year, Mr. Joh. Günther Schneider, the teacher of the Quinta, departed in God, whereupon I was transferred by order of the Count's Consistory to the Quinta class. When confirmation from my gracious Superiors arrived, I was duly installed, for which, this having been my wish, I give my thanks to God.

By order of the Most Honored Superintendent I have put this down for the record.

Ohrdruf, December 29, 1700   JOHANN CHRISTOPH BACH

THE ORGANS AT ST. MICHAEL'S IN OHRDRUF

10. Specifications of the organs (David, p. 79)

MAIN ORGAN

Oberwerk	Rückpositiv	Pedal
1. Principal 8'	1. Principal 4'	1. Principal 16'
2. Quintadena 16'	2. Stillgedakt 8'	2. Subbass 16'
3. Grob Gedakt 8'	3. Flöte 2'	3. Oktav 8'
4. Oktave 4'	4. Nassat 3'	4. Mixtur 3f. 4'
5. Quinta 3'	5. Sesquialtera 2f.	5. Fagott 16'
6. Klein Oktave 2'	6. Oktave 1'	6. Corneto 2'
7. Mixtur 4f. 2'		
8. Cymbel 2f. 1'		
9. Trompeta 8'		

SMALL ORGAN

1. Principal 8'
2. Grob Gedakt 16': C–c''', without C#, D#, F#, G# (short octave)
3. Klein Gedakt 4'
4. Flöte 2'
5. Cymbel
Pedal stops unknown

The main organ was built in 1675 by Caspar Lehmann of Suhl and expanded in 1688 by Heinrich Brunner of Sandersleben. Its compass was C–c'''. From 1695 to 1700 the organ was defective: Johann Christoph Bach reported on September 3, 1697 (BJ 1926, p. 152), that "almost nothing good could be played, particularly on the Rückpositiv." The small organ, a sixteenth-century instrument, was renovated and had a pedal added in 1683 by Brunner. Both instruments and the church itself were completely destroyed by fire in 1753.

Lüneburg and Weimar

1700–1703

BACH IS A MEMBER OF THE METTENCHOR

11. Excerpt from the Lüneburg school records, listing fees paid to matins choir members, May 1–29, 1700 (Küster, p. 93)

	rthl.	gr.
Frank [prefect]	1	—
Köhler [adjunct]	1	—
Koch	1	—
Hochgesang min[or]:	—	16
Schmersahl	—	16
Hochgesang Maj[or]:	—	12
Schmidt	—	12
Erdmann	—	12
Bach	—	12
Schön	—	8
Vogel	—	8
2 on the wait list (*Expect*[*antes*]:)	—	8

Members of the select matins choir received, in addition to the monthly fees, free tuition, room, and board at the St. Michael's School. Bach and Erdmann appear on the April and May choir lists (subsequent lists from June 1700 through 1702 are missing). These lists indicate that Bach and Erdmann, who had just arrived from Ohrdruf, were not placed on the wait list, but immediately received the third highest fee.

Cantor August Braun generally assigned at least two singers to each voice (discant, alto, tenor, and bass); specific vocal assignments are not exhibited on the lists for April and May 1700. According to the obituary (No. 306), however, Bach was "well received" in Lüneburg "because of his uncommonly fine soprano voice."

JOHANN ADAM REINKEN'S ORGAN AT
ST. CATHERINE'S IN HAMBURG

12. **Specifications of the organ** (Niedt, vol. 2, pp. 176–77; David, p. 82)

Hauptwerk (HW)	*Rückpositiv (RP)*	*Oberwerk (OW)*
Principal 16'	Principal 8'	Principal 8'
Quintadena 16'	Gedackt 8'	Hohlflöte 8'
Bordun 16'	Quintadena 8'	Flöte 4'
Octava 8'	Octava 4'	Gemshorn 2'
Spitz-Flöte 8'	Block-Flöte 4'	Nasat 3'
Quer-Flöte 8'	Hohl-Flöte 4'	Scharff 6f.
Octava 4'	Quint-Flöte 1½'	Wald-Flöte 2'
Octava 2'	Sifflet 1'	Trompeta 8'
Rausch-Pfeiffe 2f.	Sesquialtera 2f.	Zincke 8'
Mixtura 10f.	Regal 8'	Trompeta 4'
Trompeta 16'	Baar-Pfeiffe 8'	
	Schallmey 4'	

Brustwerk	*Pedal (P)*	
Principal 8'	Principal Bass 32'	Gross-Posaune 32'
Octava 4'	Principal 16'	Posaune 16'
Scharff 7f.	Octava 8'	Krumhorn 8'
Quintadena 4'	Gedackt 8'	Trompeta 8'
Wald-Pfeiffe 2'	Octava 4'	Schallmey 4'
Dulcian 16'	Nachthorn 4'	Ducian 16'
Regal 8'	Rausch-Pfeiffe 2f.	Principal 16'
	Cymbel 3f.	Cornett-Bass 2'
	Mixtur 5f.	

Tremulants (HW, RP); 4 Cymbel Sterne, Tympani, Vogelgesang;
couplers (OW/HW, RP/HW, HW/P).

*Originally built in 1543 by Hans Stellwagen (43 stops), the organ was later
expanded. In 1670 Reinken added two pedal towers with a Principal 32'
made of "the best English pewter." Jakob Adlung reports in* Musica Mechanica
Organoedi *(Berlin, 1768), p. 187, that in recalling the instrument as being
"in all parts exceptional," Bach "could not find enough praise" for "the beauty
and variety of timbre" of the 16 reed stops. His Mühlhausen and Weimar organ
designs included the addition of a 32' stop in order to achieve "the best gravity";
see Nos. 31 and 40.*

    *Adlung gives the following explanation of these terms: "Since, then, when
there is more than one manual there are, as it were, several organs together,*

distinctions are made among them according to size and according to position. *What belongs to the upper manual is called the* Oberwerk *{upper organ}; what is before us is called the* Brustwerk *{breast organ} or* Brust; *what is sometimes constructed behind the {organist's} back is called the* Rückpositiv *{back positive}. These* Rückpositivs *were formerly much more in use than they are now, when everything is included in one case, which, moreover, is much better. Meanwhile the usage has crept in among us of calling small organs, or the least important manual in an organ, with that which belongs to it, the* Rückpositiv. *When there are more than two manuals, one is sometimes called* das mittlere Werk *{the middle organ}.*

"*One manual ordinarily contains the noblest and most penetrating stops, and is accordingly sometimes called the* Hauptmanual *{principal manual}, the* Hauptwerk *{principal organ}, the* Werk κατ᾽ ἐξοχήν *{the chief organ}, whether it lies above or below. For example, in the organ at St. Stephen's in Bremen there are three manuals, of which one is called the* Werk, *the second the* Oberwerk, *and the third the* Brust. *The* Oberwerk *is not always to be considered the most important; it just lies at the top. The most important stops, with which one may improvise in full polyphony, are in the* Werk, *and so on.*"

From this we see that the terminology was by no means uniform or clear. Adlung states that the Oberwerk *lies at the top; but in the immediately preceding sentence he has explained that at St. Stephen's in Bremen the second of three manuals is called the* Oberwerk. *Very roughly,* Hauptwerk *or* das Werk *may be said to correspond to the modern* Great, Brust *or* Brustwerk *to the* Swell *(but without the shutters that give that department its name), and* Rückpositiv *to the* Choir.

BACH IS BRIEFLY EMPLOYED AT THE WEIMAR COURT

13. Excerpts from the ducal treasury register, 1703 (*BD* II, no. 6)

To the Lackey Baach

6 fl. 18 gr.   for the Reminiscere Quarter, 1703. Receipt No. 813
6 fl. 18 gr.   for the Trinitatis Quarter, 1703. Receipt No. 814

The "Reminiscere" quarter covered the period January to March; the "Trinitatis," April to June. Cf. No. 17, note.

Arnstadt

1703–1707

THE JOHANN FRIEDRICH WENDER ORGAN IN
THE NEW CHURCH

14. **Specifications of the organ** (Wenke, p. 47)

Oberwerk (OW)	*Brustpositiv (BP)*	*Pedal (P)*
Principal 8'	Principal 4'	Principal Bass 8'
Viol di Gamba 8'	Stillgedackt 8'	Sub Bass 16'
Quintadena 8'	Spielpfeife 4'	Posaunen Bass 16'
Grobgedackt 8'	Quinta 3'	Cornet Bass 2f.
Quinta 6'	Sesquialtera 2f	
Octava 4'	Nachthorn 4'	
Mixtur 4f.	Mixtur 3f.	
Gemshorn 8f.		
Cymbel 2f.		
Trompet 8'		

Tremulant (OW), couplers (BW/OW, OW/P), Zymbel Stern

The organ was built during 1701–3 by J. F. Wender of Mühlhausen.

15. **Excerpt from the records of the consistory of the Count of Arnstadt** (*BD* II, no. 7)

Upon the command of the Consistory of the Count here, Mr. Johann Sebastian Bach, Court Organist to the Prince of Saxe-Weimar, was called hither to inspect the new organ in the New Church, and the costs come to the following amounts: 2 thlr. 16 gr. to Georg Christoph Weller for the hire of the horses and messenger's pay, 4 thlr. to Mr. Bach as compensation, and 1 fl. for the time that he was here, for food and lodging, making a total of 8 fl. 13 gr.

Signed, Arnstadt, July 13, 1703   MARTIN FELDTHAUS

On the back, this document bears the following notation: 3 fl. 13 gr. to Mr. Bach for having to try the new organ and play it the first time, July 13, 1703.

The reference to Bach's position seems to be in error. Bach served for a short time in 1703 in the capelle of the prince's brother, the reigning duke in Weimar, but, as far as we know, not in the capacity of court organist.

BACH IS APPOINTED ORGANIST

16. **Certificate of Bach's appointment** (*BD* II, no. 8)

Whereas our Noble and Most Gracious Count and Master, Anton Günther, one of the Four Counts of the Empire, has caused you, Johann Sebastian Bach, to be accepted and appointed as organist in the New Church, now, therefore, you are, above all, to be true, faithful, and obedient to him, His above-mentioned Noble Grace, the Count, and especially to show yourself industrious and reliable in the office, vocation, and practice of art and science that are assigned to you; not to mix into other affairs and functions; to appear promptly on Sundays, feast days, and other days of public divine service in the said New Church at the organ entrusted to you; to play the latter as is fitting; to keep a watchful eye over it and take faithful care of it; to report in time if any part of it becomes weak and to give notice that the necessary repairs should be made; not to let anyone have access to it without the foreknowledge of the Superintendent; and in general to see that damage is avoided and everything is kept in good order and condition. As also in other respects, in your daily life to cultivate the fear of God, sobriety, and the love of peace; altogether to avoid bad company and any distraction from your calling and in general to conduct yourself in all things toward God, High Authority, and your superiors, as befits an honorloving servant and organist. For this you shall receive the yearly salary of 50 fl.; and for board and lodging 30 thlr., to be paid you, in exchange for your receipt, as follows: 25 fl. from the beer taxes, 25 fl. from the Church treasury, and the remaining 30 thlr. from the Hospital.

This certificate has been executed by authority and given under the customary signature and seal of the Count's Chancellery.

[Seal] Consistory of the
Signed, August 9, 1703   Count of Schwarzburg, etc.

The hospital is the Hospital of St. George and St. James, a home for old people, where Bach also played the organ for services.

BACH'S SALARY, 1703–1707

17. **Two receipts from the church treasury** (*BD* I, nos. 94–95)

a. Three florins, 2 gr. 7½ pf. for the half quarter, namely, from August 9 to the Day of the Holy Cross of this year, were properly paid to the undersigned as salary for the organist of the New Church by Mr. Johann Schellhase from the church's cash box, receipt of which is hereby acknowledged.

Joh. Seb. Bach.

Arnstadt, on September 28, 1703   *Organ*[ist] *at the New Church*

b. Six florins, 5 gr. 3 pf. for the quarter of St. Lucy's were properly paid to the undersigned as salary for the organist of the New Church from the church's cash box, receipt of which is hereby acknowledged.

Joh. Seb. Bach.

Arnstadt, on December 19, 1703   *Organ*[ist] *at the New Church*

Traditional paydays were the Thursdays before Reminiscere Sunday (in March) and Trinity Sunday (in June), and the Thursdays after the Day of the Holy Cross (September 14) and St. Lucy's Day (December 13). The quarterly receipts for the years 1704–7 indicate no changes in Bach's compensation.

BACH COMPOSES A PIECE OF PROGRAM MUSIC

18. *Capriccio sopra la lontananza de il fratro dilettissimo*, BWV 992, movement titles (*NBA* V / 10, pp. 3–8)

[1] *Adagio.* Is a coaxing by his friends to dissuade him from his journey. [2] Is a picturing of various calamities that might overtake him in foreign parts. [3] *Adagiosissimo.* Is a general *Lamento* of the friends. [4] Here come the friends, since they see that it cannot be otherwise, and take leave of him. [5] *Aria di Postiglione* [Air of the Postilion], *Allegro poco.* [6] *Fuga all' imitazione di Posta* [Fugue in imitation of the post-(horn)].

The conjecture that the heading of this work relates to Bach's brother Johann Jacob, who left Thuringia between 1703 and 1707 to join the Swedish army, is questionable. The traditional adjustment to the Italian title ("del suo fratello dilettissimo") is not authentic and was made only in order to fit the hypothesis. Not only does the piece display no martial characteristics ("alla battaglia"), but also the departure of a recruit by postal coach seems rather unlikely. The Latin *frater* may pertain to any kind of fraternal (professional) relationship, which, however, remains unidentified. A companion piece that names its dedicatee, the Capriccio "in honorem Johann Christoph Bachii Ohrdruf[iensis]," BWV 993, seems to date from approximately the same time—the Arnstadt years, if not before.

BACH IS INVOLVED IN A BRAWL

19. Excerpts from the proceedings of the Arnstadt consistory (*BD* II, no. 14)

a.   *Actum* [minutes], August 5, 1705

Johann Sebastian Bach, organist here at the New Church, appeared and stated that, as he walked home yesterday, fairly late at night, coming from the direction of the castle and reaching the market square, six students were sitting on the "Langenstein" (Long Stone), and as he passed the town hall, the student Geyersbach went after him with a stick, calling him to account: Why had he [Bach] made abusive remarks about him? He [Bach] answered that he had made no abusive remarks about him, and that no one could prove it, for he had gone his way very quietly. Geyersbach retorted that while he [Bach] might not have maligned him, he had maligned his bassoon at some time, and whoever insulted his belongings insulted him as well; he had carried on like a dirty dog's etc., etc. And he [Geyersbach] had at once struck out at him. Since he had not been prepared for this, he had been about to draw his dagger, but Geyersbach had fallen into his arms, and the two of them tumbled about until the rest of the students who had been sitting with him, namely, Schüttwürfel, Hoffmann—the others would name them—had rushed toward them and separated them so that he [Bach] could continue on his way home. He had said to Geyersbach, to his face, that he would straighten this out tomorrow, and it would not be becoming to him and his honor to duel with him [Geyersbach]. Since he [Bach] did not deserve such treatment and thus was not safe on the street, he humbly requested that said Geyersbach be duly punished, and that he [Bach] be given appropriate satisfaction and accorded respect by the others, so that henceforth they would let him pass without abuse or attack.

To be submitted to the Consistory   C Z A [scribe]

b.   *Actum,* August 14, 1705

The student Geyersbach is read the organist Bach's statement against him.

Ille [he, i.e., Geyersbach, the defendant]: Denies that he attacked the plaintiff Bach. Rather, having been invited by the shoemaker Jahn for the christening feast of his child, and while giving a serenade with the girls who were sponsors, Bach, tobacco pipe in his mouth, was crossing the street, whereupon Geyersbach asked same whether he admitted to having called him a greenhorn bassoonist [*Zippel Fagottist*]. Inasmuch as he could not deny this, he, Bach, proceeded to draw his dagger; he, Geyersbach, had to defend himself; otherwise he would have suffered some harm.

Denies that he maligned Bach as claimed, though it could be that he struck out when Bach went at him with his dagger.

Bach: Maintains that it was Geyersbach who had begun to insult and strike, thus making it necessary for him to reach for his dagger, not having anything else with which to defend himself.

Geyersbach: Does not remember having maligned Bach.

Hoffmann, asked to state the truth. He did not know how the two got at each other. But since he saw that Geyersbach reached out against Bach's dagger, Bach, however, still holding it at its scabbard and Geyersbach having fallen in the course of their wrestling, so that an accident might have occurred in that Geyersbach might have fallen onto the dagger, he stepped between the two of them, urging them to let go of each other and go home. Upon this, Geyersbach, who had held the dagger with both hands, gave it up, saying that he had had better intentions toward Bach, but felt differently now, whereupon Bach replied that he would pursue the matter.

Schüttwürfel: He must have been called to witness in error, for he had not been present but had been at home.

Resolved: To report back next Wednesday.

c.   *Actum,* August 19, 1705

The organist Bach is informed that because the student Geyersbach denied during the last hearing that he had initiated the brawl and alleged that Bach pulled his dagger first, he will be obliged to render proof that the said student had given first cause.

Ille: He would offer proof through his cousin Bachin, provided that her testimony, coming from a female person, be deemed sufficient.

Nos [we, i.e., members of the consistory]: He might very well have refrained from calling Geyersbach a *Zippel Fagottist;* such gibes lead in the end to unpleasantness of this kind, especially since he had a reputation for not getting along with the students and of claiming that he was engaged only for simple chorale music, and not for concerted pieces, which was wrong, for he must help out in all music making.

Ille: He would not refuse, if only there were a *Director musices.*

Nos: Men must live among *imperfecta;* he must get along with the students, and they must not make one another's lives miserable.

Resolved: The cousin is to be summoned, and both are to report again next Friday.

d.   *Actum,* August 21, 1705

Barbara Catharina Bachin: Reports, after being admonished to state the truth, that a few days ago, when she was about to cross the market square with her cousin, there were several students, coming from a christening feast, who were sitting on the "Long Stone." Geirsbach [*sic*] seeing them, at once got up and stepped in front of Bach, asking why he had maligned his bassoon; whosoever maligned his belongings, maligned him, and that is what a dirty dog's etc. would do. Whereupon Geirsbach hit Bach in the face, and Bach drew his dagger, but did not hurt him with it. Then they tumbled about, and Geirsbach dropped a stick; the other students gathered around, refereeing, and took Bach by the hand, prompting him to go on, since if they had some arguments with one another, this was taken care of; also, to her knowledge, Bach had no tobacco pipe in his mouth.

Eodem [to this point]: On the basis of the Bachin's examination, as stated above, the student Geyersbach is informed that it is to be concluded from the same that he initiated the incident, since he not only addressed Bach first but also was the first to strike out.

Ille: Admits that he struck out, but Bach used his dagger against him, his vest still showing the holes resulting from the punctures.

Nos: If he had some argument with Bach, it would have been better to settle it through others, and not to pursue it in public on the street.

Resolved: Since none of the ministers were available, the two might go off for the time being. If a verdict was reached, they would be duly informed.

BACH HAS DISCIPLINARY PROBLEMS

20. **Rebuke to Bach for his prolonged absence and improper playing: excerpt from the consistory proceedings** (*BD* II, no. 16)

Actum [minutes]: February 21, 1706

The organist in the New Church, Bach, is interrogated as to where he has lately been for so long and from whom he obtained leave to go.

Ille [i.e., Bach, the defendant]: He has been to Lübeck in order to comprehend one thing and another about his art, but had asked leave beforehand from the Superintendent.

Dominus Superintendens [The Reverend Superintendent]: He had asked for only four weeks, but had stayed about four times as long.

Ille: Hoped that the organ playing had been so taken care of by the one he had engaged for the purpose that no complaint could be entered on that account.

Nos [i.e., the consistory]: Reprove him for having hitherto made many curious *variationes* in the chorale, and mingled many strange tones in it, and for the fact that the Congregation has been confused by it. In the future, if he wished to introduce a *tonus peregrinus,* he was to hold it out, and not to turn too quickly to something else or, as had hitherto been his habit, even play a *tonus contrarius.* In addition, it was quite disagreeable that hitherto no concerted music had been performed [*bissher gar nichts musiciert worden*], for which he was responsible, because he did not wish to get along with the students; accordingly he was to declare whether he was willing to play for concerted music as well as chorales sung by the students. For a capellmeister could not be engaged just for his sake. If he did not wish to do so, he should but state that fact *categorice* so that other arrangements could be made and someone engaged who would.

Ille: If he were provided with a competent conductor [*Director*], he would perform well enough.

Resolved: He is to declare himself within eight days.

Eodem [to this point]: The student Rambach [the prefect, or choir leader] appears, and he is similarly reproved for the *désordres* that have hitherto taken place in the New Church between the students and the organist.

Ille: The organist Bach had previously played rather too long, but after his attention had been called to it by the Superintendent, he had at once fallen into the other extreme and made it too short.

Nos: Reprove him [Rambach] for going into the wine cellar on the last preceding Sunday during the sermon.

Ille: Was sorry, and it would not happen again, and the clergy had already given him hard looks on that score. The organist should not complain about him for the conducting, since it was not he but young Schmidt who took care of it.

Nos: He should behave in the future quite differently and better than he had hitherto, or the favor meant for him would be withdrawn. If he had anything to state against the organist, he should report it to the proper place, and not take the law into his own hands, but behave himself so that one could be satisfied with him, which he promised. Thereupon the servant of the chancellery was instructed to tell the Rector that he is to have Rambach go into detention for two hours each day, four days in succession.

Tonus contrarius *is not a specific term. Even the word* tonus *may be taken to mean either tone or mode. It is clear only that the substance of the reproach is that Bach introduced unexpected elements into his harmonic and melodic texture, such as passing tones, short cadenzas, chromatic progressions, cross relations, and sudden modulations.*

    The word musiciren, *in the general usage of the time, meant to perform concerted music for voices and instruments.*

21. **Rebuke to Bach for inviting a female visitor into the choir loft: excerpt from the consistory proceedings** (*BD* II, no. 17)

Actum, November 11, 1706

It is pointed out to the organist Bach that he is to declare whether he is willing to make music with the students as he has already been instructed to do, or not; for if he considers it no disgrace to be connected with the Church and to accept his salary, he must also not be ashamed to make music with the students assigned to do so, until other instructions are given. For it is the intention that the latter shall practice, in order one day to be the better fitted for music.

Ille: Will declare himself in writing concerning this matter.

Nos: Thereupon ask him further by what right he recently caused the unfamiliar maiden [*frembde Jungfer*] to be invited into the choir loft and let her make music there.

Ille: Has told Magister Uthe about it.

Spitta suggests that the "unfamiliar maiden" may have been Maria Barbara Bach, Johann Sebastian Bach's cousin, whom he married on October 17 of the following year. However, since she had been a resident of Arnstadt for many years, she could hardly have been referred to as unfamiliar.

Mühlhausen

1707–1708

22. Excerpts from the proceedings of parish meetings
(*BD* II, nos. 19–20)

a.   *Actum* [minutes], May 24, 1707

Dom. Senior Consul Dr. Conrad Meckbach: It would be remembered how the post of organist at the Church of St. Blasius had been made vacant by the decease of Mr. Johan Georg Ahle, and that accordingly it would now be necessary to fill it again; therefore the following questions were submitted:

Whether consideration should not first be given to the man named Pach [*sic*] from Arnstadt, who had recently done his trial playing at Easter?

Conclusum. And an equitable agreement should be worked out with him. To this end, the said person should be bidden to appear here. Mr. Bellstedt to be entrusted with this commission.

b.   *Actum,* June 14, 1707

Mr. Gottfried Stüler, Mr. A. E. Reiss, Mr. J. C. Stephan, deputies of the Parish of St. Blasius being present:

There appeared Mr. Joh. Seb. Bache [*sic*] and was questioned as to whether he wished to assume the vacant post of organist of the Church of St. Blasius, and what he would ask for the position.

Mr. Bach requires:

   85 gulden, which he received at Arnstadt
       and the emoluments in kind as received by Mr. Ahle, to wit:
   54 bushels of grain,

2 cords of wood, 1 beech and 1 other,
6 times threescore fagots, in place of the acreage.
Delivered to the door.

Under these conditions he would accept a call. Hoped, furthermore, that to facilitate his departure and removal hither, he would receive the assistance of a wagon to move his effects.

Asks finally that the position be offered him in writing.

[Signed by the deputies named above, who conducted the meeting, and 15 others.]

c.   *Actum,* June 15, 1707

Joh. Dieterich Petersheim reported that Mr. Seb. Vockerodt, Mr. Christian Strüler, Mr. Haserodt said they had no pen or ink, and were so dismayed at the calamity [a recent fire] that they could not think about music—whatever the other gentlemen did would satisfy them.

23. Announcement of Bach's appointment (*BD* II, no. 21)

We, the sworn Burgomasters of Mühlhausen, Free City of the Holy Empire, and Members of the Council of the Parish of St. Blasius's, herewith make known that, as the post of organist there is open, having become vacant through the death of our late friend and colleague Mr. Joh. Georg Ahle, we have called hither, in order to fill the said post, Mr. Joh. Sebastian Bach of the Bonifacius Church at Arnstadt, and have engaged him as our organist in the said Church of St. Blasius, on the conditions that he be loyal and true above all to the Magistrate of this town, not alone defend our common city from all harm but also work for its best interests, show himself willing in the execution of the duties required of him and be available at all times, particularly attend to his service faithfully and industriously on Sundays, Feast Days, and other Holy Days, keep the organ entrusted to him at least in good condition, call the attention of those serving at any time as the appointed supervisors to any defects found in it and industriously watch over its repairs and *music*, be zealous in observing all the requirements of a decent and respectable life, also avoid unseemly society and suspicious *compagnie;* and just as the said Mr. Bach has obligated himself by a handshake to show his agreement with all the foregoing and to conduct himself accordingly, so we have promised to give him, as his yearly salary:

85 gulden in money and the following emoluments in kind:
54 bushels of grain,

2 cords of wood, 1 beech and 1 oak or aspen,

6 times threescore fagots delivered to the door instead of acreage,

and have accordingly had the present certificate of appointment executed, with the seal of the Chancellery affixed.

[seal] Parishioners of Mühlhausen

Done June 15, 1707   Imperial Free City of the Holy Empire

BACH LEAVES ARNSTADT

24. **Bach's request for his dismissal: excerpt from the consistory
proceedings** (*BD* II, no. 25)

Actum, June 29, 1707

Then appears Mr. Johann Sebastian Bach, hitherto organist at the New
Church, and reports that he has been called as organist to Mühlhausen
and that he has accepted the call. Thereupon expressed his most obedient thanks to the Council for his past employment and requests his
dismissal, wishing to return herewith the keys of the organ to the
Council, from whom he had received them.

25. **Bach assigns his remaining salary to his cousin Johann Ernst
Bach: excerpt from the Arnstadt town archives** (*BD* II, no. 35)

I report herewith to the Secretary that Mr. Sebastian Baach, at present
organist in Mühlhausen, received his dismissal in July of last year,
1707, and assigned his salary then for the Crucis Quarter [the third
quarter of the year], which was then owed him, to his cousin, the present organist of the New Church, against the latter's receipt for the
same, so that the term of the present organist of the New Church
should begin with the Luciae Quarter for 1707, and his salary should be
arranged, by Your Honors' leave, accordingly. This is hereby attested.

MARTIN FELDHAUSS

BACH MARRIES MARIA BARBARA, NÉE BACH

26. **Excerpt from the Arnstadt marriage register** (*BD* II, no. 28)

Anno 1707, *Dom*[*inica*] XV *p*[*ost*] *Tr*[*initatis*]

Mr. Johann Sebastian Bach, duly appointed organist at the Church of
St. Blasius in the Imperial Free City of Mühlhausen, still single, young-

est surviving son and lawful issue of the late Mr. Johann Ambrosius Bach, musician to the Prince of Saxe-Eisenach, and Mistress Maria Barbara, youngest daughter and lawful issue of the late Master Johann Michael Bach, organist in Gehren. Were united in marriage in Dornheim on October 17. The fees were remitted.

BACH'S FIRST PUBLICATION

27. *Gott ist mein König*, cantata, BWV 71: title page (*BD* II, no. 30)

Congratulatory Church Motet as given when the Solemn Divine Service in the Principal Church B.M.V. with God's blessing the Council was changed on the 4th of February in the year 1708 and the Government of the Imperial Free City of Mühlhausen was joyously entrusted to the fatherly care of the new council, namely to the most noble, steadfast, most learned and most wise gentleman, Mr. Adolff Strecker, and the noble, steadfast, and most wise gentleman, Mr. Georg Adam Steinbach, both most deserving Messrs. burgomasters as well as the other most highly respected members, most dutifully furnished by Johann Sebastian Bach, Organist of St. Blasius, Mühlhausen. Printed by Tobias David Brückner, Printer to a most noble Council.

BACH IS PAID FOR HIS TOWN COUNCIL
ELECTION CANTATAS

28. Excerpts from the Mühlhausen town treasury register for 1708–1710 (*BD* II, nos. 30, 31, 43)

a. Feb. 11 [1708] Mr. Bach for the composition of the council piece 3 rthl.

b. Feb. 7 [1709] Mr. Baach from Weimar for the composition of the council piece 4 rthl.
Travel Expenses.
Mr. Baach from Weimar 2 rthl.

c. Feb. 20 [1710] Mr. Baach for the council piece 9 fl. 3 gr. [= 6 rthl.]

d.   To the printer Tobias David Brückner   f.   gr.   pf.
Feb. 11 [1708] for the printing of the council piece,
                    on account   6   2   —

27. *Gott ist mein König,* cantata, BWV 71: title page

| Mar. 3 | paid in cash 6 rthl. | 9 | 3 | — |
| | already received 4 rthl. | 6 | 2 | — |

To the bookbinder
Feb. 25 [1708] for the trimming of the council piece   —   8   —

e.   To the printer Tobias David Brückner
12 Mar. [1709] for the printing of the council piece   16   16   —
and the congratulatory poem, 11 rthl.

f.   To the printer Tobias David Brückner
27 Feb. [1710] for the poem to the council piece   1   —   4

The "council piece" for 1708 is BWV 71; the works for 1709–10 have not survived (in 1710 only the cantata text was printed). Although the 1710 payment does not specify "Bach from Weimar," it matches the 1709 payment exactly, including travel expenses. It is unlikely that Bach's Weimar successor, Johann Friedrich Bach, wrote the 1710 cantata, since he had not been asked to provide a composition in 1709. Moreover, in 1712, another outsider, this time G. P. Schmidt of Nordhausen, was commissioned for the cantata.

THE ORGAN OF ST. BLASIUS'S CHURCH

29.   **Specifications of the organ** (*BD* I, pp. 154f.)

Oberwerk (OW)	*Rückpositiv (RP)*	*Brustwerk (BW)*	*Pedal (P)*
Principal 8′	Gedackt 8′	Principal 2′	Untersatz 32′
Oktave 4′	Salcional 4′	Mixtur 3f.	Principal 16′
Oktave 2′	Spitzflöte 2′	Schallmey 8′	Subbass 16′
Cymbel 2f.	Sesquialtera 2f.	Quinte 1½	Oktave 8′
Mixtur 4f.	Principal 4′	Terz 1 ⅗′	Oktave 4′
Violdigamba 8′	Quintatön 8′	Flöte 4′	Mixtur 4f.
Gedackt 4′	Quintflöte 1½′	Stillgedackt 8′	Posaune 16′
Quinte 3′	Oktave 2′		Trompete 8′
Fagott 16′ (C–c)	Cymbel 3f.		Cornetbass 2′
Quintatön 16′			Rohrflötenbass 1′
Sesquialtera 2f.			

Tremulant (all manuals), couplers (BW/HW, RP/HW, HW/P), Cymbelstern, Pauke [Glockenspiel planned but not built].

The organ was rebuilt in 1708–9 by Johann Friedrich Wender of Mühlhausen, to Bach's design. Compass C, D–d'''' (pedal to d').

30. **Bach's suggested improvements to the organ: excerpt from the proceedings of a parish meeting** (*BD* I, no. 83)

Actum, February 21, 1708

Dom. Consul Senior Dr. Meckbach: The new organist, Mr. Bach, had observed various defects in the organ of the Church of St. Blasius and had submitted in writing a project for remedying them and perfecting the instrument. He read [the proposal given below] and asked:

(1) Whether the work should be carried out as projected; (2) That *Commissarii* be appointed to make the agreement; and (3) Someone having offered to purchase the small organ in the choir loft, whether the committee should be charged to come to terms with the interested party.

    Conclusum:
ad 1. *Affirmatur*
ad 2. *Denominati* Mr. Bellstedt, Mr. Reiss, Mr. Sebastian Vockerodt, with instructions to come to as close an agreement as possible and, if need be, to give the organ builder the small organ in lieu of [an additional payment of] 50 thlr., if he should not agree to complete the entire organ for 200 thlr.

31. **Bach's "Project for New Repairs to the Organ"** (*BD* I, no. 83)

Disposition of the renovation of the organ at St. Blasius's.

(1) The lack of wind must be made up by the addition of three good new bellows to take care of the *Oberwerck,* the *Rückpositiv,* and the new *Brustwerck.*
(2) The four old bellows now present must be adapted, with stronger wind pressure, to the new 32-foot Sub-Bass and the other bass stops.
(3) The old wind chests must all be taken out and freshly supplied with such wind conduction that one stop alone and also all the stops together can be used without alteration of the pressure, which has never been possible in the past and yet is very necessary.
(4) Then follows the 32-foot Sub-Bass or so-called *Untersatz* of wood, which gives the whole organ the most solid foundation [*die beste Gravität*]. This stop must now have its own wind chest.
(5) The Trombone Bass must be supplied with new and larger pipes [*corpora*], and the mouthpieces must be quite differently arranged so that this stop can produce a much more solid tone [*eine viel bessere Gravität*].

(6) The new chimes [*Glockenspiel*] desired by the parishioners to be added to the Pedal, consisting of 26 bells of 4-foot tone; which bells the parishioners will acquire at their own expense, and the organ builder will then install them.

(7) As regards the Upper Manual, instead of the Trumpet (which will be taken out) a *Fagotto* of 16-foot tone will be installed, which is useful for all kinds of new ideas [*inventiones*] and sounds very fine [*delicat*] in concerted music [*in die Music*].

(8) Further, in place of the *Gemshorn* (which is likewise to be taken out) there is to be a *Viol di Gamba* 8 foot, which will concord admirably with the 4-foot *Salicinal* already included in the *Rückpositiv. Item,* instead of the 3-foot *Quinta* (which is also to be taken out)

(9) a 3-foot *Nassat* could be installed. The other stops now included in the Upper Manual can remain, as also the entire *Rückpositiv,* although all of these must be tuned again anyway in the course of the repairs.

(10) Now, as far as the most important matter is concerned, the new little *Brustpositiv,* the following stops could be included in it.

In front, three Diapasons [*Principalia*], namely:

(a) *Quinta* 3′,
(b) *Octava* 2′, } of good 14-ounce tin;
(c) *Schalemoy* [= *Schalmei, chalumeau*] 8′,
(d) *Mixture,* three ranks
(e) *Tertia,* with which, by drawing a few other stops, one can produce a fine and complete *Sesquialtera;*
(f) *Fleute douce* 4′; and finally a
(g) *Stillgedackt* 8′, which accords perfectly with concerted music and, made of good wood, should sound much better than a metal *Gedackt.*

(11) Between the manuals of this *Brustpositiv* and the *Oberwerck* there must be a coupler.

And finally, in addition to a complete tuning of the whole organ, the tremulant must be regulated so that it flutters at the proper rate [*mensur*].

BACH LEAVES MÜHLHAUSEN

32. Bach's request for his dismissal (*BD* I, no. 1)

To the Everywhere Honored and Most Highly Esteemed Parishioners of the Church of St. Blasius

A Humble Memorial

YOUR MAGNIFICENCE, HONORED AND NOBLE SIRS, HONORED AND
LEARNED SIRS, HONORED AND WISE SIRS, MOST GRACIOUS PATRONI
AND GENTLEMEN!

The manner in which Your Magnificence and my Most Respected
Patrons most graciously engaged my humble self for the post of organist of the Church of St. Blasius when it became vacant a year ago, and
your graciousness in permitting me to enjoy a better living, I must
ever acknowledge with obedient thanks. Even though I should always
have liked to work toward the goal, namely, a well-regulated church
music, to the Glory of God and in conformance with your wishes, and
would, according to my small means, have helped out as much as possible with the church music that is growing up in almost every township,
and often better than the harmony that is fashioned here, and therefore
have acquired from far and wide, not without cost, a good store of the
choicest church compositions, just as I have also fulfilled my duty in
delivering the project for remedying the faults of the organ and should
gladly have discharged every other duty of my office—yet it has not
been possible to accomplish all this without hindrance, and there are,
at present, hardly any signs that in the future a change may take place
(although it would rejoice the souls belonging to this very Church); to
which I should humbly add that, however simple my manner of living,
I can live but poorly, considering the house rent and other most necessary expenses.

Now, God has brought it to pass that an unexpected change should
offer itself to me, in which I see the possibility of a more adequate
living and the achievement of my goal of a well-regulated church music
without further vexation, since I have received the gracious admission
of His Serene Highness of Saxe-Weimar into his Court Capelle and
Chamber Music.

Accordingly, I have felt I must bring my intention in this matter,
with obedient respect, to the notice of my Most Gracious Patrons, and
at the same time beg them to content themselves for the time being
with the modest services I have rendered to the Church and to furnish
me at the earliest moment with a gracious dismissal. If I can contribute
anything further to the service of Your Honors' Church, I will do so
more in deed than in words, remaining forever,

Honored Sir, Most Gracious Patrons and Gentlemen, Your Honors'
most obedient servant

Mühlhausen, June 25, Anno 1708   JOH. SEB. BACH

33. **Bach's dismissal, as recorded in the proceedings of a parish meeting** (*BD* I, p. 21)

Actum, June 26, 1708

D. Cons. Dr. Meckbach: The organist Pach received a call to Weimar and accepted the same, and accordingly made written request for his dismissal.

He submitted: Since he could not be made to stay, consent must doubtless be given to his dismissal, but in notifying him it should be suggested that he help bring to completion the project that had been undertaken.

34. **Excerpt from the minutes of St. Blasius's Church on Bach's successor, Johann Friedrich Bach** (*BD* II, no. 37)

Action taken in the Parish Meeting of July 4, 1708

Present: Dom. Cons. Meckbach, Dom. Cons. Stephan, Cons. Grabe, Mr. J. H. Bellstedt, Mr. A. E. Reiss, Mr. Plathner, Mr. Vockerodt, Mr. Tilesius, Mr. Eisenhardt, Mr. Volckerodt, Mr. Vogeler. It was pointed out that there had presented himself for the vacant post of organist Mr. Pache's cousin, also named Pache [Johann Friedrich Bach], a student.

It was asked whether he should be engaged and at what salary.

Agreed, but negotiations should be carried on with him on the basis of Mr. Ahle's agreement, and this task was entrusted to Mr. Reiss.

Ahle had been Bach's predecessor, but at a lower salary.

Weimar

1708–1717

35. **The duke's order for Bach's salary and compensation: excerpt from the ducal archives at Weimar** (Küster, pp. 186f.)

By the grace of God, Wilhelm Ernst, Duke of Saxony, Jülich, Cleves, and Berg, also Engern and Westphalia etc.

Steadfast, dear, and loyal councilor,
Whereas we agreed to appoint our chamber musician and court organist, Johann Sebastian Bach of Mühlhausen, we also decree for his annual salary and allowances, at our pleasure,

> one hundred and fifty florins, in cash,
> eighteen bushels of grain [wheat],
> twelve bushels of barley,
> four cords of wood [*Flossholz*], and
> thirty pails [*Eimer*] of beer from our castle brewery here, beverage-tax-free,

beginning with the approaching quarter of the Holy Cross, and additionally ten florins for moving costs. Thus, also on behalf of our dear beloved minor cousin, we desire that you would arrange with our princely treasury that all this, especially the salary and allowance as divided into the usual quarters, be extended to him against his receipts and that it be properly accounted for as an expense. This represents our will, and we are most favorably inclined toward you. Given Weimar, at the Wilhelmsburg, on June 20, 1708.

WILHELM ERNST

Recipient of the order was the privy councilor and president of the Weimar superior consistory, Johann Christoph von Hoffmann. Flossholz is high-quality wood from the Thuringian Forest, sent downstream.

BACH'S COMPSENSATION AT WEIMAR, 1708–1717

36. **Monetary present for Bach on his arrival, July 14, 1708** (*BD* II, no. 38)

> 10 fl.   To the newly arrived Court Organist from Mühlhausen, Johann Sebastian Bach, a benevolent entry allowance.

37. **Fees for instrument repairs: excerpt from the ducal treasury register of 1709–10** (*BD* II, no. 49)

> – fl. 12 gr.   To the Court Organist, Mr. Bach, for repairing 2 harpsichords, Dec. 9, 1709
>
> 1 fl. 3 gr.   To the Court Organist, Mr. Bach, for repairing one harpsichord, Dec. 17, 1709
>
> 2 fl. 6 gr.   To the Court Organist, Mr. Bach, for repairing one harpsichord, Feb. 6, 1710

38. **The duke's order for a salary increase: excerpt from the ducal archives at Weimar** (Küster, pp. 192f.)

By the grace of God, Wilhelm Ernst, Duke of Saxony, Jülich, Cleves, and Berg, also Engern and Westphalia etc.

Dear and loyal, after we have graciously added, from this date, fifty florins to the annual salary, at our pleasure, and thus a better income of our chamber musician and court organist here, Johann Sebastian Bach, upon his humble request, because the salary and allowance of his predecessor, Johann Effler, will cease completely and revert to our princely treasury. Thus we herewith desire for us and also for our dear beloved cousin, Herr Ernst August, as guardian of our dear beloved cousin, Herr Ernst August, Duke of Saxony, Liebden, etc., that you would take notice of this and, beginning with [the] Trinity [quarter], provide him with this most gracious increase, divided into the usual quarters, always with his previous salary against his receipts, and duly accounted for. This represents our will. Dated Weimar, at the Wilhelmsburg, on June 3, 1711.

WILHELM ERNST

In 1708, Bach's original salary of 150 fl. exceeded that of his predecessor as court organist, Johann Effler, by 20 fl. and, except for certain allowances, equaled that of the vice capellmeister, Johann Wilhelm Drese. After the increases of 1711 to 200 fl. and 1714 to 250 fl., Bach's pay exceeded the vice capellmeister's. When, after Bach's departure, Johann Wilhelm Drese succeeded his father as capellmeister, he received a salary of only 200 fl., and the court organist's salary for Bach's successor, Johann Martin Schubart, reverted to 130 fl.

39. **Excerpts from the "Complete Chamber Accounts from Michaelmas," ducal archives for 1710–17** (*BD* II, nos. 38–41, 71, 81)

a. *1710–1711:*

> *Salary:* 150 fl. to the Court Organist J. S. Bach.
> *Allowance of Wood:* 6 fl. 15 gr. to the Court Organist Bach, i.e., 3 cords of timber @ 1 rthl. 23 gr.
> *Castle Church:* 12 gr. for coal to tide the Court Organist over the winter.

b. *1711–1712:*

> *Salary, Castle Capelle:* 200 fl. to the Court Organist Bach {formerly only 150 fl., because of the 50 fl. increase}.
> *Allowance of Wood:* 8 fl. 12 gr. to the Court Organist in lieu of 4 cords of timber.
> *Prince's Gift:* 2 fl. to the Court Organist Bach.

c. *1712–1713:*

> *Salary, Castle Capelle:* 203 fl. 15 gr. 9 pf. to the Chamber Musician and Court Organist Johann Sebastian Bach. Every quarter 50 fl.; Trinitatis 53 fl. 15 gr. 9 pf., in accordance with the Prince's command of February 24.
> *Allowance of Wood:* 8 fl. to the Chamber Musician and Court Organist Joh. Sebast. Bach in lieu of 4 cords of timber @ 2 fl.
> *Prince's Gift (St. William's Day):* 2 fl. to the Court Organist Bach.
> *Court Capelle and Castle Church:* 12 gr. for coal for the organist, Dec. 16, 1712.

d. *1713–1714:*

> *The Prince's Castle Capelle:* 232 fl. 10 gr. 6 pf. to the Concertmaster and Court Organist Joh. Seb. Bach.
>
> | | |
> |---|---|
> | 53 fl. 15 gr. 9 pf.—Crucis | |
> | 53 fl. 15 gr. 9 pf.—Luciae | *1713* |
> | 62 fl. 10 gr. 6 pf.—Rem. | |
> | 62 fl. 10 gr. 6 pf.—Trin. | *1714* |

incl. 15 fl. increase in accordance with the Prince's command under Nos. 182–185.

Allowance of Wood: 12 fl. to the Concertmaster etc., in lieu of 6 cords of timber @ 2 fl., to wit:

$$\left.\begin{array}{l} \text{2 fl.—Crucis} \\ \text{2 fl.—Luciae} \end{array}\right\} \textit{1713}$$

$$\left.\begin{array}{l} \text{4 fl.—Rem.} \\ \text{4 fl.—Trin.} \end{array}\right\} \textit{1714,}\ \text{incl. 1 cord increase}$$

Prince's Gifts: 2 fl. to the Court Organist Bach.

Court Capelle and Castle Church: 18 gr. for coal for the Organist, Oct. 16, 1714 [*recte:* 1713?] and Feb. 20, 1714.

e. *1714–1715:*

For Mournful Occasions: 12 fl. to the Concertmaster and Org. Bach 12 fl.

Prince's Castle Capelle: To the Concertmaster and Court Organist Bach 250 fl. per annum @ 62 fl. to 10 gr. 6 pf. per quarter.

Allowance of Wood: 16 fl. 12 gr. to the Concertmaster and Court Organist Joh. Sebastian Bach for 8 cords of timber.

Prince's Gifts: for St. William's Day, May 28, 1715: 2 fl. to the Court Organist Bach.

Court Capelle and Castle Church: 2 fl. 6 gr. to the dealer Johann Christian Hindorff for 2 strings, which the Concertmaster caused to be ordered June 21, 1715.

Printed Matter: 13 fl. 15 gr. for 6 reams of writing paper and 12 reams of printing paper for the Church Cantatas, July 9, 1715.

f. *1715–1716:*

Salary, Castle Capelle: 250 fl. to the Concertmaster Bach.

Allowance of Wood: 18 fl. 6 gr. to the Concertmaster etc. for 8 cords of timber.

Prince's Gift: 2 fl. to the Court Organist Bach.

Castle Capelle: 12 gr. for coal for the organist, Nov. 26, 1715.

g. *1716–1717:*

Salary, Castle Capelle: 250 fl. to the Concertmaster Bach.

Allowance of Wood: 18 fl. 6 gr. to the Concertmaster etc. for 8 cords of timber.

Prince's Gift: 2 fl. to the Court Organist Bach.

Castle Capelle: 12 gr. for coal for the organist, November 1, 1716.

THE ORGAN IN THE CASTLE CHAPEL

40. **Specifications of the organ** (David, p. 88)

Hauptwerk (HW)	*Unterwerk (UW)*	*Pedal (P)*
Principal 8'	Principal 8'	Groß Untersatz 32'
Quintadena 16'	Viol di Gamba 8'	Sub-Bass 16'
Gemshorn 8'	Gedackt 8'	Posaun Bass 16'
Grobgedackt 8'	Trompeta 8'	Violin Bass 16'
Quintadena 4'	Klein Gedackt 4'	Principal Bass 8'
Octava 4'	Octava 4'	Trompeta Bass 8'
Mixtur 6f.	Wald-Flöthe 2'	Cornett-Bass 4'
Cymbel 3f.	Sesquialtera 4f.	
Glocken Spiel		

Tremulant (HW, UW), couplers (UW/HW, HW/P), Cymbel Stern

The organ was renovated in 1712–13 and 1719–20 by Heinrich Nicolaus Trebs of Weimar.

BACH'S ELDEST SON, WILHELM FRIEDEMANN,
IS BAPTIZED

41. **Entry in the church records** (*BD* II, no. 51)

To the wife of Mr. Court Organist Joh. Sebastian Bach, Maria Barbara, also née Bach, a son born on November 22 [1710], baptized on the 24th. Name: Wilhelm Friedemann. The Godparents:

1. Wilhelm Ferdinand Baron von Lyncker, princely Saxon gentleman-in-waiting here.
2. Mrs. Anna Dorothea Hagedorn, wife of Mr. Gottfried Hagedorn, Candidate of Laws, from Mühlhausen.
3. Mr. Friedemann Meckbach, Doctor of Laws, from Mühlhausen.

BACH WRITES A TESTIMONIAL FOR THE ORGAN
BUILDER HEINRICH NICOLAUS TREBS

42. **Bach's letter on behalf of Trebs** (*BD* I, no. 84)

Whereas Mr. Heinrich Trebs, the bearer, an organ builder experienced
in his art, requests me to give him a testimonial concerning the work
he has done in this principality, I have neither been able nor desired to
refuse him, since he merits it too well; accordingly I assure the gracious
reader of this letter that he has applied his most praiseworthy industry
to the work he has done in these parts, and I, as one appointed to
inspect the same, have found that both in the fulfillment of the contract
and in subsequent work he has proven himself a reasonable and conscientious man, for he made us the lowest price and he afterwards performed the work agreed upon with the greatest industry.

JOH.SEBAST. BACH

Weimar, February 16, 1711   *Court Organist and Chamber Musician*

BACH GIVES INSTRUCTION TO THE
DUKE'S PAGE

43. **Entries in the private account books of Duke Ernst August**
(*BD* II, no. 53)

2 fl. 6 gr. in the form of 1 cord of timber to the organist Bach for
instruction by the same on the Clavier, July 28, 1711.
1 fl. 6 gr. in the form of ½ cord of the same to the above-named for
instruction, Feb. 25, 1712.

*Adam Friedrich Wilhelm von Jagemann, the duke's page, received dance lessons
as well, from Adam Immanuel Weldig, falsettist and master of the pages.*

BACH PRESENTS A GUEST PERFORMANCE
IN WEISSENFELS

44. **Excerpt from the state archive** (*BD* II, no. 55)

The following persons bidden to the Ducal residence-town for service
in connection with His Most Serene Highness's birthday are to be
lodged here on Feb. 21 and 22 [1713]

. . .

Mr. Johann Sebastian Bach, Court Organist in Weimar, board 16 gr. daily.

In all likelihood, the hunting cantata BWV 208 was written for and performed on this occasion. Bach was later appointed honorary court capellmeister to the Duke of Weissenfels (see Nos. 155 and 174).

BACH SIGNS AN AUTOGRAPH ALBUM WITH A
FOUR-PART PERPETUAL CANON

45. Canon for four voices, BWV 1073: album entry
(*BD* I, no. 147; *NBA* VIII/1, p. 3)

To contribute this little item at this place to the Honored Owner [of this book] in the hope of friendly remembrance is the wish of

JOH. SEBAST. BACH
Court Organist and Chamber Musician
to His Saxon Highness

Weimar, August 2, 1713

BACH AUDITIONS IN HALLE AND TURNS DOWN
AN APPOINTMENT

46. Excerpts from the account book of the Church of Our Lady in Halle, for 1713–1714 (*BJ* 1994, p. 32)

a. *Main entry*

Legal costs and copyist's fee for the organist's contract, in duplicate	12gr.
General expenses	
To the organist, Mr. Bach, for the performance of the trial music and travel expenses	12 rthl.
To the keeper of the Inn of the Golden Ring	7 rthl.
To the courier to the organist in Weimar, fee and waiting money	1 rthl. 12 gr.

b. *Itemized bill from the Inn of the Golden Ring*

Expenses Mr. Pach [*sic*] has incurred		
For food	2 rthl.	16 gr.
For beer		18 gr.

45. Canon for four voices, BWV 1073

For brandy		8 gr.
For heat	1 rthl.	4 gr.
For lodging and light	2 rthl.	
For tobacco		4 gr.
Summa	7 rthl.	2 gr.

[*signed:*] Joh. Sebast. Bach   J. H. Eberhardt

47. Bach's receipt for travel expenses (*BJ* 1994, p. 32)

Twelve thaler have been paid to me, the undersigned, by the Church *Collegio* B[*eatae*] M[*ariae*] Virg[*ini*]s for travel expenses, which is hereby gratefully attested.

Dated Halle, December 15, 1713.   [Johann Sebastian Bach]

Bach's signature has been cut out, apparently by a souvenir hunter.

48. Text of the proffered agreement (*BD* II, no. 63)

We, the undersigned fathers and members of the Council of Eight of the Church of Our Lady here, for ourselves and our successors in the Church Council, hereby make known and testify that we have herewith appointed and accepted the honorable and learned Mr. Johann Sebastian Bach as organist of the Church of Our Lady, on condition that he be faithful and regular in attendance upon us and our Church, strive for a virtuous and exemplary life, above all cling faithfully all his life long to the unchanged Augsburg Confession, the Formula of Concord, and other symbolic confessions of faith, keep diligently to the altar of this Church and be devoutly obedient to the Word of God, and thus demonstrate to the entire Congregation his confession of faith and Christian character.

Further, as concerns the performance of his official duties, he is obliged:

(1) On all high holidays and feast days, and any others as they occur, and on the eves of such days, and every Sunday and Saturday afternoon, as well as at the regular Catechism sermons and public weddings, to play the large organ in furtherance of divine service to the best of his ability and zeal, and in such manner that at times the small organ and the regal also may be played, particularly on high feasts for the chorales and the concerted music. He is also

(2) Ordinarily—on high and other feasts, as well as on every third Sunday—to present with the Cantor and the Choir Students, as well as with the Town Musicians and other instrumentalists, a moving and well-sounding sacred work; and on extraordinary occasions—on second and third holidays [of the three each celebrated at Christmas, Easter, and Pentecost]—to perform short concerted pieces with the Cantor and the Students, and also at times with some violins and other instruments; and to conduct everything in such a way that the members of the Congregation shall be the more inspired and refreshed in worship and in their love of harkening to the Word of God. But especially he is

(3) Obliged to communicate in good time to the Chief Pastor of our Church, the Councilor of the Consistory, Dr. Heinecke, for his approval, the texts and music chosen, for which purpose he is herewith referred to the Councilor of the Consistory. Further he is

(4) To take care to accompany attentively the regular chorales and those prescribed by the Minister, before and after the Sermons on Sundays and feast days, as well as at Communion and at Vespers and on the eves of holidays, slowly and without unusual embellishment, in four or five parts, on the Diapason, to change the other stops at each verse, also to use the Fifth and the Reeds, the Stopped Pipes, as well as syncopations and suspensions, in such manner that the Congregation can take the organ as the basis of good harmony and unison tone, and thus sing devoutly and give praise and thanks to the Most High.

(5) Accordingly he is hereby entrusted with the large and small organs, as well as the Church regal and other instruments belonging to

the Church, specified in an inventory to be made out for him, and he is instructed to take good care that the former are kept in good condition as regards their bellows, pipes, stops, and other appurtenances, and in good tune, without dissonance; and if anything should become weak or faulty to report the same at once to the Superintendent or, if its importance warrants, to the Church Council, so that it may be repaired and greater damage averted. But the regal, which was bought from the Church Treasury, as well as the other musical instruments, are to be used only for divine service in our Church, and on no account to be lent to other churches, much less for festivities, without our consent; and if any of them are lost, or broken as a result of negligence, the damage is to be made good by him.

For these his efforts he is to receive annually from the Church receipts a salary of 140 thlr., as well as 24 thlr. for his lodging and 7 thlr. 12 gr. for wood; also, for the composition of the Catechism music 1 thlr. each time, and for each wedding music 1 thlr. In return for which he promises not to accept any secondary employment during the present engagement, but to attend exclusively and industriously to his duties in this Church, while, however, he is free to seek other income, through teaching or otherwise, so long as he can do this without neglecting the said duties. In witness whereof we have had this Certificate of Appointment executed *in duplo* under the great seal of this Church, have signed both copies with our own hands, as has been done by the Organist, and have given him one copy and kept the other for the Church records.

Done at Halle, December 14, 1713

Signed [seal] ANDREAS OCKEL   [seal] AUGUSTUS BECKER
                    [SEAL] A. MATTHESIUS, DM.
[seal] FRIDRICH ARNOLD REICHHELM   [seal] CHRISTOPHER SEMLER
                    [seal] CHRISTIANUS KNAUT
[SEAL] CT. W. MÖSCHEL   [SEAL] JOHANN GOTTHILF KOST

49. **Bach's letter to A. Becker, church board member, requesting changes in the agreement** (*BD* I, no. 2)

MOST NOBLE, MOST HONORED SIR,
Your most honored letter with the *vocation in duplo* I have duly received. I am much obliged to you for having sent it, and as I hold it a piece of good fortune that the whole Honorable *Collegium* have wished to vote for my humble self, I shall be the more inclined to follow the Divine

beckoning revealed by this *vocation;* yet I must beg you, Most Honored Sir, not to take it amiss that I cannot at once notify you of my final decision, for the reasons, first, that I have not yet received my definite dismissal and, second, that in one or another respect I should like to have some changes made, in respect of the *salarium* as well as of the duties; concerning all of which I will inform you in writing in the course of this week. Meanwhile, I am returning the one copy, and since I have not yet received my definite dismissal, you will not take it amiss, my Most Honored Sir, that I am at the moment not yet able to engage myself elsewhere by signing my name before I am really released from service here. And as soon as we can agree upon the *station,* I shall appear at once in person and show by my signature that I am really willing to engage myself in Your Honors' service. Meanwhile, I beg you, Most Honored Sir, not to be weighed down by my request to make my most humble respects to all the gentlemen of the Church Board, and to make my excuses to them that at the present moment time has not allowed me to give any categorical decision, both because of certain obligations at Court in connection with the Prince's birthday and because the church services in themselves did not permit it; but it shall be given this week formally and without fail. I accept what you have been so kind as to send me with all respect, and hope that the Honored Church Board will also be graciously pleased to remove the few difficulties that may still arise. In the hope of a prompt and happy issue, I remain,

Most Noble, Most Honored Sir, Your most loyal servant

Weimar, January 14, 1714   JOH. SEBAST. BACH

Bach apparently received an unsatisfactory reply and declined the call to Halle.

50. **Bach's letter refuting an accusation of unfair dealings**
   (*BD* I, no. 4)

MOST NOBLE, MOST THOROUGHLY LEARNED, AND MOST
   HONORED SIR!

That the Most Honored Church Board is astonished at my declining the desired post of organist to which, as you think, I aspired, astonishes me not at all, since I see that they have given the matter so very little thought. You say I applied for the said post of organist, but I do not know of any such thing. This much I do know, that I presented myself and that the most Honored *Collegium* applied to me; for I, after presenting myself, should immediately have taken my leave if the request and courteous invitation of Dr. Heineccius had not compelled me to compose and to perform the piece you know of. Moreover, it is not to be assumed that one will go to a place where one's situation is worsened; but this I could not learn accurately in a fortnight or three weeks, since I am wholly of the opinion that even after many years one cannot rightly know one's livelihood in a place where one must count incidental fees as part of one's income, let alone in a fortnight; and that is more or less the reason why I at first accepted and then, on request, in turn rejected the appointment. But it is by no means to be inferred from all these circumstances that I should have played such a trick upon the Honored Church Board in order to induce my most Gracious Master to increase my salary, since the latter already shows so much graciousness toward my service and art that I do not have to journey to Halle in order to have my salary increased. Accordingly I regret that the assurance of the Honored Church Board has thus had a somewhat uncertain outcome, and add the following: Even if I had received just as good a salary in Halle as here, should I not then have been bound to prefer the prior service to the other one? You, as one learned in the law, can best judge of this and, if I may ask you to, can present this my justification to the Honored Church Board. I remain, in turn,

Your Honor's obedient

JOH. SEB. BACH

Concertmeister and Court Organist

WEIMAR, MARCH 19, 1714

À Monsieur.

Monsieur A. Becker Licentié en Droit.

Mon très honoré Ami à Halle. p. couvert.

BACH IS PROMOTED TO CONCERTMASTER
AT WEIMAR

51. **Excerpt from "Reports concerning the Office of the Princely Court Marshal of Weimar at the Wilhelmsburg," by T. B. Bormann, court secretary** (*BD* II, no. 66)

On Friday, March 2, 1714, His Serene Highness the Reigning Duke most graciously conferred upon the quondam Court Organist Bach, at his most humble request, the title of Concertmaster, with official rank below that of Vice-Capellmeister Drese, for which he is to be obliged to perform new works monthly. And for rehearsals of those, the musicians of the capelle are required to appear upon his demand.

BACH'S DAY-TO-DAY ACTIVITIES AT WEIMAR

52. A note concerning rehearsals (BD II, no. 66)

NB. Rehearsing of the musical pieces at home or in one's lodgings was changed on March 23, 1714, and it was expressly ordered that this should always take place in the church chapel.

This arrangement went into effect two days before Bach presented his first work as concertmaster, the cantata Himmelskönig, sei willkommen, *BWV 182, on March 25, 1714.*

53. A list of the Castle Capelle members, 1714–16
(*BD* II, no. 80; Spitta I, p. 855)

22. Court Secretary, Master of the Pages, and Bass boards at court	Gottfried Ephraim Thiele
25. Bassoonist	Bernhard George Ulrich
27. Chamber Servant and Trumpeter gets board money	Johann Christoph Heininger
28. Castle Steward and Trumpeter receives board money	Johann Christian Biedermann
29. Trumpeter has board money	Johann Martin Fichtel
30. Trumpeter accepts board money	Johann Wendelin Eichenberg
31. Trumpeter enjoys board money	Johann Georg Beümelburg
32. Trumpeter	Conrad Landgraf
33. Kettledrummer is given board money	Andreas Nicol
20. Capellmeister receives daily 1 small loaf of bread and 1 measure of beer from the cellar	Salomo Drese
21. Vice Capellmeister	[Johann Wilhelm] Drese
29. Concertmaster and Court Organist	Johann Sebastian Bach
30. Secretary and Tenor	[Andreas] Aiblinger
31. Tenor and Court Cantor	[Johann] Döbernitz
32. Court Cantor and Bass, also col-l[ega] quint[us] [fifth teacher]	[Christoph] Alt
33. Alto	[Christian Gerhard] Bernhardi

34. Soprano   [Johann Philipp] Weichard
    goes along to the free table
35. Soprano   [Johann Christian] Germann
36. Chamber Musician   Johann Andreas Ehrbach
37. Musician and Violinist   [Andreas Christoph] Eck
38. Violinist and Musician   Johann Georg Hoffmann
    lives in Jena. But when he is
    here he boards at Court.
39. Court Secretary and Musician,   August Gottfried Denstedt
    also Violinist
    [Additionally:] Six Choir Boys

The first group (nos. 22–33) is from a list of employees serving the court of the reigning duke Johann Ernst. The second group (nos. 20–39) is from a list of court employees serving both dukes, Johann Ernst and Ernst August.

54. **Payments for strings and music paper: excerpts from the ducal register** (*BD* II, no. 71)

> 2 fl. 6 gr. For 1 ream of sturdy paper [*Doppel-Papier*] for the Concertmaster's music, October 5, 1714
> 2 fl. 6 gr. To the merchant Johann Christian Hindorff for 2 bundles of strings ordered by Concertmaster Bach, June 21, 1715
> 2 fl. 6 gr. For 1 ream of sturdy paper for Mr. Concertmaster Bach, May 16, 1716

BACH'S SON CARL PHILIPP EMANUEL
IS BAPTIZED

55. **Entry in the records of the Town Church for 1714**
    (*BD* II, no. 67)

A little son, born March 8. Name: Carolus Philippus Imanuel
Godparents:

1. Mr. Secretary Adam Imanuel Weltzig, at present Master of the Pages and Chamber Musician at the Court of the Prince of S. Weissenfels.
2. Mr. Georg Philipp Telemann, Capellmeister to the Imperial Free City of Frankfurth on the Mayn.
3. Mrs. Catharina Dorothea Altmann, Widow of the late Mr. Christian Friedrich Altmann, Chamberlain to the Princely Court of Schwarzburg in Arnstadt.

BACH'S SON JOHANN GOTTFRIED BERNHARD
IS BAPTIZED

56. Entry in the records of the Town Church for 1715
(*BD* II, no. 74)

To the wife of Mr. Johann Sebastian Bach, p[rincely] S[axon] Chamber
Musician, Concertmaster, and Court Organist, Maria Barbara née Bach,
a little son born on May 11, baptized on the 12th. Johann Gottfried
Bernhard. [Godparents:]

1. Mr. Johann Andreas Schanert, Registrar of the Court of Hohenlohe in
   Ohrdruf.
2. Mr. Johann Bernhard Bach, p[rincely] S[axon] Chamber Musician as well
   as Court and Town Organist in Eisenach.
3. Mrs. Dorothea Emmerling, wife of Mr. Emmerling, princely
   Schwarzburg chef in Arnstadt.

BACH RECEIVES A SALARY INCREASE

57. Excerpt from the Weimar state archives (*BD* II, no. 73)

On March 20, 1715, notice given to the two Capellmeisters, Drese
Senior and Junior, upon the order of His Most Serene Highness the
Reigning Duke, that henceforth, in the distribution of perquisites and
honoraria, the Concertmaster Bach is to receive the portion of a Capellmeister, and the Steward of the Castle, Biedermann, a chamber musician's portion, and that forthwith the incoming New Year's money is
to be given them in such measure.

BACH EXAMINES THE NEW CHRISTOPH CUNTZIUS
ORGAN IN HALLE

58. Bach's acknowledgment of the church board's invitation
(*BD* I, no. 5)

MOST NOBLE, MOST HIGHLY HONORED SIR!
For the quite exceptional and most gracious confidence of your noble
self and of all your noble *Collegium,* am most deeply obliged; and as it
is always my greatest *plaisir* to offer to Your Honor my most obedient
service, I shall now be all the more zealous in waiting upon Your Honor

at the appointed [time] and then to give satisfaction, so far as in me lies, in the desired examination. I beg you accordingly, without giving yourself too much trouble, to communicate this my decision to the Honorable *Collegium,* and at the same time to convey to them my most obedient regards, and to assure them of my sense of respectful obligation for their very special confidence.

Since, moreover, Your Honor has been good enough to take great pains in my behalf not only in the present instance but heretofore as well, I acknowledge this with obedient thanks, and assure you that it shall ever be my greatest pleasure to call myself

Your Honor's and My Most Especially Highly Honored Sir's

Most obedient servant
JOH. SEB. BACH
Concertmaster

Weimar, April 22, 1716

59. Report on the organ by Johann Kuhnau, Christian Friedrich Rolle, and Bach (*BD* I, no. 85)

Judgment of the Organ of the Church of Our Lady at Halle

Whereas it has pleased the Most Honorable *Collegium Marianum* of the Town of Halle to request the undersigned, in writing, to appear on the 29th of April last, the day before yesterday, and to scrutinize and examine in all its parts the large new organ in the Church of Our Lady, constructed by the Grace of God and to His Glory by the organ builder Mr. Christoff Cuncius, and to note down whatever we should find of good or bad therein, and in general make known our judgment thereupon; accordingly, in most dutiful response to this gracious request and the trusting confidence expressed in our experience and skill, we made our appearance here on the appointed day and, after having had the high summons repeated to us orally, undertook in God's Name the examination of the new organ in the said Church.

Wherein:

(1) We have found the bellows chamber large enough for the bellows, and well protected against bad weather; but have also noted that since the window faces west the bellows must be exposed to excessive heat from the sun, and accordingly a curtain or some other protection against the sun will be needed for the time when the organ is not in use.

(2) As for the bellows themselves, which are 10 in number (although the builder promised only 9 in the contract, perhaps because he

thought *quod superflua non noceant* [there would be no harm in abundance], and that the even number was preferable to the odd for the sake of the arrangement of the bellows, which are set opposite each other), they might still demonstrate the required capacity and the industry of the builder, but the wind would not drive the liquid in the wind gauge we applied to the 35th or 40th degree otherwise required in organs of such size and found in other organs having a good wind supply, but only to the 32nd or 33rd. Accordingly, when the Great Organ was played a certain faltering in the bellows was to be noted. Now this might be endured if only the *Ober Werck,* on the middle manual, did not falter—for this is counted among the serious defects.

(3) Next, however, as concerns the wind chests, we found no visible defect, and they also withstood the test of having the keys of both manual and pedal keyboards pressed down at the same time without our noticing any leakage except a little in the middle manual; which, however, is caused by the fact that the upper boards [*Stöcke*] are not screwed in too firmly, and can easily be corrected. And under the ventils there have been placed not double or triple springs, such as poor builders often use to prevent squealing, but single ones throughout. This fact should make the clavier rather easy to play. Nevertheless, it will be necessary for the touch to be made even a little lighter, and yet the quick rebound of the keyboards [i.e., keys] must not be hindered, still less any squealing be brought about. Which, then, the builder has agreed to bring to this state.

(4) As far as the housing of the organ is concerned, greater space for it would indeed have been desirable, so that everything would not have had to be placed so close together, and everything could have been gotten at more conveniently.

(5) For the rest, all the stops specified in the contract are present, and they are made of the materials there mentioned, except that instead of the specified metal 16-foot *Gemshorn Bass* a wooden 32-foot *Untersatz* or Sub-Bass has been provided, the size of the pipes of which should make up for the absence of the metal.

Furthermore, the following finished and usable stops have been provided over and above the contract:

Spitzflöte	2 foot	⎫
Quinta	3 foot	⎪
Octava	2 foot	⎬ of metal [a tin and lead alloy (Adlung)]
Nachthorn	4 foot	⎪
Quinta open	6 foot	⎭

On the other hand, the following have been omitted:

The *Fagott Bass,* of tin	8 foot
Gedackt, metal	4 foot
Waldflöte, ditto	2 foot
Rohrflöte, ditto	12 foot

Likewise, he has provided two 3-rank Cymbals instead of the two 2-rank ones called for.

(6) And while it shall not be discussed in what proportions the metals were alloyed, it is altogether easy to see that (as is commonly done) for the stops that do not meet the eye there has been more saving of tin than of lead; also in this organ the metal of the pipes could or should have been somewhat heavier.

The pipes that form the façade of the organ ought to shine with a bright light, and presumably the best part of the good tin was used for them; the fact that they do not shine thus must not be blamed on the builder, but on the soot that has fallen upon them. On the other hand, it is his fault if the sound especially of the big pipes cannot be heard clearly, since there are shortcomings as regards the good voicing that should obtain; which defect has shown in various such pipes, among others in the 32-foot Sub-Bass and Trombone Bass, as well as in other reed stops. Now, Mr. Cuncius has not only promised, as he will have to tune the pipes more exactly here and there, since we have found them fairly out of tune in all three keyboards, to adopt the system of passably good temperament he upon occasion showed us, but also, as concerns better voicing of some pipes desired, to attend to the correction of that matter. Although it would have been better if this had been attended to before the examination; and if we could have inspected the parts that are still missing—namely, the coupler; two tremulants; two stars; a movable sun in the Upper Positive; and the bird song.

This, then, is what we, the undersigned, in obedience to our duty and in the interest of truth must report concerning this organ. We may add that we hope it may always be heard with pleasure and last steadily for many years; to the Glory of the Most High and the especial renown of our Most Noble Patrons, as well as of the whole worthy town, in peace and tranquillity, to the encouragement of divine worship.

Halle, Philippi Jacobi Day [May 1], 1716

> [seal] JOHANN KUHNAU   [seal] CHRISTIAN FRIEDRICH ROLLE
> [seal] JOH. SEBAST. BACH

Kuhnau was cantor of St. Thomas's in Leipzig; Rolle was organist in Quedlin-
burg. According to Adlung, the organ had no fewer than 47 stops for the three
manuals and 18 stops for the pedal.

60. **"Menu of the Dinner of the Most Worshipful Council on the Occasion of the Dedication of the New Organ," Sunday, May 3, 1716** (Terry, p. 109f.)

1 piece of Bœuf à la mode [*Bäffallemote*]
Pike with a sardelle *beu* [*probably bleu* (blue, i.e., boiled)]
1 smoked ham
1 dish of peas
1 dish of potatoes
2 dishes of spinach and chicory [? *Zerzigen*]

1 roast quarter of mutton	Warm asparagus salad
Boiled pumpkin	Lettuce
Fritters	Radishes
Preserved lemon rind	Fresh butter
Preserved cherries	Roast veal

61. **Reimbursement of travel costs: excerpts from the account books of the Church of Our Lady** (*BD* I, no. 108)

Six thlr. along with a sealed little parcel have truly been paid to me the undersigned by Mr. Becker, Lic. for travel expenses, which is hereby gratefully attested. Dated Halle, May 2, anno 1716.

JOHANN SEBASTIAN BACH
Princely Saxe-Weimar
Concertmaster and Court
Organist, etc. etc.

BACH AND JOHANN ANTON WEISE WRITE A
TESTIMONIAL FOR THE ORGAN BUILDER
JOHANN GEORG SCHRÖTER

62. **Statement by Bach and Weise on behalf of Schröter**
(*BD* I, no. 86)

Whereas we, the undersigned, have tested the new organ, built by Mr. Johann Georg Schröter in the St. Augustine's of Lutheran Confession at Erffurth, having been appointed *Examinatores* for this purpose, and have found after sufficient investigation that it has been built faithfully and well, in accordance with the contract; and, in addition, the said Mr. Schröter has requested us not to fail to give him a testimonial to the industry he has devoted to this work; now, therefore, we have sought to gratify this wish herewith, as is fair, and must add, to his credit, that (as has already been mentioned) he has faithfully fulfilled the terms of the contract drawn up for this work; moreover, it is but right for him to be congratulated on the fact that the first organ he has completed as a master builder has turned out so well, and accordingly it is not to be doubted, in respect to such further work as he shall undertake, that he will likewise complete it industriously and untiringly, applying the knowledge that God has lent him. This much we neither could nor would refuse him, out of respect for the truth.

Given at Erffurth, July 13, 1716

JOHANN SEBASTIAN BACH   JOHANN ANTON WEISE
Concertmeister and Court Organist   *Organ Builder,*
to the Prince of Saxe-Weimar   *of Arnstadt*

BACH PRESENTS A PASSION PERFORMANCE
IN GOTHA

63. **Excerpt from the private ducal account book for 1717**
    (Glöckner, p. 35)

    12 rthl. to the Concertmaster Bach, on April 12, rept. no. 13

    Receipt no. 13 has not survived. On Good Friday, March 26, 1717, Bach substituted for the court capellmeister Christian Friedrich Witt, who fell ill in January and died on April 3, 1717.

64. **Excerpt from the ducal account book for 1716–1717**
    (Glöckner, p. 35)

    1 fl. 4 gr. For 20 Passion booklets that were delivered to the princely court chapel, paid to the printer Christoph Reyher, on April 12, 1717. No. 2447

    The Passion librettos are lost.

65. **Accompanying invoice** (Glöckner, p. 35)

    Upon gracious princely command, 20 bound booklets for the Passion to be performed this year were delivered to the princely court chapel for the Princely Saxon Capellmeister, Mr. Witt; if one copy is 1 gr. 3 pf., these 20 copies cost 1 fl. 4 gr.

CHRISTOPH REYHER,
Court Printer

Gotha, on April 2, 1717

BACH TAKES ON HIS COUSIN JOHANN LORENZ BACH
AS A STUDENT

66.   Excerpt from J. L. Bach's letter of application, 1717
(*BD* II, no. 82)

Since my youth, I have pursued studies at the Latin School . . . as well as tutelage in music under the direction of my father, to the extent that for 5 years here and elsewhere, since I remained for several years with the Princely Concertmaster and Chamber Musician at Weimar, I practiced and qualified in vocal and instrumental music such that I trust myself to take on the desired cantorate with due pleasure of my superiors and their parish. . . .

J. L. Bach, of Schweinfurt, left the Ohrdruf Lyceum in September 1713 for Weimar.

BACH AND LOUIS MARCHAND COMPETE
AT THE DRESDEN COURT

67.   A later account by Johann Abraham Birnbaum, 1739
(*BD* II, no. 441)

. . . Suppose I were to mention a man who in his time was considered the greatest master in all France on the clavier and the organ, against whom the Hon. Court Composer not too long ago fully maintained the honor of Germans, as well as his own honor. This man was *Mons. Marchand,* who while he was in Dressden, and the Hon. Court Composer was also there, was challenged by the latter, in a courteous letter sent at the suggestion and command of some important personages of the Court there, to a trial and comparison of their respective talents at the clavier, and who agreed to appear as proposed. The hour arrived when two great virtuosi should match their strengths. The Hon. Court Composer, together with those who were to be the judges of this musical contest, waited for the other contestant anxiously, but in vain. It finally developed that he had vanished from Dressden early in the day by the fast stagecoach. Doubtless the famous Frenchman found his talents too weak to withstand the powerful assaults of his expert and valiant opponent. Otherwise he would not have sought refuge in so hasty a flight.

There is no documentation for the event that took place in the fall of 1717; Bach's letter to Marchand (BD I, no. 6) is lost. The source for this report can only be Bach himself, under whose watchful eye Birnbaum's defense of the composer (No. 344) was written. See also the version of the story in the obituary (No. 306).

BACH IS JAILED AND UNFAVORABLY DISMISSED
FROM HIS WEIMAR POST

68. Excerpt from the court secretary's report (*BD* II, no. 84)

On November 6, [1717], the quondam concertmaster and organist Bach was confined to the County Judge's place of detention for too stubbornly forcing the issue of his dismissal and finally on December 2 was freed from arrest with notice of his unfavorable discharge.

BACH TITLES A COLLECTION OF ORGAN
CHORALES FOR THE ECCLESIASTICAL YEAR

69. *Orgel-Büchlein,* BWV 599–644: title page (*BD* I, no. 148)

Little Organ Book (with 48 realized chorales), In which a beginner at the organ is given instruction in developing a chorale in many divers ways, and at the same time in acquiring facility in the study of the pedal since in the chorales contained therein the pedal is treated as wholly obbligato.

In Praise of the Almighty's will
and for my neighbor's greater skill

Autore
Joanne Sebast. Bach
P[leno] t[itulo] Capellae Magistro
S[erenissimi] P[rincipis] R[egnantis]
Anhaltini Cotheniensis

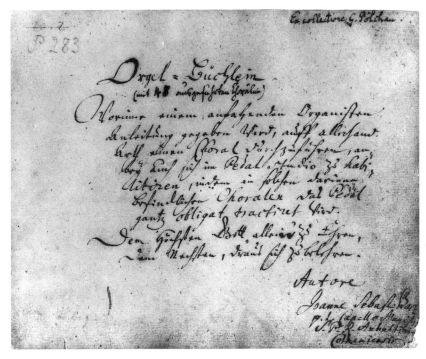

69. *Orgel-Büchlein,* BWV 599–644: title page

This appended title page is undated, but it was written in Cöthen and its style resembles that of the Inventions (No. 92). Pleno titulo means "with full title." The vast majority of chorale settings were composed in Weimar.

Cöthen

1 7 1 7–1 7 2 3

70. **Excerpts from the record of the Princely Capelle and trumpeters' wages** (*BD* II, no. 86)

a. Dec. 29 [1717]   thlr.   gr.

The newly arrived Capellmeister Mr. Johann Sebastian Bach receives monthly 33 rth. 8 gr. and has duly received that amount from August 1 [1717]

b. August 7 [post-dated entry]

To the same a most gracious recompense upon taking up   50   –
the appointment [*bey der Capitulation*]

c. Dec. 29

For the months of August, Sept., Oct., Nov., and December   166   16
1717 until January 1, 1718, according to the register, fol.
1, no. 245

d. Feb. 5 [1718]

For the month of January   33   8

e. [February] 28

For the months of February and March, Joh. Seb. Bach   66   16

f. April 2   For the month of April   33   8

g. [April] 30   For the month of May   33   8

h. May 6   For the month of June for the journey to Carls-   33   8
bad

Bach's annual salary of 400 thlr., the second-highest paid to a Cöthen court official, was twice as much as his predecessor Augustin Stricker had received.

THE JOHANN SCHEIBE ORGAN OF ST. PAUL'S
CHURCH IN LEIPZIG

71. **Specifications of the organ** (*BD* I, p. 167)

Hauptwerk	*Brustwerk*	*Hinterwerk (Echo)*
Gross-Principal 16'	Principal 8'	Lieblich getackt 8'
Gross-Quinta-Tön 16'	Viol di Gamb 8'	Quinta-Tön 8'
Klein Principal 8'	Grob getackt 8'	Fleute deuce 4'
Schalmo [Chalumeau] 8'	Octav 4'	Quinta decima 4'
Fleute Allemande 8'	Rohr-Flöte 4'	Decima nona 3'
Gems-Horn 8'	Octav 2'	Holl-Flöte 2'
Octav 4'	Nassat 3'	Viola 2'
Quinta 3'	Sedecima 1'	Vigesima nona 1½'
Quint-Nassat 3'	Schweitzer-Pfeiffe 1'	Weit-Pfeiffe 1'
Octavina 2'	Largo [Larigot]	Mixtur 3f.
Wald-Flöte 2'	Mixtur 3f.	Helle Cymbal 2f.
Grosse Mixtur 5–6f.	Helle Cymbal 2f.	Sertin [Sordune] 8'
Cornetti 3f.		
Zinck 2f.		

Pedal		
Gross Principal Bass 16'	Mixtur-Bass 5–6f.	Sub-Bass 16'
Gross Quinta-Tön-Bass 16'	Gross hell-Quinten-Bass 6'	Posaunen-Bass 16'
Octav-Bass 8'	Jubal-Bass 8'	Trompeten-Bass 8'
Octav-Bass 4'	Nacht-Horn-Bass 4'	Holl-Flöten-Bass 1'
Quint-Bass 3'	Octav-Bass 2'	Mixtur-Bass 4f.

The organ, built in 1716–17 by Johann Scheibe, would be the largest and most modern instrument later available to Bach in Leipzig. Scheibe, the father of Johann Adolph Scheibe, also built the organs in St. John's (which Bach examined in 1744; the report is lost) and in Zschortau (see No. 235).

72. **Bach's report on the organ** (*BD* I, no. 87)

Since at the request of his Most Noble Worship Dr. Rechenberg, at this time *Rector Magnificus* of the Most Worshipful Academy [University] at

Leipzig, I undertook the examination of the organ in St. Paul's Church, which has been in part newly built and in part repaired, I have accomplished the same to the best of my ability, taken note of any defects, and wished in general to make the following observations concerning the whole organ, to wit:

(1) As regards the whole structure of the organ, it is on the one hand not to be denied that this structure is very closely confined, and thus it will be hard to get at every part, in case there should in time be something to repair, but on the other hand Mr. [Johann] Scheibe, as the contractor for the said organ, excuses this on the grounds that in the first place the organ case was not built by him, and so he had to get on as best he could within the given space, and in the second place he was not granted the additional space he requested in order to arrange the structure more conveniently.

(2) The usual principal parts of an organ—namely, the wind chests, bellows, pipes, roller boards, and other items—are well and carefully made, and there is nothing further to be said about them except that the wind must be made equal throughout, to forestall occasional sudden blasts of wind. The roller boards should, indeed, be enclosed in frames, so as to avoid any howling in bad weather, but since Mr. Scheibe, as is his custom, has made them with [specially prepared] tables and gives assurance that the latter will achieve what would otherwise have to be achieved by frames, this has been allowed to pass.

(3) The items listed in the Disposition as well as in all the contracts are present in both number and kind, except for two reeds, namely, *Schallmey* 4 foot and *Cornet* 2 foot, which, pursuant to the instructions of the Honorable *Collegium*, have had to be omitted, and in their place the *Octava* 2 foot has been placed in the *Brustwerck* and the *Hohlflöte* 2 foot in the *Hinterwerck*.

(4) The existing defects that have shown themselves in respect to inequality of voicing must and can be remedied at once by the organ builder, so that, in particular, the lowest pipes of the Trombone and Trumpet Bass[es] shall not speak so coarsely and noisily, but rather produce and maintain a clear and firm tone, and the other pipes that are unequal shall be carefully corrected and made even, which can perfectly well be done when the whole organ is once more thoroughly tuned, and this in better weather than we have been having.

(5) The touch of the organ should indeed be somewhat lighter, and the keys not go down so far, but since, on account of the too close construction, this condition could not be changed, it must be accepted as it is—however, it can still be played so that one does not have

to fear that one will stick fast in the middle of playing.

(6) Since the organ builder has also had to make a new wind chest for the *Brustwerck,* above and beyond what was called for in the contract, because the old wind chest, which was to have served instead of the new one, has in the first place a [one-piece] soundboard [*Fundament-Brett*], and is thus wrong and unacceptable; and in the second place it contains, according to the old custom, a short octave, and the remaining keys, which are missing, could not be installed so that all three manuals might be made equal, but would instead have caused a *déformité*—accordingly it was highly necessary that a new wind chest should be made, the defects avoided that would otherwise have been troublesome, and a fine *conformité* maintained. Therefore, and without my reminder, the organ builder should be reimbursed and held harmless for the parts he has constructed over and above the contract specifications.

Whilst, furthermore, the organ builder has asked me to point out to the Honorable Council that there has been a desire to count as covered by his payment items not covered in his agreement, such as the sculptural work, the gilding, also the fees received by Mr. Vetter for the inspection, and possibly other similar items, and that he was in fact not obliged to provide for the same, nor had such treatment ever been customary (else he would have made a better estimate)—thus he very humbly prays that he not be put to any losses on this account.

Now, finally, it cannot remain unmentioned that (1) the window, i.e., that part of it which extends behind the organ, should be shielded on the inside by a little wall, or by a heavy piece of sheet iron, to avoid further threatened damage from the weather.

(2) It is customary and most important that the organ builder should guarantee his work for one year, so as to remove completely any further defects that may show themselves, and this he would be most ready to do, if only he were granted the promptest and fullest compensation for the expenses he has incurred over and above those provided for in the contract.

This, then, would be what I have found it necessary to report in examining the organ, having the honor of being ever at the service of Your Honorable Magnificence Dr. Rechenberg and the whole Honorable *Collegium,* and remain

Your Honor's most obedient and devoted

JOH. SEB. BACH
Capellmeister to the Prince of Anhalt
Cöthen, etc.

Leipzig, December 17, Anno 1717

Bach was dismissed from Weimar on December 2. Reading No. 74 seems to indicate that the first rehearsal of the Cöthen Capelle in his house took place on December 10. Accordingly he must already have moved to Cöthen before making this report.

73. Receipt for Bach's examination fee: from the university archives (*BD* I, no. 109)

That I have received from His Most Noble Magnificence, Herr Dr. Rechenberg, at present Rector Magnificus, on behalf of the Worshipful University of Leipzig for examining and testing the organ in St. Paul's Church, and for pointing out any defects that may occur, 20 rthl., say twenty reichsthaler, as recompense, such I herewith have wanted to attest and acknowledge, along with obedient gratitude. Dated Leipzig, December 18, 1717.

JOH. SEB. BACH
Capellmeister, etc.

BACH IS REIMBURSED FOR VARIOUS EXPENSES

74. Rent for 1717–1718: excerpt from the account books of the Court Capelle (*BD* II, no. 91)

1 October [1718].

> To the Capellmeister Bach, one year's rent for the Capelle
> (*Collegium Musicum*) from December 10, 1717, to the same date
> 1718,   12 rth.

75. Rehearsals and harpsichord maintenance (*BD* II, no. 91)

October 13 [1719].

> To the same [J. S. Bach], for rehearsals held in his house and for
> maintaining the harpsichord, from December 10, 1718, to
> Dec. 10, 1719.   12 [thlr.]

76. Visiting musicians: excerpts from the court account books (*BD* II, no. 93)

a. October 20 [1718]

> To the same [J. S. Bach], for paying the discantist from
> Rudolstadt who performed here   16 [thlr.]

b. [December 16, 1718]

For the bass singer Riemenschneider, who was here for several
weeks,   40 [thlr.]
For the Concertmaster Lienigke of Merseburg,   16 [thlr.]
For [the organist Johann Gottfried] Vogler from Leipzig,   16 [thlr.]
For the discantist [Emanuel] Prese,   6 [thlr.]
To Capellmeister Bach paid in the presence of the Hon.
Councilors   78 [thlr.]

c. [August] 24 [1719]

To the Capellmeister Bach, for paying a discantist   20 [thlr.]

*The visiting musicians listed under the December 1718 date may have partici-
pated in the performance of BWV Anh 5 and BWV 66a on the occasion of
Prince Leopold's birthday, December 10, 1718.*

**77. Purchase of a harpsichord in Berlin: excerpt from the court
account books** (*BD* II, no. 95)

March 1 [1719] To Capellmeister Bach for the harpsichord
built in Berlin and travel expenses   130 [thlr.]

*The instrument is listed in a 1784 inventory as "The grand harpsichord with
2 manuals, by Michael Mietke in Berlin, 1719; defect."*

BACH'S SON LEOPOLD AUGUSTUS IS BAPTIZED,
WITH NOBLE GODPARENTS APPOINTED

78. Excerpt from the Castle Church record (*BD* II, no. 94)

November 17, 1718. The Prince's Capellmeister, Mr. Johann Sebastian
Bach, and his wife, Maria Barbara, had a son baptized in the Castle
Church, born on the 15th of this month; Name, Leopold Augustus.
The godparents were (1) His Highness the Prince Leopold, reigning
Prince of Anhalt. (2) His Highness the Prince Augustus Ludwig,
Prince of Anhalt. (3) Her Highness the Duchess Eleonora Wilhelmina,
Duchess of Saxe-Weimar. (4) The Hon. Mr. Christoph Jost von
Zanthier, His Highness's, the reigning Prince Leopold's, privy coun-
cilor. (5) The Hon. Mrs. Juliana Magdalene, His Highness's, the reign-
ing Prince Leopold's, Mr. Gottlob von Nostiz's wife.

BACH COMPILES A COLLECTION OF PIECES FOR
HIS ELDEST SON

79. *Clavier-Büchlein für Wilhelm Friedemann Bach:* title page
    (*BD* I, no. 149)

Little Clavier Book for Wilhelm Friedemann Bach, begun in Cöthen
on January 22 A[nn]o 1720.

DEATH OF BACH'S WIFE, MARIA BARBARA

80. **Burial notice from the Cöthen register of deaths**
    (*BD* II, no. 100)

July 7 [1720] the wife of Mr. Johann Sebastian Bach, Capellmeister to
His Highness the Prince, was buried. The entire school [choir] paid,
however, only 2 thlr. paid to the school.

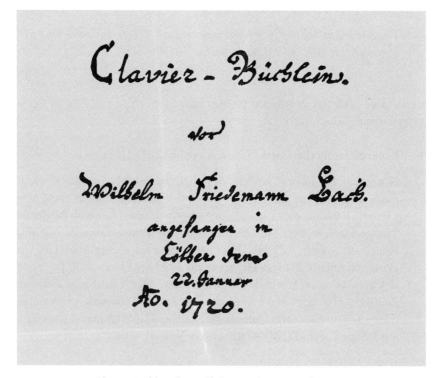

79. *Clavier-Büchlein für Wilhelm Friedemann Bach:* title page

Bach was absent at the time, with Prince Leopold in Carlsbad, Bohemia.

BACH APPLIES FOR THE ORGANIST'S POST AT
ST. JACOBI CHURCH IN HAMBURG

81.   **Excerpts from the minutes of St. Jacobi Church** (*BD* II, no. 102)

Anno 1720, September 12. Heinrich Friese, the organist and clerk of this Church, died. Whereupon

Anno 1720, November 21. The Pastor, with the two gentlemen of the Congregation, as well as the four Beadles [*Herren in der Beede*] namely— Mr. Bernhard Cropp and Mr. Fridericus Wahn, Trustees of the Sepulcher, and Mr. Johan Luttas and Mr. Johan Caspar Weber, Annual Trustees—were together in the Church chamber, where, the formalities having been discharged, Mr. Bernhard Cropp pointed out that various persons had entered their names for the choice of an organist, which the four Beadles herewith presented, namely:

Mr. Matthias Christoph Wideburg [formerly Capellmeister at Gera]; Mr. Heinrich Zinck, Organist at Itzeho; Mr. Vincent Lübec Junior; Mr. Johann Joachim Heitmann; Mr. Johann Sebastian Bach; Mr. Frenkel, Organist at Ratzeburg; Mr. Lüders; Mr. Hertzog.

When these names had been read, Mr. Beckhoff, in the name of the gentlemen present, replied; hereupon various points were discussed, namely:

(1) How many of the above eight persons should be admitted to trial?

Conclusum: All the competent ones should be admitted to trial, if they requested to be.

(2) What persons should be asked hither to give their *judicium* thereupon?

Conclusum: It was found necessary that, in addition to the Honorable Cantor, three organists should be asked to assist at the same—namely, Mr. Johann Adam Reinike {*sic*} of St. Catherine's, Mr. Andreas Kniller of St. Peter's, and Mr. Georg Preuss of the Holy Spirit—and everything should be done again this time according to the procedure of November 26, Anno 1674.

(3) At what time the trial should take place, so that the competent persons might present themselves for it?

Conclusum: The same could most conveniently take place on November 28, being Thursday, after the hour of prayers.

(4) The question was raised whether it was desired that money should be given for the organist's post; on which point it was decided that:

There were many reasons not to introduce the sale of an organist's post, because it was part of the ministry of God; accordingly the choice should be free, and the capacity of the candidates should be more considered than the money. But if, after the selection had been made, the chosen candidate of his own free will wished to give a token of his gratitude, the latter could be accepted for the benefit of the Church and the Holy Sepulcher, entered in the books, and used again where it was needed.

[On November 23, 1720, Bach was summoned to return to the service of his Prince. On November 28, four of the candidates gave their trial performance.]

Anno 1720, December 19. There appeared in the large Church Chamber, in response to the kind invitation that had gone out, the Pastor, Mr. Erdmann Neumeister, Mr. Walther Beckhoff and Mr. Henning Lochau, present Trustees of our beloved Congregation, Mr. Bernhard Crop and Mr. Friederich Wahn, Trustees of the Sepulcher, Mr. Johan Luttas and Mr. Johann Caspar Weber, Annual Trustees. Whereupon, the formalities having been discharged, the Senior Trustee of the Sepulcher stated that it was known by all how on November 28, after the trial and the report of the Cantor and the organists invited therefor, the choice had been set for December 12. But Mr. Luttas had sought a postponement until he should receive a letter from Mr. Johann Sebastian Bach, Capellmeister at Cöthen, in which the Pastor and Gentlemen of the Congregation had acquiesced. Since Mr. Luttas had now received a letter, he had already communicated the same to the Pastor and Gentlemen of the Congregation, and it was thereupon read aloud in full. Whereupon it was resolved in God's Name to proceed to the choice, and thus Johann Joachim Heitmann was chosen by a majority vote, *viva voce,* as organist and clerk of the St. Jacobi Church, which was also indicated to him by the Church servant, and he was asked to appear at the Church Chamber; meanwhile, the Pastor and the Gentlemen of the Congregation took their leave. When he thereupon appeared, he was notified of the said choice by the Beadles, and he expressed for his part his thanks for the kindness shown him, whereupon everyone went home.

The documents further reveal that Heitmann showed his gratitude by the payment of 4,000 marks. It should be noted that certain offices at Hamburg, such as that of the council's cake baker, were sold to the highest bidder as a matter of principle; a second class of offices were bestowed with the expectation of payment; and only a small class, including those of the higher teachers, the librarian, the council musicians and trumpeter, were simply elected.

82. Johann Mattheson's later account of the appointment process, from *Der musicalische Patriot,* 1728 (*BD* II, no. 253)

I remember, and a whole large congregation will probably also remember, that a few years ago a certain great virtuoso, whose merits have since brought him a handsome Cantorate, presented himself as candidate for the post of organist in a town of no small size, exhibited his playing on the most various and greatest organs, and aroused universal admiration for his ability; but there presented himself at the same time, among other unskilled journeymen, the son of a well-to-do artisan, who was better at preluding with his thalers than with his fingers, and he obtained the post, as may be easily conjectured, despite the fact that almost everyone was angry about it. This took place just at Christmas time, and the eloquent chief preacher, who had not concurred in the Simoniacal deliberations, expounded in the most splendid fashion the gospel of the music of the angels at the birth of Christ, in which connection the recent incident of the rejected artist gave him quite naturally the opportunity to reveal his thoughts, and to close his sermon with something like the following pronouncement: he was firmly convinced that even if one of the angels of Bethlehem should come down from Heaven, one who played divinely and wished to become organist of St. Jacobi, but had no money, he might just as well fly away again.

BACH ASSEMBLES THE BRANDENBURG CONCERTOS

83. *Six Concerts avec plusieurs Instruments,* BWV 1046–1051: title page (*BD* I, no. 150)

Six concertos with several instruments dedicated to His Royal Highness, Monseigneur Christian Ludwig, Margrave of Brandenburg &c. &c. &c., by His very humble and very obedient servant Johann Sebastian Bach, Capellmeister of His Most Serene Highness, the Reigning Prince of Anhalt-Cöthen

This collection represents a fair copy of concerto scores of earlier origin.

83. *Six concerts avec plusieurs instruments,* BWV 1046–1051: title page

84. Bach's dedication to the Margrave of Brandenburg
(*BD* I, no. 150)

To His Royal Highness My Lord Christian Ludwig, Margrave of Brandenburg &c. &c. &c.

YOUR ROYAL HIGHNESS,

As I had a couple of years ago the pleasure of appearing before Your Royal Highness, by virtue of Your Highness's commands, and as I noticed then that Your Highness took some pleasure in the small talents that Heaven has given me for Music, and as in taking leave of Your Royal Highness, Your Highness deigned to honor me with the command to send Your Highness some pieces of my composition: I have then in accordance with Your Highness's most gracious orders taken the liberty of rendering my most humble duty to Your Royal Highness with the present concertos, which I have adapted to several instruments; begging Your Highness most humbly not to judge their imperfection with the rigor of the fine and delicate taste that the whole world knows Your Highness has for musical pieces; but rather to infer from them in benign consideration the profound respect and the most humble obedience that I try to show Your Highness therewith. For the rest, Sire, I beg Your Royal Highness very humbly to have the goodness to continue Your Highness's gracious favor toward me, and to be assured that nothing is so close to my heart as the wish that I may be employed on occasions more worthy of Your Royal Highness and of Your Highness's service—I, who without an equal in zeal am,

Sire, Your Royal Highness's most humble and obedient servant

Coethen, March 24, 1721   JEAN SEBASTIEN BACH

BACH VISITS THE COURT OF SCHLEIZ

85. Excerpts from the court account book (*BD* II, no. 107)

16 fl. 18 gr.	to the Capellmeister of Cöthen, paid August 7 [1721]
3 fl. 14 gr. 8 pf.	for the Capellmeister Bach in the Inn of the Blue Angel, paid August 11
20 gr.	passage fare from here to and from Gera, paid to the Postmaster on August 13

The cantor of the court chapel at Schleiz, Johann Sebastian Koch, had been choir prefect in Mühlhausen between 1709 and 1711 and most likely knew Bach from those years.

BACH IS MARRIED AGAIN, TO
ANNA MAGDALENA, NÉE WILCKE

86. Excerpt from the Castle Church register (*BD* II, no. 110)

On December 3, 1721, Mr. Johann Sebastian Bach, widower, Capellmeister here to His Highness the Prince, and Mistress Anna Magdalena, legitimate youngest daughter of Mr. Johann Caspar Wülcken, Court and Field Trumpeter of the Music of His Highness the Prince of Saxe-Weissenfels, were married at home, by command of the Prince.

For September 21, 1721, a few weeks before their marriage, the register of the Castle Church shows Anna Magdalena Wilcke to be on the roster of court singers in Cöthen. Along with Bach she is listed among the godparents of J. C. Hahn, son of a footman to the prince, as "Miss Magdalena Wilckens, singer at the princely court here" (BD II, no. 108).

SALARIES FOR BACH AND HIS WIFE, 1721–1723

87. Excerpts from the Cöthen Capelle accounts (*BD* II, no. 86)

a. *For 1721–1722:*
For Bach 400 rth. again; in addition, his wife is to have 26 rth. 16 gr. monthly

b. *For 1722–1723:*

His wife the same from October 10 to May 1, according to the book, p. 2, 166 th. 16 gr.

When Bach remarried, in 1721, the prince granted his wife an annual salary of 200 thaler, and within a year she received 300 thaler (more than any of the other court functionaries except chamber councilor, court minister, and capellmeister), bringing the combined income of Johann Sebastian and Anna Magdalena to some 700 thaler—as much as they were to have in Leipzig, where it was "very expensive" to live (cf. No. 152).

BACH COMPILES A COLLECTION OF PIECES FOR
HIS WIFE

88. *Clavier-Büchlein für Anna Magdalena Bach:* title page

Little Clavier Book for Anna Magdalena Bach. Anno 1722.

BACH WARDS OFF A LAWSUIT BY THE
LÄMMERHIRT HEIRS

89. Bach's petition to the Erfurt town council (*BD* I, no. 8)

To the Most Noble, Steadfast, Most Learned and Most Wise Town Mayors, Burgomasters, Syndic, and Other Members of the Council, My Most Especially Gracious Honored Patrons in Erffurth.

MOST NOBLE, STEADFAST, MOST LEARNED, ALSO MOST WISE SIRS, ESPECIALLY MOST HIGHLY ESTEEMED GENTLEMEN AND PATRONI!

It is already known to Your Honors how I and my brother Joh. Jacob Bach (who is in the Royal Swedish service) come to be partial heirs in the Lemmerhirt estate. Since I now hear unofficially that the other honorable joint heirs are disposed to open a lawsuit concerning this estate, and since this would not suit either me or my absent brother, for I am not disposed to contest the Lemmerhirt will at law, but am satisfied with what is bestowed and conferred upon me therein, on account of which I herewith for myself and *sub cautione rati* in the name

88. *Clavier-Büchlein für Anna Magdalena Bach:* title page

of my brother wish to renounce and enter formal *protestation* against any legal proceedings, now therefore I have accordingly considered it necessary to notify Your Honors obediently of this fact, with the most humble request that you will graciously receive this my renunciation and protestation, and will kindly cause the *quotas* still due me and my brother from the inheritance, from what already lies on deposit as well as from whatever may be deposited in the future, to be remitted, which high *faveur* I acknowledge with most obedient thanks, and remain therefore

Your Honors' most devoted servant

JOH. SEB. BACH

Cöthen, March 15,　　　*Capellmeister to His Highness the Prince of*
Anno 1722　　　　　　*Anhalt-Cöthen*

Bach's petition was successful: the proceedings were apparently never begun, and the legacies were paid. Bach's share was approximately 550 thlr.

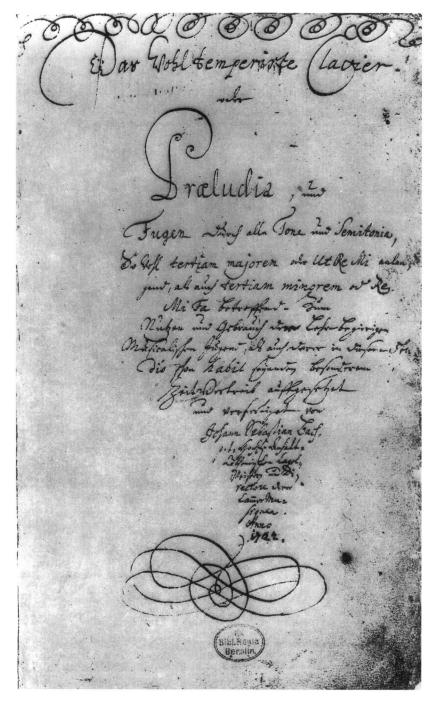

90. *Das Wohltemperirte Clavier,* Book I, BWV 846–869: title page

BACH COMPLETES 24 PRELUDES AND FUGUES

90. *Das Wohltemperirte Clavier,* Book I, BWV 846–869: title page

The Well-Tempered Clavier, or, preludes and fugues through all the tones and semitones, both as regards the *tertia major* or *Ut Re Mi* and as concerns the *tertia minor* or *Re Mi Fa.* For the use and profit of the musical youth desirous of learning as well as for the pastime of those already skilled in this study, drawn up and written by Johann Sebastian Bach p.t. Capellmeister to His Serene Highness, the Prince of Anhalt-Cöthen, etc., and Director of His chamber music. Anno 1722.

It is quite unlikely that Bach had the second set (BWV 870–893), which was not completed until many years later, in mind when he wrote the first. The somewhat complicated description of what we know simply as major and minor modes was necessitated by the fact that these terms had not yet come into general use.

BACH REPAIRS THE PRINCE'S HARPSICHORDS

91. Excerpts from the Cöthen Capelle accounts (*BD* II, no. 115)

a. *September 12, 1722:*
To the Capellmeister Bach for repairs to the Prince's *Cimbalo,* without the strings, 1 th.

b. *December 30, 1722:*
The same for quilling the big *Clavecin,* including the strings, 1 th. 8 gr.

c. *March 20, 1723:*
To the Capellmeister Bach, who had to quill this *Clavecin,* 1 th.

BACH COMPILES 15 TWO-PART INVENTIONS AND
15 THREE-PART SINFONIAS

92. Inventions and Sinfonias, BWV 772–801: title page
(*BD* I, no. 153)

Upright Instruction
wherein the lovers of the clavier, and especially those desirous of learn-ing, are shown a clear way not alone (1) to learn to play clearly in two

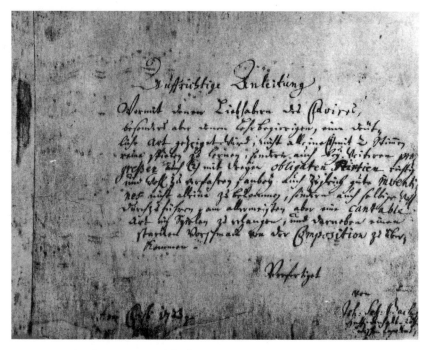

92. Inventions and Sinfonias, BWV 772–801: title page

voices but also, after further progress, (2) to deal correctly and well with three *obbligato* parts; furthermore, at the same time not alone to have good *inventiones* [ideas] but to develop the same well and, above all, to arrive at a singing style in playing and at the same time to acquire a strong foretaste of composition. Produced by

Joh. Seb. Bach
Capellmeister to His Serene Highness
the Prince of Anhalt-Cöthen

Anno Christi 1723

The pieces in this volume, all of which were also included in the Little Clavier Book for Friedemann Bach (No. 79), were apparently written before those of The Well-Tempered Clavier, *which is represented there only by a few preludes.*

Leipzig
1723–1730

BACH IS APPOINTED CANTOR AND MUSIC
DIRECTOR AT ST. THOMAS'S

93. A summary account from Johann Salomon Riemer's *Chronicle of Leipzig* (Wustmann, pp. 434–35; *BD* II, nos. 123, 142)

a. *1722:*

On June 5 died Mr. Johann Kuhnau, *Director musices* at the two principal churches of St. Thomas and St. Nicholas, and the same in St. Paul's Church of the University, and no less Cantor at the St. Thomas School, aged 62 years and 2 months, a learned man, expert in art, who not only had a good understanding of Hebrew, Greek, and Latin but also, in addition to his music, was a finished mathematician, and no less, before he became Cantor, had been a well-learned lawyer.

On August 9 the test for the Cantorate was passed by Mr. Telemann. Although he had sought the same both orally and in writing, as well as the *Directorium* at a Worshipful University, yet after he had received an increase of a few hundred thaler in Hamburg, his application was withdrawn.

b. *1723:*

On February 7, Quinquagesima Sunday, Mr. Sebastian Bach, then Capellmeister at Cöthen, passed his test for the post of the Cantorate made vacant by the death of the late Mr. Kuhnau. Some time before this, four others had passed their tests, namely, (1) [Christian Friedrich Rolle] the Capellmeister of Altenburg [*recte:* Magdeburg], [2] Mr. Graupner, the Capellmeister of Darmstadt, and [3] Mr. Georg Balthasar Schott, *Dir. musices* in the New Church.

On May 30 [*recte:* June 1] Mr. Johann Sebastian Bach, formerly Capellmeister at Cöthen, entered upon the Cantorate he had obtained.

In listing the candidates, Riemer omitted Georg Friedrich Kauffmann of Merseburg.

94. Deliberations excerpted from the proceedings of the town council (*BD* II, nos. 119, 121, 127)

a. *December 21, 1722:*

Those who were to be subjected to examination for the Cantorate had recently been named; others had presented themselves, namely, Capellmeister Graupner in Darmstadt and Bach in Cöthen; [Johann Friedrich] Fasch, on the other hand, declared that he could not teach, along with his other duties, and the candidate from Merseburg [Kauffmann] requested again that he be admitted to examination.

Resolved: Rolle, Kaufmann, and also Schotte should be admitted to examination, especially with regard to the teaching.

b. *January 15, 1723:*

Court Councilor and Burgomaster Dr. Lange stated that the Capellmeister of Darmstadt, Mr. Graupner, had presented himself and would do his auditioning on Sunday; he had a good name everywhere, as various letters showed, but precaution should be taken to see that he could obtain dismissal from his Court. His attention had been called to this, but he had declared that he was under no hard and fast obligation, and had explained what impelled him to make the change. The question was now only, if his trial playing should go off well, whether the Cantorate should be conferred upon him, and whether His Honor the Landgrave ought not to be written to beforehand. . . .

Episcopal Councilor Dr. Born: Since Mr. Graupner had such a good name, so that Kauffmann even considered him better than himself, he [Dr. Born] was also inclined toward Graupner, and he suggested for consideration the question of whether the students of the St. Thomas School should not be obligated to offer themselves for use, in case they were needed, no matter where they happened to be. . . .

Dr. Hölzel: Rolle was said to surpass Telemann, and he might also be heard; he seconded Episcopal Councilor Dr. Born's vote and was inclined to favor Graupner.

Commissioner Wagner: Voted, on the grounds given, for Graupner, with the added conditions that he submitted for consideration the question of whether Rolle and Bach should also be admitted to examination.

c. *April 9, 1723:*

The man who had been favored for the Cantorate, namely, Graupner, could not obtain his dismissal—the Landgrave of Hesse-Darmstadt simply would not dismiss him. The others in view were the Capellmeister at Cöthen, Bach; Kauffmann in Merseburg; and Schotte here, but none of the three would be able to teach also, and in Telemann's case consideration had already been given to a division [of the duties].

Appeals Councilor Plaz: The latter suggestion he considered for several reasons somewhat questionable; since the best could not be obtained, mediocre ones would have to be accepted; many good things had once been said about a man in Pirna.

95. **Newspaper report on Bach's audition, in the Hamburg *Relationscourier,* datelined Leipzig, February 2, 1723; reprinted by other papers** (*BD* II, no. 124)

On Sunday last [February 7] in the morning the Hon. Capellmeister of Cöthen, Mr. Bach, gave his test here at the Church of St. Thomas for the hitherto vacant cantorate, the music of the same having been amply praised on that occasion by all knowledgeable persons. Mr. Schott, Director of the Collegium Musicum here, also presented his test in the New Church on the Feast of Purification [February 2], and the vacant position mentioned above will now be filled very soon by the Hon. and Most Wise [Town] Council.

Bach performed two cantatas, before and after the sermon: Jesus nahm zu sich die Zwölfe, BWV 22, *and* Du wahrer Gott und Davids Sohn, BWV 23. *The town council covered Bach's travel expenses rather generously (20 rthl.), suggesting that he had been specifically invited by them (cf.* BD II, no. 125).

96. **Letter of Bach's dismissal, from the Prince of Cöthen** (*BD* II, no. 128)

By the Grace of God, We, Leopold, Prince of Anhalt, etc., make known herewith to one and all in what manner We have had in Our service and under Our patronage the Respectable and Learned Johann Sebastian Bach, since August 5, 1717, as Capellmeister and Director of Our Chamber Music. Whereas We have at all times been well content with his discharge of his duties, but the said Bach, wishing now to seek his fortune elsewhere, has accordingly most humbly petitioned Us to grant him a most gracious dismissal, now therefore We have been pleased graciously to grant him the same and to give him highest recommendation for service elsewhere. In witness whereof We have executed this discharge with Our Own signature and caused Our Princely seal to be affixed thereto.

Done at Cöthen, April 13, 1723

97. Bach's preliminary pledge to the town council (*BD* I, no. 91)

Whereas I, the undersigned, have presented to the Noble and Most Wise Council of the Town of Leipzig my candidacy for the vacant post of Cantor to the St. Thomas School in that place, and have respectfully requested that I be considered in this connection, now, therefore, I hereby pledge myself that if my request be granted and the said post be entrusted to me, I will not only within three or, at the most, four weeks from this date make myself free of the engagement given me at the Court of the Prince of Anhalt-Cöthen, and convey to the said Council the certificate of dismissal I receive, but also, when I actually enter upon the duties of the said post of Cantor, conduct myself according to the School Regulations now in effect or to be put into effect; and especially I will instruct the boys admitted into the School not only in the regular classes established for that purpose but also, without special compensation, in private singing lessons. I will also faithfully attend to whatever else is incumbent upon me, and furthermore, but not without the previous knowledge and consent of a Noble and Wise Council, in case someone should be needed to assist me in the instruction in the Latin language, will faithfully and without ado compensate the said person out of my own pocket, without desiring anything from a Noble and Most Wise Council or otherwise. In witness whereof I have executed this pledge under my hand and seal.

JOHANN SEBASTIAN BACH
Capellmeister to the Prince of Anhalt-

Done at Leipzig, April 19, 1723 *Cöthen, &c.*

Since the dismissal from Cöthen had actually been granted six days earlier, which Bach must have known, the present document was probably only signed, but not drawn up, by him.

98. Proceedings of the three councils of Leipzig on Bach's election (*BD* II, no. 129)

Dominus Consul Regens Dr. Lange related, in joint assembly of all three Councils, that it was known that for the position of Cantor at St. Thomas's Mr. Telemann had been thought of, and he had promised to do everything, but had not kept his promise. Thereupon attention had been turned, though only privately, to Mr. Graupner, Capellmeister at Darmstadt, who, however, had reported that he could not obtain his dismissal. Thereupon Bach, Hoffman [*recte:* Kauffmann], and Schott had presented themselves. Bach was Capellmeister in Cöthen and excelled on the clavier. Besides music he had the teaching equipment [*Information*]; and the Cantor must give instruction in the *Colloquia Corderi* [a textbook of piety, letters, and behavior] and in grammar, which he was willing to do. He had formally undertaken to give not only public but also private instruction. If Bach were chosen, Telemann, in view of his conduct, might be forgotten.

Dominus Consul Dr. Platz: Since the vacancy had existed for such a long time, there was reason to proceed to the election. It was to be hoped that the third [candidate] would be the right one. He must accommodate himself to the instruction of the youth. Bach was fitted for this and willing to do it, and accordingly he [Platz] cast his vote for him.

Dominus Consul Dr. Steger: Expressed his thanks for the careful procedure, and it had been explained how the delay had come about and why Mr. Bach should be taken. Bach was as much of a person as Graupner. He had declared himself ready to prove his loyalty not only as Cantor but also as Instructor in the St. Thomas School. As Fourth Instructor he was willing to make arrangements with the other *Praeceptores* who were to replace him [when necessary]. He [Steger] voted for Bach, and he should make compositions that were not theatrical.

The other Council members likewise cast their votes for Bach, whereupon *Dominus Consul Regens:* It was necessary to be sure to get a famous man, in order to inspire the [University] students. Bach should seek his dismissal, and he [Lange] hoped that it would turn out well; whereupon this meeting was at an end.

Graupner wrote to the Leipzig council on May 4, 1723, that Bach is "a musician just as strong on the organ as he is expert in church works and Capelle pieces," who "will honestly and properly perform the functions entrusted to him."

99. **Notifications of Bach's election: excerpt from the records of the St. Thomas School, May 5, 1723** (*BD* II, no. 133)

Then appeared Mr. Johann Sebastian Bach, hitherto Capellmeister at the Court of the Prince of Anhalt-Cöthen, in the Council Chamber, and after he had taken his place behind the chairs, *Dominus Consul Regens Dr. Lange* stated that various candidates had presented themselves for service as Cantor of the St. Thomas School; but since he had been considered the most capable for the post, he had been unanimously elected, and he should be introduced by the Superintendent here, and the same should be given him as the deceased Mr. Kuhnau had had.

Ille [he, i.e., Bach]: Expressed his most obedient thanks for the fact that he had been thought of, and promised his full loyalty and industry.

Further: At the instructions of the Honorable and Learned Council, the Honorable Superintendent Dr. Deyling was notified by me that the quondam Anhalt Capellmeister at Cöthen, Mr. Johann Sebastian Bach, had been unanimously elected to the post of Cantor at the St. Thomas School here, of which fact it had been thought necessary to notify him so that he might have the goodness to attend to everything in connection with the Presentation, and so forth.

Ille: Expressed his thanks for the said notification, and he would not fail to attend to the Presentation and whatever was necessary.

Further: I likewise notified the Honorable Pastor of St. Thomas's, Licentiate Weise, of the fact of the election of Mr. Johann Sebastian Bach as Cantor of the St. Thomas School; he expressed his most obedient thanks for the notification and invoked God's blessing upon the choice.

100. Bach's final pledge to the town council (*BD* I, no. 92)

Whereas the Honorable and Most Wise Council of this Town of Leipzig has engaged me as Cantor of the St. Thomas School and has desired an undertaking from me in respect to the following points, to wit:

(1) That I shall set the boys a shining example of an honest, retiring manner of life, serve the School industriously, and instruct the boys conscientiously;

(2) Bring the music in both the principal churches of this town into good estate, to the best of my ability;

(3) Show to the Honorable and Most Wise Council all proper respect and obedience, and protect and further everywhere as best I may its honor and reputation; likewise if a gentleman of the Council desires the boys for a musical occasion unhesitatingly provide him with the same, but otherwise never permit them to go out of town to funerals or weddings without the previous knowledge and consent of the Burgomaster and Honorable Directors of the School currently in office;

(4) Give due obedience to the Honorable Inspectors and Directors of the School in each and every instruction that the same shall issue in the name of the Honorable and Most Wise Council;

(5) Not take any boys into the School who have not already laid a foundation in music, or are not at least suited to being instructed therein, nor

do the same without the previous knowledge and consent of the Honorable Inspectors and Directors;

(6) So that the churches may not have to be put to unnecessary expense, faithfully instruct the boys not only in vocal but also in instrumental music;

(7) In order to preserve the good order in the churches, so arrange the music that it shall not last too long, and shall be of such a nature as not to make an operatic impression, but rather incite the listeners to devotion;

(8) Provide the New Church with good scholars;

(9) Treat the boys in a friendly manner and with caution, but, in case they do not wish to obey, chastise them with moderation or report them to the proper place;

(10) Faithfully attend to the instruction in the School and whatever else it befits me to do;

(11) And if I cannot undertake this myself, arrange that it be done by some other capable person without expense to the Honorable and Most Wise Council or to the School;

(12) Not go out of town without the permission of the Honorable Burgomaster currently in office;

(13) Always so far as possible walk with the boys at funerals, as is customary;

(14) And shall not accept or wish to accept any office in the University without the consent of the Honorable and Learned Council;

Now, therefore, I do hereby undertake and bind myself faithfully to observe all of the said requirements, and on pain of losing my post not to act contrary to them, in witness whereof I have set my hand and seal to this agreement.

Done in Leipzig, May 5, 1723   JOHANN SEBASTIAN BACH

101. The examiner's certificate of Bach's theological competence: excerpt from the records of the St. Thomas School, May 8, 1723 (*BD* II, no. 134)

Dn. Jo. Sebastianus Bach ad quaestiones a me propositas ita respondit ut eundem ad officium Cantoratus in Schola Thomana admitti posse censeam. [Mr. Jo. Sebastian Bach replies to the questions propounded by me in such wise that I consider that the said person may be admitted to the post of Cantor in the St. Thomas School.]

DR. JO. SCHMID [the examiner]
Consentit DR. SALOMON DEYLING [Superintendent]

THE BACH FAMILY MOVES TO LEIPZIG

102. Report in the Hamburg *Staats- und Gelehrte Zeitung,* datelined Leipzig, May 29, 1723, on Bach's arrival in Leipzig
(*BD* II, no. 138)

This past Saturday at noon, four wagons loaded with household goods arrived here from Cöthen; they belonged to the former Princely Capell-meister there, now called to Leipzig as *Cantor Figuralis.* He himself arrived with his family on 2 carriages at 2 o'clock and moved into the newly renovated apartment in the St. Thomas School.

BACH IS FORMALLY INSTALLED AND COMMENCES
HIS DUTIES

103. Excerpt from *Acta Lipsiensium Academica,* 1723
(*BD* II, no. 139)

The 30th instant [May], being the First Sunday after Trinity, the new Cantor and Director of the *Collegium Musicum,* Mr. Johann Sebastian Bach, who has come hither from the Prince's Court at Cöthen, produced his first music here, with great success.

The title "Director of the Collegium Musicum" *may be either an academic version of Bach's title* Director Musices *or a reference to the fact that Bach also directed music at the university. In his memorandum to the king, dated December 31, 1725, Bach states that he had begun his university service on Whitsunday, two weeks before the service mentioned above.*

104. Excerpt from the town council proceedings, June 1, 1723
(*BD* II, no. 145)

A Noble and Most Wise Council of this Town caused the new Cantor in the St. Thomas School, Mr. Johann Sebastian Bach, to be presented and introduced in the usual manner, and for this purpose ordered Com-missioner [*Baumeister*] Gottfried Conrad Lehmann, as Director of the said School, and me, the Chief Town Clerk, to go thither, where we were received downstairs by the Rector, Magister Ernesti, and led into the upper auditorium, in which the Pastor of St. Thomas's Church, Licentiate Weiss, was already present and announced to us that the Superintendent Dr. Deyling, in sending him the order of the Consistory in this connection, had delegated his duties to him. Thereupon all the teachers of the School assembled in the said room, and we all sat down on the chairs set out for us, so that Lic. Weiss sat at the top, and next to him Commissioner Lehmann and I, and opposite us the said teachers of the School in order. The students performed a piece outside the door, and at its conclusion all filed into the auditorium. Thereupon I made the bestowal of the office as follows:

Whereas it had pleased the Almighty God to call from this world the Instructor and Cantor ordained for this School, Mr. Johann Kuhnau, and in his place a Noble and Most Wise Council had elected Mr. Johann Sebastian Bach, formerly Capellmeister at the Court of His Highness the Prince of Anhalt-Cöthen, accordingly nothing remained but that the said person should be properly introduced to and installed in the said office, which accordingly was done herewith, in the name of the Holy Trinity, by the aforementioned Council as the Patron of this School; and the new Cantor was admonished faithfully and industriously to discharge the duties of his office, show the authorities and his superiors due respect and willingness, cultivate good relations and friendship with his colleagues, conscientiously instruct the youth in the fear of God and other useful studies, and thus keep the School in good repute. The resident students and the others who attend the School were likewise admonished to give obedience and show respect to the new Cantor, and the speech was concluded with a good wish for the welfare of the School.

Now, according to the usual custom, the Cantor should have made his reply to this, but Lic. Weiss spoke up [mentioning] that a decree had been issued by the Consistory, which he therewith exhibited, to the Superintendent, by virtue of which the new Cantor was to be presented to the School and installed, and he added an admonition to the Cantor to the faithful observance of his office, and a good wish. Commissioner Lehmann, who extended his congratulation to the new Cantor, at once pointed out that this installation by the Consistory, or by one appointed by it for the purpose, had not taken place before, and was an innovation, which must be brought to the attention of a Noble Council, to which I also thereupon agreed. But the aforementioned Lic. Weiss justified himself, saying that he had not known this and had done in this connection only what he had been instructed to do.

Before these remarks had been made, the new Cantor expressed his most obliged thanks to a Noble and Most Wise Council, in that the same had been most graciously pleased to think of him in conferring this office, with the promise that he would serve the same with all fidelity and zeal, would show due respect to his superiors, and in general so conduct himself that his greatest devotion should always be observed. Whereupon the other instructors of the School congratulated him, and the occasion was concluded with another musical piece.

When we then arrived at the Council Hall and there reported what had taken place, it was considered necessary to speak with the Superintendent about it, and I was appointed to do this, which action I accomplished on the afternoon of the same day, when the latter made it known that the explicit content of the decree that he had received had been that the new Cantor should be installed and introduced by him, and since he had been prevented from doing so, he had charged Lic. Weiss to do it and he hoped that the latter had not departed from his text. He had no intention of making the slightest encroachment upon the proper rights of a Noble and Most Wise Council, but must also obey the decree of the Consistory; accordingly he would mention it at the session on the morrow, and another time a specific understanding on this point must be arranged. If a Noble Council had had a different custom in similar cases, it was not to be blamed for wishing to hold to it.

CARL FRIEDRICH MENSER
Chief Town Clerk
Signed with his own hand

Nota. When, immediately upon our entrance, Lic. Weiss reported to us how the Superintendent had laid upon him the duty of installing the new Cantor, and we pointed out to him how the custom was otherwise, he said that he would let it go at that; and yet the above-described action was taken by him.

105. Report in the Hamburg *Relationscourier,* June 10, 1723, of Bach's first Leipzig performance (*BD* II, no. 140)

Leipzig on June 3 [1723]
This past Sunday, the Princely Capellmeister, Mr. Bach, who had been called hither from Cöthen by the Honorable and Most Wise Council of this town to fill the vacant post of Mr. Kuhnau, *Directoris Chori Musici,* who died here last year, presented, in entering upon his office, his music before and after the sermon.

Performance at St. Nicholas's of the cantata Die Elenden sollen essen, *BWV 75, which consists of two parts.*

106. Dr. Salomon Deyling's Report on Bach to the consistory
(*BD* II, no. 175)

YOUR MAGNIFICENCES, MOST WORTHY AND MOST LEARNED, ESPE-
CIALLY MOST HIGHLY ESTEEMED SIRS AND PATRONS!

Whereas I reported to Your Honors under the date of June 29 of last
year that the new Thomas Cantor here, Mr. Joh. Seb. Bach, would
not offer the [non-musical] instruction, but had persuaded the Third
Colleague, for a certain compensation, to take upon himself the school
labors in his stead, I have in time obtained further information and
have found that the said Third Colleague has in fact not only taken
over the school teaching assigned to the Cantor, but that the Cantor
Bach, in cases when the Third Colleague has had to be absent for illness, or on account of other hindrances, has also visited the class and
has dictated an exercise to the boys for them to work on. This I have
wished to call to Your attention, Most Highly Esteemed Sirs and
Patrons, ever remaining, Your Noble Magnificences as well as Most
Reverend Sirs,

Your prayerful and most obedient

DR. DEYLING

Leipzig, February 20, 1724   Signed with his own hand

*On June 29, 1723, Dr. Salomon Deyling had sent a report to the consistory,
which yields no additional information but is referred to in this report and in
the reply from the consistory that follows.*

107. The consistory's reply (*BD* II, no. 177)

*To Dr. Salomon Deyling, P[rofessor] P[ublicus], Pastor, and Superintendent
here in Leipzig, etc.*

We have read the report that the addressee sent us concerning the
Cantor of the St. Thomas School here, Johann Sebastian Bach.
    Since the installation and introduction of the said new Cantor, per-
formed by him through the Pastor at the Church of St. Thomas, Lic.
Christian Weiss, is in accordance with the Electoral Saxon Church Regulations,
    Therefore the matter must rest at that. After all, we agree that, in
accordance with the proposal made, the teaching duties of the same
may be left for the time being to the Third Colleague, and we herewith

request the latter in the name of His Most Serene Highness, etc., to conduct himself accordingly.

Given at Leipzig,　　　　The Ordained Members of the Electoral
March 22, 1724　　　　　　Consistory of that Place

BACH'S INCOME, 1723–1750

108. Excerpts from the Leipzig account books on Bach's salary (*BD* II, no. 137)

[thlr. gr.]

21	21	[For the first (Reminiscere) quarter, 1723] To Mr. Johann Sebastian Bach, Cantor
21	21	[For the second (Trinity) quarter, 1723] To Mr. Johann Sebastian Bach, Cantor
21	21	[For the third (Holy Cross) quarter, 1723] To Mr. Johann Sebastian Bach, Cantor
21	21	[For the fourth (St. Lucy) quarter, 1723] To Mr. Johann Sebastian Bach, Cantor

Bach's fixed annual salary amounted to little more than 100 thlr., paid quarterly, 1723–50. However, he received free housing and additional income from weddings and funerals as well as regular payments from various special funds established by the electoral government, the city, and wealthy Leipzig citizens. In 1730 Bach estimated his annual income to be about 700 thlr. (see his letter to Erdmann, No. 152). The records are incomplete; the following are representative examples.

109. Excerpts from the Leipzig account books on other compensation paid to Bach (*BD* I, nos. 139, 136, 146, 167, 144, and Szeskus, p. 406)

a. *Annual payments from the Lobwasser legacy, 1723–50, receipt of June 1748:*

Legatum Lobwasserianum
J. S. Bach　　　　　　　　　　　　　　　　　　rec[eived]. 2 fl.–

b. *Payments (twice annually) from the Sinner legacy, 1723–50, receipt of Easter 1748:*

Jo. Sebast. Bach.　　　　　　　　　　　　　　acc[epted]. 5 rthl.

c. *Payments (twice annually) from the Mentzel endowment, excerpt from the account book of the Mentzel legacy, 1734–50:*

| [Easter] | 1 thlr. 8 gr. Mr. Capellmeister Bach accepted Joh. Seb. Bach. |
| [St. Michael's Day] | 1 thlr. 8 gr. Mr. Bach -acc[epted]. J. S. Bach |

d. *Payment for regular Memorial Services from the Rettenbach legacy:*

3 [thlr.] 8 [gr.]   To the Cantor John. Sebastian Bach, for the Rettenbach memorial service, 1723

Identical payments were made for 1724–50. E. Rettenbach had in 1668 established an endowment fund, the income of which was to be used for the singing of motets and hymns four times a year in memory of members of various family members: on January 18, Jacob Handl's motet Ecce quomodo moritur; *on April 24, the hymn* Herr Jesu Christ, meins Lebens Licht; *on September 9, the hymn* Freu dich sehr, o meine Seele; *and on October 26, the hymn* Herzlich lieb hab ich dich, o Herr.

e. *Payment from the Bose legacy*

rec[eived]. Joh. Seb. Bach.   1 thlr. 8 gr. 9 pf.

Annual performance on the name day of the donor of the motet Turbabor sed non perturbabor, *under the direction of the cantor.*

f. *Payment for the "Old Service" at St. Paul's (University) Church:*

[c. October 30, 1733]	thlr.	gr.	pf.
To the Capellmeister Bach for the music	1	—	—
To the town musicians	1	12	—

Complete records are preserved only for 1733–34 and 1743–44 in the account books of rector August Friedrich Müller, recipient of Bach's congratulatory cantata BWV 205 (1725). However, from 1723 to 1750 Bach continued the practice of his predecessors Schelle and Kuhnau in providing cantata performances four times a year (on the first days of Christmas, Easter, and Pentecost, as well as on the Reformation Festival) at the University Church, by repeating—approximately one hour later—the music presented earlier at St. Thomas's or St. Nicholas's. Bach's total annual income from the University amounted to 13 rthl. 10 gr. including fees for both the "Old Service" and the Quartal-Orationes *(quarterly orations); the fees had remained unchanged since the time of Schelle. See also Nos. 119–120.*

110. Payments to Bach for maintaining church instruments
(*BD* II, nos. 160–61)

a. *Excerpt from the account book of St. Thomas's, 1723:*

2 [thlr.] 19 [gr.] 6 [pf.]
To the Cantor, Joh. Sebastian Bach, for preservation and repair of church instruments

b. *Excerpt from the account book of St. Nicholas's, 1723:*

2 [thlr.] 19 [gr.] 6 [pf.]
To the Cantor, Joh. Sebastian Bach, for preservation and repair of church instruments, September 28, 1723

The regular annual payments varied considerably, depending on what was required, amounting to as much as 12 thlr. 17 gr. 6 pf. for 1729–30 at St. Thomas's.

BACH'S OLDEST SONS, WILHELM FRIEDEMANN
AND CARL PHILIPP EMANUEL, ARE ENROLLED
IN THE ST. THOMAS SCHOOL

111. Excerpt from the school register (*BD* II, no. 149)

June 14 [1723]   Wilhelm Friedemann Bach, of Weimar, f[ather] Mr. Joh. Sebastian Bach, the Cantor here, is 12 years old, comes into the Third Class.
ditto   Carl Philipp Immanuel Bach, born in the same place and to the same father, comes into the Fifth Class.

BACH WRITES A TESTIMONIAL FOR A STUDENT,
GEORG GOTTFRIED WAGNER

112. Bach's statement on behalf of Wagner (*BD* III, p. 627, no. 56a)

As the bearer of this, Mr. Johann [*recte:* Georg] Gottlieb Wagner, student of theology, has asked me, the undersigned, for an attestation of his abilities in music, I have not wanted to decline, especially since such will be needed for his further advancement. I state therefore that the said Mr. Johann Gottlieb Wagner has not only perfected himself in the practice of various instruments such as clavier, violin, etc., but also distinguished himself in the art of composition, so that in both respects he has already given good and praiseworthy proof. I think it unnecessary to make further statements and have no doubt that Mr. Wagner, granted the opportunity to present himself, will give the best verification for this, my short attestation.

J S Bach
Capellmeister of the
Principality of Anhalt Cöthen,
Dir. Musices, *and Cantor at*
the School of St. Thom.

Written at Leipzig,
November 20, 1723.

BACH PERFORMS AT SERVICES IN LEIPZIG FOR
THE FIRST SUNDAY IN ADVENT

113. "Order of the Divine Service in Leipzig" for November 28, 1723 (*BD* I, no. 178)

Order of the Divine Service in Leipzig
on the First Sunday in Advent: Morning

(1) Preluding
(2) Motet
(3) Preluding on the Kyrie, which is performed throughout in concerted manner [*musiciret*]
(4) Intoning before the altar
(5) Reading of the Epistle
(6) Singing of the Litany
(7) Preluding on [and singing of] the Chorale
(8) Reading of the Gospel [*crossed out:* and intoning of the Creed]
(9) Preluding on [and performance of] the principal music [cantata]
(10) Singing of the Creed [Luther's Credo hymn]
(11) The Sermon
(12) After the Sermon, as usual, singing of several verses of a hymn
(13) Words of Institution [of the Sacrament]
(14) Preluding on [and performance of] the music [probably the second part of the cantata]. After the same, alternate preluding and singing of chorales until the end of the Communion, *et sic porrò* [and so on].

Entered in the autograph score of the cantata "Nun komm, der Heiden Heiland," BWV 61.

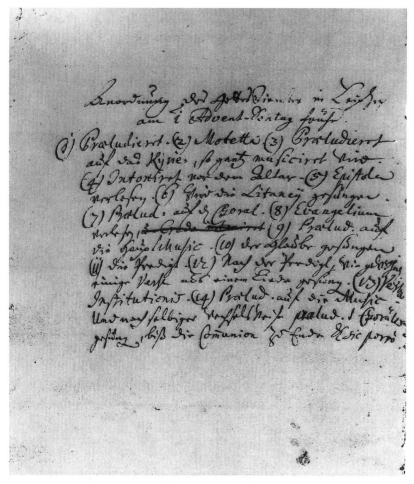

113. "Order of the Divine Service in Leipzig" for November 28, 1723

ON PASSION PERFORMANCES IN LEIPZIG, 1722–1738

114. Entries in the diary of St. Thomas's sexton, Johann Christoph Rost, 1722–1738 (*BD* II, no. 180)

On Good Friday of the year 1721, in the vesper service, the Passion was performed for the first time in concerted style [*musiciret*]. At a quarter to 2 o'clock all bells were rung, and when the ringing was finished, the hymn "Da Jesus an dem Creutze stund" was sung from the choir gallery. Then the *Musicirte Passion* began immediately, half of which was performed before the sermon. This half was completed with the hymn verse "O Lamm Gottes unschuldig," during which the priest ascended to the pulpit. After he reached the pulpit, [the congregational hymn] "Herr Jesu Christ, dich zu uns wendt" was sung. After the sermon the other half of the music began, and when it was finished the motet "Ecce quomodo moritur justus" was sung [by the choir]; then the Passion verse was intoned and prayer said; finally [the congregational hymn] "Nun danket alle Gott" was sung. In 1723 it was done in the same way.

In 1723 the vesper service was held for the first time at St. Nicholas's. The sermon, which was sponsored by Mrs. Kopp, was given by Superintend. D. [theol.] Deyling.

In 1724 the Passion by the Cantor [*St. John Passion,* BWV 245] was performed for the first time at St. Nicholas's; at St. Thom. only hymns were sung, as used to be done before.

1725. at St. Thom. [*St. John Passion,* BWV 245]

1726. at St. Nichol. [Reinhard Keiser, *St. Mark Passion*]

1727. at St. Thom. [*St. Matthew Passion,* BWV 244]

1728. at St. Nichol. [*St. John Passion,* BWV 245]

1729. St. Thomas's [*St. Matthew Passion,* BWV 244]

1730. St. Nicholas's [anonymous *St. Luke Passion,* BWV 246]

1731. St. Thomas's [*St. Mark Passion,* BWV 247]

1732. St. Nichol.

1733. was the mourning period for the King.

1734. St. Thomas's

1735. St. Nicholas's

1736. St. Thomas's, with both organs. [*St. Matthew Passion,* BWV 244]

1737. St. Nichol.

1738. St. Thom.

[1739. St. Thomas's; performance canceled, see No. 208]

[1740. St. Nicholas's]

[1741. St. Thomas's; *St. Matthew Passion,* BWV 244]

[1742. St. Nicholas's]

[1743. St. Thomas's]

[1744. St. Nicholas's]

[1745. St. Thomas's]

[1746. St. Nicholas's]

[1747. St. Thomas's]

[1748. St. Nicholas's]

[1749. St. Thomas's: *St. John Passion,* BWV 245]

[1750. St. Nicholas's]

Johann Kuhnau's St. Mark's Passion *was performed in 1721; it is not known which works were presented in 1722 and 1723. The incomplete performance schedule for 1724–50 is based on evidence provided by the extant sources.*

115. Excerpts from the proceedings of the council, April 3, 1724 (*BD* II, no. 179)

Mr. Johann Sebastian Bach, Cantor of the St. Thomas School, was notified of the decision previously made by the Honored and Learned Council that the Passion Music for Good Friday should be given alternately in St. Nicholas's and in St. Thomas's. But since the title of [the libretto to] the music sent around this year revealed that it was to take place again in St. Thomas's, and since the Superintendent of St. Nicholas's had requested of the Honored and Learned Council that this time the above-mentioned Passion music should be given in St. Nicholas's, therefore, the Cantor should for his part act accordingly.

Hic: He would comply with the same, but pointed out that the booklet was already printed, that there was no room available, and that the harpsichord needed some repair, all of which, however, could be attended to at little cost; but he requested at any rate that a little additional room be provided in the choir loft, so that he could place the persons needed for the music, and that the harpsichord be repaired.

Senatus: The Cantor should, at the expense of the Honored and Most Wise Council, have an announcement printed stating that the music was to take place this time in St. Nicholas's, have the necessary arrangements in the choir loft made, with the aid of the sexton, and have the harpsichord repaired.

116. Flier announcing the change of a performance site, 1724 (*BD* II, no. 179)

Since, after completed printing of the Passion texts, a Noble and Wise Council decided that their future performance should, God willing, take place at St. Nicholas's Church and should, as usual, also henceforth alternate with the music for feast days and Sundays, it was thus made to be known to the Messrs. listeners [*Herren Auditoribus*].

BACH AND HIS WIFE PRESENT GUEST
PERFORMANCES AT THE CÖTHEN COURT, 1724–1728

117. Excerpts from the court account books
   (*BD* II, nos. 184, 199, and 241)

   a. 1724, July 18.   To the Director Musices Bach and his
                               wife, who performed, in settlement   rthl. 60

   b. 1725, Dec. 15.   To the Leipzig Cantor Bach and his
                               wife, who gave a number of perform-
                               ances here   rthl. 30

   c. 1728, Jan 5.   To the Leipzig Cantor Bach, in settlement   rthl. 24

The performances are related to Bach's obligations as honorary Cöthen Capell-
meister. The 1724 payment included out of pocket expenses for board and lodg-
ing. While the nature of the occasion in 1724 is unknown, the 1725
performance relates to the birthdays of Princess Charlotte and Prince Leopold,
the one in 1728 to New Year's Day festivities.

BACH GIVES TWO ORGAN RECITALS AT
ST. SOPHIA'S IN DRESDEN

118. Report in the Hamburg *Relationscourier,* September 27, 1725
   (*BD* II, no. 193)

Dresden, 21 September 1725. When the *Capell-Director* from Leipzig,
Mr. Bach, came here recently, he was very well received by the local
virtuosos at the court and in the city since he is greatly admired by all
of them for this musical adroitness and art. Yesterday and the day
before, in the presence of the same, he performed for over an hour on
the new organ in St. Sophia's Church preludes and various concertos,
with intervening soft instrumental music [*Doucen Instrumental-Music*]
in all keys.

The organ at St. Sophia's (with 31 stops, two manuals, and pedal) was built
1718–1720 by Gottfried Silbermann. Bach's Dresden visit enabled him to
submit his first letter of complaint (No. 119a) personally to the court.

119. Three letters of complaint to the king (*BD* I, no. 10–12)

a. *To His Most Serene Highness, the Most Mighty Prince and Lord, Frederick Augustus, King in Poland, . . . My Most Gracious King, Elector, and Master.*

YOUR MOST SERENE HIGHNESS, MOST MIGHTY KING AND ELECTOR, MOST GRACIOUS MASTER!

May Your Royal Majesty and Serene Electoral Highness most graciously deign to permit it to be pointed out, with most humble obedience, how the Directorship of Music of the Old and New Divine Service at a Worshipful University at Leipzig, with the compensation and incidental fees of the same, has always been connected with the Cantorate of St. Thomas's here, even during the life of my predecessor, but during the vacancy that followed the death of the latter it was given to the organist of St. Nicholas's, [Johann Gottlieb] Görner, and on my entering upon my new post the directorship of the so-called Old Service was again left to me, but the compensation therefore was later withdrawn and given with the directorship of the New Service to the above-mentioned organist of St. Nicholas's; and although I have duly addressed myself to a Worshipful University, and made application that the old arrangement should be left intact, yet the best I have been able to obtain is an offer of half the salary, 12 gulden.

Whereas, however, Most Gracious King and Elector, a Worshipful University has expressly required that I furnish the music for the Old Service, and has accepted me for it, and I have until now performed this office; whereas the salary that has been attached to the directorship of the New Service was never previously connected with the latter but specifically with the Old Service, just as the direction of the New Service at its inception was connected with the Old Service; and whereas, while I did not wish to dispute the directorship of the New Service with the organist of St. Nicholas's, yet the withdrawal of the salary, which, in fact, always belonged to the Old Service even before the New was instituted, is deeply disturbing and slighting to me: and whereas Church *Patroni* are not in the habit of changing the disposition of the regular compensation earmarked and provided for a servant of the Church, either by withdrawing it entirely or by decreasing it, in spite of which I have had to perform my office in respect to the above-mentioned Old Service for over two years already without compensation—accordingly my most obedient prayer and entreaty goes forth to

Your Royal Majesty and Serene Electoral Highness that Your Majesty may issue most gracious commands that a Worshipful University at Leipzig shall leave the arrangement as it was formerly, and grant me the directorship of the New Service in addition to the directorship of the Old, and particularly the full compensation for the Old Service and the incidental fees accruing from both. For this Most High and Royal Favor, I shall remain all my life long

   Your Royal Majesty's and Your Serene Electoral Highness's most humble and obedient servant

Leipzig, September 14, 1725   JOHANN SEBASTIAN BACH

b. YOUR MOST SERENE HIGHNESS, MOST MIGHTY KING AND ELECTOR, MOST GRACIOUS MASTER!

Since at the most gracious command of Your Royal Majesty—upon my most humble supplication in the matter in which I was the complainant and the University of this place was the defendant—the said University has submitted the most humble report required of it and has duly notified me of its submission, and I, on the other hand, consider it necessary to protect my future position: accordingly my most humble and obedient request goes forth to Your Royal Majesty and Serene Electoral Highness that You will have a copy of the said report in this matter sent to me and will most graciously deign to withhold Your Majesty's Most High Decision until I have made the most necessary comments upon it; I shall not fail to hasten the same as much as possible, and to remain my life long in deepest submission

   Your Royal Majesty's and Your Serene Electoral Highness's most humble and obedient servant

Leipzig, November 3, 1725   JOHANN SEBASTIAN BACH

c. YOUR MOST SERENE HIGHNESS, MOST MIGHTY KING AND ELECTOR, MOST GRACIOUS MASTER!

That Your Royal Majesty and Serene Electoral Highness has most graciously deigned to cause to be sent to me a copy of the reply of the University here to my complaint against them in respect to the *Directorium Musices* of the Old and New Divine Service in St. Paul's Church and the salary belonging to the former, hitherto withheld—this I acknowledge with most humble thanks. Although I had thought that the University would at once take proper steps to satisfy my demands, and grant my fully justified request without further ado, I perceive that on the contrary it has been at great pains to take various exceptions to the same, and to excuse itself, saying that:

(1) I had without ground claimed that the directorship of the music of the Old and New Divine Service was necessarily connected with the office of Cantor of St. Thomas's, whereas the University found itself *in libertate naturali* as regards the conferring of the above-mentioned directorship, although it did not dispute my right to the directorship of the Old Service, or deny the fact that by virtue of an established custom it had paid me an honorarium for the same. Further, that

(2) my assertion that I had had to do my work until now for nothing was the stranger since it was clear from the Rector's Accounts that at all the *Quartal-Orationes* as well as at the three high feast days and at the Feast of the Reformation a special and ample honorarium, of 13 thlr. 10 gr., had been tendered me and I had hitherto always received the same. Further,

(3) that I had hitherto frequently not attended the *Quartal-Orationes* in person, but, according to the records of these occasions submitted, had caused the singing of the motets to be directed by Prefects. Likewise

(4) that the Cantor of St. Thomas's, on account of his official Sunday and holiday duties, was by no means in a position to take over in addition the directorship of the music in the University Church without detriment and disorder, since he had to direct the music in the Churches of St. Thomas and St. Nicholas at almost the same time; especially

(5) it was very carefully pointed out that my predecessor received for the *Directorium Musices* of the New Service a quite new and additional gratuity of 12 fl.; furthermore

(6) so many difficulties had arisen, caused by the Council in reference to the pupils of the St. Thomas School and the Town and Professional Pipers [*Stadt- und Kunst-Pfeiffer*] that the University had to make use of the assistance of its own students and to think of some other person who could without hindrance assume the direction of the music in person, and better maintain a good relation with the students, who refused to stand by the Cantor without compensation; to which was also added the fact that

(7) during the long vacancy in the office after the death of the previous Cantor, the University entrusted the *Directorium Musices* for the New Service to Johann Gottlieb Görner and assigned to him the new salary of 12 fl. intended for this post, which salary had no relation to the former direction of the Old Service, but was newly instituted.

At bottom, however, Most Gracious King, Elector, and Master, these exceptions taken by the University will not stand and are easily disposed of. For, to begin with

(1) as concerns the connection of the New Service and the Old, it was not my contention that such a connection was necessary, but only that the *Directorium* of the latter had always been combined with the former; and just as the power and freedom to connect or separate the two is not for me to question, but may be left to the proper authorities, so I accept, on the other hand, the fact that the *Directorium* of the Old Divine Service, according to established custom, is yielded and conceded to me in the [University's] most humble report. If this is true, however, the *Directorium* of the music at the *Promotiones Doctorales* [conferring of doctoral degrees] and other solemn University occasions in St. Paul's, together with the honorarium for the same, cannot be denied me, since all this, before the New Service was established, used to belong indisputably, at least as far as the music was concerned, to the Old Service, and [this] was the accepted practice. Next

(2) I am not a little surprised that the University dares to refer to an ample honorarium of 13 thlr. 10 gr. that I am said to have received from it, and to contradict me by denying that I have done the work for nothing until now, seeing that the honorarium is something separate and apart from the salary of 12 fl., and a gratuity does not exclude the salary. Actually, however, my complaint concerns not the honorarium but the salary, which was always customary and belonged to the Old Service, but which has hitherto been denied me, in the amount of 12 fl. Indeed, as may be seen from the very Rector's Accounts cited by the University, even this honorarium, which is supposed to have amounted to 13 thlr. 10 gr., has not been paid to me in full, but instead I have been paid by the two Beadles, as they will be able to testify on oath, not more than 16 gr. 6 pf. every quarter, instead of the 20 gr. 6 pf. stated in the Rector's Accounts, and at the three high feast days, as well as at the Feast of the Reformation, each time not more than 1 thlr., instead of 2 thlr. 12 gr., making a total of only 6 thlr. 18 gr. instead of 13 thlr. 12 gr. annually. Nor did my predecessors, Schelle and Kuhnau (as the affidavits executed by their widows, herewith as Exhibits A and B, will show) receive any more for the quarterly and feast day music, or sign receipts for any more, and yet in the extract from the Rector's Accounts concerning them a much higher amount was set down. The fact

(3) that I have frequently not attended the *Quartal-Orationes* in person, and that the record of October 25, 1725, shows as much, will be

found of little significance; for just as the month and date show that the record was made only after I had complained about the University, while before that time there was nothing to record against me, so it will be found that such absence has not occurred more than once or twice, and this for legitimate reasons, since I had to be away, and particularly on the one occasion had something to attend to in Dresden. Furthermore, the Prefects are assigned to the said quarterly ceremonies, so that the latter were never taken care of by my predecessors Schelle and Kuhnau themselves, but the singing of the motets was always attended to and directed by the Prefects. Still less can

(4) there be any deeper merit in the urging of the University that it is not possible for the music in the Churches on both sides to be taken care of by one person; for according to this, a reference to the organist of St. Nicholas's, Görner, will be found even more important, and the direction of the music in both Churches even less possible for him, since the organist not only has to wait for the end of the concerted music before and after the sermon at the same time in St. Nicholas's and in St. Paul's but must also play the organ right through to the very last hymn, whereas the Cantor can leave after he has attended to the concerted music and need not be present for the hymns to the end of the service; and thus the late Kuhnau in his time attended to both quite well without detriment or confusion; moreover, in the church where no *musica formalis* is to be provided, the ordinary music can quite well be directed by Vicars and Prefects. Now, particularly

(5) as concerns the disputed 12 fl., the University will never be able to assert on good grounds that gave these 12 fl. to my predecessor Kuhnau for the direction of the music as a new, added gratuity. The truth of the matter is that these 12 fl. have been from time immemorial the salary for providing the music for the Old Service, and my predecessor, to avoid the disadvantageous consequences to be feared from a separation of the directorships, directed the music for the New Service for nothing, and never demanded a penny for it, nor did he ever rejoice in any alleged new gratuity of 12 fl. Indeed, receipts for these 12 fl. were regularly signed not alone by Kuhnau but by Schelle and even earlier, before anybody ever thought of the New Service. And since the affidavits of the Widows Schelle and Kuhnau, Exhibits A and B, clearly state that the 12 fl. were always the salary for the provision of music for the Old Service, accordingly the University will not be able to refuse to disclose these receipts. Similarly

(6) the question of whether there was not a good relation with the students in the direction of the New Service, and they did not wish to

lend the Cantor their aid for nothing, cannot prejudice the salary attached to the music for the Old Service; for as there is no desire either to concede or to deny this, and it is known that the Students who are lovers of music are always willing and glad to present themselves, so for my part there has never been any unpleasantness with the Students, and they regularly take part in both the vocal and the instrumental music under my direction unhesitatingly and up to this moment gratis and without compensation. Moreover

(7) if the *Directorium Musices* for the New Service should remain for the time being, so far as Görner is concerned, *in statu quo,* and although no one desires to cast doubt on the fact that for this new arrangement a new salary could be established, yet the salary of 12 fl. hitherto assigned to him is not at all a newly instituted item, or intended as something new for this new directorship, but on the contrary the same was withdrawn from the *Directorium Musices* of the Old Service and only later, while the Cantorate of St. Thomas's was vacant, when Görner was appointed to the new *Directorium,* assigned to this new *Directorium.*

This has been stated before, and, indeed, among those who have hitherto had to do with the music in the Churches on both sides, all this is notorious, and it can be confirmed, furthermore, and made still more widely known by their testimony. However, I am compelled to add this further special circumstance: that two years ago, when I took occasion to speak about the *Directorium* with the *Rector Magnificus* of the June term, as he wanted to disprove my point out of a handwritten account book, which was presumably a book of the Rector's Accounts, it happened that on the page to which the book was opened my eye must fall upon the entry and the clearly written words that told of the payment of 12 fl. *Salarium* to Schelle *pro Directorio Musices,* and I at once showed the same to the *Rector Magnificus* of the June term, and pointed it out to him.

Finally, the University has already conceded and offered me through Dr. Ludovici, who held the post of Rector last summer, half of the salary of 12 fl., and this it would certainly not have done if it had not been convinced that the matter was well grounded. Accordingly the change strikes me all the harder when it now does not wish to hear of any salary at all, and wishes to withdraw it from me altogether; also, after I had expressly mentioned the fact of this offer in my most humble Memorial, the University in its reply has passed over this point and made no answer to it, and thus through this silence the basis of my claim and the reasonableness of my cause are confirmed by the

University anew and, as it itself is convinced, silently conceded to be true.

Since, then, the University, by its own admission and by the Rector's Accounts cited by it under points ☉ and ☽, gives me 3 thlr. 10 gr. annually for the *Quartal-Orationes,* and a special honorarium of 10 thlr. annually for the three high feast days and the Feast of the Reformation, making altogether 13 thlr. 10 gr., by virtue of established custom;

Since I should thus have received, from the time I entered upon my University functions at Whitsunday, 1723, up to the end of the year 1725 (that is, in two and three-quarters years), a total of 36 thlr. 18 gr. 6 pf., but have not received that much, and instead only 11 thlr. for music on as many feast days, and 7 thlr. 13 gr. 6 pf. for II *Quartal-Orationes,* making a total of 18thlr. 13 gr. 6 pf., and accordingly am still owed 18 thlr. 5 gr.;

Since I still have due me the regular annual salary of 12 fl. for a period of two and three-quarters years, i.e., 33 fl.;

And since the University has wished to come to an agreement about the salary and has already offered to pay half of it, and thus has *eo ipso* not held my claim to be unjust or unfounded but on the contrary conceded it, and since it has passed over the last point in silence, in its most humble report, and has accordingly once more tacitly admitted it, and for the rest has not been able to interpose the slightest reply of any importance;

Therefore my most humble prayer is addressed to your Royal Majesty and Serene Electoral Highness, most graciously to command the University not only to leave the arrangements as they were, and to assign to me in the future the full salary of 12 fl. for the Old Service, with the incidental fees for the *Promotiones Doctorales* and other *Actus Solemnes* formerly attached to it, but also to pay me the outstanding honorarium of 18 thlr. 5 gr. and the remaining regular salary of 33 fl., and to make good all the expenses I have had in this respect; or, in case the University should not be convinced by what has hitherto been adduced, to disclose the receipts executed by Schelle and Kuhnau both for the special honorarium and for the regular salary. This high favor I shall all my life long acknowledge with most humble thanks and remain

Your Royal Majesty's and Your Serene Electoral Highness's most humble and obedient servant

Leipzig, December 31, 1725   Johann Sebastian Bach

120. The king's decision (*BD* II, no. 202)

By the Grace of God, Frederick Augustus, King in Poland, Duke of Saxony, Jülich, Cleves, Berg, Engern, and Westphalia, Elector.

WORTHY AND MOST LEARNED, DEAR LOYAL AND FAITHFUL!

We have had duly brought to Our Attention and read to Us what you have most obediently reported to Us under date of October 29 of last year, in accordance with Our Command issued to you on September 17 of the same year, relating to the most humble request of the Cantor at St. Thomas's in Leipzig, Johann Sebastian Bach, about the *Directorium Musices* of the so-called Old and New Services in the St. Paul's Church of that place. But you receive enclosed herewith what the said Cantor, having received a copy of the said report, has further represented and requested.

Since We now see that the *Directorium Musices* of the Old Service is an old affair and has no relation to the New Service:

Accordingly We let the matter rest at that, and, since you have also offered to leave the *Directorium* to him, in respect to the Old Service, and to pay him regularly the fees intended for the same, acquiesce therein and, not unjustly, in the special arrangements you have made concerning the New Service.

And thus Our Desire is that you will make good your offer but, for the rest, under the circumstances, reject the request of the said Cantor. This is Our Will.

Given at Dresden, January 21, 1726

Although Bach failed to expand his musical responsibilities for the University he continued to serve as Music Director in charge of the "Old Service" at the University Church as well as the Quartal-Orationes *throughout his Leipzig cantorate; see No. 109f.*

BACH WRITES TO A FORMER SCHOOLMATE,
GEORG ERDMANN

121. Bach's letter to Erdmann (*BJ* 1985, p. 85)

NOBLE AND MOST HONORED SIR AND (IF STILL PERMISSIBLE) ESTEEMED MR. BROTHER

On this favorable occasion it is my obligation to inquire about Your Honor's well-being and sincerely wish its lasting continuation. The scant oral message from the bearer of these lines gave me such pleasure that I have the burning desire to receive more extensive details regarding the recent circumstances duly becoming to your merits. I therefore am emboldened to submit to Your Honor to what extent my curiosity may be gratified. If accordingly you will be disposed toward remembering a devoted erstwhile schoolmate and travel companion and comply with his humble request, grateful indebtedness will oblige Your Honor's humble servant

Leipzig. July 28, 1726   JOH: SEBAST: BACH

Erdmann had been a school comrade of Bach's in Ohrdruf and at the St. Michael's School in Lüneburg. (See No. 11.)

BACH WRITES A TESTIMONIAL FOR AN ORGANIST, JACOB ERNST HÜBNER

122. Bach's letter on behalf of Hübner (*BD* III, p. 628, no. 56b)

Since by special request the bearer of this, Mr. Jacob Ernst Hübner from Löbau, has asked the undersigned to furnish him with written testimony concerning his proficiency in music, especially on the keyboard, I did not want to decline such a just demand but fairly state that he is in good command of the fundaments (those particularly required) for the organist's service. The examples of proof that he has given me were fully satisfactory. In his possible future advancement, no doubt he will, with further work at the organ, show his ability to new advantage and demonstrate the present testimony to represent nothing but the truth. Written at Leipzig, July 20, 1726.

> JOHANN SEBASTIAN BACH
> *Princely Anhalt-Cöthen Capellmeister,*
> *also Direct. Chori Musici at Leipzig,*
> *and Cantor at S. Thomas's*

BACH FINDS A NEW CANTOR, GEORG GOTTFRIED WAGNER, FOR THE TOWN OF PLAUEN

123. Bach's acknowledgment of the council's request (*BD* I, no. 14)

MOST NOBLE, STEADFAST, AND MOST LEARNED, ALSO MOST WISE SIRS, MOST GRACIOUS PATRONS!

The special and most gracious confidence of which Your Honors have most kindly consented to give me evidence in the letter delivered to me makes it my duty not alone to express herewith my most humble obligation but also to exert every effort to show by deeds how I make it my greatest pleasure, Most Noble and Most Wise Sirs, to show you herewith my devotion. But since this is an affair that cannot be set in motion at once, in that it will take a little time to choose a candidate with the requisite qualities, Your Honors will be most graciously pleased to delay the filling of the Cantor's post until some suitable candidate is found. For my part, I shall not fail to contribute everything possible, in order on the one hand to justify, so far as possible, the most gracious confidence reposed in me and on the other to see that this vacancy is filled as soon as possible, so that all the *désordres* and omissions may be avoided that must otherwise be feared. Accordingly, I present my most obedient respects and remain, with all consideration,

Most Noble, Steadfast, and Most Learned, also Most Wise Sirs, Your Most Noble and Wise Honors' obedient servant

Leipzig, September 14, Anno 1726   JOH. SEBAST. BACH

124. Bach's report of finding a suitable candidate (*BD* I, no. 15)

HONORED AND MOST NOBLE, HONORED AND MOST LEARNED, STEADFAST, AND ALSO HONORED AND MOST WISE SIRS, HONORED AND MOST GRACIOUS PATRONS!

In accordance with my recent promise to you, Most Noble and Wise Sirs, I have looked for a suitable candidate, and have found a person who is well versed both *in humanioribus* and particularly *in musicis*. To give you a slight foretaste, he is thoroughly at home *in compositione* and has given various samples of his work here with good success. Furthermore, he plays a good organ and clavier, is accomplished on the violin, violoncello, and other instruments, sings a bass that is, though not too strong, quite mannerly, and his qualities in general are such that I believe he could well be used for the vacant post. It therefore depends entirely on Your Honors' gracious command, Most Noble and Wise Sirs, when and how Your Honors will graciously deign to admit the said person to examination. I accordingly await your further immediate orders so that I may be able really to show how I live in the earnest endeavor to make it my greatest pleasure to serve Your Most Noble and Wise Honors in this matter and to remain, with due respect,

Most Esteemed, Most Noble, Honored and Most Learned, Steadfast, and also Honored and Most Wise Sirs, Your Honors' obedient servant

Leipzig, September 26, Anno 1726   JOH. SEBAST. BACH

125. Bach's inquiry about the council's decision (*BD* I, no. 16)

HONORED AND MOST NOBLE, STEADFAST, HONORED AND MOST LEARNED, ALSO HONORED AND MOST WISE SIRS, HONORED AND MOST GRACIOUS PATRONS!

Presumably the person proposed by me, Georg Gottfried Wagner by name (eldest son of the Cantor of Wurtzen, still living), who has mostly resided in Leipzig from his earliest years to the present, and that respectably, and has laid the foundations for his humane studies as a student in our St. Thomas School here, and also has embarked in this place upon higher studies by zealously attending University classes, wherefore I presume not without reason that he has done his part in them, will by now have approached Your Honors with a most obedient letter.

While, then, Honored and Most Wise Sirs, it is entirely up to you to ordain how and in what manner you will most graciously deign to admit *Mons.* Wagner to examination, I await in this matter your very gracious notification, in order to be able to show in deeds some token of my interest and my desire to be of service, and accordingly I present once again my respects, and remain with all devotion,

Honored and Most Noble, Steadfast, Honored and Most Learned, also Honored and Most Wise Sirs, Honored and Most Gracious Patrons, Your most obedient servant

Leipzig, October 21, 1726   JOH. SEB. BACH

P.S. The said Mr. Wagner is still single and unmarried.

126. Bach's letter of introduction for Wagner (*BD* I, no. 17)

HONORED AND MOST NOBLE, STEADFAST, HONORED AND MOST LEARNED, ALSO HONORED AND MOST WISE SIRS, HONORED AND MOST GRACIOUS PATRONS!

The bearer of this letter, *Mons.* Wagner, has wished, in accordance with Your Honors' disposition, to present himself herewith to you most humbly, and orally to beg Your Honors' further patronage in connection with the examination to come. And since I do not doubt that he will so seek to distinguish himself that you, Honored and Noble Sirs, will be fully satisfied, and my humble self will be upheld thereby, I hope that you, Honored and Noble Sirs, will give him most gracious consideration before any others. The offer made me to show Your Honors' most gracious *faveur* to me or my family, when occasion offers, I acknowledge with the humblest and most grateful devotion, and I shall not fail ever to remember to make, when the occasion arises, my most humble petition to Your Noble and Esteemed Honors. With heartfelt wishes for a happy outcome of the forthcoming selection of a new Cantor, I remain forever,

Honored and Most Noble, Steadfast, Honored and Most Learned, also Honored and Most Wise Sirs, My Highly Esteemed Patrons, ever Your most obedient and willing servant

Leipzig, November 15, 1726   JOH. SEBAST. BACH

Wagner was chosen cantor and served for almost thirty years.

BACH PUBLISHES HIS FIRST INSTRUMENTAL WORK

127. *Clavier-Übung,* Part I, BWV 825: title page

Keyboard Practice, consisting of preludes, allemandes, courantes, sarabandes, gigues, minuets, and other galanteries, composed for music lovers, to refresh their spirits, by Johann Sebastian Bach, Actual Capellmeister to His Highness the Prince of Anhalt-Cöthen and Directore Chori Musici Lipsiensis. Partita I. Published by the Author. 1726.

Partitas II–VI were published with nearly the same title: II and III in 1727, IV in 1728, V and VI in 1730. The six partitas were issued together as Opus I, again with practically the same title, in 1731; Prince Leopold of Anhalt-Cöthen having died on November 19, 1728, Bach eliminated the reference to this prince, but added his recently acquired title: "Actual Capellmeister to the Court of Saxe-Weissenfels."

128. A dedicatory poem to the newborn prince, Emanuel Ludwig, which accompanied a copy of the publication *(BD* I, no. 55)

To His Most Serene Highness, Prince and Lord, Emanuel Ludewig, Heir to the Prince of Anhalt, Duke of Saxony, Engern, and Westphalia, Count of Ascania, Lord of Bernburg and Zerbst, &c., these modest musical beginnings are dedicated out of most humble devotion by Johann Sebastian Bach.

> Serene and Gracious Prince, though cradle cov'rings deck thee,
>   Yet doth thy Princely glance show thee more than full-grown.
> Forgive me, pray, if I from slumber should awake thee
>   The while my playful page to thee doth homage own.

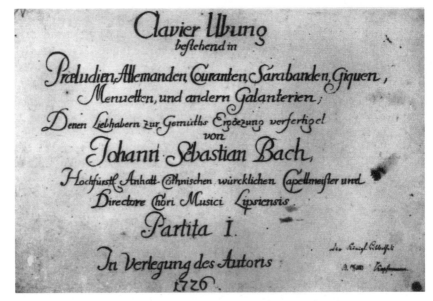

127. *Clavier-Übung*, Part I, BWV 825: title page

It is the first fruit of my strings in music sounding;
  Thou the first son round whom thy Princess's arms have curled.
It shall for thee and for thy honor be resounding,
  Since thou art, like this page, a firstling in this world.
The wise men of our time affright us oft by saying
  We come into this world with cries and wails of woe,
As if so soon we knew the bitterness of staying
  E'en this short time in weary travail here below.
But this do I turn round about, instead proclaiming
  That thy sweet childish cries are lovely, clear, and pure;
Thus shall thy whole life be with gladness teeming—
  A harmony complete of joys and pleasures sure.
So may I, Prince of all our hopes, e'er entertain thee,
  Though thy delights be multiplied a thousandfold,
But let, I pray, the feeling evermore sustain me
  Of being, Serene Prince, Thy humblest servant

BACH

*The prince, son of Prince Leopold by his second wife, was born on September 12,
1726. The poem's author is unknown.*

BACH WRITES TESTIMONIALS FOR A MUSICIAN,
CHRISTOPH GOTTLOB WECKER

129. Bach's letter of recommendation for Wecker (*BD* I, no. 18)

To the . . . Burgomasters, Town Magistrates, and all the Officials . . . of the Town of Chemnitz.

HONORED AND MOST NOBLE, HONORED AND MOST LEARNED, HONORED AND MOST WISE SIRS, PARTICULARLY MOST HIGHLY ESTEEMED PATRONI!

As the report has been received that the Cantor until now in the service of Your Honors wishes to undertake a change, and undoubtedly Your Honors have already given your most wise thought to the question of filling the vacant post with a capable person, I am almost afraid that I shall come too late with my most humble petition to Your Honors. But if as I hope the matter is still *in statu quo,* and Your Honors are not yet supplied with another capable person, then I address to you, Most Esteemed Sirs, a most humble petition that you will most graciously deign to grant to the bearer of this letter, Mr. Christoph Gottlob Wecker, the trial hearing that he requests and, according to the results of the said trial hearing, will very graciously grant him your most gracious patronage. If Your Honors find me capable of pleasing Your Honors with my service, I beg only to receive Your commands; I shall not fail to show, with the greatest *plaisir,* that I have the honor ever to be,
　　Most Noble Sirs and My Most Highly Esteemed Patrons, Your most obedient servant

JOH. SEBAST. BACH
*Capellmeister to the Prince of Anhalt-Cöthen
and Director Chori Musici Lipsiensis
and Cantor of the St. Thomas School*

Leipzig, February 26, 1727

Bach's intervention in this case was unsuccessful. See also the following letter.

130. Bach's cover letter to Wecker sent with a testimonial
(*BD* I, no. 120)

*Monsieur
Monsieur Cristoffle Gottlob Wecker, Candidat en Droit, et Musicien bien renomé a Schweidnitz.*

MONSIEUR, MON TRES HONORÉ AMY,

You will not take it amiss that an absence of three weeks has prevented me from answering your kind letter before this. From the letter I see that the good Lord seems to guide your footsteps toward a position. In this I wish for you a Divine *fiat,* and it would give me pleasure if my modest testimonial, which goes to you herewith, should contribute something toward that end. With the Passion music you request I should be glad to oblige you if it were not needed by myself this year. I am furthermore obliged to you for having troubled yourself in connection with the Hauckwitz debt, which is still owed me, and therefore seek every opportunity (especially if it should come to actual payment) to show myself *réellement* thankful. If you find anything else in which I am capable of serving you, I beg that you will notify me; I will show with all *dexterité* that I am ever to be called,

Monsieur, Mon tres honoré Amy, votre tres dedié serviteur

JOH. SEB. BACH

Leipzig, March 20, 1729

P.S. The latest is that the dear Lord has now also provided for honest Mr. Schott [organist of the New Church], and bestowed on him the post of Cantor in Gotha; wherefore he will say his farewells next week, as I am willing to take over his *Collegium* [*Musicum*].

See the "Announcement of the Musical Concerts at Leipzig," No. 187.

131. Bach's testimonial on behalf of Wecker (BD I, no. 60)

The bearer, Mr. Christoph Gottlob Wecker, *LL. Candidatus* as well as *in Musicis peritus,* has asked me, the undersigned, to give him a testimonial concerning on the one hand the deportment he has shown in this place and on the other the knowledge he possesses *in Musicis.* Since, then, I can testify this much concerning him: that his conduct has been such as to give full satisfaction; and specifically that his knowledge *in Musicis* has made him a welcome guest everywhere, particularly since he has a good command of various instruments and no less can well afford to make himself heard *vocaliter,* and equally he has been able to give creditable assistance in my church and other music; therefore, I have executed this testimonial with my own hand, and leave the rest to him to prove to you.

JOH. SEBAST. BACH
Capellmeister to the Prince of Saxe-Weissenfels
as well as to the Prince of Anhalt-Cöthen,
Director Chori Musices Lipsiensis and Cantor

Leipzig, March 20, 1729   *at St. Thomas's here*

BACH COMPOSES A CANTATA, BWV ANH. 9,
FOR THE BIRTHDAY OF KING AUGUST II

132. Excerpts from Christoph Ernst Sicul's *Das frohlockende Leipzig,* 1727 (*BD* II, no. 220)

May 12, 1727

Since the general day of joy did not permit the people of Leipzig who rejoiced at it to acquiesce in the above-described solemnities; so various private persons as well as all the Royal foundationers and resident students took pains to exhibit in various ways their most humble joy.

For the foundationers, after eight o'clock in the evening, when they were told by the Court Messenger that it was now time, performed a piece of music that had been composed by the Capellmeister and Town Cantor, Mr. Johann Sebastian Bach, and that the latter personally directed.

On this occasion the following text had been chosen for the *Drama musicum.*

Aria tutti
Entfernet euch, ihr heitren Sterne, &c.

The principal copy of the same, which was to be presented to His Royal Majesty, the foundationers had had bound in deep scarlet velvet, with gilt tassels and gold fringes, but printed on white satin, and it was carried by the Orator of the same, named Haupt, who had been chosen by lot, upon a silver platter.

The procession itself was arranged in the following order: (1) The Seniors of the 15 tables in the refectory and a 16th in addition, with wax torches; (2) two marshals with marshal's batons; (3) the said Haupt with the copy on a silver vessel, accompanied by two others; (4) the tablemates of 4 tables with burning torches; (5) the *Chorus Musicus,* which made itself heard during the marching with trumpets and kettledrums, along with other instruments; (6) the rest of the foundationers, also with torches.

When, then, they arrived in this order before His Royal Majesty in the marketplace, the bringers of the poems were led by the two marshals up to the front of the Antechamber, and the Orator had to make and present his compliments to His Excellency the Chief Cupbearer, Von Seiffert; through whom His Royal Majesty most graciously expressed His Most Gracious Thanks to them for the most humble devotion that they intended to demonstrate by a serenade for His High Birthday, and assured them of His Royal Favor on each and every occasion.

During this ceremony, and before the return of those delegated for the purpose, everything had been set in readiness for the music, which was then executed to the Most Gracious Contentment, amid a great concourse of people, behind an adequate *barrière* formed by the soldiery in attendance upon His Royal Majesty. Whereupon all the foundationers, as the offerers of the said evening music, returned in the aforesaid order, down the Cather Street, then by the Menke house, and after inspection of the illumination at that place, went back into the *Collegium Paulinum* [the University], where they closed their solemnity with the burning of the remainders of their torches in the square of the *Collegium,* amid much crying of "Vivat!"

Drama musicum or Dramma per musica was the original designation of Bach's secular cantatas in dialogue form. The music for BWV Anh. 9 is lost.

BACH COMPOSES A CANON FOR
LUDWIG FRIEDRICH HUDEMANN

133. Canon for four voices, BWV 1074: reprint of album entry (NBA VIII/1, p. 3)

Canon for 4 voices, dedicated to Mons. Houdemann and composed by J. S. Bach.

The canon, dating from before August 18, 1727, is reproduced from Mattheson's Der vollkommene Capellmeister *of 1739. For his comments, see No. 329. For a poem in praise of Bach by Hudemann, see No. 308.*

BACH WRITES A TESTIMONIAL FOR A STUDENT,
FRIEDRICH GOTTLIEB WILD

134. Bach's testimonial on behalf of Wild (BD I, no. 57)

Whereas Mr. Friedrich Gottlieb Wild, *Cand*[*idatus*] *jur*[*is*], and noted musician, has asked the undersigned to furnish him with a letter of recommendation concerning his achievements in his studies as well as concerning the noble art of music,

Accordingly I have thought it no more than my Christian duty to testify to the fact that the said *Mons.* Wild, during the four years that he has lived here at the University, has always shown himself to be diligent and hardworking, in such a manner that he not only has helped

133. Canon for four voices, BWV 1074

to adorn our church music with his well-learned accomplishments on the *Flaute traversiere* and *Clavecin* but also has taken special instruction from me in the clavier, thorough bass, and the fundamental rules of composition based thereupon, so that he may on any occasion be heard with particular approval by musicians of attainment. I consider him, by virtue of his conduct in this and other respects, worthy of all encouragement, and add my wish that this sincere and conscientious testimonial may be of use to him in securing the advancement he deserves.

JOH. SEBAST. BACH
*Capellmeister to the Prince of Anhalt-Cöthen and
Director Chori Musici Lipsiensis*

Leipzig, May 18, 1727

BACH COMPOSES AN ODE OF MOURNING, BWV 198,
FOR QUEEN CHRISTIANE EBERHARDINE

135. A statement Bach refused to sign (*BD* II, no. 227)

Whereas a Worshipful University at Leipzig has not been willing to permit that the Music of Mourning ordered from me by Mr. von Kirchbach for the memorial oration of the same in St. Paul's on the occasion of the recent death of Her Royal Majesty in Poland and Electoral Highness in Saxony, Our Dearly Beloved Queen Consort, should be performed, but has finally consented on the following conditions: that Mr. von Kirchbach is to come to terms with the *Director Chori Musici* of a Worshipful University in the said Church, and I am to sign a pledge.

Now, therefore, I recognize that this is purely a favor, and hereby agree that it is not to set any precedent (and that I shall dispatch a document acknowledging this), likewise that I am never to make any claim to the directorship of the music in the said St. Paul's, much less contract with anyone for music for such solemnities or otherwise without the consent and permission of a Worshipful University here, but on the contrary will always conduct myself in accordance with the most gracious order issued at Leipzig under date of January 21, 1726.

Leipzig, October 11, 1727

After the death of Queen Christiane Eberhardine, consort of the king and elector, on September 6, 1727, H. C. von Kirchbach, a university student, obtained the king's permission for a commemorative service in St. Paul's. He commissioned J. C. Gottsched, an eminent poet of the time, to write an ode of mourning and Bach to set it to music. Görner, the Director Chori Musici Academici, *complained to the university about this encroachment upon his prerogatives, and several attempts were made to procure Bach's signature to the above paper. Bach, however, could not be induced to sign; Görner was paid 12 thlr., and the performance met with no further obstacle.*

136. A report on the performance, in Christoph Ernst Sicul's *Das thränende Leipzig,* 1727 (*BD* II, no. 232)

October 17, 1727

In solemn procession, while the bells were rung, the Town Officials and the Rector and Professors of the University entered St. Paul's, where many others were present, namely, princely and other persons of rank, as well as not only Saxon but also foreign Ministers, Court and other Chevaliers, along with many ladies.

When, then, everyone had taken his place, there had been an improvisation on the organ, and the Ode of Mourning written by Magister Johann Christoph Gottsched, member of the *Collegium Marianum,* had been distributed among those present by the Beadles, there was shortly heard the Music of Mourning, which this time Capellmeister Johann Sebastian Bach had composed in the Italian style, with *Clave di Cembalo* [harpsichord], which Mr. Bach himself played, organ, violas di gamba, lutes, violins, recorders, transverse flutes, &c., half being heard before and half after the oration of praise and mourning.

BACH INSISTS ON CHOOSING THE HYMNS FOR THE SERVICE

137. The consistory's instructions to Dr. Salomon Deyling
(*BD* II, no. 246)

Greeting:

MOST REVEREND, MOST LEARNED, ESPECIALLY BELOVED COL-
LEAGUE, GRACIOUS SIR AND GOOD FRIEND!

Whereas the *Diaconus substitutus* of the Church of St. Nicholas of this place has submitted the accompanying complaint about the Cantor of the St. Thomas School, Johann Sebastian Bach, concerning the singing of the hymns at the vesper sermons;

Now, therefore, in the name of the Most Serene and Mighty Prince and Lord, Frederick Augustus, King in Poland, etc., Duke in Saxony, Jülich, Cleves, Berg, Engern, and Westphalia, Archmarshal and Elector of the Holy Roman Empire, Landgrave in Thuringia, Margrave of Meissen, also Upper and Lower Lausitz, Burgrave of Magdeburg, Prince and Count of Henneberg, Count of the Mark, of Ravensberg and Barbey, Lord of Ravenstein, Our Most Gracious Lord, we require of the same

That he shall inform the Cantor that when the ministers who are preaching cause it to be announced that particular hymns are to be sung before or after the sermon, he shall be governed accordingly and have the same sung. On this point we have not wished to keep silent, and are willing to be at his service.

	The Members of the Consistory of the
Given at Leipzig,	Elector and Prince of Saxony
September 8, 1728	in this Place

138. Bach's protest to the council (*BD* I, no. 19)

YOUR MAGNIFICENCES, MOST NOBLE, MOST DISTINGUISHED, STEAD-
FAST, HONORED AND MOST LEARNED, ALSO MOST WISE, MOST
HIGHLY ESTEEMED GENTLEMEN AND PATRONI!

Your Magnificences and You, Most Noble and Most Distinguished Sirs, will graciously deign to remember how, on the occasion of my acceptance of the call to the Cantorate of the St. Thomas School here, which

is entrusted to me, I was instructed by Your Magnificences and You, Most Noble and Most Distinguished Sirs, to abide in all things strictly by the customs hitherto followed at the public divine service, and not to make any innovations; and how you graciously assured me that you would favor me in this matter with Your High Protection. Among these customs and practices was the ordering of the hymns before and after the sermons, which was always left solely to me and my predecessors in the Cantorate to determine, in accordance with the gospels and the *Dresdener Gesangbuch* [a hymnal] based on the same, as seemed appropriate to the season and the circumstances, and, as the honorable ministry can attest, no conflict ever arose about this. Contrary to this practice, however, the Subdeacon of St. Nicholas's, Magister Gottlieb Gaudlitz, has taken it upon himself to attempt an innovation and has sought, in place of the hymns chosen in accordance with the established use, to introduce others, and when I hesitated, because of possible consequences to be feared, to comply with this, he lodged a complaint against me with the Most Worshipful Consistory, and worked out an order addressed to me by the terms of which I should have had to cause to be sung whatever hymns the preachers should choose. Now, it seems the less proper for me to carry out such an arrangement without the previous knowledge of Your Magnificences and You, Most Noble and Most Honored Sirs, as the high *Patroni* of the churches in this town, since hitherto the ordering of the hymns has remained for so long undisturbed as a function of the Cantorate, and the said Mr. Gaudlitz himself admits, in the document that has been addressed by him to the Most Worshipful Consistory and a copy of which is attached as Exhibit A, that on the few occasions when he has had his way, I, as the Cantor, have been asked for my approval. It may be added that when, in addition to the concerted music, very long hymns are sung, the divine service is held up, and all sorts of disorder would have to be reckoned with; not to mention the fact that not a single one of the clergymen except Magister Gaudlitz, the Subdeacon, wishes to introduce this innovation. This matter I have felt necessary to bring obediently to the attention of Your Magnificences and You, Most Noble and Most Distinguished Sirs, with the humble request that you will protect me in respect to the old practices concerning the hymns and their ordering. Wherefor I shall remain my life long,

Your Magnificences and Most Noble and Most Distinguished Sirs, Your most obedient

Leipzig, September 20, 1728   JOHANN SEBASTIAN BACH

The original complaint by Gaudlitz referred to by both the consistory and Bach adds nothing to the information given in the above documents. Whether the council took any action is not known. But the subject came up again in a memorandum from the consistory to Deyling, No. 149, which seems to indicate that Bach's view prevailed.

BACH PERFORMS THE FUNERAL MUSIC FOR
PRINCE LEOPOLD

139. Excerpt from the Cöthen court accounts (*BD* II, no. 259)

To Capellmeister Bach, his wife and son [presumably Wilhelm Friedemann] from Leipzig, called hither, also to the musicians from Halle, Merseburg, Zerbst, Dessau, and Güsten, who have helped attend to the funeral music for His Late Serene Highness, Prince Leopold, on the occasion of the interment, March 23, 1729, and the funeral sermon, March 24, 1729, as settlement including board money, [paid] 230 thlr.

BACH DISTRIBUTES PUBLICATIONS BY
COLLEAGUES

140. Excerpt from the Leipzig *Post-Zeitungen,* April 18, 1729 (*BD* II, no. 260)

The musical amateurs are informed that the recently published treatise by Mr. Capellmeister [Johann David] Heinichen of Dresden, titled *Der General-Bass in der Composition,* will at the instigation of good friends be found at the following locations in Germany under commission, namely: in Hamburg from Mr. Capellmeister Mattheson; in Hesse-Darmstadt from Mr. Capellmeister Graupner; in Wolfenbüttel from Mr. Concertmeister Simonetti; in Berlin from the royal chamber musician, Mr. [Peter] Glösch; in Leipzig from Mr. Capellmeister Bach; in Freiberg from the organist and mathematician Mr. [Elias] Lindner; and in Dresden from the book's author. However, because the latter had to arrange for the transport of the copies to the said foreign locations at major expense, the Messrs. amateurs will approve of paying an additional 2, 4, and up to 6 gr. for postage, depending on distance, for each copy over and above the very civil price of 2 rthl. NB. From the abovementioned Capellmeister Bach may also be obtained Mr. Johann Gottfried Walther's *Musicalisches Lexicon,* Litera A [first installment], for 2 gr.

PROPOSALS FOR ADMISSION TO THE
ST. THOMAS SCHOOL

141. A letter from Dr. Christian Ludwig Stieglitz, school board chairman (*BD* II, no. 262)

Through past departures, nine spaces for alumni at the School of St. Thomas are vacated, for which there have been applications in writing, listed in the enclosed specification, *sub A. no. 1,* in part with statements by the Mr. Rector or Co-Rector, as well as *sub No. 2,* those not in writing, based on Mr. Capellmeister and Cantor Bach's suggestion. As for the orally observed opinion of Mr. Bach, grade *sub. B. and C.,* those named are competent in singing; for the others no such *dispositio* has been found. In enclosure *sub D.,* however, the same takes occasion to point out that, with respect to singing in services of all five churches, there is need for 44 boys. Since many of those used so far have left the School and the churches can in no way be served by current alumni, the same begs that the Mr. Rector consider, to the extent possible, the unavoidable need for reflecting upon such subjects as are competent in music and singing, to fill the vacant places. Hereafter, the Mr. Rector submitted his grade, *sub E and F,* as to how he had judged the boys who had been subjected to his examination. For a clearer distinction, the names of those boys who, in both grades, were found the most competent, were marked with prefixed double strokes in red. A Most Wise Council will kindly resolve which of all of these will be taken on as alumni. Leipzig, May 18, 1729.

DR. CHRISTIAN LUDWIG STIEGLITZ
as Chairman

142. Exhibit B: Bach's report (*BD* I, no. 63)

The boys who wish to be admitted to fill present vacancies in the School of St. Thomas as resident students are as follows:

1. Those who can be used in music

Sopranos
(1) Christoph Friedrich Meissner, of Weissenfels, aged 13 years, has a good voice and fine proficiency.
(2) Johann Tobias Krebs, of Buttstädt, aged 13 years, has a good strong voice and fine proficiency.
(3) Samuel Kittler, of Bellgern, aged 13 years, has a fairly strong voice and good proficiency.
(4) Johann Heinrich Hillmeyer, of Gehrings Walde, aged 13 years, has a strong voice as well as good proficiency.

(5) Johann August Landvoigt, of Gaschwitz, aged 13 years, has a passable voice; his proficiency is fair.

(6) Johann Andreas Köpping, of Grossboden, aged 14 years, has a fairly strong voice; his proficiency is *mediocre*.

(7) Johann Gottlieb Krause, of Grossdeuben, aged 14 years, whose voice is somewhat weak and proficiency indifferent.

(8) Johann Georg Leg, of Leipzig, aged 13 years, whose voice is somewhat weak and proficiency slight.

Altos

(9) Johann Gottfried Neucke, of Grima, aged 14 years, has a strong voice and quite fine proficiency.

(10) Gottfried Christoph Hoffmann, of Nebra, aged 16 years, has a *passable* alto voice, but his proficiency is still rather poor.

2. Those who have no musical accomplishments
   (1) Johann Tobias Dieze
   (2) Gottlob Michael Wintzer
   (3) Johann David Bauer
   (4) Johanna Margarethe Pfeil's son
   (5) Gottlob Ernst Hausius
   (6) Wilhelm Ludewig's son Friedrich Wilhelm
   (7) Johann Gottlieb Zeymer
   (8) Johann Gottfried Berger
   (9) Johann Gottfried Eschner
   (10) Salomon Gottfried Greülich
   (11) Michael Heinrich Kittler of Prettin

JOH. SEBAST. BACH
Direct. Musices and Cantor of St. Thomas's

143. Exhibit C: An amendment by Bach (*BD* I, no. 64)

Gottwald Pezold of Aurich, aged 14 years, has a fine voice and his proficiency is passable.

Johann Christoph Schmid of Bendleben, aged 19 years, has a fairly strong tenor voice and hits the notes very prettily.

144. Exhibit D: Organization of the St. Thomas Choir
(*BD* I, no. 180)

At St. Nicholas's the 1st choir requires:	At St. Thomas's the 2nd choir:	At the New Church the 3rd choir:
3 Sopranos	3 Sopranos	3 Sopranos
3 Altos	3 Altos	3 Altos
3 Tenors	3 Tenors	3 Tenors
3 Basses	3 Basses	3 Basses

The 4th choir:
2 Sopranos   2 Altos
2 Tenors   2 Basses
And this last choir must also take care of St. Peter's.

145. Two additions by Bach to his report (*BD* I, nos. 65–66)

a. Carolus Heinrich Scharff, aged 14 years, has a fair alto voice and moderate proficiency in *Musicis*.

J. S. BACH,
[May 21, 1729?]   *Cantor* etc.

b. The above-named Wünzer has a somewhat weak voice, and little proficiency as yet, but he should (if private practice is diligently maintained) become usable in time.

JOH. SEBAST. BACH
Leipzig, June 3, 1729   *Cantor* etc.

G. M. Wintzer (see No. 142) was apparently reexamined.

BACH COMPOSES SERVICE MUSIC FOR THE
TOWN COUNCIL ELECTION

146. Excerpt from the files of the town scribe, August 22, 1729 (*BD* II, no. 264)

Have ordered from Mr. Superintendent, D. [theol.] Deyling, the sermon for the inauguration of the new Council, on this coming Monday; likewise the doorkeeper ordered the music from Mr. Cantor.

BACH WRITES A TESTIMONIAL FOR A STUDENT,
JOHANN GOTTLIEB GRAHL

147. Bach's testimonial on behalf of Grahl (*BD* III, p. 629, no. 66a)

Since the bearer of this, Mr. Johann Gottlieb Grahl, student of theology and highly proficient in music, has asked the undersigned to furnish him with a few lines regarding his deportment here and his diligence and resulting qualification in music, I wish to state, in order to comply, that no one may be easily found who would not agree with me in complete satisfaction, and that his capacity in the art of music will give itself the best attestation. Leipzig, September 12, 1729.

JOH: SEB: BACH.
*Princely Saxe-Weissenfels Court Capellmeister and
Direct. Chori Musici
at Leipzig.*

BACH WRITES A TESTIMONIAL FOR
JOHANN CHRISTIAN WEYRAUCH

148. Bach's testimonial on behalf of Weyrauch (*BD* I, no. 67)

Whereas the bearer, Mr. Johann Christian Weyrauch, *J*[*uris*] *U*[*triusque*] *C*[*andidatus*], has requested me, the undersigned, to give him an official testimonial concerning his knowledge *in musicis,* now, therefore, I have felt it my duty not to fail to gratify his wish in this respect, considering that he not only masters various instruments but can also well afford to make himself heard *vocaliter,* has given many examples of his skill, and also can show on request what he has done in the art of composition. I do not doubt that he will be able to prove the accuracy of all this in person.

JOH. SEB. BACH
*Capellmeister to the Elector of S.-W. and
Director Chori Musici Lipsiensis*

Leipzig, January 14, 1730

THE CONSISTORY FORBIDS THE USE OF
UNFAMILIAR HYMNS

149. The consistory's letter to Dr. Deyling (Bitter II, pp. 231f.)

Greeting:

MOST REVEREND, MOST LEARNED, ESPECIALLY BELOVED COL-
LEAGUE, GRACIOUS SIR AND GOOD FRIEND!

Whereas attention has been called to the fact that in the public divine services during the past Advent Season the chanting of the Nicene Creed has been omitted and it has been desired to sing and introduce new hymns, hitherto unknown, but such an arbitrary procedure is not to be tolerated,

Now, therefore, in the Name of the Most Serene and Mighty Prince and Lord, Frederick Augustus, King in Poland, etc., Duke in Saxony, Jülich, Cleves, Berg, Engern, and Westphalia, Archmarshal and Elector of the Holy Roman Empire, Landgrave in Thuringia, Margrave of Meissen, also Upper and Lower Lausitz, Burgrave of Magdeburg, Prince and Count of Henneberg, Count of the Mark, of Ravensberg and Barbey, Lord of Ravenstein, Our Most Gracious Lord, we herewith require of the same

That he shall arrange that in the churches of this town, too, matters shall be regulated accordingly, and new hymns, hitherto not customary, shall not be used in public divine services without his, or if need be our, previous knowledge and approbation.

On this point we have not wished to keep silent.

The Members of the Consistory of the
Elector and Prince of Saxony

Given at Leipzig, February 16, 1730   in that Place

Whereas No. 137 makes direct reference to Bach, it is unclear whether he prompted this new controversy.

BACH IS REPROACHED, AND HE RESPONDS
AT LENGTH

150. Excerpts from the minutes of the council meetings
(*BD* II, nos. 280–81)

a. August 2, 1730

The St. Thomas School had many times been the subject of deliberation and the plans and projects were at hand, but they would need to be investigated further. In which connection it should be remembered that when the Cantor came hither he received a dispensation concerning the teaching; Magister Pezold attended to the functions poorly enough; the third and fourth classes were the nursery for the whole school, and accordingly a competent person must be placed in charge of them; the Cantor might take care of one of the lowest classes; he did not conduct himself as he should (without the foreknowledge of the burgomaster in office [he] sent a choir student to the country; went away without obtaining leave), for which he must be reproached and admonished; at present it must be considered whether the said classes should not be provided with a different person; Magister Kriegel was

said to be a good man, and a decision would have to be made about it.
Court Councilor Lange: Everything was true that had been mentioned against the Cantor, and he could be admonished and the place filled with Magister Kriegel.
Court Councilor Steger: Not only did the Cantor do nothing, but he was not even willing to give an explanation of that fact; he did not hold the singing class, and there were other complaints in addition; a change would be necessary, a break would have to come some time, and he would acquiesce in the making of other arrangements.
Diocesan Councilor Born: Adhered to the above votes.
Dr. Hölzel: Likewise.
Commissioner Dr. Falckner: Likewise.
Commissioner Kregel: Likewise.
Syndic Job: Likewise, since the Cantor was *incorrigible.*
Commissioner Sieber: Likewise.
Commissioner Winckler: Likewise.
Commissioner Hohmann: Likewise.
I [the clerk]: Likewise.

Hereupon it was resolved to restrict the Cantor's [incidental] income.

b. August 25, 1730
   The Vice Chancellor and Burgomaster, Dr. Born, reports: He has spoken with the Cantor, Bach, but he shows little inclination to work, and the question is whether the class ought not to be given to Magister Krügel instead of Petzold, without additional salary.
   Resolved: Arrangements to that effect are to be made.

   Although Bach's memorandum, which follows, was written two days before this meeting, it had presumably not yet been brought to the council's attention.

151. **Bach's "Short But Most Necessary Draft for a Well-Appointed Church Music, with Certain Modest Reflections on the Decline of the Same": memorandum to the Leipzig town council**
   (*BD* I, no. 22)

A well-appointed church music requires vocalists and instrumentalists.
   The vocalists in this place are made up of the pupils of the St. Thomas School, being of four sorts, namely, sopranos [*Discantisten*], altos, tenors, and basses.

In order that the choruses of church pieces may be performed as is fitting, the vocalists must in turn be divided into 2 sorts, namely, concertists and ripienists.

The concertists are ordinarily 4 in number; sometimes also 5, 6, 7, even 8; that is, if one wishes to perform music for two choirs [*per choros*].

The ripienists, too, must be at least 8, namely, two for each part.

The instrumentalists are also divided into various kinds, namely, violinists [*Violisten,* i.e., string players], oboists, flutists, trumpeters, and drummers. N.B. The violinists also include those who play the violas, the violoncellos, and the violones.

The number of the *Alumni* [resident students] of the St. Thomas School is 55. These 55 are divided into 4 choirs, for the 4 churches in which they must partly perform concerted music with instruments [*musiciren*], partly sing motets, and partly sing chorales. In the 3 churches, namely, St. Thomas's, St. Nicholas's, and the New Church, the pupils must all be musical. St. Peter's receives the residue [*Ausschuss*], namely, those who do not understand music and can only just barely sing a chorale.

Every musical choir should contain at least 3 sopranos, 3 altos, 3 tenors, and as many basses, so that even if one happens to fall ill (as very often happens, particularly at this time of year, as the prescriptions written by the school physician for the apothecary must show) at least a double-chorus motet may be sung. (N.B. Though it would be still better if the group were such that one could have 4 subjects on each voice and thus could provide every choir with 16 persons.)

Hence the number of those who must understand music comes to 36 persons in all.

The instrumental music consists of the following parts, namely:

2 or even 3 for the	*Violino 1*
2 or 3 for the	*Violino 2*
2 for the	*Viola 1*
2 for the	*Viola 2*
2 for the	*Violoncello*
1 for the	*Violon[e]*
2, or, if the piece requires, 3, for the	*Hautbois*
1, or even 2, for the	*Basson*
3 for the	*Trompetten*
1 for the	*Paucken*

total 18 persons at least, for the instrumental music. N.B. If it happens that the church piece is composed with flutes also (whether they are recorders [*à bec*] or transverse flutes [*Traversieri*], as very often happens for variety's sake, at least 2 more persons are needed. Making altogether 20 instrumentalists.

The number of persons appointed to play the church music is 8, namely, 4 town pipers [*Stadt Pfeifer*], 3 professional fiddlers [*Kunst Geiger*], and one associate. Modesty forbids me to speak at all truthfully of their qualities and musical knowledge. Nevertheless it must be remembered that they are partly *emeriti* and partly not at all in such practice [*exercitio*] as they should be. This is the plan for them:

Mr. Reiche [aged 63]	for the	1st *trumpet*
Mr. Genssmar [45]	————	2nd *trumpet*
vacant	————	3rd *trumpet*
vacant	————	*kettledrums*
Mr. Rother [65]	————	1st *violin*
Mr. Beyer [49]	————	2nd *violin*
vacant	————	*viola*
vacant	————	*violoncello*
vacant	————	*violon*[e]
Mr. Gleditsch [46]	————	1st *oboe*
Mr. Kornagel [41]	————	2nd *oboe*
vacant	————	3rd *oboe* or *taille*
The associate	————	*bassoon*

Thus there are lacking the following most necessary players, partly to reinforce certain voices, and partly to supply indispensable ones, namely:

2 *violinists* for the 1st *violin*
2 *violinists* for the 2nd *violin*
2 that play the *viola*
2 *violoncellists*
1 *violonist*
2 for the *flutes*

The lack that shows itself here has had to be supplied hitherto partly by the *studiosi* [of the University] but mostly by the *alumni* [of the St. Thomas School]. Now, the *studiosi* have shown themselves willing to do this in the hope that one or the other would in time receive some kind of reward and perhaps be favored with a *stipendium* or *honorarium* (as was indeed formerly the custom). But since this has not occurred, but on the contrary, the few slight *beneficia* formerly devoted to the *chorus musicus* have been successively withdrawn; the willingness of the *studiosi,* too, has disappeared, for who will do work or perform services

151. Bach's "Short But Most Necessary Draft for a Well-Appointed Church Music": memorandum to the Leipzig town council

for nothing? Be it furthermore remembered that, since the 2nd *violin* usually, and the *viola, violoncello,* and *violone* always (in the absence of more capable subjects) have had to be played by students, it is easy to estimate how much the chorus has been deprived of in consequence. Thus far only the Sunday music has been touched upon. But if I should mention the music of the Holy Days (on which days I must supply both the principal churches with music), the deficiency of indispensable players will show even more clearly, particularly since I must give up to the other choir all those pupils who play one instrument or another and must get along altogether without their help.

Moreover, it cannot remain unmentioned that the fact that so many poorly equipped boys, and boys not at all talented for music, have been accepted [into the school] to date has necessarily caused the music to decline and deteriorate. For it is easy to see that a boy who knows nothing of music and who cannot indeed even form a second in his throat can have no natural musical talent; and *consequenter* can never be used for the musical service. And that those who do bring a few precepts with them when they come to school are not ready to be used immediately, as is required. For there is no time to instruct such pupils first for years until they are ready to be used, but on the contrary: as soon as they are accepted, they are assigned to the various choirs, and they must at least be sure of *measure* and *pitch* in order to be of use in divine service. Now, if each year some of those who have accomplished something *in musicis* leave the school and their places are taken by others who either are not yet ready to be used or have no ability whatsoever, it is easy to understand that the *chorus musicus* must decline.

For it is notorious that my honored predecessors, Messrs. Schell[e] and Kuhnau, already had to rely on the help of the *studiosi* when they wished to produce a complete and well-sounding music which, indeed, they were enabled to this extent to do, that not only some vocalists, namely, a bass, a tenor, and even an alto, but also instrumentalists, especially two violinists, were favored with separate *stipendia* by a Most Noble and Most Wise Council and thus encouraged to reinforce the musical performances in the churches. Now, however, that the state of music is quite different from what it was, since our artistry has increased very much, and the taste [*gusto*] has changed astonishingly, and accordingly the former style of music no longer seems to please our ears, considerable help is therefore all the more needed to choose and appoint such musicians as will satisfy the present musical taste, master the new kinds of music, and thus be in a position to do justice to the composer and his work. Now the few *beneficia,* which should have been increased rather than diminished, have been withdrawn entirely from the *chorus musicus.* It is, anyhow, somewhat strange that German musicians are expected to be capable of performing at once and *ex tempore* all kinds of music, whether it come from Italy or France, England or Poland, just as may be done, say, by those virtuosos for whom the music is written and who have studied it long beforehand, indeed, know it almost by heart, and who, it should be noted, receive good salaries besides, so that their work and industry is thus richly rewarded; while, on the other hand, these are not taken into consideration, but they [German musicians] are left to look out for their own wants, so that many a one, for worry about his bread, cannot think of improving— let alone distinguishing—himself. To illustrate this statement with an example one need only go to Dresden and see how the musicians there are paid by His Royal Majesty. It cannot fail, since the musicians are relieved of all concern for their living, free from *chagrin* and obliged each to master but a single instrument; it must be something choice and excellent to hear. The conclusion is accordingly easy to draw: that with the stopping of the *beneficia* the powers are taken from me to bring the music into a better state.

In conclusion I find it necessary to append the enumeration of the present *alumni,* to indicate the proficiency of each *in musicis* and thus to leave it to riper reflection whether in such circumstances the music can continue to be maintained, or whether its still greater decline is to be feared. It is, however, necessary to divide the whole group [*coetus*] into three classes.

Accordingly those who are usable are as follows:

> (1) Pezold, Lange, Stoll, *Praefecti.* Frick, Krause, Kittler, Pohlreüter, Stein, Burckhard, Siegler, Nitzer, Reichhard, Krebs *major* and *minor,* Schönemann, Heder, and Dietel.

The names of the motet singers, who must first have further training in order to be used eventually for concerted music [*Figural Music*] , are as follows:

> (2) Jänigke, Ludewig *major* and *minor,* Meissner, Neücke *major* and *minor,* Hillmeyer, Steidel, Hesse, Haupt, Suppius, Segnitz, Thieme, Keller, Röder, Ossan, Berger, Lösch, Hauptmann, and Sachse.

Those of the last sort are not *musici* at all, and their names are:

> (3) Bauer, Gross, Eberhard, Braune, Seyman, Tietze, Hebenstreit, Wintzer, Össer, Leppert, Haussius, Feller, Crell, Zeymer, Guffer, Eichel, and Zwicker.

Total: 17 usable, 20 not yet usable, and 17 unfit.

JOH. SEB. BACH
Director Musices

Leipzig, August 23, 1730

The Alumni discussed in this document represent the resident students of the St. Thomas School, whose number was limited to 55. They were required to earn their stipends by taking part in the School's choral activities. Not included in Bach's memorandum are the nonresident students (Externi) who, like Bach's own sons and Gotthelf Engelbert Nietzsche (b. 1714, prefect from 1736; see No. 186), lived with their families in Leipzig, outnumbered the alumni by a very wide margin, and participated in the School's program of music lessons. The most capable among them were selected to take part in the performing activities (some of them even with benefits, a specified by the School regulations), but their variable numbers as well as those of the University students are not indicated by Bach.

BACH SEEKS ANOTHER POSITION

152. Bach's letter to Georg Erdmann, Imperial Russian Residence agent in Danzig (*BD* I, no. 23)

MOST HONORED SIR,

Your Honor will have the goodness to excuse an old and faithful servant for taking the liberty of disturbing you with the present letter. It must be nearly four years since Your Honor favored me with a kind answer to the letter I sent you; I remember that at that time you graciously asked me to give you some news of what had happened to me, and I humbly take this opportunity of providing you with the same. You know the course of my life from my youth up until the change in my fortunes that took me to Cöthen as Capellmeister. There I had a gracious Prince, who both loved and knew music, and in his service I intended to spend the rest of my life. It must happen, however, that the said *Serenissimus* should marry a Princess of Berenburg, and that then the impression should arise that the musical interests of the said Prince had become somewhat lukewarm, especially as the new Princess seemed to be unmusical; and it pleased God that I should be called hither to be *Director Musices* and Cantor at the St. Thomas School. Though at first, indeed, it did not seem at all proper to me to change my position of Capellmeister for that of Cantor. Wherefore, then, I postponed my decision for a quarter of a year; but this post was described to me in such favorable terms that finally (particularly since my sons seemed inclined toward [university] studies) I cast my lot, in the name of the Lord, and made the journey to Leipzig, took my examination, and then made the change of position. Here, by God's will, I am still in service. But since (1) I find that the post is by no means so lucrative as it was described to me; (2) I have failed to obtain many of the fees pertaining to the office; (3) the place is very expensive; and (4) the authorities are odd and little interested in music, so that I must live amid almost continual vexation, envy, and persecution; accordingly I shall be forced, with God's help, to seek my fortune else-where. Should Your Honor know or find a suitable post in your city for an old and faithful servant, I beg you most humbly to put in a most gracious word of recommendation for me—I shall not fail to do my best to give satisfaction and justify your most gracious intercession in my behalf. My present post amounts to about 700 thaler, and when there are rather more funerals than usual, the fees rise in proportion; but when a healthy wind blows, they fall accordingly, as for example last year, when I lost fees that would ordinarily come in from funerals to an amount of more than 100 thaler. In Thuringia I could get along better on 400 thaler than here with twice that many, because of the excessively high cost of living.

Now I must add a little about my domestic situation. I am married for the second time, my late first wife having died in Cöthen. From the first marriage I have three sons and one daughter living, whom Your Honor will graciously remember having seen in Weimar. From the second marriage I have one son and two daughters living. My eldest son is a *Studiosus Juris,* and of the other two [from the first marriage], one is in the *prima* class [the last class of school] and the other in the *secunda,* and the eldest daughter is also still unmarried. The children of my second marriage are still small, the eldest, a boy, being six years old. But they are all born musicians, and I can assure you that I can already form an ensemble both *vocaliter* and *instrumentaliter* within my family, particularly since my present wife sings a good, clear soprano, and my eldest daughter, too, joins in not badly. I shall almost transgress the bounds of courtesy if I burden Your Honor any further, and I therefore hasten to close, remaining with most devoted respect my whole life long

Your Honor's most obedient and devoted servant

Leipzig, October 28, 1730   JOH. SEBAST. BACH

Leipzig
1 7 3 1–1 7 4 0

153. Bach's testimonial on behalf of Johann Adolph Scheibe
(*BD* I, no. 68)

Whereas the bearer, Mr. Johann Adolph Scheibe, *LL. Studiosus* and most zealous student of music, has requested me, the undersigned, to give him a testimonial concerning his knowledge *in musicis,* now, therefore, I have been glad to do so and at the same time to testify that he is thoroughly at home not only on the clavier and violin but also in composition, and accordingly I do not doubt that he will be in a position adequately to attend to whatever office God may assign to him.

JOH. SEBAST. BACH
Capellmeister to the Prince of Saxe-Weissenfels
Direct. Chori Musici Lipsiensis

Leipzig, April 4, 1731

Scheibe, son of the organ builder Johann Scheibe, was the author of the letter, No. 343, that precipitated the famous controversy that is reflected in Nos. 344–47 and summarized in No. 348.

154. Bach's testimonial on behalf of Johann Christoph Dorn
(*BD* I, no. 69)

The bearer, *Mons.* Johann Christoph Dorn, student of music, has requested the undersigned to give him a testimonial to his knowledge *in musicis.*

Since I have found, after examining him, that he has a fair command of the clavier as well as of other instruments, and is thus in a position to render service to God and the public weal, I must not refuse his reasonable request, but rather testify that as his years increase it may well be expected that with his good native talent he will develop into a quite able musician.

JOH. SEB. BACH

Capellmeister to the Prince of Sax-Weissenfl. and

Direct. Chori Musici Lipsiensis

Leipzig, May 11, 1731

BACH PUBLISHES PARTITAS NOS. 1–6

155. *Clavier-Übung,* Part I, BWV 825–830: title page

Keyboard Practice, consisting of preludes, allemandes, courantes, sarabandes, gigues, minuets, and other galanteries, composed for music lovers, to refresh their spirits, by Johann Sebastian Bach, Actual Capellmeister to the Court of Saxe-Weissenfels and Directore Chori Musici Lipsiensis. Opus 1. Published by the Author. 1731. Leipzig, Commissioned from the daughter of the late Boethius, under the town hall.

See note to No. 127.

155. *Clavier-Übung,* Part I, BWV 825–830: title page

BACH RECEIVES LIQUOR TAX REVENUES

156. Bach's receipt to the liquor tax collector (BD I, no. 117)

That I have duly received from Mr. Johann Paul Latzer, regularly appointed Assessment and Liquor Tax Collector of His Royal Majesty in Poland and His Serene Electoral Highness in Saxony, for the period from Low Sunday, 1731, to the same, 1732, in accordance with the Electoral Saxon Regulation of November 9, 1646, the tax amount for three barrels [of beer, an impost remitted to the higher school and church officials] @ 40 gr., making altogether 5 thlr., say five thaler: this I have been in duty bound most obediently to acknowledge and at the same time duly to give a receipt for the same.

JOH. SEB. BACH
Direct. Musices and Cantor at St. Thomas's

Leipzig, Low Sunday, 1732
D S Deyling S mpp
Th Wagner mpp

BACH EXAMINES A REBUILT ORGAN IN KASSEL

157. Excerpt from the Kassel *Polizey- und Commerzienzeitung,* September 22, 1732 (*BD* II, no. 316)

The great and costly organ in the Collegiate Church of St. Martin, or the so-called Great Church, on which work has been going on for almost three years, has finally been adapted to the mode of today and brought to perfection. When this organ, in accordance with the orders of High Authority, has been examined by the famous Organist and Music Director Mr. Bach of Leipzig, with the help of the Court and Town Organist here, Mr. Carl Möller, in the hope that it will pass the desired test, it is to be played fully next Sunday [September 28, 1732], please God, in public assembly, and inaugurated with musical harmony. It is wished that the said work, chiefly intended for the Glory of God, may serve to inspirit the congregation as a whole and each person in particular.

158. Excerpt from the account books (*BD* II, no. 318)

To the Capellmeister Mr. Bach from Leypzig, who examined the organ and tried it out, 50 thlr. granted as *honorarium* and 26 thlr. traveling expenses, which have been paid to the same per order, and duly receipted . . . 76 thlr.

Board for the Capellmeister Mr. Bach and wife for the time during which they were lodged here, paid to Mr. Holtzschue per order, and duly receipted . . . 84 thlr.

BACH HOLDS COLLEGIUM MUSICUM CONCERTS

159. Announcement from the *Nachricht auch Frag u. Anzeiger,* Leipzig, January 6, 1733 (*BJ* 1984, p. 175)

Tonight at 8 o'clock is the Bachian Concert [*Bachische Conzert*] at the Zimmermann Coffeehouse on Catharine Street.

160. Special announcement of the resumption of concerts following a mourning period, June 1733 (*BD* II, no. 331)

His Royal Highness and Electoral Grace having given kind permission [*Concession*] for the continuation of the temporarily suspended Collegia Musica, tomorrow, Wednesday, June 17, the beginning will be made by Bach's Collegium Musicum at Zimmermann's Garden on the Grimmische Steinweg, at 4 o'clock in the afternoon, with a fine concert. It will be maintained week by week, with a new harpsichord [*Clavicymbel*], such as had not been heard here before, and lovers of music as well as virtuosos are expected to be present.

After the death of Elector Friedrich Augustus I on February 1, 1733, Saxony observed an official mourning period of several months. Concerted church music was not permitted from Estomihi Sunday until the Fourth Sunday after Trinity; it was resumed on July 2.

BACH DEDICATES HIS MASS IN B MINOR TO
THE DRESDEN COURT AND ASKS THE ELECTOR
TO GRANT HIM A TITLE

161. *Missa* (Kyrie and Gloria), BWV 232: performing parts, title wrapper (*BD* I, no. 166)

To His Royal Majesty and Electoral Highness of Saxony, demonstrated with the enclosed Mass—for 21 [voices], 3 violins, 2 sopranos, alto,

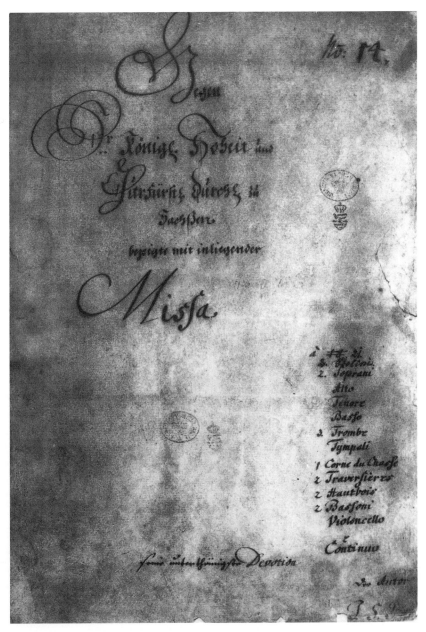

161. *Missa* (Kyrie and Gloria), BWV 232: performing parts, title wrapper

tenor, bass, 3 trumpets, tympani, 1 hunting horn, 2 transverse flutes, 2 oboes, 2 bassoons, violoncello, and, continuo—his most humble devotion, the author, J. S. Bach

162. Bach's letter accompanying the Mass (*BD* I, no. 27)

To His Most Serene Highness, the Prince and Lord, Frederick Augustus, Royal Prince in Poland and Lithuania, Duke in Saxony, . . . My Most Gracious Lord.

MY MOST GRACIOUS LORD, MOST SERENE ELECTOR, MOST GRACIOUS LORD!

To Your Royal Highness I submit in deepest devotion the present small work of that science which I have achieved in *musique,* with the most wholly submissive prayer that Your Highness will look upon it with Most Gracious Eyes, according to Your Highness's World-Famous Clemency and not according to the poor *composition;* and thus deign to take me under Your Most Mighty Protection. For some years and up to the present moment, I have had the *Directorium* of the Music in the two principal churches in Leipzig, but have innocently had to suffer one injury or another, and on occasion also a diminution of the fees accruing to me in this office; but these injuries would disappear altogether if Your Royal Highness would grant me the favor of conferring upon me a title of Your Highness's Court Capelle, and would let Your High Command for the issuing of such a document go forth to the proper place. Such a most gracious fulfillment of my most humble prayer will bind me to unending devotion, and I offer myself in most indebted obedience to show at all times, upon Your Royal Highness's Most Gracious Desire, my untiring zeal in the composition of music for the church as well as for the orchestra, and to devote my entire forces to the service of Your Highness, remaining in unceasing fidelity Your Royal Highness's most humble and most obedient servant

Dressden, July 27, 1733   JOHANN SEBASTIAN BACH

After his death on February 1, 1733, Augustus the Strong was automatically succeeded as elector of Saxony by his only legitimate son, Frederick Augustus II (1696–1763), who, as Augustus III, was elected king of Poland on October 5, 1733, and crowned at Cracow on January 17, 1734.

BACH JOINS WITH THE ORGANIST AND RECTOR
IN PROTESTING THE NONPAYMENT OF FEES

163. Letter from Bach, Johann Schneider, and Johann Matthias Gesner to the council (*BD* I, no. 28)

To Their Magnificences, the Most Noble, Most Learned, and Most Wise Gentle-men, the Honorable Burgomasters, Proconsul, and all the Eminent Members of a Highly Esteemed Council of this place, our Particularly Highly Esteemed Masters and Eminent Patrons.

YOUR MAGNIFICENCES, MOST NOBLE, MOST LEARNED, MOST WISE, AND MOST HIGHLY ESTEEMED SIRS AND EMINENT PATRONS!

May it please Your Magnificences and You, Most Noble Sirs, graciously to learn herewith how Mr. Johann Friedrich Eitelwein, a merchant of this place, on August 12 of this year got married outside of Leipzig and accordingly thinks himself justified in withholding the fees regularly due us on this account and, disregarding many courteous reminders, has refused to give them to us. Now, since the said fees make up the most part of our compensation and hitherto no one has tried to get us to give them up, accordingly we are obliged most humbly to request Your Magnificences and You, Most Noble Sirs, to take us under Your Protection in this matter, and by Your Decision and forethought to maintain us in the enjoyment of our old rights and regular *salarium,* and to command the said Mr. Eitelwein to restore to each of us in proportion the legally assigned share in the marriage fees, together with the costs incurred in this connection—just as we, with all due respect and esteem, remain,

Your Magnificences and Most Noble Sirs and Our Most Highly Esteemed Masters and Eminent Patrons, Your most obediently devoted

JOHANN SEBASTIAN BACH   JOHANN SCHNEIDER
Dir. Musices and Cantor   *Organist*
M. JOHANN MATTHIAS GESNER
Rector of the St. Thomas School, on behalf of the Students of this School

Leipzig, August 25, 1733

164. Letter from Bach, Schneider, and Gesner to the consistory
(*BD* I, no. 29)

To the Electoral and Princely Saxon Consistory here in Leipzig, &c.

We cannot omit bringing most humbly to your attention herewith, Your Most Noble Magnificences and You, Most Reverend and Most Noble Sirs, how the merchant and dealer of this place, Mr. Johann Friedrich Eitelwein, received permission by most gracious command to marry his betrothed, Mistress Sieber, without publication of banns. Now, when the said most gracious command was produced, His Most Reverend Magnificence, the Superintendent here, Dr. Salomon Deyling, granted the wish of the bridegroom for the issuance of instructions for the wedding to the pastorate at Plausig; accordingly we notified Mr. Eitelwein of our fees, and we should certainly have believed that he would acknowledge the fairness of the same. But we have had to learn, not without astonishment, that Mr. Eitelwein, on the illegal and untenable excuse that he would give nobody nothing [*sic*], wishes to refrain from making the payment due and will not admit the validity of any representations. Therefore, and since we, on the other hand, cannot acquiesce for these reasons, namely:

(1) These fees are due us in lieu of salary;

(2) In similar cases it has always been the rule that he who wishes to get married outside of Leipzig is nevertheless obligated to pay the usual honorarium to the church officials and students; moreover,

(3) As can be seen from Exhibit A, herewith, it was ordered by the High Authority of the land that the regular fees were to be paid nonetheless *in loco domicilii* [in the place of the residence]; and especially

(4) Since the bride and bridegroom are resident here, the fees cannot be withheld from us; moreover, finally,

(5) on account of the precedent, an arbitrary discontinuance of this sort must not be tolerated; and, above all,

(6) by order of the Electoral General Articles of the Church, §20, and according to Article 22 of the same, last section, it is expressly stated that no part of the receipts of servants of the Church and the School must be withheld from them;

Now, therefore, we turn to the justice-loving kindness of Your Most Noble Magnificences and You, Most Reverend and Most Noble Sirs, most humbly praying that Your Honors will deign to protect us most forcefully in the receipts that are established for our support, and to have Mr. Eitelwein commanded by the Council in Leipzig to pay us the usual fees without further delay and to reimburse us for all the costs to which we have been put. We reverence this high decision with humble thanks and remain with the most devout submission, . . .

Your humble and most obedient

JOH. SEBAST. BACH   JOH. SCHNEIDER   M. JOH. MATTHIAS GESNER
Dir. Mus. & Cantor at   *Org. at St. Nicholas's* *On behalf of the Students*
St. Thomas's   *of the St. Thomas School*
[September. . . , 1733]

The consistory, which received this letter on September 23, instructed the council of Leipzig, on November 11, to "notify Eitelwein to pay the usual fees most promptly, failing which he must be held to it by appropriate means."

BACH ANNOTATES HIS BIBLE

165. Excerpts from Bach's marginal comments in his copy of Abraham Calov's edition of the Lutheran Bible (Wittenberg, 1681) (Cox, pp. 18, 22)

a. *Beside the beginning of Calov's commentary to Exod. 15:20:*
NB. First section for two choirs to be performed to the honor of God.

b. *Beside the outline of 1 Chron. 26:*
NB. This chapter is the true foundation for all church music that is pleasing to God. etc.

c. *Beside Calov's commentary on 1 Chron. 29:21:*
NB. A splendid example [showing] that, besides other forms of worship, music especially has also been ordered by God's spirit through David.

d. *Beside the text of 2 Chron. 5:13:*
NB. With a devotional music God is always in his presence of grace [*Gnaden-Gegenwart*].

These manuscript comments with musical connotations were made, along with many entries of a more general nature, after Bach acquired this Bible in 1733.

BACH COMPOSES A PERPETUAL CANON

166. Canon for two voices, BWV 1075: album entry

(*BD* I, no. 167; NBA VIII/1, p. 3)

Perpetual canon for 2 [voices].

> To contribute this as a memento for
> his good friend [*Pathen*] was the wish of

Leipzig, January 10, 1734   JOH. SEB. BACH

This canon, as well as one by Carl Philipp Emanuel, was written for one of Bach's godchildren. The most plausible dedicatee is the son of Bach's Weimar cousin, Johann Gottfried Walther, Jun. (b. 1712).

BACH WRITES A TESTIMONIAL FOR A STUDENT,
PAUL CHRISTIAN STOLLE

167. Bach's testimonial on behalf of Stolle (*BJ* 1978, p.73)

Since the bearer of this, Mr. Paul Christian Stolle, student of theology, has asked me, the undersigned, to give him a formal testimonial of his demeanor and industry as an alumnus of almost ten years at our School of St. Thomas, I am most happy to comply. I wish to bear out truly that he not only proved himself throughout to be a devout, diligent,

166. Canon for two voices, BWV 1075

and loyal alumnus but also demonstrated his eagerness and zeal in mastering music and the keyboard through private study.

Leipzig, April 5, 1734.   JOHANN SEBASTIAN BACH.
                                                              Saxe-Weissenfels Capellmeister,
                                                              Direct. Chori Mus. *at Leipzig*
                                                              Cantor at St. Thomas's

LORENZ CHRISTOPH MIZLER DEDICATES HIS
ACADEMIC THESIS TO BACH AND OTHERS

168. Mizler's dedication of his thesis, "Dissertatio quod Musica ars sit pars eruditionis philosophicae" (*BD* II, no. 349)

To the most celebrated composers [*melothetis*] in Germany, the most famous and most eminent gentlemen, Johann Mattheson, Capellmeister of the Duke of Schleswig-Holstein, etc., Johann Sebastian Bach, Director of the Chorus musicus in Leipzig and Capellmeister of his Highness the Prince of Weissenfels, Johann Benedict [*recte:* Georg Heinrich] Bümler, Capellmeister to his Highness the Prince of Brandenburg-Ansbach, as well as Johann Samuel Ehrmann, Director of the Chorus musicus in Ansbach and very best of friends, I present this dissertation, which has been duly approved, adjudicated, and defended.

169. Excerpt from Mizler's preface, dated June 28, 1734

Likewise your instruction in practical music [*musica practica*], most celebrated Bach, have I used with great profit, and I regret that it is not possible for me to enjoy it further.

Mizler had been a student at the University of Leipzig beginning April 1731, with a leave of absence in 1733; he taught there from 1737 to 1743.

BACH'S COLLEGIUM MUSICUM CELEBRATES THE
KING'S NAME DAY

170. Announcement in the *Leipziger Zeitungen,* August 3, 1734 (*BD* II, no. 350)

On the occasion of the high name day of His Royal Majesty in Poland, and His Electoral Highness in Saxony, today in the afternoon at 4 o'clock, the Bachian Collegium Musicum will humbly perform a solemn music, with trumpets and timpani, at Zimmermann's garden, in front of the Grimma gate.

The identity of the work performed is not known.

BACH PERFORMS A DRAMMA PER MUSICA
BEFORE THE KING AND QUEEN

171. *Preise dein Glücke, gesegnetes Sachsen,* cantata, BWV 215: printed text, title page (*BD* II, no. 351)

When His Most Serene Highness, the Most Mighty Prince and Lord Frederick Augustus, King in Poland and Grand Duke of Lithuania, Reuss, Prussia, Mazovia, Samogitia, Kiovia, Volhynia, Podolia, Podlachia, Liefland, Smolensko, Severia, and Czernicovia &c. &c., Duke of Saxony, Jülich, Cleves, and Berg, also Engern and Westphalia, Archmarshal and Elector of the Holy Roman Empire, Landgrave in Thuringia, Margrave of Meissen, also Upper and Lower Lausitz, Burgrave of Magdeburg, Prince and Count of Henneberg, Count of the Marck, Ravensberg, and Barby, Lord of Ravenstein &c. &c., together with His Most Serene Consort, graced with Their Most High Presences the Town of Leipzig at the Michaelmas Fair of 1734, the students at the University in that place wished on October 5, being the day on which His Majesty in the preceding year of 1733 had been chosen King in Poland and Grand Duke of Lithuania, to demonstrate their most submissive devotion in an evening serenade.

172. **Bach's receipt for his payment** (*BD* I, no. 119)

That there has been duly paid to me, the undersigned, by the Registrar Eberhardt, 50 thlr., say fifth thaler, for the provision of the music recently offered to His Royal Majesty, is hereby acknowledged and receipt therefor gratefully given.

JOH. SEB. BACH
Direct. Chori Musici and Cantor of St. Thomas's
Leipzig, October 14, 1734

173. **Report of the festivities in the Leipzig town chronicle** (Wustmann, pp. 259–60; *BD* II, no. 352)

On the 5th [of October], the Coronation Day of His Royal Majesty was celebrated in the greatest gala style. While Their Majesties were at

Als der
**Allerdurchlauchtigste, Großmächtigste-
Fürst und Herr,**

HERR

Friedrich August,

**König in Pohlen und Groß-Hertzog von Litthauen,
Reußen, Preußen, Mazovien, Samogitien, Kiovien, Volhy-
nien, Podolien, Podlachien, Liefland, Smolensko, Severien und Czernicovien, ꝛc. ꝛc.
Hertzog zu Sachsen, Jülich, Cleve und Berg, auch Engern und Westphalen,
des Heil. Röm. Reichs Ertz-Marschall und Churfürst, Landgraf in Thüringen,
Marggraf zu Meissen, auch Ober- und Nieder-Lausitz, Burggraf zu Magdeburg,
Gefürsteter Graf zu Henneberg, Graf zu der Marck, Ravensberg und Barby,
Herr zu Ravensstein, ꝛc. ꝛc.**

Nebst
Dero Allerdurchlauchtigsten

Gemahlin

mit Ihrer allerhöchsten Gegenwart die Stadt Leipzig
an der Michaelis-Messe 1734. beglückten,
Wolten
am 5ten October, als am Tage, an welchem

Ihro Majestät

im verwichenen 1733ten Jahre
zum
König in Pohlen und Groß-Hertzog von Litthauen
gewehlet worden,
durch eine Abend-Music
ihre allerunterthänigste Devotion bezeugen
Die auf dasiger Universität Studirende.

171. *Preise dein Glücke, gesegnetes Sachsen,* cantata, BWV 215: printed text, title page

their noon dinner, and when their healths had been drunk, a signal was
given from the Apel house to the tower of the Castle, from there to the
tower of St. Thomas's, and finally from there to the Castle, that the
pieces [of artillery] should make a brave sound, [although] the *Connest-
ables* were not able to load them. At seven in the evening a cannon was
fired as a signal, and then the whole town was illuminated. The Rathhaus tower and the balcony were very splendidly decked out with many
variegated lamps; the towers of St. Thomas's and St. Nicholas's were
beautifully and properly illuminated from the balcony to the belfries,
and this could be seen for some miles out into the country. Amid all
this a picture dealer had written a verse in his window:

> O dearest King,
> 'This little I sing:
> I'm a sinner, and poor,
> May God help me endure.
> Debts oft bring me incarceration
> But tonight I have illumination.

His example was followed by a certain book printer who was his neighbor, and who had printed the following verses, framed by a heart:

> I love my King with heart devout,
> I have a lot of pain from gout,
> My poverty makes me cry out.
> My name is Johann Gottlieb Bauch.

The innkeeper of The Black Goat [*Zum schwarzen Bocke*] had put up the
following illumination: a country road, on which many wagons and
carriages were riding to and fro, with this inscription:

> As many years as shocks of oats—
> This is the wish that's offered by
> The innkeeper of The Black Goat.

And the illumination lasted until twelve o'clock. Many people came in
from the country to see it, and at seven o'clock in the morning one
could still see some lamps burning. About nine o'clock in the evening
the students [at the University] here presented Their Majesties with a
most submissive evening serenade [*Preise dein Glücke*] with trumpets
and drums, which the Hon. Capellmeister, Johann Sebastian Bach,
Cantor at St. Thomas's, had composed. For this, six hundred students
carried wax tapers, and four Counts acted as marshals in presenting the
music. The procession made its way up to the King's residence. When
the musicians had reached the *Wage* [weigh house], the trumpets and

drums went up on it, while others took their places in another choir at the Rathhaus. When the text was presented, the four Counts were permitted to kiss the Royal hands, and afterward his Royal Majesty together with his Royal Consort and the Royal Princes did not leave the windows until the music was over, and listened most graciously and liked it well.

BACH PUBLISHES HIS *FRENCH OVERTURE* AND
ITALIAN CONCERTO

174. *Clavier-Übung,* Part II, BWV 831 and 971: title page (*BD* I, no. 168)

Second part of the Keyboard Practice, consisting of a Concerto after the Italian Taste and an Overture after the French Manner, for a harpsichord with two manuals. Composed for music lovers, to refresh their spirits, by Johann Sebastian Bach, Capellmeister to His Highness the Prince of Saxe-Weissenfels and *Directore Chori Musici Lipsiensis.* Published by Christoph Weigel, Junior.

For a contemporary review of the Italian Concerto *by Johann Adolph Scheibe, see No. 331. It is unclear whether Bach had to pay the musicians from this amount. Cf. No. 201.*

BACH WRITES TO MÜHLHAUSEN ON BEHALF OF
HIS SON JOHANN GOTTFRIED BERNHARD

175. Bach's letter to Tobias Rothschier, senior of the town council (*BD* I, no. 30)

To the Most Honored and Most Learned Sir, Mr. Tobias Rothschier, Eminent Juris consult and Highly Respected Member and Highly Deserving Senior of the Most Honored and Most Wise Council of the Imperial Free City of Mühl-hausen, in Mühlhausen.

MOST NOBLE, MOST LEARNED, AND MOST ESPECIALLY HIGHLY HON-ORED MR. SENIOR, MOST ESTEEMED PATRON!

It is reported that Mr. Hetzehenn, Town Organist in Mühlhaussen, recently died there, and that his post has to date not been filled. Now, since my youngest son, Johann Gottfried Bernhard Bach, has already

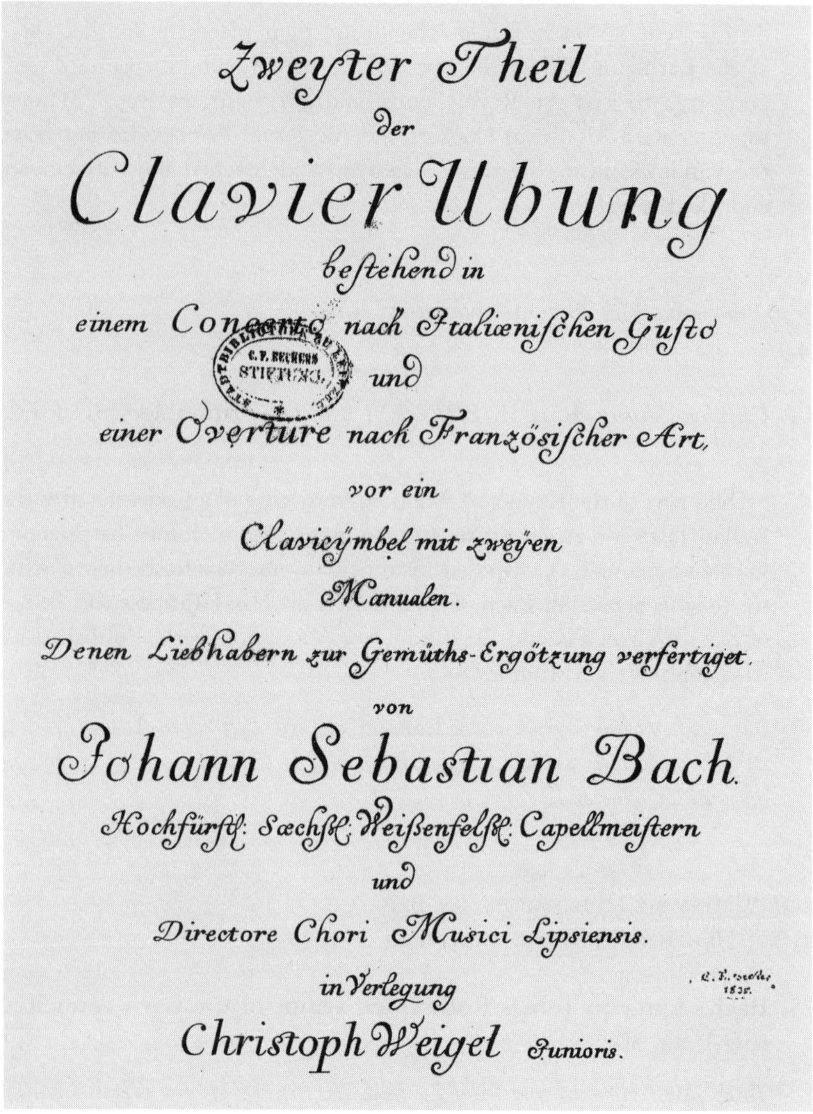

Zweyter Theil
der
Clavier Übung
bestehend in

einem Concerto nach Italiænischen Gusto
und

einer Overture nach Französischer Art,

vor ein

Clavicymbel mit zweyen

Manualen.

Denen Liebhabern zur Gemüths-Ergötzung verfertiget.

von

Johann Sebastian Bach.

Hochfürstl: Sæchsl: Weißenfelsl: Capellmeistern

und

Directore Chori Musici Lipsiensis.

in Verlegung

Christoph Weigel Junioris.

174. *Clavier-Übung,* Part II, BWV 831 and 971: title page

acquired such skill in music that I am firmly convinced that he is fully equipped and able to attend to this newly vacant post of town organist, therefore I beg Your Honor, in most grateful deference, to be good enough to give my son the benefit of your highly valued intercession in respect to the acquisition of the above-mentioned post, and thus to make me your debtor and my son happy, that I may have reason to assure myself of your favor now as in the past, and can assure you in return that I remain forever with unchanged devotion

Your Honor's and My Most Particularly Highly Honored Mr. Senior's most devoted servant

JOH. SEBAST. BACH

Leipzig, May 2, 1735   *Formerly Organist of St. Blas. in Mühlhausen*

176. Bach's letter to Burgomaster Christian Petri (*BD* I, no. 31)

To His Magnificence, the Most Noble, Respected and Most Learned Gentleman, Mr. Christian Petri, Eminent Councilor and Jurisconsult, likewise Highly Respected Burgomaster and Senior, My Most Honored Patron in Mühlhausen.

Postage paid in full

YOUR MAGNIFICENCE, MOST NOBLE, RESPECTED AND MOST LEARNED, MOST HIGHLY ESTEEMED COUNCILOR, BURGOMASTER AND SENIOR, EMINENT PATRON!

The invaluably high *faveur* that Your Noble Magnificence has again been most graciously pleased to show to an old and faithful servant on the occasion of the most humble letter I sent through the merchant Mr. Hagedorn obliges me to express to Your Most Noble Magnificence herewith my most humble thanks. Now, since my own and my son's duty will require that with our most humble personal attendance we shall show our most obedient and respectful sense of obligation and at the same time give some modest evidence of my son's musical proficiency, we now await only the most gracious command and *ordre* of Your Most Noble Magnificence to present ourselves for the examination to be permitted by you, remaining, in the greatest possible respect and homage,

Your Magnificence and Most Noble Sir, My Most Highly Esteemed Councilor, Burgomaster, and Senior, likewise Eminent Patron, Your most obedient and devoted servant

Leipzig, May 21, 1735   JOHANN SEBASTIAN BACH

The examination was successful. On October 30, 1736, however, Johann Sebastian had to write a new letter of application for his son (No. 188).

BACH WRITES A TESTIMONIAL FOR A STUDENT,
JOHANN LUDWIG KREBS

177. Bach's testimonial on behalf of Krebs (*BD* I, no.71)

The bearer, Mr. Johann Ludwig Krebs, having requested the undersigned to oblige him with a testimonial concerning his accomplishments at our School, I would not deny him the same, but wish to declare that I am convinced of having trained in him a man of such parts, and one who has so distinguished himself here particularly *in musicis,* having qualified himself in respect to the clavier, the violin, and the lute, as well as composition, that he need have no hesitation in letting himself be heard, although this will be more fully revealed in practice. I wish him accordingly Divine Support in his advancement, and herewith recommend him again most heartily.

Leipzig, Aug. 24, 1735

JOH. SEB. BACH
Capellm. and Direct. Musices

BACH COMPOSES AND ARRANGES THE MUSIC
FOR A PUBLISHED HYMNAL

178. *Musicalisches Gesang-Buch* of Georg Christian Schemelli (Leipzig, 1736): title page

Musical Hymn Book, wherein 954 spiritual songs and arias, old as well as new, with well-set melodies, in soprano and bass are to be found. Specially dedicated to the Evangelical congregations of the diocese of Naumburg-Zeitz and with a foreword by the Most Reverend Mr. Friedrich Schulz, Preacher at the Castle, Superintendent of the Bishopric, and Official of the Episcopal Consistory at Zeitz, edited by Georg Christian Schemelli, cantor at the castle in that place. With most gracious permission. Not to be reprinted, either with or without music. Leipzig 1736. Published by Bernhard Christoph Breitkopf, Bookprinter.

179. Excerpt from Schemelli's preface

The melodies to be found in this musical song book have been in part quite newly composed and in part improved in the thorough bass by the most noble Mr. Johann Sebastian Bach, Electoral Saxon Capellmeister and *Director Chori Musici* in Leipzig.

Musicalisches Gesang-Buch,

Darinnen

954 geistreiche, sowohl alte als neue
Lieder und Arien, mit wohlgesetzten
Melodien, in Discant und Baß,
befindlich sind;
Vornemlich denen Evangelischen Gemeinen
im Stifte Naumburg-Zeitz gewidmet,
und
mit einer Vorrede Sr. Hochehrw.
Herrn Friedrich Schulzens,
Schloßpredigers, Stifts-Superint. und des
Stifts-Consistorii Assessors zu Zeitz,
herausgegeben von
George Christian Schemelli,
Schloß-Cantore daselbst.

Mit Allergnädigster Freyheit,
weder mit, noch ohne Noten nachzudrucken.

Leipzig, 1736.
Verlegts Bernhard Christoph Breitkopf, Buchdr.

178. *Musicalisches Gesang-Buch* (Leipzig, 1736): title page

BACH DISPUTES RECTOR JOHANN HEINRICH ERNESTI
ABOUT THE RIGHT TO APPOINT THE PREFECTS

180. A later summary account from Johann Friedrich Köhler's *Historia Scholarum Lipsiensium* (Leipzig, 1776) (*BD* III, no. 820)

With Ernesti [Rector of the St. Thomas School] Bach fell out completely. The occasion was the following. Ernesti removed the General Prefect [Gottfried Theodor] Krause for having chastised one of the younger students too vigorously, expelled him from the School when he fled [to avoid the public whipping to which Ernesti had sentenced him] and chose another student [who also bore the surname Krause, his Christian names being Johann Gottlieb] in his place as General Prefect—a prerogative that really belongs to the Cantor, whom the General Prefect has to represent. Because the student chosen was of no use in the performance of the church music, Bach made a different choice. The situation between him and Ernesti developed to the point of charge and countercharge, and the two men from that time on were enemies. Bach began to hate those students who devoted themselves completely to the *humaniora* and treated music as a secondary matter, and Ernesti became a foe of music. When he came upon a student practicing on an instrument, he would exclaim "What? You want to be a beer-fiddler, too?" By virtue of the high regard in which he was held by the Burgomaster, Stieglitz, he managed to be released from the duties of the special inspection of the School and to have them assigned to the Fourth Colleague. Thus when it was Bach's turn to undertake the inspection, he cited the precedent of Ernesti and came neither to table nor to prayers; and this neglect of duty had the worst influence on the moral training of the students. From that time on, though there have been several incumbents of both posts, little harmony has been observed between the Rector and the Cantor.

181. Bach's first complaint to the Leipzig town council (*BD* I, no. 32)

To Their Magnificences, the Most Noble, Most Distinguished, Respected and Most Learned, likewise Most Wise Gentlemen, the Burgomaster and Members of the Most Worshipful Town Government at Leipzig, My Most Esteemed Masters and Patrons.

YOUR MAGNIFICENCES, MOST NOBLE, MOST DISTINGUISHED, RESPECTED AND MOST LEARNED SIRS, MOST WISE AND MOST HIGHLY ESTEEMED GENTLEMEN AND PATRONI!

May it please Your Magnificences and You, Most Noble and Most Distinguished Sirs, most graciously to be informed as follows: Although according to the Regulations of a Noble and Most Wise Council concerning the School of St. Thomas here it is for the Cantor to choose as Prefects from among the schoolboys those whom he considers capable, and in choosing them he must keep in mind not only that they must have a good clear voice but also that the Prefects (especially the one who sings in the First Choir) must be able to take over the direction of the chorus when the Cantor is ill or absent; and although such action has hitherto been taken without the concurrence of the Rector and by the Cantors alone, and only thus; nevertheless, the present Rector, Magister Johann August Ernesti, has, as a new departure, sought to effect the replacement of the Prefect of the First Choir without my previous knowledge and consent, and accordingly has recently appointed Krause, hitherto Prefect of the Second Choir, to be Prefect of the First Choir. He has further refused to withdraw this appointment despite all the protests that I, in perfect good will, have made to him. But since my acceptance of this situation, which is in violation of the above-mentioned School Regulations and traditional usage, would prejudice the rights of my successors and work to the detriment of the *chorus musicus,* there accordingly goes forth to Your Magnificences and to You, Most Noble and Most Distinguished Sirs, my most humble request graciously to resolve this dispute between the Rector and me, in my official capacity, and—since the said usurpation of the replacement of the Prefects by the Rector might lead to disharmony and be to the disadvantage of the students—to instruct Magister Ernesti, in accordance with Your Honors' signal benevolence and foresight as concerns St. Thomas's, that he is to leave the replacement of the Prefects, in accordance with previous practice and the customs and regulations of the School, to me alone, and thus to uphold me most graciously in my office. Expecting your most gracious decision, I remain with most obedient respect, Your Magnificences and Most Noble and Most Distinguished Sirs,

Your most obedient

Leipzig, August 12, 1736   JOH. SEBAST. BACH

182. Bach's second complaint to the council (*BD* I, no. 33)

To their Magnificences, the Most Noble, Most Distinguished, Steadfast and Most Learned, also Most Wise Gentlemen, the Burgomaster and Members of the Most Worshipful Town Government of the Town of Leipzig, My Most Highly Esteemed Masters and Patrons.

YOUR MAGNIFICENCES, MOST NOBLE, MOST DISTINGUISHED, RESPECTED AND MOST LEARNED SIRS, ALSO MOST WISE AND MOST HIGHLY ESTEEMED GENTLEMEN AND PATRONI!

Although I yesterday importuned Your Magnificences and You, Most Noble Sirs, with a most humble memorial concerning the encroachments that the Rector, Mr. Ernesti, has with the greatest impropriety made, through the replacement of the Prefect, upon the functions entrusted to me at the St. Thomas School here, as Director *Chori Musici* and Cantor, and although I have thus already most humbly entreated Your Most Gracious Protection—yet I find myself obliged once more most dutifully to call the attention of Your Magnificences and of You, Most Noble Sirs, to the fact that, although I had informed the said Rector, Mr. Ernesti, that I had already delivered my complaint in this matter to you, and was awaiting authoritative determination of the matter by Your Magnificences and You, Most Noble Sirs, he nevertheless, disregarding the respect he owes to the Most Noble and Most Wise Council, yesterday made bold again to give all the students to understand that no one was to dare, on pain of expulsion and whipping, to take the place of Krause, the boy mentioned in my most humble memorial of yesterday, who is incapable of the direction of a *chorus musicus* (but whom he wishes to force on me by all means as Prefect of the First Choir), either in the chanting or in directing the usual motet. Accordingly it came about that in yesterday afternoon's service at St. Nicholas's, to my great shame and public humiliation, there was not a single pupil, for fear of the threatened penalty, willing to take over the chanting, much less the direction of the motet. Indeed, the very service would have been upset as a result if a former pupil at the St. Thomas School, named Krebs, had not fortunately taken over the same, at my request, in place of one of the present students. Now, since, as was sufficiently stated and commented upon in my previous most humble memorial, the replacement of the Prefects is, by the regulations and traditions of the School, not a function of the Rector; and since the latter, in his *modus procedendi,* has greatly transgressed, has done me deep injury in the discharge of my office, and has sought to weaken, nay destroy, all the authority that I must have over the students in connection with the church and other music, which authority was entrusted to me by the Most Noble and Most Wise Council when I entered upon my office; and since it is to be feared that if such irresponsible conduct continues the services may be disturbed and the church music fall into the most serious decay, and the School, too, within a short time, suffer such deterioration as shall make it impossible for many years to bring it back to its former estate—therefore my most obedient and earnest entreaty once again goes forth to Your Magnificences and You, Most Noble Sirs, since I cannot, by virtue of my office, remain silent, to instruct the Rector as promptly as possible, since there is peril in delay, henceforth not to disturb me in the discharge of my office, nor to discourage the students in their obedience to me by his unjust warnings and threats of such dire punishment, but rather to see to it, as is his duty, that the School and the *chorus musicus* should be improved and not deteriorated. Expecting most gracious action and protection in my office, I remain with most obedient respect, Your Magnificences and Most Noble Sirs, Your wholly obedient

Leipzig, August 13, 1736   JOHANN SEBASTIAN BACH

183. Bach's third complaint to the council (*BD* I, no. 34)

Memorandum

The full and true account concerning the student Krause, whom the Rector wishes to force upon me as First Prefect, is as follows:

The said Krause last year had already earned such a bad reputation for his disorderly living and for the debts into which it had brought him that a meeting was held about him, at which he was expressly told that although he had fully deserved to be turned out of school for his profligate way of living, he would, in view of his needy situation (since he had himself confessed having contracted debts of over 20 thaler) and on his promise to mend his ways, be given three months' grace, and then, depending on whether he had changed his way of living, he would be given further notification as to whether he would be suffered to remain or actually expelled. Now, the Rector has always shown a particular liking for the said Krause and accordingly asked me in conversation to let him have a post of Prefect, but I remonstrated, saying that he was not at all suited to such a post. Yet the Rector replied that I should do it anyway, so that the said Krause might get out of debt, and thus a disgrace to the School might be avoided, particularly as his time would soon be up and thus one would be rid of him with good grace. Accordingly, I wished to do the Rector a favor and gave Krause the post of Prefect in the New Church (where the students have nothing to sing but motets and chorales, and have nothing to do with other *Concert Musique,* since the latter is taken care of by the organist), having in mind the fact that the years of his agreement were all gone but one, and it need not be feared that he would ever get to conduct the Second

Choir, much less the First. But when later the Prefect of the First Choir, named Nagel, from Nürnberg, at the time of the singing for last New Year's, complained that because of a weak constitution he would not be able to hold out, it was necessary to make a change in the Prefects before the regular time, to put the Prefect of the Second Choir into the First, and, of necessity, the much discussed Krause into the Second. But since he made various mistakes in the time, as the Co-Rector (who inspects the Second Choir) told me, for when the said mistakes were investigated the blame for them was placed by the other students solely and entirely on the Prefect, on account of his beating the time incorrectly; and since, in addition, I recently in the singing class made a test myself of his time, which he failed so badly that he could not accurately give the beat in the two principal kinds of time—namely, even, or four-quarter, and uneven, or three-quarter—but now made an even measure of three-quarter, and *vice versa* (as all the students can testify); and since I am accordingly fully convinced of his incompetence; therefore it was impossible for me to entrust the post of Prefect of the First Choir to him, especially since the concerted pieces that are performed by the First Choir, which are mostly of my own composition, are incomparably harder and more intricate than those sung by the Second Choir (and this only on Feast Days), so that I must be chiefly guided, in the choice of the same, by the *capacité* of those who are to perform them. Thus, and although various other reasons could be given to prove even more strongly the *incapacite* of the said Krause, I consider that the *raisons* already given are sufficient to show that the complaint I have lodged with Your Most Noble and Most Wise Council is justified, and requires a prompt and speedy remedy.

Leipzig, August 15, 1736   Joh. Seb. Bach

184. Ernesti's reply to the council (*BD* II, no. 382)

Your Magnificences, Most Noble, Most Learned, and Most Honorable Sirs and Patroni!

Your Magnificences and You, Most Noble Sirs, were gracious enough to have communicated to me yesterday what the Cantor of the St. Thomas School here has brought against me, and instructed me therewith to state as promptly as possible what I had to say in response. Now, the complaint brought by him really concerns not me alone but the Director of the School, the Appeals Councilor Stiglitz, as well, since it was with his consent and by virtue of the power vested in him, according to the School Regulations of Your Most Noble and Most

Wise Council, that the Prefect Krause, arbitrarily and unjustly dismissed by the Cantor, was restored to his post. Yet I must obey the command of Your Magnificences and You, Most Noble Sirs, and, since the said Director of the School is away at the moment, I must report and explain the true nature of the affair in good conscience, so that the Cantor may be told to drop his unjust complaint and to show the proper obedience and respect to his superiors.

To begin with, I cannot sufficiently express my astonishment that the said Cantor can take it upon himself to represent to Your Magnificences that the posts of Prefect in the four choirs have hitherto always been filled, without the concurrence of the Rector, solely by the Cantor, since the opposite procedure is clearly prescribed by the School Regulations, according to which (p. 74) the Cantor shall accept eight boys, including the Prefect, *with the consent of the Rector,* and in addition *shall always present the Prefects to the Director* and beg the latter's consent (p. 78), which last-named step, however, the Cantor has never taken.

It is true that in the filling of a post of Prefect the Cantor has the most important part, inasmuch as he must judge their ability in singing. But since the Prefects are responsible to the Rector, since complaints about them are to be made to him, and they are to be punished by him at his discretion (p. 73), and the money they collect by singing is delivered to him, and not to the Cantor, so that he may keep a record of it and distribute it at stated times; now therefore he, too, who must know more about their behavior than the Cantor, must judge whether a post of this kind can be entrusted to them without danger. It has accordingly always been the custom here, during my Rectorate no less than before, for the Cantor to send me through the Prefect the singers he had chosen, with the inquiry as to whether I had any objection to one or another—a custom he followed even as recently as in the disputed case. Indeed, there are precedents in which the Cantor, having skipped over a meritorious student out of personal prejudice, has been instructed not to skip over the said student.

Now, by the gracious leave of Your Magnificences and You, Most Noble Sirs, I will report what has taken place in the case of the disputed post of Prefect, that you may judge therefrom whether I have made the slightest encroachment upon his rights, and whether I have not on the contrary done everything that can be required of an honest and peace-loving man.

After the post of First Prefect had become vacant, about eight weeks ago, the Cantor himself filled it by naming the first student, then Second Prefect, Jo. Gottl. Krause. To this I had the less objection since (1) he had so conducted himself in the posts of Second and Third Prefects that there had been no complaint about him, and the School Regulations expressly provide (p. 77) *that for this post of First Prefect the first student is always to be chosen,* or else the next following one, although only with notice to the Director, if the former is not capable enough *in musicis.* But this latter circumstance could not obtain this time, since he had already held the post of Prefect in the other three choirs, and the post of Second Prefect requires much more musical ability than that of First, since on the mornings and afternoons of Feast Days the Second Prefect has to conduct the music in the churches subject to the inspection of the Co-Rector, while the First Prefect, on the contrary, never conducts. Then, when the said Krause had already been filling this post for several weeks, the Cantor on July 10 sent me the Second Prefect, Küttler, giving me notice that he would be forced to make a change concerning the First Prefect, and he wished to make him Second again, and Küttler First in his place. To this I made the reply that he must know whether he was equal to it or not, and if that was how things were, I could not but agree; but I wished that he had tested him more carefully in the beginning. Your Magnificences, and You, Most Noble Sirs, can see from this, too, that he conceded the necessity of my concurrence in the replacing of the Prefects.

The dismissed Prefect complained to me about this, because he was being dismissed through no fault of his own, but I referred him to the Cantor, telling him that, since he felt he had been dismissed for another reason, he should address him politely and tell him that I should be very pleased if he could remain in his post. When he thereupon humbly approached him several times and, having been unable to accomplish anything, begged him only to state the reason why he was being dismissed, the Cantor finally let it slip out thoughtlessly that *he had dismissed him on my, the Rector's, account,* for at the time when I had suspended [G. T.] Krause (the one who later ran away) until he should submit to his punishment, I had told him [J. G. Krause] that he should for the time being fill the post of First Prefect; and in this I had encroached upon his [the Cantor's] rights, since it was he who appointed the Prefects, and not the Rector.

Now, whether I have thereby taken it upon myself alone to fill the post of First Prefect, as Mr. Bach claims—this Your Magnificences and You, Most Noble Sirs, can easily judge. When I spoke with the Director two days later, that is, on July 12, I reported the affair to him, and received from him the decision that Your Magnificences and You, Most Noble Sirs, will yourselves recognize as most fair. Since [he said] the

Cantor had given no reason but this one and, in doing so, had been so thoughtless as to let the affair become known among the students, he could not consent to the dismissal of the First Prefect, but the latter must remain in his post. I thereupon summoned the Cantor, to speak with him about the affair, and he likewise admitted that it was for the aforementioned reason that he wished to make this change. I therefore pointed out to him that to suspend was not to dismiss, and that it was not in the least likely that I should have filled a post that was not empty. Neither the Director nor I would give our consent under these circumstances, and I acquainted him with the decision of the Director, and forbade him to dismiss the Prefect.

Now, thereupon he should indeed not have undertaken the actual dismissal without receiving a different decision from the Director and me, and he should have addressed himself, if he was not satisfied, to the Director. But he nevertheless carried through the dismissal of the Prefect, as I observed Sunday in church. I should therefore have been sufficiently justified in restoring the dismissed Prefect to his post; but I wished to spare his dignity before the student body, with whom, as it is, his authority is inadequate, so that consequently he has had to rely on mine on several occasions. I accordingly wrote him a letter, in which I pointed out to him how greatly he had transgressed by taking upon himself such a change, in the above-described circumstances, in order to revenge himself for what he considered an encroachment upon his rights, so that now even the innocent must suffer; and although I could at once reinstate the dismissed Prefect, I would rather, in order that his authority might not be impaired, see him reinstate him himself, for in that way we should both be satisfied. Thereupon, on July 17, he sent the Co-Rector to me to say that he had read my letter with pleasure, and he himself would be glad if the affair could be settled in a friendly manner. Through the intervention of the Co-Rector it finally even came to pass that he promised to reinstate the dismissed Prefect at the first singing lesson. But it later turned out that he was making sport of the Co-Rector as well as of me. For the promised and agreed-upon reinstatement did not occur. I sent him a reminder and received the reply that he wished to go away for a fortnight, and I should just have patience until his return, when it would be done. In this, too, I acquiesced. But after his return ten days went by, and still nothing happened. So finally last Saturday I wrote him another letter, in which I asked what I was to make of this delay; it seemed to me that he was really not inclined to keep his promise. I therefore wished to give him notice herewith that if he did not reinstate the Prefect on that very day I would most certainly reinstate him myself Sunday morning, by authority of the order I had previously received from the Director, which he had in the meanwhile renewed. But to this he answered not a single word either directly or indirectly, much less did what was required of him.

Now, may Your Magnificences and You, Most Noble Sirs, yourselves judge of this behavior toward the Director and me, and whether I was not fully entitled to make the reinstatement. I therefore ordered the two Prefects each to take up his former post again; and since this order was given upon the instruction and with the consent of the Director, [I said that] any one other than Krause who should take upon himself the duties of the First Prefect would be considered to be disobeying not only me but the Director as well, which would necessarily result in severe punishment, of which I wished to give everyone due warning. As soon as the First Prefect, at my instruction, reported this to the Cantor, the latter ran at once to the Superintendent, bringing up the same unjustified charge against me that he has now preferred with Your Magnificences and You, Most Noble Sirs, after having failed to obtain the decision he desired from the Superintendent; and declared at the same time that he would lay the matter on the following Wednesday (that is, the day before yesterday) before the Consistory. Now, although the Superintendent gave him no decision, except to say that he would inquire of me about the nature of the affair, and that the affair itself could not be settled either by him or by the Consistory without previous communication with the *Patroni* and the Director—yet, on the pretense of having received an order from the Superintendent, he forced the Second Prefect, Küttler, to leave St. Nicholas's and go with him to the First Choir in St. Thomas's, from which he with great commotion chased away the Prefect Krause, who was already singing. I went from the Church to the Superintendent to learn whether he had given any such order, but heard that he had said nothing but what I have already reported. I thereupon related the whole story to him, as I have told it here to Your Magnificences and You, Most Noble Sirs; and he fully approved my conduct in the matter, and agreed that things should remain as they were under the order of the Director until the latter should return and settle the matter, since it was more fitting that the Cantor should give in *ad interim* to the Director and Rector than vice versa. I acquainted the Cantor with this decision, but received the answer that he would not budge in this matter, *no matter what the cost.* Now, since after lunch the two Prefects had each gone again to the places to which I had assigned them, he again chased Krause out of the choir loft with much shouting and noise, and ordered the student Claus to sing in the Prefect's place, which he did, excusing himself to me after church for doing so. How, then, can the Cantor state that it was no student of the School but a University student who sang? As for the Second Prefect, Küttler, he sent him away from the table, in the evening, for having obeyed me.

From all this Your Magnificences and You, Most Noble Sirs, will perceive that the complaint of the Cantor is unjustified, pretending as it does that I have newly taken it upon myself to appoint the Prefect in the First Choir without his previous knowledge or consent, and have made the Prefect of the Second Choir Prefect of the First. It is not so great a thing to appoint a Prefect that I should cause anyone vexation over it, and I have never claimed the privilege, and never will claim it; even though I do claim the right of concurrence given to me by the School Regulations, and hope to be sustained in that claim. The Cantor has perverted the whole *Status Controversiae,* which consists in the following: whether I had not the right to reinstate, with the foreknowledge and consent of the Director, a Prefect whom he had removed simply to spite the Rector and against the will and consent of the Director and Rector, since the Cantor was not willing to reinstate him himself, after having promised to do so and thereby conceded that the boy is not incompetent, which appears, even without that concession, from the foregoing. I pray accordingly that Your Magnificences and You, Most Noble Sirs, will dismiss the Cantor with his untimely and unfounded complaint, and will insist that he abide by the arrangements made with the foreknowledge of the Director; and will earnestly reprimand him for his disobedience and insubordination to the Director and me, and order him not to do such things again without the consent of his superiors and against the School Regulations of a Most Noble and Most Wise Council, and in general to attend to his duties more industriously.

This is not the place to complain to Your Magnificences and You, Most Noble Sirs, about him, which, however, I reserve for another occasion; but I cannot avoid instancing this one fact: that not alone his unpleasantness but also the misfortune suffered by poor Gottfr. Theodor Krausse, who later ran away, is to be attributed solely to the negligence of the Cantor. For if he had gone to the wedding service as he should have, since there was nothing wrong with him, instead of thinking it was beneath his dignity to conduct at a wedding service where only chorales were to be sung (for which reason he has absented himself from several such wedding services, including the recent one for the Krögels, in connection with which, as I could not help hearing, the musicians in service to Your Magnificences and You, Noble Sirs, complained to other people)—then the said Krause would have had no opportunity to indulge in those excesses, both in the Church and outside, upon which such harsh penalties are laid by a Most Noble and Most Wise Council itself. I hope all the more that Your Magnificences and You, Noble Sirs, will grant my most humble request, since the authority and honor of the Director, who represents a Most Noble and Most Wise Council at the School, and whose authority is the Council's own authority, and my own as well are at stake. But Your Magnificences and You, Noble Sirs, know better than I can say how necessary the authority of a Rector is to him, and that a Rector without authority is not only a useless but even a harmful man. For this favor, as well as for all others shown me, I shall at all times remain, Your Magnificences and Noble Sirs, Your most obedient servant

Leipzig, August 17, 1736   M[agister] JO. AUG. ERNESTI

185. Bach's fourth complaint to the council (*BD* I, no. 35)

To Their Magnificences, the Most Noble, Most Distinguished, Steadfast and Most Learned, also Most Wise Gentlemen, the Burgomasters and Members of the Most Worshipful Town Government of the Town of Leipzig, My Most Highly Honored Masters and Patrons.

YOUR MAGNIFICENCES, MOST NOBLE, STEADFAST AND MOST LEARNED, ALSO MOST WISE, AS WELL AS MOST HIGHLY HONORED GENTLEMEN AND PATRONI!

There will still be present to Your most gracious memory, Your Magnificences and You, Most Noble Sirs, what I felt compelled to report to Your Honors concerning the *disordres* that were caused eight days ago during the public divine service by the actions of the Rector of the St. Thomas School here, Mr. Ernesti. Since the same thing took place today, both in the morning and in the afternoon, and, to avoid a great commotion in the Church and a *turbatio sacrorum,* I had to make up my mind to conduct the motet myself and to have the intonation taken care of by a University student, and the situation is becoming worse and worse, so that without the most vigorous intervention on the part of You, My High Patrons, I should hardly be able to maintain my position with the students entrusted to me, and accordingly should be blameless if further and perhaps irreparable disorders should result from it; now, therefore, I have not been able to avoid calling this in proper fashion to the attention of Your Magnificences and You, Most

Noble Sirs, with the most humble request that Your Honors will deign to put a prompt stop to these activities on the part of the Rector and, by hastening the principal decision I have prayed for, will, in accordance with Your Honors' well-known zeal for the good of the community, prevent the results otherwise to be feared, such as further public annoyance in the Church, disorder in the School, and reduction of the authority with the students that is necessary to my office and other evil consequences. I remain, Your Magnificences and Most Noble Sirs, Your obedient

Leipzig, August 19, 1736   J OHANN S EBASTIAN B ACH

In writing this letter, Bach evidently had no knowledge of the contents of Ernesti's reply, written only two days before.

186. Ernesti's rebuttal of Bach's third complaint (*BD* I, no. 383)

Memorandum

The account communicated to me, concerning the student [J. G.] Krause and the arbitrary taking from him, without sufficient cause, of the post of Prefect, is neither *complete*—as is shown by the report I delivered two days after that account had been drawn up, namely, on August 17, which if necessary I could confirm by the testimony of the Co-Rector and of many students, and to which I should be prepared to swear with good conscience—nor *truthful*. Mr. Bach cannot instance anything but his [i.e., Krause's] incompetence, because he thinks not only that he will be conceded the right to pass such a judgment but also that it will be held in this case to be correct and unbiased. But just as I have been able to cite other evidence that his testimony in this connection is not always to be relied upon, and it seems likely that an old specie thaler has made a soprano out of a boy that was no more a soprano than I am, so I am completely convinced that his account of this matter is wholly incorrect, and give assurance on my honor that from the very beginning I should never have said a word to this change if that account had been tinged with the slightest probability.

If the boy is unequal to the post of First Prefect, then he is most certainly unequal to the other posts as well. For the Prefects all have the same duties, which consist of the following:

(1) They conduct the motets in church—that is, whichever of them is the leading student in the School, whether he be First or Second Prefect—and this very Krause is now in that position according to the order in the School;

(2) They begin the hymns in church;

(3) They each conduct a choir at the New Year's singing in the homes.

The difference is only that the First Prefect does the last of these things also at Michaelmas, and at weddings leads the singing of a few motets at table, conducting the same; but the Second Prefect conducts the concerted music of the Second Choir on Feast Days, which the First Prefect does not do. So if the pieces that are performed by the First Choir are more intricate—which is the only argument he brings up or can bring up—the fact is that Mr. Bach conducts them, and not the Prefect. The former Prefect, Nagel, never did anything but play the violin. And how does it happen, then, that he now wants to have a First Prefect who can conduct a difficult piece in the First Choir, since he never had one before, or at least never took care to have one, if he had a liking for the person in other ways. For before, when he was away, he regularly had the organist of the New Church, Mr. Schott or Mr. Gerlach, conduct, as the latter, if necessary, will bear witness. Of course, it is better if the Prefect can do it. But if he is incompetent, as he pretends, why:

(1) Did he not stick to that reason, since I had already consented to his becoming Second Prefect again in that case? And why did he tell the students and, *nota bene,* me, too, right to my face in my room when I interrogated him about it, that it was on my account, and because he had been told that I had said something prejudicial to his rights, that he *not just refused to let him become First Prefect,* for he had already been in that post for four weeks and more, but *wished to remove him from it.* This is the reason I bestirred myself about it, since it is not advisable to suffer that he should do such things, and make known his intentions to the students.

(2) If he had first found him unsure of the meter in those four weeks, and not in the six years he had had him in his singing class, as might have been expected, he should not have given him any Prefect's post at all. For if he is unsure of the meter in the First Choir, he will certainly be so in the Second, and thus it was in violation of the demands of his office and his conscience for him to get the Co-Rector to tell me and promise me on his behalf that, in accordance with the letter I had written him on the previous day, he would reinstate him at the first singing class. The test he gave two days after this promise, upon being goaded to it once again, as before, by the runaway [G. T.] Krause, was a trap. The students I have questioned say that he made only one single slip, and corrected himself at once. It would have been a great wonder, in my opinion, if he had not made a slip, since Mr. Bach had the intention and desire that he should make one.

Any claim that I asked the Cantor to make the student [J. G.] Krause a Prefect is completely false. The fact of the matter is as follows: As we were riding home together from Magister Kriegel's wedding, before the New Year, about Advent time, he asked me whether this Krause should also become a Prefect, for it was time that the usual singing classes that are given before the New Year by the Prefects should begin; and he would have to become the *Fourth* (N.B.: not *Third,* as Mr. Bach writes, for the first three Prefects at the time were Nagel, Krauss, and Nitsche—how easily one betrays oneself in a lie!). What made him hesitate was that Krause was in other ways a loose-living dog. To this I replied that the last statement was doubtless true, and he had had debts of 20 thaler two years ago (of which 12 thaler were for a suit of clothes), as I had found noted by Mr. Gesner in the account book. But since Mr. Gesner, after discussing the matter with me, had pardoned him on account of his excellent talent, and since the debts were now largely paid off, he could not be skipped over, if he were otherwise competent, for the post of Prefect. To this he answered, as God is my witness, "Oh, I suppose he's competent enough!"; and thus he became in succession Third, Second, and First Prefect, and I can testify on my honor that I never received any complaint about him. The mistakes that were made in church took place before he became Fourth Prefect. The Superintendent told me recently that *since he had ordered an investigation on account of the frequent disorder in church there had been no further trace of it.* But this disorder took place right after New Year's, before Krause sang the intonation in any of the churches. How can Mr. Bach have decided that he was responsible for it?

M[*agister*] Jo. Aug. Ernesti
R[*ector*]

Leipzig, September 13, 1736

For the continuation of the dispute, see Nos. 192–196.

BACH HOLDS WEEKLY CONCERTS AT ZIMMERMANN'S COFFEEHOUSE

187. "Announcement of the Musical Concerts at Leipzig" in Lorenz Christoph Mizler's *Neu eröffnete musikalische Bibliothek,* I / 1 (Leipzig, [September] 1736) (*BD* II, no. 387)

Both of the public musical Concerts or Assemblies that are held here weekly are still flourishing steadily. The one is conducted by Mr. Johann Sebastian Bach, Capellmeister to the Court of Weissenfels and *Musik-Direcktor* at St. Thomas's and at St. Nicholas's in this city, and is held, except during the Fair, once a week in Zimmermann's coffeehouse in the Catherine Street, on Friday evenings from 8 to 10 o'clock; during the Fair, however, twice a week, on Tuesdays and Fridays, at the same hour. The other is conducted by Mr. Johann Gottlieb Görner, *Musik-Direcktor* at St. Paul's and Organist at St. Thomas's. It is also held once weekly, in the Schellhafer Hall in the Closter-Gasse, Thursday evenings from 8 to 10 o'clock; during the Fair, however, twice weekly, namely, Mondays and Thursdays, at the same time.

The participants in these musical concerts are chiefly students here, and there are always good musicians among them, so that sometimes they become, as is known, famous virtuosos. Any musician is permitted to make himself publicly heard at these musical concerts, and most often, too, there are such listeners as know how to judge the qualities of an able musician.

BACH WRITES TO SANGERHAUSEN ON BEHALF
OF HIS SON JOHANN GOTTFRIED BERNHARD

188. Bach's first letter to the Sangerhausen town council
(*BD* I, no. 37)

To Mr. Klemm, Gentleman, Most Respected Member of a Most Noble and Most Wise Council of the Town of Sangerhausen, My Most Particularly Esteemed Patron, in Sangerhausen.

MOST DISTINGUISHED AND MOST HIGHLY ESTEEMED MR. KLEMM,

My *amitie* of many years' standing with your late honored father permits me to hope that you, Most Esteemed Sir, will not take it amiss that I particularly beg of you the gracious continuation of the same. To this end, then, and in this confidence, I have dared to take the liberty (since I have heard that the Organist of the Lower Church has died and the vacancy will probably soon be filled) of obediently asking you, Most Esteemed Sir, not only for your gracious patronage on behalf of a person who is very close to me, but also to show me in this matter the special *faveur* of sending me most kindly a gracious note on the salary of the vacant post. And just as I hope and wish that my request as well as the addition to it may find a favorable reception, so I remain with most devoted gratitude at all times Your Honor's wholly obedient servant

Leipzig, October 30, 1736   JOH. SEBAST. BACH

189. Bach's second letter to the Sangerhausen town council
(*BD* I, no. 38)

MOST NOBLE AND MOST HIGHLY ESTEEMED SIR,

The gracious reception with which my recent letter to Your Honor met could be observed in almost every line of your most kind reply, especially as my first request was so favorably received by Your Honor. Since, then, I owe for it an expression of my deepest gratitude, I assure Your Honor that I will seek every occasion to demonstrate my ever-eager devotion in return. I should have sent Your Honor written acknowledgment of my obligation by return of post if I had not been waiting for a second note (which Your Honor, in your most valued letter, most graciously promised to send). But since this, owing to Your Honor's many other affairs, has so far failed to appear, I have thought it my duty not to delay any longer my answer to Your Honor's most valued letter. And since I take it that Your Honor, with your most valued recommendation and intercession on behalf of the person I have in mind, has already had so much gracious forethought that at the proper time an examination will be most graciously open to him along with other suitable candidates, I accordingly have no further reluctance to inform Your Honor that the person proposed by me is one of my sons. Now, although Your Honor has not yet been able to inform me fully as to the actual salary, yet I have such confidence in Your Most Noble and Most Worshipful Council as to be sure that it will not allow a person elected by it to suffer want. And who knows whether a Divine Decree is not here at work, by virtue of which Your Most Noble Council is now better in a position, by choosing one of my children, to keep the promise made to my humble self almost 30 years ago, in the conferring of the post of organist [*Figural Organist*] then vacant, since at that time a candidate was sent to you by the highest authority of the land, as a result of which, although at that time, under the régime of the late Burgomaster Vollrath, all the votes were cast for my humble self, I was nevertheless, for the aforementioned *raison,* not able to have the good fortune of emerging with success. Your Honor will please not take it unkindly that I disclose my fate at that time on this occasion; only the fact that the first *entrée* of my written *correspondence* found such gracious *ingress* brings the thought to me that perhaps Divine Providence is taking a hand here. May Your Honor further remain a gracious patron of me and my family, and believe not only that the good Lord will reward you but also that I and my family will be our life long Your Honor's wholly obedient servant

Leipzig, November 18, 1736   JOH. SEB. BACH

The vacancy Bach refers to occurred when the organist, Gottfried Christoph Gräffenhayn, died in early July 1702. Bach's son received the post but could not hold it, as it appears from Bach's letters of 1738, Nos. 203 and 204.

BACH IS APPOINTED ROYAL COURT COMPOSER

190. "Certificate for Johann Sebastian Bach as compositeur to the royal court orchestra" (*BD* II, no. 388)

Whereas His Royal Majesty in Poland and Serene Electoral Highness of Saxony, etc., has most graciously conferred upon Johann Sebastian Bach, on the latter's most humble entreaty and because of his ability, the title of *Compositeur to the Royal Court Orchestra*.

Now, therefore, the present certificate relating to the same has been prepared with His Royal Majesty's Most August Signature and the imprint of the Royal Seal.

Done at Dresden, November 19, 1736

G. W. MENTZEL

On the 28 instant the original was
dispatched to His Excell. Baron
von Keyserling

A[ugustus]. R[ex].

[seal] De Brühl

Initialed by the king, certified by Prime Minister von Brühl, the appointment certificate was sent to Bach via Hermann Carl von Keyserlingk, a noble family friend.

BACH PLAYS AN ORGAN RECITAL IN DRESDEN

191. Excerpt from the *Dresdner Nachrichten* (*BD* II, no. 389)

On December 1, 1736, the famous Capellmeister to the Prince of Saxe-Weissenfels and *Director Musices* at Leipzig, Mr. Johann Sebastian Bach, made himself heard from 2 to 4 o'clock on the new organ in the church of Our Lady, in the presence of the Russian Ambassador, Von Keyserlingk, and many Persons of Rank, also a large attendance of other persons and artists, with particular admiration, wherefore also His Royal Majesty most graciously named the same, because of his great ability in composing, to be His Majesty's Composer.

The large organ, built by Gottfried Silbermann, had 35 sounding stops for the three keyboards and 8 (ranging from 32-foot to 4-foot and including a mixture) for the pedal. Bach's recital took place on the Saturday before the First Sunday in Advent; the instrument had been dedicated only on the previous Sunday, November 25 (cf. Werner Müller, Gottfried Silbermann [Leipzig, 1982], pp. 258–70).

BACH'S DISPUTE WITH ERNESTI CONTINUES

192. Decree of the town council (*BD* I, no. 99)

A Noble and Most Wise Council of the Town of Leipzigk has had to learn with displeasure how misunderstandings have arisen at the St. Thomas School with respect to the appointment of the Prefect of the Resident Students [*Inquilinorum*], commonly called General Prefect. But since it is clearly stated in the School Regulations, Chapter 13, § 8, and Chapter 14, § 1 and § 4, that

The Cantor is to accept the eight boys for each of the four choirs with the consent of the Rector, and from them to choose four Choir Prefects with the foreknowledge and approval of the Director,

And that for the General of *Inquilinorum* Prefect the first student or, if he be not sufficiently capable *in musicis,* the next one is to be chosen,

Moreover, according to the said School Regulations Chapter 2, § 17, Chapter 6, § 1 and § 7, neither the Rector nor the Cantor nor even all the preceptors together have the power on their own authority to exclude a student from the School or from the enjoyment of this or that benefit;

Now, therefore, they are bound to conduct themselves accordingly, and to refrain from suspending by themselves one or another of the students from an office once entrusted to them, or even to exclude them, or to give instructions to the entire student body under pain of exclusion [*sub poena exclusionis*], unless they have previously fulfilled the requirements of § 7 of Chapter 6; and the Cantor is no less bound to refrain from entrusting the obligations of the Prefects to anyone other than a regular student. Likewise the Prefects, if need be, are to be punished in such wise that they shall not become the objects of scorn on the part of those over whom they are given a certain degree of supervision by § 4 of Chapter 14, and accordingly never to be subject to public whipping. Furthermore, those preceptors to whom by Chapter 4, § 9, of the aforesaid School Regulations the inspection of the choirs in public services as well as in wedding services is assigned will see to it that they strictly perform their duties in this respect, and thus avoid such excesses as Gottfried Theodor Krause has been convicted of;

Which is to be kept strictly in mind, when, at the coming Easter, Johann Gottl. Krausse's stay at the school is over, in filling the post of First Prefect; and in general the School Regulations—particularly, in case of any disagreements, § 4 of the First Chapter and § 11 and § 12 of the Second Chapter—shall be precisely adhered to.

This document authenticated by the affixing of the usual Town Seal.

[Seal]

Leipzig, February 6, 1737

193. Bach's first appeal to the consistory (*BD* I, no. 39)

Their Magnificences, the Most Noble, Most Reverend, Most Distinguished, Respected and Most Learned Members of the Most Worshipful Royal and Electoral Saxon Consistory at Leipzig, My Most Honored Masters and High and Mighty Patroni.

YOUR MAGNIFICENCES, MOST NOBLE, MOST REVEREND, MOST DISTINGUISHED, RESPECTED AND MOST LEARNED, MOST HIGHLY ESTEEMED MASTERS AND HIGH PATRONI!

The Rector of the St. Thomas School here, Magister Johann August Ernesti, has recently taken it upon himself to force upon me against my will an incompetent Prefect in the First Choir, which is formed by students of the said School; and when I neither could nor would accept this, the said Magister Ernesti gave orders to all the students, on pain of expulsion, that none of them was to sing or conduct the motet in church without this Prefect arbitrarily appointed by him; and he accomplished so much by this action that the following Sunday, at the afternoon service, not a single student, for fear of the threatened punishment, was willing to take over the singing or to conduct the motet; indeed, the services would have been disturbed if I had not finally succeeded in inducing a University student to attend to it.

Since then not only have I been very much injured and disturbed in the fulfillment of my office by this undertaking of the Rector's, but also the respect that the students owe me has been withdrawn, and I have thus been deprived of my rightful standing with them; and this although:

(1) according to Chapter 14, § 4, of the School Regulations of the Honorable Council here, set up for the St. Thomas School, the choice of the *praefecti chororum* from among the schoolboys belongs to me, without the concurrence of the Rector, and has always been so made

not only by me but by my predecessors; there being sensible reasons for this, since the Prefects according to the said School Regulations must take the place of me, the Cantor, and must conduct, because I cannot be in all the churches at once, and I have special duties of inspection and supervision over the First Choir, and consequently must know best with whom I can be sure of making out well; furthermore since

(2) the Rector's forbiddance of the students not [sic] to sing under any other Prefect is highly improper, considering that if the students are not to give me their obedience in the singing, it is impossible to accomplish anything fruitful; and accordingly, lest this beginning be taken as a precedent, I have high grounds for taking action;

Now, therefore, I am obliged to address Your Magnificences and You, Most Honorable Sirs, with regard to this troublous situation, and accordingly my most humble petition is submitted to you:

To uphold me in my office, and accordingly to impress it earnestly upon the Rector, Magister Ernesti, that he is not to hinder me any further in the discharge of the same, and that he is to refrain in the future from appointing Prefects without my knowledge and consent, and from any forbiddance of the School boys not [sic] to give me their obedience in singing; and most graciously to give the Superintendent or one of the Clergymen at St. Thomas's appropriate instructions, without undue stipulation, to exhort the School children to give me again the respect and obedience due me, and thus to enable me further to discharge my office.

As, in my reasonable request I hope and wait for Your High Protection and Aid, so I shall remain, as always, with all respect,

Your Magnificences and Most Noble, Most Reverend, and Most Distinguished Sirs, Your most obedient

JOHANN SEBASTIAN BACH
*Composer of the Court Capelle of His Royal
Majesty in Poland, and Dir. Chori Musici
in this Place*

Leipzig, February 12, 1737

The original date, November 1736, was erased and the later date substituted, in this document and in the text of No. 194. On February 13, 1737, the consistory sent a communication to Dr. Salomon Deyling, superintendent of the diocese of Leipzig and assessor of the consistory, and to the council, saying that Bach had "complained to the Consistory about the Rector, and the Council should investigate the matter and seek to dispose of it without delay, and see to it that in the public services no disturbance or commotion should occur." In April

1737, Ernesti, Bach, and Deyling were notified of some action, the nature of
which we do not know, taken by the council.

194. Bach's second appeal to the consistory (*BD* I, no. 40)

To Their Magnificences the Most Reverend, Most Noble, Most Distinguished,
Respected and Most Learned Sirs, the Members of the Most Worshipful Royal
and Electoral Saxon Consistory at Leipzig, My Most Highly Esteemed Masters
and Patroni.

YOUR MAGNIFICENCES, MOST REVEREND, MOST NOBLE, RESPECTED
AND MOST LEARNED, AND MOST HIGHLY ESTEEMED MASTERS AND
PATRONI!

Your Magnificences and You, Most Noble, also Most Reverend and
Most Distinguished Sirs, will most graciously deign to remember how
I, under date of February 12 of this year, complained about the Rector
of the St. Thomas School, Magister Johann August Ernesti, concerning
the hindrance offered me in the discharge of my duties and concerning
the injunction laid upon the students not to obey me and the resultant
humiliation to me, and how I most humbly sought Your Honors' protection and aid.

Now, since that time a Noble and Honorable Council has sent me a
decree, of which a copy is attached as Exhibit A; but on the one hand
it does not give me satisfaction in respect to the humiliation to which
I was subjected by the said Rector, and on the other it does me, indeed,
great harm:

For in the first place I have been very greatly injured in my dignity
by the threat to the students publicly made by the Rector, in open
church services, and in the presence of all the students of the highest
class, of expulsion and forfeiture of his bond for any student who should
be tempted to obey my orders, for which reason I request, not without
reason, the restoration of my honor. And, in the second place, the said
decree of the Council is based upon a set of School Regulations promulgated in 1723, about which the facts are as follows: they differ in many
respects from the old School Regulations, and to my great disadvantage
in the discharge of my office as well as in the fees accruing to me, but
they have therefore never been acknowledged as valid; and indeed,
when it was suggested that they be published, the blessed late Rector
Ernesti opposed this step on the ground that they must first of all be
sent to the Most Worshipful Consistory, and the decision of the latter
concerning them must be awaited. Now, since their ratification has, to

my knowledge, never taken place and I can accordingly not be governed by these new and to me unfavorable School Regulations, particularly since they would greatly diminish the fees accruing to me, and the decision must still be based upon the old School Regulations; therefore, the said decree of the Council, which is based on the new Regulations, cannot dispose of the matter. And particularly that part cannot be maintained according to which I should not have the power to suspend or even expel a boy from any office in the choirs once given to him [here a few words are missing in the original]; for cases arise in which a change must be made on the spot and no lengthy investigation can be undertaken into such trivial disciplinary and school matters, while in every elementary school the power to make such changes in matters concerning music is given to the Cantor, since it would be impossible to control the boys or to do justice to one's office if they knew that there was nothing one could do to them.

I have accordingly thought it necessary to bring these matters to the attention of Your Magnificences, Most Reverend, Most Noble, and Most Distinguished Sirs, and my most humble petition herewith once again goes forth to you:

To uphold me in preserving the necessary dignity in the discharge of my office; to forbid the Rector Ernesti any and all unwarranted encroachments; also to take the necessary steps to see that my honor before the students, which has been violated as a result of the said Rector's conduct, shall be restored; and to protect me against the new School Regulations, to the extent that they injure me and prevent me from discharging the duties of my office.

For the assistance shown me in this matter I shall always remain with due respect,

Your Magnificences and Most Reverend, Most Noble, and Most Distinguished Sirs, Your obedient

JOHANN SEBASTIAN BACH

Leipzig, August 21, 1737   *ipse concepi* [I drew this up myself]

On August 28, 1737, the consistory informed Deyling and the council of Bach's letter of August 21 and ordered that a report on the matter be made within a fortnight. Almost six weeks later, on October 4, the council decided "to let the matter rest for a while yet." "The blessed late Rector Ernesti" was Johann Heinrich Ernesti, the predecessor of Johann Matthias Gesner, who in turn was the predecessor of Bach's opponent, Johann August Ernesti. The document, though signed by Bach, is written in another hand, and by adding ipse concepi *Bach testifies to its authenticity.*

195. Bach's appeal to the king (*BD* I, no. 41)

To His Most Serene Highness, the Mighty Prince and Lord, Frederick Augustus, King in Poland, Grand Duke in Lithuania, Reuss, Prussia, Mazovia, Samogitia, Kyovia, Vollhynia, Podolia, Podlachia, Lieffland, Smolensk, Severia, and Czernienhovia, Duke of Saxony, Jülich, Cleves, Berg, Engern, and Westphalia, Archmarshal and Elector of the Holy Roman Empire, Landgrave of Thuringia, Margrave of Meissen, also of Upper and Lower Lausiz, Burgrave of Magdeburg, Prince and Count of Henneberg, Count of the Marck, Ravensberg, and Barby, Lord of Ravenstein, My Most Gracious King, Elector, and Master.

Your Most Serene Highness, Most Mighty King and Elector, Most Gracious Lord!

That Your Royal Majesty has most graciously deigned to confer upon me the title of Court Composer, this I shall gratefully appreciate with the most humble thanks all my life long. Just as I confide, therefore, with humblest assurance, in Your Royal Majesty's most gracious protection, so also I venture to ask for it most obediently in my present afflictions.

My predecessors, the Cantors at the St. Thomas School here, have always had the right, according to the traditional School Regulations, to appoint the Prefects of the *chorus musicus,* and this for the good reason that they could know most surely which person was most suited to the post; and this special right I, too, have enjoyed for a considerable time and without its being disputed by anybody.

Nonetheless, the present Rector, Magister Johann August Ernesti, has had the effrontery recently to fill the post of Prefect, without my concurrence, by appointing a person whose ability *in musicis* is very poor; and when, noticing his weakness and the resulting disorder in the music, I saw myself compelled to make a change, and choose a more capable person in his place, the said Rector, Ernesti, not only stubbornly opposed my purposes but also, to my great injury and humiliation, forbade all the boys, in general assembly and on pain of whipping, to give their obedience in the arrangements I had made. Now, although I have sought to maintain my well-founded prerogatives by submitting the enclosed Exhibit A to the Magistrate here and have also begged the Royal Consistory here for satisfaction for the injuries I had sustained, through Exhibit B, yet from the latter I have had no reply, and from the former only the order of which a copy is enclosed as Exhibit C. Since, however, Most Gracious King and Lord, the rights I have hitherto enjoyed are completely cut off by the terms of this enclosure, which is based on a set of School Regulations newly promulgated in the year 1723, by which I cannot be bound, above all because, even if they would otherwise be valid, they have never been ratified by the Consistory here;

Now, therefore, I entreat Your Royal Majesty in humblest submission most graciously to order:

(1) The Council here to uphold me without injury in my *jus quaesitum* in respect to the appointment of the *praefecti chori musici* and to protect me in the exercise of that right, and

(2) The Consistory here to compel the Rector Ernesti to apologize for the abuse to which he has submitted me, and also, if Your Majesty please, to instruct Dr. Deyling to exhort the whole student body that all the School boys are to show me the customary respect and obedience that are due me.

This Most High Royal Favor I acknowledge eagerly, with undying gratitude, and remain in deepest submission Your Royal Majesty's most humble, most obedient

Leipzig, October 18, 1737　　　　　　　JOHANN SEBASTIAN BACH

196. The king's decree (*BD* II, no. 406)

To the Worthy and Most Learned, Our Dear Loyal and Faithful Members of the Consistory at Leipzig, concerning the Court Composer Bach:

By the Grace of God, Frederick Augustus, King in Poland, Duke of Saxony, Jülich, Cleves, Berg, Engern, and Westphalia, Elector.

WORTHY AND MOST LEARNED, DEAR LOYAL AND FAITHFUL!

Whereas Our Court Composer, Johann Sebastian Bach, has complained to Us about the present Rector of the St. Thomas School in Leipzig, Magister Johann August Ernesti, that he has had the effrontery to fill the post of Prefect without his concurrence, and with a person whose ability *in musicis* is very poor, and when, noticing the latter's weakness and the resulting disorder in the music, he [the Cantor] saw himself compelled to make a change and to choose a more accomplished person in his place, the said Rector Ernesti not only opposed his purpose but also, to his great injury and humiliation, forbade all the boys, in general assembly and on pain of whipping, to give their obedience in the arrangements the Cantor had made; and what he accordingly requests is indicated by the enclosure;

We therefore desire herewith that you shall take such measures, in response to this complaint, as you shall see fit. This is Our Will.

Dated Dressden,   JACOB FRIEDRICH SCHILLING
December 17, 1737   ANDREAS HEINRICH BEYER

On February 5, 1738, the consistory again requested Deyling and the council to draw up within a fortnight the report asked for on August 28, 1737. Thereafter the flood of documents in this long-drawn-out case comes an end; the outcome is unknown. Spitta notes that the king came to Leipzig for the Easter Fair, and assumes that at this time he intervened personally to settle the affair in favor of his court composer. Nos. 199–200 show that Bach performed music in the king's honor on this occasion.

BACH WRITES TESTIMONIALS FOR A STUDENT,
BERNHARD DIETRICH LUDEWIG

197. Bach's first testimonial on behalf of Ludewig (*BD* I, no. 73)

Whereas the bearer, Mr. Bernhard Dieterich Ludewig, *Theol. Candidatus* and student of music, has requested me, the undersigned, to give him a testimonial concerning his performance in this town; now, therefore, I am heartily glad not only to comply with his request but also to state in his praise that he has not only acquitted himself well in his *studium Theologicum* but also in various years frequented my Collegium musicum with diligence, untiringly participated in the same, playing various instruments as well as making himself heard many times *vocaliter,* and has in general so distinguished himself that I have been impelled not only to entrust the younger members of my family [*meine kleine Familie*] to his conscientious instruction but also to instruct him regularly myself in those things which he did not yet know *in Musicis.* Thus I do not doubt that he will confirm in person what I have stated in writing.

JOH. SEB. BACH
*Royal Polish & Electoral Saxon Composer
& Director Chori Musici*
Leipzig, March 4, 1737   *Lipsiensis etc.*

198. Bach's second testimonial on behalf of Ludewig (*BD* I, no. 74)

Whereas the bearer, Mr. Bernhard Dieterich Ludewig, *S. Th. Studiosus* and student of music, has requested me, the undersigned, to write him a formal testimonial concerning the diligent instruction he has given my children and the assistance he has lent to both church and other music, vocally as well as instrumentally, now, therefore, I not only am heartily glad to accomplish this but wish to certify that I have been fully satisfied with the diligence he has shown my children, as well as that his ability *in Musicis* has given me much pleasure. And samples of his work, in one [direction] as well as in another, will fully confirm and verify this my testimonial. I wish him in his endeavors divine grace and support.

JOHANN SEBAST. BACH
Royal Polish and Electoral Saxon
Composer, etc.

Leipzig, October 10, 1737

BACH PRESENTS A CANTATA FOR THE VISIT
OF THE KING AND THE BETROTHAL
OF PRINCESS AMALIA

199. Excerpt from Johann Salomon Riemer's *Chronicle of Leipzig*
     (*BD* II, no. 425)

On April 28, 1738, at 9 o'clock in the morning, Baron Woldemar of Schmettau made a solemn address in St. Paul's Church of this city on the occasion of the forthcoming marriage of Her Royal Highness the Princess Amalia to His Majesty the King of the Two Sicilies. At 9 o'clock in the evening the students at the University here offered a fine evening serenade with many wax tapers, and, to the sound of trumpets and drums, in front of the Apel house on the Marketplace, a most humble *Drama*, which had been composed and was performed by the Capellmeister, Mr. Joh. Sebastian Bach, whereupon the Count of Zierotin, the Baron of Schmettau, and the Lords of Leipnitz and Marschall had the honor of offering the Cantata to Their Royal Majesties and to Their Royal Highnesses the Two Princesses, and of being allowed to kiss their hands.

200. *Willkommen! Ihr herrschenden Götter der Erden,* cantata, BWV
     Anh. 13: printed text, title page (*BD* II, no. 424)

When His Most Serene Highness, the Most Mighty Prince and Lord Frederick Augustus, King in Poland, Grand Duke of Lithuania, Reuss, Prussia, Mazovia, Samogitia, Kiovia, Vollhynia, Podolia, Podlachia, Liefland, Smolensko, Severia, and Czernicovia &c. &c., Duke of Saxony,

Als der
Allerdurchlauchtigste, Großmächtigste
Fürst und Herr,

HERR
Friedrich August,

König in Pohlen,

Großherzog in Litthauen, Reußen, Preußen, Mazovien,
Samogitien, Kyovien, Vollhynien, Podolien, Podlachien,
Liefland, Smolensko, Severien, Czernicovien ꝛc.

Herzog zu Sachsen, Jülich, Cleve, Berg, Engern und Westphalen,
des heil. Rom. Reichs Erzmarschall und Churfürst, Landgraf in Thüringen, Marggraf zu Meissen, auch Ober = und Niederlausitz, Burggraf zu Magdeburg, Gefürsteter Graf
zu Henneberg, Graf zu der Mark, Ravensberg, Barby und Hanau,
Herr zum Ravenstein ꝛc. ꝛc.

nebst Dero
Frau Gemahlinn Königlichen
Majestät,

und

Der Durchlauchtigsten ältesten Prinzeßinn
Königlichen Hoheit,

mit Ihrer allerhöchsten Gegenwart,
die Stadt Leipzig, an der Ostermesse 1738 beglückten,

wollten am 27 April,

durch eine Abendmusik,

ihre alleruntertähnigste Devotion bezeigen
Die auf dasiger Universität Studirenden.

Leipzig,
gedruckt bey Bernhard Christoph Breitkopf.

200. *Willkommen! Ihr herrschenden Götter der Erden,* cantata,
BWV Anh. 13: printed text, title page

Jülich, Cleves, and Berg, also Engern and Westphalia, Archmarshal and Elector of the Holy Roman Empire, Landgrave in Thuringia, Margrave of Meissen, also Upper and Lower Lausitz, Burgrave of Magdeburg, Prince and Count of Henneberg, Count of the Marck, Ravensberg, Barby and Hanaus, Lord of Ravenstein &c. &c., together with Her Royal Majesty, His Consort, and Her Royal Highness, the Eldest Princess, honored the Town of Leipzig with Their Presences at the Easter Fair of 1738, the Students at the University of that place wished on April 27 to demonstrate their most submissive devotion in an Evening Serenade. Leipzig, printed by Berhard Christoph Breitkopf.

The music of this dramma per musica *does not survive. The performance date appears variously as April 27 (printed text), April 28 (Riemer), and April 29 (another contemporary source).*

201. Bach's receipt for his payment (*BD* I, no. 122)

Fifty-eight thaler for the evening music offered to His Royal Majesty, etc., on April 27, 1738, were paid to me by a Worshipful University in Leipzig this day, which I herewith acknowledge and for which I duly give this receipt. Leipzig, May 5, 1738

50 rthl. for me, and	JOHANN SEBASTIAN BACH
8 rthl. for the Town Pipers	*Royal Polish and Electoral Saxon*
	Court Composer

JOHANN ELIAS BACH ORDERS GIFTS FOR BACH
AND HIS WIFE, ANNA MAGDALENA

202. J. E. Bach's letter, from his correspondence book, April 1738 (*BD* II, no. 423)

If possible, I would be glad to have for my honored cousin [*Herrn Vetter*] a bottle of the brandy made with yeast and a few, *notabene,* yellow carnations for our honored aunt [*Frau Muhme*], a great connoisseur of gardening. I know for certain that this would give great delight and ingratiate me all the more with both, wherefore I beg for this again and remain as above.

Johann Elias Bach (1705–1755), a son of Johann Sebastian's first cousin Johann Valentin, came to Leipzig in 1738 in order to study theology at the university. During his stay in Leipzig, he served as secretary to Bach. An agreement between the two stipulated that Johann Elias was free to leave only on three months' notice. A number of first drafts and copies of letters by Johann Elias have survived. For details, see Odrich-Wollny.

BACH WRITES ABOUT DEBTS INCURRED BY HIS
SON JOHANN GOTTFRIED BERNHARD

203. Bach's letter to Johann Friedrich Klemm (*BD* I, no. 42)

MOST NOBLE, MOST HIGHLY ESTEEMED MR. KLEMM,

Your Honor will not take it unkindly that absence has prevented me from answering your most esteemed letter earlier than this, since I returned only two days ago from Dressden. With what pain and sorrow, however, I frame this reply, Your Honor can judge for yourself as the loving and well-meaning father of Your Honor's own most beloved offspring. Upon my (alas! misguided) son I have not laid eyes since last year, when I had the honor to enjoy many courtesies at Your Honor's hands. Your Honor is also not unaware that at that time I duly paid not only his board but also the Mühlhausen draft (which presumably brought about his departure at that time), but also [*sic*] left a few ducats behind to settle a few bills, in the hope that he would now embark upon a new mode of life. But now I must learn again, with greatest consternation, that he once more borrowed here and there and did not change his way of living in the slightest, but on the contrary has even absented himself and not given me to date any inkling as to his where-abouts.

What shall I say or do further? Since no admonition or even any loving care and *assistance* will suffice any more, I must bear my cross in patience and leave my unruly son to God's Mercy alone, doubting not that He will hear my sorrowful pleading and in the end will so work upon him, according to His Holy Will, that he will learn to acknowl-edge that the lesson is owing wholly and alone to Divine Goodness.

Since now I have opened my heart to Your Honor, I am fully confi-dent that you will not impute the evil conduct of my child to me, but will be convinced that a devoted father, whose children are close to his heart, seeks to do everything to help to further their welfare. This it was that impelled me, at the time Your Honor had the vacancy, to recommend him for it as best I could, in the hope that the more civi-lized Sangerhausen way of living and his eminent patrons would equally move him to a different behavior, and on this account I again express herewith my most dutiful thanks to Your Honor as the author of his advancement. Nor do I doubt that Your Honor will seek to move Your Most Noble Council to delay the threatened change until it can be learned where he is keeping himself (God who knoweth all things is my Witness that I have not seen him again since last year), so that it can be ascertained what he has decided to do in the future: to remain, and change his way of living; or to seek his fortune elsewhere. I would not willingly have Your Most Noble Council burdened with this request, but for my part would only pray for patience until such time as he turns up, or it can be learned otherwise whither he has gone.

Since, moreover, various *creditores* have presented their claims to me, and I can hardly agree to pay these claims without my son's oral or written confession of them (in which I am supported by all laws), therefore I most obediently request Your Honor to have the goodness to obtain precise information as to his whereabouts, and then you only need to be good enough to give me definite notification so that one last effort may be made to see whether with God's help his impenitent heart can be won over and brought to a recognition of his mistakes. Since, furthermore, he has hitherto had the good fortune to lodge with Your Honor, I will at the same time pray you to inform me whether he took with him the little furniture he had, or what there may be of it still on hand. Awaiting a most prompt reply, and wishing you a more joyous holiday than I shall have, I remain, with my most humble respects to your Honored Wife, Your Honor's most devoted servant

Leipzig, May 24, 1738   JOH. SEB. BACH

204. Bach's letter to Anna Margarete Klemm (*BD* I, no. 43)

MOST NOBLE AND MOST HIGHLY ESTEEMED MRS. KLEMM,

The Honored Lady will not take it unkindly that I cannot accede as she would wish to her letter accompanying the statement of claims sent me; because in the first place it is necessary that I should be shown my (alas! misguided) son's written acknowledgment in his own handwriting, before I make a decision, and I must also know whether he has not yet returned home, in order to take appropriate steps. He has not been with me again since my trip to Sangerhausen last year, as I can give assurance with God and my family as my witnesses. If the Honored Lady should learn where he is staying, and then give me definite information on that score, I should not only acknowledge it with all thanks but take pains to reimburse her. Awaiting a most prompt reply, I remain, Most Noble and My Most Highly Esteemed Mrs. Klemm,

Your most devoted servant

Leipzig, May 26, 1738   JOH. SEB. BACH

Inquiries about Johann Gottfried Bernhard's whereabouts were made—in vain—in the autumn of the same year. On January 28, 1739, he matriculated as a student of law in the University of Jena. He died on May 27 of the same year, at the age of 24.

BACH PUBLISHES A COLLECTION OF
ORGAN WORKS

205. Johann Elias Bach's invitation for subscribers: excerpt from a letter to Cantor Johann Wilhelm Koch in Ronnenberg (*BD* II, no. 434)

Thus it happens also that my honored Cousin will bring out some clavier pieces that are mostly for organists and are exceedingly well composed, and they will doubtless be ready for the coming Easter Fair, and make some 80 folios; if my Brother can obtain some subscribers for them, let him accept them at a price of ———, for others, later, will have to pay more . . .

    Most devoted greetings from my honored Cousin and his whole family, and especially from me.

January 10, 1739

206. *Clavier-Übung,* Part III, BWV 552, 669–689, and 802–805: title page (*BD* I, no. 169)

Third Part of the Keyboard Practice, consisting of various preludes on the catechism and other hymns for the organ. For music lovers and especially for connoisseurs of such work, to refresh their spirits, composed by Johann Sebastian Bach, Royal Polish and Electoral Saxon Court Composer, Capellmeister, and Directore Chori Musici in Leipzig. Published by the Author.

For a contemporary review of the work, see No. 333.

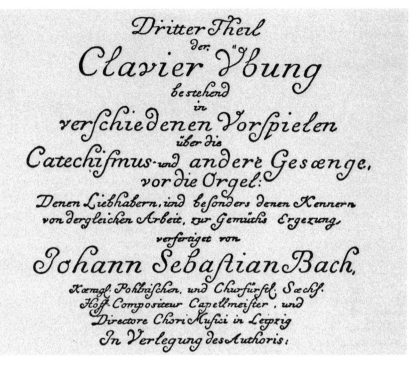

206. *Clavier-Übung,* Part III, BWV 552, 669–689, and 802–805: title page

COLLEGIUM MUSICUM IS DEFINED, WITH A
REFERENCE TO BACH

207. Entry in Johann Heinrich Zedler's *Grosses Universal Lexicon,* vol. 22 (Leipzig, 1739), col. 1488 (*BJ* 1984, p. 175)

MUSICUM COLLEGIUM is a gathering of certain musical connoisseurs who, for the benefit of their own exercise in both vocal and instrumental music and under the guidance of a certain director, get together on particular days and in particular locations and perform musical pieces. Such collegia are to be found in various places. In Leipzig, the Bachian Collegium Musicum is more famous than all others.

BACH IS CAUTIONED BY THE COUNCIL ABOUT A
PASSION PERFORMANCE

208. Excerpt from the Leipzig town council archives (*BD* II, no. 439)

Upon a Noble and Most Wise Council's order I have gone to Mr. Bach here and have pointed out to the same that the music he intends to perform on the coming Good Friday is to be omitted until regular permission for the same is received. Whereupon he answered: it had always been done so; he did not care, for he got nothing out of it anyway, and it was only a burden; he would notify the Superintendent that it had been forbidden him; if an objection were made on account of the text, [he remarked that] it had already been performed several times. This I have accordingly wished to communicate to a Noble and Most Wise Council.

ANDREAS GOTTLIEB BIENENGRÄBER
Clerk

Leipzig, March 17, 1739   With my own hand

BACH'S COUSIN AND PRIVATE SECRETARY,
JOHANN ELIAS BACH, CORRESPONDS

209. Excerpt from a letter to Cantor Johann Wilhelm Koch: draft (*BD* II, no. 448)

. . . and I certainly hoped to have the honor of speaking to my Brother soon, which I wished the more eagerly since just at that time something extra fine in the way of music was going on, my honored Cousin from Dressden [Wilhelm Friedemann Bach], who was here for over four weeks, having made himself heard several times at our house along with the two famous lutenists Mr. Weise [Sylvius Leopold Weiss] and Mr. [Johann] Kropffgans.
August 11, 1739

210. Invitation to Koch, on behalf of Bach, to attend a performance of the Collegium Musicum: draft (*BD* II, no. 455)

But, since we are speaking of baptizing children, I should mention here that my honored Cousin sends his most obedient thanks to the Cantor in Ronneburg and his Lady for the christening gift, which was consumed with good wishes for their health; he wishes for nothing better than the eagerly awaited opportunity to make you an appropriate return, and begs you at the same time not to take it amiss that, on account of the accumulation of work, he cannot thank you with a note of his own this time, since he will begin the Collegium Musicum this Friday and will perform some music in the first week of the Fair for the birthday of His Royal Majesty; it will certainly be worth listening to, and if my Brother could get away, he would certainly not regret having been in the audience. Concerning Your Honor's first letter, I must report in most obedient reply that the church piece he sent back was duly received, together with the 10 [gr.?], and also that the work of my honored Cousin, engraved on copper, is now ready, and may be obtained from him @ 3 rthl. per copy.

September 28, 1739

Bach had stood as godfather to Koch's daughter at her baptism in Ronneburg on September 9, 1739. The work, engraved on copper, is Part III of the Clavier-Übung, *whose imminent publication Johann Elias Bach had announced to Koch (see No. 202).*

211. Excerpt from the draft of a letter asking his sister to send wine for Bach: draft (*BD* II, no. 458)

Further, I will repeat my earlier request for the new sweet wine. The good Lord will presumably send you a fine vintage this year, and accordingly I beg you, my dear Sister, most earnestly, to decoct [*abkochen*] 10 or 12 measures of new sweet wine for me, and send it to me by the express man Herrin, since I would but too gladly give our honored Cousin this pleasure, having enjoyed many favors in his house for going on two years already.

October 5, 1739

212. Excerpt from a thank-you letter, on behalf of Bach, to Johann Leberecht Schneider in Weissenfels, November 11, 1739 (*BD* II, no. 462)

P.S. From my honored Cousin and his whole household I am to send you most obedient respects, and to inform you most gratefully that one had intended to show Your Honor his indebtedness, but since the Doctor advised strongly against it in this weather, of which Mrs. [Johanna Christina] Krebs [Anna Magdalena Bach's sister] will also have news, I am once more to give you my honored Cousin's most obedient thanks for your most kind invitation, which perhaps when he is fully restored to health he will have the honor of accepting.

213. Excerpt from a second thank-you letter to J. L. Schneider, November 14, 1739 (*BD* II, no. 462)

P.S. My Honored Cousin and his Lady send Your Honor and Mrs. Krebs with many greetings once again their thanks for your overwhelming courtesy, and since the former, upon his safe return, found a bit of work awaiting him, he will send you his own written thanks either tomorrow or next Wednesday.

BACH WRITES OUT THOROUGH-BASS RULES, 1740–1745

214. "Some Most Necessary Rules of Thorough Bass by J. S. B." (*BD* I, no. 183)

Scales

The scale of the major 3rd is: a tone [tonic], 2nd a whole tone, 3rd a whole, 4th a half, 5th a whole, 6th a whole tone, 7th a whole, 8ve a half tone; the scale of the minor 3rd is: a tone [tonic], 2nd a whole tone, 3rd a half, 4th a whole, 5th a whole, 6th a half, 7th a whole, 8ve a whole; hence the following rule can be derived: the 2nd is large in both scales, the 4th always small [*sic*], the 5th and 8ve perfect, and the 6th and 7th are like the 3rd.

The chord consists of 3 tones, namely, the 3rd, whether large or small, the 5th, and the 8ve; e.g., for C, C-E-G.

Some Rules of Thorough Bass

(1) Every principal note has its own chord, whether natural [*eigenthümlich*] or borrowed.

(2) The natural chord of a fundamental [or bass] note consists of the 3rd, 5th, and 8ve.

N.B. Of these three intervals none can be altered except the 3rd, which can be large or small, and is accordingly called major or minor.

(3) A borrowed chord is formed by intervals other than the usual ones appearing over the fundamental note:

$$\text{e.g.} \quad \begin{matrix} 6 \\ 4, \\ 2 \end{matrix} \quad \begin{matrix} 6 \\ 3, \\ 6 \end{matrix} \quad \begin{matrix} 6 \\ 5, \\ 3 \end{matrix} \quad \begin{matrix} 5 \\ 4, \\ 8 \end{matrix} \quad \begin{matrix} 7 \\ 5, \\ 3 \end{matrix} \quad \begin{matrix} 9 \\ 7, \\ 3 \end{matrix} \quad \text{etc.}$$

(4) A ♯ or ♭ alone over the note means that for a ♯ one plays the major 3rd and for a ♭ the minor 3rd, but the other intervals remain unchanged.

(5) A 5 alone or an 8 alone means the whole chord.

(6) A 6 alone is accompanied in three ways: (1) with the 3rd and the 8ve; (2) with the 3rd doubled; (3) with the 6th doubled and the 3rd.

N.B. When the major 6th and minor 3rd both appear over the note, the 6th must not be doubled, because it sounds bad; instead, the 8ve and the 3rd must be added.

(7) 2 over a note is accompanied by the 5th doubled, and now and then by both the 4th and the 5th; and not seldom occasionally [*sic*] [also with the 4th and 6th].

(8) The ordinary 4th, especially when it is followed by the 3rd, is combined with the 5th and 8ve. But if there is a line through the 4 [4, indicating an augmented 4th], the 2nd and 6th are played with it.

(9) The 7th is also accompanied in three ways: (1) with the 3rd and 5th; (2) with the 3rd and 8ve; (3) the 3rd is doubled.

(10) The 9th seems to have an identity with the 2nd, and is in itself a doubling of the 2nd, but the difference is that it requires a completely different accompaniment, namely, the 3rd and 5th, or occasionally the 6th instead of the 5th, but very seldom.

(11) With $\frac{4}{2}$ the 6th is played, or occasionally the 5th instead of the 6th.

(12) With $\frac{5}{4}$ the 8ve is played, and the 4th resolves downward to the 3rd.

(13) With $\frac{6}{5}$ the 3rd is played, whether it be major or minor.

(14) With $\frac{7}{5}$ the 3rd is played.

(15) With $\frac{9}{7}$ the 3rd is played.

The other precautions that must be observed will explain themselves better in oral instruction than in writing.

BACH REPORTS ON CANDIDATES FOR AN
ASSISTANT'S POST AT THE ST. THOMAS SCHOOL

215. Bach's report (*BD* I, no. 76)

Upon the order of His Excellency, the Vice-Chancellor, the three candidates have come to me, and I have found them as follows:

(1) Magister Röder excused himself from the examination because he had changed his mind and accepted a position as tutor in a noble family in Merseburg.

(2) Magister Irmler has a very fine way of singing, but lacks somewhat in aural judgment.

(3) Mr. Wildenhayn plays somewhat on the clavier, but, by his own confession, has no skill at singing.

Leipzig, January 18, 1740   JOH. SEB. BACH

BACH WRITES A TESTIMONIAL FOR A STUDENT,
CHRISTIAN FRIEDRICH SCHEMELLI

216. Bach's testimonial on behalf of Schemelli (*BD* I, no. 77)

Whereas the bearer, Mr. Christian Friedrich Schemelli, *Phil. Studiosus,* has requested me, the undersigned, to give him a testimonial concerning the diligence he has shown *in musicis,* accordingly I have not wished to deny him the same, but rather to bear witness that at all times, for as long as he frequented our St. Thomas School, he showed all possible diligence therein, and I was able to make very good use of him in the choirs as a soprano.

JOHANN SEBAST. BACH
Royal Polish and Electoral Saxon
Leipzig, February 24, 1740   *Court Composer*

Schemelli was the son of Georg Christian Schemelli, cantor in Zeitz and editor of the 1736 Musical Hymn Book, *to which Bach contributed (No. 178–179). C. F. Schemelli was born in 1713, and was at the school from 1731 to 1734—that is, between the ages of eighteen and twenty-one. Bach's reference to him as a soprano at the end of this testimonial, is significant as an explicit reference to his use of falsetto singers.*

JOHANN ELIAS BACH CORRESPONDS FURTHER

217. Letter to Cantor Johann Georg Hille inquiring about a songbird (*BD* II, no. 477)

To Cantor Hille in Glaucha, close by Halle.

MOST NOBLE SIR, MOST HIGHLY ESTEEMED MR. CANTOR, MOST WORTHY PATRON!

I had the particular distinction a few years ago of making Your Honor's personal acquaintance in the home of my honored Cousin Capellmeister Bach, and now I am also afforded the desired occasion to wait upon you in writing. For the said Capellmeister, when he came back from Halle during Lent of this year, reported to his beloved wife, together with many kindnesses, that Your Honor possessed a linnet which, as a result of the skillful instruction of its master, made itself heard in particularly agreeable singing. Now, since the honored lady my Cousin is a particular lover of such birds, I have felt I should inquire whether Your Honor would be of a mind to relinquish this singing bird to her for a reasonable sum, and to send it to her by some sure means. I can certainly assure you not only that the favor you would thus confer would, apart from a cheerful payment, be reciprocated if possible, but also that I *en particuliaire* will ever be, with much respect,

Your Honor's most obedient servant

June 1740   [JOHANN ELIAS BACH]

218. Excerpt from a letter to Simon von Meyer acknowledging a gift of carnations for Anna Magdalena Bach: draft
(Odrich-Wollny, no. 44)

I have two most esteemed communications of Your Honor's to answer, and I must further most humbly voice twofold thanks that Your Honor has most graciously granted my impertinent request, and has deigned to present me, or rather the honored lady my Cousin [*meine Frau Muhme*] with the six most beautiful carnation plants. With an extended description of the joy that was given thereby to the said lady my Cousin I will not burden Your Honor, but will mention only this: that she values this unmerited gift more highly than children do their Christmas presents, and tends them with such care as is usually given to children, lest a single one wither. She also wishes her most honorably obedient thanks therefore (to talk in womanish style) to be conveyed, and hopes for an occasion to show Your Honor her gratitude in deeds.

October 10, 1740

Leipzig
1 7 4 1–1 7 5 1

219. Excerpt from a letter of Johann Elias Bach to Johann Wilhelm Koch, January 28, 1741 (*BD* II, no. 484)

I had not wanted to reply at all to the first kind letter, which a carrier brought me, because I could send neither the requested *Basso Solo* nor the *collegium Russian[um]*. As to the former, my cousin gave me hope that he would let it be copied, but because this has not happened so far, I unfortunately cannot delight my dear brother [*Herrn Bruder*] at this time. Also I cannot blame my cousin, since he has lent the copied parts to a bass singer by the name of Büchner, who has not returned them. But he won't allow the score out of his hands, for he has lost many things this way. Meanwhile, I should respectfully compliment you and, at the same time, return on his behalf and with many thanks the canons sent to him. There is no magic [*Hexerei*] involved here, as he put it, and he has written a comment on the large ones. They also got a bit wet through the fault of the carrier, for it rained heavily that day, which I hope my dear brother will excuse.

A propos, if my dear brother will be so kind as to cover the copying costs for the *Basso Solo* in the amount of 12 gr., I promise herewith that I will take care of the matter. However, I ask for a prepaid order.

"Basso Solo" apparently represents an unspecified solo cantata by Bach; the bass singer was probably Johann Polykarp Büchner, court singer at Weissenfels. Nothing is known about the canons.

BACH RESOLVES A CANON BY TEODORO RICCIO

220. Resolution of a puzzle canon: album supplement
(*BJ* 1982, pp. 126–27)

Resolution of Ricci's canon, by J. S. Bach.

The Ansbach capellmeister Teodoro Riccio (c. 1540–1600) entered a riddle canon, dated April 27, 1597, in an autograph album that later was in the possession of Johann Friedrich Mentz (1673–1749), professor of philosophy and in 1735 and 1743 rector of the University of Leipzig. Mentz apparently asked Bach to provide a solution, which Bach then entered in the album (undated) on a separate leaf.

BACH ACKNOWLEDGES A GIFT OF VENISON
FROM JOHANN LEBERECHT SCHNEIDER

221. Bach's letter to Schneider: draft or copy (*BD* I, no. 44)

à Mons.
Mons. Jean Leberecht Schneider, Consulent de la Chambre des Finances de Son Altesse Serenissime le Duc de Weissenfels &c.
Weissenfels.

220. Resolution of a puzzle canon

MOST NOBLE SIR, MOST PARTICULARLY HIGHLY ESTEEMED SIR CON-
SULENT!

Although of Your Honor's invaluable favor I never entertained the
slightest doubt, yet Your Honor recently deigned most graciously to
give me another proof of it. I and my whole household acknowledge
the same with most obedient thanks and wish only for an opportunity
to prove our desire to thank Your Honor in deeds. The fine roast venison has been, in the meantime, consumed by us, with a wish for Your
Honor's good health, but we should have enjoyed it still more if we
could have done so in Your Honor's agreeable *compagnie*. Since, however,
our wish was not fulfilled this time, we hope at least that we shall in
the near future have the privilege of seeing Your Honor here with us in
Leipzig, remaining, with most obedient respects to Your Most Worthy
Mamma, and with proper esteem, ever

Your Honor's and My Most Particularly Highly Esteemed Sir *Consulent*'s most obedient servant

Leipzig, July 1741   JOH. SEB. BACH

ANNA MAGDALENA BACH FALLS ILL

222. Johann Elias Bach's letter informing Bach of his wife's illness: draft or copy (*BD* II, no. 489)

a Mons.
Mons. Bach, compositeur de la
Musique de Sa Maj. le Roi de Pologne
e Electeur de Saxes etc. etc.
pres[entement] a Berlin.
To be delivered in care of the Court Councilor, Dr. Stahl.

MOST NOBLE SIR, MOST HIGHLY ESTEEMED COUSIN,

At the good report of Your health that Your Honor was good enough
to send to Your Honor's beloved household a few days ago, we all
heartily rejoice and hope that we shall find you just as happy and well
when we kiss you upon your return as you are now during your absence.
This return we hope to see accomplished soon because our most lovable
Mama [*unsere liebwertheste Frau Mama*] has been very ailing for a week
now, and we do not know whether perhaps, as a result of the violent
throbbing of her pulse, a creeping fever or some other evil consequence
may arise; to which is added the fact that St. Bartholomew's Day and
the Council Election here will occur in a few weeks, and we should not

know how we should conduct ourselves in respect to the same in Your Honor's absence. It is indeed painful to us to have to disturb Your Honor somewhat by such news in your present peace and contentment, but since unavoidable necessity required it, we have good confidence that our most worthy Papa and Cousin respectively will not take the same amiss. To this is added a hearty greeting from the whole household to Your Honor and to my honored younger Cousin, and especially most obedient respects from me, who, with all conceivable respect, remain my life long,

Most Noble Sir, Your Honor's most obedient servant and cousin

August 5, 1741   [JOHANN ELIAS BACH]

223. Johann Elias Bach's letter updating Bach on his wife's condition: draft or copy (*BD* II, no. 490)

MOST ESTEEMED SIR COUSIN,

Our honored Cousin has been good enough to send to his beloved wife another good report, to the relief of us all, and to set the date of his departure; but great as was the pleasure we derived from this, just so great must be the pain we feel about the increasing weakness of our most honored Mama, for the latter has for a fortnight now not had a single night with one hour's rest, and cannot either sit up or lie down, so that during last night I was called, and we could not help thinking that, to our great sorrow, we would lose her. The most pressing need therefore forces us to give our most dutiful report of the same, in order that Your Honor may perhaps (if I do not presume!) hasten his journey and rejoice us all with his desired presence, with which wish, and with heartiest greetings from the whole household, I, *en particulierement,* with appropriate respect and zeal remain my life long, etc.

August 9, 1741   JOHANN ELIAS BACH

224. Anna Magdalena Bach's letter of regret to Johann Leberecht Schneider, in Weissenfels: draft (*BD* II, no. 493)

MOST NOBLE SIR, MOST HIGHLY RESPECTED SIR CHAMBERLAIN, HIGHLY ESTEEMED PATRON!

Your most highly honored letter of September 8, Most Noble Sir, for good reason worked such a change in my spirits that it almost if not completely made me forget the most acute pains of the body, since in it you give me and my household the strongest assurance of Your Honor's invaluable favor and deign to wish to go even further and demonstrate the same in a specific manner. If I had willingly cast aside an offer so much desired, I should be deserving that the special favor and the benevolent forethought shown me should be wholly withdrawn. For the pleasure that I may always promise myself in advance from a visit to our beloved Weissenfels with Your Honor and my family can anyway never be compared with any other possible joys. But my past and continuing sickly condition robs me, alas, of such pleasant hours, and the advice of my family forbids me to undertake such a journey, on which, in their opinion, might hinge either a noticeable improvement or the complete ruin of my health. Nothing remains for me, therefore, but to beg Your Honor most obediently once again not to take my disobedience amiss or to hold it against me. For the same results not from lack of respect toward Your Honor, which, regardless, ever remains unchanged, but rather from a desire to spare my health, which the very Laws of Nature oblige us to do. If, meanwhile, Your Honor should kindly grant the repeated prayer of my beloved husband, to which I now add my own, and should graciously honor our house with Your Honor's most esteemed and most desired presence at the coming St. Michael's Fair, I assure Your Honor that for us all the greatest honor and pleasure would spring therefrom, and we should certainly conclude that we were boundlessly distinguished by the undeserved benevolence of Your Honor, with which wish and hope I remain my life long, with most obedient compliments to Your Honor's most beloved and honored Mamma,

Your Honor's and, My Most Highly Honored Sir Chamberlain and Highly Esteemed Patron, Your most humbly devoted servant

Leipzig, September . . . , 1741   Maria Magdalena Bach

In this draft, Johann Elias gave Anna Magdalena Bach the wrong first name. It should be noted that she recovered from her illness and in February of the following year gave birth to her last child, Regina Susanna.

Bach's Goldberg Variations Are Published

225. *Clavier-Übung,* Part IV, *Aria mit verschiedenen Veraenderungen,* BWV 988: title page (*BD* I, no. 172)

Keyboard Practice, consisting of an Aria with Divers Variations, for the Harpsichord with 2 Manuals. Composed for Music Lovers, to Refresh

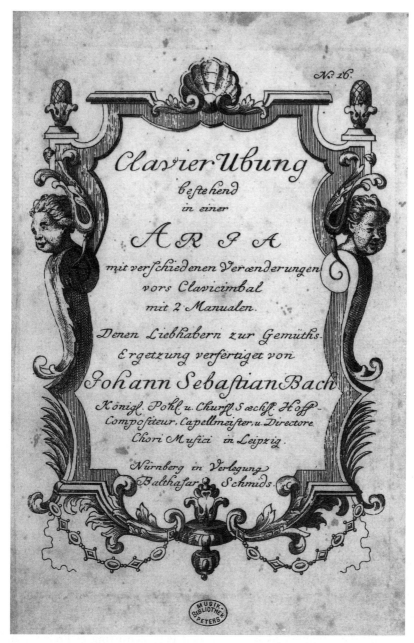

225. *Clavier-Übung,* Part IV, *Aria mit verschiedenen Veraenderungen,*
BWV 988: title page

their Spirits, by Johann Sebastian Bach, Royal Polish and Electoral Saxon Composer, Capellmeister, and Directore Chori Musici in Leipzig. Nürnberg: Published by Balthasar Schmid.

BACH IS THANKED BY HIS COUSIN
JOHANN ELIAS BACH

226. J. E. Bach's letter to Bach: draft or copy (*BD* II, no. 511)

I most dutifully report to Your Honor that the goodness of my God brought me happily to Zöschau on the second inst[ant] and has given me here such gracious patrons that I have already found it fitting to decline many favors, as was fitting; meanwhile, I can positively assure my most highly esteemed Cousin that nevertheless I will not be induced by this to forget the great kindness I enjoyed for several years in his household, but will on the contrary always remember it with grateful feelings and will, if possible, show myself grateful for it in deeds; and to the same end I will not cease to pray the Almighty daily in warm entreaty for the welfare of Your Honor's whole highly cherished household, and particularly to beg fervently for the lasting health of Your Honor. In the meantime, however, I return with many thanks the Roquelaur [coat] and fur boots most kindly lent me, which benefited me greatly on my journey, although they did not encounter rain or any other damage, and with my most obedient and devoted compliments to my most highly cherished Cousins, mother and daughter, as well as sons, I remain with appropriate respect,

Your Honor's etc. most obedient servant and cousin

November 7, 1742   [JOHANN ELIAS BACH]

BACH COMPLETES 24 MORE
PRELUDES AND FUGUES

227. *Das Wohltemperirte Clavier,* Book II, BWV 870–893: title page

The Well-Tempered Clavier's Second Part, consisting of Preludes and Fugues through all the tones and semitones, written by Johann Sebastian Bach, Royal Polish and Electoral Saxon Court Composer, Capellmeister and *Directore Chori Musici* in Leipzig.

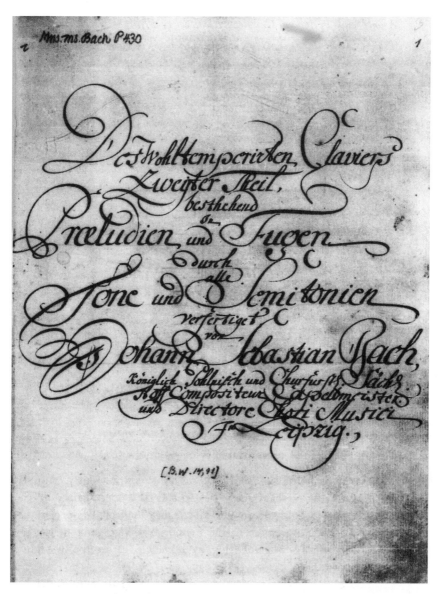

227. *Das Wohltemperirte Clavier,* Book II, BWV 870–893: title page
(in the hand of J. C. Altnickol)

A copy made by Johann Christoph Altnickol in 1744; the work was actually completed c. 1738–42.

BACH PARTICIPATES IN A BOOK AUCTION

228. Auction receipt (*BD* I, no. 123)

These *Teütsche und herrliche Schrifften des seeligen Dr. M. Lutheri* (which stem from the library of the eminent Wittenberg general superintendent and theologian Dr. Abraham Calov, which he supposedly used to compile his great German Bible; also, after his death, they passed into the hands of the equally eminent theologian Dr. J. F. Mayer), I have acquired at an auction for 10 thlr., anno 1742, in the month of September.

JOH. SEBAST. BACH

Here Bach acquired the principal German edition of Luther's collected works, 10 parts in 7 volumes (Altenburg, 1661–64); see also the listing in his estate, No. 279. Bach already owned a copy of Calov's "great German Bible" (see No. 165).

BACH PERFORMS SERVICES UNDER TERMS OF
THE NATHAN LEGACY

229. Bach's receipt for memorial service payment (*BD* I, no. 124)

Mr. Martin Simon Hille, mentioned several times previously, as present Inspector of the Nathan legacy, has on this date once again duly paid me the usual 5 gulden from the said legacy for [scholars of?] the St. Thomas School in respect to the memorial service sung in the said church; in witness whereof I hereby acknowledge receipt by signing with my own hand.

JOH. SEB. BACH
Leipzig, October 26, 1742   *Royal Court Composer*

230. Bach's receipt for St. Sabina's Day funeral song (*BD* I, no. 127)

The provisions of the annual legacy, called the Nathan legacy, have been completely fulfilled by the present Inspector Mr. Christoph Eulenberg, after the death of the former Inspector Mr. Hille, by the payment of the five Meissen gulden provided for in respect to the singing of a funeral song on St. Sabina's Day [Aug. 29]. In witness whereof I hereby testify and acknowledge receipt.

Leipzig October 27, 1744   JOH. SEB. BACH

The legacy was established by Sabine Nathan of Leipzig (d. 1612), from which the St. Thomas cantor and his choirboys received annual payments.

BACH WRITES TESTIMONIALS FOR
TWO STUDENTS

231. Bach's testimonial on behalf of Johann Georg Heinrich
(*BD* I, no. 79)

Whereas the bearer, Mr. Johann Georg Heinrich, *J*[*uris*] *U*[*triusque*] *Studiosus,* has requested me, the undersigned, to give him an impartial testimonial concerning the diligence and conduct he has shown among us here at the St. Thomas School; now, therefore, I have not wished to deny him the same, but rather to testify that he has always conducted himself as a diligent and willing student, and, moreover, in the private lessons he has had with me has devoted himself with much zeal to the *studium musicum,* so that I am persuaded that his ability will give satisfaction.

JOH. SEB. BACH
Royal Polish and Electoral Saxon
Court Composer

Leipzig, May 13, 1742

J. G. Heinrich apparently resubmitted Bach's testimonial two years later, for he changed the original date to 1744.

232. Bach's testimonial on behalf of Christian Gottlob Wunsch
(*BD* I, no. 78)

Whereas *Mons.* Christian Gottlob Wunsch, native of Joachim Stein, near Radmeritz, in the Upper Lausitz, *Stud. Jur.* and student of music, has requested me, the undersigned, to give him an official testimonial concerning the two years of instruction he has had from me in music, and particularly on the clavier; now, therefore, I have not been able to refuse him the same, but must rather testify with good reason to the truth, namely, that (without missing a single lesson devoted to the

Stud[*ium*] *Mus*[*icum*]) he has expended great diligence and effort to make himself fit to be of useful service in the future to God and the *res publica.* Accordingly, I am confident that on the proper occasion he will show that he has not spent the time without profit.

JOH. SEBAST. BACH
Royal Polish and Electoral Saxon
Court Composer

Leipzig, December 16, 1743

BACH RECEIVES LIQUOR TAX REVENUES

233. Bach's receipt to the liquor tax collector (*BD* I, no. 125)

That I have duly received from Mr. Christian Friedrich Henrici, regularly appointed Assessment and Liquor Tax Collector of His Royal Majesty in Poland and His Serene Electoral Highness in Saxony, in accordance with the Electoral Saxon Regulation of November 9, 1646, for the period from Low Sunday, 1742, to the same, 1743, the tax amount for three barrels @ 40 groschen, making altogether 5 thlr., say five thaler, in legal tender coins: this I herewith acknowledge and with due thanks give a receipt for the same.

Low Sunday, 1743, at Leipzig   JOH. SEBAST. BACH

See also No. 156.

BACH AUDITIONS CARL FRIEDRICH PFAFFE FOR
ASSISTANT TOWN PIPER

234. Bach's report on Pfaffe (*BD* I, no. 80)

At the command of a Most Noble and Most Worthy Council, Carl Friedrich Pfaffe, hitherto apprentice to Your Honors' Town Pipers, has taken his trial examination in the presence of the other Town Musicians; whereupon it was found that he performed quite well and to the applause of all those present on all the instruments that are customarily employed by the Town Pipers—namely, Violin, *Hautbois, Flute Travers., Trompette, Waldhorn,* and the remaining bass instruments—and he was found quite suited to the post of assistant that he seeks.

Leipzig, July 24, 1745   JOHANN SEBASTIAN BACH

BACH EXAMINES THE NEW JOHANN SCHEIBE
ORGAN IN ZSCHORTAU

235. Bach's report on the organ (*BD* I, no. 89)

Whereas the Most Noble Gentleman, Mr. Heinrich August Sahrer von Sahr, Hereditary Liege Lord and Magistrate at Zschortau and Binsen, as Most Respected Church Patron of the Church at Zschortau, has requested me, the undersigned, to go through and examine the organ, newly built in the said Church by Mr. Johann Scheibe, of Leipzig; and I accordingly, in the presence of the said Lord of Sahr, have gone through the same piece by piece, tried it out, and carefully compared it with the contract placed before me, drawn up between the Inspectors and Mr. Scheibe under the date of June 30, 1744; and I have found not only that the contract has been fulfilled in each and every part, and everything has been capably carefully, and well built, and that apart from a few little shortcomings, which Mr. Scheibe attended to on the spot at the trial, there are nowhere any major defects, but on the contrary the following stops, over and above the contract, have been found, and proved to be well made and good, namely:

1. *Quinta Thön*	of wood	16 foot	5. A *Coupler* for the manual
2. *Viola di Gamba*		8 foot	and pedal
3. *Fleute travers.*		4 foot	
4. *Super Octava,*	of metal,	1 foot	

Now, therefore, I have wished according to request, in the interests of truth and for the builder's good name, to testify by request [*sic*] to the same over my own signature and with my own seal affixed.

JOH. SEBAST. BACH
Royal Pol. and Elect. Sax.
Court Composer

Given at Zschortau, August 7, 1746

BACH EXAMINES THE ZACHARIAS HILDEBRANDT
ORGAN OF ST. WENCESLAS'S IN NAUMBURG

236. Report on the organ, by Bach and Gottfried Silbermann
(*BD* I, no. 90)

Whereas Your Most Noble and Most Wise Council of the Town of Naumburg has been graciously pleased to show us, the undersigned, the honor of having us inspect the organ in the Church of St. Wenceslas, which has been completely repaired and almost completely rebuilt by Mr. Hildebrandt, and to examine [this organ] in the light of the contract made in this respect for the same, which has been handed to us; accordingly, we have conscientiously and dutifully done so, and it has developed that:

Every part specified and promised by the contract—namely, manuals, bellows, wind chests, channels, pedal and manual action, with the various parts, registers, and stops pertaining thereto, both open and stopped, as well as reed—is really there;

Likewise each and every part has been made with care, and the pipes are honestly delivered in the material specified; nor should it remain unmentioned that an extra bellows and a stop named *Unda Maris,* not mentioned in the contract, have been provided. But it will be necessary that Mr. H. be requested to go through the entire organ once more, from stop to stop, and watch out for more complete equality both of voicing and of key and stop action. Once again we affirm that this is our conscientious and dutiful testimony, and we have signed this with our own hands and put hereunto our customary seals.

JOH. SEBASTIAN BACH
Royal Polish and Electoral Saxon
Court Composer
Naumburg, on September 27, 1746

GOTTFRIED SILBERMANN
Royal Polish and Electoral
Saxon Court and Official
Organ Builder

According to Adlung, the organ had three keyboards, with 41 sounding stops, and a pedal with 12 stops (ranging from 32-foot to 2-foot and including a 7-rank mixture); it cost 10,000 thaler.

BACH COMPOSES A CANON ON THE HARMONIC TRIAD

237. Canon for eight voices, BWV 1072: reprint of an album entry (*BD* III, p. 53; *NBA* VIII/1, p. 3)

Eight-part canon in contrary motion, for two choirs.
The harmonic triad [*Trias harmonica*]:

The date of this play on a single chord is not known. Since we owe its preservation to F. W. Marpurg, whose knowledge of Bach's works dates from the last years of the latter's life, it seems likely that the canon was written at that time—perhaps on the occasion of Marpurg's visit to Bach (see No. 357). The notation is reproduced from Marpurg's Treatise on the Fugue *of 1753–54. According to Marpurg, "The late Mr. Capellmeister Bach as author has given this canon the title 'Trias Harmonica, the harmonic triad, for no other harmony than this is contained therein' " (p. 97).*

BACH'S "SCHÜBLER" CHORALES FOR ORGAN ARE
PUBLISHED IN 1746

238. *Sechs Choräle,* BWV 645–650: title page (BD I, no. 175)

Six Chorales of Various Sorts, to be performed on an Organ with 2 Manuals and Pedal, composed by Johann Sebastian Bach, Royal Polish and Electoral Saxon Court Composer, Capellmeister and Direct. Chor. Mus. Lips. Published by Joh. Georg Schübler at Zella at the Thuringian Forest. To be had in Leipzig from the Capellmeister Bach, from his Sons in Berlin and Halle, and from the Publisher in Zella.

238. *Sechs Choräle,* BWV 645–650: title page

The publication date is unknown. According to the address given for W. F. Bach, it must have occurred after his move from Dresden to Halle (April 1746), but most probably only sometime in 1748.

BACH VISITS FREDERICK THE GREAT

239. Report in the *Spenersche Zeitung,* Berlin, May 11, 1747 (*BD* II, no. 554)

One hears from Potsdam that last Sunday [May 7] the famous Capellmeister from Leipzig, Mr. Bach, arrived with the intention to have the pleasure of hearing the excellent Royal music at that place. In the evening, at about the time when the regular chamber music in the Royal apartments usually begins, His Majesty was informed that Capellmeister Bach had arrived at Potsdam and was waiting in His Majesty's antechamber for His Majesty's most gracious permission to listen to the music. His August Self immediately gave orders that Bach be admitted, and went, at his entrance, to the so-called Forte and Piano, condescending also to play, in His Most August Person and without any preparation, a theme—for the Capellmeister Bach, which he should execute in a fugue. This was done so happily by the aforementioned Capellmeister that not only was His Majesty pleased to show his satisfaction thereat, but also all those present were seized with astonishment. Mr. Bach found the theme propounded to him so exceedingly beautiful that he intends to set it down on paper as a regular fugue and have it engraved on copper. On Monday, the famous man let himself be heard on the organ in the Church of the Holy Spirit at Potsdam and earned general acclaim from the listeners attending in great number. In the evening, His Majesty charged him again with the execution of a fugue, in six parts, which he accomplished just as skillfully as on the previous occasion, to the pleasure of His Majesty and to the general admiration.

BACH WRITES A TESTIMONIAL FOR
JOHANN CHRISTOPH ALTNICKOL

240. Bach's testimonial on behalf of Altnickol (*BD* I, no. 81)

That the bearer, Mr. Johann Christoph Altnickol, has since Michaelmas 1745 uninterruptedly taken part in the *chorus musicus,* performing now as violinist, now as violoncellist, but mostly as vocal bass, and has thus made up for the lack of bass voices at the St. Thomas School (which is owing to the fact that because of too early departure they cannot come to maturity), is hereby attested with my own hand.

Leipzig, May 25, 1747   JOH. SEBAST. BACH

See also the letters Bach wrote to Naumburg on behalf of his pupil and future son-in-law of his, Nos. 253 and 254.

BACH JOINS THE SOCIETY FOR MUSICAL SCIENCES AND COMPOSES TWO WORKS FOR THE SOCIETY

241. **Report in Lorenz Christoph Mizler's *Neu-eröffnete musikalische Bibliothek*, IV/1 (Leipzig, 1754) pp. 107–8**

Johann Sebastian Bach, Capellmeister and Music Director in Leipzig, joined the Society in the year 1747, in the month of June.

In the fifth packet [circulating among the members] of the Society, the late Capellmeister Bach presented a triple canon with six voices to be resolved.

242. **Canon for six voices, BWV 1076: reprint from 1746 portrait version** (*NBA VIII* / I, p. 3)

Triple canon for 6 voices, by J. S. Bach

242. Canon for six voices, BWV 1076

On the portraits of Bach painted by Haussmann, Bach is shown holding this canon, which was also printed separately for distribution among the members. The canon forms part of the series of fourteen Canons, BWV 1087; see also No. 251.

243. *Einige canonische Veraenderungen über das Weynacht-Lied, "Vom Himmel hoch da komm ich her,"* BWV 769: title page
(*BD* I, no. 176)

A few canonic variations on the Christmas hymn "From heaven high to earth I come," for the organ with 2 manuals and pedal, by Johann Sebastian Bach, Royal Polish and Electoral Saxon Court Composer, Capellm. and Direct. Chor. Mus. Lips. Nürnberg, published by Balth. Schmid, No. xxviii.

BACH PUBLISHES THE *MUSICAL OFFERING*,
DEDICATED TO FREDERICK THE GREAT

244. *Musikalisches Opfer,* BWV 1079: title page (*BD* I, no. 173)

Musical Offering to His Royal Majesty in Prussia &c. Most submissively dedicated by Johann Sebastian Bach.

245. Bach's dedication (*BD* I, no. 173)

MOST GRACIOUS KING!

In deepest humility I dedicate herewith to Your Majesty a musical offering, the noblest part of which derives from Your Majesty's Own August Hand. With awesome pleasure I still remember the very special Royal Grace when, some time ago, during my visit in Potsdam, Your Majesty's Self deigned to play to me a theme for a fugue upon the clavier, and at the same time charged me most graciously to carry it out in Your Majesty's Most August Presence. To obey Your Majesty's command was my most humble duty. I noticed very soon, however, that, for lack of necessary preparation, the execution of the task did not fare as well as such an excellent theme demanded. I resolved therefore and promptly pledged myself to work out this right Royal theme more fully and then make it known to the world. This resolve has now been carried out as well as possible, and it has none other than this irreproachable intent, to glorify, if only in a small point, the fame of a Monarch whose greatness and power, as in all the sciences of war and peace, so especially in music, everyone must admire and revere. I make

Einige canonische Veraenderungen
über das
Weynacht-Lied:
Vom Himmel hoch da
komm ich her.
vor die Orgel mit 2. Clavieren
und dem Pedal
von
Johann Sebastian Bach
Königl: Pohl: und Chur Sæchß: Hoff Compositeur
Capellm. u. Direct. Chor Muf. Lips.
Nürnberg in Verlegung Balth: Schmids

N. XXVIII

243. *Einige canonische Veraenderungen über das Weynacht-Lied,*
"*Vom Himmel hoch da komm ich her,*" BWV 769: title page

Muſicaliſches

Opfer

Sr. Königlichen Majeſtät in Preußen ꝛc.

allerunterthänigſt gewidmet

von

Johann Sebaſtian Bach.

244. *Musikalisches Opfer,* BWV 1079: title page

bold to add this most humble request: may Your Majesty deign to dignify the present modest labor with a gracious acceptance, and continue to grant Your Majesty's Most August Royal Grace to

Your Majesty's most humble and obedient servant,

Leipzig, July 7, 1747   THE AUTHOR

246. Entry in Johann Gottlob Immanuel Breitkopf's account books (*BD* II, no. 556)

> July 10, 1747. For the printing of a title on behalf of Mr. Capellmeister Bach, called Musical Offering, 200 copies royal [paper]   2 rthl. 12 gr.

247. Excerpt from a letter by Lorenz Christoph Mizler to Meinrad Spiess, September 1, 1747 (*BD* II, no. 557)

On my return by way of Leipzig spoke to Mr. Capellmeister Bach, who told me of his Berlin journey and the story of the fugue he played before the king, which will shortly be engraved in copper and a copy of which will appear in the packet of the Society. I have already seen the beginning of it.

Spiess, like Bach a member of the Leipzig-based Society of Musical Sciences, learned from Mizler, the society's secretary, that the new publication would be put in one of the packets regularly circulated among the society's membership (see No. 241).

248. Publication announcement in the *Extract der eingelauffenen Nouvellen,* Leipzig, September 30, 1747 (*BD* III, p. 656, no. 558a)

Since the Royal Prussian Fugue Theme, as announced on May 11 of the current year by the Leipzig, Berlin, Frankfurt, and other gazettes, has now left the press, it shall be made known that the same may be obtained at the forthcoming Michaelmas Fair from the author, Capellmeister Bach, as well as from his two sons in Halle and Berlin, at the price of 1 imperial taler. The elaboration consists 1.) in two fugues, one with three, the other with six obbligato parts; 2.) in a sonata for transverse flute, violin, and continuo; 3.) in diverse canons, among which is a *fuga canonica.*

BACH LEASES A CLAVIER TO A NOBLEMAN AND
PROVIDES LESSONS

249. Two Bach receipts for loan payments (*BD* I, nos. 132, 135)

a.   *Receipt*

That I, the undersigned, have again been paid by Ignatz Ratsch, Steward of the Count, etc., von Würben, the sum of one thaler, eight groschen, in advance for lending the clavier for a month from October 5 to November 5, I hereby acknowledge.

Leipzig, October 5, 1747   JOH. SEBAST. BACH

b.   *Receipt*

That I, the undersigned, have again been paid for the clavier for [illegible word] by Ignatz Ratsch, Steward of the Count, etc., von Werben, one r[eichs]thaler, eight groschen, I hereby duly acknowledge.

Leipzig, December 5, 1747   JOH. SEBAST. BACH
Id est 1 rthlr. 8 gr.

Eugen Wenzel, count of Wrbna-Freudenthal and a student at the University of Leipzig, rented an instrument for at least six months, June through December 1747, during which time he also received instruction from Bach.

250. Bach's receipt for a lesson (Trautmann, p. 84)

Receipt

That I, the undersigned, have again been paid by Ignatz Ratsch, Steward of the Count, etc., of Würben, the sum of six thaler for the clavier lesson given to the Count, I hereby properly acknowledge.

Leipzig, December 18, 1747   JOH. SEBAST. BACH.
That is 6 thlr.

BACH DEDICATES A CANON TO
JOHANN GOTTFRIED FULDE

251. Canon for five voices, BWV 1077 (*BD* I, no. 174; *NBA* VIII/1, p. 4)
Double canon upon the subject.

Symbolum [motto]:	With these notes to recommend
Christ will crown the Cross-bearers	himself to the Gentleman owning this book was the wish of
Leipzig, October 15, 1747	J. S. BACH

The subject is the same as in No. 242. On the motto, see the commentary on pp. 19–20.

251. Canon for five voices, BWV 1077

BACH WRITES MORE TESTIMONIALS FOR
JOHANN CHRISTOPH ALTNICKOL

252. Bach's testimonial on behalf of Altnickol (*BD* I, no. 82)

Since the bearer of this, Mr. Johann Christoph Altnickol, candidate in music, has asked me, the undersigned, to furnish him with a verified testimonial concerning the industry he has shown in the art of music, I have taken pleasure in carrying it out and attest that not only did the said Mr. Altnickol act for four years diligently as assistant for our *Chorus Musicus,* but he also has shown, in addition to his vocal performance, such outstanding work on various instruments as one could desire from an accomplished musician. A number of fine church compositions of his have found no less ample approval in our town. Inasmuch as he is in a position to administer commendably the office of a *Director Musices* or Organist, I have no doubt that God will induce favorably disposed patrons, who will not fail to consider his expertise and provide him, as the occasion arises, with their recommendation to promote his prospects in every possible manner. In sum, he is a disciple of whom I need in no way be ashamed.

Leipzig, January 1, 1748   JOH. SEB. BACH.
                                Royal Polish and Electoral Saxon
                                Court Compositeur *and*
                                Director Chori Musices *at Leipzig*

253. Bach's letter to the Naumburg town council recommending Altnickol (*BD* I, no. 47)

MOST NOBLE, HONORED AND MOST DISTINGUISHED, STEADFAST, HONORED AND MOST LEARNED AS WELL AS MOST WISE SIRS, MOST DEVOTEDLY AND HIGHLY TO BE ESTEEMED SIRS!

I still recall with the greatest pleasure the gracious confidence that a Most Noble and Most Wise Council of the Town of Naumburg placed in my humble self: once when my modest opinion was required in connection with the repair of your organ, and was then most kindly found acceptable; the other time when, by kind invitation, I duly attended in person the acceptance and trial of this organ. This confidence in me makes me so bold as to flatter myself that I shall receive from Your Honors' invaluable favor toward me the granting of a request. For in the absence of my dear former *ecolier* Mr. Johann Christoph Altnickol, at present organist and schoolmaster in Greiffenberg, I make bold to apply most humbly in his name and on his behalf for Your Honors' vacant post of organist, which is now about to be filled again. I assure you, Most Noble and Most Wise Sirs, that in the said Mr. Altnickol you will find a candidate who will fully satisfy your desires. For since he has already been in charge of an organ for some time, and has a good knowledge of playing and conducting, and especially understands perfectly how to treat an organ well and take proper care of it, which qualities are inevitably required of a good organist; since over and above this he has a quite exceptional ability in composition, in singing, and on the violin; therefore I am convinced that you, Most Noble and Most Wise Sirs, will never regret having honored the said candidate with your choice and having granted me my request. For my part I shall count this beneficence shown him as having been granted to me myself, and call myself while I live, with the greatest respect,

Most Noble, Honored and Most Distinguished, Steadfast, Honored and Most Learned as well as Most Wise Sirs, Your most obedient servant

JOH. SEB. BACH

Leipzig, July 24, 1748   *Royal and Electoral Court Composer*

For the report on the organ referred to by Bach, see No. 236.

254. Bach's letter to the burgomaster of Naumburg recommending Altnickol (*BD* I, no. 48)

MOST NOBLE SIR, MOST HIGHLY ESTEEMED SIR COMMISSIONER,

To Your Honor I first express my most obliged and obedient thanks for so kind a reception of my recent letter, and no less for the fact that Your Honor most graciously sent me assurance through the Treasurer, Mr. Sonnenkalb, that my humble request was to be granted. I shall my life long and with the greatest reverence admire this particularly high favor shown me. I make bold, however, to burden Your Honor once again with the enclosed; for when I first heard of the vacancy in the organist's post in Naumburg, and at once made up my mind to make humble application myself on behalf of Mr. Altnickol to Your Most Noble Honor and a Most Respected Council of the Town of Naumburg, I wrote at once about it, as well as about my decision, to the said former *ecolier* of mine, and reminded him at the same time to follow up as soon as possible my request with his own. Now, since Your Honor has let me know through the Treasurer, Mr. Sonnenkalb, that Mr. Altnickol's own declaration would be required, it is all the more agreeable to me that I have anticipated Your Honor's request, and am already in a position to convey herewith the memorial that he has sent me. If, then, Your Honor will extend to this communication, too, Your Honor's high protection, I shall consider myself obliged my life long to call myself

Your Honor's and My Most Highly to be Esteemed Sir Commissioner's and Councilor's most obedient and obliged servant

Leipzig, July 31, 1748   JOH. SEBAST. BACH

Altnickol received the appointment and shortly thereafter married Bach's daughter Elisabeth Juliana Friederica.

BACH WRITES A TESTIMONIAL FOR THE ORGAN
BUILDER HEINRICH ANDREAS CUNTZIUS

255. Bach's testimonial on behalf of Cuntzius (*BJ* 1977, p. 137)

Since Mr. Cuntzius, recognized for his art as an organ and instrument maker in Halle, has asked me, the undersigned, for a verified attestation of his skill in the construction of organs and other instruments, I could not refrain from executing such herewith. I therefore state that the work of said Mr. Cuntzius on organs and instruments is good and proper to the point of no possible reservation, and that one could wish only that all such work were carried out so capably, so that neither the House of God nor the connoisseurs of such musical instruments would henceforth be deluded by incompetents.

Leipzig, January 12, 1748   JOH. SEB. BACH,
                                                   Royal Polish and Electoral Saxon
                                                   Court Compositeur, *Capellmeister and*
                                                   Director Chori Musices *at Leipzig*

BACH WAITS IMPATIENTLY FOR A HARPSICHORD
FROM JOHANN GEORG MARTIUS

256. Bach's dunning letter to Martius (*BD* III, p. 627, no. 45c)

MR. MARTIUS
My patience is now at its end. How long do you think I must wait for the harpsichord? Two months have passed, and nothing has

changed. I regret to write thus to you, but I cannot do otherwise. You must bring it in good order, and within five days, else we shall never be friends.

Adieu

Leipzig, March 20, 1748   JOH. SEBAST. BACH

BACH WRITES TO JOHANN ELIAS BACH

257. Bach's letter concerning a copy of the "Prussian Fugue" (*BD* I, no. 49)

Monsieur J. E. Bach, Chanteur et Inspecteur du Gymnase a Schweinfourth.
p[ar] l'occasion

HONORED AND MOST NOBLE, MOST ESTEEMED COUSIN,

As time is short, I will say much in a few words, by invoking God's grace and support for a blessed vintage as well as for the blessed event soon to be expected. I cannot oblige you at present with the desired copy of the Prussian Fugue [from the *Musical Offering*], the edition having been exhausted just today, since I had only 100 printed, most of which were distributed *gratis* to good friends. But between now and the New Year's Fair I shall have some more printed, and if then my honored Cousin is still of a mind to have a copy, he need only give me notice on occasion, sending me a thaler at the same time, and his wish shall be fulfilled. In conclusion, with best greetings again from us all, I remain

Your Honor's devoted

Leipzig, October 6, 1748   J. S. BACH

P.S. My Son in Berlin already has two male heirs: the first was born just about the time we had (alas!) the Prussian Invasion [1745], and the second is about two weeks old.

Par l'occasion (on occasion) is a reference to the postal schedule.

258. Bach's letter concerning a cask of wine (*BD* I, no. 50)

A Monsieur,
Monsieur J. E. Bach, Chanteur et Inspecteur des Gymnasiastes de la Ville
Imperialle a Schweinfourth
Franquè Coburg

MOST NOBLE AND MOST ESTEEMED COUSIN,

That you and also your dear wife are still well I am assured by the agreeable note I received from you yesterday accompanying the excellent little cask of must you sent me, for which I send you herewith the thanks I owe you. It is, however, greatly to be regretted that the little cask was damaged, either by being shaken up in the wagon or in some other way, for when it was opened for the usual customs inspection here it was almost two-thirds empty, and according to the inspector's report contained no more than six quarts [*Kannen*]; and it is a pity that even the least drop of this noble gift of God should have been spilled. But, while I heartily congratulate my honored Cousin on the rich vintage he has garnered, I must acknowledge my inability, *pro nunc*, not [*sic*] to be in a position to make an appropriate return. But *quod differtur non auffertur* [deferred is not canceled], and I hope to have occasion to acquit my debt in some way. It is indeed to be regretted that the distance between our two cities does not permit us to pay personal visits to each other. Otherwise I should take the liberty of humbly inviting my honored Cousin to the marriage of my daughter Liessgen [Lizzy], which will take place in the coming month of January 1749, to the new organist in Naumburg, Mr. Altnickol. But since, owing to the remoteness I have mentioned and the unfavorable season, it will presumably not be possible for our honored Cousin to be with us personally, I will at least ask him the favor of assisting them with a Christian wish; whereupon I send best regards to my honored Cousin and remain, with best greetings to you from us all, Your Honor's wholly devoted and faithful cousin and most willing servant

Leipzig, November 2, 1748   JOH. SEB. BACH

P.S. Magister [Johann Abraham] Birnbaum was buried, as much as 6 weeks ago. *P[ro]. M[emoria]*. Although my honored Cousin kindly offers to oblige with more of the *liqueur,* I must decline his offer on account of the excessive expenses here. For since the carriage charges cost 16 groschen, the delivery man 2 groschen, the customs inspector 2 groschen, the inland duty 5 groschen, 3 pfennig, and the general duty 3 groschen, my honored Cousin can judge for himself that each quart costs me almost 5 groschen, which for a present is really too expensive.

BACH COMPOSES TWO CANONS FOR
AUTOGRAPH ALBUMS

259. Canon for seven voices, BWV 1078: album entry
(*BD* I, no. 177; *NBA* VIII/1, p. 4)

Canon upon Fa Mi in 7 parts, at the distance of a full measure
Fa Mi and Mi Fa are the whole of music

Leipzig, March 1, 1749

Sir Owner, You hardly fail to know that to remember a faithful friend means happiness; accordingly take the cultivator of the good art as your true friend.

The canon inscription contains acrostics for the names FABER and BACH. The capital letters I T stand for Isenaco-Thuringum *("from Eisenach in Thuringia"). The name FABER is also expressed by the note names F A B[♭] E and the R of* repetatur *("repeat"). In solmization, F and B♭ are called Fa; A and E, Mi.* Tempus *means, in the old terminology, a measure comprising one breve.*

    The canon was dedicated to Benjamin Gottlob Faber, a medical student at Leipzig University in the late 1740s and a friend of the Bach family.

    This canon survives in secondary sources only, in a copy by Johann Philipp Kirnberger and in Friedrich Wilhelm Marpurg, Abhandlung von der Fuge *(Berlin, 1754).*

260. Canon for two voices, BWV 1086: album entry (*NBA* VIII / 1, p. 4)

Perpetual canon, "Discordant Concord." By J. S. Bach.

This canon survives in an entry by Johann Gottfried Müthel, along with a canon of his own, in an album for his student Johann Conrad Arnold. Müthel's dedication reads, "When, dearest Mr. Arnold, you occasionally leaf through this book, remember kindly your former teacher, who will remain to the end of his life, with much esteem and love, Your true and sincere friend. Johann Gottfried Müthel. Riga, March 16, 1778."

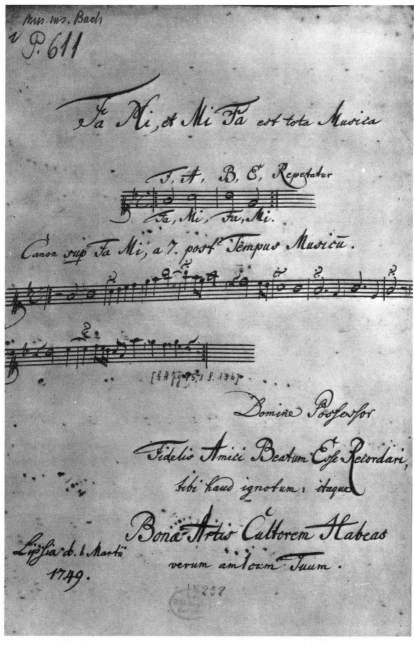

259. Canon for seven voices, BWV 1078: copy by J. P. Kirnberger

260. Canon for two voices, BWV 1086: album entry by J. G. Müthel

Bach Receives a Commission from
Count Johann Adam von Questenberg

261. **Excerpt from a letter to the count from Franz Ernst Wallis,
Leipzig, April 2, 1749** (*BJ* 1981, p. 26)

Your Excellency will not take offense at my failing to answer forthwith
Your kind communication from the 19th of last month. I have above
all been concerned to perform my assignment in good order, carrying
it out so that I may hope Your Excellency will be content with what has
been accomplished. Immediately after receipt of Your gracious letter, I
inquired in different places about Mr. Bach's residence and, the information having been obtained, the Lieutenant went to him in person in
order to transmit the messages, as reported in the letter. He was greatly
pleased to receive news from Your Excellency, as his generous benefactor, and asked me to forward the enclosed letter. However, he sent it to
me on Saturday, which, the mail having gone out, was late, so I had to
wait until today to give Your Excellency my humble report. The letter
of the *Herr Musique-Director* will convey the various matters that Your
Excellency has wanted to know.

BACH SELLS A FORTEPIANO

262. Bach's receipt for his payment (*BD* III, p. 633, no. 142a)

That to me, the undersigned, the payment of 115 rthl., written out one hundred and fifteen rthl. in *Lui blanc* [= 23 louis d'or], for an instrument called *Piano et Forte* which shall be delivered to His Excellency Count [Jan Klemens von] Branitzky in Bialastock [Bialystok, Poland], was properly handed over by Mr. [Barthelemy] Valentin here, I herewith attest. Leipzig, May 6, 1749.

Joh. Sebast. Bach.
Royal Polish and
Electoral Saxon Court Compositeur

BACH WRITES TESTIMONIALS FOR A STUDENT,
JOHANN NATHANAEL BAMMLER

263. Bach's first statement on behalf of Bammler, from the town archive, Eilenburg (*BJ* 1997, p. 38)

That the bearer, Mr. Johann Nathanael Bammler, has for ten years been an alumnus of the St. Thomas School; that he also has shown himself to be a diligent alumnus in letters as well as in music, is hereby attested and, at the same time, mentioned that as a prefect he applied himself well both *vocaliter* and *instrumentaliter.*

Leipzig, April 12, 1749   JOH. SEBAST. BACH
C[*antor*].

264. Bach's second statement on behalf of Bammler, from the town archive, Eilenburg (*BJ* 1997, p. 40)

That the bearer, Mr. Johann Nathanael Bammler of Kirchberg, *studiosus* of theology, has for ten years been an alumnus here at the St. Thomas School and conducted himself during that time as a faithful, diligent, and devout disciple, and has also equipped himself in letters and particularly in music so that I could fully entrust him with the prefect's office for the choirs, as he directed the church music of the second choir for three years and, for his last year in school, likewise served as prefect of the first choir, too, and conducted not only the motets but also, in my absence, the entire church music. This is hereby affirmed with my own hand.

Leipzig, December 11, *Anno* 1749   JOH: SEBAST: BACH.

GOTTLOB HARRER IS SUGGESTED AS AN
EVENTUAL SUCCESSOR TO BACH

265. Letter of introduction from Count Heinrich von Brühl, the Saxon prime minister, to Vice Chancellor Jacob Born for Harrer (*BD* II, no. 583)

MOST NOBLE, MOST ESTEEMED MR. VICE CHANCELLOR,

The bearer, who is the composer of my Capelle, Harrer, is the candidate I recommended to Your Honors when I was in Leipzig for the future filling of the post of *Capell-Director* there, upon the eventual occasion of the decease of Mr. Bach.

Since the said person is willing to perform in person a sample of the music of his composition there, and thus to show his ability in music, I have wished to beg Your Honors most kindly, not only to grant the said Harrer permission for the same, but also to give him every kindly assistance toward the attainment of his goal.

Your Honors may be assured that I for my part will neglect no opportunity whereby I shall be able to give a sincere token of that esteem with which I remain constantly Your Honors' devoted servant

Dresden, June 2, 1749   G[RAF] V[ON] BRÜHL

P.S. Since I do not doubt that the trial music to be performed by Mr. Harrer will meet with approbation, it would be agreeable to me if a certificate were to be issued to him, for his greater assurance that in the said eventuality he will not be passed over.

266. Excerpt from Johann Salomon Riemer's *Chronicle of Leipzig* on Harrer's trial performance (*BD* II, no. 584)

1749. On June 8, by order of a Noble and Most Wise Council of this Town, most of whom were present, the trial performance for the future appointment as Cantor of St. Thomas's, in case the Capellmeister and Cantor Mr. Sebastian Bach should die, was given in the large musical concert room at the Three Swans on the Brühl by Mr. Gottlob Harrer, *Capell-Director* to His Excellency the Privy Councilor and *Premier Ministre* Count von Brühl, with the greatest applause.

BACH THANKS COUNT WILHELM OF SCHAUMBURG-LIPPE
IN BÜCKEBURG FOR A MEMENTO

267. Bach's letter thanking the count (*BD* I, no. 54)

A sa Haut Excellence Illustrissime Monseigneur le Comte Regnante de Schaum-
bourg Comte et Noble Seigneur de la Lipps à Bükebourg

MOST HONORED IMPERIAL COUNT
GRACIOUS COUNT AND LORD!

Your Merciful Imperial Highness will graciously permit my pen to
present this message to Your noble eyes, inasmuch as I feel deeply
obliged to convey my humble thanks for the precious memento Your
Imperial Highness has sent me. Since Your Imperial Highness has
deemed to honor one of my family to be in the service of Your Highness, I send with this my son, hoping that he may be able to offer Your
Imperial Highness complete satisfaction. It is my humble desire that
both I and my son may further partake in Your gracious mercy,
remaining throughout my life, Most Noble Imperial Count, Your
Highness's

humble and obedient servant

Leipzig, October 27, 1749   JOHANN SEBASTIAN BACH

BACH SUPPORTS JOHANN GEORG SCHRÖTER IN A CONFLICT
WITH RECTOR JOHANN GOTTLIEB BIEDERMANN

268. Excerpt from a communication by Georg Friedrich Einike, cantor and music director at Frankenhausen (*BD* II, no. 592)

When Magister Biedermann [Rector in Freiberg] had published his
Programma de Vita musica, the late Capellmeister Bach some time thereafter sent a copy of it to Mr. Schröter, Organist in Nordhausen, and
requested him to review it and refute it, since he knew and could find
no one in these parts more capable of doing so.

Mr. Schröter at once declared himself ready to do so, prepared his
review, and sent it to Mr. Bach in Leipzig, leaving it to him whether
to have it included in the learned journals [doubtless an allusion to
Mizler's *Musikalische Bibliothek*] or in some other weekly. Mr. Bach
thereupon wrote me, on December 10, 1749:

"Schröter's criticism is well written, and to my taste, and it will soon
make its appearance in print. . . . Mr. Mattheson's [*Panacea, Being a*

Supplement to his Musical] *Mithridates* has made a big impression, as I am credibly informed. If further *refutationes* should follow, as I suspect, I do not doubt that the author's [i.e., Biedermann's] dirty ear [*Dreckohr*] will be cleansed and made more fit to listen to music."

Some time later, Capellmeister Bach sent on a few printed copies of the said review; but in such form that, as the copy herewith shows, it no longer resembled Mr. Schröter's original in the least but had many additions and many changes. Mr. Schröter, when he saw this gruesome mixture, could not help being offended about it and, under the date of April 9, 1750, bade me inform Mr. Bach "that the violent changes made in his criticism had offended him deeply"; further, "that his consolation in the matter was that no reader who was familiar with his way of writing or thinking, from other sources, could consider him the author of such a mixture, not to mention the unhappy title *Christian Reflections upon,* etc. For although his hastily written article contained nothing un-Christian, yet such a title was in no way suited to the matter in hand."

This message I conveyed word for word, in writing, to Capellmeister Bach, who, under the date of May 26, 1750, sent me the following answer:

"To Mr. Schröter please extend my compliments until such time as I am able to write, since I wish to disclaim the blame for the changes in his criticism, as they are not at all my fault; on the contrary, the same are entirely the fault of the man who took care of the publication."

Hereupon followed Mr. Schröter's answer of June 5, 1750:

"The Capellmeister Bach remains at fault, no matter how he twists or turns, now or in the future. But he can put a good and prompt end to this matter if he will (1) openly acknowledge that he is the author of the *Christian Reflections.* N.B. *mut[andis]* [changing whatever is to be changed]; (2) expose the fact that Rector Biedermann's principal aim, despite his title, was not at all directed to the praise of music and its kindred arts, and that the two and a half sheets of *Flosculi in laudem Musices* ["Flowerets in Praise of Music"] represent only a torn covering through which his unfriendly attitude toward the innocent art of music is clearly to be seen; (3) at the same time the unknown author of the *Reflections,* which are claimed to be 'honest,' must be challenged to identify himself.

"Indeed, such an action on the part of a Capellmeister would do Mr. Bach unusual honor, give our Mr. Mattheson an unexpected and well-merited pleasure, and contribute to the further growth of the noble art of music. This well-intended proposal is made, with the request that it be transmitted with most obedient compliments to Leipzig, by C. G. Schröter."

In accordance with my duty I could not do otherwise than to notify Capellmeister Bach accordingly. But since his death followed so soon afterward, I did not have the honor of receiving a reply from him.

This communication, containing fragments of letters by Bach which are not preserved otherwise, was printed by Mattheson in his Seven Dialogues of Philosophy and Music *(Hamburg, 1751). Schröter, the central figure in the correspondence, was an outstanding organist, writer, and instrument maker. E. L. Gerber, in his* Tonkünstler-Lexicon, *while acknowledging his ability as an organist, adds that "his manner could not possibly please those who knew Bach's* legato *manner of playing, for he played everything* staccato." *His ability as an organ builder appears from the testimonial of July 13, 1716, of which Bach was a co-signer. Schröter played an important part in the development of the piano. He was, like Bach, a member of the Musical Society, and wrote a summary account of the Scheibe controversy (No. 348).*

Dreckohr *is a pun on which Mattheson fastidiously comments (in French): "A base and disgusting expression, unworthy of a Capellmeister; a poor allusion to the word:* Rector."

BACH UNDERGOES EYE SURGERY

269. Reports in the *Berlinische Privilegirte Zeitung,* April 4 and April 7, 1750 *(BD* II, nos. 598–99)

a. Leipzig, April 1:

This Saturday past, and again last night, the Chevalier Taylor gave public lectures at the concert hall in the presence of a considerable assembly of scholars and other important persons. The concourse of people who seek his aid is astonishing. Among others, he has operated upon Capellmeister Bach, who by a constant use of his eyes had almost entirely deprived himself of their sight, and that with every success that could have been desired, so that he has recovered the full sharpness of his sight, an unspeakable piece of good fortune that many thousands of people will be very far from begrudging this world-famous composer and for which they cannot sufficiently thank Dr. Taylor. Owing to the numerous engagements the latter is obliged to discharge here, he will not be able to proceed to Berlin before the end of this week.

b. Leipzig, April 4:

Several people have so far called each day to seek the Chevalier Taylor's help. Among the many persons of both sexes and of various ranks and ages whom his skill has afforded council and consolation, his cures of the *medico* Dr. Koppen, of Capellmeister Bach, and of the merchant Herr Meyer have been so particularly successful as to do him honour. The many patients who call upon him have caused him to postpone his departure until next Tuesday morning, when he proposes to leave for Potsdam, and to reach Berlin the following day.

270. Excerpt from *The History of the Travels and Adventures of the Chevalier Taylor, Ophthalmiater, . . . Written by Himself* (1761), describing the operation (*BD* III, no. 712)

I have seen a vast variety of singular animals, such as dromedaries, camels, etc., and particularly at Leipsick, where a celebrated master of music, who had already arrived to his 88th year, received his sight by my hands; it is with this very man that the famous Handel was first educated, and with whom I once thought to have had the same success, having all circumstances in his favor, motions of the pupil, light, etc., but, upon drawing the curtain, we found the bottom defective, from a paralytic disorder.

In January 1750, when the operation took place, Bach was in his 65th (not 88th) year. The man with whom Handel had studied was Zachow, who had died in 1712.

BACH'S DEATH

271. Excerpt from the Leipzig burial register (*BD* II, no. 609)

1750. Thursday, July 30. A man, 67 years [*sic*], Mr. Johann Sebastian Bach, Capellmeister and Cantor of the St. Thomas School, died Tuesday. 4 minor children. Hearse *gratis.*

272. Announcement read from the pulpit of St. Thomas's, July 31, 1750 (*BD* II, no. 611)

Peacefully and blissfully departed in God the Esteemed and Highly Respected Mr. Johann Sebastian Bach, Court Composer to His Royal Majesty in Poland and Serene Electoral Highness in Saxony, as well as

Capellmeister to the Prince of Anhalt-Cöthen and Cantor in the St. Thomas School, at the Square of St. Thomas's; his dead body was this day in accordance with Christian usage committed to the earth.

The conflicting burial dates (Thursday, July 30 or Friday, July 31) are not reconcilable, but the second date seems more probable. Not only was the pulpit announcement made with reference to the second day of penance in 1750 (= Friday, July 31), but also the special tax due on Bach's oaken coffin was collected on July 31.

273. Death notice from the *Spenersche Zeitung,* Berlin, August 6, 1750 (*BD* II, no. 612)

Leipzig, July 31. Last Tuesday, that is, the 28th instant, the famous musician Mr. Joh. Seb. Bach, Royal Polish and Electoral Saxon Court Composer, Capellmeister of the Princely Court of Saxe-Weissenfels and of Anhalt-Cöthen, *Director Chori Musici* and Cantor of the St. Thomas School here, in the 66th year of his age, from the unhappy consequences of the very unsuccessful eye operation by a well-known English oculist. The loss of this uncommonly able man is greatly mourned by all true connoisseurs of music.

BACH'S SUCCESSOR AS CANTOR IS CHOSEN
AND INSTALLED

274. Excerpts from the proceedings of the Leipzig inner town council, July 29, 1750 (*BD* II, nos. 614, 615)

a.   *July 29, 1750*

The Cantor of the St. Thomas School in Leipzig, or rather the Choir Director, Bach, had likewise died, whereupon the following had presented themselves:

The son of the deceased, Mr. Bach, in Berlin.

Mr. Johann Trier, a student of theology and of music, possibly in regard to a post as organist.

Mr. Joh. Gottlieb Görner, Organist of St. Thomas's.

Mr. Gottlob Harrer, Director to His Excellency the *Premier Ministre,* Count Brühl, which candidate is strongly recommended by the said *Premier Ministre.*

Yesterday there presented themselves:

Mr. August Friedrich Graun, Cantor of the *Gymnasium* at Merseburg.
Mr. Johann Ludwig Krebs, Castle Organist at Zeitz.

The Vice Chancellor and Burgomaster, Dr. Born: He could hardly disregard
the recommendation, and therefore would cast his vote for Harrer.

The Councilor of the War Office, Burgomaster Stieglitz: The School needed
a Cantor and not a Capellmeister, although he must understand music.
Harrer had made excellent promises and had declared himself agreeable
to everything required of him. Partly on this account, therefore, and
partly in consideration of the high recommendation, he would cast his
vote for him. The Commissioner and Pro-Consul Dr. Masian also voted
for Harrer.

Comm. Dr. Trier	
Comm. Dr. Winkler	
Comm. Dr. Platz	
Comm. Winkler	} Likewise
Privy Councilor Richter	
Comm. Leistner	
Comm. Thomae	

b.   *Aug. 8, 1750*

His Magnificence the Consul Regens, Court Councilor Dr. Küstner,
laid the following matters before the assembly of the Three Councils:

I

It was known that the Court Clerk Mr. Engelschall had recently
departed this life, as a result of which one of the most important posts
had become vacant . . . [there follows a lengthy explanation of a proposal for filling this vacancy].

II

Consequent upon the death of the Cantor in the St. Thomas School,
Mr. Bach, the filling of his post must also be thought of. Six persons
had announced their candidacy, among whom the *Seniores* had chosen

Mr. Gottlob Harrer, who is the Director of the Capelle of
His Excellency, the Hon. Prem. Ministre Count von Brühl

and who had not only given a performance but also brought a recommendation from the said high Minister, had spent some time in Italy
and learned composition there, and who was willing to give the instruction that was expected of a Cantor. The others were all skillful musi-

cians, to be sure, but whether they were capable of the instruction was to be doubted. The question was then for the gentlemen to decide whom they wished to appoint Cantor of the St. Thomas School.

The Vice Chancellor and Burgomaster, Dr. Born: Thanked the governing Burgomaster for the care he had taken, and since neither post could long remain vacant, he wished to be brief and expeditious and to give his vote
1) for the Court Clerk of the City Courts, to Mr. Fleischer, and
2) for the Cantor of the St. Thomas School, to Mr. Harrer.

The Privy Councilor of the War Office and Burgomaster, Dr. Stieglitz: No delay could be afforded in filling these two positions.
1) The office of the court clerk . . . [there follows an appraisal of the situation].
2) Mr. Bach had been a great musician, it is true, but not a school teacher, so that a person must be sought to fill his place as Cantor of the St. Thomas School who would be skillful in both capacities; he believed that both could be found in Mr. Harrer, who had stated that he was master of both the Latin and the Greek languages, and had promised to accept willingly his subordinate place; therefore he wished to give him his vote for the post of Cantor of the St. Thomas School.

Commissioner Thomä	voted for 1) Mr. Fleischer [clerk]
Captain Richter	2) Mr. Harrer [cantor]
Councilor Hohmann	
Dr. Schubart	
Mr. Schmid	
Mr. Winkler	
Court Councilor Mencke	
Mr. Rimmel	
Dr. Küstner	

275. **Excerpt from Johann Salomon Riemer's** *Chronicle of Leipzig* **on the installation of the new cantor** (*BD* II, no. 624)

On September 29, that is, on Michaelmas, Mr. Gottlob Harrer, as Cantor called to St. Thomas's, held his installation music in both the principal churches and on the following October 2 was introduced in the customary fashion to the School here in the place of the late Mr. Johann Sebastian Bach.

BACH'S WIDOW, ANNA MAGDALENA, PETITIONS
THE LEIPZIG TOWN COUNCIL AND THE UNIVERSITY

276. Anna Magdalena Bach's petition to the council for a death benefit (*BD* II, no. 617)

YOUR MAGNIFICENCES, MOST NOBLE, STEADFAST AND MOST
LEARNED, AS WELL AS MOST WISE AND MOST HIGHLY ESTEEMED
SIRS!

Whereas it has pleased the inscrutable counsel and will of our otherwise
so loving Father in Heaven to take from his earthly life, a few days ago,
my dear husband, the Director of Music and Cantor of the St. Thomas
School here, in blessed death, and thus to leave me in the most sad
estate of a widow; and whereas it has for a long time been the custom
at the St. Thomas School for the widows of deceased Cantors to receive
a half-year's grace after the death of their husbands, and such was
enjoyed by my predecessor the Widow Kuhnau, and before her by the
Widow Schall [Schelle]; now, therefore, I make bold humbly to address
Your Magnificences and You, Most Noble and Most Wise Sirs, with
the most obedient prayer that Your Honors will deign, by virtue of
Your Honors' inborn condescension and world-famous kindness, most
graciously to have the same high favor shown to me also; for which I
shall strive to be my life long, with all conceivable respect,

Your Magnificences' and, Most Noble, Most Honored, and Most
Wise Sirs, Your most obedient servant

ANNA MAGDALENA BACH

Leipzig, August 15, 1750 *Widow*

277. Anna Magdalena Bach's first petition to the university for guardianship of her children (*BD* II, no. 625)

RECTOR MAGNIFICUS, MOST WORTHY, MOST NOBLE, MOST LEARNED
IN THE LAW, MOST EXPERT, MOST DISTINGUISHED AND MOST WISE
SIRS, HIGH PATRONS!

Your Magnificence and You, Most Worthy and Most Noble Sirs, will
most graciously deign to permit it to be humbly brought to your attention that on July 28 of the current year my late husband, named Johann
Sebastian Bach, sometime Cantor at the St. Thomas School here, died
and left me with five [*recte:* four] minor children. Now, since it is
incumbent upon a mother, if she does not herself know whom to propose as guardian for her children, to apply within a certain time for the

appointment of a guardian, my most humble prayer goes forth to Your Magnificence and to You, Most Worthy and Most Noble Sirs, to have the graciousness to appoint and ordain at the earliest moment a guardian for my minor children.

For which I shall forever be, with all respect, Your Magnificence's and, Most Worthy and Most Noble as well Most Wise Sirs, Your humble and most obedient

ANNA MAGDALENA BACH
Widow

Leipzig, October 17, 1750

278. Anna Magdalena Bach's second petition to the university for guardianship of her children (*BD* II, no. 626)

RECTOR MAGNIFICUS, MOST WORTHY, MOST NOBLE, MOST LEARNED IN THE LAW, MOST EXPERT, MOST DISTINGUISHED AND MOST WISE SIRS, HIGH PATRONS!

Your Magnificence and You, Most Worthy and Most Noble Sirs, will remember that on the 17th of this month I most humbly applied for the appointment and ordination of a guardian for my children. Since, however, I have decided, with the consent of a Worshipful University, on the promise not to marry again, to take upon myself the guardianship of my children, namely: Johann Christoph Bach, 18 years old, Johann Christian Bach, 15 years old, Johanna Carolina Bach, 12 years old, Regina Susanna Bach, 9 years old,

Now, therefore, there goes forth to Your Honors my most duly humble prayer not only properly to constitute me the guardian of my said children but also, in regard to the forthcoming division of the estate of my deceased husband, to appoint Mr. Görner, *Director Musices* of a Worshipful University and Organist of St. Thomas's here, as co-guardian with me, but only as concerns the division.

For which I remain, in humility, Your Magnificence's and, Most Worthy and Most Noble Sirs, Your most humble

ANNA MAGDALENA BACH
Widow

Leipzig, October 21, 1750

The document bears this note: *"Resolved, October 21, 1750. Both to be done."*

J. S. Bach, who never became a citizen of Leipzig and throughout his life remained a citizen of Eisenach, had a special relationship with the University of Leipzig not only because of his regular service for the University (see No. 109f), but also because two of his sons had studied law there, Wilhelm Friede-

mann in the years 1729–33 and Carl Philipp Emanuel 1731–34. This gave his family the privileged status and legal protection of "university relatives" (Universitäts-Verwandte). *It is for this reason that the widow petitioned the rector and that the University functioned as probate court for Bach's estate.*

BACH'S ESTATE

279. "Specification of the Estate Left by the Late Mr. Johann Sebastian Bach, Formerly Cantor at the St. Thomas School in Leipzig, Departed in God July 28, 1750" (*BD* II, no. 627)

SPECIFICATIO

Ch. I

One share in a mine called Ursula Erbstolln at Klein

Vogtsberg, value		60 rthl.	— gr.	— pf.
	Total	60 rthl.	— gr.	— pf.

Ch. II: In Cash

(a) In Gold

One triple ducat		8 rthl.	6 gr.	— pf.
4 double ducats		22	—	—
1 *ditto* in the form of a medal		5	12	—
28 single ducats		77	—	—
41 ducats	Total	112 rthl.	18 gr.	— pf.

(b) In Silver Money
    (α) In Specie Thaler, Guilders, and Half-Guilders

77 species thaler		102 rthl.	16 gr.	— pf.
24 old guilders		16	—	—
1 half-guilder		—	8	—
	Total	119 rthl.	— gr.	— pf.

    (β) In the Form of Medals

No. 1. 1 triple species thaler		4 rthl.	— gr.	— pf.
No. 2. 1 double species thaler		2	16	—
No. 3. 2 species thalers at 1 rthl. 12 gr.		3	—	—
No. 4. 1 double species thaler		2	16	—
No. 5. 1 species thaler		1	8	—
No. 6. 2 species thaler with hooks		2	16	—
No. 7. 2 square species thaler		2	16	—
No. 8. 4 species thaler		5	8	—
No. 9. 2 guilders		1	8	—
No. 10. 1 piece		—	4	—
	Total	25 rthl.	20 gr.	— pf.

Ch. III: Debts Outstanding

A debt owed by Mrs. Krebs		58 rthl.	— gr.	— pf.
ditto Unruh		4	—	—
ditto Haase		3	—	—
	Total	65 rthl.	— gr.	— pf.

Ch. IV: Petty Cash on Hand

Petty cash		36 rthl.	— gr.	— pf.
	Total	36 rthl.	— gr.	— pf.

out of which some of the liabilities, which are specified on p. 8 a and b under Liabilities, Chs. I and II [see below, p. 255], have been discharged.

Ch. V: Silverware and Other Valuables

1 pair of candlesticks	16 oz. [32 *loth*] @ 1 rthl.	16 rthl.	— gr.	— pf.
1 pair *ditto*	13½ oz. @ 1 rthl.	13	12	—
6 matching cups	31½ oz. @ 22 gr.	28	7	—
1 *ditto*, smaller	5 oz. @ 1 rthl.	5	—	—
1 *ditto*, chased	6 oz. @ 1 rthl., 2 gr.	6	12	—
1 *ditto*, still smaller	5 oz. @ 22 gr.	4	14	—
1 goblet with cover	14 oz. @ 1 rthl., 2 gr.	15	4	—
1 big coffee pot	18 oz. @ 1 rthl., 2 gr.	19	12	—
1 *ditto*, smaller	10 oz. @ 1 rthl., 2 gr.	10	20	—
1 big tea pot	14 oz. @ 1 rthl., 2 gr.	15	4	—
1 sugar bowl with spoons	13 oz. @ 1 rthl.	13	—	—
1 *ditto*, smaller	7 oz. @ 1 rthl.	7	—	—
1 *tabatière* with a cup	6 oz. @ 1 rthl., 8 gr.	8	—	—
1 *ditto*, engraved	4 oz. @ 1 rthl., 8 gr.	5	8	—
1 *ditto*, inlaid		1	8	—
2 saltcellars	5½ oz. @ 1 rthl.	5	12	—
1 coffee dish	5½ oz. @ 1 rthl.	5	12	—
2 dozen knives, forks, and spoons in a case	24 oz. @ 1 rthl.	24	—	—
1 place setting, knife and spoon in a case	4½ oz. @ 20 gr.	3	18	—
1 gold ring		2	—	—
1 *ditto*		1	12	—
1 *tabatière* made of agate set in gold		40	—	—
	Total	251 rthl.	11 gr.	— pf.

Ch. VI: Instruments

1 veneered *Clavecin,* which if possible is to remain in the family		80 rthl.	— gr.	— pf.
1 *Clavesin*		50	—	—
1 *ditto*		50	—	—
1 *ditto*		50	—	—

1 *ditto,* smaller	20	—	—
1 *Lauten Werck* [lute-harpsichord]	30	—	—
1 *ditto*	30	—	—
1 Stainer violin	8	—	—
1 less valuable violin	2	—	—
1 *violino piccolo* [small violin]	1	8	—
1 *braccia* [viola]	5	—	—
1 *ditto*	5	—	—
1 *ditto*	—	16	—
1 *Bassetgen* [little bass]	6	—	—
1 violoncello	6	—	—
1 *ditto*	—	16	—
1 viola da gamba	3	—	—
1 lute	21	—	—
1 *Spinettgen* [little spinet]	3	—	—
Total	371 rthl.	16 gr.	— pf.

Ch. VII: Pewter

1 big bowl	1 rthl.	8 gr.	— pf.
1 *ditto,* smaller	—	16	—
1 *ditto*	—	16	—
1 *ditto,* smaller	—	8	—
1 *ditto*	—	8	—
1 small bowl	—	6	—
1 *ditto*	—	6	—
1 *ditto,* still smaller	—	4	—
1 *ditto*	—	4	—
1 *ditto*	—	4	—
1 wash basin	—	8	—
2 dozen plates, each @ ¾ lb.; @ 4 gr. lb.	3	—	—
4 pitchers with tin mounting	1	8	—
Total	9 rthl.	— gr.	— pf.

Ch. VIII: Copper and Brass

2 flatirons with plate [*Platt-Glocken nebst Eisen*]	3 rthl.	— gr.	— pf.
3 pair brass candlesticks	2	—	—
1 brass coffee pot	—	16	—
1 *ditto,* smaller	—	16	—
1 *ditto,* still smaller	—	6	—
1 brass coffee tray	—	16	—
1 copper kettle	—	8	—
1 *ditto,* smaller	—	8	—
Total	7 rthl.	22 gr.	— pf.

Ch. IX: Clothing, &c.

1 silver dagger [*Degen*]	12 rthl.	— gr.	— pf.
1 stick with silver mounting	1	8	—
1 pair silver shoe buckles	—	16	—
1 coat of *gros du tour,* which has been turned	8	—	—

	rthl.	gr.	pf.
1 funeral coat of *drap des dames*	5	—	—
1 cloth coat	6	—	—
Total	**32 rthl.**	**— gr.**	**— pf.**

Ch. X: Linen

	rthl.	gr.	pf.
11 shirts	— rthl.	— gr.	— pf.

Ch. XI: Home Furnishings

	rthl.	gr.	pf.
1 dresser	14 rthl.	— gr.	— pf.
1 linen chest	2	—	—
1 wardrobe	2	—	—
1 dozen black leather chairs	2	—	—
½ dozen leather chairs	2	—	—
1 writing desk with drawers	3	—	—
6 tables	2	—	—
7 wooden bedsteads	2	8	—
Total	**29 rthl.**	**8 gr.**	**— pf.**

Ch. XII: Theological Books

In Folio

	rthl.	gr.	pf.
Calovius, Writings, 3 volumes	2 rthl.	— gr.	— pf.
Luther's Works, 7 volumes	5	—	—
The same, 8 volumes	4	—	—
His Table Talk	—	16	—
His [recte: Chemnitz's] Examination of the Council of Trent	—	16	—
His Psalm Commentary, 3rd Part	—	16	—
His House *Postilla*	1	—	—
Müller's [Evangelical] Chain of Conclusions	1	—	—
Tauler's Sermons	—	4	—
Scheubler's [Spiritual] Gold Mine, II Parts 2 vols.	1	8	—
Pintingius [*Bünting*], Travel Guide to the Holy Scriptures,	—	8	—
Olearius, Principal Key to the Entire Holy Scriptures, 3 vols.	2	—	—
Josephus, History of the Jews	2	—	—

In Quarto

	rthl.	gr.	pf.
Pfeiffer, Apostolic School of Christians	1	—	—
His Evangelical Treasury	—	16	—
Pfeiffer's School of Marriage	—	4	—
His Apple of the Evangelical Eye	—	16	—
His Kernel and Sap of the Holy Scriptures	1	—	—
Müller's Sermons on the Injuries of Joseph	—	16	—
His Chain of Conclusions	1	—	—
His Atheism	—	4	—
His Judaism	—	16	—
Stenger's Postilla	1	—	—
His Foundations of the Augsburg Confession	—	16	—
Geyer's Time and Eternity	—	16	—
Rambach's Reflection	1	—	—

His Reflection on the Counsel of God	—	16	—
Luther's House *Postilla*	—	16	—
Frober's Psalm	—	4	—
Various Sermons	—	4	—
Adam's Golden Apple of the Eye	—	4	—
Meiffart's [Christian] Admonition	—	4	—
Heinisch's Revelation of St. John	—	4	—
Jauckler's Plumb Line of Christian Teachings	—	1	—

In Octavo

Francke's House *Postilla*	—	8	—
Pfeiffer's Evangelical School for Christians	—	8	—
His Anti-*Calvin*	—	8	—
His Christianity	—	8	—
His Anti-*Melancholicus*	—	8	—
Rambach's Reflection on the Tears of Jesus	—	8	—
Müller's Flame of Love	—	8	—
His Hours of Refreshment	—	8	—
His Counsel of God	—	4	—
His Defense of Luther	—	8	—
Gerhard's School of Piety, 5 vols.	—	12	—
Neumeister's Table of the Lord	—	8	—
His Doctrine of Holy Baptism	—	8	—
Spener's Zeal against Popery	—	8	—
Hunnius' Purity of Religious Instruction	—	4	—
Klinge's Warning against Desertion of the Lutheran Religion	—	4	—
Arnd's True Christianity	—	8	—
Wagner's Leipzig Hymn Book, 8 volumes	1	—	—

	Total	38 rthl.	17 gr.	— pf.

SUMMARY

Fol. 1. *a.* Ch. I	One Share	60 rthl.	— gr.	— pf.
Fol. 1. *a.* Ch. II.	In Cash:			
	(*a*) In Gold	112	18	—
Fol. 1. *a.* Ch. II.	(*b*) In Silver Money:			
	(α) In thaler, guilders, and			
	half-guilders	119	—	—
Fol. 1. *b.* Ch. II.	(β) In the form of medals	25	20	—
Fol. 1. *b.* Ch. III.	Debts Outstanding	65	—	—
Fol. 2. *a.* Ch. IV.	Petty Cash on hand, out			
	of which some of the			
	liabilities, specified on			
	Fol. 8 *a* and *b,* under			
	Liabilities, Chs. I and			
	II, were paid	36	—	—
Fol. 2. *a.* and *b.* Ch. V.	Silverware and other Valu-			
	ables	251	11	—
Fol. 3. *a.* Ch. VI.	Instruments	371	16	—

Fol. 3. *b*. Ch. VII.	Pewter	9	—	—
Fol. 3. *b*. and 4. *a*. Ch. VIII.	Copper and Brass	7	22	—
Fol. 4. *a*. Ch. IX.	Clothing, etc.	32	—	—
Fol. 4. *b*. Ch. X.	Linen, 11 shirts	—	—	—
Fol. 4. *b*. Ch. XI.	House Furnishings	29	8	—
Fol. 5. *a*. & *b.*, 6. *a*. & *b*.				
Ch. XII.	Theological Books	38	17	—

Grand total	1122 rthl.	16 gr.	— pf.
[*recte:*	1159]		

†

LIABILITIES

as extracted from the account books, of which some have been paid out of the money
listed in Ch. IV, p. 2 [see above, p. 251].

Ch. I: Statements

[18 items are listed, by number only.]	Total	143 rthl.,	21 gr.,	6 pf.

Ch. II: Other Necessary Expenses

For necessary things	1 rthl.	8 gr.	— pf.
Paid to Mr. Schübler	2	16	—
To the maid	4	—	—
For the appraisal	1	—	—

Total	9 rthl.	— gr.	— pf.

SUMMARY

Fol. 8. *a*. & *b*. Ch. I.	Statements	143 rthl.	21 gr.	6 pf.
Fol. 8. *b*. Ch. II.	Other Necessary Expenses	9	—	—

Grand total	152 rthl.	21 gr.	[6] pf.

Anna Magdalena Bach, widow
Dr. Friedrich Heinrich Graff, Trustee
Catharina Dorothea Bach
Wilhelm Friedemann Bach, for myself, and on behalf of my brother, Carl Philipp Emanuel
  Bach, and also as Trustee of my above-named sister
Gottfried Heinrich Bach
Gottlob Sigismund Hesemann, Trustee for the above-mentioned Bach
Elisabeth Juliana Friderica Altnickol, née Bach
Johann Christoph Altnicol, on behalf of myself and as spouse of and Trustee for my wife,
  Elisabeth Juliana Friderica, née Bach
Johann Gottlieb Görner, as Guardian, in the distribution of the paternal estate, for
  Johann Christoph Friedrich Bach
  Johann Christian Bach
  Johanna Carolina Bach
  Regina Susanna Bach

In an account of the distribution of the estate, dated November 11, 1750, which
in general adds nothing to our knowledge of Bach's possessions, it is stated that

"the youngest son, Mr. Johann Christian Bach, received 3 claviers with a set of pedals from the late departed during his lifetime, and still has them, and accordingly these were not listed in the Specificatio, *since he says he received them as a present from the deceased, and he has given the names of several witnesses of this fact. . . ."*

On the books (including their original German titles and extant exemplars), see Robin A. Leaver, Bach's Theological Library: A Critical Bibliography (Stuttgart, 1983).

BACH'S *ART OF FUGUE* IS PUBLISHED
POSTHUMOUSLY

280. A note written on the proof sheets by Johann Christoph Friedrich Bach [Leipzig, 1750] (*BD* III, no. 631)

"Canon p[er]. Augmentationem contrario motu."
NB: The late Papa had the following heading engraved on the plate, "Canon per Augment: in Contrapuncto all ottave," but he had crossed it out on the proof plate and put it in the above-noted form.

The engraver of the plates was J. G. Schübler (cf. No. 238). The payment due to him in 1750 (No. 279, under "Liabilities") apparently relates to his work on The Art of Fugue.

281. *Avertissement* by Carl Philipp Emanuel Bach in the *Critische Nachrichten aus dem Reiche der Gelehrsamkeit,* May 7, 1751 (*BJ* 1992, pp. 101–2)

Berlin.

The heirs of the late Mr. Johann Sebastian Bach, the great composer, erstwhile Royal Polish and Electoral Saxon Capellmeister and Music Director in Leipzig, have resolved to save from oblivion a work he left in manuscript and to issue it under the title *Die Kunst der Fuge, in 24 Exempeln entworfen durch Johann Sebastian Bach, ehemahligen Capellmeister, und Musikdirector in Leipzig* [The Art of Fugue, designed in 24 Examples, by Johann Sebastian Bach, former Capellmeister and Music Director in Leipzig]. Because of a dearth of well-executed examples, the mystery of fugue has for some time been rather scantily maintained. Great masters have often guarded it jealously. Those who were impelled to gain from them some insight had to gain it by ear, as it were. While the rules we were given were good and abundant, the needed examples were lacking. Yet one knows how fruitless instruction is without illustration, and experience shows what unequally greater advantage one draws from practical elaborations rather than from meager theoretical direction. The present work, which we announce to the public, is throughout practical and indeed accomplishes what many skillful men have suggested in their writing over the years. It is sufficient for the connoisseur to know that it comes from the famous Bach at Leipzig, whose recent death will be felt by admirers of true merit for some time to come. Those who have a concept of what is possible in art and who desire original thought and its special, unusual elaboration will receive from it full satisfaction. Such fugues as show no casual chance in their connection of notes, no unnecessary notes, and only well-justified, artful imitation are quite rare in our time. Nor does one believe it is saying too much to call this work a perfect work, since it contains all good manners of fugues and counterpoints, in two parts, three parts, four parts; with one, two, or more themes, inverted, retrograde, written in augmentation or in diminution; at the octave, tenth, twelfth; perpetual canons or canons in various other species, etc. All these manifold fugues are composed upon *one and the same principal theme, and in the same key,* namely, *D Minor* or *D La Re* with the minor third. Those who are knowledgeable in the history of music will admit that such a work, in which the entire study of fugue is so thoroughly elaborated upon a single theme, has so far nowhere appeared. Since all the parts involved are singable throughout, and one is as strongly worked out as the other, each part has been given its own system, with the appropriate clef, in score. What special understanding, however, one can attain of the art of composition by studying scores, both with respect to harmony and melody, those who have been fortunate in proving themselves will demonstrate with their examples. Nevertheless, everything has at the same time been arranged for use at the harpsichord [*Clavier*] or organ. The last pieces are two fugues for two keyboard instruments [*Clavier oder Flügel*] and a fugue with three themes, in which the author, writing the third theme, has displayed his name *Bach.* The conclusion is made with an appendix of a four-part church hymn, which the late author, during his last days, already deprived of his eyesight, dictated to the pen of a friend. Since this work comprises 70 copper plates in folio, and thus was very costly to produce, it is offered by subscription. *This will be valid from now until the Leipzig Michaelmas Fair and will be accepted in the principal bookstores of Germany upon the payment of 5 reichsthaler.* After that time, the work will not be sold under 10 reichsthaler. Copies will be surrendered after the period set for prepayment to the Subscribers without any further payment or cost, upon return of the certificate received on prepayment. The persons undertaking this [edition] obligate themselves to spare nothing concerning engraving, print, and paper to satisfy the public in these respects as well. Prepayment will be received at the *Haude und Spenerische* Bookstore.

282. Publication announcement by Carl Philipp Emanuel Bach in the *Leipziger Zeitungen,* June 1, 1751 (*BJ* 1992, p. 101)

It is herewith made to be known that *Avertissements* for the Art of Fugue in 24 examples, composed by Joh. Seb. Bach, former Capellmeister and Director of Music at Leipzig, are to be had in the most numerous and excellent bookstores in Germany. Since the work comprises about 70 plates and incurred much expense, a subscription price of 5 thaler for the volume, which is described with more detail in the *Avertissements,* will be accepted in the best bookstores, as well as from the Widow [Anna Magdalena] Bach in Leipzig, from Mr. Music-Director [Wilhelm Friedemann] Bach in Halle, from the Royal Chamber Musician [Carl Philipp Emanuel] Bach in Berlin, and from the organist [Johann Christoph] Altnicol in Naumburg. This subscription period extends until the forthcoming Leipzig Michaelmas Fair, at which time the work will be delivered without further cost against the subscription receipt.

283. *Die Kunst der Fuge,* BWV 1080: title pages (*BD* III, no. 645)

a. *Manuscript title page* (c. 1745)

The Art of *Fuga,* by Mr. Joh. Seb. Bach.

In the hand of Johann Christoph Altnickol, added as a supplement to the autograph score of the first version of the work, which was completed c. 1742.

b. *Title page of the first edition (1751)*

The Art of Fugue, by Mr. Johann Sebastian Bach, late Capellmeister and Music Director at Leipzig.

284. "Notice" on the back of the title page of the first edition, 1751 (*BD* III, no. 645)

The late Author of this work was prevented by his disease of the eyes, and by his death, which followed shortly upon it, from bringing the last Fugue, in which at the entrance of the third subject he mentions himself by name [in the notes B A C H, i.e., B♭ A C B♮], to conclusion;

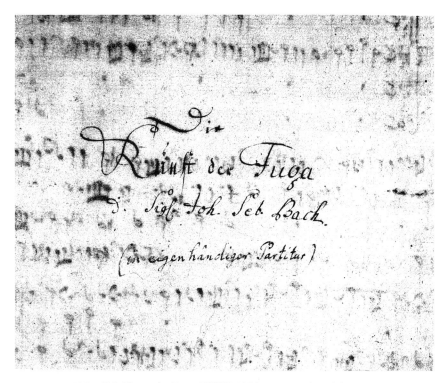

283a. *Die Kunst der Fuge*, BWV 1080: manuscript title page
(in the hand of J. C. Altnickol)

283b. *Die Kunst der Fuge*, BWV 1080: title page of the first edition

accordingly it was wished to compensate the friends of his muse by including the four-part church chorale added at the end, which the deceased man in his blindness dictated on the spur of the moment to the pen of a friend.

This notice was later replaced by an extended foreword by Friedrich Wilhelm Marpurg (No. 374).

285. A later note appended by Carl Philipp Emanuel Bach to the unfinished fugue, undated [Hamburg, 1780s] (*BD* III, no. 631)

NB. While working on this fugue, in which the Name BACH appears in the countersubject, the author died.

See facsimile, No. 298.

Bach's Music Manuscripts

Introductory Note

The documentation of "Bach's Life in His Own Writings" (Part II of this volume) makes no particular reference to what actually constitutes the vast bulk of Bach's writings. Telling and informative as we may consider the numerous letters, reports, testimonials, receipts, and other writings that relate to Bach's life and work, they cannot detract from the most significant documents penned by Bach, the manuscripts that record his music. Primarily because Bach's estate was divided after his death and much was subsequently lost, we will never know for sure how many works he actually composed over his creative life. Moreover, many works—especially keyboard and other instrumental compositions—have not come down to us in autograph sources. Yet what did survive in manuscript amounts to well over 20,000 pages of scores and performing parts, most of them autograph scores and copyists' performing parts prepared from the scores. The majority of these Bach manuscripts extant today are preserved in the Staatsbibliothek zu Berlin, Preußischer Kulturbesitz (D-SBB), which in the nineteenth century (when it was the Royal Prussian Library) systematically acquired Bach sources, most important among them the manuscripts from the estate of Carl Philipp Emanuel Bach.[1]

Bach's music hand shows a remarkably perfected kind of penmanship, and the character of his musical autographs has often been described as reflecting the qualities inherent in the music itself. The speed and care with which a manuscript was prepared varied according to its function, and the handwriting varies as well. Thus, one can differentiate between non-calligraphic and

---

1. Paul Kast, *Die Bach-Handschriften der Berliner Staatsbibliothek* (Tübingen, 1958), catalogs the Berlin holdings. Gerhard Herz, *Bach Sources in America* (Kassel, 1984), lists autographs and other Bachiana in American collections.

calligraphic manuscript types that represent sketches, drafts, composing scores, revision copies, and fair copies.[2] Whether hasty or careful, Bach's music notation shows a unique individuality that remained constant throughout the composer's life, but certain of its features, such as clefs, note symbols, and spacing, changed somewhat over the decades. And since Bach dated only a few of his works, his changing handwriting style often provides important clues about their time of origin.

FACSIMILES

The facsimiles on the following pages represent thirteen autograph pages of various manuscript types, arranged in chronological order.[3] These samples (together with the facsimiles of the several canon autographs in this volume) are complemented by handwriting specimens from three principal copyists whose work is frequently encountered among the manuscripts of Bach's music: Anna Magdalena Bach, his wife and collaborator; and Johann Andreas Kuhnau and Christian Gottlob Meissner, two students at the St. Thomas School who assisted Bach during his early Leipzig years.

2. For a classification of the handwriting types see Robert L. Marshall, *The Compositional Process of J. S. Bach: A Study of the Autograph Scores of the Vocal Works* (Princeton, N.J., 1972), vol. 1, pp. 3–30.

3. For a survey of Bach's handwriting with critical commentary see Yoshitake Kobayashi, "Die Notenschrift Johann Sebastian Bachs: Dokumentation ihrer Entwicklung," *NBA* IX/2 (Kassel, 1989).

286. *Wie schön leuchtet der Morgenstern,* organ chorale prelude, BWV 739; fair copy (1705 or earlier)

Berlin, Staatsbibliothek, Preußischer Kulturbesitz: *Mus. ms. Bach P 488,* f. 1ʳ

287. *Gott ist mein König,* cantata, BWV 71/1: fair copy (1708)

Berlin, Staatsbibliothek, Preußischer Kulturbesitz: *Mus. ms. Bach P 45,* f. 2ʳ

288. *Ich hatte viel Bekümmernis,* cantata, BWV 21: soprano part
(1714)

Berlin, Staatsbibliothek, Preußischer Kulturbesitz: *Mus. ms. Bach St 354*

289. *Bereitet die Wege, bereitet die Bahn,* cantata, BWV 132/1: composing score (1715)

Berlin, Staatsbibliothek, Preußischer Kulturbesitz: *Mus. ms. Bach P 60,* f. 1ʳ

290. Sonata in G Minor for Violin Solo, BWV 1001/2: fair copy
(1720)

Berlin, Staatsbibliothek, Preußischer Kulturbesitz: *Mus. ms. Bach P 967,* f. 2ᵛ

291. Magnificat, in E-flat Major, BWV 243a/1: composing score (1723)

Berlin, Staatsbibliothek, Preußischer Kulturbesitz: *Mus. ms. Bach P 38*, f. 1ʳ

292. *Sie werden aus Saba alle kommen,* cantata, BWV 65/1: sketches for opening chorus (1724) entered below final chorale of BWV 81.

Berlin, Staatsbibliothek, Preußischer Kulturbesitz: *Mus. ms. Bach P 147,* f. 7^r

293. Suite in G Minor for Lute, BWV 995/1: fair copy (c. 1727–1732)

Brussels, Bibliothèque Royale Albert I: *Fétis 2910*, f. 1ʳ

294. *Der Geist hilft unsrer Schwachheit auf,* motet, BWV 226: composing score (1729)

Berlin, Staatsbibliothek, Preußischer Kulturbesitz: *Mus. ms. Bach P 36,* f. 1ʳ

295. *St. Matthew Passion*, BWV 244/1, second version: fair copy (1736)

Berlin, Staatsbibliothek, Preußischer Kulturbesitz: *Mus. ms. Bach P 25,* f. 2ʳ

296. *The Well-Tempered Clavier,* Book II, Prelude in G Minor, BWV
885/1: fair copy (1739–1742)

London, British Library: *Add. MS 35021,* f. 12[r]

297. Mass in B Minor, *Symbolum Nicenum,* BWV 232/13: revision copy (1748–1749)

Berlin, Staatsbibliothek, Preußischer Kulturbesitz: *Mus. ms. Bach P 180,* f. 51ʳ

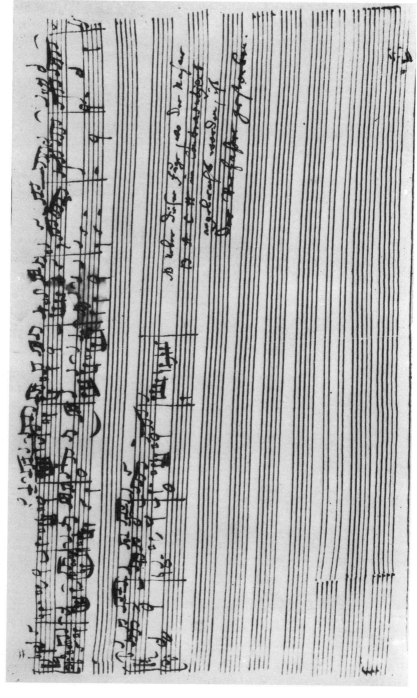

298. *The Art of Fugue*, BWV 1080/19: unfinished fugue, composing score (1748–1749)

Berlin, Staatsbibliothek, Preußischer Kulturbesitz: *Mus. ms. Bach P 200*, adnex 3, f. 5ʳ

299. Trio Sonata in C major for Organ, BWV 529/2: copied by Anna Magdalena Bach (c. 1727)

Berlin, Staatsbibliothek, Preußischer Kulturbesitz: *Mus. ms. Bach P 272*, f. 29ᵛ

300. *Himmelskönig, sei willkommen,* cantata, BWV 182 (Leipzig version): alto part, copied by Johann Andreas Kuhnau (1724), with emendations by Bach

Berlin, Staatsbibliothek, Preußischer Kulturbesitz: *Mus. ms. Bach St 47a*

301. *Herr Gott, dich loben alle wir,* cantata, BWV 130: alto part, copied by Christian Gottlieb Meissner (1724), with emendations by Bach

Houghton Library, Harvard University: bMS Eng 870 (35a)

PART III

Early
Biographical
Documents
on
Bach

Early Biographical Documents
on Bach

GENEALOGY

Introductory Note

The Bach family has been properly called a clan. When Johann Sebastian Bach's father died, the boy, not quite ten years old, found refuge in his elder brother's home. In later years, when he, in turn, had become firmly established, younger members of the clan came to stay with him, or in his vicinity. The first relative he took into the household that he had set up with Maria Barbara Bach, the cousin he had married, was Johann Bernhard Bach (Genealogy No. 41, Family Tree No. 43), who was the second son of the very brother in whose home Johann Sebastian had lived. This nephew had been going to school in Ohrdruf, but (as he himself explained) he had a poor memory, and his father had not considered it advisable for him to continue at school. Accordingly the boy was sent to his uncle, then "Concertmeister at Weimar, who was a very famous and able master on the clavier," and here the young Bernhard actually "advanced satisfactorily on the clavier as well as in composition." He later appears on the payroll of the Cöthen Capelle as a music copyist. After Johann Sebastian moved to Leipzig, Johann Ernst Bach (Genealogy No. 34, Family Tree No. 36) came to study at the St. Thomas School and Johann Elias Bach (Genealogy No. 39, Family Tree No. 41) at the university. The latter served during his years in Leipzig as secretary to his famous cousin.[1]

Johann Sebastian took an active interest in the history of his family, or at least of the musical members of it, for according to Carl Philipp Emanuel he was the author of the first draft of the present genealogy. This translation is

1. For a complete list of family members studying with Johann Sebastian Bach, see below, pp. 314–17.

based on two extant copies, both reprinted, which are virtually identical concerning events up to 1735—the year of the original from which both seem to have been made (see No. 303, entry 18). One, copied by Anna Carolina Philippina Bach, daughter of Carl Philipp Emanuel, was sent by the latter to Forkel in 1774, with his own additions and corrections, and these instructions: "Pray put this into good order, and do with it as you will. The first draft was written by my late father many years ago. With a clean pen, additions can be made to the family tree if something should be missing" (see also No. 394). The other copy seems to have been made by Johann Elias, and was preserved in the family of his brother, Johann Lorenz. It contains a few details not included in Carl Philipp Emanuel's copy. The text given here embodies all the information contained in both copies. All additions to the original version of 1735 are given in italics, those from Johann Lorenz's copy being enclosed in parentheses. A few dates have been supplied by the present editors, from other sources, in brackets.

Where Johann Sebastian gathered the information included in the Genealogy, and whether he also owned a family tree, we do not know. As noted earlier, Carl Philipp Emanuel sent a family tree to Forkel together with the Genealogy. Another, described as the family tree "of the famous Capellmeister [C. P. E.] Bach in Hamburg," was included in Johann Matthias Korabinsky, *Beschreibung der königlichen ungarischen Haupt-, Frey-, und Krönungsstadt Pressburg,* vol. 1 (Pressburg, 1784), pp. 110ff., because the Bachs were considered a Hungarian family. Still another tree (reprinted on page 285) was published in the *Allgemeine Musikalische Zeitung* (Leipzig, 1823). Since its numbers differ from those of the Genealogy, they have been added to the latter in brackets, to make it easier to find one's way through the maze of Bach family relations.

302. The Historical Bach Family Tree: two versions

a. [See p. 284]

Johann Elias / Johann Lorenz Bach version, the so-called Emmertsche Tafel *(ink and watercolor, c. 1750–60); for details, see Kock, pp. 13–34.*

b. [See p. 285]

Schematic version of lithographed tree published in the Allgemeine Musikalische Zeitung, *12 (1823); source: drawing—now lost—from the estate of Johann Sebastian Bach's student Johann Christian Kittel (1732–1809). The numbering systems used in the a and b versions are basically identical, differing only with respect to the youngest generation.*

303. "Origin of the Musical Bach Family": genealogical notes by Bach (1735), with additions by Carl Philipp Emanuel Bach and others (*BD* I, no. 184)

Additions by Carl Philipp Emanuel Bach are shown in italics, those by Johann Elias/Johan Lorenz Bach in parentheses, and those by the editors in brackets.

No. 1. Veit Bach, a white-bread baker in Hungary, had to flee Hungary in the sixteenth century on account of his Lutheran religion. Hence, after having converted his property into money, so far as might be, he moved to Germany; and, finding adequate security for the Lutheran religion in Thuringia, settled at Wechmar,[2] near Gotha, and continued in his baker's trade there. He found his greatest pleasure in a little cittern [*Cythringen*], which he took with him even into the mill and played upon while the grinding was going on. (*How pretty it must have sounded together! Yet in this way he had a chance to have time drilled into him.*) And this was, as it were, the beginning of a musical inclination in his descendants. He died the [8th of March 1619].

No. 2. Johannes Bach, son of the preceding, at first took up the trade of baker. But, having a particular bent for music, he was taken in as an apprentice by the Town Piper at Gotha. At that time the old Castle of Grimmenstein was still standing, and his master, according to the custom of the time, lived in the tower of the castle. He also remained in service to the aforesaid for some time after his apprenticeship was up; but after the destruction of the castle (which took place in Anno 15—),[3] his father Veit, in addition, having died in the meantime, he moved to Wechmar, married Mistress Anna Schmied, daughter of an innkeeper in Wechmar, and took possession of his father's property. From the time of his first settling there, he was frequently called to Gotha, Arnstadt, Erffurth, Eisenach, Schmalkalden, and Suhl to assist the town musicians of those places. Died in 1626 at the time of the rampant contagion. His wife, however, lived on for nine years as a widow, dying in 1635.

No. 3. His brother, [Caspar] Bach, became a carpet maker, and had three sons who learned music and who were sent on a journey to Italy by the reigning Count of Schwarzburg-Arnstadt, at the latter's expense, the better to cultivate music. Of these three brothers the youngest

2. The family name "Bach" is traceable in Wechmar, a small town located between Arnstadt and Gotha (and like Ohrdruf part of the county of Hohenlohe), also before 1550. However, relationships to Veit Bach cannot be established; cf. Kock, 243–48.

3. The correct date is 1567, which indicates that the story cannot be quite accurate.

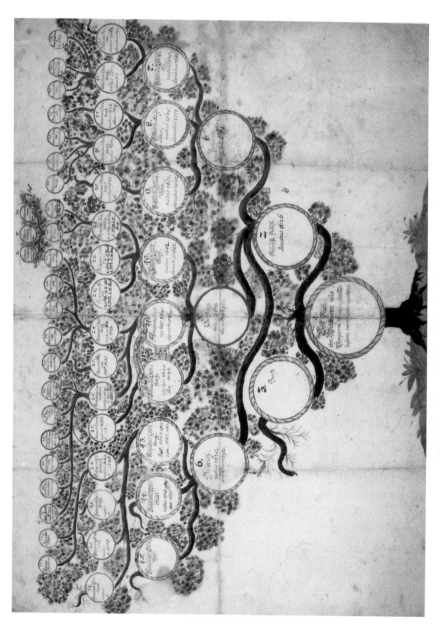

302a. The Historical Bach Family Tree, c. 1750–60

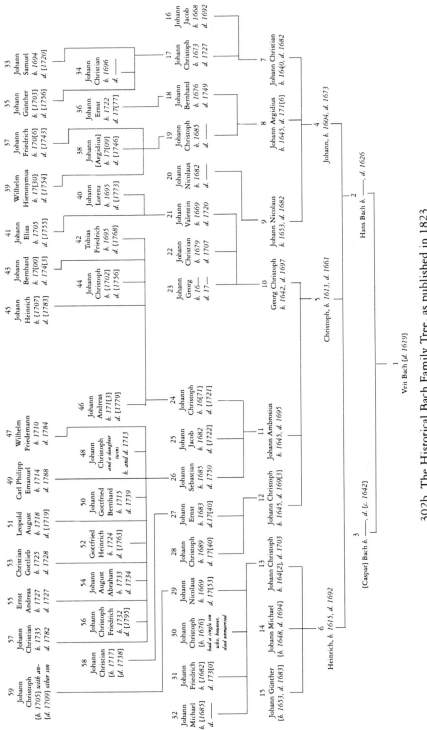

302b. The Historical Bach Family Tree, as published in 1823
(corrections and emendations are shown in brackets)

became blind as a result of an accident, and was called Blind Jonah; and of him many adventures used to be related. Now, since he died unmarried, it is presumably from his two brothers that the members of the family and bearers of the name were descended who formerly lived in Mechterstädt (lying between Eisenach and Gotha) and the places round about. The Capellmeister Johann Ludewig Bach, who died in Meinungen Anno 1730 [recte: died 1731] *and was born in 1677*, and whose late father, Jacob Bach, was Cantor in Suhl, *and was born in 1655*, was of this branch; likewise the Cantor of the Minster in Brunswick, Stephan Bach, who died a few years ago. (His brother ———— [Johannes Poppo] Bach was a minister in Lähnstädt, not far from Weimar.) There are also said to be some bearers of the name among the inhabitants of the lands of the Lords of Seebach, particularly in Opfershausen, but whether they belong to the branch of the family just mentioned is not known. *The son of the Capellmeister of Meinungen is still living there, as Court Organist and Court Painter; his son is engaged as his assistant in both capacities. Both father and son are excellent portrait painters. The latter visited me last summer and painted my portrait, catching the likeness excellently.*

No. 4. Johannes Bach, eldest son of Hans Bach, mentioned under No. 2 above, was born in Wechmar, Anno 1604, on November 26. Now, as his father, Hans Bach, often took him along when he was called to the various places mentioned above, it came about that on one occasion the old Town Piper in Suhl, named Hoffmann, persuaded the father to let his son be apprenticed to him, which was done; and the boy remained there for five years as apprentice and two years as journeyman. From Suhl he betook himself to Schweinfurth, where he became Organist. Anno 1635 he was called to Erfurth as Director of the Town Musicians, and he actually went there; after a few years he obtained the additional post of Organist *of the Prediger-Kirche*. Died in 1673. Was twice married: first to Mistress Barbara Hoffmann, daughter of his beloved master, by whom he had one stillborn son, whom the mother followed in death half an hour later; and second to Mistress Hedewig Lemmerhirt, daughter of Mr. Valentin Lemmerhirt, Member of the Council in Erfurth, by whom he had the sons listed under Nos. 7, 8, and 9 below.

No. 5. Christoph Bach, second son of Hans Bach, referred to under No. 2 above, was also born in Wechmar, Anno 1613, on April 19. He, too, made a study of instrumental music. Was at first in the service of the Court of Weimar; thereafter was appointed to the musical Compagnie of Erffurth, and finally to that of Arnstadt, where he died Anno 1661, on September 12. Was married to Mistress Maria Magdalena Grabler, a native of Plettin, in Saxony, by whom he had the three sons listed under Nos. 10, 11, and 12 below. She died in Arnstadt 24 days after the death of her husband, Christopher, that is, on October 6, 1661.

No. 6. Heinrich Bach, third son of Hans Bach, noted above under No. 2, was, like his elder brother Christoph, in the Compagnie at Arnstadt, and held in addition the post of Town Organist there. He was also born in Wechmar, Anno 1615, on December 16. Died at Arnstadt, Anno 1692. Was married to Mistress Eva Hoffmann of Suhl, presumably a sister of the Barbara Hoffmann mentioned under No. 4. *Was a good composer and of lively disposition.*

No. 7. Joh. Christian Bach, eldest son of Johann Bach (No. 4). Was born in Erffurth in 1640. Died there as Director of the Town Musicians Anno 1682. His two sons are listed under Nos. 16 and 17.

No. 8. Joh. Egydius Bach, the other son of Johann Bach (No. 4), was born in Erffurth in 1645. At his death there, Anno 1717 [*recte:* 1716], he held the posts of Director of the Town Musicians and Organist of St. Michael's Church. His two sons follow below under Nos. 18 and 19.

No. 9. Johann Nicolaus Bach, third son of Johann Bach (No. 4), was born in Erffurth in 1653. He was a very good player on the viola da gamba and belonged to the Town Compagnie there. He died of the plague in 1682, leaving a posthumous son, Joh. Nicolaus (No. 20).

No. 10. Georg Christoph Bach was the first son of Christoph Bach (No. 5), born Anno 1642 on September 6. Was called as Cantor to Schweinfurth, and died there Anno 16— *(April 24, 1697).* His sons are listed under No. 21. *N. B. Further information is lacking.*

No. 11. Johann Ambrosius Bach, second son of Christoph Bach (No. 5), was Court and Town Musician in Eisenach. Born in Erffurth, Anno 1645, on February 22. Died in Eisenach, Anno 1695. Was married to Mistress Elisabetha Lemmerhirt, daughter of Mr. Valentin Lemmerhirt, member of a Noble Council in Erfurth; by her he had eight children, namely, six sons and two daughters. Of these, three sons and the youngest daughter died unmarried; three sons and the eldest daughter survived the parents and were married (as follows in Nos. 22, 23, and 24).

No. 12. Johann Christoph Bach, twin brother of the aforesaid Ambrosius, and third son of Christoph Bach [No. 5], was Court and Town Musician in Arnstadt. He married Mistress Martha Elisabetha Eisentraut, daughter of Mr. Franz Eisentraut, former Sexton in Ohrdruf, and had by her the two sons mentioned below under Nos. 25 and 26.

N.B. These twins are perhaps the only ones of their kind ever known. They loved each other extremely. They looked so much alike that even their wives could not tell them apart. They were an object of wonder on the part of great gentlemen and everyone who saw them. Their speech, their way of thinking—everything was the same. In music, too, they were not to be told apart: they played alike and thought out their performances in the same way. If one fell ill the other did, too. In short, the one died soon after the other.

No. 13.[4] Joh. Christoph Bach, first son of Heinrich Bach (No. 6), was born at Arnstadt, Anno [1642]. He died in Eisenach, where he was Court and Town Organist, in 1703. He was a profound composer. He married Mrs. [Maria Elisabeth], née Wiedemann, the eldest daughter of Mr. [Johann] Wiedemann, Town Scribe in Arnstadt, and had by her the four sons given below under Nos. 27, 28, 29, and 30. *This is the great and expressive composer.*

No. 14.[5] Joh. Michael Bach, the second son of Heinrich Bach (No. 6), was also born at Arnstadt, Anno [1648]. He was Town Clerk and Organist in the Bailiwick of Gehren. Was, like his elder brother, an able composer. Left, at his death, a widow, namely, the second daughter of the Town Scribe Wiedemann of Arnstadt, and four unmarried daughters, but no son. [Died 1694.]

No. 15. Joh. Günther Bach, third son of Heinrich Bach (No. 6), acted as assistant to his father. Was a good musician and a skillful builder of various newly invented musical instruments. He died without male heirs Anno 16— [1683].

No. 16. Johann Jacob Bach, eldest son of Johann Christian Bach (No. 7), born in Erfurth in 1668. At his death, in 1692, he was unmarried, and serving as a Town Musician's Journeyman to the late Johann Ambrosius Bach [Johann Sebastian's father] in Eisenach.

---

4. J. G. Walther made the following entry in his *Musicalisches Lexicon,* 1732: "Bach (Joh. Christoph), for 38 years Organist at Eisenach, was the father of the three brothers, namely [1] the Organist at Jena, Mr. Joh. Niclas, who was born Anno 1669, October 10, succeeded to this position in the town just mentioned Anno 1695, and is particularly known for the claviers he builds; [2] the musician formerly living in Rotterdam, but now in England who is called Joh. Christoph and gives instruction on the clavier, having also sojourned previously for considerable time in Erfurt and Hamburg; and [3] the Organist at St. Blasius's Church in Mühlhausen, named Johann Friedrich, who died Anno 1730. Has composed various fine pieces for the clavier, and particularly for voices, which, however, have not been printed. Died March 31, 1703, in the sixtieth year of his life."

5. Note in Walther's *Musicalisches Lexicon:* "Bach (Joh. Michael), the brother of the aforementioned Joh. Christoph at Eisenach, former Organist and Town Clerk at Gehren, a hamlet and bailiwick at the Thuringian Forest, first father-in-law of Mr. Johann Sebastian Bach, has composed many church pieces and excellent sonatas [*starcke Sonaten*] and clavier pieces, but which likewise [see the preceding note] have not been printed."

No. 17. Johann Christoph Bach, second son of Joh. Christian Bach (No. 7). Born in Erffurth in 1673. Died in Gehren, where he was Cantor, in the year 1727. His children follow under Nos. 31, 32, and 33.

No. 18.⁶ Joh. Bernhard Bach, eldest son of Johann Egydius Bach (No. 8), was born in Erffurth Anno 1676. He is still living at the present time (that is, 1735), being Chamber Musician and Organist in Eisenach, as successor to Joh. Christoph Bach (No. 13). His only son is given below under No. 34.

No. 19. Joh. Christoph Bach, the other son of Joh. Egydius Bach (No. 8), was born in Erffurth in 1685. He still holds the post of Director of the Town Musicians in Erffurth. His sons follow under Nos. 35, 36, and 37.

No. 20. Joh. Nicholaus Bach, a posthumous son of Joh. Nic. Bach (No. 9), became a surgeon, and now lives 10 miles beyond Königsberg, in Prussia, in the Bailiwick of ———, but has a whole house full of children.

No. 21. Joh. Valentin Bach, son of Georg Christoph Bach (No. 10), (*was born Anno 1669, on January 6, at 3 o'clock in the afternoon. On May 1, 1694, he was accepted as Town Musician in Schweinfurth⁷ and there he died, Anno 1720, on August 12. His sons follow under Nos. 38, 39, 40.*) The names of his brothers are: [Joh. Christian and Joh. Georg].⁸

No. 22 [24].⁹ Joh. Christoph Bach, eldest son of Joh. Ambrosius Bach (No. 11). Was born in (*Eisenach*) in the year (*1671*). Died in Ohrdruf, where he was Organist and Schoolmaster, in 17—(*February 22, 1721*).

No. 23 [25]. Joh. Jacob Bach, second son of Joh. Ambros. Bach (No. 11). Was born in Eisenach Anno 1682. Learned the craft of Town Piper with the successor of his father, Mr. Heinrich Halle. After a few years, namely, Anno 1704, he entered the service of the Royal Swedish Army, as oboist *in the Guards.* Fate led him, with his Most Gracious King, Charles XII, after the unfortunate battle of Pultava, to the Turkish

---

6. Note in Walther's *Musicalisches Lexicon:* "Bach (Joh. Bernhard), eldest son of Mr. Aegydius Bach, former Senior of the Council Musicians of Erffurt, born November 23, 1676, became first Organist at the Merchants Church {*Kauffmanns-Kirche*}, went Anno 1699 in a similar function to Magdeburg, and Anno 1730 to Eisenach, where he still lives as Chamber Musician to His Highness the Prince."

7. Carl Philipp Emanuel's copy of the Genealogy calls him Cantor in Schweinfurth, presumably by mistake.

8. The Family Tree (Nos. 301a–b) supplies these names, which are missing in all copies of the Genealogy, under Nos. 22 and 23.

9. The numbers in brackets from this point on refer to the Family Tree, No. 302b.

town of Bender [on the Dniester, in Bessarabia]. There he remained with his King for eight or nine years; and then, a year before the King's return, he received permission to retire to Stockholm as Royal Chamber and Court Musician. There he died, Anno 17— [1722], without issue. *From Bender he journeyed to Constantinople, and there had instruction on the flute from the famous flutist Buffardin, who had traveled to Constantinople with a French Ambassador. This information was furnished by Buffardin himself when he once visited J. S. Bach in Leipzig.*

No. 24 [26].[10] Joh. Sebastian Bach, youngest son of Joh. Ambrosius Bach [No. 11], was born in Eisenach in the year 1685, on March 21. Became

(1) Court Musician, in Weimar, to Duke Johann Ernst, Anno 1703;
(2) Organist in the New Church at Arnstadt, 1704 [*recte:* 1703];
(3) Organist in the Church of St. Blasius in Mühlhausen, Anno 1707;
(4) Chamber and Court Organist in Weimar, Anno 1708;
(5) Concertmaster as well, at the same Court, Anno 1714;
(6) Capellmeister and Director of the Chamber Music at the Court of the Serene Prince of Anhalt-Cöthen, Anno 1717;
(7) Was called hence, Anno 1723, to become Music Director and Cantor at the St. Thomas School, in Leipzig; where, in accordance with God's Holy Will, he still lives and at the same time holds the honorary position of Capellmeister of Weissenfels and Cöthen (*as well as Royal Polish Court-Composer*). His family is listed below under *Nos. 45 to 57* [*recte: 45 to 50*]. *He died (from a stroke at Leipzig) in 1750 on July 28 (30).*

No. 25 [27]. Joh. Ernst Bach, first son of Joh. Christoph Bach (No. 12), born Anno 1683, on August 5, is Organist in Arnstadt in the Upper Church. His children are listed under Nos. [not included]. †[11]

No. 26 [28]. Joh. Christoph Bach, second son of Joh. Christoph Bach [No. 12], lives in Plankenhayn, and supports himself by conducting a general store *{Materialisten Kram}*, and is married but has no children. Born Anno 1687, September 12.

No. 27 [29].[12] Joh. Nicholaus Bach, now [1735] the Senior of all the living Bachs, is the eldest son of Joh. Christoph Bach (No. 13). Is Organist both at the University and at the Town Church in Jena. (*Was born in October 1669.*) † [1753.]

---

10. For Walther's biographical note on Johann Sebastian Bach, see No. 304.
11. Crosses were added, mostly by C. P. E. Bach, to indicate those members of the family who were dead at the time of writing—that is, in 1774, at the latest.
12. See also p. 288, n. 4.

No. 28 [30].[13] Joh. Christoph Bach, second son of Joh. Christoph Bach (No. 13), is also devoted to music. But has never taken on a regular position, seeking his greatest plaisir, rather, in traveling. †

No. 29 [31]. Joh. Friedrich Bach was the third son of Joh. Christoph Bach (No. 13). He died in the year 172– [1730], while holding the post of Organist of the Church of St. Blasius in Mühlhausen, in succession to J. S. Bach—without issue.

No. 30 [32]. Joh. Michael Bach, fourth son of Joh. Christoph Bach (No. 13), learned the art of organ builder; but he later journeyed to the Northlands and never returned, so that nothing further is known about him.

No. 31 [33]. Joh. Samuel Bach, eldest son of J. C. Bach (No. 17), died at an early age in Sondershausen, where he served as musician.

No. 32 [34]. Joh. Christian Bach, second son of J. C. Bach (No. 17), was also a musician, and also died at an early age in Sondershausen.

No. 33 [35]. Joh. Günther Bach, third son of J. C. Bach (No. 17), is a good tenor, and is now engaged as Schoolmaster at the Congregation of the Merchants' Church [*Kaufmanns Gemeinde*] in Erffurth.

No. 34 [36]. Joh. Ernst Bach, only son of Joh. Bernh. Bach (no. 18), was born Anno 1722. Will devote himself to music along with his [academic] studies. *Is Capellmeister of Weimar, but now lives away from the Court, very happily and quietly attending to his duties as Organist in Eisenach. Still receives a pension from the Court, and has sons, but presumably unmusical ones.*

No. 35 [37]. Joh. Friedrich Bach, eldest son of J. C. Bach (No. 19), is Schoolmaster in Andisleben.

No. 36 [38]. Joh. Egydius[14] Bach, second son of J. C. Bach (No. 19), is Schoolmaster in Gross Munra.

No. 37 [39]. Wilhelm Hyeronimus Bach, third son of J. C. Bach (No. 19).

No. 38 [40]. Joh. Lorenz Bach, eldest son of Joh. Valent. Bach (No. 21), *(born at Schweinfurth, Sept. 10, 1695)* is Organist at Lahme in Franconia.

---

13. Ibid.
14. The Family Tree gives this name erroneously as August.

No. 39 [41]. Joh. Elias Bach, second son of J. Valent. *(No. 21), (born at Schweinfurth on February 12, 1705, at 3 o'clock in the morning)* now Cantor in Schweinfurth. † *(divinity student, died as cantor and inspector in Schweinfurt)*

No. 40 [42].[15] Tobias Friedrich Bach, eldest son of Joh. Xtoph Bach (No. 22), is Cantor in Udestädt, not far from Erffurth. Born in 1695 *(on July 21).*† *His son has succeeded him.*

No. 41 [43]. Joh. Bernhard Bach, second son of the J. C. Bach just mentioned (No. 22), succeeded his late father as Organist in Ohrdruff. Born 169– *(November 24, 1700).* † *(Died June 12, 1743.)*

No. 42 [44]. Joh. Christoph Bach, third son of J. C. Bach (No. 22), is Cantor and Schoolmaster in Ohrdruff; born in the year 1—— (1702). † *(Died November 2, 1756.)*

No. 43 [45]. Joh. Heinrich Bach, fourth son of J. C. Bach (No. 22), is in the service of the Count of Hohenlohe as Musician and Cantor in Öhringen; was born in 17—(07).

No. 44 [46]. Joh. Andreas Bach, fifth son of J. C. Bach (No. 22), is in the military service of the Prince of Gotha as oboist. Born 17— *(September 7, 1713). He was later Organist in Ohrdruff, and is now dead.*[16]

No. 45 [47]. Wilhelm Friedemann Bach, eldest son of Joh. Seb. Bach (No. 24) is now [1735] Organist of St. Sophia's in Dresden. Born in 1710 on November 22. *Became Music Director and Organist in Halle, gave up his post, and lives without any position.*

No. 46 [49]. Carl Philipp Emanuel Bach, second son of Joh. Seb. Bach (No. 24). Is now living at Frankfurt-on-the-Oder as a student at the University and giving clavier instruction. Born March 14, 1714. *Cetera scis [the rest you know].*[17]

No. 47 [50]. Joh. Gottfried Bernhard Bach, third son of Joh. Seb. Bach (No 24), is Organist in Mühlhausen at St. Mary's or Upper Church. Born May 11, 1715. *Died 1739 in Jena.*

---

15. Johann Elias's copy inserts under No. 40: "J. Heinrich Bach, third son of Joh. Valentin, with those in Carl Philipp Emanuel's; the latter are used here.

16. Johann Elias' copy simply remarks: "He is now Organist in Ohrdruff."

17. A later addition in Johann Elias' copy reads "He was Capellmeister in Berlin, went from Berlin to Hamburg, there became Music Director on November 3 [1767], died in Hamburg, December 15 [14], 1788, at 10 o'clock in the night."

No. 48 [52]. Gottfried Heinrich Bach, fourth son of Joh. Seb. Bach (No. 24). Was born February 26, Anno 1724, likewise inclined toward music, particularly *clavier-playing. He had great talent, which, however, remained undeveloped. He died in 1761* [1763] *in Leipzig, or Naumburg.*[18]

No. 49 [56]. Joh. Christoph Friedrich Bach, fifth son of Joh. Seb. Bach (No. 24), was born June 21, 1732. *Is now Concertmaster to the Count of Bükeburg. Has a musical wife, and children who are musical.*

No. 50 [57].[19] Joh. Christian Bach, sixth son of Joh. Seb. Bach (No. 24), born in 1735 on the 5th of September. *Went, after our late father's death, to his brother C. P. E. in Berlin, who gave him his upbringing and his education. Journeyed in 1754 to Italy. Is now in England in the service of the Queen—between us, he has managed differently from honest Veit.*[20]

---

18. The latter is correct.
19. Altogether, Johann Sebastian Bach had the following children:

• with Maria Barbara (b. October 20, 1684 in Gehren, d. July 7, 1720 in Cöthen)

(1) Catharina Dorothea, baptized December 29, 1708, d. January 14, 1774

(2) Wilhelm Friedemann (No. 45), b. November 22, 1710, d. July 1, 1784

(3–4) Twins, Maria Sophia and Johann Christoph, b. February 23, 1713; son d. at birth, daughter buried March 15, 1713

(5) Carl Philipp Emanuel (No. 46), b. March 8, 1714, d. December 14, 1788

(6) Johann Gottfried Bernhard (No. 47), b. May 11, 1715, d. May 27, 1739

(7) Leopold Augustus, b. November 15, 1718, d. September 28, 1719

• with Anna Magdalena (b. September 22, 1701 in Zeitz, d. February 27, 1760 in Leipzig)

(8) Christiana Sophia Henrietta, b. spring 1723, d. June 29, 1726

(9) Gottfried Heinrich (No. 48), baptized February 27, 1724, buried February 12, 1763, at Naumburg

(10) Christian Gottlieb, baptized April 14, 1725, d. September 21, 1728

(11) Elisabeth Juliana Friderica, baptized April 5, 1726, d. August 24, 1781

(12) Ernestus Andreas, baptized October 30, 1727, d. November 1, 1727

(13) Regina Johanna, baptized October 10, 1728, d. April 25, 1733

(14) Christiana Benedicta, baptized January 1, 1730, d. January 4, 1730

(15) Christiana Dorothea, baptized March 18, 1731, d. August 31, 1732

(16) Johann Christoph Friedrich (No. 49), baptized June 23, 1732, d. January 26, 1795

(17) Johann August Abraham, baptized November 5, 1733, d. November 6, 1733

(18) Johann Christian (No. 50), baptized September 7, 1735, d. January 1, 1782

(19) Johanna Carolina, baptized October 30, 1737, d. August 18, 1781

(20) Regina Susanna, baptized February 22, 1742, d. December 14, 1809

20. Carl Philipp Emanuel's remark: *"inter nos, machte es anders als der ehrliche Veit"* has been interpreted as a disapproving allusion to Johann Christian's having embraced Roman

No. 51 [59].[21] Joh. Christoph Bach, eldest son of Joh. Nicolaus Bach (No. 27).

No. 52. (*Johann Christian*) Bach, second son of Joh. Nic. Bach (No. 27).

No. 53. Joh. Heinrich Bach, only son of Joh. Xtoph Bach (No. 28). He is a good clavier player. D[ied ca.]. 173[5]–.

BIOGRAPHICAL ACCOUNTS

304. "Bach (Joh. Sebastian)," entry in Johann Gottfried Walther's *Musicalisches Lexicon* (Leipzig, 1732) (*BD* II, no. 323)

Bach (Joh. Sebastian), Son of Mr. Joh. Ambrosius Bach, late Court and Town Musician at Eisenach; born in that place Anno 1685, March 21; learned the first *principia* on the clavier from his eldest brother, Mr. Johann Christoph Bach, formerly organist and schoolmaster at Ohr-druff; became organist, first, Anno 1703, in Arnstadt at the New Church, and Anno 1707 in Mühlhausen, at St. Blasius's Church; came Anno 1708 to Weimar, where he became Chamber Musician to His Serene Highness and Court Organist, and Anno 1714 Concertmaster; Anno 1717 Capellmeister to the Court of Cöthen; and Anno 1723, after the death of the late Mr. Kuhnau, Music Director in Leipzig; also Capellmeister to the Court of Saxe-Weissenfels. Of his excellent clavier works there have appeared, in copper engraving: Anno 1726 a Partita in B♭ major, under the title "*Clavier-Übung,* consisting of Preludes, Allemandes, Courantes, Sarabandes, Gigues, Minuets, etc." This was followed by the 2nd, in C minor; the 3rd, in A minor; the 4th, in D major; the 5th, in G major; and the 6th, in E minor, with which, presumably, the Opus ends. The Bach family is said to have originated in Hungary, and all those who have borne this name, so far as is known, are said to have devoted themselves to music; which perhaps springs from the fact that even the letters B' A' C" H' are melodic in their

---

Catholicism. But in such a use *"der ehrliche Veit"* means something like "simple old Veit." What Carl Philipp Emanuel probably meant to express was pride in the success and fame of his former pupil, Johann Christian, in contrast to Veit, the baker, who had amused himself by plucking a few notes on his poor little instrument. For Johann Christian had risen to the post of Music Master to the English Queen, was in great demand and highly paid as a teacher, directed one of the finest orchestras in the world, and dominated musical life in the English capital much as Handel had before him.

21. The Family Tree leaves space for a son of Johann Ernst. Johann Christoph Bach (No. 51) is the last member of the family represented in the tree.

arrangement.[22] (This *remarque* is the discovery of the Leipzig Mr. Bach [for correction, see No. 305].)

305. Manuscript additions in Walther's personal copy of his *Lexicon* (*BD* II, no. 323)

When on Sept. 14, 173[1] he played the organ at Dresden's St. Sophia's Church in the presence of all court musicians, the following verses were made about him:

A pleasant brook [*Bach*] may well the ear's delight inspire, . . . [see No. 307]

The 2nd Part of the *Clavier-Übung* consists of a Concerto in F major after the Italian Taste, and an Ouverture in B minor for a harpsichord with two manuals. These two pieces take up 14 large folios, and at the Easter Fair of 1735 they have come to light through copper engraving by Joh. Weigel's publishing house.

(His three sons from his first marriage are all good musicians. The 1st, Wilhelm Friedemann, is born Nov. [22] 1711 [*recte:* 1710], and since 173[3] organist at St. Sophia's Church in Dresden; the 2nd, Carl Philipp Emanuel, is born in March 1713 and stays in Frankfort-on-the-Oder; the 3rd, Johann Gottfried Bernhard, is born May 11, 1714, and lives now (1738) in Jena; where he died on May 30 [*recte:* 27], 1739, from a hot fever.)

[Regarding B'A'C"H':] (This *remarque* is the discovery of the Jena Mr. Bach [i.e., Johann Nicolaus, 1669–1753].)

OBITUARY

Introductory Note

Most of Bach's pupils were practical musicians like Bach himself, eager to become players and composers worthy of a post as organist, cantor, or capell-meister. Lorenz Christoph Mizler (1711–1778) must have cut a strange figure

22. "Walther relates that he [Bach] had observed that the notes B♭, A, C, and [B]♯ are melodious in their order; the last is by the Germans signified by the letter H: taking, therefore, this succession of notes for a point or subject, he wrought it into a fugue, as above is mentioned. Mr. John Christian Bach being applied to for an explanation of this obscure passage in Walther's memoir of his father gave this account of it, and in the presence of the author of this work wrote down the point of the fugue." [cf. *BD* III, no. 817.]
SIR JOHN HAWKINS 1776

among them. He was not much of a composer, being chiefly interested in theoretical and scientific matters. He studied at the University of Leipzig from 1731 to 1734 and took lessons from Bach during these years. He was given the master's degree for a dissertation showing "that musical art was a part of the education of a philosopher" (see Nos. 168–69). He continued his studies at Wittenberg and returned to Leipzig to give courses in philosophy, mathematics, and music. In 1743 he became the court mathematician of a Polish count, and later he moved to Warsaw, where he achieved high honors. In 1747 he received the M.D. degree from Erfurt University.

Mizler founded in 1738 the Society of the Musical Sciences (*Societät der musicalischen Wissenschaften*), an academy of outstanding musicians who had theoretical as well as practical accomplishments to their credit. Among the members were Handel, the only honorary member of the society; Telemann, who had been the first choice of the Leipzig councilors for the post ultimately given to Bach; Carl Heinrich Graun, the capellmeister of the Prussian court; and others. Bach, apparently after long hesitation, became a member in July 1747 (No. 241). In accordance with the laws of the society, he contributed his Canonic Variations[23] and a canon for distribution among the members.[24]

In 1736, Mizler began the publication of the *Neu-eröffnete Musikalische Bibliothek* (Newly Opened Musical Library), later called simply *Lorenz Mizlers Musikalische Bibliothek*—one of the first musical periodicals—which appeared at irregular intervals. It contained various references to Bach, for whom Mizler showed great reverence throughout his life,[25] and to the society. In Vol. 1, 1737, pp. 9–10, Mizler had written, ". . . Where can one find so excellent a lutenist as Mr. Weiss in Dresden? Where can other nations show such clavier-players as Handel and our Mr. Bach here . . . ?" (*BD* II, no. 404).

Mizler also contributed a sketch of his life to Mattheson's *Ehrenpforte* (Hamburg, 1740), containing the following sentences:

> His principal purpose is to make of music a scientific or scholarly pursuit [*in die Gestalt einer Wissenschaft zu bringen*] . . . .
>
> In composition his success was based on reading good books, listening to good music, perusal of many scores by good masters, and also on his association with Capellmeister Bach. He especially acknowledges that he has found much of value that he has been able to put to good use in the writings of the famous Capellmeister Mattheson.

23. See the translation of the title page, No. 243.

24. The canon (see No. 242) was included in the fifth "package" sent around among the members.

25. See his notes on Bach's thorough-bass playing (No. 327) and on Part III of the *Clavier-Übung* (No. 333), and his refutations of Scheibe (No. 346).

"Very well said!" remarks Mattheson, who has introduced Mizler on a rather polemic note, in which he speaks about his own inability to "blow the geometers' mathematical horn with them." But he cannot let it go at that, and annotates Mizler's remarks as follows: "The latter [Bach] was certainly and in truth just as little instrumental in teaching him the supposed mathematical bases of composition as the man to be named next [Mattheson himself]. This I can guarantee" (*BD* II, no. 470).

In the last installment ever issued (Vol. IV, Part I, 1754), there appeared an obituary, "Monument to Three Late Members of the Musical Society"; the last of these members was Bach. The authors of this obituary, the only comprehensive one bestowed upon Bach, are not named, but Carl Philipp Emanuel Bach later stated[26] that he had written it himself with the help of Johann Friedrich Agricola, another of Bach's pupils, who was at the time composer to the Prussian court.[27] Mizler himself was the author of the last four sentences, and the obituary was followed by a mourning ode, entitled *Singgedicht* ["Poem for a Cantata"], written by one of the members of the society, a truly pitiful doggerel. The obituary itself, however, remains the richest and most trustworthy early source of information on Bach's career.

306. **"The World-Famous Organist, Mr. Johann Sebastian Bach, Royal Polish and Electoral Saxon Court Composer, and Music Director in Leipzig," obituary by Carl Philipp Emanuel Bach and Johann Friedrich Agricola (1750,[28] published 1754)**
(*BD* III, no. 666)

Johann Sebastian Bach belongs to a family that seems to have received a love and aptitude for music as a gift of Nature to all its members in common. So much is certain, that Veit Bach, the founder of the family, and all his descendants, even to the present seventh generation, have been devoted to music, and all save perhaps a very few have made it their profession. This Veit had been expelled from Hungary in the sixteenth century for religious reasons and had later settled in Thuringia. Many of his descendants have also made their homes in that province. Among the many members of the Bach family who have excelled in practical music, as well as in the building of new musical instruments, the following, in addition to our Johann Sebastian, are particularly noteworthy for their composition: (1) Heinrich Bach, an

---

26. Letters to J. N. Forkel (Nos. 394–95).

27. See also his notes on Bach written for Adlung's *Musica Mechanica Organoedi* (1768), (No. 358). A note on Agricola is included in Forkel's biography of Bach (p. 457).

28. Mizler reported from Warsaw in March, 1751 (*BD* III, no. 637) that he had received Bach's obituary. Hence it must have been written by the end of 1750.

organist in Arnstadt, who died in 1692; (2) and (3) his two sons: Johann Christoph, Organist of the Court and Town of Eisenach, who died in 1703, and Johann Michael, Organist and Clerk in the district of Gehren, Johann Sebastian's first father-in-law; (4) Johann Ludewig Bach, Capellmeister to the Duke of Meiningen; (5) Johann Bernhard Bach, Chamber Musician and Organist in Eisenach, who entered into eternity in 1749. Of all these men we still have works at hand, bearing witness to their strength in vocal as well as instrumental composition. The aforesaid Johann Christoph, particularly, was strong in the invention of beautiful ideas as well as in the expression of the meaning of the words. His writing was, so far as the taste of his day permitted, *galant* and singing as well as remarkably polyphonous. To the first point, a motet written seventy-odd years ago, in which, apart from other fine ideas, he had the courage to use the augmented sixth, may bear witness; and the second point is borne out just as remarkably by a church piece composed by him for 22 obbligato voices, without the slightest violence to the purest harmony, as by the fact that both on the organ and on the clavier he never played in fewer than five real parts. Johann Bernhard wrote many fine *ouvertures* in the manner of Telemann.

It would be a matter for astonishment that such excellent men should be so little known outside their native land if one did not remember that these honest Thuringians were so well satisfied with their native land and with their station in life that they did not even dare to wander far to seek their fortune. They gladly preferred the approval of the rulers in whose domains they were born, and the approval of a throng of their faithful countrymen, who were close at hand, to the uncertain manifestations of praise that they might gather, at great pains and expense, from a few (perhaps even envious) foreigners. Meanwhile, the obligation we have of establishing and keeping fresh the memory of worthy men will sufficiently excuse us to those who may have found this little excursion into the musical history of the Bach family too lengthy. We return to our Johann Sebastian.

He was born in the year 1685, on March 21, in Eisenach. His parents were Johann Ambrosius Bach, Court and Town Musician there, and Elisabeth (née Lemmerhirt), daughter of a town official in Erfurth. His father had a twin brother named Johann Christoph, who was Court and Town Musician in Arnstadt. The two brothers were so much alike in every respect, even as concerns their health and their knowledge of music, that when they were together they could be distinguished only by their clothing.

Johann Sebastian was not yet ten years old when he found himself bereft of his parents by death. He betook himself to Ohrdruff, where his eldest brother, Johann Christoph, was Organist, and under this brother's guidance he laid the foundations for his playing of the clavier. The love of our little Johann Sebastian for music was uncommonly great even at this tender age. In a short time he had fully mastered all the pieces his brother had voluntarily given him to learn. But his brother possessed a book of clavier pieces by the most famous masters of the day—Froberger, Kerl, Pachelbel—and this, despite all his pleading and for who knows what reason, was denied him. His zeal to improve himself thereupon gave him the idea of practicing the following innocent deceit. This book was kept in a cabinet whose doors consisted only of grillwork. Now, with his little hands he could reach through the grillwork and roll the book up (for it had only a paper cover); accordingly, he would fetch the book out at night, when everyone had gone to bed and, since he was not even possessed of a light, copy it by moonlight. In six months' time he had these musical spoils in his own hands. Secretly and with extraordinary eagerness he was trying to put it to use, when his brother, to his great dismay, found out about it, and without mercy took away from him the copy he had made with such pains. We may gain a good idea of our little Johann Sebastian's sorrow over this loss by imagining a miser whose ship, sailing for Peru, has foundered with its cargo of a hundred thousand thaler. He did not recover the book until after the death of his brother [1721]. But did not this very passion to improve himself in music and the very industry applied to the aforesaid book perhaps by coincidence provide the first basis for the cause of his own death?—as we shall later hear.

After the death of his brother,[29] Johann Sebastian betook himself, in company with one of his schoolfellows, named Erdman, who not many years since departed this life as Baron and Imperial Russian Resident Minister in Danzig, to the St. Michael *Gymnasium* in Lüneburg.

In Lüneburg, our Bach, because of his uncommonly fine soprano voice, was well received. Some time thereafter, as he was singing in the choir, and without his knowledge or will, there was once heard, with the soprano tones that he had to execute, the lower octave of the same. He kept this quite new species of voice for eight days, during which he could neither speak nor sing except in octaves. Thereupon

29. Johann Sebastian actually went to Lüneburg in 1700, whereas his brother did not die until more than twenty years later.

he lost his soprano tones and with them his fine voice.

From Lüneburg he journeyed now and again to Hamburg, to hear the then famous Organist of St. Catherine's, Johann Adam Reinken. And here, too, he had the opportunity to go and listen to a then famous band kept by the Duke of Celle, consisting for the most part of Frenchmen; thus he acquired a thorough grounding in the French taste, which, in those regions, was at the time something quite new.

In the year 1703 he came to Weymar, and there became a musician of the Court. The next year he received the post of Organist in the New Church in Arnstadt. Here he really showed the first fruits of his application to the art of organ playing and to composition, which he had learned chiefly by the observation of the works of the most famous and proficient composers of his day and by the fruits of his own reflection upon them. In the art of the organ he took the works of [Nicolaus] Bruhns, Reinken, Buxtehude, and several good French organists as models. While he was in Arnstadt, he was once moved by the particularly strong desire to hear as many good organists as he could, so he undertook a journey, on foot, to Lübeck, in order to listen to the famous Organist of St. Mary's Church there, Diedrich Buxtehude. He tarried there, not without profit, for almost a quarter of a year, and then returned to Arnstadt.

In the year 1707 he was called as Organist to the Church of St. Blasius in Mühlhausen. But this town was not to have the pleasure of holding him long. For in the following year, 1708, he undertook a journey to Weymar, had the opportunity to be heard by the reigning Duke, and was offered the post of Chamber and Court Organist in Weymar, of which post he immediately took possession. The pleasure His Grace took in his playing fired him with the desire to try every possible artistry in his treatment of the organ. Here, too, he wrote most of his organ works. In the year 1714 he was named Concertmaster at the same Court. Now, the functions connected with this post then consisted mainly in composing church pieces and performing them. In Weymar he also trained various competent organists, among whom Johann Caspar Vogler, his second successor there, deserves to be especially noticed.

After the death of Zachau [1713], Music Director and Organist at the Market Church in Halle, Bach received a call to take his post. He did indeed journey to Halle and produced his trial work there. But he found reasons to reject this post, which thereupon was filled by [Gottfried] Kirchhof.

The year 1717 gave our already so famous Bach a new opportunity to achieve still further honor. Marchand, the clavier player and organist famous in France, had come to Dresden, had let himself be heard by the King with exceptional success, and was so fortunate as to be offered a highly paid post in the Royal service. The Concertmaster in Dresden at the time, [Jean-Baptiste] Volumier, wrote to Bach, whose merits were not unknown to him, at Weymar, and invited him to come forthwith to Dresden, in order to engage in a musical contest for superiority with the haughty Marchand. Bach willingly accepted the invitation and journeyed to Dresden. Volumier received him with joy and arranged an opportunity for him to hear his opponent first from a place of concealment. Bach thereupon invited Marchand to a contest, in a courteous letter in which he declared himself ready to execute *ex tempore* whatever musical tasks Marchand should set him and, in turn, expressed his expectation that Marchand would show the same willingness—certainly a proof of great daring. Marchand showed himself quite ready to accept the invitation. The time and place were set, not without the foreknowledge of the King. Bach appeared at the appointed time at the scene of the contest, in the home of a leading minister of state, where a large company of persons of high rank and of both sexes was assembled. There was a long wait for Marchand. Finally, the host sent to Marchand's quarters to remind him, in case he should have forgotten, that it was now time for him to show himself a man. But it was learned, to the great astonishment of everyone, that Monsieur Marchand had, very early in the morning of that same day, left Dresden by a special coach. Bach, who thus remained sole master of the scene of the contest, accordingly had plentiful opportunity to exhibit the talents with which he was armed against his opponent. And this he did, to the astonishment of all present. The King had intended to present him on this occasion with 500 thaler; but through the dishonesty of a certain servant, who believed that he could use this gift to better advantage, he was deprived of it, and had to take back with him, as the sole reward of his efforts, the honor he had won. Strange Fate! A Frenchman voluntarily abandons a permanent salary offered to him, amounting to more than a thousand thaler, and the German, to whom the former by his flight certainly seemed to have conceded the preference, cannot even obtain possession of the one special gift intended for him by the favor of the King. For the rest, our Bach willingly credited Marchand with the reputation of fine and very proper playing. Whether, however, Marchand's Musettes for Christmas Eve, the composition and playing of which is said to have contributed most to his fame in Paris, would have been able to hold the field before connoisseurs against Bach's multiple fugues: that may be decided by those who heard both men in their prime.

In this same year, after our Bach had returned to Weymar, the reigning Prince Leopold of Anhalt-Cöthen, a great connoisseur and amateur of music, called him to be his Capellmeister. He entered forthwith upon the duties of this post, which he filled for almost six years, to the greatest pleasure of his gracious Prince. During this time, about the year 1722, he made a journey to Hamburg and was heard for more than two hours on the fine organ of St. Catherine's before the Magistrate and many other distinguished persons of the town, to their general astonishment. The aged Organist of this Church, Johann Adam Reinken, who at that time was nearly a hundred years old, listened to him with particular pleasure. Bach, at the request of those present, performed extempore the chorale *An Wasserflüssen Babylon* at great length (for almost half an hour) and in different ways, just as the better organists of Hamburg in the past had been used to do at the Saturday vespers. Particularly on this, Reinken made Bach the following compliment: "I thought that this art was dead, but I see that in you it still lives." This verdict of Reinken's was the more unexpected since he himself had set the same chorale, many years before, in the manner described above; and this fact, as also that otherwise he had always been somewhat inclined to be envious, was not unknown to our Bach. Reinken thereupon pressed him to visit him and showed him much courtesy.

The town of Leipzig chose our Bach in the year 1723 as its Music Director and Cantor at the St. Thomas School. He heeded this call, although he was loath to leave his gracious Prince. Providence seemed to wish to remove him from Cöthen before the death of the Prince, which, contrary to all expectations, occurred shortly thereafter, so that he should at least no longer be present at this melancholy event. But he had the sad satisfaction of preparing in Leipzig the funeral music for the Prince whom he had so dearly loved, and of performing it in person in Cöthen [March 23–24, 1729].

Not long thereafter, the Duke of Weissenfels appointed him to be his Capellmeister; and in the year 1736 he was named Royal Polish and Electoral Saxon Court Composer, that is, after he had let himself be heard variously at Dresden, playing the organ publicly and with great success before the Court and the connoisseurs of music of that city.

In the year 1747 he made a journey to Berlin and on this occasion had the opportunity of being heard at Potsdam by His Majesty the King in Prussia. His Majesty himself played him a theme for a fugue, which he at once developed, to the particular pleasure of the Monarch, on the pianoforte. Hereupon His Majesty demanded to hear a fugue with six obbligato voices, which command he also fulfilled, to the astonishment of the King and the musicians there present, using a theme of his own. After his return to Leipzig, he set down on paper a three-voiced and a six-voiced so-called *ricercar* together with several other intricate little pieces, all on the very theme that had been given him by His Majesty, and this he dedicated, engraved on copper, to the King.

His naturally somewhat weak eye sight, further weakened by his unheard-of-zeal in studying, which made him, particularly in his youth, sit at work the whole night through, led, in his last years, to an eye disease. He wished to rid himself of this by an operation, partly out of a desire to be of further service to God and his neighbor with his other spiritual and bodily powers, which were still very vigorous, and partly on the advice of some of his friends, who placed great confidence in an oculist who had recently arrived in Leipzig. But the operation, although it had to be repeated, turned out very badly. Not only could he no longer use his eyes, but his whole system, which was otherwise thoroughly healthy, was completely overthrown by the operation and by the addition of harmful medicaments and other things, so that, thereafter, he was almost continuously ill for full half a year. Ten days before his death his eyes suddenly seemed better, so that one morning he could see quite well again and could also again endure the light. But a few hours later he suffered a stroke; and this was followed by a raging fever, as a victim of which, despite every possible care given him by two of the most skillful physicians of Leipzig, on July 28, 1750, a little after a quarter past eight in the evening, in the sixty-sixth year of his life, he quietly and peacefully, by the merit of his Redeemer, departed this life.

The works we owe to this great composer are in the first place the following, which have been made generally available by means of copper engraving:

(1) First Part of the *Clavier Uebungen,* consisting of six suites;
(2) Second Part of the *Clavier Uebungen,* consisting of a concerto and an overture for a harpsichord with 2 manuals;
(3) Third Part of the *Clavier Uebungen,* consisting of various preludes on some church hymns for the organ;
(4) An Aria with 30 Variations for 2 manuals;
(5) Six three-voiced preludes on as many hymns for the organ;
(6) Some Canonic Variations on the hymn *Vom Himmel hoch da komm ich her;*

(7) Two fugues, a trio, and several canons, on the above-mentioned theme given by His Majesty the King in Prussia; under the title *Musical Offering;*

(8) *The Art of the Fugue.* This is the last work of the author, which contains all sorts of counterpoints and canons, on a single principal subject. His last illness prevented him from completing his project of bringing the next-to-the-last fugue to completion and working out the last one, which was to contain four themes and to have been afterward inverted note for note in all four voices. This work saw the light of day only after the death of the late author.

The unpublished works of the late Bach are approximately as follows:[30]

(1) Five full annual cycles [*Jahrgänge*] of church pieces, for all the Sundays and holidays;

(2) Many oratorios, Masses, Magnificats, several Sanctus, secular cantatas [*dramata*], serenades, music for birthdays, name days, and funerals, wedding cantatas [*Brautmessen*]; and also several comic vocal pieces;

(3) Five Passions, of which one is for double chorus;

(4) Some double-chorus motets;

(5) A lot of free preludes, fugues, and similar pieces for organ, with obbligato pedal;

(6) Six trios for the organ with obbligato pedal;

(7) Many preludes on chorales for the organ;

(8) A book of short preludes on most of the church hymns, for the organ;

(9) Twice twenty-four preludes and fugues, in all keys, for the clavier;

(10) Six toccatas for the clavier;

(11) Six [English] suites for the same;

(12) Six more of the same, somewhat shorter [French suites];

(13) Six sonatas for the violin, without bass;

(14) Six of the same for the violoncello;

(15) Various concertos for one, two, three, and four harpsichords;

(16) Finally, a mass of other instrumental pieces of all sorts and for all kinds of instruments.

Our Bach was twice married. The first time with Mistress Maria Barbara, youngest daughter of the above-mentioned Johann Michael Bach, a worthy composer. By this wife he begot seven children, namely, five sons and two daughters, among whom were a pair of twins. Three of these children are still living, namely, the eldest, unmarried daughter, Catharina Dorothea, born in 1708; Wilhelm Friedemann, born in 1710, now Music Director and Organist at the Market Church in Halle; and Carl Philipp Emanuel, born in 1714, Royal Prussian Chamber Musician. After thirteen years of blissful married life with his first wife,

---

30. See the footnotes to Forkel's list of works, pp. 466–73.

the misfortune overtook him, in the year 1720, upon his return to Cöthen from a journey with his Prince to Carlsbad, of finding her dead and buried, although he had left her hale and hearty on his departure. The news that she had been ill and died reached him only when he entered his own house.

He took for his second wife, in Cöthen, in the year 1721, Mistress Anna Magdalena, youngest daughter of Mr. Johann Caspar Wülken, Court Trumpeter to the Duke of Weissenfels. Of thirteen children, namely, six sons and seven daughters, whom the latter bore him, the following six are still alive;

(1) Gottfried Heinrich, born in 1724;
(2) Elisabeth Juliane Fridrike, born in 1726 and married to the Organist of St. Wenceslas's in Naumburg, Mr. Altnikol, a skilled composer;
(3) Johann Christoph Friedrich, born in 1732, now Chamber Musician to the Imperial Count of Schaumburg-Lippe;
(4) Johann Christian, born in 1735;
(5) Johanna Carolina, born in 1737;
(6) Regina Susanna, born in 1742.
The widow is also still living.

This is the brief description of the life of a man who contributed quite exceptionally to the honor of music, of his fatherland, and of his family.

If ever a composer showed polyphony in its greatest strength, it was certainly our late lamented Bach. If ever a musician employed the most hidden secrets of harmony with the most skilled artistry, it was certainly our Bach. No one ever showed so many ingenious and unusual ideas as he in elaborate pieces such as ordinarily seem dry exercises in craftsmanship. He needed only to have heard any theme to be aware—it seemed in the same instant—of almost every intricacy that artistry could produce in the treatment of it. His melodies were strange, but always varied, rich in invention, and resembling those of no other composer. His serious temperament drew him by preference to music that was serious, elaborate, and profound; but he could also, when the occasion demanded, adjust himself, especially in playing, to a lighter and more humorous way of thought. His constant practice in the working out of polyphonic pieces had given his eye such facility that even in the largest scores he could take in all the simultaneously sounding parts at a glance. His hearing was so fine that he was able to detect the slightest error even in the largest ensembles. It is but a pity that it was only seldom he had the good fortune of finding a body of such performers as could have spared him unpleasant discoveries of this nature. In conducting he was very accurate, and of the tempo, which he generally took very lively, he was uncommonly sure.

So long as we can be offered in contradiction no more than the mere suggestion of the possible existence of better organists and clavier players, so long we cannot be blamed if we are bold enough to declare that our Bach was the greatest organist and clavier player that we have ever had. It may be that many a famous man has accomplished much in polyphony upon this instrument; is he therefore just as skillful, in both hands and feet—just as skillful as Bach was? This doubt will not be considered unfounded by anyone who ever had the pleasure of hearing both him and others and is not carried away by prejudice. And anyone who looks at Bach's organ and clavier pieces, which, as is generally known, he himself performed with the greatest perfection, will also not find much to object to in the sentence above. How strange, how new, how expressive, how beautiful were his ideas in improvising! How perfectly he realized them! All his fingers were equally skillful; all were equally capable of the most perfect accuracy in performance. He had devised for himself so convenient a system of fingering that it was not hard for him to conquer the greatest difficulties with the most flowing facility. Before him, the most famous clavier players in Germany and other lands had used the thumb but little. All the better did he know how to use it. With his two feet, he could play things on the pedals that many not unskillful clavier players would find it bitter enough to have to play with five fingers. He not only understood the art of playing the organ, of combining the various stops of that instrument in the most skillful manner, and of displaying each stop according to its character in the greatest perfection, but he also knew the construction of organs from one end to the other. This latter knowledge he demonstrated particularly on one occasion, among others, at the trial of a new organ in the church not far from which his earthly remains now lie. The builder of this instrument was a man who was in the last years of his long life. The trial was perhaps one of the most exacting ever made. Accordingly, the complete approval that our Bach expressed about the instrument did no slight honor both to the organ builder and, because of certain circumstances, to Bach himself.[31]

31. Agricola, co-author of the present Obituary, indicates in his notes to Adlung's *Musica Mechanica Organoedi* (excerpts in No. 358 that it was the organ of St. John's in Leipzig that was "declared faultless by Capellmeister Bach and Mr. Zacharias Hildebrand after perhaps the most severe examination that any organ ever received." This organ was built by Johann Scheibe, father of Johann Adolph Scheibe, who had criticized Bach on various occasions. (Cf. Nos. 343–48.)

No one could draw up or judge dispositions for new organs better than he. But despite all this knowledge of the organ, he never enjoyed the good fortune, as he used to point out frequently with regret, of having a really large and really beautiful organ at his constant disposal. This fact has robbed us of many beautiful and unknown inventions in organ playing that he would otherwise have written down and displayed in the form in which he had them in his head. In the tuning of harpsichords, he achieved so correct and pure a temperament that all the tonalities sounded pure and agreeable. He knew of no tonalities that, because of impure intonation, one must avoid. Not to mention other talents that were his.

Of his moral character, those may speak who enjoyed association and friendship with him and were witnesses to his uprightness toward God and his neighbor. He joined the Society of Musical Sciences in the year 1747, in the month of June, at the suggestion of Hofrath Mizler, whose good friend he was and to whom he had given instruction in clavier playing and composition while the latter was still a student in Leipzig. Our lately departed Bach did not, it is true, occupy himself with deep theoretical speculations on music, but was all the stronger in the practice of the art. To the Society he furnished the chorale *Vom Himmel hoch da komm ich her* fully worked out, which was thereupon engraved on copper. He also presented to the Society the canon reproduced in Table IV, p. 16,[32] and he would undoubtedly have done much more had not the shortness of time—he was a member for only three years—prevented him from doing so.

32. See No. 242.

PART IV

*Bach
as Viewed
by His
Contemporaries*

Bach as Viewed by
His Contemporaries

POEMS OF PRAISE

307. "A pleasant brook [Bach]," by Micrander [Johann Gottlob Kittel] (1731) (*BD* II, no. 294)

On Sept. 14 at 3 o'clock in the afternoon, Mr. Joh. Sebastian Bach, the princely Anhalt-Cöthen Capellmeister and Cantor at St. Thomas's in Leipzig, who had arrived here only a few days earlier, let himself be heard on the organ at St. Sophia's Church in the presence of all the Court musicians and virtuosos in a fashion that compelled the admiration of everyone; hence a poetic pen came across the following thoughts:

> A pleasant brook may well the ear's delight inspire,
>   As through the woods, between high cliffs, it finds its way;
> But surely one must rank that other Bach far higher
>   Who with his hurrying hand so wondrous sure doth play.
> 'Tis said, when Orpheus did his lyre strings awake,
>   All creatures in the forest answered to the sound;
> But sure, 'twere better that such praise of Bach we spake,
>   Since he, whene'er he plays, doth each and all astound.

Kittel's pseudonym, Micrander, *means "little man." The poem was published in a Dresden newspaper report on an organ recital given by Bach. On September 13, 1731, the day immediately preceding the recital, the designated new Saxon court capellmeister, Johann Adolf Hasse, presented the premiere of his opera* Cleofide, *a performance that Bach presumably attended. The organ at St. Sophia's was built by Gottfried Silbermann. See also No. 218.*

308. "If in dim ages past," by Ludwig Friedrich Hudemann (1732) (*BD* II, no. 294)

> If in dim ages past the sound of Orpheus' lute
> Just as it did touch men, touch'd ev'ry creature mute,
> Then, O Great Bach, must your success be even higher,
> Since your art none but thinking men can ever fire.
>
> And surely this does fit experience full well:
> For mortals oft like animals are seen to dwell,
> When their too empty souls fail your deserts to see,
> And they no more than beasts in pow'r of judgment be.
>
> Scarce do you send your tones to my attentive ear,
> It seems the choir of all the Muses that I hear;
> An organ chord by you must even put to shame
> The serpent's tongue of envy and of sland'rous blame.
>
> Apollo long ago gave you the laurel crown,
> And of your name in marble etched the great renown,
> But you alone, through your strings' living harmony
> Preparest, perfect Bach, your immortality.

Hudemann—according to Walther—was "a legal scholar who has not only taken great strides in the theory of music, but is also not inexperienced in execution, and occasionally uses his pen for composition, his fingers for playing, his throat for singing; also, in addition to his thorough knowledge of many languages, writes neat Latin as well as German poetry, and particularly a galant *letter in Italian and French." The present poem may have been written in acknowledgment of the intricate canon Bach dedicated to Hudemann in 1727; see No. 133.*

309. "O day, come often!" an anonymous birthday poem (manuscript, c. 1735) (*BD* II, no 374)

> O day, come often! Joyous day return
> When GOD gave you to us, and Bach was born!
> We thank Him, praying that He long your life may spare,
> For seldom does the world receive a gift so rare.

The manuscript is appended to correspondence between Johann Gottfried Walther and Heinrich Bokemeyer. The author is unknown, but a similarity of wording suggests a connection with No. 310.

310. "Vivat: J S B," an anonymous congratulatory poem engraved on a crystal goblet (c. 1735) *(BD* II, no. 375)

VIVAT: J S B

 Dearest Bach!

 Clamors   ah!

 Hopes for life

That you alone can give them.

Therefore, hear their longing ah!

Dearest  Bach.

Crystal goblet (Bachhaus Eisenach)

It is not known who presented Bach with the goblet, which was probably made in Dresden.

311. "Sonnet on the Late Cappellmeister Bach," by Georg Philipp Telemann (January 1751) *(BD,* no. 636)

> Let Italy go on her virtuosi vaunting
>   Who through the sounding art have there achieved great fame—

On German soil they also will not be found wanting,
  Nor can they here be held less worthy of the name.
Departed Bach! Long since your splendid organ playing
  Alone brought you the noble cognomen "the Great,"
And what your pen had writ, the highest art displaying,
  Did some with joy and some with envy contemplate.

Then sleep! The candle of your fame ne'er low will burn;
The pupils you have trained, and those they train in turn
  Prepare your future crown of glory brightly glowing.
Your children's hands adorn it with its jewels bright,
But what shall cause your true worth to be judged aright
  Berlin to us now in a worthy son is showing.

Telemann (1681–1767) was, next to Handel and Hasse, the most famous among German musicians of his time. In 1701 he began to study at Leipzig University and shortly afterward was appointed organist at the New Church in Leipzig. Among the students he founded a collegium musicum—*the same that Bach was later to conduct; and he wrote music for St. Thomas's as well as for the Leipzig opera. It is not surprising, then, that, after the death of Kuhnau, the Leipzig councilors thought of him before all others as a suitable candidate for the post of cantor of St. Thomas's, which he declined (cf. No. 93). From 1708 to 1712 he served as concertmaster and capellmeister at Eisenach. He knew Bach at this time, and in 1714 he became Carl Philipp Emanuel's godfather (cf. No. 55 and Carl Philipp Emanuel's letter to Forkel, No. 395). From 1712 to 1718 he was capellmeister at Frankfurt-on-the-Main, and then held a similar post in Hamburg, where, on his death, Carl Philipp Emanuel succeeded him.*

BACH THE TEACHER

Introductory Note: An Overview of Bach's Pupils

Of major composers, Bach was one of the most active, dedicated, and prolific teachers. He saw his first pupils in Arnstadt, when he was about twenty. The vast majority, however, clustered around him in Leipzig—obviously attracted by the opportunity to combine academic studies at Germany's largest and most prestigious university with private instruction in music. Many of Bach's numerous students later became leading figures in the dissemination of his music and teachings, some of them prominent composers and influential authors of theoretical treatises. As a matter of fact, German music theory after 1750 was clearly dominated by figures from Bach's circle.

The documents related to Philipp David Kräuter (see below), which are especially valuable for Bach studies, provide welcome information about a broad range of financial, teaching, living, and working arrangements. For Bach's closer pupils, formal instruction appears to have been less important than the overall experience of nearly total immersion in a unique musical enterprise. While the exact number of Bach's private pupils cannot be determined, the following list presents the names of all those whose student relationship to Bach is evidenced by testimonials and other documentation as well as by historical reports and references. Students of the St. Thomas School who merely participated in the regular musical exercises conducted by Bach are not included.

KEY

B; B*	Bach testimonial; B* included in this volume
D; D*	Other documentation (letter, receipt, archival reference); D* in this volume
W	Johann Gottfried Walther, *Musicalisches Lexicon* (Leipzig, 1732); with manuscript emendations (*BD* III, p. 654, no. 324)
G	Ernst Ludwig Gerber, *Historisch-Biographisches Lexikon der Tonkünstler* (Leipzig, 1790–92)
F*	Johann Nikolaus Forkel, *Ueber Johann Sebastian Bachs Leben, Kunst und Kunstwerke* (Leipzig, 1802); see this volume, Part VI.

Arnstadt
>   Schubart, Johann Martin (1690–1721) – D, W
>   Vogler, Johann Caspar (1696–1763) – D*, G, F*

Mühlhausen
>   *Continuing:* Schubart and Vogler

Weimar
>   *Continuing:* Schubart
>   *New:*
>> Bach, Johann Bernhard (1700–1743) – D
>> Bach, Johann Lorenz (1695–1773) – D*
>> Bach, Wilhelm Friedemann (1710–1784) – D, G, F*
>> Baumgarten, Johann Christoph (1687–1770) – D
>> Dretzel, Cornelius Heinrich (1698–1775) – D
>> Gmelin, Samuel (1695–1752) – D
>> Jagemann, Adam Friedrich Wilhelm von (1695–1714) – D*
>> Johann Ernst, Prince of Sachsen-Weimar (1697–1715) – D

Kräuter, Philipp David (1690–1741) – D*
Krebs, Johann Tobias (1690–1762) – D, W
Ziegler, Johann Gotthilf (1688–1747) – W, G

Cöthen

Continuing: J. B. Bach and W. F. Bach
New:

Bach, Carl Philipp Emanuel (1714–1788) – D, G, F*

Leipzig

Continuing: W. F. Bach and C. P. E. Bach
New:

Abel, Carl Friedrich (1723–1787) – D
Agricola, Johann Friedrich (1720–1774) – D, G, F*
Altnickol, Johann Christoph (1719–1759) – B*, G, F*
Bach, Gottfried Heinrich (1724–1763) – D
Bach, Johann Christian (1735–1782) – D, G, F*
Bach, Johann Christoph Friedrich (1732–1795) – D, G,F*
Bach, Johann Elias (1705–1755) – D*
Bach, Johann Ernst (1722–1777) – D
Bach, Johann Gottfried Bernhard (1715–1739) – D
Bach, Johann Heinrich (1707–1764) – D
Bach, Samuel Anton (1713–1781) – D
Bammler, Johann Nathanael (1722–1784) – B*
Barth, Christian Samuel (1735–1809) – G
Dietrichstein, Franz Ludwig, Count (1715–1765) – D
Doles, Johann Friedrich (1715–1797) – D, G
Flemming, Adam Heyno Heinrich, Count (1716–1746) – D
Folger, Carl August (1730–?) – D
Freudenberg, Siegismund (1704–?) – D
Fritzsche, Christian Gottlieb (c. 1730–?) – D
Gabler, Christian Friedrich (1730–1800) – D
Geier, Benjamin Gottlieb (1710–1762) – D
Gerber, Heinrich Nicolaus (1702–1775) – D, G*
Gerlach, Theodor Christian (1694–1768) – D
Gerlach, Carl Gotthelf (1704–1761) – D
Goldberg, Johann Gottlieb (1727–1756) – G, F*
Gräbner, Christian Heinrich (1705–1769) – D
Grahl, Johann Gottlieb (1703–1762) – B*
Große, Johann Michael (1713–1791) – D
Haase, Johann Gottlob (c. 1720–17?) – D, [B]
Hartwig, Karl (1709–1750) – D

Heinrich, Johann Georg (1721–?) – B*
Hochberg, Heinrich Ludwig Carl, Count (1714–1765) – D
Homilius, Gottfried August (1714–1785) – F*
Hübner, Jacob Ernst (fl. 1726–33) – B*
Kirnberger, Johann Philipp (1721–1783) – D, G, F*
Kittel, Johann Christian (1732–1809) – D, G, F*
Krebs, Johann Ludwig (1713–1780) – B*, W, G, F*
Landvoigt, Johann August (1715–1766) – [B]
Ludewig, Bernhard Dieterich (1707–1740) – B*
Meissner, Christian Gottlob (1707–1760) – D
Mempell, Johann Nicolaus (1713–1747) – D
Mizler, Lorenz Christoph (1711–1778) – D*, G
Müthel, Johann Gottfried (1728–1788) – G, F*
Nagel, Maximilian (1714–1748) – D
Naumann, Gottlieb Daniel (1710–1782) – D
Nichelmann, Christoph (1716–1762) – D, G
Nicolai, David (1702–1764) – D
Raden, Gottlob Ludwig (1718–1764) – D
Reimann, Johann Balthasar (1702–1749) – G
Ritter, Johann Christoph (1715–1767) – D
Scheibe, Johann Adolph (1708–1776) – D*, B*
Schemelli, Christian Friedrich (1713–1761) – D*, B*
Schimert, Peter (1712–1785) – D
Schneider, Johann (1702–1788) – D*, W
Schübler, Johann Georg (1720–?) – D
Sojka, Matthias (1740–1817) – [B]
Sonnenkalb, Johann Friedrich Wilhelm (1732–1785) – D
Stolle, Paul Christian (1706–1779/80) – B*
Straube, Rudolph (1717–1785) – D, G
Transchel, Christoph (1721–1800) – G, F*
Trier, Johann (1716–1790) – D
Vitzthum zu Eckstädt, Ludwig Siegfried, Count (1716–1777) – D
Voigt, Johann Georg (1728–1765) – D
Wagner, Georg Gottfried (1698–1756) – B*, W, G
Wecker, Christoph Gottlob (1706–?) – B*
Weyrauch, Johann Christian (1694–?) – B*
Wild, Friedrich Gottlieb (c. 1706–1723) – B*
Wrbna (Würben) und Freudenthal, Eugen Wenzel Joseph, Count
    (1728–1789) – D*
Wunsch, Christian Gottlob (1720–1754) – B*, D

312. **Studying with Bach in Weimar: excerpts from the files of the Augsburg Evangelical Scholarchat on Philipp David Kräuter** (*BD* II, no. 58; *BD* III, p. 649, nos. 53a, 53b, 58a; Krautwurst, pp. 180–81)

    a. *Kräuter's plan discussed by the school board, Augsburg, December 12, 1711:*

Philipp David Kräuter plans to travel to Weimar in March of next year, where he will receive instruction from the famous musician Bach.

    b. *Kräuter sends a report to the school board, Weimar, 1712:*

HIGH AND NOBLE, GRACIOUS, MOST WISE AND MOST ESTIMABLE MEMBERS OF THE SCHOLARCHAT, BENEVOLENT AND HONORED SIRS!

With your accustomed kindness, you will not take exception to my liberty in sending you these lines to offer my humble thanks for the 50 florins allotted to me prior to my voyage; may God make rich amends. I shall report, according to your kind instruction, how I have used these funds and how I have duly arranged with my new teacher, Mr. Bach in Weimar, for a year's board and tutelage. The traveling expense was between 25 and 26 florins, since the roads were very bad and I had to give the coachman almost twice the normal compensation. I gave 4 florins to Mr. Bach for half the month of April, since I was concerned that he might count the entire month as part of the year that now is to commence with the month of May. He had initially asked for 100 reichsthaler to cover the year, but I was able to lower it to 80 thlr., against which he will offer me board and tuition. He is an excellent and sterling man, both in composition and in instruction on keyboard and other instruments. It is assuredly six hours per day of guidance that I am receiving, primarily in composition and on the keyboard, at times also on other instruments. The rest of the time I use by myself for practice and copying work, since he shares with me all the music I ask for. I am also at liberty to look through all of his pieces. Thus nothing should be wanting for my project, devoted to the glory of God, if My Noble and Gracious Magnificences and Benevolent Sirs would be so obliging as to yield to my renewed petition to comply with Mr. Bach's request, mentioned above, of 80 thaler, from which, however, 20 florins still in my possession could be subtracted. I asked the same how he wished payment to be made, and he responded that it should not matter but preferably occur monthly or quarterly. Since, however, I have not received final instructions from Your Noble and Gracious

Sirs as to the manner of payment but must obtain those from Mr. Federlin as intermediary, I have begged Mr. Bach's patience until such time. Meanwhile, I shall do what I can myself for obligations, New Year's gratuity, and needs beyond sustenance for the time granted to me. To this end I shall gladly apply—in view of the welcome opportunity for honest and thorough learning—my savings, however small, as well as my hard earnings from the cantorate and private lessons, after having taken care of the necessary expenses for clothes, linen, instruments, and house and travel needs, hoping that dear God will keep me in good health so that I may eventually serve the nation's high patrons to the extent that they might help support my livelihood.

My humble petition, therefore, is submitted to My Estimable Sirs that I may again partake, through gracious resolve as to my stipend and your dispositions, in the renown of your munificence and benevolence. With God's help, I will in turn dedicate myself to such learning as may convince My Sirs that magnanimous charity would not have been extended to one unworthy of it; will beseech the mercy of God for your abiding health, long life, prosperity, and blissful reign; and remain in lifelong due devotion Your Noble Graces'

| Weimar, the 30th of April | Obedient servant |
| in the year 1712 | PHILIPP DAVID KRÄUTER |

c. *Kräuter asks for an extension, Weimar, April 10, 1713*

. . . first, only then would I be able to perfect myself more and more in composition and on the clavier and other instruments as well, and to go a long way in my art with God's help. 2. Because the Weimar Prince here, who is not only a great lover of music but himself an incomparable violinist, will return to Weimar from Holland after Easter and spend the summer here, I could hear much fine Italian and French music, particularly profitable to me in composing concertos and ouvertures. 3. By Whitsuntide the castle organ here will be in as good a condition as possible; hence I could familiarize myself more completely with the structure of an organ, in order to be able to judge if this or that would be useful for an organ, if all repair work were executed well and not superficially, and at the same time how much, approximately, one or two ranks of pipes would cost, all of which I consider rather worthwhile. Also, especially after the new Weimar organ is ready, Mr. Bach will play on it incomparable things; thus I shall be able to see, hear, and copy a great deal.

d. *Kräuter's petition is discussed by the school board, Augsburg, April 27, 1713:*

Phil. Dav. Kräuter requests in writing that he be allowed to stay a bit longer in Weimar with Mr. Bach, beyond the year that has already passed.

Granted to him for the motives and reasons put forth in his petition.

Kräuter (1690–1741) studied with Bach from March 1711 to September 1713, on a scholarship provided by the Augsburg Scholarchat. Shortly after his return, in December 1713, he was appointed cantor and music director at St. Anne's Church in Augsburg.

313. Excerpt from a letter of application for an organist post in Görlitz, by Johann Caspar Vogler, Leipzig, December 25, 1729 (*BD* II, no. 266)

I herewith report that I [have been] a pupil of the famous Mr. Bach, who is now music director in Leipzig and who, as he himself told me, has not yet been personally in Görlitz but whose reputation is perhaps known there. As regards virtue on the organ and speed of hands and feet, I come closest to him here in Saxony, which can best be demonstrated by an actual presentation.

Vogler mailed this letter from Leipzig, where he was an applicant for the post of organist at St. Nicholas's. He was not chosen, because, according to the minutes, "he made the church [people] mad and played too fast."

314. On Bach's teaching of composition, by Johann Philipp Kirnberger (1782) (*BD* III, no. 867)

Johann Sebastian Bach always writes, in all his works, a thoroughly pure style, and every piece of his has a completely unified character. Rhythm, Melody, Harmony—in short, everything that makes a composition truly beautiful—he has, as his practical works testify, fully in his power. His method is the best, for he proceeds steadily, step by step, from the easiest to the most difficult, and as a result even the step to the fugue has only the difficulty of passing from one step to the next. On this ground I hold the method of Johann Sebastian Bach to be the best and only one. It is to be regretted that this great man never wrote anything theoretical about music, and that his teachings have reached posterity only through his pupils. I have sought to reduce the method of the late Joh. Seb. Bach to principles, and to lay his teachings before the world to the best of my powers, in my "Art of Pure Writing" [*Die Kunst des reinen Satzes in der Musik*].

315. The education of Bach's pupil Heinrich Nicolaus Gerber, by Ernst Ludwig Gerber (1790) (*BD* III, no. 950)

Gerber *(Heinrich Nicolaus)* was Court Organist to the Prince of Schwarzburg in Sondershausen, born at Wenigen-Ehrich in the Schwarzburg domains, on September 6, 1702. He was a worthy man in his field, and my father. I would therefore have to make myself reproaches on two grounds if, out of a mistaken sense of modesty, I did not accord to him the same justice that I grant to so many others in these pages.

. . . After he had spent two years at preparatory studies [with Cantor Irrgang at Bellstedt], his father sent him to the school in Mühlhausen, which was then counted among the best in Thuringia and where many worthy men were engaged as teachers of the various branches of knowledge. Only in music did darkness still cover the earth there, and this darkness was half a century thicker, even, than that which the late Mr. [Johann Lorenz] Albrecht, 50 years later, so often and so loudly bemoaned in his writings. The only musical genius living there was a drunken organist [Johann Friedrich Bach] (for when he was sober he accomplished just as little as his fellow citizens), of the Bach family. His [Gerber's] only desire was to delight in this man's singing style of performance. But even this was made hard for him by the fact that the students were forced to go to a church other than that at which Bach was organist. But he still assured one in his old age that he had learned his style of organ playing from this Bach alone. However, since this man, leading the sort of life he did, was not able to give instruction, young Gerber was left to his own devices and to the little he had learned from Cantor Irrgang.

Fed up with this dry kind of life, he asked his father to send him to school at Sondershausen. This happened in the year 1721. But there, too, taste was only beginning to awaken. . . . When there was nothing left for him to draw from the sources there, he went to Leipzig, partly to study law and partly to study music with the great Sebast. Bach. He [Gerber] was received there as a student in the University, under the Rectorate of Dr. Börner, on May 8, 1724. In the first half year, as he arranged his courses, he had heard much excellent church music and many a concert under Bach's direction; but he had still lacked any opportunity that would have given him courage enough to reveal his desires to this great man; until at last he revealed his wish to a friend, named Wilde [Friedrich Gottlieb Wild; see No. 134], later organist in Petersburg, who introduced him to Bach.

Bach accepted him with particular kindness because he came from Schwarzburg, and always thereafter called him *Landsmann* [compatriot]. He promised to give him the instruction he desired and asked at once whether he had industriously played fugues. At the first lesson he set his Inventions before him. When he had studied these through to Bach's satisfaction, there followed a series of suites, then *The Well-Tempered Clavier.* This latter work Bach played altogether three times through for him with his unmatchable art, and my father counted these among his happiest hours, when Bach, under the pretext of not feeling in the mood to teach, sat himself at one of his fine instruments and thus turned these hours into minutes. The conclusion of the instruction was thorough bass, for which Bach chose the Albinoni violin solos; and I must admit that I have never heard anything better than the style in which my father executed these basses according to Bach's fashion, particularly in the singing of the voices. This accompaniment was in itself so beautiful that no principal voice could have added to the plea-sure it gave me.

Having spent two years in Bach's school, with an industry appro-priate to the excellence of such a teacher, and having finished his courses [at the University], he returned to his father in the country. Here he employed two years of leisure to put into order and apply the manifold good and beautiful things he had brought with him from Leipzig. At the same time he began to build, with the help of a cabinet maker, a small organ with pedals, containing 12 stops. . . .

[In 1728 he received his first call—the beginning of a successful career.] . . . The continual persecution at the hands of recruiting officers to which, on account of his youth, he was exposed almost until 1740 prevented him from getting to know the world outside his fatherland. He permitted himself but a single journey in 1737, to his beloved teacher Bach in Leipzig.

[He died in 1775.]

316. Johann Philipp Kirnberger and Bach, by Friedrich Ludwig Aemilius Kunzen and Johann Friedrich Reichardt (1793) (Kunzen and Reichardt, p. 112)

When Kirnberger went to Leipzig in order to study counterpoint under the tutelage of the great Sebastian Bach, and to learn to write in pure four-part style, he exerted himself so strenuously that he fell ill with a fever and for eighteen weeks had to keep to his room. But he neverthe-less continued, in his hours of respite from the fever, to work out all kinds of themes, and when Sebastian observed this extraordinary industry, he offered to come up to Kirnberger's room, since it might be bad for Kirnberger to go out and the sending back and forth of the papers was somewhat inconvenient. When Kirnberger one day gave his Master to understand that he could never adequately repay him for his kindness and his pains, Bach, who without doubt foresaw the future merits of his pupil in preserving the pure style of writing, and who loved the art for its own sake and not just for the advantages connected with it, said, "Do not, my dear Kirnberger, speak of gratitude. I am glad that you wish to study the art of tones from its roots up, and it depends only on you to learn for yourself so much of it as has become known to me. I require nothing of you but the assurance that you will transplant that little in turn in the minds of other good students who are not satisfied with the ordinary lirum-larum, etc."

317. **A reminiscence by the last of Bach's pupils, Johann Christian Kittel (1808) (Kittel, pt. 3, p. 33)**

One of his most capable pupils always had to accompany on the harpsichord. It will easily be guessed that no one dared to put forward a meager thorough-bass accompaniment. Nevertheless, one always had to be prepared to have Bach's hands and fingers intervene among the hands and fingers of the player and, without getting in the way of the latter, furnish the accompaniment with masses of harmonies that made an even greater impression than the unsuspected close proximity of the teacher.

REPORTS AND REVIEWS

Introductory Note

Little publicity attended musicians of the early eighteenth century unless they wrote for the stage. The small newspapers of the time contained little about music, and the few musical magazines that were just then putting in a cautious appearance were devoted to questions of theory or aesthetics rather than to musical news. The following references to Bach, accordingly, are taken from widely divergent sources in the literature of his day. A few come from theoretical books; others from magazines (or, rather, books published in installments); others from books not devoted chiefly to music; still others from occasional letters and dedications.

Equally varied is the list of their authors. It includes Gerber, a churchman who wrote a history of Divine Service in Saxony; Gesner, a rector of the St. Thomas School, who drew a sketch of Bach in a note to an edition of Quintilian; and Bellermann, another schoolmaster, who refers to Bach in one of his annual school reports. There are, furthermore, some pupils of Bach and an occasional visitor to his home. And, finally, a few professional writers on music are represented: Mizler and Scheibe, whose names have already appeared in this work, and Johann Mattheson.

Mattheson undoubtedly was the most colorful figure among all these. Born in Hamburg in 1681 as the son of a tax collector, he was given an excellent education, which included singing, playing on five instruments, composing, dancing, drawing, arithmetic, fencing, horseback riding, languages, and law. In his eighteenth year he sang the leading part in his own first opera. In 1703 he was invited to Lübeck as a candidate to succeed Buxtehude, but he preferred not to marry Buxtehude's daughter—which, according to a custom of the time, he would have had to do to obtain it. He was a friend of Handel's, although on one famous occasion they fought a duel. Mattheson himself had a successful and remunerative career, serving in various musical capacities and carrying out diplomatic missions. He died in Hamburg, where he had spent the larger part of his life, in 1764.

In addition to being a competent composer, Mattheson was the most prolific musical writer of his time. Although given to parading his knowledge, he was basically a sensible and progressive man. He introduced the terms "major" and "minor" into German musical theory, and he fought successfully for the abandonment of solmization. His *Critica Musica* of 1722 may be called the very first musical periodical in any language. His *Musicalische Ehrenpforte* (1740) was a valuable collection of biographies and autobiographies. And his larger theoretical works, including particularly *Der vollkommene Capellmeister* (1739), are among the most comprehensive documents of contemporary theory.

Mattheson was continually involved in polemics. Ambitious and conceited, he took delight in appraising the output of other musicians and theorists and in criticizing every weakness he could spot. For better or for worse, he was the first professional music critic.

318. The first reference to Bach in print, from *Das beschützte Orchestre,* by Johann Mattheson (1717) (*BD* II, no. 200)

I have seen things by the famous organist of Weimar, Mr. Joh. Sebastian Bach, both for the church and for the fist [i.e., vocal and keyboard pieces], that are certainly such as must make one esteem the man highly.

319. On Bach's declamation, by Johann Mattheson (1725)
(*BD* II, no. 200)

In order that good old Zachau may have company, and not be quite so alone, let us set beside him an otherwise excellent practicing musician of today, who for a long time does nothing but repeat:
"I, I, I, I had much grief, I had much grief, in my heart, in my heart. I had much grief, etc., in my heart, etc., etc., I had much grief, etc., in my heart, etc., I had much grief, etc., in my heart etc., etc., etc., etc., etc. I had much grief, etc., in my heart, etc., etc." Then again: "Sighs, tears, sorrow, anguish (rest), sighs, tears, anxious longing, fear and death (rest) gnaw at my oppressed heart, etc." Also: "Come, my Jesus, and refresh (rest) and rejoice with Thy glance (rest), come, my Jesus (rest), come, my Jesus, and refresh and rejoice . . . with Thy glance this soul, etc."

The quotations are from Bach's cantata Ich hatte viel Bekümmernis, *BWV 21. Mattheson uses repeat signs where we have used "etc."*

320. On Bach the keyboard player, by Georg Ludwig Heinrich Schwanenberger (1727) (*BD* II, no. 239)

I could wish that you should once hear Mr. Bach on the organ, for neither you nor anyone else in Braunschweig could hold your head before him; I never heard anything like it, and I must completely change my whole style of playing, for it is worth nothing. And in thorough bass, too. I will, if God pleases and keeps me healthy, be uncommonly industrious, for I am eager to learn his style.

321. On Bach, Frescobaldi, and Carissimi, and on three famous B's (Buxtehude, Bachelbel, and Bach), by Martin Heinrich Fuhrmann (1729) (*BD* II, nos. 268–69)

a. When I was at the Easter Fair in Leipzig recently . . . I had the good fortune to hear the world-famous Mr. Bach. I thought the Italian Frescobaldi had polished off the art of keyboard playing all by himself, and [Giacomo] Carissimi was a most valued and cherished organist. But if one were to put the two Italians with their art on one side of the scales and the German Bach on the other, the latter would far outweigh them, and they would be lifted straight up into the air. I later heard the well-known Mr. Kirchhof play the organ in Halle, and his fingers so mastered the charms of music that I cried out, "What a shame that the hands of these two keyboard players in Leipzig and Halle must some day turn to dust!"

b. We have the learned musical trefoil in B, consisting of three incomparable virtuosi whose family names bear a B on their shields: Buxtehude, Bachhelbel, and Bach in Leipzig; these men mean as much to me as Cicero did to the Romans.

322. On holdings of Buxtehude and Bach manuscripts, by Johann Gottfried Walther (August 6, 1729) (*BD* II, no. 263)

Now I have to add that . . . with regard to the work of German organists, especially the famous Buxtehude and Bach, I can serve the connoisseur in a manner already mentioned, since I have many, in fact more than altogether 200 pieces, from both of them. The ones of the former I received mainly from the late Mr. Werckmeister, in Mr. Buxtehude's own hand and in German tablature; the ones of the latter, however, from the author himself, who for nine years was here as court organist, and who was my cousin and a sponsor, along with me, as godfather.

323. On the difficulty of partitas by Graupner and Bach, by Johann Mattheson (1731) (*BD* II, no. 304)

Let no one think, by the way, that this aria is being offered as an example of a technical[ly advanced] etude [*Hand-Sachen*]: for such pieces are of quite a different sort. Let a student of art but compare it with, say, a Suite from among Capellmeister Graupner's so-called *Partien* for Clavier, or from my *Harmonisches Denkmahl,* or from Capellmeister Bach's *Partitas,* and he will easily find out the difference. Etudes need to be practiced, and anyone who ventured to read them off at sight would be undertaking something very foolhardy, thinking that with his juggler's tricks he could impose on his listeners' credulity—were he the arch-harpsichordist himself.

324. On large-scale Passion music, by Christian Gerber (1732) (Gerber, p. 283)

Fifty and more years ago it was the custom for the organ to remain silent in church on Palm Sunday, and on that day, because it was the beginning of Holy Week, there was no music. But gradually the Passion story, which had formerly been sung in simple plainchant, humbly and reverently, began to be sung with many kinds of instruments in the most elaborate fashion, occasionally mixing in a little setting of a Passion Chorale that the whole congregation joined in singing, and then the mass of instruments fell to again. When in a large town this Passion music was done for the first time, with twelve violins, many oboes, bassoons, and other instruments, many people were astonished and did not know what to make of it. In the pew of a noble family in church, many Ministers and Noble Ladies were present, who sang the first Passion Chorale out of their books with great devotion. But when this theatrical music began, all these people were thrown into the greatest bewilderment, looked at each other, and said, "What will come of this?" An old widow of the nobility said, "God save us, my children! It's just as if one were at an Opera Comedy." But everyone was genuinely displeased by it and voiced just complaints against it. There are, it is true, some people who take pleasure in such idle things, especially if they are of sanguine temperament and inclined to sensual pleasure. Such persons defend large-scale church compositions as best they may, and hold others to be crotchety and of melancholy temperament—as if they alone possessed the wisdom of Solomon, and others had no understanding.

These remarks, which appeared five years after the first performance of Bach's St. Matthew Passion, *most likely do not refer to that work (cf. Friedrich Smend,* Bach in Köthen, *pp. 156f).*

325. On the German style in clavier music, by Johann Adolph Scheibe (1737) (Scheibe, p. 148)

In some types of clavier pieces there is a clear distinction between the German style and others. In foreigners we find that neither the structure, nor the ornamentation, nor the working out of these pieces is so perfect as in the Germans. For they know how to exploit this instrument with the greatest strength and according to its true nature better than all other nations. The two great men among the Germans, Mr. Bach and Mr. Handel, illustrate this most strikingly.

326. On a fugue subject by Bach, by Johann Mattheson (1737) (*BD* II, no. 408)

Now, how long the so-called subject of a fugue may be, in measures, is to some extent arbitrary, and something will appear on this question at the conclusion of this chapter. But in general it is held that the sooner and faster an answer follows its subject, the better is the effect of the fugue. One often finds the most excellent workings-out upon the fewest notes, or shortest fugue subjects; almost as the best sermons can be made on three or four words of text.

Who would believe that these eight short notes [from the Sonata for Violin Solo, BWV 1003] would be so fruitful as to bring forth a counterpoint of more than a whole sheet of music paper, without unusual extension, and quite naturally? And yet the skilled and in this species particularly fortunate Bach has set just this before the world; indeed, he has in addition introduced the subject here and there in inversion.

327. On Bach's thorough-bass playing, by Lorenz Christoph Mizler (1738) (*BD* II, no. 432)

Whoever wishes truly to observe what delicacy in thorough bass and very good accompanying mean need only take the trouble to hear our Capellmeister Bach here, who accompanies every thorough bass to a solo so that one thinks it is a piece of concerted music and as if the melody he plays in the right hand were written beforehand. I can give a living testimony of this since I have heard it myself.

328. On Bach's playing and conducting, by Johann Matthias Gesner (1738) (*BD* II, no. 432)

To Marcus Fabius Quintilianus

You would think but slightly, my dear Fabius, of all these [the accomplishments of the citharists], if, returning from the underworld, you could see Bach (to mention him particularly, since he was not long ago my colleague at the Leipzig St. Thomas School), either playing our clavier [*polychordum*], which is many citharas in one, with all the fingers of both hands, or running over the keys of the instrument of instruments [*organon organorum*], whose innumerable pipes are brought to life by bellows, with both hands and, at the utmost speed, with his feet, producing by himself the most various and at the same time mutually agreeable combinations of sounds in orderly procession. If you could see him, I say, doing what many of your citharists and six hundred of your tibia players together could not do, not only, like a citharist, singing with one voice and playing his own parts, but watching over everything and bringing back to the rhythm and the beat, out of thirty or even forty musicians [*symphoniaci*], the one with a nod, another by tapping with his foot, the third with a warning finger, giving the right note to one from the top of his voice, to another from the bottom, and to a third from the middle of it—all alone, in the midst of the greatest din made by all the participants, and, although he is executing the most difficult parts himself, noticing at once whenever and wherever a mistake occurs, holding everyone together, taking precautions everywhere, and repairing any unsteadiness, full of rhythm in every part of his body—this one man taking in all these harmonies with his keen ear and emitting with his voice alone the tone of all the voices. Favorer as I am of antiquity, the accomplishments of our Bach, and of any others who may be like him, appear to me to effect what not many Orpheuses, nor twenty Arions, could achieve.

The original is in Latin; Charles Burney made an incomplete translation, some details of which are used here.

329. On Bach's canon for Hudemann, by Johann Mattheson (1739) (*BD* II, no. 466)

The famous Bach, whom I mention now as before with all honor, particularly on account of his great manual dexterity, also made such an intricately contrived piece some years ago and had it engraved on copper, dedicating it to a great musical connoisseur and musician, a really highly learned teacher of laws, who has done me the honor of being among the auditors at my melopoetic lectures. This is how it looks:

Canon a 4.

dedié

A Monsieur Houdemann

et

composé

par J. S. Bach

This is a puzzlelike circular canon; in Italian, *canone enimmatico;* in Latin, *canon aenigmaticus*. In it more than one clef is given at the beginning and at the end, but, on the other hand, there is no indication (such as §) of the order in which the four voices are to enter. And for the very reason that this has been withheld by the composer, the guessing of the puzzle is made all the harder for the executants. There are such canons in which upon the return each voice must enter one tone lower. Ah! what ingenuities!

Since the above puzzle arrived from Leipzig on August 18, 1727, while we were in the midst of our lectures, every member of the company that was present had to set himself at it, and seek to find the solution. For, as anyone can see, the doors were closed; it was what is rightly called *canon clausus*.

One hit upon this solution; another upon that; until at length two, of whom one now has the best organist's post in Gröningen and has already stepped forward with a published work, while the other became a distinguished official in the government at Hamburg, but alas! died not long since in the full flood of his good fortune and merits at the Imperial Court [—these two, I say] agreed as follows, cherishing the idea that the task, if everything must remain the same in contrary motion (as they suspected they were to conclude from the inverted clefs at the end), must assume the form given below.

Whether and in what degree these solvers have hit the mark, the Author himself may best judge, and not blame me if his intention has not been guessed—at the thought of which I shudder. I have never devoted any more time and trouble to it than was required for the mere copying of the above, and should rather have spared myself that, too, if I did not believe that the quotation of the little piece might contribute to many a reader's instruction or reflection.

See also Mattheson's 1717 biographical sketch (No. 318). For a facsimile of the canon, BWV 1074, see No. 133.

330. On the greatest masters of the organ, by Johann Mattheson (1739) (*BD* II, no. 465)

Finally, concerning the best-known and greatest masters of the organ, it may be said in general that Germany produces the most famous organists. The fame of Frescobaldi and [Bernardo] Pasquini in former times spread from Rome across the Alps; but no miracles have been mentioned in this chapter in connection with other Italians. It is a strange thing, since in general Italy has always been, and still wishes to be, an eminent school of music. But one could see from the arrangements of their organs that they do not lay as much store by them as the Germans do.

About the one organ in Trent a great fuss is made. But the organist of that very place is said to have been astonished when he heard Signor Sassone (as the Italians called Handel) play on it while he was passing through. Flanders, Holland, and Brabant, on the other hand, have given the world many a fine organist and in fact used to be the nursery gardens for the same. Frescobaldi, for example, spent many years in Flanders. Whether the situation is still the same there I cannot say, for lack of precise information.

In particular, no one could easily surpass Handel in organ playing, unless it be Bach in Leipzig; for which reason, these two must stand at the head of the list, out of their alphabetical order. I have heard them at the height of their powers, and often played with the former in Hamburg as well as in Lübeck. He had a pupil in England, named Babel [William Babell] of whom it is said that he surpassed his master.

In addition to these the following are famous: Böhme [Georg Böhm] in Lüneburg, Callenberg in Riga, [Nicholas] Clerambault in Paris, Green [Maurice Greene] in London, Hoffmann in Breslau, Küntze in Lübeck, Lübeck in Hamburg, Lüders in Flensburg, Rameau formerly in Clermont, Raupach in Stralsund, Rosenbusch in Itzehoe, [Christian] Pezold in Dresden, Stapel in Rostock, Vogler and Walther in Weymar, etc. etc. etc. No one whose name is not included here is by any means excluded, nor are those who are here named given any preference on that account over others whose powers are either unknown to me or have not occurred to me readily.

In a review of Mattheson's Der vollkommene Capellmeister, *Lorenz Christoph Mizler remarks, "To the above-named I will add but two fine organists. One is Mr. Schröter in Nordhausen, who is not only a practical but also a learned composer and organist; the other Mr. Schneider, Organist of St. Nicholas's Church in Leipzig, whose preludes on the organ are of such good taste that in this field, except for Mr. Bach, whose pupil he has been, there is nothing better to be heard in Leipzig. It is but a pity that in such a famous place, where the Muses have taken up their seat, there are at the same time so few connoisseurs and lovers of a true music" (BD II, no. 565).*

331. On the *Italian Concerto*, by Johann Adolph Scheibe (1739) (*BD* II, no. 463)

Finally I must briefly mention that concertos are also written for one instrument alone, without any accompaniment by others—especially clavier concertos or lute concertos. In such pieces the basic structure is kept the same as in concertos for many instruments. The bass and the middle voices, which are added now and then to fill out the texture, must represent the subordinate parts. And those passages which above all form the essence of the concerto must be most clearly differentiated from the rest. This can very well be done if, after the principal idea of a fast or slow movement is concluded with a cadence, new and distinct ideas enter and these in turn give way to the principal idea in varying keys. By such means, a piece of this sort for one instrument becomes quite similar to one for many instruments. There are some quite good concertos of this kind, particularly for clavier. But preeminent among published musical works is a clavier concerto of which the author is the famous Bach in Leipzig and which is in the key of F major. Since this piece is arranged in the best possible fashion for this kind of work, I believe that it will doubtless be familiar to all great composers and experienced clavier players, as well as to amateurs of the clavier and music in general. Who is there who will not admit at once that this clavier concerto is to be regarded as a perfect model of a well-designed solo concerto? But at the present time we shall be able to name as yet very few or practically no concertos of such excellent qualities and such well-designed execution. It would take as great a master of music as Mr. Bach, who has almost alone taken possession of the clavier, and with whom we can certainly defy foreign nations, to provide us with such a piece in this form of composition—a piece that deserves emulation by all our great composers and that will be imitated all in vain by foreigners.

332. On florid expression, by Johann Adolph Scheibe (1739) (Scheibe, pp. 645–46)

Having stated above that lavish decoration or florid expression really has to do with melody, I must now make this somewhat more clear. It will readily be seen what I mean by florid expression, for it is nothing but the performance of a musical idea in a different and more lively form than it should really have according to the principal melodic notes, or according to the concatenation of the piece. It is a new and ornamental alteration of a short melodic idea in order to render it more emphatic or even more lofty, without hurt to the harmony. But since the circumstances of such a florid or unliteral expression vary, there are accordingly many species of the same. If I were permitted to decorate my pages with musical notation, I should have occasion enough at this point to show my readers many choice examples of florid expression, especially if I wished to leaf through the excellent works of a Hasse, of a Graun, of a Telemann, and of various other great men of our times, but above all of a Bach, who is a particularly great master in this respect.

333. On Part III of the *Clavier-Übung*, by Lorenz Christoph Mizler (1740) (BD II, no. 482)

Capellmeister Bach has also published here: "Third Part of the *Clavier-Übung* consisting of various preludes on the catechism and other hymns for the organ. For music lovers, and especially for connoisseurs of such work, for the refreshment of their spirits, composed by Johann Sebastian Bach, Royal Polish and Electoral Saxon Court Composer, Capellmeister and *Directore Chori Musici* in Leipzig. Published by the Author."

The work consists of 77 copper plates in folio, very cleanly engraved and neatly printed on good strong paper. The price is 3 rthlr. The author has here given new proof that in this field of composition he is more practiced and more fortunate than many others. No one will surpass him in it, and few will be able to imitate him. This work is a powerful refutation of those who have made bold to criticize the composition of the Honorable Court Composer.

334. On meeting Bach, by Johann Francisci (1740) (*BD* II, no. 469)

In the year 1725 I again had a great desire to see the famous Leipzig. Accordingly, I journeyed thither, having received permission to do so, in company with a merchant from here, and arrived during the Easter Fair. I had the good fortune to make the acquaintance of the famous Capellmeister Bach, and to profit by observing his ability.

335. On traveling to Leipzig to hear Bach, by Johann Balthasar Reimann (1740) (*BD* II, no. 471)

During this time I traveled to Leipzig at the expense of an eminent patron here in Hirschberg in order to hear the famous Joh. Sebast. Bach. This great artist received me amiably and so enchanted me with his uncommon dexterity that I have never regretted the journey.

Reimann (1702–1749) was, in Johann Mattheson's words, "a very agreeable melody maker on the clavier as well as on paper." The period he refers to as "this time" is 1729–1740.

336. On Bach warming up, by Theodor Leberecht Pitschel (1741) (*BD* II, no. 449)

You know, the famous man who has the greatest praise in our town in music, and the greatest admiration of connoisseurs, does not get into condition, as the expression goes, to delight others with the mingling of his tones until he has played something from the printed or written page, and has [thus] set his powers of imagination in motion. . . . The able man whom I have mentioned usually has to play something from the page that is inferior to his own ideas. And yet his superior ideas are the consequences of those inferior ones.

Pitschel (1716–1743) belonged to the circle of J. C. Gottsched in Leipzig.

337. On being acquainted with Bach, by Johann Christian Voigt (1742) (*BD* II, no. 514)

I said to him that one must begin slowly, so as to preserve a uniform tempo, and the second and third time it would go better. He answered unpleasantly that these good sirs might well have stayed at home with their *Parthien;* there were enough good things already for the clavier, by Italians and Frenchmen, as well as the beautiful *Clavier-Uebungen* by the well-known Bach, which were certainly well written. I was not too lazy to look for Mr. Bach's clavier pieces and show them to him. But if he had not already hacked at the keyboard he now began to do so in earnest, and fell into a discourse about Mr. Bach: whether I knew him; he had heard that I was a Thuringian and born in Mühlhausen, and Mr. Bach had been organist in Mühlhausen. I replied that I did indeed well remember having seen him, but that I did not know him any more, since at that time I had been only twelve years old; that I had not been back there in 30 years; that Mr. Bach had succeeded to the post after the death of Mr. Ahle, and this had been in 1707. But in 1708 he had moved to Weymar. He had specified a peal of chimes for St. Blasius's Church, but when it was almost finished he had been called, although to the great regret of the Council in Mühlhausen, to be a chamber musician in Weymar [see No. 25].

338. On Bach's pedal playing, by Constantin Bellermann (1743) (*BD* II, no. 522)

Bach of Leipzig, author of profound music, is not inferior to those mentioned above [Mattheson, Keiser, Telemann]. Like Handel among the English, he deserves to be called the miracle of Leipzig, as far as music is concerned. For if it pleases him, he can by the use of his feet alone (while his fingers do either nothing or something else) achieve such an admirable, agitated, and rapid concord of sounds on the church organ that others would seem unable to imitate it even with their fingers. When he was called from Leipzig to Cassel to pronounce an organ properly restored, he ran over the pedals with this same facility, as if his feet had wings, making the organ resound with such fullness, and so penetrate the ears of those present like a thunderbolt, that Frederick, the legitimate hereditary Prince of Cassel, admired him with such astonishment that he drew a ring with a precious stone from his finger and gave it to Bach as soon as the sound had died away. If Bach earned such a gift for the agility of his feet, what, I ask, would the Prince have given him if he had called his hands into service as well?

Bellermann was rector at Minden. The present excerpt was originally written in Latin. Regarding Bach's visit to Kassel, see Nos. 157–158.

339. A dedication to Bach, from the *Third Half-Dozen Sonatinas for the Clavier,* by Georg Andreas Sorge (1742) (*BD* II, no. 526)

MOST HONORED, STEADFAST AND MOST LEARNED, ESPECIALLY MOST HIGHLY ESTEEMED MR. COURT COMPOSER, &C., MOST HIGHLY VALUED PATRON!

Many will wonder, perhaps, that I have had the boldness to dedicate the present Sonatinas to Your Honor, who is so great and world-renowned a virtuoso and Prince of Clavier Players. But such cannot yet have learned that the great musical *Virtu* that Your Honor possesses is ornamented with the excellent *Virtu* of amiability and unfeigned love of your neighbor. It is true, there are here and there distinguished artists and worthy virtuosi, but many of them are full of such conceit and culpable self-love that they consider all those over whose heads they can keep their gaze raised as nothing, and quite cast out the love of one's neighbor that is commanded from on high. I am one of those who have met with a quite different and better assurance from Your Honor. . . . And perhaps even in these light pieces there is a passage or an idea that will cause Your Honor to break into a friendly smile. I need mention nothing further in this direction, but must only beg Your Honor, most obediently, to accept with a gracious hand this little work as a sign of my quite special respect for Your Most Esteemed Person and incomparable Composition, and to continue to be of most gracious and friendly disposition toward me and to wish me well, for I remain, with cordial wishes for all possible happiness and welfare, and with great respect,

Your Honor's and my most particularly highly esteemed Mr. Court Composer's etc., and highly esteemed Patron's most obedient servant

THE AUTHOR

Sorge (1703–1778) was the author of numerous musical and theoretical works. The former included twenty-four preludes and double fugues in all the keys, a Clavier-Übung *(1742) consisting of six sonatas "in the Italian taste" to*

which the work dedicated to Bach formed a continuation; and the latter, works on temperament and organ building, as well as an "Entrance Hall [Vorgemach] to Musical Composition" (1745–47). See also No. 342.

340. On Bach's instructions for playing chorales, by Johann Gotthilf Ziegler (1746) (*BD* II, no. 542)

As concerns the playing of chorales, I was instructed by my teacher, Capellmeister Bach, who is still living, not to play the songs merely offhand but according to the sense [*Affect*] of the words.

The post of organist at the Church of Our Lady in Halle, which Bach declined in 1714, then went to Gottfried Kirchhoff. When he died, in 1746, Ziegler wrote a letter of application in which the above passage occurs: but the choice of the town councilors fell upon Wilhelm Friedemann Bach, who served as organist from 1747 to 1764.

341. On Bach's criticism of Gottfried Silbermann's system of temperament, by Georg Andreas Sorge (1748) (*BD* II, no. 575)

In a word, Silbermann's system of temperament cannot be maintained under the conditions of present-day practice. That all this is nothing but the truth I call all nonpartisan musicians who are expert in the matter to witness, especially the world-famous Mr. Bach in Leipzig. It is therefore to be wished that that superior man [Silbermann], who has acquired so much honor and fame, as well as a good bit of money, with his excellent art, should change his mind about temperament, improve his otherwise beautiful and well-constructed organs in respect to temperament, and thus add to his fame the very important portion that is still lacking to it. . . . The 4 bad triads are of a rough, wild, or, as Capellmeister Bach in Leipzig says, barbaric nature intolerable to a good ear.

342. On Bach's adroitness in preluding chorales, from the preface to the *First Part of Preludes to Well-Known Chorale Tunes,* by Georg Andreas Sorge (1750) (Wolff, p. 115)

Next to the knowledge of figured bass, to which my "Vorgemach der musicalischen Composition" [Lobenstein, 1745–1747] gives sufficiently comprehensive and detailed instructions, nothing is more important to the organist than that he be adroit in preluding to the various chorales, according to their particular content, so that the congregation will be stimulated to sing the subsequent chorale with appropriate devotion. The preludes on the Catechism Chorales by Mr.

Capellmeister Bach in Leipzig are examples of this kind of keyboard piece that deserve the great renown they enjoy. But because works such as these are so difficult as to be all but unusable by young beginners and others who may lack the considerable proficiency they require, I have prepared, at the suggestion of my good friends as well as my own pupils, the following eight simple preludes, to be played only on the manuals, and I herewith publicly present them to those members of our musical youth who are eager to learn and to all devotees of this type of playing.

CRITICISM AND DEFENSE: A CONTROVERSY

Introductory Note

What Bach's contemporaries thought about him is strikingly illustrated in the controversy the highlights of which are given here. The dispute was touched off by a criticism of Bach published by Johann Adolph Scheibe.

Scheibe had been a pupil of Bach's. In 1729 he had applied for the post of organist at St. Thomas's, and Bach had been one of the judges who picked Görner in preference to him. Perhaps the defeat rankled, and it is possible that Scheibe was voicing his resentment in the criticism that he published anonymously in his *Critischer Musikus.*

In it he accused Bach, as many a contemporary may have done, of writing in an overladen style. But the criticism is not particularly severe, and does not really smack of personal resentment. Doubtless it was the anonymity that Scheibe had foolishly assumed that made the Bach worshipers spring into action, counterattacking with considerably more vehemence and personal invective than the attack itself had shown.

The first reproof to Scheibe was administered by a teacher of rhetoric at Leipzig University, Johann Abraham Birnbaum, who, according to Mizler, possessed a good grasp of music and played the clavier decently. His essay was first published as a pamphlet and then reprinted in Mizler's *Musikalische Bibliothek.* Scheibe, too, reprinted it, with numerous footnotes. From then on, the matter became the object of rebuttal and surrebuttal in a series of increasingly lengthy papers.

Scheibe repeated some of his original statements in a letter published by Mattheson, and drew a reply from Mizler. Scheibe then resorted to writing thinly veiled parodies on Bach and Mizler, but also made various attempts to do justice to Bach in print (see Nos. 325, 331, and 332).

A considerable part of this tempest in a teapot centered on the single word *Musikant,* which had originally designated simply a musician, without any derogatory connotation. But just at this time it had begun to assume the meaning of a mere practical and somewhat humble musician, like "fiddler," as opposed to "violinist," in modern usage. Since no exact equivalent exists in English, we have kept the word wherever it appears.

343. "Letter from an Able *Musikant* Abroad" [by Johann Adolph Scheibe], May 14, 1737 (*BD* II, no. 400)

... Finally, Mr. ———— is the most eminent of the *Musikanten* in ————. He is an extraordinary artist on the clavier and on the organ, and he has until now encountered only one person with whom he can dispute the palm of superiority. I have heard this great man play on various occasions. One is amazed at his ability, and one can hardly conceive how it is possible for him to achieve such agility, with his fingers and with his feet, in the crossings, extensions, and extreme jumps that he manages, without mixing in a single wrong tone, or displacing his body by any violent movement.

This great man would be the admiration of whole nations if he had more amenity [*Annehmlichkeit*], if he did not take away the natural element in his pieces by giving them a turgid [*schwülstig*] and confused style, and if he did not darken their beauty by an excess of art. Since he judges according to his own fingers, his pieces are extremely difficult to play; for he demands that singers and instrumentalists should be able to do with their throats and instruments whatever he can play on the clavier. But this is impossible. Every ornament, every little grace, and everything that one thinks of as belonging to the method of playing, he expresses completely in notes: and this not only takes away from his pieces the beauty of harmony but completely covers the melody throughout. All the voices must work with each other and be of equal difficulty, and none of them can be recognized as the principal voice. In short, he is in music what Mr. von Lohenstein was in poetry. Turgidity has led them both from the natural to the artificial, and from the lofty to the somber; and in both one admires the onerous labor and uncommon effort—which, however, are vainly employed, since they conflict with Nature.

344. "Impartial Comments on a Questionable Passage in the Sixth Number of *Der Critische Musicus*," by Johann Abraham Birnbaum (1738) (*BD* II, no. 409)

To the Most Honored Sir, Mr. Johann Sebastian Bach, Royally Appointed Court Composer and Capellmeister to His Royal Majesty in Poland and Serene

Electoral Highness in Saxony, as well as Director of Music and Cantor at the St. Thomas School in Leipzig, the author dedicates, with great devotion, these pages concerning him.

Quid verum atque decens curo, et rogo, et omnis in hoc sum.

[The search of truth and decency hath fill'd my breast, Hath every thought and faculty possess'd.]

HORACE [*Epist.* I, i, 11.]

The person is still to be born who will have the quite exceptional good fortune to please everyone. For it is not to be denied: we should wait in vain, in a world of which imperfection is all too characteristic, for a man who, as the embodiment of all perfections, would be worthy to receive the approval of everyone. We have reason enough, then, to be satisfied if, in the inseparable combination of good and evil, the former clearly outweighs the latter.

Praise and blame are the usual judgments of men who have both elements before them. If both are to be weighed by justice, truth above all should speak for them. But how great may be the number of those who on this account know how to make a fundamental determination of true perfections? If all those who make it their chief concern to judge the actions and omissions of others possessed the ability needed for this purpose, there is no denying that everyone would get his just deserts. The number of base flatterers and ill-advised faultfinders would, on the other hand, be smaller than it is.

Now, daily experience teaches that both praise and blame are the most dangerous stones over which the judgments of most people stumble. Little reflection will be needed in order to discover more than one reason for this. Sometimes it is a lack of deep insight into the matters to be praised or blamed. Things are judged by people who do not understand them. At times one is blinded by too partisan emotions. Such a judgment always does violence to truth. Sometimes an arbitrary and spoiled taste makes laws for reason to obey. What conforms to this taste is alone recognized as worthy of praise. What is in conflict with it, on the other hand, is summarily and unjustly discarded. Often one is misled by the general opinion. One speaks then more in accordance with the opinion of others than from one's own conviction. Thus it cannot be otherwise: people and things of quite exceptional qualities are deprived of the value that properly attaches to them.

Such, approximately, were the thoughts that crossed my mind when the Sixth Part of the *Critische Musicus* came to my eyes. I read therein a letter that contained both praise and blame for persons some of whom are really the most eminent masters in Germany and Saxony, and some want to pass for such. Since the writer does not give his name, although he utters his opinions pretty freely on one thing and another, a certain curiosity was aroused in me to inquire a little more closely into who the author of this letter might be. And I did not consider this curiosity so very unjustified. I believed that knowledge about [the identity of] a person who lays his opinions before the world would lead to a more accurate investigation of his abilities and his insight into what he was judging; and that this would provide an opportunity the better to test the value of the opinions themselves. I thus fell into various suspicions, some of which may perhaps not have been unfounded. At least certain special circumstances concerning the said letter revealed very clearly that one should not aim long at the target [(*Ziel-*)*Scheibe*] if one wished to hit the bull's-eye.

I have already pointed out that the purpose of the letter is to judge both the merits and the shortcomings of certain composers and musical experts. 'Tis but a pity that the judgments do not always coincide with the truth, and smack too strongly of prejudice. As evidence of this, the following passage may serve.

[Here Birnbaum quotes Scheibe's criticism of Bach (No. 343) in full.]

I have chosen this passage from among various others principally because partly the love of truth and partly also the particular esteem for the truly great master in music whom it concerns oblige me to defend his honor. The man in question is the *Royal Polish and Electoral Saxon Court Composer and Capellmeister, Mr. Johann Sebastian Bach in Leipzig.*

The author of these lines praises the Hon. Court Composer in one place, and finds fault with him all the more sharply in another. On closer investigation I have found the praise given him to be incomplete and the blame groundless. I shall demonstrate both these conclusions more clearly.

The Hon. Court Composer is called the most eminent of the *Musicanten* in Leipzig. This expression smacks too strongly of the mean and low, and does not fit the titles "extraordinary artist," "great man," "the admiration of whole nations," which are applied to the Hon. Court Composer in what follows. The term *Musicanten* is generally used for those whose principal achievement is a form of mere musical practice. They are employed for the purpose (indeed, they often devote themselves voluntarily to it) of bringing pieces written by others into sound by means of musical instruments. As a matter of fact, not even all the men of this sort, but only the humblest and meanest of them, usually bear this name, so there is hardly any difference between *Musicanten* and beer-fiddlers. If one of those musical *practici* is an extraordinary artist on an instrument, he is called not a *Musicant* but a virtuoso. And least of all does this disdainful name apply to great composers and those who have to conduct choruses. Now, let the reasonable reader himself decide whether the praise that is due the Hon. Court Composer can be fully expressed by calling him the most eminent of the *Musicanten.* This is in my opinion equivalent to wishing to pay a special tribute to a thoroughly learned man by calling him the best member of the last class of schoolboys. The Hon. Court Composer is a great composer, a master of music, a virtuoso on the organ and the clavier without an equal, but in no sense a *Musicant.* Perhaps, however, the author will wish to excuse himself by saying that on this occasion he departed from the ordinary usage of language and took the word *Musicant* in a far nobler sense. But this would help him little. For supposing he had had good grounds for departing from the ordinary usage of language which I am far from granting—then he should at least have instructed the reader, by a clear definition, concerning the new meaning. Indeed, he would not even have needed to employ this word. For there is no lack of expressions in the German language that indicate far more emphatically what should have been said.

In the words that immediately follow, the author praises the Hon. Court Composer as "an extraordinary artist on the clavier and the organ." I could state in this connection that "artist" [*Künstler*] sounds much too much like a handicraftsman, and that to speak thus is just as contrary to the usage of language once introduced as it would be to call philosophers, orators, and poets "artists" in thinking, speaking, and verse making. But this is a trifle. And I would have left it quite unmentioned if the use of a word that has such an inappropriate meaning, in place of which a far more emphatic one could have been used with little trouble, did not give grounds for suspecting that the author was not really in earnest about discussing the quite extraordinary ability of the Hon. Court Composer in the terms it deserves. It would have sounded much more emphatic if he had said, expressing himself in the manner of musical talk: "he is extraordinarily strong on the clavier and the organ," or "he is an extraordinary virtuoso on both."

The author writes further that "the Hon. Court Composer has until now encountered only one person with whom he can dispute the palm of superiority." Just who may be meant by this is unknown to me, as well as to many others. The author would have put many people under obligation, and could have satisfied their justifiable curiosity, if he had given more precise information about this man. But I doubt whether he will ever be in a position to do so. If he is aiming at a certain great master of music in a foreign realm, who, it is said, has in accordance with the usage of his country received the dignity of a doctorate in music because of his quite special ability, I will invoke the testimony of some impartial connoisseurs of music who on their journeys have also had the good fortune of hearing this great man, and have praised his ability uncommonly, but nevertheless have frankly stated that *there was only one Bach in the world, and no one could equal him.* Accordingly, it may be said that the Hon. Court Composer has still encountered *no one* with whom he could dispute the palm of superiority.

Then the author divulges more precisely what he found worthy of praise and admiration in this man whom he heard play on various occasions. He admires the uncommon agility of his hands and feet; he considers it inconceivable that it is possible in the fastest and most violent movements of both hands and feet, and with such wide jumps, not to "mix in a single wrong tone" or to "displace the body." Now, all this is just and correct; yet such a judgment would also have been pronounced by a man who did not have a thorough knowledge of music. But since the author wishes to be regarded as a man whose judgment is far above the common taste, it seems to me very curious that he did not mention in addition circumstances that are far more important than this—circumstances that could easily strike a real connoisseur of true musical perfections. Why does he not praise the astonishing mass of unusual and well-developed ideas? the developments of a single subject through the keys with the most agreeable variations? the quite special adroitness, even at the greatest speed, in bringing out all the tones clearly and with uninterrupted evenness? the uncommon fluency with which he plays in the most difficult keys just as quickly and accurately as in the simplest? and in general an amenity that is everywhere joined with art? To discuss such remarkable perfections, which indisputably belong to the Hon. Court Composer alone, and to emphasize them as they deserve, would have been better worth the author's trouble.

But even the little that the author observes about the perfections of the Hon. Court Composer would almost have led him to believe that the latter would be "the admiration of whole nations," if the author had not been led away from this good idea by false notions of certain errors that are supposed to be of such a nature as to detract from the fame of the Hon. Court Composer. Suddenly he changes his language;

and the praise that has hitherto been given to this great man now changes into an even stronger faultfinding, which, however, as will appear from what follows, is ungrounded.

He reproaches Bach's pieces, to begin with, with a lack of "amenity" (that is, melody without dissonances), or as others say, who have no better understanding of the matter, "because they do not please the ear." Now, to refute this accusation a noteworthy passage in the English *Spectator* [in the 24th (later 29th) Essay of the First Volume, p. 161 (April 3, 1711, by Joseph Addison)] would suffice almost by itself. This passage reads: "Music is not design'd to please only Chromatick Ears, but all that are capable of distinguishing harsh from agreeable [*recte:* disagreeable] Notes"—that is, those who know how to introduce a dissonance skillfully and resolve it adroitly. The true amenity of music consists in the connection and alternation of consonances and dissonances without hurt to the harmony. The nature of music demands this. The various passions, especially the dark ones, cannot be expressed with fidelity to Nature without this alternation. One would be doing violence to the everywhere accepted rules of composition if one wished to slight it. Indeed the well-founded opinion of a musical ear that does not follow the vulgar taste values such alternation, and rejects on the other hand the insipid little ditties that consist of nothing but consonances, as something of which one very soon becomes tired. How carefully the Hon. Court Composer sees to this alternation, and how poignantly pleasing his harmony is, is clearly to be seen from his pieces. And this is confirmed by the complete approval of those whose musical hearing is not spoiled by I know not what newfangled taste. Consequently the faultfinding of the author is groundless. And this conclusion will remain valid until he shall be able to refute the given definition of "amenity," and replace it by a better one.

The Hon. Court Composer is further accused of "taking away the natural element in his pieces by giving them a turgid and confused style." This is as severe as it is obscure. What does "turgid" mean in music? Is it to be taken in that sense in which in rhetoric that style of writing is called turgid in which the most splendid ornaments are lavished on matters of slight import, so that their worthlessness is only the more brought to light thereby; in which useless splendor of all kinds is invoked from outside the subject without having the essential beauty clearly in view; in which the desire for decoration leads one to hit upon contemptible, forced, and inconsequential trifles and to confuse important ideas with childish notions? If so, I concede that such mistakes may be made in music by those who either do not understand the rules of composition or do not know how to employ them properly. But even to think such a thing of the Hon. Court Composer, let alone to say it, would be the greatest abuse. For this composer does not lavish his splendid ornaments on drinking songs, lullabies, or other insipid *galanteries*. In his church compositions, overtures, concertos, and other musical works, one finds decorations that are always appropriate to the principal ideas he has wished to develop. The author has therefore made a statement for which there is no basis, since it is obscure and cannot be proved; accordingly the comparison he makes shortly thereafter between the Hon. Court Composer and Mr. von Lohenstein is itself an idea that belongs among the reprehensible ornaments, and thus to the turgid style of writing.

What does the word "confused" mean in music? One must certainly call upon the definition of what "confused" means in general, if one wishes to guess what the author's meaning may be. This much I know: that "confused" means that which has no order, and of which the individual parts are so strangely thrown about and mixed up among one another that one cannot see where each really belongs. If that is what the author understands by the word, then he must hold, in respect to the Hon. Court Composer, that there is no order in his pieces, and everything in them is so mixed up that one cannot discover what they are about. If this is the author's judgment in earnest, I must almost believe that a certain confusion has taken place in *his* thoughts that prevents him from knowing the truth. Where the rules of composition are most strictly observed, there without fail order must reign. Now, I hope that the author will never consider the Hon. Court Composer as a violator of these rules. It is certain, by the way, that the voices in the works of this great master of music work wonderfully in and about one another, but without the slightest confusion. They move along together or in opposition, as necessary. They part company, and yet all meet again at the proper time. Each voice distinguishes itself clearly from the others by a particular variation, although they often imitate each other. They now flee, now follow one another without one's noticing the slightest irregularity in their efforts to outdo one another. Now, when all this is performed as it should be, there is nothing more beautiful than this harmony. If, however, the clumsiness or negligence of the instrumentalists or singers brings about confusion, it is truly very tasteless to attribute such mistakes to the composer. In music, anyway, everything depends on performance. The most wretched melodies often please the ear if they are well played. On the other hand, a piece in whose composition one can see the most beautiful harmony and melody can certainly not please the ear if those who are to perform it are unable and unwilling to fulfill their obligations. If then, as has been sufficiently demonstrated, there is nothing either turgid or confused to be found in the works of the Hon. Court Composer, the natural element— that is the necessary agreeable melody and harmony—cannot be taken away from them by this means. Instead, the praiseworthy efforts of the Hon. Court Composer are directed toward the end of presenting this natural element to the world, through his art, in its highest splendor.

But that is just what the author will not concede. He says explicitly that the Hon. Court Composer "darkens the beauty of his works by an excess of art." This sentence contradicts the nature of true art, which is what is here being discussed. The essential aims of true art are to imitate Nature, and, where necessary, to aid it. If art imitates Nature, then indisputably the natural element must everywhere shine through in works of art. Accordingly it is impossible that art should take away the natural element from those things in which it imitates Nature— including music. If art aids Nature, then its aim is only to preserve it, and to improve its condition; certainly not to destroy it. Many things are delivered to us by Nature in the most misshapen states, which, however, acquire the most beautiful appearance when they have been formed by art. Thus art lends Nature a beauty it lacks, and increases the beauty it possesses. Now, the greater the art is—that is, the more industriously and painstakingly it works at the improvement of Nature—the more brilliantly shines the beauty thus brought into being. Accordingly it is impossible that the greatest art should darken the beauty of a thing. Can it be possible, then, that the Hon. Court Composer, even by the use of the greatest art he applies in the working out of his musical compositions, could take away from them the natural element and darken its beauty?

Up to this point the author has attempted to make Bach's works repulsive to delicate ears. Now he sets out to issue a warning against them to the rest-loving fingers of instrumentalists, and to the throats of singers, which have been spoiled over a long period. He represents them as being very difficult to play, since the Hon. Court Composer, in writing them, "judged only according to his own fingers." He accordingly considers the demand "that singers and instrumentalists should be able to do with their throats and instruments whatever he can play on the clavier" as impossible. I grant that the pieces written by the Hon. Court Composer are very difficult to play, but only for those who are not willing to train their fingers to fluent motion and correct fingering. Incidentally, he is not unjust when, in writing these pieces, he judges according to his own fingers. His reasoning can only be as follows: that which I have achieved by industry and practice, anyone else with tolerable natural gift and ability can also achieve. And for this very reason the alleged impossibility falls to the ground. One can do anything if only one really wishes to, and if one industriously strives to convert natural abilities, by untiring zeal, into finished skills. If it is not impossible for the Hon. Court Composer to play pieces on the clavier with two hands, perfectly and without the least error, in which both principal and inner voices have their proper share of work, how should it be impossible to a whole chorus, consisting of so many persons each of whom has to pay attention only to one part? The objection that the accuracy needed for this task and the maintenance of the steady tempo throughout are impossible when many persons take part is untenable. It is true that there are difficulties, but that does not mean that they are insurmountable. If a whole army can be trained to the point where at a given command many thousands of men are seen to move as if they were one, the same accuracy must be all the more surely possible to a musical chorus consisting of far fewer persons. The clearest proof of this possibility, even in musical choruses, we see in the well-appointed musical forces of royal and princely personages. No one who has had the good fortune to be present at a concert given by the famous Capelle of the greatest court in Saxony will doubt the truthfulness of this assertion.

But this does not dispose of the author's claim that Bach's pieces are impossible to play or sing. He reproaches them further with the fact that the Hon. Court Composer writes out "every ornament, every little grace, and everything that one thinks of as belonging to the method of playing, complete in notes." Either the author notes this as something characteristic of the Hon. Court Composer alone, or else he holds it to be a failure in general. If the former, he errs mightily. The Hon. Court Composer is neither the first nor the only man to write thus. From among a mass of composers whom I could cite in this respect, I will mention only [Nicolas de] Grigny and [Pierre] Du Mage, who in their *Livres d'orgue* have used this very method. If the latter, I can find no reason why it should deserve the name of fault. On the contrary, I consider it, for reasons that cannot be disregarded, as a necessary measure of prudence on the part of the composer. To begin with, it is certain that what is called the "manner" of singing or playing [the addition of ornaments] is almost everywhere valued and considered desirable. It is also indisputable that this manner can please the ear only if it is applied in the right places but must on the contrary uncommonly offend the ear and spoil the principal melody if the performer employs it at the wrong spot. Now, experience teaches further that usually its application is left to the free whim of singers and instrumentalists. If all such men were sufficiently instructed in that which is truly beautiful in the manner; if they always knew how to employ it where it might serve as a true ornament and particular emphasis of the main melody; in that case it would be superfluous for the composer to write down in notes once more what they already knew. But only the fewest have a sufficient knowledge, and the rest, by an inappropriate application of the manner, spoil the principal melody and indeed often introduce such passages as might easily be attributed, by those who do not know the true state of affairs, to an error of the composer. Therefore every composer, including the Hon. Court Composer, is entitled to set the wanderers back on the right path by prescribing a correct method according to his intentions, and thus to watch over the preservation of his own honor. As a result of this explanation, the opinion of the author that this procedure "takes away from the Hon. Court Composer's pieces the beauty of harmony and makes the principal melody unattractive" falls of its own weight to the ground.

The last exception the author wishes to take to the pieces by the Hon. Court Composer amounts to this: that "all the voices work with each other and are of equal difficulty, and none of them can be recognized as the principal voice" (by which presumably the upper voice is meant). Now, the idea that the melody must always be in the upper voice and that the constant collaboration of the other voices is a fault is one for which I have been able to find no sufficient grounds. Rather, is it the exact opposite that flows from the very nature of music. For music consists of harmony, and harmony becomes far more complete if all the voices collaborate to form it. Accordingly this is not a failing but rather a musical perfection, and I am very much astonished that the author could consider this a failing, since it is characteristic of the Italian taste, nowadays everywhere so highly admired, especially in church works. The author need only look into the works of *Praenestinus* [Palestrina], among the old composers, or [Antonio] Lotti and others among the more modern ones, and he will find not only that all the voices are continuously at work but also that each one has a melody of its own that harmonizes quite well with the others.

I therefore leave the question open whether the author of the passage I have now examined, on closer examination of the stated reasons, may not soon find that he infringed upon the reputation and the merits of so great a man and may not have reason to regret his unjust opinion.

Undoubtedly he was too hasty, and perhaps he did not really know the Hon. Court Composer. If he had known him, I am convinced, he would have bestowed upon him the same praise that in this letter he awards to the famous Mr. Graun. By changing only a single word, he would thus have been able to say, "The great Augustus bestows his favor upon him and rewards his deserts; this suffices for his praise. Whoever is loved by so great and wise a prince must certainly possess true skill." If he had considered this, he would not have made bold to find fault with a man whose slightest perfection he is not fit to imitate. Indeed, he would have kept in mind that it is no art to find fault, but that to do better is always what is furthest removed from those who always find so much to reproach in others. I, together with all other true admirers of the *great Bach,* wish the author in the future more salutary thoughts and, after the completion of his musical journeys, the happy beginning of a new life that may be free of all unnecessary desire to find fault.

345. A reply by Scheibe, February 18, 1738 (*BD* II, no. 413)

. . . I am not at all put out about an essay recently issued in Leipzig against the above-mentioned writing. I regret only that it smacks too strongly of the partiality and injustice of its author and that the latter has revealed in it only too clearly how little he knows the true basis of music, and its real beauty. Even one who knows nothing would have to admit this at the first glance at this essay, and my readers will realize it even more when I describe for them the disorderly statements that make up this wondrous defense of one of the greatest *Musikanten* of our time. Indeed, this famous man has been more injured than exalted by this flattering essay in praise of him, and his qualities have been ruthlessly submitted to the most exacting examination by the fact that he is set above all other *Musikanten* and that it is expressly maintained that there is only one Bach in the world.

But before I bring these pages to a definite end, I must explain one thing with which I have been at various times reproached and even most violently condemned. It is represented to be the greatest error that I should use the word *Musikant* in such a noble sense. I am even accused of insulting, through its use, those great masters of music to whom I have applied this term, since it is supposed to apply only to the meanest or at most the mediocre heroes of music. I would not be subjected to these reproaches, however, if the word *Musikant* were looked at without prejudice, and if an effort were made to understand its true meaning. . . .

Actually, *Musikanten* should be ashamed not to wish to be taken for what they really are. They wish to cultivate music and make a name for themselves, and thus earn fame, honor, money, and their daily bread; and yet (what folly!) they do not wish to be called *Musikanten.* According to this, a philosopher would have to be ashamed to bear the name of his science. A lawyer would also have to discard his title, and in the end new titles would have to be found in all the branches of learning to indicate what and who the people are who cultivate them. And how will men in the end satisfy the mad rapacity of their pride?

Surely this remarkable and contemptible pride is partly responsible for the fact that the good name of music and *Musikanten* has fallen so low, and falls still further every day. If all *Musikanten* knew what it takes to be a real *Musikant,* what his true qualities are, and how he can win true esteem, they would rather consider it an honor to bear the title that the ancient Greeks considered one of the most honorable and that they often applied to their greatest philosophers.

346. Refutations of Scheibe, by Lorenz Christoph Mizler (1738–1739) (*BD* II, nos. 420, 336)

. . . The twenty-sixth and last number [of the *Critische Musikus*] finally seeks to defend the author, claiming that he is right in calling even the greatest musicians *Musicanten.* He adduces grounds that are not pertinent. He says one should regard the word without prejudice. Now, what should a prejudice mean in this case? Prejudices have validity in the usage of a language just as they may be cited in a court or faculty of law, if they are not contrary to reason. There is, then, nothing unreasonable about calling humble folk who earn their living at music *Musicanten.* Since this belongs to an old usage of speech, a reasonable man must not depart from it, particularly if the new meaning has in it something of the ludicrous. Horace says, quite reasonably: *usus norma loquendi,* i.e., in speaking one must be governed by the usage of speech. In such matters it does no good to reason too subtly. It suffices that people do not speak thus. None of what the author further presents to justify himself is pertinent. For words are symbols that denote concepts with which they are associated. The association with concepts was arbitrary at first, but became obligatory through general introduction and can therefore no longer very well be changed. One may say "the *Musicanten* in the tavern at Golitz," but not "the Royal Court *Musicanten* in Dressden"; rather, "the Royal *Capelle,*" "the virtuosi." There are, indeed, many other words: "a man expert in music," "an artist in tones," "a composer," "a good singer," "a violinist," "a virtuoso on the violin," and so forth; so this particular low word need not be used. The word *Musicus* has also, as a matter of fact, acquired German nationality, although it has a Latin ending, there being other such words in the German language. However, since the author lays so much store by this word, we shall always call him a *Musicant,* but otherwise we shall use the word properly.

The other matter we wish to discuss concerns the animus of the Critical *Musicant* against Capellmeister Bach. In this letter, on page 11 [of Johann Mattheson's *Kern melodischer Wissenschaft* (Hamburg, 1737], it is stated that "Bach's church compositions are always more artificial and laborious, but by no means of such effect, conviction, and reasonable reflection as the works of Telemann and Graun."

I still cannot avoid the idea that the Critical *Musicant* must either not have listened carefully to anything by Capellmeister Bach or not yet have had any mature knowledge of music when he did hear it. Mr. Telemann and Mr. Graun are excellent composers, and Mr. Bach has written works of just the same quality, but if Mr. Bach at times writes the inner parts more fully than other composers, he has taken as his model the music of twenty or twenty-five years ago. He can write otherwise, however, when he wishes to. Anyone who heard the music that was performed by the students at the Easter Fair in Leipzig last year, in the Most High Presence of his Royal Majesty in Poland, which was composed by Capellmeister Bach, must admit that it was written entirely in accordance with the latest taste, and was approved by everyone. So well does the Capellmeister know how to suit himself to his listeners.

347. A satire, by "Cornelius" [Scheibe] (1739) (*BD* II, no. 442)

To the Critical Musikus

MY DEAR SIR,

I am one of those *Musikanten* who have striven with the greatest care to achieve extreme facility in playing an instrument, and an admirable ability at composing in the most intricate style. I could prove by the testimony not only of all the inhabitants of the town that has the honor to contain me within its walls, but also of all the chiefs of the musical *Capellen* in the surrounding villages and hamlets, that I am the greatest of all artists on the cittern [*Cithrinchen*] and that, over and above this, I compose so intricately and wonderfully that listening to my pieces makes people quite bewildered. Everything is intermingled. Everything is so completely worked out that one cannot tell one voice from another, nor can one ever recognize the principal melody or understand the words. Let it be said, however, to anyone who would make bold to find fault with my ability, to cast doubt upon my merits, or in any way to belittle my fame, that I am the greatest citharist and the greatest composer in the world. It is certain that if I had lived in the time of the ancient Greeks (whom our writers praise so highly in their papers), I should be remembered with greater fame than any of the ancient philosophers and *Musikanten.*

You know now who I am, and with whom you have to deal. But I must also explain to you at this point why I now write to you. I have never concerned myself with learned matters. I have also read very few musical writings or books. Your pages, too, would have remained unknown to me if my brother-in-law, the town clerk, had not induced me by many representations to look through them. I have always been of the opinion that a *Musikant* had enough to do with his art itself, without concerning himself with the writing of extensive books, or with learned and philosophical investigations, and wasting his time in such fashion. For that reason, too, I cannot really approve of your undertaking, and, to tell the truth, you would be wiser to stick to the practice of music, seeking to contrive some fine new instrument or composition and distinguish yourself thus. Since, however, you are intent on writing about music, it is my intention to reveal to you herewith how you are to conduct yourself in referring to my person. First, however, you may consider it no small honor that I have decided, with the help of a learned man who is my good friend, to prepare these lines addressed to you. I myself have never taken the time to learn how to write an extensive letter, and I have been able up to now to dispense very well with this pedantry. Notes, my dear Sir, I can write perfectly and in great quantities so that you would be astonished if you saw my intricate scores.

But now to the matter in hand. I have found in the course of reading through your pages that you have taken the liberty to write about great artists in music very bitingly, and that you have even been so foolhardy as to ridicule and find fault with many excellent works of art which have caused no little severe and arduous brain work. Since, however, as I have firmly convinced myself, I am undoubtedly the greatest artist in music, I cannot forbear to warn you that you are in the future not to make bold to find fault with me, or to condemn or make ridiculous the manifold counterpoints, canons, circular songs, and all the other intricate forms of music writing that, as I have found, you have perversely called "turgid." All these things are particularly close to my heart. And my greatest pleasure and joy come when I have made a piece in which I have introduced, if not all, at least most of these artifices. What good are those bare songs that can be understood at once and remembered and sung from memory? I reserve my praise for a piece in which everything is finely intermingled, so that the listener is astonished and cannot conceive in what variegated curlicues everything is interwoven with everything else, since no melody and in fact nothing can be remembered. These are the true masterpieces. In them one may recognize a composer.

Shame on you, Sir, that you once attacked such remarkable works of art. And do not make bold to express any longer your false and annoying opinion, or to maintain it, or to go so far as to use it to belittle me. I assure you that I will not let such insult stand. Though I cannot write against you myself, I will persuade one of my good friends to defend me against you. The learned man who is now writing you this letter according to my indications and ideas will protect me against you, you may be sure. Don't let things come to that, for you might very easily rue it. I am a man of my word, and what I have once decided to do, that I invariably carry out.

I shall see how you conduct yourself. If you accept my suggestions, you will always have a good friend in me; but if you go against my will, then you may be very sure that you and all your followers will be most violently pursued by him who until then calls himself,

Sir, Your Honor's servant,

W., December 30, 1737 [*sic*]   "CORNELIUS"

The copy of Scheibe's Critischer Musikus *in the New York Public Library bears a notation in an eighteenth-century hand: "This letter is a satire on Mr. Bach." Scheibe himself, however, claimed that it was the expression of a fictitious character who combined the follies of various musicians.*

348. A summary account of the controversy, by Christoph Gottlieb Schröter (1746) (*BD* II, no. 552)

Concerning the "letter" in the Sixth Number [of Scheibe's *Critischer Musikus*], one soon became aware of a new battle of pens, because the Critical Musician had found fault with certain persons expert in music, and especially had cast reflections on the famous Capellmeister Bach. For although it was claimed on p. 41 that the letter had been written by a traveling musician to a master of music, and the latter had requested its inclusion, yet it was soon learned that the *Criticus* had framed this excessively fine piece of satirical writing himself. . . .

Perhaps those who have not read the critical pages and other writings in the matter will be anxious to know whether Capellmeister Bach has remained silent in the face of them. *Answer:* Since he was not in a position, on account of the piling up of his official duties, to answer the Critical Musician properly, Magister Birnbaum undertook the task, and wrote *Impartial Comments on a Questionable Passage in the Sixth Part of* Der critische Musicus. *In 8. One sheet and six pages.*

These *Impartial Comments* were incorporated by Magister Mizler in his *Musicalische Bibliothek,* Fourth Part, pp. 62–73. But modestly as the aforementioned Magister Birnbaum addressed the Critical Musician— all the more immodest and confused was the subsequent *Reply to the* Impartial Comments, *etc., written by Johann Adolph Scheibe. Hamburg, 1738 2½ sheets in 8.*

This ill-conceived *Reply* is to be found as a supplement to the First Part of the *Critischer Musicus.* Thereupon one was much pleased to see *Magister Johann Abraham Birnbaum's Defense of his* Impartial Comments, *etc., Against Joh. Adolph Scheibe's* Reply *to the Same, 1738. Six sheets in 8.*

With this well-conceived *Defense,* Magister Birnbaum gave new proof of his native modesty and thoroughness. And although on pages 75 and 76 the opinion given of the knowledge necessary to a finished composer is a little too sparing, yet the learned author may easily be forgiven for such a small oversight, since music is only his avocation. In reply to this *Defense* the Critical Musician has not published any special answer, but in the Second Part he has in various places again betrayed his injurious stubbornness. All impartial readers can see from this diffuse report that what he published in the Sixth Number was not a permissible satire but a shameful libel. Since in the face of the anger thus aroused he has not adopted any modest or well-grounded position, but instead has heaped injury upon injury, it is to be feared that with his defamatory style of writing he will bring still more dis- turbance upon himself, which hardship no one, because of his other good qualities, wishes to see visited upon him.

Actually, Scheibe had not failed to have the last word: in 1745 he had reprinted Birnbaum's Defense *with 164 polemic footnotes (BD II, no. 441).*

PART V

*Bach
in the
Second Half
of the
Eighteenth Century*

Bach in the
Second Half of the
Eighteenth Century

Introductory Note

The group of writers represented here is not quite as variegated as that of the authors of the Reports and Reviews given above. It does include J. M. Schmidt, a Leipzig theologian, who mentions Bach twice in a treatise dealing, as the subtitle indicates, with the Comprehension of God and His Will through Music; but the other authors were mostly professional musicians. Bach's pupils form a sizable group among them: his son Carl Philipp Emanuel; Johann Friedrich Agricola; Johann Philipp Kirnberger; Carl Friedrich Abel; Heinrich Nicolaus Gerber, speaking through his son Ernst Ludwig, the lexicographer who took up the task of musical biography where Johann Gottfried Walther had left off; and Johann Christian Kittel. Outsiders, however, are equally conspicuous: Johann Joachim Quantz and his pupil Frederick the Great; Friedrich Wilhelm Marpurg, Royal *Lotterie-Director* and assiduous writer on music; Johann Friedrich Daube, an outstanding propagator of Rameau's theories of harmony; Jakob Adlung, author of an invaluable treatise on organ building; Johann Nikolaus Forkel, who wrote the first monograph on Bach; and finally Johann Friedrich Reichardt, Agricola's successor as capellmeister in Berlin, a fluent writer in words as well as tones, who looked back on Bach with the critical eye of a more "advanced" period.

349. On the merits of Bach, by Johann Friedrich Agricola (August 28, 1750) (*BD* II, no. 620)

One need consider only the Masses of [Gottfried Heinrich] Stölzel, who died recently, the Masses and Magnificats of Bach, who died a few days ago in Leipzig, the countless church compositions, especially the choruses of the venerable Telemann, who is still living, and the Psalms by Handel and many other ingenious men: one will find that there are Germans who can easily measure up to [Giacomo Antonio] Perti. Besides, specialists assure us that Perti is by no means a wizard of fugal writing. Fux, Telemann, Bach, Handel, Graun, and others among the Germans have accomplished much more. All these composers stick to the point in fugal works; they are not as superficial as the Italians, who are in the habit of producing sham fugues.

[. . .]

The correspondent [Filippo Finazzi] is intending finally to diminish the merits of the famous and now deceased Mr. Bach. He generously pretends to let him pass for great, but this could not be in earnest. He denies his music the effect of pleasure for the listener who would not savor such difficult harmony. Yet, assuming the harmonies of this great man were so complex that they would not always achieve the intended result, they would nevertheless serve for the connoisseur's genuine delight. Not all learned people are able to understand a Newton [*Newton* = Isaac Newton], but those who have progressed far enough in profound science to be able to understand him will find the greater gratification and real benefit in reading his work. In short, Bach was a real ornament to the Germans, and his memory, which his works make immortal, will, with those knowledgeable in music, bring our country lasting glory; let an Italian castrato [Finazzi] say what he will.

350. On Bach's eminence in the development of organ playing, by Johann Joachim Quantz (1752) (*BD* III, no. 651)

As early as the last century, in fact from the middle of the same, a few famous men—some of whom had themselves visited Italy or France and profited thereby, while some took the works and the taste of distinguished foreigners as models—began to strive for an improvement of musical taste. The organists and clavier players—among the latter especially Froberger and after him Pachhelbel [*sic*], and among the former Reinken, Buxtehude, Bruhns, and some others—were almost the first to contrive the most tasteful instrumental compositions of their period for their instruments. But particularly the art of organ playing, which had to a great extent been learned from the Netherlanders, was already at this time in a high state of advancement, thanks to the abovementioned and some other able men. Finally the admirable Johann Sebastian Bach brought it to its greatest perfection in recent times.

We can only hope that now, after his death, owing to the small number of those who still devote sufficient industry to it, it will not again fall into decline or even decay.

351. On strict and free fugue, by Friedrich Wilhelm Marpurg (1753) (*BD* III, no. 655)

The true fugue is of two sorts, distinguished according to their treatment of the fugue subject:

(A) A strict fugue, *fuga obligata,* is one in which no other material than the subject is treated throughout, i.e., in which the subject, after the exposition (if not entirely, then at least in part) makes its appearance in one entry after another, so to speak, and in which, consequently, all the counterpoints and interludes are derived from the principal subject or from the counterpoint that first appears against the answer, by means of division, augmentation, diminution, contrary motion, etc.; all this, however, being bound together through imitation and a coherent and solid harmony. When such a strict fugue is worked out at length, and all kinds of other artifices (made possible by the many kinds of imitation, double counterpoint, canon, and change of key) are introduced in it, such a piece is called by the Italian name of *Ricercare* or *Ricercata*— an art fugue, a master fugue. Such is the nature of most of the fugues by the late Capellmeister Bach.

(B) A free fugue, *fuga libera, soluta, sciolta,* is a fugue in which the principal subject is not continuously treated; that is, in which it does not make its appearance in one entry after another, although often enough, and in which, when the principal subject is abandoned, a brief, well-chosen interlude is worked out by imitation and transposition— which has a similarity to the principal subject or to the counterpoint that first appears against the answer, and is related to the same, even though it is not always derived from it. Such is the nature of most of the fugues by Handel.

352. On keyboard fingering, by Carl Philipp Emanuel Bach (1753) (*BD* III, no. 654)

My late father told me about having heard great men in his youth who did not use the thumb except when it was necessary for large stretches. Since he lived at a time in which there gradually took place a quite remarkable change in musical taste, he was obliged to think out a much more complete use of the fingers, and especially to use the thumb (which apart from other uses is quite indispensable especially in the difficult keys) in such manner as Nature, as it were, wishes to see it used. Thus it was raised suddenly from its former idleness to the position of the principal finger.

Since this new fingering is such that it enables one to bring out all kinds of things at the proper time, I am using it . . . as a basis.

353. Dedication for the *Treatise on the Fugue,* Part II, by Friedrich Wilhelm Marpurg (1754) (*BD* III, no. 658)

Dedication to the most Worthy Brothers, Mr. Wilhelm Friedemann Bach, Music Director and Organist in Halle, and Mr. Carl Philipp Emanuel Bach, Royal Prussian Chamber Musician.

MOST NOBLE, HIGHLY TO BE ESTEEMED SIRS,

I take the liberty of laying before Your Honors the principles of an art that owes its improvement particularly to the excellent efforts of your famous Father. One need not look back even half a century to discover the happy moment when a beginning was made of combining imaginative harmonic changes with an agreeable and unified melody. At the very time when the world was beginning to degenerate in another direction, when light melody making was gaining the upper hand and people were becoming tired of difficult harmonies, the late Capellmeister was the one who knew how to keep to the golden mean, and taught us how to combine an agreeable and flowing melody with the richest harmonies.

Experience shows, Sirs, that a happy combination of these two elements has remained the property of your family. If the inheritance of a famous name is a factor that predisposes the world in one's favor, it is even far more excellent to increase this advantage by one's own merits. The charmingly learned and ever new tones of your fertile Muse have long been the delight of the Church, the Court, and the Town in turn; and if that taste is still considered the fairest by which the heart and the understanding are set into gentle motion together with the ear, the inventions of your minds must inspire the emulation of the most distant posterity. But I leave this material for your praise to a more gifted pen than my own, and rest content with recognizing your merits. I had in any case only the intention of submitting this Second Part of my treatise to your judgment. I have had the less hesitation in doing so since the first part was fortunate enough to meet with Your Honors' kind approval. I grasp this opportunity, Sirs, to thank you publicly for it and to declare to you the lively esteem with which I have the honor to be

Your Honors' most wholly obedient servant,

Berlin, February 1, 1754　　　　　　　　　　　THE AUTHOR

Part I of Marpurg's Treatise *was dedicated to Georg Philipp Telemann.*

354. On the depth of Bach's compositional art, by Johann Michael Schmidt (1754) (*BD* III, no. 659)

a. Man is indeed the Lord of Tone, but his song is not ready as soon as he opens his mouth to sing, as the song of the birds is. He must first add poetry to his [inarticulate] song, or learn a song from others. To the extent that he does the former, often and skillfully, he is called a composer. If he wishes to become great and famous, he must possess, in addition to knowledge of rules already discussed, all the powers of understanding in considerable degree; he must be able to think deeply and in intricate combinations. To be convinced of this, just look at the chorale, published in copper engraving, by Bach, who has now been received into the choir of angels: *Vom Himmel hoch da komm ich her.* I cannot persuade myself that the most difficult demonstration in geometry requires much deeper and more extensive reflection than this labor must have demanded.

b. Not many years ago it was reported from France that a man had made a statue that could play various pieces on the *Fleuttraversiere,* placed the flute to his lips and took it down again, rolled its eyes, etc. But no one has yet invented an image that thinks, or wills, or composes, or even does anything at all similar. Let anyone who wishes to be convinced look carefully at the last fugal work of the above-praised Bach, which has appeared in copper engraving, but which was left unfinished because his blindness intervened, and let him observe the art that is contained therein; or what must strike him as even more wonderful, the chorale that he dictated in his blindness to the pen of another: *Wenn wir in höchsten Nöthen seyn.* I am sure that he will soon need his soul if he wishes to observe all the beauties contained therein, let alone wishes to play it to himself or to form a judgment of the author. Everything that the champions of materialism put forward must fall to the ground in view of this single example.

355. On Bach's thorough-bass playing, by Johann Friedrich Daube (1756) (*BD* III, no. 680)

For the complete practical application of thorough bass it is necessary to know three species: (1) the simple or common; (2) the natural, or that which comes closest to the character of a melody or a piece; (3) the intricate or compound.

The excellent Bach possessed this third species in the highest degree; when he played, the [written-out] upper voice had to shine. By his exceedingly adroit accompaniment he gave it life when it had none. He knew how to imitate it so cleverly, with either the right hand or the left, and how to introduce an unexpected countertheme against it, so that the listener would have sworn that everything had been conscientiously written out. At the same time, the regular accompaniment was curtailed very little. In general his accompanying was always like a *concertante* part most conscientiously worked out and added as a companion to the upper voice so that at the appropriate time the upper voice would shine. This right was even given at times to the bass, without slighting the upper voice. Suffice it to say that anyone who missed hearing him missed a great deal.

356. On Bach's organ chorales, by Jakob Adlung (1758) (*BD* III, no. 693)

Bach (Joh. Sebastian) . . . wrote beautiful chorales while he was still Court Organist in Weimar and others later as Capellmeister in Köthen, and finally continued in this with industry as Music Director in Leipzig as well as Court Composer to the King in Poland and Elector of Saxony. He was born in 1685, and Walther gave his life at length, so far as it was possible at that time. The 30th of July 1750 was for him the fatal day on which he exchanged the temporal for the eternal. . . .*

His chorales are full of art. Most of them were given out in written form, but in the latest years some of them appeared in copper engraving, such as the Six Chorales of Various Sorts for an Organ with two Manuals and Pedal, published by Joh. Georg Schübler in Zelle at the Thuringian Forest, and *Vom Himmel hoch da komm ich her,* for two manuals and pedals, four leaves in folio, published by Schmid at Nürenberg, etc.

---

*In 1750 he had his cataracts couched, which perhaps contributed to his death. [Adlung's note]

357. Bach's views on variety and declamation in fugal composition, by Friedrich Wilhelm Marpurg (1760) (*BD* III, no. 701)

a. *On variety*

Just consider how many times the principal subject must be heard in a fugue. If, in addition, it must be heard constantly in the same keys, whether in a higher or lower octave, with nothing else in between, always in the same way, is it then possible to stifle one's disgust? Truly that is not the way the greatest fugue maker of our time, old Bach, thought. How many ingenious transpositions of the principal subject, how many splendidly assorted subsidiary ideas you will find there!

I myself once heard him, when during my stay in Leipzig I was discussing with him certain matters concerning the fugue, pronounce the works of an old and hardworking contrapuntist *dry and wooden,* and certain fugues by a more modern and no less great contrapuntist—that is in the form in which they are arranged for clavier—*pedantic;* the first because the composer stuck continuously to his principal subject, without any change; and the second because, at least in the fugues under discussion, he had not shown enough fire to reanimate the theme by interludes. It seems to me that the examples and judgments of so great a man as old Bach, who (so to speak) shook all sorts of paper intricacies out of his sleeve, any one of which would make many a man sweat for days, and most likely in vain, besides—old Bach's judgments, I say, contribute considerably to the confirmation of a principle of musical practice that is already confirmed by feeling.

b. *On declamation*

To look for strict and accurate adherence to the rules of noble declamation in a multi-voiced fugue, as if it were a cavatina, would come close to an injustice. Indeed, it would be an obvious injustice if one were to require it throughout the entire fugue without exception. But who actually did ever require the latter? Never ever, not even he [Kirnberger] in his entire critique. However, I hope that Legation Secretary Mattheson will readily agree with me that a correct and exact declamation observed in a fugal subject or subjects, if there are several, will give the fugue in its entirety infinitely more transparency and clarity rather than the opposite. I recall with great pleasure a certain fugue by the late Mr. J. S. Bach to the words: *Nimm, was dein ist, und gehe hin* ["Take what is thine and go away" BWV 144/1]. (The text was not dramatic, one could thereby imagine a choir of admonishers.) This fugue evoked a most unusual attentiveness and particular delight even among most of the musically inexperienced listeners, which certainly did not come from the contrapuntal artifices but from the superb declamation that NB. the composer applied to the subject and, by way of a little special play, to the phrase *gehe hin.* The truthfulness, natural character, and exactly commensurate correctness of the declamation was immediately picked up by everyone's ears. I could well refer to several similar fugues by others but in particular by the aforementioned great master. I admit, however, that it is often difficult and also not always and continuously possible to pay close attention to the declamation in the subjects of a fugue, especially if the subject is to be used for certain contrapuntal artifices. At the same time, many a harmonic artificiality might well be clarified by correct declamation.

358. Notes quoting Bach in Jakob Adlung's *Musica mechanica organoedi,* by Johann Friedrich Agricola (1768)
(*BD* III, nos. 739–44)

a. *On reed stops*

In many old organs of Germany, e.g., in St. Catherine's Church in Hamburg, and in others, and even in many new, splendid organs of France, the reeds are present in fairly large numbers. The greatest organist and expert on organs in Germany, and perhaps in Europe, the late Capellmeister Bach, was a great friend of the reeds; he for one must have known what could be played on them, and how. Is the convenience of some organists and organ builders really reason enough to scorn such stops [because they are apt to get out of tune easily], to call them names, and to eliminate them?

In the organ of St. Catherine's in Hamburg there are 16 reeds. The late Capellmeister, Mr. J. S. Bach in Leipzig, who once made himself heard for two full hours on this instrument, which he called excellent in all its parts, could not praise the beauty and variety of tone of these reeds highly enough. It is known, too, that the famous former Organist of this Church, Mr. Johann Adam Reinken, always kept them in the best tune.

b. *On stops of low pitch*

The late Capellmeister Bach in Leipzig gave assurance that the 32-foot *Principal* and the pedal *Trombone* in the organ of St. Catherine's in Hamburg spoke evenly and quite audibly right down to the lowest C. But he also used to say that this *Principal* was the only one as good as that, of such size, that he had heard.

c. *On the length of keys*

. . . It is good to have the manuals [i.e., the length of the keys] as short as possible. For when there are three or four, the player can go from one to the other with much more ease if the manuals are short. He can remain in a straight sitting position even if he wishes to play on the fourth or even fifth manual. Whereas he must get a backache if he wishes to play for any length of time even on the third manual (reckoning from the bottom up) of some organs, having long manuals. Anyone who is in the habit of placing his fingers properly will know that he need never stretch a finger out straight in playing. Why then does he need such long manuals? As far as the width of the keys is concerned, it is known that particularly in Brandenburg the keys are made narrower than elsewhere, but no man yet has got his fingers stuck between the semitones. Are there giants, then, in Thuringia? A certain organist who wore very wide shoes had had the pedals of his organ, on which he could not play much anyway, spread so far apart that anyone else, wishing to play anything more on these pedals than the bass tone already represented by the little finger of the left hand, could easily have ruptured himself. The French very rightly make even the keys of their harpsichords shorter than is done in Germany; but no one has yet complained about it. The semitones must anyway be a little narrower at the top than at the bottom. That is how the late Capellmeister Bach required them to be, and he, for the above-mentioned reasons, also liked short keys on the organ.

d. *On Silbermann's pianofortes*

. . . Mr. Gottfried Silbermann had at first built *two* of these instruments [pianofortes]. One of them was seen and played by the late Capellmeister, Mr. Joh. Sebastian Bach. He praised, indeed admired, its tone; but he complained that it was too weak in the high register and too hard to play [i.e., the action was too heavy]. This was taken greatly amiss by Mr. Silbermann, who could not bear to have any fault found in his handiworks. He was therefore angry at Mr. Bach for a long time. And yet his conscience told him that Mr. Bach was not wrong. He therefore decided—greatly to his credit, be it said—not to deliver any more of these instruments, but instead to think all the harder about how to eliminate the faults Mr. J. S. Bach had observed. He worked for many years on this. And that this was the real cause of this postponement I have the less doubt since I myself heard it frankly acknowledged by Mr. Silbermann. Finally, when Mr. Silbermann had really achieved many improvements, notably in respect to the action, he sold one again to the Court of the Prince of Rudolstadt. Shortly thereafter His Majesty the King of Prussia had one of these instruments ordered, and, when it met with His Majesty's Most Gracious approval, he had several more ordered from Mr. Silbermann. Mr. Silbermann also had the laudable ambition to show one of these instruments of his later workmanship to the late Capellmeister Bach, and have it examined by him; and he received, in turn, complete approval from him.

e. *Bach's Lute-Harpsichord*

The author of these notes remembers, about the year 1740, in Leipzig, having seen and heard a lute-harpsichord [*Lautenclavicymbel*] designed by Mr. Johann Sebastian Bach and executed by Mr. Zacharias Hildebrand[t], which was of smaller size than the ordinary harpsichord, but in all other respects was like any other harpsichord. It had two sets of gut strings, and a so-called little octave [*Octävchen*] of brass strings. It is true that in its regular setting (that is, when only one stop was drawn) it sounded more like the theorbo than like the lute. But when the stop that on harpsichords is called the Lute stop . . . was drawn with the Cornet stop, it was almost possible to deceive even professional lute players. Mr. Friderici [Christian Ernst Friederici] also made similar instruments, but with some changes.

Johann Lorenz Albrecht (1732–1773), the editor of Adlung's manuscript, whose text Agricola is annotating, had condemned the smaller dimensions; Albrecht was organist at the Church of the Blessed Virgin in Mühlhausen, which is in Thuringia, and may have been Agricola's target in his mocking reference to "giants." Besides Hildebrandt, Johann Nicolaus Bach, in Jena, also built lute-harpsichords.

359. On Bach's renown, by Carl Philipp Emanuel Bach (1773)
(*BD* III, no. 779)

No master of music was apt to pass through this place [Leipzig] without making my father's acquaintance and letting himself be heard by him. The greatness that was my father's in composition, in organ and clavier playing, was far too well known for a musician of reputation to let the opportunity slip of making the closer acquaintance of this great man if it was at all possible.

360. King Frederick's recollection of Bach's visit, by Gottfried van Swieten (1774) (*BD* III, no. 790)

He [Frederick the Great] spoke to me among other things of music, and of a great organist named Bach, who has been for a while in Berlin.

This artist is endowed with a talent superior, in depth of harmonic knowledge and power of execution, to any I have heard or can imagine, while those who knew his father claim that he, in turn, was even greater. The King is of this opinion, and to prove it to me he sang aloud a chromatic fugue subject that he had given this old Bach, who on the spot had made of it a fugue in four parts, then in five parts, and finally in eight parts.

That Bach ever improvised in more than six parts may be doubted. On his visit to the Prussian court, he improvised a fugue in six parts, though not on the king's theme, and he improvised a fugue on the king's theme, though not in six parts. (See Wilhelm Friedemann's report as given by Forkel in his biography, chapter 2 [pp. 429–30]. The "great organist" referred to is Wilhelm Friedemann.

361. On Bach's four-part writing, by Johann Philipp Kirnberger (1774) (BD III, no. 767; Kirnberger, pt. 1, pp. 156–57)

But the highest purity of writing does not suffice to make the four-part song perfect; each voice must have an individual and flowing melody of its own, and, at the same time, all the voices must combine agreeably.

First, then, each voice must have its own individual and flowing melody. It must not be thought that one has made a four-part setting if one lets several voices proceed in octaves with one another. There is perhaps in the whole science of writing nothing more difficult than this: not only to give each of the four voices its own flowing melody, but also to keep a uniform character in all, so that out of their union a single and perfect whole may arise. In this the late Capellmeister Bach in Leipzig perhaps excelled all the composers in the world; that is why his chorales as well as his larger works are to be most highly recommended to all composers as the best models for conscientious study. Even experienced composers will the more easily persuade themselves of this fact by trying to set to the bass and soprano of one of his chorales an alto and tenor, and to make these voices just as singable and as good in expression as the other two.

362. On Bach's contrapuntal daring, by Johann Philipp Kirnberger (1774) (BD III, no. 767; Kirnberger, pt. 1, pp. 216–18)

At times, even four tones in succession may be dissonant. When the movement is fast and the melody light and easily grasped this may pass; only in slow tempo it would be intolerable. But even in fast tempo it must not occur often, particularly if other voices were to rush along in similar manner; for it makes the music highly confused. It is better in this matter to take as a model Capellmeister Graun, the most euphonious and thoughtful writer of beautiful vocal melody, than Handel or J. S. Bach. The latter was the most daring in this respect, and therefore his things require a quite special style of performance, exactly suited to his manner of writing, for otherwise many of his things can hardly be listened to. Anyone who does not have a complete knowledge of harmony must not make bold to play his difficult things; but if one finds the right style of performance for them, even his most learned fugues sound beautiful.

363. On Bach's tuning, by Friedrich Wilhelm Marpurg (1776) (*BD* III, no. 815)

Mr. Kirnberger has more than once told me as well as others about how the famous Joh. Seb. Bach, during the time when the former was enjoying musical instruction at the hands of the latter, confided to him the tuning of his clavier, and how that master expressly required of him that he tune all the thirds sharp.

364. On Bach's invention of the viola pomposa, by Johann Nikolaus Forkel (1782) (*BD* III, no. 856)

When a violinist played a violin solo, the connoisseur of music did not quite know for a long time how he should be accompanied. The harpsichord or the pianoforte would indeed have been the most appropriate instruments for this purpose, but the violinist believed that his solo would be too much obscured by such full, harmonic accompaniment. He therefore preferred to be accompanied by a violoncello alone, or even to have his bass played on a second violin. The former instrument, namely, the violoncello, was in too distant a relation to the violin, and left too much room between to make the accompaniment advantageous for the violinist, or sufficiently harmonious for the connoisseur of harmony. The latter instrument was too close to the solo instrument, on the other hand, and even went above it at times. In order to find a way out of this situation, and to avoid both extremities, the former Cappellmeister in Leipzig, Mr. Joh. Seb. Bach, invented an instrument that he called *viola pomposa*. It is tuned like a violoncello but has one string more at the top, is somewhat larger than a viola, and is so attached with a ribbon that it can be held on the arm in front of the chest.

365. Reminiscences of the Bach family and the Collegium Musicum, by Jacob von Stählin (1784) (*BJ* 1973, p. 89)

I am charmed by the memory of the famous Emanuel Bach, our mutual friendship, and almost daily conversations in Leipzig, where I occasionally played a solo or concert at the Collegium Musicum created by his father. Of the three Bach sons in my conversations, the eldest [Wilhelm Friedemann], who recently died in Dresden [*recte:* Berlin], was the elegant one, and a bit affected. The second (yours in Hamburg), natural, profound, pensive, and funny in company, was named Carl and referred to by his brothers as the black Bach [*der schwarze Bach*]; and the third, the windy one [*der Windige*] (who died a short while ago in London), often played duets with me on the traverso. You will oblige me if you take the first opportunity to witness this illustrious virtuoso and to convey my distinguished esteem, which I will forever retain for this worthy friend: recalling our acquaintance renders a pleasant memory of our conversations in Leipzig during almost four years.

This is from a letter dated St. Petersburg and addressed to his son Peter in Hamburg. Stählin, a historian and member of the Academy of Sciences in St. Petersburg, had studied at the University of Leipzig in 1732–36. Hence, the "windy Bach" could only have been Johann Gottfried Bernhard (1715–1739), not Johann Christian, who was born in 1735 and was the Bach son living in London.

366. On Bach's significance, by Christian Friedrich Daniel Schubart (1784–1785) (*BD* III, no. 903)

Sebastian Bach.

Unquestionably the Orpheus of the Germans! Immortal in himself, and immortal through his great sons. Hardly ever did the world grow a tree such as this imperishable cedar that soon produced such enduring fruit. Sebastian Bach was a genius of the highest order. His spirit was so original, so vast, that centuries would be needed to measure up to it. He performed on the keyboard instruments, the clavichord and harpsichord, with equal power of invention, and at the organ—who would be his equal! His hand was gigantic. He would reach a twelfth with the left hand and embellished it with the middle fingers. He performed runs on the pedal with utmost accuracy. He used the stops in such subtle variety that the listener was overwhelmed by the whirl of his magic. His hand never tired and bore up under days of playing the organ. He was as strong on the harpsichord as at the organ and mastered all aspects of music with the force of an Atlas. He was as conversant in the whimsical as he was with the grave style. He was virtuoso as much as composer. What Newton was as philosopher [*Welt-weiser*], Bach was as musician [*Tonkünstler*]. He wrote very many works, for the church as well as for the chamber, yet all in such a complex style that his pieces are most rarely heard today. The annual cycles he composed for the church service are rarely to be found, though they are an inexhaustible treasure for the musician. One encounters in them such bold modulations, such great harmony, such novel melodic passages, that the original genius of a Bach cannot fail to be recognized. Yet the craving for smallness that is gaining more and more ground among a new generation has almost completely lost the taste for such gigantic works. Precisely this can be said about his organ works. Hardly ever has someone written pieces for the organ with such profundity, such genius, such perception of art as shown by him. But it takes a great master to perform them, for they are so difficult that there are no more than two or three people in Germany who could render them without fault. A fantasy, sonata, concerto, or chorale elaboration for organ in Bach's compositions covers, as a rule, six staves, two for the upper manual, two for the lower, and two for the pedal. The stops, which have to be pulled quickly, are usually indicated. The pedal writing is extraordinarily busy, and the phrases, running passages, and other ornate details of organ texture are so formidably written that one often has to think about a section for hours. Moreover, there are stretches of tenths or twelfths for the left and right hand that only a giant can accomplish.

Bach's keyboard works do not show the charm of those written now but make up for it by strength. How much our keyboard players of today could learn from this immortal man, if they were not more interested in the easy response from insects of fashion than in that, so much more important, from great connoisseurs of art! Bach's works are not transcribed from those for other instruments but are true keyboard works. He thoroughly understood the nature of the instrument; his writing strengthens the hand and fills the ear. Both hands are equally occupied, so that the left does not slacken when the right grows strong. And he commands such a wealth of ideas that none but his own great son can measure up to him. With all these favorable qualities, Bach also combined the rarest gift of instruction. The greatest organ and keyboard performers in all of Germany were trained under his guidance, and if Saxony has proved so much stronger in this respect than other German provinces, it is indebted to this great man alone.

367. On a performance in Hamburg of the Credo from Bach's B Minor Mass, by Carl Friedrich Cramer (1786) (*BD* III, no. 911)

Hamburg. In the four concerts given this year to benefit the local Medical Institute for the Poor, performed with great success, among other works, were a commemoration and coronation music by Handel, Armida by Salieri, Alceste by Gluck, a Magnificat and Sanctus by C. P. E. Bach, and a Credo by Johann Sebastian Bach. On this occasion one had the opportunity to perceive the different manner in the works of these famous composers, and to admire especially the five-part Credo of the immortal Sebastian Bach, one of the most outstanding musical works ever heard, in which, however, the vocal parts must be presented in sufficient numbers, if it is to show its full effect. Our good singers proved again, especially in the Credo, their known skill in performing securely the most difficult passages, and in all four concerts some of the lady dilettantes (*Liebhaberinnen*) offered the large audiences, by their excellent voices and tasteful rendition, the greatest pleasure.

368. On the compositional styles of Bach and Carl Philipp Emanuel Bach, by Carl Friedrich Abel (1787 or earlier) (*BD* III, no. 943)

If Sebastian Bach and his admirable son Emanuel, instead of being music directors in commercial cities, had been fortunately employed to compose for the stage and public of great capitals, such as Naples, Paris, or London, and for performers of the first class, they would doubtless have simplified their style more to the level of their judges; the one would have sacrificed all unmeaning art and contrivance, and the other have been less fantastical and *recherché;* and both, by writing in a style more popular, and generally intelligible and pleasing, would have extended their fame, and been indisputably the greatest musicians of the eighteenth century.

This passage was first printed by Charles Burney in A General History of Music *in 1789. In his article on Bach in Rees's* Cyclopaedia, *Burney reprints the passage without change, but credits Abel as its author. Abel was the son of a colleague of Johann Sebastian Bach's in the Cöthen Capelle, and himself a pupil of J. S. Bach in Leipzig. He became the foremost virtuoso on the viola da gamba in his time and, with Johann Christian, founded the Bach-Abel concerts, fashionable in London for over twenty years. In Burney's words, "he loved his bottle" and "by excess of drinking," when he was ill, "put an end to his complaint and to his life."*

369. On the fugues of Handel and Bach, by Charles Burney (1789) (*BD* III, no. 942)

The very terms of *Canon* and *Fugue* imply restraint and labor. Handel was perhaps the only great Fuguist exempt from pedantry. He seldom treated barren or crude subjects; his themes being almost always natural and pleasing. Sebastian Bach, on the contrary, like Michel Angelo in painting, disdained facility so much, that his genius never stooped to the easy and graceful. I never have seen a fugue by this learned and powerful author upon a *motivo* that is natural and *chantant;* or even on an easy and obvious passage that is not loaded with crude and difficult accompaniments.

370. On Bach composing without use of a keyboard, by Ernst Ludwig Gerber (1790) (*BD* III, no. 948)

. . . And this astonishing facility, this fingering never used before him, he owed to his own works; for often, he said, he had found himself compelled to make use of the night in order to be able to bring to realization what he had written during the day. This is all the easier to believe since it was never his habit in composing to ask advice of his clavier. Thus, according to a certain tradition, he wrote his *Tempered Clavier* (consisting of fugues and preludes, some of them very intricate, in all the 24 keys) in a place where ennui, boredom, and the absence of any kind of musical instrument forced him to resort to this pastime.

Gerber hints that Bach composed The Well-Tempered Clavier *while in detention, in Weimar. But this cannot be true of the entire work, since some of its pieces are included in the* Clavier-Büchlein *for Wilhelm Friedemann, begun in 1720, in what is surely their earlier form. Cf. note to No. 69.*

371. On Bach's pedal technique, by Ernst Ludwig Gerber (1790) (*BD* III, no. 948)

On the pedals his feet had to imitate with perfect accuracy every theme, every passage that his hands had played. No appoggiatura, no mordent, no short trill was suffered to be lacking or even to meet the ear in less clean and rounded form. He used to make long double trills with both feet, while his hands were anything but idle.

372. On Bach's keyboard and vocal works, by Johann Friedrich Reichardt (1796) (*BD* III, no. 996)

Bach (Johann Sebastian), instrumental and vocal composer, organist and clavier player. Born at Eisenach, March 21, 1685, died at Leipzig, July 28, 1750.

Never did a composer, not even the best and deepest of the Italians, exhaust all the possibilities of our harmony as did this great artist. He employed every proper harmonic art and every improper harmonic artifice, in earnest and in jest, with such boldness and individuality that the greatest harmonists, if called upon to supply a single missing measure in one of his greater works could perhaps not be sure of having supplied it exactly as Bach had done. His works for clavier and organ will remain, as long as those splendid instruments endure, the higher school of organists and clavier players, just as he himself, as a practicing artist, was the highest model for organists and clavier players. He invented the convenient and sure fingering and the significant style of performance, with which he cleverly combined the ornamental manner of the French artists of the time, and thus made the perfecting of the clavier important and necessary, in which task Silbermann was so fortunately at his side.

His vocal works, although they are full of invention and of the most learned writing, and full, too, of strong and genuine traits as regards expression, yet betray too great a lack of genuine good taste, of knowledge of language and poetry, and thus have entirely the conventional form of their period, so that they can hardly maintain their currency. Yet they, too, remain for all times true studies for thoughtful and industrious artists, and excellent practice pieces for choirs.

373. On Bach's central position among German composers, by Augustus Frederic Christopher Kollmann and Johann Nikolaus Forkel (1799) (*BD* III, no. 1023)

. . . An English organist at the Royal German Chapel (the same who is now planning to edit Joh. Seb. Bach's Well-Tempered Clavier [A. F. C. Kollmann]) then had a leaf engraved in copper, on which the German composers known to him were presented. Joh. Seb. Bach appears in the center: immediately around him are shown Handel, Graun, and Haydn. The rays of the sun are represented by other German composers, as follows:

. . . Our worthy Haydn is supposed to have seen this piece himself, and it is said that he was not unfavorably impressed by it, nor minded the proximity to Handel and Graun, nor considered it at all wrong that Joh. Seb. Bach was the center of the sun and hence the man from whom all true musical wisdom proceeded.

On *The Art of Fugue*

Introductory Note

The Art of Fugue was originally published with a short prefatory Notice (No. 284). In the hope of giving the work wider circulation, a new issue was prepared in which the Notice gave way to Friedrich Wilhelm Marpurg's extended preface. Marpurg (1718–1795), then at the beginning of his career, became one of the leading theorists of his time. He was among the first writers to expound Rameau's theories in German, and his *Abhandlung von der Fuge* (1753–54), whose second part is dedicated to Bach's sons Wilhelm Friedemann and Carl Philipp Emanuel (No. 353), inspired by his study of *The Art of Fugue* (see No. 351), was the most detailed treatise on the subject in its time. He was personally acquainted with Bach and one of his most fervent admirers and champions.

374. Preface to the 1752 edition, by Friedrich Wilhelm Marpurg (*BD* III, no. 643)

If I have agreed to furnish the esteemed heirs of the late Capellmeister Bach with a preface to accompany the present work, it is with the more pleasure because I am thus afforded the opportunity of publicly renewing the expression of my respect for the ashes of this famous man. And this I do, moreover, with the greatest ease since I can spare myself the trouble of resorting to the conventional ornaments of rhetoric. The name of the composer is sufficient recommendation for a work of this nature. One would have to lack confidence in the insight of musical connoisseurs if one were to tell them that in this work are contained the most hidden beauties possible to the art of music. To be an excellent musician and not to appreciate the virtues of the late Bach is a contradiction. In the minds of all those who had the good fortune to hear him, there still hovers the memory of his astonishing facility in invention and improvisation; and his performance, equally excellent in all keys, in the most difficult passages and figures, was always envied by the greatest masters of the keyboard.

But if one looks into his works, one could also draw the conclusion, taking into consideration everything that has ever come to pass in music past or present, that no one has surpassed him in thorough knowledge of the theory and practice of harmony, or, I may say, in the deep and thoughtful execution of unusual, ingenious ideas, far removed from the ordinary run, and yet spontaneous and natural; I say natural, meaning those ideas which must, by their profundity, their connection, and their organization, meet with the acclaim of any taste, no matter of what country. A melody which agrees only with canons of taste obtaining at a particular time and place has value only so long as that taste prevails. Let it but suit the fancy to take more pleasure in a different turn of expression, and that taste falls by the wayside. Natural and cogent thoughts maintain their worth in all times and places. Such thoughts are to be found in all the pieces that ever flowed from the pen of the late Mr. Bach. The present work testifies anew to this fact. Nothing could be more regrettable than that, through his eye disease, and his death shortly thereafter, he was prevented from finishing and publishing the work himself. His illness surprised him in the midst of the working out of the last fugue, in which, with the introduction of the third subject, he identifies himself by name. But we are proud to think that the four-voiced chorale fantasy added here, which the deceased in his blindness dictated ex tempore to one of his friends, will make up for this lack, and compensate the friends of his Muse. That all the various types of fugues and counterpoints in this work are based upon the same principal subject in D minor, or *D la Re* with the minor third, and that all the voices therein continuously sing, each one being worked out as thoroughly as the others—these things are immediately manifest to every connoisseur of the art. A particular merit of this work is the fact that everything contained in it is set in score. But the advantages of a good score have for a long time been incontestable.

To me, however, this work has given the occasion to examine more closely the nature of the fugue, and to compare with it the rules which have in the meanwhile been drawn up governing its construction. My desire to devote so much as in me lies to the propagation of music has brought me to the decision to lay before the world for its consideration, at the earliest moment, my observations on the subject. Since the rules of fugue have generally been treated together with the other principles of musical composition, many music lovers who do not have at hand the great and lengthy works on composition may thus find satisfaction. But that the rules of fugue cannot be so universally known and so general as, for example, those for the making of a minuet, experience proves. Formerly, skill in fugue was so indispensable in a composer that no one could have attained a musical post who had not worked out a given subject in all kinds of counterpoint and in a regular fugue. In those days, no one would have had the face to claim a place among the virtuosos with a piece put together of borrowed bits, juggler's tricks, and street tunes. It was held that, in a fugue of twenty-four measures, more profundity and science might prevail than in a concerto four yards long; and that it required far more art to set down on paper an uninterrupted song, without a host of halts and starts, than a melody that stopped for all sorts of capers in order to appeal to taste, as it is called. For this reason, the fugue was reckoned among the most splendid ornaments of church and chamber music. Although one may still discover an example here and there in the former, from the latter it has completely disappeared.

The musical mechanic, the man who is permitted to play only works not his own, and who may not do any thinking and writing on his own account, knows the fugue only by name. The contemporary composer, who considers the fugue the child of ancient aberration, gives the mechanic no opportunity to make his listeners sensible of the charms of a fugue. Thus the manly element which should prevail in music remains quite absent from it; for it may be believed without further testimony that the composer who has made himself particularly acquainted with fugues and counterpoints—however barbaric this last word may sound to the tender ears of our time—will let something of their flavor inform all his other works, however *galant* they are meant to be, and will set himself against the spreading rubbish of womanish song. It is to be hoped that the present work may inspire some emulation, and assist the living examples of so many righteous people whom one sees now and then at the head of a musical body, or in its ranks, to restore in some measure, in the face of the hoppity melodification of so many present-day composers, the dignity of Harmony.

During the Leipzig Easter Fair, 1752   MARPURG

375. A laudatory note, by Johann Mattheson (1752) (*BD* III, no. 647)

Johann Sebastian Bach's so-called *Art of Fugue,* a practical and splendid work of 70 plates in folio, will one day throw all French and Italian fugue makers into astonishment—at least to the extent that they can really penetrate and understand it, not to speak of playing it. How would it be, then, if every foreigner and every compatriot risked his louis d'or on this rarity? Germany is and will most certainly remain the true land of the organ and the fugue.

376. An offer to publishers for the plates, by Carl Philipp Emanuel Bach (September 14, 1756) (*BD* III, no. 683)

Berlin. Publishers of practical musical art works are hereby notified of my decision to sell directly, at a reasonable price, the cleanly and accurately engraved copper plates of the fugal work (announced some years ago) by my late father, Capellmeister Joh. Seb. Bach. The number of the same comes to sixty-odd, and they amount to about a hundredweight. Of the intrinsic value of this work it is unnecessary to say much, since the respect of connoisseurs of this kind of work for my late father, especially in the fugue, of whatsoever nature and form, is still not extinct. But I may be permitted to observe this much: that it is the most perfect practical fugal work, and that every student of the art, with the help of a good theoretical instruction book, such as the one by Marpurg, must necessarily learn from it to make a good fugue, and thus needs for his instruction no oral teacher, who often charges dear enough for imparting the secret of the fugue.

This work has been sold hitherto at 4 reichsthaler the copy. However, only about 30 copies have been disposed of, since it is not yet everywhere known; and as my obligations in the service of His Majesty do not permit me to indulge in much or lengthy correspondence, and thus to make it everywhere known as it should be, that is the reason I have decided to free myself of any concern with it. Gentlemen who are interested may address me in writing, here in Berlin, and may rest assured that I will transfer the plates, without causing any delay or complications, upon the first acceptable offer anyone makes me, so that through his wider circle of acquaintances the work may become known everywhere, to the benefit of the public.

377. On the whereabouts of the remainder of the autograph, by Carl Philipp Emanuel Bach (Wolff, p. 423)

Mr. Hartmann has the real thing [*das eigentliche*].

The identity of "Herr Hartmann" is unclear. This undated note—now lost—was originally attached to the title wrapper of the autograph score and appendices in C. P. E. Bach's possession.

ON THE FOUR-PART CHORALES

Introductory Note

Between the publication of *The Art of Fugue* in 1752 and the first editions of *The Well-Tempered Clavier* in 1801, Bach's name appeared on the title pages of only two issues—both collections of his chorales. The first was published by F. W. Birnstiel in Berlin in two parts, each comprising a hundred chorales, in 1765 and 1769, as "Johann Sebastian Bach's Four-Part Chorales, collected by Carl Philipp Emanuel Bach." The story of this edition as well as of the later one, published by J. G. I. Breitkopf, unfolds on the following pages.

Bach's sons, with the possible exception of Johann Christian (who is rumored to have referred to Johann Sebastian as "the old wig"), held his father's work in high esteem, but Carl Philipp Emanuel was the only one among them who actively worked to increase Johann Sebastian's fame and make his works more generally known. Among Bach's pupils, Kirnberger was the most active writer on Bach's behalf. Heading the Berlin group of theorists, he attempted to form a system out of Bach's teachings. In this he was handicapped by his own innate pedantry, but it was his self-effacing insistence that led to the improved reprint of the chorales, which did much to pave the way for a fuller recognition of Bach's greatness.

378. Foreword to the first edition, by Carl Philipp Emanuel Bach (Birnstiel: Berlin, 1765) (*BD* III, no. 723)

The preparation of this collection was entrusted to me by the publishers after several sheets had already been printed. Thus it happened that four chorales were included that are not the product of my father's pen. These four chorales will be found under Nos. 6, 15, 18, and 31. The rest of the chorales, in this part as well as in the following ones, were all written by my late father, and originally set out on four staves for four singers. They have been presented on two staves to accommodate lovers of the organ and the clavier, since they are easier to read in that form. If it is desired to sing them in four voices, and some of them should go beyond the range of certain throats, they can be transposed. In those places where the bass goes so low, in relation to the other voices, that it cannot be played without pedals, one plays the higher octave, and one takes the octave below when the bass crosses above the tenor. The late author, because of the latter circumstance, reckoned on a 16-foot instrument, which always played along with these songs, for the bass. To accommodate those whose sight is weak, and to whom certain settings might appear incorrect, the progression of the voices has been indicated where necessary by single and double oblique lines.

I also hope to contribute much of profit and of pleasure through this collection, without having to quote anything in praise of the harmony of these songs. The late author is not in need of my recommendation. One was accustomed to see nothing but masterpieces come from him. Nor can the term be withheld from this volume by connoisseurs of the art of writing when they contemplate with appropriate attention the quite special arrangement of the harmony and the natural flow of the inner voices and the bass, which are what above all distinguish these chorales. How useful such contemplation may be to those who are anxious to learn the art of writing! And who nowadays denies the advantage of that instruction in writing by which the beginning is made with chorales instead of stiff and pedantic counterpoint? Finally I can assure lovers of sacred songs that this collection will represent a complete Chorale Book. This part will be followed by two others, and together they will contain over 300 songs.

379. "Note to the Public," by Carl Philipp Emanuel Bach (May 29, 1769) (*BD* III, no. 753)

Mr. Birnstiel in Berlin has recently, with as much impudence as ignorance of music, issued the Second Part of Johann Sebastian Bach's Four-Part Chorales, of which I am the true compiler, without giving me the slightest notice of that fact. I have looked at them a little and have found a great mass of errors of all sorts in them. Vexation and disgust kept me from going through everything, because I ended up by finding mistakes such as even a beginner in composition would not easily make. I am in a position to point out the errors to anyone who calls upon me to do so and to show him my original by way of contrast.

Since through this edition the honor of the great deceased as well as my own honor as compiler have been most sharply offended, I herewith openly proclaim my innocence and warn the public most sincerely not to be taken in by buying this Second Part. In particular I beg all friends of my late father to place every obstacle in the way of the advertising of these works, which have been mutilated, to his shame, after his death; the more so since this collection can now do incomparably more harm, whereas it could have been of uncommon benefit to students of the art of writing, as a practical textbook of the most excellent models. But—how rich we are nowadays in textbooks that lack correct principles and models!

380. Excerpt from a letter of Carl Philipp Emanuel Bach to Johann Philipp Kirnberger (July 21, 1769) (*BD* III, no. 754)

. . . With the same intentions as your own, I wish to see a decent edition of the chorales of my late father. I am agreeable to anything. You be the negotiator.

(1) The Second Part must be thoroughly cleaned of the mistakes indicated;

(2) I will take care of the Third and Fourth Parts, and you will be good enough to look through the whole carefully;

(3) On all three parts to come, as well as on the First Part, my name

must appear, and I will take the responsibility for everything. The principal point is that I be paid in advance. . . .

381. **Excerpts from five letters of Johann Philipp Kirnberger to Johann Gottlob Immanuel Breitkopf**
(*BD* III, nos. 821–23, 848, 880)

a. May 10, 1777
. . . I have all the available chorales of J. Seb. Bach, which were once issued by Mr. [Friedrich Wilhelm] Birnstiel in two Parts, but full of mistakes, and I have in addition 200 more, which makes more than 400 in all, which my Serene Princess [Amalia] received from Capell-meister Bach in Hamburg and for which she paid him. Mr. Bach in Hamburg has no right to publish these chorales any more, but I have this right alone, for which reason I have been pressed on all sides to have them printed. But I have no desire to do so at my expense. If you wish to take them over yourselves, I should be glad to come to an arrangement with you, since it would be a great loss if the chorales were not preserved for posterity. . . .

b. June 7, 1777
. . . As regards the Bach chorales, of which there are now over 400, which were gathered by Mr. Bach of Hamburg, and mostly written out by him, and which I now possess, it is very close to my heart that the chorales should be preserved for musical posterity. I am far from having any idea of making a profit in the world through a book dealer or publisher, and accordingly I have no thought of selling them. But out of love for knowledge and for their great value to young students, I will give them all to you for nothing, if only they may see the light of day in fine printed form. All profits that may accrue from this shall be your own and not mine; in exchange I ask only for a few copies as a present, as well as a couple for Mr. Bach, who requested them from me if the chorales should appear in print through my efforts—although I sent him 12 *Frieder. d'or* cash for them, which I received as a gift from my Most Gracious Princess. . . .

c. June 19, 1777
. . . But first I must tell you how the First and Second Parts were issued by Birnstiel. At the time when Marpurg was in the most miserable and wretched circumstances, he made an agreement with Birnstiel to give him the Bach chorales, demanding for the delivery and correction of

one chorale 12 gr., which made 4 rthl. to the sheet. Before this part was finished, he [Marpurg] was appointed through my efforts to the new *Lotterie* Office, so Birnstiel was forced to ask the Hamburg Bach, who at that time was still here, to send him the rest of the First Part. He agreed, but demanded for each chorale 1 rthl. 8 gr., instead of 12 gr., so that a sheet amounted to 12 rthl. [*recte:* 10 rthl. 16 gr.]. Birnstiel finished the First Part in anxiety and stress, and had no desire to go on with the Second Part at this high price.

At this point he brought me your MS., which he claimed to have bought for 30 rthl., and asked me to undertake the corrections. Mr. Bach was still here, and I declined (1) so as not to get into any trouble with Mr. Bach, and (2) because I did not have courage enough to take over the corrections, the manuscript being very faulty. Mr. Bach went to Hamburg, and thereupon Mr. Birnstiel persuaded the late Agricola, who took care of the corrections of the Second Part, but overlooked various errors; and thus Mr. Bach had the opportunity to revenge himself on Birnstiel for the profit he had missed, by inserting a notice in the *Hamburger Zeitung* about the Second Part, accusing it of being full of mistakes and even stating that some of the chorales were not by his late father. This was so damaging to Birnstiel that his entire Second Part became so much waste paper.

Now to come to myself: I have always wished to have all the chorales by the late Bach that could be gathered together. Accordingly I requested my Gracious Princess to buy the remainder from Mr. Bach for me, and this she did. Mr. Bach demanded 12 louis d'or, received them, and sent to me what I have sent to you for your examination, together with the letter he sent me, which contains his note concerning the publication. I promised him that I would have it published under my supervision and with my correction, with both the parts that had been brought out by Birnstiel, as a complete Chorale Book. And you will see from his letter that this would have been done with his permission.

But other affairs have hitherto kept me from considering it. Now, however, since it would mean a great deal to me to see them in print, for the general profit of all young students because of their excellent writing, and since it is decreed that I am to have no profit in this world for my worries and efforts, I will yield them to you, just as you receive them, without the slightest payment, only to see them in print to the eternal memory of J. Seb. Bach. It is understood, however, that all the ones published by Birnstiel must be included, which will bring the number to more than 400 items. If you wish of your own free will to send me a token of your appreciation, I will accept it with much thanks; but if not, to see them in print will put me under the same obligation toward you as if you had paid me any amount for them. . . .

If the chorales should be published by you, I will take the corrections upon myself, for I do not trust anybody in Leipzig to understand the matter, not even Mr. [Johann Adam] Hiller—as I conclude from his published things. . . .

Breitkopf received the chorales, deliberated for over a year, and finally returned the manuscript. Several years later, Kirnberger took the question up again:

d. March 27, 1781

. . . The beautiful collection of J. Seb. Bach's Four-Part Chorales that you had before you I still have lying here untouched; it is a crying shame that they are not being published for posterity. I will present them to you for art's sake, and to the eternal memory of Bach, if you will have them printed, and just give me one copy on good paper. . . .

Breitkopf ended by graciously accepting Kirnberger's offer, and promised publication on a subscription basis. But no further action was taken. Six years after his first letter to Breitkopf, Kirnberger finally became impatient:

e. June 14, 1783

. . . Again and again you have put me off with the promise that Bach's chorales would, in fulfillment of the condition on which I presented them to you, appear in print; but I see that this remains a mere empty promise, and therefore I am now expecting to have returned to me my Joh. Seb. Bach chorales without delay; for which reason, unless I receive them within a fortnight, I shall consider the lack of a reply from you as notice that I shall have to make a formal demand upon you for the Bach chorales.

On July 27, Kirnberger died. A year later the new edition was finally produced, with the help of Carl Philipp Emanuel Bach.

382. Subscription notice, by Johann Gottlob Immanuel Breitkopf, July 1781 (*BD* III, no. 849)

Mr. Joh. Phil. Kirnberger in Berlin, who owns the beautiful collection of J. Seb. Bach's four-part chorales and who wishes that they be preserved for posterity in print since they are unique models of pure part writing and an inexhaustible source for young composers, will turn them over to me, the undersigned, with the condition that I render them in print. I gladly resolve to fulfill this condition, if Seb. Bach, this father of the art, would find enough friends in Germany that the necessary cost will be sufficiently covered by subscription or advance order. They will be published in convenient format on strong writing paper, in four parts. The subscription price for each part will be 1 thaler and, with the delivery of each part, prepayment for the subsequent one will be collected. Subscription orders can be filled in all reputable bookstores of Germany until Easter 1782. If this time passes fruitlessly, the entire project will be called off. Those who order five or more copies in advance will receive ten percent off for their effort.

383. A supportive announcement of the publication, by Johann Friedrich Reichardt (before October 2, 1781) (*BD* III, no. 853)

Mr. Kirnberger, who a few years ago earned such merit again in serving music by issuing Hans Leo Hassler's four-part Psalms and Christian Songs Written in Fugal Manner [*Psalmen und Christliche Gesänge . . . fugweis componirt*], is planning to edit an even more important work with the publishers Breitkopf in Leipzig. It consists of the chorales by Johann Sebastian Bach and is to appear successively in four installments, for prepayment to Breitkopf of one thaler each. The editor of this journal of art is also willing to accept subscriptions. If any work has ever deserved serious support by German friends of art, it is this one. The contents: chorales—greatest work of German art; the creator of harmony: Johann Sebastian Bach—greatest harmonist of all times and nations; the editor: Johann Philipp Kirnberger—most discerning artistic adjudicator of our time.

384. Foreword to the second edition, by Carl Philipp Emanuel Bach (Breitkopf: Leipzig, 1784) (*BD* III, no. 897)

This collection of the chorales has been looked through once again by me with great care after the earlier edition, and cleansed of the mistakes that had crept into it. They were delivered to the present publisher by Mr. Kirnberger (to whom I had given them as early as the year 1771), shortly before his death. In this new printing the spurious chorales mistakenly included in the earlier edition have been omitted, and those that have been printed, in this part as well as in the parts to follow, were all written by my late father. [The rest of this revised Foreword is identical with that of the first edition.]

ON THE TRANSMISSION AND DISSEMINATION OF
MANUSCRIPTS AND PRINTS

Introductory Note

Only a small portion of Bach's music—almost exclusively, keyboard works
from the Leipzig period—was published during the composer's lifetime, and,
with the exception of the two editions of four-part chorales, no major composition by Bach was published in the half century after his death. The distribution of manuscript copies therefore, assumed a decisive role in the
dissemination of Bach's music for the entire eighteenth century, a fact that
largely accounts for the many idiosyncrasies in the transmission of his output.

The original sources (autograph composing scores, autograph fair copies,
and copies made by assistants under the composer's eye and for his own use)
were, for the most part, kept in Bach's personal library and in 1750 passed
on to his heirs, primarily the four musical sons and Anna Magdalena Bach.
The division of his estate into many parts subsequently resulted in considerable losses, whose extent is hard to estimate, but the lost items certainly
made up nearly two-fifths of his vocal oeuvre and included, for example, two
annual cycles of church cantatas (see also the summary work list in the Obituary, No. 306). Of the sons, only C. P. E. Bach served as a careful curator of
his portion of the paternal heritage, which appears in a detailed catalog of
his own musical estate (see *BD* III, no. 957, and the facsimile edition of the
1790 *Verzeichniss des musikalischen Nachlasses des verstorbenen Capellmeisters Carl
Philipp Emanuel Bach,* ed. Rachel Wade [New York, 1981]). By contrast, his
elder brother Wilhelm Friedemann put most of his holdings up for auction
in 1778 (see No. 391); only a few items of this material survive.

The special emphasis placed from the very beginning on Bach's organ and
clavier works reflects his compositional activities and reputation as a keyboard virtuoso. Numerous copies were made by students and colleagues, but
the scope of the dissemination soon went beyond the narrower Bach circle.
Already before 1750, some of his works were available in Austria, Italy,
France, and England. By 1800 the time was ripe for publication projects
involving both keyboard and vocal works (see No. 392).

385. Excerpt from a letter of Padre Giovanni Battista Martini to Johannes Baptist Pauli, listing manuscripts and prints (Bologna, April 14, 1750) (*BD* II, no. 600)

. . . I have received together: a toccata, allemande, corrente, and fugue
for harpsichord by Sig. Gio. Sebastiano Bach; a fugue for harpsichord

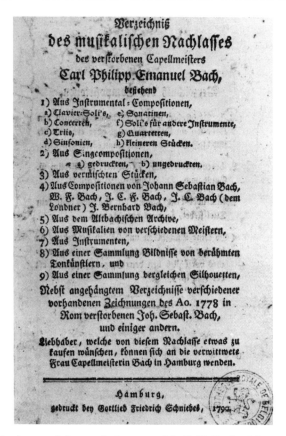

Verzeichniß
des musikalischen Nachlasses
des verstorbenen Capellmeisters
Carl Philipp Emanuel Bach,
bestehend
1) Aus Instrumental-Compositionen,
  a) Clavier-Soli's,   e) Sonatinen,
  b) Concerten,   f) Soli's für andere Instrumente,
  c) Trio,   g) Quartetten,
  d) Sinfonien,   h) kleineren Stücken.
2) Aus Singcompositionen,
  a) gedruckten, b) ungedruckten.
3) Aus vermischten Stücken,
4) Aus Compositionen von Johann Sebastian Bach,
  W. F. Bach, J. C. F. Bach, J. C. Bach (dem
  Londner) J. Bernhard Bach,
5) Aus dem Altbachischen Archive,
6) Aus Musikalien von verschiedenen Meistern,
7) Aus Instrumenten,
8) Aus einer Sammlung Bildnisse von berühmten
  Tonkünstlern, und
9) Aus einer Sammlung dergleichen Silhouetten,
Nebst angehängtem Verzeichnisse verschiedener
vorhandenen Zeichnungen des Ao. 1778 in
Rom verstorbenen Joh. Sebast. Bach,
und einiger andern.
Liebhaber, welche von diesem Nachlasse etwas zu
kaufen wünschen, können sich an die verwittwete
Frau Capellmeisterin Bach in Hamburg wenden.

Hamburg,
gedruckt bey Gottlieb Friedrich Schniebes, 1790.

Catalogue of the musical estate of C. P. E. Bach: title page

titled Fugue for the King of Prussia, also by Bach; the same fugue
written out in 6 parts; a sonata for violin, transverse flute, and basso
continuo; several canons by the same; two duets for harpsichord, all of
it by the aforementioned Sig. Bach. I consider it to be superfluous to
describe the singular merit of Sig. Bach, for he is thoroughly known
and admired not only in Germany but throughout our Italy. I will say
only that I think it would be difficult to find someone in the profession
who could surpass him, since these days he could rightfully claim to
be among the first in Europe.

*The manuscripts (BWV 830) and prints (BWV 1079) have survived in the
Padre Martini Collection of the* Civico Museo Bibliographico Musicale,
Bologna *(see BD II, no. 597b and NBA VIII/1, p. 66f.).*

386. Excerpt from the will of Johann Caspar Vogler (Weimar, July 15, 1766) *(BD III, no. 728)*

... Likewise, the mentioned Mr. Court Organist's entire supply of music, by J. S. Bach and other famous musicians, is to be sold at a favorable price, and the Messrs. connoisseurs can be served, upon request, with a corresponding catalog.

On the surviving part of Vogler's collection see Hans-Joachim Schulze, Studien zur Bach-Überlieferung im 18. Jahrhundert *(Leipzig, 1984), pp. 66–68.*

387. Excerpt from a letter of Carl Philipp Emanuel Bach to Christoph Gottlieb von Murr, offering chorale preludes (Berlin, after 1765) *(BD III, no. 725)*

I have, from the hand of my late father and composed by him, 60 chorale elaborations, none of which belongs to those printed by Birnstiel. These 60 chorales were actually written for organ, *manualiter* and *pedaliter,* though they can very well be performed on the harpsichord. They are all arranged on two systems or staves. Most of them are kept brief, the *cantus firmus* being carried straight through one of the parts. Between phrases, small rests may appear in the *cantus firmus,* while the other parts continue. Many are more extensively worked out, in that some of them can barely be accommodated on two leaves. All of them call for organ alone, without including another instrument or voice. They are not yet known; since I am aware, however, that (wherever they will be desired) they will fall into good hands, friendly to my dear late father, I will let go of them and make them available in clean copy. They are all masterpieces, with even more work and art than shown in the samples delivered. For the communication and copy, in good friendship, I ask for no more than 40 thaler in good gold, or 8 louis d'or. Does my dear friend own my late father's Art of Fugue?

The description of the 60 chorale preludes suggests the Orgel-Büchlein *(No. 69), although the latter contains only 46 pieces.*

388. Note mentioning Bachiana at Montecassino, by Christian Traugott Weinlig (Naples, October 14, 1768) *(BD III, no. 750)*

In such entertaining manner we went into the evening, visited some of the Messrs. *Patres,* and finally the Brother organist, on whose desk there was music from our old German Bach.

Today the library of the Benedictine monastery at Montecassino contains no historical Bach materials.

389. Excerpts from letters of Carl Philipp Emanuel Bach to Johann Nikolaus Forkel, offering manuscripts and original editions (Hamburg, 1774) (*BD* III, nos. 793–795)

a. *August 26, 1774*

Herewith you will receive the two books, for the proper payment of which I send you my best thanks. With one of them you will find the six engraved chorales [BWV 645–650] bound in the back. The inscribed annotations are from the hand of the late author. In addition you will receive six pieces by J. S. and as many by W. F. The former six contain fine preludes, of special value to the beginner, [BWV 933–938] and the latter include the requested piece for two keyboards. Close to a dozen trios by J. S. and some pedal pieces by him are available. This is all I have. It is annoying that my late father's things drift to and fro like this; I am too old and too occupied to hold them together.

b. *October 7, 1774*

In somewhat of a rush, I take pleasure in sending you, my dear friend, the remainder of my *Sebastianoren*, namely 11 trios, 3 pedal pieces, and *Vom Himmel hoch* [BWV 769], etc. In case you already have this latter chorale, please return it when convenient. The 6 *Clavier Trios* [BWV 1014–1019], whose respective numbers belong together, are among the best works of my dear departed father. They still sound excellent and give me much joy, although they date back more than fifty years. They contain some *Adagii* that could not be written in a more singable manner today. Since they are badly worn, you will be so kind as to use them with great care.

Today Bach's personal annotated copy of the "Schübler Chorales," BWV 645–650 (No. 238) may be found in the Scheide Library at Princeton University.

390. Note from James Hutton presenting an autograph of the Goldberg Variations to Mr. Glen (1776) (*BD* III, no. 817)

Bach, An Aria with 2 Var. for the Harpsichord or Organ, 3 pages. . . . An exact Copy of a Composition of the Learned Professor of Music J. S. Bach, with which he presented me in his own writing in the year 1749 on my going from Vienna to Leipzig, professedly to hear his astonishing performance on the organ.—As a token of respect J[ames]

H[utton] has for Mr. Glen, he begs his acceptance of this copy. . . .
N. B. My long intimacy with the late Sir John Hawkins induced me
to give him a copy to insert in his History of Music.

*James Hutton (1715–1795) is said to have visited Germany several times
between 1739 and 1756. Hawkins published three movements from the Goldberg Variations, BWV 988 / 1, 9–10, in* A General History of the Science
and Practice of Music *(London, 1776). The autograph of the Goldberg
Variations is lost.*

391. **Excerpt from a letter of Wilhelm Friedemann Bach to Johann
Joachim Eschenburg asking him to auction off music and
books (Berlin, July 4, 1778)** (*BD* III, no. 831)

A propòs, did Your Honor give Your *Musicalia* into auction? My departure from Braunschweig was so hasty that I could not compile a catalog
of my relinquished music and books. I do remember the Art of Fugue
by my father and Quantz's manual for the flute. Your Honor has kept
in good faith [*en honethomme*] the other church *Musiquen* and annual
cycles, as well as books, and promised me to convert them, with the
advice of a knowledgeable musician, into cash through auction.

*No details are known about an auction sale of Bachiana in Brunswick (Eschen-
burg's place of residence) or elsewhere. However, No. 392d refers to the dis-
counted sale (12 rather than 100 rthl.) of the chorale cantata cycle that was
once in W. F. Bach's possession.*

392. **Four letters of Johann Nikolaus Forkel to the Leipzig publisher
Hoffmeister & Kühnel (Göttingen, 1801–1803)**
(Stauffer, 3–7, 23–25, 41–43, 73–75)

a. May 4, 1801
Honored Sirs,
It would have been my duty to reply long since to your letter regarding
the publication of J. Seb. Bach's works. But I believed, as I received it,
that I would be coming to Leipzig at Eastertime and could then tell
you personally of my pleasure at your project. The trip has had to be
postponed, so that it will not take place until about Whitsunday. Since
I have received the first fascicle of your edition [*Oeuvres complettes de Jean
Sebastian Bach* (Leipzig 1801–)], however, and can judge from it how
you are going about the task, I cannot refrain from giving you my
candid opinion in writing even before my appearance in person, in the

hope that you will not take really well-intentioned candor amiss. Much pleased as I was at first about your project, I now regret just as much that your choice fell upon an editor who, unfortunately:

1. *did not know how to make a sensible selection of works.*

The *toccata* is one of the earliest works of J. S. Bach, and in no way a masterpiece. Like every other man, Bach had to start out as a bungler before he could become a master. His student exercises, by means of which he little by little made of himself the great master he afterwards became, do not deserve to be included in an edition of his works any more than the school exercises of one who later became a great scholar would be included in his *Opera*.

2. *used poor and very old copies of the works as his sources.*

As Seb. Bach gradually perfected himself, he gave many of his works more perfection. This is particularly true of the Inventions and *The Well-Tempered Clavier.* As time went on, he discarded every superfluous and every tasteless element that still adhered to them from earlier years, and made them so tasteful and so completely melodious that in their later form they became masterpieces, which they had not been originally. I see with regret that it is from one of the very oldest copies that the Inventions as well as the first prelude of *The Well-Tempered Clavier* have been engraved. A scholar who wants to publish an edition of one of the old classics takes pains to procure several manuscripts and compare them, so that, when he has enough knowledge and judgment about them, he may include only the best readings in his edition. Why didn't your editor do likewise?

3. *did not know how to distinguish among the so-called ornaments.*

Seb. Bach was so conscientious in this matter that, in his improved works, every type of ornament is carefully distinguished, and each is indicated with its specific sign. Your editor seems, however, to have hardly an inkling of the necessity for making such distinctions, and obviously knows neither the nature of the ornaments customarily introduced in the music of the Bach school nor the signs used to indicate them. How can such a man take upon himself the editing of such classic works as those of S. Bach? And finally,

4. *must understand very little about harmony.*

I am amazed at the errors which appear in the Inventions, errors which a musical school-boy hardly would have let stand. And this is to be the edition of the works of the most classic of all German composers?

My most honored Sirs, if you will listen to the advice of an honorable man who loves art, suppress this first fascicle, seek out a man who is knowledgeable in these matters, and re-issue it in more correct form.

If you do not do this, your whole venture will miscarry, and neither you nor the German nation will be honored by it. What connoisseur of music can avoid a feeling of horror when, instead of the masterpieces he had expected, he finds such school-boy stuff?

You cannot therefore take it amiss if, as a true musical patriot, I shortly publish in various journals these opinions, which I have expressed so candidly to you. One must not make a public scandal out of the works of a master like Seb. Bach, either through their bungled disfigurement, or through the passing off of his student works as representative. And no true connoisseur will remain silent in the face of such conduct.

Please excuse my frankness. I shall have more to say about this matter when I see you. I remain respectfully and devotedly, honored sirs,

Your most obedient and faithful servant,

FORKEL

b. February 15, 1802

Messrs. *Hoffmeister* and *Kühnel* in *Leipzig.*
Postage Paid Mühlhausen

According to all appearances, you have, my esteemed friends, found another disturber of your project, after having happily got rid of Mr. [Hans Georg] Nägeli in Zurich. For along with your esteemed letter I received the day before yesterday another, in which the proposal is made to me that from among all the works of S. Bach I should make such a selection as would form a useful Method for clavier-players, and lead them from the beginning to the highest peaks of the player's art. This man wants to have this Method accompanied by an appropriately instructive text, and proposes that I should furnish both. Now, although this point of view does not afford a prospect quite as broad as yours, your firm might suffer a considerable loss if this project should be realized and if your investment were not covered by a sufficient number of subscribers who could be counted on to continue to the end. Since I do not wish to obstruct your undertaking in any way, I will delay my reply to the aforesaid proposal until I learn your own opinion of it.

I cannot return to you any of the Second Part of the *Well-Temp. Clav.,* partly because I must first get some other matters out of the way— partly, too, because a brief glance has shown me that again there is a good deal to correct. But you shall have the work as soon as possible, one gathering at a time, so that your work will not be held up. About the nature of my participation in the dissemination of Bach's works I am myself not yet clear. If you are to issue an essay of mine along with any of the latest fascicles, as you apparently wish to do, I do not know under what pretext this should be done, since the project is not mine but yours. Even for the changes I have suggested I cannot with propriety take responsibility before the public, but at most only before you. It would be up to you to take the responsibility for having accepted the changes I suggested. At long last I have hit upon another idea about which I wish to know your opinion.

I believe, namely, that the most appropriate way to further the whole project and to inform a large public about its value would be if now or in the near future a little essay *on the life and works of J. S. Bach* could be placed in the hands of this larger public. Since for more than 20 years I have been gathering material for such a work, and am certainly better acquainted with the subject than anyone else in Europe, I should be willing, in this good cause, to put aside the other work I have planned in order to undertake this task, if you should find it possible to venture the publication. After a rough survey it seems to me that this work might amount to some 10 or 12 sheets. If it were clearly printed and perhaps ornamented with a well-engraved portrait of S. Bach, it would not only sell well, but also surely be of value to the larger project. I hope you will let me have your opinion on this matter as soon as possible.

So far as the further revision of the Bach works is concerned, I will leave the compensation for my work up to you. You must know best what circumstances permit you to pay. So let me have your proposal. Incidentally, all of Bach's works (and I do not say this out of self-interest), even the engraved ones, need correction, for even in the latter there are many engraving errors. Now if these remain and new ones occur, the result will always be incorrect works—a circumstance you must certainly seek to avoid. Even my own copies, which are in the main wholly correct, must be looked through very carefully if they are to serve for the engraving. There are individual wrong notes everywhere, which I have always played correctly because I have a precise knowledge of the material, and which for this reason have remained uncorrected.

Is Mr. Hoffmeister now with you or in Vienna? I greet you cordially, and am, as ever,

Yours,
FORKEL

This letter contains the first mention of Forkel's Bach biography.

c. July 16, 1802

Praemissis Praemittendis [Premising those things which are to be premised]

At last you receive the enclosed manuscript. A few sheets are still missing, which, because they contain difficult matter, namely the characterization of Bach's genius, I must polish as much as possible and therefore must keep here for the moment. But now the whole thing is finished, and even these last few sheets shall be sent off not later than a week from today. Thus you can have the printing started right away. In this connection, I beg you to look around for a really good copy-reader and tell him that everything throughout the book is to be set according to [Johann Christoph] Adelung's [*Grundsätze der deutschen*] *Orthographie* [Leipzig, 1782].

If, as I gather, you wish to print the work in Roman rather than in Gothic characters, it is all the same to me. My only wish is that it be printed in a clean and sharp typeface, and on good paper. The format must be large quarto, like Zelter's Fasch.

I have dedicated it to [Baron Gottfried] v[an] Swieten, because in Vienna we debated a great deal about our Bach, and because it may be altogether a good idea to gain his interest in this way in the whole project.

As soon as the little book is finished, I will send it to London to be translated into English by one of my friends [probably A. F. C. Kollmann; see Part VI]. It really ought to be published in French, too. Since with works of art as great as those of Seb. Bach one cannot count much on humble art-lovers, connoisseurs will have to be sought out all over Europe, and I really believe that this is the only means of giving your project some momentum and getting it distributed.

Do you plan to insert a well-engraved portrait of Bach as a frontispiece? If so, it must be a fine one.

Now that I am rid of this work you shall soon receive the English and French *Suites*. Until now it has been impossible for me to get at them—my head has been so constantly full of Bach.

See to it that everything is done in proper fashion, and farewell. I am as ever

Yours most faithfully,
FORKEL

P.S. You will certainly have to publish the corrected Two-Part Inventions, and the sooner you do it the more credit it will throw upon your enterprise. At the same time you could abandon the *Toccata.* It is a very early and imperfect piece. Altogether I must urge you to take care that your edition may turn out to be a correct and critical one, if you wish to achieve a wide distribution for it. Thus I sincerely advise you, for example, to be cautious: if any of the already published fascicles should be required in England or France, by all means withhold the *Toccata* and the Two-Part Inventions. Everywhere there are at least a few connoisseurs whose judgments remain the most influential in the end.

I send you and Mr. Hoffmeister my cordial greetings.

d. April 24, 1803

Praemissis Praemittendis

To your esteemed communication of March 28, I have the honor of replying as follows:

As regards the church pieces of Sebastian: I had Wilh. Friedm. B.'s whole cantata cycle in my house, the one that so beautifully treats chorale melodies. Friedem. Bach was at the time in sore straits, and asked a price, for outright purchase of the cycle, of 20 *Louis d'or,* and simply for the right to look through the works, 2 *Louis d'or.* I was at the moment not rich enough to be able to put out 20 *Louis d'or* at one time, but the 2 *Louis d'or* I could manage. Had I wished to have them all copied out in the space of that half-year, it would have cost me more than 20 *Louis d'or.* I therefore decided to copy out a few of the very best pieces in this cycle myself, for the 2 *Louis d'or* I was paying. I now possess therefore only two cantatas based on chorales: Es ist das Heil uns kommen her, etc., etc., and Wo Gott der Herr nicht bei uns hält [BWV 9 and 178]. Both works are extraordinarily beautiful. The whole [chorale cantata] cycle, for which I should have had to pay 20 *Louis d'or,* was later sold out of necessity for 12 Thaler. But I do not know what has become of it.

If you now want to have both my pieces, nothing would be more reasonable than that you should reimburse me for the fee I paid, and then let me have an engraved copy free of charge. . . .

I remain most cordially

Yours,

FORKEL

LETTERS OF CARL PHILIPP EMANUEL BACH TO
JOHANN NIKOLAUS FORKEL

393. Excerpts from three letters concerning portraits and music of Bach (*BD* III, nos. 785a, 785b, and 792)

a. Hamburg, April 20, 1774

. . . When I send you these Psalms, which I will do as soon as I receive them at the time of the fair, I shall have the pleasure of sending you a recently executed copper engraving of my late father's portrait, clearly done and a fair likeness. I have my father's portrait, drawn in pastels, in my gallery of musical pictures, in which there are more than 150 professional musicians. I had it brought here by water from Berlin, since such paintings with dry colors do not bear well being shaken up over the axle; otherwise I should very gladly have sent it to you for copying. . . .

b. Hamburg, July 12, 1774

. . . further you will receive my late father [engraved] in copper and my Passion . . .

c. Hamburg, August 9, 1774

. . . My late father's portrait costs nothing. The music by him you received you may return at your convenience, since I do not need it so urgently. There are no more copies to be had of the things of my father's that were engraved; even the plates are no longer in existence. What I have—namely, the First and Third Parts [of the *Clavier-Übung*]—I shall be glad to let you have, bound, for copying, or even for purchase. The material of both of them used to cost 6 thlr. If you do not wish to copy them, I will let you have both parts, cleanly bound and in very good condition, for 8 thlr. I have the manuscript of the deceased, and I can get along with that, and you have the copy he used to have for his own use. But you must not feel any compunction about it. . . .

For the extensive correspondence between Bach and Forkel, see The Letters of C. P. E. Bach, *trans. & ed. Stephen L. Clark (Oxford, 1997). The contents of C. P. E. Bach's famous portrait gallery (see No. 393a) occupy 36 pages of his estate catalogue (1790). The earliest engraved portrait of Bach, by Samuel Gottlieb Kütner (1774), exists in several copies (see frontispiece), but the pastel mentioned here and also at the end of No. 395 has not survived.*

394. Letter on Bach's personal and artistic traits (*BD* III, no. 801)

A little inflammatory fever and a funeral music have prevented me from sending you before this the enclosed 6 solos and 4 concertos of mine. More later. My first Essay [*Versuch*] is also enclosed. It costs only 3 rthlr. Give me the pleasure of your visit here soon, and then we shall settle our account.

The account of my father's life [i.e., the obituary by C. P. E. Bach and J. F. Agricola] in Mizler is, through my help, the most complete.

The list of clavier pieces he wrote as given therein omits 15 two-part Inventions and 15 three-part *Sinfonie,* also 6 short Preludes. As to the church works of the deceased, it may be mentioned that he worked devoutly, governing himself by the content of the text, without any strange misplacing of the words, and without elaborating on individual words at the expense of the sense of the whole, as a result of which ridiculous thoughts often appear, such as sometimes arouse the admiration of people who claim to be connoisseurs and are not.

No one has ever tried out organs so severely and yet at the same time honestly as he. He understood the whole art of organ building in the highest degree. When an organ builder had worked conscientiously, and incurred losses by his work, he would persuade the employers to make amends. No one understood registration at the organ as well as he. Organists were often terrified when he sat down to play on their organs and drew the stops in his own manner, for they thought that the effect could not be good as he was planning it; but then they gradually heard an effect that astounded them. [*Marginal note:*] These sciences perished with him.

The first thing he would do in trying an organ was this: he would say, in jest, "Above all I must know whether the organ has good lungs," and, to find out, he would draw out every speaking stop, and play in the fullest and richest possible texture. At this the organ builders would often grow quite pale with fright.

The exact tuning of his instruments as well as of the whole orchestra had his greatest attention. No one could tune and quill his instruments to please him. He did everything himself. The placing of an orchestra he understood perfectly. He made good use of any space. He grasped at first glance any peculiarity of a room. A remarkable illustration of that fact is the following:

He came to Berlin to visit me; I showed him the new opera house. He perceived at once its virtues and defects (that is, as regards the sound of music in it). I showed him the great dining hall; we went up to the gallery that goes around the upper part of that hall. He looked at the ceiling, and without further investigation made the statement that the architect had here accomplished a remarkable feat, without intending to do so, and without anyone's knowing about it: namely, that if someone went to one corner of the oblong-shaped hall and whispered a few words very softly upward against the wall, a person standing in the corner diagonally opposite, with his face to the wall, would hear quite distinctly what was said, while between them, and in the other parts of the room, no one would hear a sound. A feat of architecture hitherto very rare and much admired! This effect was brought about by the arches in the vaulted ceiling, which he saw at once.

He heard the slightest wrong note even in the largest combinations. As the greatest expert and judge of harmony, he liked best to play the viola, with appropriate loudness and softness. In his youth, and until the approach of old age, he played the violin cleanly and penetratingly, and thus kept the orchestra in better order than he could have done with the harpsichord. He understood to perfection the possibilities of all stringed instruments. This is evidenced by his solos for the violin and for the violoncello without [accompanying] bass. One of the greatest violinists told me once that he had seen nothing more perfect for learning to be a good violinist, and could suggest nothing better to anyone eager to learn, than the said violin solos without bass.

Thanks to his greatness in harmony [i.e., counterpoint], he accompanied trios on more than one occasion on the spur of the moment and, being in a good humor and knowing that the composer would not take it amiss, and on the basis of a sparsely figured continuo part just set before him, converted them into complete quartets, astounding the composer of the trios.

When he listened to a rich and many-voiced fugue, he could soon say, after the first entries of the subjects, what contrapuntal devices it would be possible to apply, and which of them the composer by rights ought to apply, and on such occasions, when I was standing next to him, and he had voiced his surmises to me, he would joyfully nudge me when his expectations were fulfilled.

He had a good penetrating voice of wide range and a good manner of singing. In counterpoints and fugues no one was as happy as he in all kinds of taste and figuration, and variety of ideas in general.

There are many adventurous stories about him. A few of them may be true, and concern youthful pranks. The deceased never liked to hear them mentioned, so pray omit these humorous things.

The family tree must be copied, and the description pertains to it.

If you come here soon, this can be done in your presence, or if you cannot, and are pressed for time, then I will attend to it soon.

In addition to the enclosed Concerto in F, I have made two sonatinas for two keyboard instruments [*Flügel*]. The latter, as well as the other sonatinas, I have for the time being not made public. For your kind attempt to help deliver my poor *Israeliten in der Wüste* [i.e., to perform the writer's oratorio], I thank you devotedly in advance.

I have scribbled out the above *Specialia Patris* without ornament, just as they occurred to me. Use them as you please, and put them into better order. To Mr. and Mme. [Christian Gottlob] Heyne my most obedient respects.

Pray continue to love

Your

[Hamburg, December 1774]   BACH

I am afraid the post may already have left. Excuse me.

Toward the end of this letter, Carl Philipp Emanuel promises a copy of the family tree and the genealogy (No. 303). He mentions the charges for these in the following letter. Accordingly, there cannot have been a long interval between the two letters, and the present undated one was probably written very late in 1774.

The enclosed work is presumably a copy of the first part of his Versuch über die wahre Art das Clavier zu spielen.

395. Letter answering questions about Bach (*BD* III, no. 803)

The account of my late father's life in Mitzler, dearest friend, was thrown together by the late Agricola and me in Berlin, and Mitzler added only that part from the words "He joined the Society" to the end. It is not worth much. The departed, like myself or any true musician, was no lover of dry, mathematical stuff.

ad 1mum [to the first (question)]: The instruction received by the departed in Ohrdruf may well have been designed for an organist and nothing more.

ad 2dum: Besides Froberger, Kerl, and Pachhelbel, he heard and studied the works of Frescobaldi, the Baden Capellmeister Fischer, Strunck [Nicolaus Adam Strungk], some old and good Frenchmen, Buxdehude, Reincken, Bruhns, and [*crossed out:* his teacher Böhm] the Lüneburg organist Böhm.

ad 3um: I do not know what took him from Lüneburg to Weimar.

ad 4tum: The departed formed his taste by adding his own efforts.

ad 5tum: Through his own study and reflection alone he became even in his youth a pure and strong fugue writer. The above-named favorites were all strong fugue writers.

ad 6tum: As a result of frequent large-scale performances of music in churches, at court, and often in the open air, in strange and inconvenient places, he learned the placing of the orchestra, without any systematic study of acoustics [*Phonurgie*]. He knew how to make good use of this experience, together with his native understanding of building design so far as it concerns sound; and these were supplemented in turn by his special insight into the proper design of an organ, the disposition of stops, and the placing of the same.

ad 7mum: If I exclude some (but, *nota bene,* not all) of his clavier pieces, particularly those for which he took the material from improvisations on the clavier, he composed everything else without instrument, but later tried it out on one.

ad 8um: Prince Leopold in Cöthen, Duke Ernst August in Weimar, and Duke Christian in Weissenfels particularly loved him, and rewarded him appropriately. In addition, he was particularly honored in Berlin and Dresden. But in general he did not have the most brilliant good fortune, because he did not do what it requires, namely, roam the world over. Yet by connoisseurs and lovers of the art he was sufficiently honored.

ad 9um: Since he himself had composed the most instructive pieces for the clavier, he brought up his pupils on them. In composition he started his pupils right in with what was practical, and omitted all the *dry species* of counterpoint that are given in Fux and others. His pupils had to begin their studies by learning pure four-part thorough bass. From this he went to chorales; first he added the basses to them himself, and they had to invent the alto and tenor. Then he taught them to devise the basses themselves. He particularly insisted on the writing out of the thorough bass in [four real] parts [*Aussetzen der Stimmen im Generalbasse*]. In teaching fugues, he began with two-part ones, and so on.

The realization of a thorough bass and the introduction to chorales are without doubt the best method of studying composition, as far as harmony is concerned. As for the invention of ideas, he required this from the very beginning, and anyone who had none he advised to stay away from composition altogether. With his children as well as with other pupils, he did not begin the study of composition until he had seen work of theirs in which he detected talent.

ad 10mum: Apart from his sons, the following pupils come to my mind: the organist Schubert, the organist Vogler, Goldberg of Count

Brühl's household, the organist Altnicol (my late brother-in-law), the organist Krebs, Agricola, Kirnberger, Müthel in Riga, Voigt in Anspach, [*sic; apparently C. P. E. Bach intended to add names*]

ad 11mum: In his last years he esteemed highly: Fux, Caldara, Händel, Kayser, Hasse, both Grauns, Telemann, Zelenka, Benda, and in general everything that was worthy of esteem in Berlin and Dresden. Except for the first four, he knew the rest personally. In his younger days he saw a good deal of Telemann, who also stood godfather to me. [*crossed out:* He esteemed him, particularly in his instrumental things, very highly.] In his judgment of works he was, as regards harmony, very severe, but otherwise he valued everything that was really good, and gave it his acclaim even if it contained human weaknesses. With his many activities he hardly had time for the most necessary correspondence, and accordingly would not indulge in lengthy written exchanges. But he had the more opportunity to talk personally to good people, since his house was like a beehive, and just as full of life. Association with him was pleasant for everyone, and often very edifying. Since he never wrote down anything about his life, the gaps are unavoidable. I cannot write any more. Farewell, and continue to love your true fr[iend]

Hamburg, January 13, 1775   BACH

The following remarks appear in the margin:

What portrait do you want for a frontispiece? The one you have is faulty. I have a beautiful original pastel, a good likeness. The cost of the family tree amounts to 2½ thaler. The present generation, as far as music is concerned, is degenerated.
With a few things by J. Xstoph I can oblige if you wish.

The names of Caldara, Keiser, Telemann, the word "both" before Graun, and possibly also Fux, were added on second thought.

A COMPARISON OF BACH AND HANDEL
[BY CARL PHILIPP EMANUEL BACH?]

Introductory Note

The centenary of Handel's birth was lavishly though somewhat prematurely celebrated in London by a series of concerts in 1784. The following year "An account of the musical performances in Westminster Abbey and the Pantheon . . . in commemoration of Handel" was published, including a life of Handel from the pen of Charles Burney, author of the four-volume *General History of Music* and various books describing his extensive travels and the state of music on the continent. A translation of the commemorative pamphlet was published in Berlin in the same year by Friedrich Nicolai, author and well-known literary critic. As a reply to a statement in Burney's account, Nicolai received the present comparison and inserted it in 1788 as an anonymous contribution in the *Allgemeine Deutsche Bibliothek,* the excellent literary magazine of which he was the editor as well as publisher.

Who could have been the author of this "very just and equitable estimate" of Bach's and Handel's "respective merits, drawn up by a man fully competent to the task," as Forkel called him? It was certainly an enthusiastic fighter for the cause of Bach, a person of literary ability, thoroughly conversant with the organ, and, not least, familiar with the English scene.

In the first edition of *The Bach Reader,* the Comparison was tentatively attributed to A. F. C. Kollmann. But one sign that was overlooked points strongly in another direction: the story of Hurlebusch's visit to Bach, "of which," says the writer of the Comparison, "I was a witness." Kollmann was born six years after Bach's death, so he cannot have witnessed this incident. Dragan Plamenac (in *The Musical Quarterly* 35 [1949]: 575–87) pointed out many striking similarities between the Comparison and a letter written by C. P. E. Bach on January 21, 1786, to J. J. Eschenburg, translator of Burney's *Account of the Musical Performances in Commemoration of Handel.* Was the writer of the Comparison, whom Forkel called "a man fully competent to the task," Emanuel himself? If so, he displayed (or rather concealed under the cloak of anonymity) strange taste and judgment in laying so much stress on impartiality as a prerequisite for making such a comparison, and in claiming this impartiality for himself. But it is not likely that anyone else living in 1788 knew such details of Bach's life as, for example, Bach's attempts to make Handel's acquaintance, related in the Comparison and repeated almost exactly by Forkel, whose information about Bach was, according to his own Preface (p. 422), based largely on what he had learned from Carl Philipp Emanuel. Whether or not, then, Carl Philipp Emanuel actually wrote the Comparison, much of its substance originated with him, and no other attribution of it can be made at this time.

396. "Excerpt from a Letter of February 27, 1788, Written at ———" (*BD* III, no. 927)

Concerning the following passage in Dr. Burney's account of the life of Handel (p. 401), I must communicate my thoughts to you:

It is my belief, likewise, that in his full, masterly, and excellent *organ-fugues,* upon the most natural and pleasing subjects, he [Handel] has surpassed Frescobaldi, and even Sebastian Bach and others of his countrymen, the most renowned for abilities in this difficult and elaborate species of composition. . . .

Comparisons of great men can be uncommonly instructive when they are undertaken by a man who himself has greatness enough to penetrate, depict, and judge their virtues. Even with individual masterpieces of famous artists it is a difficult undertaking to compare their relative values exactly and determine them correctly; but how far is this difficulty increased when one puts the entire talents of two excellent artists both into the scales? How deep is the knowledge, how fine the artistic feeling in the field in which the two men were great, which this task requires! *De artifice non nisi artifex judicare potest* [None but the artist can judge the artist]. Great geniuses, therefore, acknowledge none but their equals as competent judges of their deserts, especially when the merits of two men are to be set side by side. But even the knowledge of art in its entire scope, fine genuine taste, and a delicate sense for every beauty, no matter how hidden—even these are not sufficient. Without the strictest impartiality, without the honest renunciation of all predilection, without the firm resolution to be just to every merit, the judge will run the risk of erring wholly. And he remains exposed to this risk as long as he does not have before him and investigate all the evidence in the case he is to judge; that is, if he expresses his one-sided opinion without knowing all the outstanding works of the masters he is to appraise. Moreover, he must compare not just the works of one sort but also the output of the same periods in the lives of the two artists, not the youthful work of the one with the product of the other's ripe maturity, or the hastily and casually assembled composition of the one with the tested and improved work of the other. The recognized masterpieces of both, to which the finishing touches have been given— these must be compared with each other.

Knowledge of art, and particularly taste, we may concede to Dr. Burney; but is he also impartial? Did he know all the works of the two famous men whom he wished to compare? On pages 400 and 401 there is nothing to be seen but partiality, and of any close acquaintance with the principal works of J. S. Bach for the organ we find in Dr. Burney's writings no trace. Moreover, to judge from his descriptions of his travels, he seems to have gathered little information about J.S.B.'s great and amazing way of playing the organ, although at the time of his travels many pupils not unworthy of their teacher were still living and among them Bach's eldest son, Wilhelm Friedemann. If Dr. Burney had had any idea of the greatness of J.S.B. as a master on the organ, he would have looked up such men wherever he could, for they would have been able to give him more detailed information about this first of all organists; and he would have discussed with them at length a phenomenon that marks an epoch in music. But no, for him Handel was the greatest organist, and why should he bother about the lesser ones? Hence his unjust and distorted comparisons. In order to prove their falsity, I too must make comparisons; but I flatter myself I shall do so with greater impartiality, after longer and more searching study, and (as I wish to make clear at the outset) on the premise that I consider Handel a great man—though not always as an instrumental composer, yet as an opera composer and still more as a church composer—and one who combined theoretical knowledge and the science of harmony with richness of ideas, invention, expression, and feeling.

Bach and Handel were born in the same year, namely 1685, and accordingly they were composing at about the same time. As an opera composer there was another great man besides Handel: Kaiser [Keiser], who, be it mentioned in passing, in the beauty, novelty, expression, and pleasing qualities of his melody, need have no fear of comparison with Handel.

Clavier pieces by Bach and Handel appeared in print at the same time, in the twenties of this century. But what a difference! In Handel's Suites there is considerable imitation of the French manner of the period, and there is not much variety; in the parts of Bach's *Clavier-Übung* all is originality and variety. The melody of the arias with variations in Handel's Suites is flat and for our times far too simple. Bach's arias with variations are still good today: they are original, and will accordingly not easily become outdated. What riches, especially in Bach's printed Aria with Variations for the harpsichord with two manuals [the Goldberg]! What diversity! What perfection of the hands and of expression this art requires!

The First Part of Handel's Clavier Suites is, except for the arias, very good. The Second Part is supposed to be more *galant,* but it is in large part ordinary and poverty-stricken.

Handel's fugues are good, but he often abandons a voice. Bach's clavier fugues can be set out for as many instruments as they have voices; no voice fails to receive its proper share, and every one is carried through properly. Handel's fugues never extend beyond four voices at the most. Bach wrote five-voiced fugues in his collections entitled *The Well-Tempered Clavier* and in all 24 keys. Indeed there is a fugue by him on the Royal Prussian theme that is for six voices *manualiter* [without pedals]. When it comes to the art of harmony, or the genius of the master who created many parts for a large work, worked them out completely, and dovetailed them into a large and beautiful whole that combined diversity and the greatness of simplicity, and this in such manner that even the amateur, if he but have some understanding of the language of the fugue (and others can have no judgment of fugues), was delighted—I doubt whether Handel's fugues will ever bear comparison with Bach's.

And what virtues are to be found in Bach's other clavier works! What life, novelty, and pleasing melody, even now, when melody has become so refined in every respect! What invention, what diversity in various styles, the learned and the *galant,* the strict and the free, whether harmony or melody reigns—on the one hand, extreme difficulty for the hands of masters, and on the other, ease even for the somewhat practiced amateur. How many fine clavier players his works have produced! Was he not the creator of a quite new treatment of keyboard instruments? Did not he give them particularly melody, expression, and the singing style in performance? He, the deepest savant of contrapuntal arts (and even artifices), knew how to subordinate art to beauty. And what a great mass of clavier pieces he wrote!

But now for the organ works of the two masters, since we can no longer set off the organ playing of one against the other. Of Bach's great pupils few are left, and if Handel trained and formed any great organists, that fact is not known. Thus they must be judged according to their works.

Now, if we weigh the organ works of the two men in the same scales, there is a difference as wide as the sky in favor of J.S.B. The proof of this statement can without any trouble be made convincing even to people who are not experts.

One may assume without fear of contradiction that the pedal is the most important part of an organ, without which it would have little of that majesty, greatness, and power that belong to it alone above all other instruments. Anyone who knows at all what the word "organ" means will grant that.

What shall we say, then, if Handel almost completely neglected and seldom used the very thing that makes an organ an organ, and lifts it so high above all other instruments? Not at all because he was completely lacking in the necessary genius, but because he was not practiced on the pedals, or because he was compelled, as an Englishman, to renounce the experience of the pedals that, as a German, he had possessed. That this is exactly what happened to him cannot be doubted by those who know that in England there are few organs with pedals and that they are not even missed there. But the situation is quite different in Germany, where one is not likely to find pedals lacking even in the smallest village organ. An organ without pedals is called a positive, and is not considered worth very much. Accordingly good organists have always been at home in Germany, and who does not know what J.S.B.'s works have contributed to the training of many great organists? It will not be unjust to conclude from what has been said that an Englishman can have no clear conception of the true and essential qualities of an organist, and must therefore not set himself up to be a judge of great organists. How little Dr. Burney forms an exception to this rule will be clear from the following reliable report that was given me about him. When he was in Hamburg, I was told, he prayed the Capellmeister Emanuel Bach (who is, of course, the son of J. Sebastian) to play on the organ of St. Michael's Church, which has a fine new instrument by Hildebrandt. When Bach told him that he could not play the pedal, he is said to have laughed and said the pedals were not essential.

Thus the English can hardly have a proper notion of a good organist; and it will seem exaggerated to them when German connoisseurs of music tell them that a good organist is a great man; that he plays the most difficult and most perfect of instruments, which requires uncommon talents, knowledge, and practice to do it full justice. And thus an Englishman will hardly ever have heard J. S. Bach's organ works properly performed anywhere on his island; for what qualities are needed to be able to play those works!

Bach's organ pieces usually—and the pieces for two manuals and pedals always—are written on three staves, one above another. The pedal is always independent of the manuals, and forms a voice in itself. At times there are even two obbligato voices in the pedal. The left hand is anything but the player of the bass; it must have the same fluency and dexterity as the right, in order to play properly parts that are so often full of lively melody.

According to the registration, Bach sometimes gives to the pedals the resplendent chief melody, which is often neither slow nor easy, while the brilliant matter is assigned to the hands; sometimes the pedal has the highest of the inner voices, sometimes the lowest. And the hands, too, must adapt themselves to the same tasks and changes.

The pedal has at times much brilliant and quick material, which, however, only practiced masters can play, and the like of which may never have been heard in England. Now, when one adds that Bach not only satisfied all these requirements with his pen but could do so also in improvisation and in the most correct possible style—what greatness does this require!

In addition to the chorale settings and variations J. S. wrote, and the preludes to them (these, too, are little known among the English, since the English style of church singing presents very little occasion for them), various trios for the organ have become known, particularly six for two manuals and pedal that are written in such *galant* style that they still sound very good, and never grow old, but on the contrary will outlive all revolutions of fashion in music. All in all, no one has written so much beautiful music for the organ as J. S. Bach.

Quantz says in one place in his printed "Method of Playing the Transverse Flute" (*Viz.,* in Ch. XVIII, § 83) that it was our admirable J. S. Bach who, in recent times, brought the art of organ playing to its greatest perfection. And Quantz was indisputably a connoisseur of art and a man of taste—taste he had developed in long travels through Germany, Italy, France, Holland, and England, during which he frequently heard all the great musicians. And especially Handel he knew very well, and admired. Quantz, together with Hasse and the Faustina—all of whom had known Handel for a long time and had often heard him play the clavier and the organ—was present in Dresden when J. S. Bach, in the thirties of this century, performed on the organ before the Court and many connoisseurs. They confirmed the opinion quoted, pronouncing him the first and most perfect of all organists and composers for this instrument. And this opinion still survives in the general estimation in Germany and foreign countries.

Of the organ works of Handel, as compared with those of Bach, nothing can be said. They are of too different a character and simply cannot be compared.

It will perhaps be said that Handel gave in to the taste of the English, and turned his back on the outstanding qualities of the organ, perhaps even for economic reasons. That may be true when, in his *Saul,* for example, he includes organ solos that are so thinly woven, of such two-voiced transparency, and so light and easy that they can be played at sight by any mediocre clavier player, and are of just as good effect on the short-toned harpsichord as on the organ with its sustained tones. But should not Handel have disposed at least one piece among his organ works in such manner that the masters across the sea, too, could tell that he measured up to their higher art? Should he not have written and left behind in Germany a single work worthy of the German organ?

Yet among all the Handel organ works I know, and (I intentionally add what Dr. Burney, as concerns Bach, omitted) however numerous the works of Handel are that I do know, I can find none that has the virtues for which the Bach works have been praised above. Everywhere the pedal lets its cards be trumped (that is, it does no more than strengthen the bass), and everything can be played on the manuals alone without any weakening of the effect.

Consider all his printed organ concertos and organ fugues. If there are unprinted ones in existence that are of quite different workmanship, let them be exhibited. But until now none of our oldest musicians has ever seen them, and it would be strange if Handel had had just his poor organ works printed. Since everything he wrote was engraved in England in such immense quantity, and sold like hot cakes, should he not have been able to bring out, along with the lighter pieces, a few organ fugues and concertos of a proper sort, in which one could have recognized the master of the organ, with all his richness of invention and brilliance of artistry? Or was this *great and loftier* work, this *Bachian* art (which so happily and inimitably united the old, dark burrowings with the brighter taste and more beautiful expression of our newer music)—was this in itself simply not to the taste of even the great Handel?

A strange circumstance in the story of his life makes it seem probable that he did not trust himself to challenge comparison with J.S.B. in this respect. In the first volume of Marpurg's "Contribution to the History of Music" [*Beyträge zur Geschichte der Musik,* p. 450], there is a passage that confirms this assumption, but it needs a brief commentary. The passage reads as follows: "Did not the great Handel avoid every occasion of coming together with the late Bach, that phoenix of composition and improvisation, or of having anything to do with him?" etc. And the commentary is: Handel came three times from England to Halle: the first time about 1719, the second time in the thirties, and the third time in 1752 or 1753. On the first occasion, Bach was Capellmeister in Cöthen, twenty short miles from Halle. He learned of Handel's presence in the latter place and immediately set out by stage coach and rode to Halle. The very day he arrived, Handel left. On the second occasion, Bach unfortunately had a fever. Since he was therefore unable to travel to Halle himself, he at once sent his eldest son, Wilhelm Friedemann, to extend a most courteous invitation to Handel. Friedemann visited Handel, and received the answer that he could not come to Leipzig, and regretted it very much. (J.S.B. was at that time already in Leipzig, which is also only twenty miles from Halle.) On the third occasion, J. S. was already dead. So Handel, it seems, was not as curious as J.S.B., who once in his youth walked at least 250 miles to hear the famous organist of Lübeck, Buxtehude. All the more did it pain J.S.B. not to have known Handel, that really great man whom he particularly respected.

Perhaps someone will think in this connection of the story of the justly famous French organist Marchand, who came to Dresden to play in contest with Bach, and retired modestly without victory to his native country, after the King with a large and brilliant company had waited for him to appear at the home of the Marshal Count von Flemming. He abandoned a salary of some 1,000 thaler, having departed by a special stagecoach. Perhaps it will be concluded that Bach was a challenging musical braggart and that the peaceful Handel had to keep out of his way. No, Bach was anything but proud of his qualities and never let anyone feel his superiority. On the contrary, he was uncommonly modest, tolerant, and very polite to other musicians. The affair with Marchand became known mainly through others; he himself told the story but seldom, and then only when he was urged.

A single example of his modesty, of which I was a witness. Bach once received a visit from Hurlebusch, a clavier player and organist who was then quite famous. The latter was prevailed upon to seat himself at the harpsichord; and what did he play for Bach? A printed minuet with variations. Thereupon Bach played very seriously, in his own style. The visitor, impressed with Bach's politeness and friendly reception, made Bach's children a present of his printed sonatas, so that they might, as he said, study them, although Bach's sons were already able to play pieces of a very different kind. Bach smiled to himself, and remained modest and friendly.

This is what I wished to say in reply to the much too sharp verdict of a music critic who, it is true, is none too competent—partly to show that we Germans do not concede to him the *jus de non appellando,* and partly to warn him and other judges of art to be more careful in the future in making comparisons of famous men; not to place them side by side in respects in which they cannot be compared; not to invent for them qualities that they do not possess and that, with their other talents, they might even do without; not to exalt a favorite at the expense of others of equally established merits; but, if comparisons are to be made, to compare *similar qualities and merits,* to examine them impartially with proper insight and correct judgment, and then to present their opinions modestly to the public, to connoisseurs, and to amateurs of art who are like connoisseurs. Only then can parallels drawn between famous artists and art works be instructive.

For the quotation from Quantz, see No. 350.

Bach played on the Silbermann organ in the Dresden St. Sophia's Church on September 14, 1731 (see note to No. 307), which was the day after the first performance of J. A. Hasse's Cleofide, the opera with which Hasse and his wife, the famous Faustina Bordoni, made their Dresden debut. It may be assumed that Quantz as well as Bach had come to Dresden for this event, and that the present passage refers to Bach's 1731 concert in St. Sophia's rather than the concert he gave on December 1, 1736, in the Church of Our Lady (see No. 151).

ANECDOTES

397. Bach and the herrings, by Friedrich Wilhelm Marpurg (Berlin, 1786) (*BD* III, no. 914)

Johann Sebastian Bach, to whom the quotation from Horace may be applied—*nil oriturum alias, nil ortum tale* [none such will ever arise, and none has arisen]—used to remember with pleasure an incident that had happened to him on a musical journey he had undertaken in his youth.

He was at school in Lüneburg—near Hamburg, where at the time a very able organist and composer, named Reinecke [Reinken], was in his prime. Since he made several trips to hear this master, it happened one day, since he stayed longer in Hamburg than the state of his purse permitted, that on his way home to Lüneburg he had only a couple of schillings in his pocket. He had not got halfway home yet when he developed a keen appetite, and accordingly went into an inn, where the savory odors from the kitchen only made the state in which he found himself ten times more painful. In the midst of his sad meditations on this subject, he heard the grinding noise of a window opening and saw a pair of herring heads thrown out onto the rubbish pile. Since he was a true Thuringian, the sight of these heads made his mouth begin to water, and he lost not a second in taking possession of them. And lo and behold! he had hardly started to tear them apart when he found a Danish ducat hidden in each head. This find enabled him not only to add a portion of roast meat to his meal but also at the first opportunity to make another pilgrimage, in greater comfort, to Mr. Reinecke in Hamburg. It is remarkable that the unknown benefactor, who must undoubtedly have watched from the window to see who would be lucky enough to find his gift, did not have the curiosity to ascertain more closely the identity and personality of the finder.

398. The unknown organist, by Friedrich Wilhelm Marpurg (Berlin, 1786) (*BD* III, no. 914)

A traveling virtuoso came to a town where there was a very able organist, in whose church there were two organs, a larger and a smaller. He struck up an acquaintance with him, and they agreed to give themselves the pleasure of leading each other astray (as the saying is) on the two organs, and of trying their powers in turn in all sorts of fantasies, duets, trios, and quartets, fugued and unfugued. The contest proceeded for a time as something like an equal match. With the harmony with which one man concluded on his organ, the other one began on his and carried the harmonic texture forward. The next player completed the rhythm of the preceding one, which had been left unfinished, and it seemed as if the four hands and four feet were being directed by one and the same head. Gradually the visiting virtuoso began to employ the more hidden arts of counterpoint and modulation. He made use of augmentation and diminution for certain ideas, combined several subjects, employed them in contrary motion, introduced an *alla stretta,* and all at once fell into the most distant of all keys. The local organist observed what the other man was doing. He sought to imitate him, and harmonic gaps were produced. He began to feel his way around, stumbled, was set straight by the traveler, and then led into new bypaths from which he in the end simply could not extricate himself. So he arose from his keyboard, ran to his opponent, whom he acknowledged to have won the contest, entreated him to continue his intricate organ playing as long as he cared to, admired him, embraced him, and said that he must be either Sebastian Bach or an angel from heaven.

It was indeed Sebastian Bach, with whom the organist would not have matched talents if he had recognized him.

399. A strange accomplishment, by Charles Burney (London, 1789) (*BD* III, no. 943)

He was so fond of full harmony that, besides a constant and active use of the pedals, he is said to have put down such keys by a stick in his mouth, as neither hands nor feet could reach.

400. Bach teases Gottfried Silbermann, by Edward John Hopkins (London, 1855) (Hopkins, p. 143)

The tradition runs that whenever Sebastian Bach observed Silbermann among his select circle of auditors, he used to say to him, in perfect good humor, "You *tune* the organ in the manner *you* please, and I *play* the organ in the key *I* please," and thereupon used to strike off a Fantasia in A-flat major; the contest invariably ending in Silbermann's retiring to avoid his own "wolf."

According to Adlung, Silbermann "would not tolerate equal temperament in his organs." Bach, on the other hand, probably was in favor of reasonably equal temperament on the organ as well as on the clavier.

401. The musical beggars, by Johann Friedrich Reichardt (Berlin, 1796) (*BD* III, no. 997)

It is said that Joh. Seb. Bach often gave himself the musical entertainment and satisfaction, with certain beggars who had a quite exceptionally complaining way of begging (consisting in a series of dissonances), of first acting as if he wished to give them something and could find nothing, during which time their complaint would rise to a higher pitch. He would then give them a few times in succession the very least possible amount, which softened their complaining only slightly. And in the end he would give them an unusually large amount, which produced a complete resolution and a wholly satisfying cadence.

402. The unresolved dissonance, by Johann Friedrich Reichardt (Berlin, 1796) (*BD* III, no. 997)

Johann Sebastian Bach once came into a large company while a musical amateur was sitting and improvising at a harpsichord. The moment the latter became aware of the presence of the great master, he sprang up and left off with a dissonant chord. Bach, who heard it, was so offended by this musical unpleasantness that he passed right by his host, who was coming to meet him, rushed to the harpsichord, resolved the dissonant chord, and made an appropriate cadence. Only then did he approach his host and make him his bow of greeting.

403. Bach and the bungler, by Carl Ludwig Hilgenfeldt (Hamburg, 1850) (Hilgenfeldt, p. 172)

Peaceful, quiet, and even-tempered though Bach was at all unpleasantnesses he encountered at the hands of third persons, so long as they concerned only his own personality, he was, however, quite another man when, no matter in what form, anyone slighted art, which was sacred to him. In such cases it doubtless happened at times that he donned his armor and gave expression to his wrath in the strongest ways. The organist of St. Thomas's, who was in general a worthy artist, once so enraged him by a mistake on the organ, during a rehearsal of a cantata, that he tore the wig from his head and, with the thundering exclamation "You ought to have been a cobbler," threw it at the organist's head.

404. Bach replies to compliments on his organ playing, quoted by Johann Friedrich Köhler (Leipzig, after 1776) (*BD* III, no. 820)

"There is nothing remarkable about it. All one has to do is hit the right notes at the right time, and the instrument plays itself."

405. A maxim, by Johann Philipp Kirnberger (Berlin, 1781) (*BD* III, no. 848)

The great J. Seb. Bach used to say, "Everything must be possible" [*es muss alles möglich zu machen seyn*], and he would never hear of anything's being "not feasible." This has always spurred me onward to accomplish many difficult things in music, by dint of effort and patience, according to my own poor powers.

406. *Io son' organista,* too, by Carl Friedrich Zelter (Göttingen, c. 1815)

It is understandable that Bach's organ playing didn't please everyone. The organist of the Garnison Church [in Potsdam] belonged among the dissatisfied and, when Bach had finished playing, sat down at the organ in order to demonstrate *io son' organista* [I am an organist] in his own manner. When the organist finished and found himself alone with the bellows operator, he said, "This one I have driven away, and he won't come back!" The Concertmaster Carl Benda has told me the story.

Manuscript annotation, c. 1815, in Zelter's interleaved personal copy, at the Houghton Library, Harvard University, of Forkel's Bach book, page 10 (see this volume, Part VI). Carl Hermann Benda was the son of Franz Benda, an eyewitness to Bach's Potsdam visit in 1747.

407. The linen draper and the portrait of Bach, by Carl Friedrich Zelter (letter to Goethe, January 24, 1829, trans. A. D. Coleridge)

Kirnberger had a portrait of his master, Sebastian Bach; it was my constant admiration, and it hung in his room, between two windows, on the wall above the piano. A well-to-do Leipzig linen draper, who had formerly seen Kirnberger, when he was a chorister at the St.

Thomas School, singing before his father's door, comes to Berlin, and it occurs to him to honor the now celebrated Kirnberger with a visit. Hardly were they seated, when the Leipziger bawls out, "Why, good Lord! you've actually got our Cantor, Bach, hanging there; we have him, too, in Leipzig, at the St. Thomas School. They say he was a rough fellow; didn't the conceited fool even go and have himself painted in a smart velvet coat?"

Kirnberger gets up quietly, goes behind his chair, and lifting it up with both hands in the guest's face, exclaims, first gently, then *crescendo,* "Out, you dog! Out, you dog!" My Leipziger, mortally frightened, seizes his hat and stick, makes with all haste for the door, and bolts out into the street. Upon this, Kirnberger has the picture taken down and rubbed, the Philistine's chair washed, and the portrait, covered with a cloth, restored to its old place. When someone inquired about the meaning of the cloth, he answered, "Leave that alone! There's something behind it." This story was the origin of the report that Kirnberger had lost his senses.

408. Johann Christian and Carl Philipp Emanuel Bach, by Johann Friedrich Reichardt (Berlin, 1796) (Reichardt, anecdote no. 18)

Christian Bach was a very lighthearted and jovial person. When one of his more serious friends once reproached him for his carefree ways, both as an artist and as a man (carefree ways with which he tossed off almost exclusively the light and passing things that were requested of him, and then threw away the money he earned by them on even more frivolous and fleeting sensual pleasures), and held up to him the example of his elder brother in Berlin, who wrote large works and knew very well how to hold on to the money he earned, Bach said, "Oh well, my brother lives to compose and I compose to live; he works for others, I work for myself."

409. Bach on his sons, by Carl Friedrich Cramer (Kiel, 1792) (*BD* III, no. 973)

The old Sebastian had three sons. He was satisfied only with Friedemann, the great organist. Even of Carl Philipp Emanuel he said (unjustly!), " 'Tis Berlin Blue! It fades easily!" He applied to the London Chrétien Bach always the verse by Gellert: "The boy progresses surely by his stupidity!" [*Der Jürge kömmt gewiss durch seine Dummheit fort!*] Actually this one of the three Bachs made the greatest progress. I have these statements direct from the mouth of Friedemann.

PART VI

*Forkel's
Biography
of
Bach*

JOHANN NIKOLAUS FORKEL

On Johann Sebastian Bach's Life, Genius, and Works

Introductory Note

Johann Nikolaus Forkel (1749–1818) deserves a place of honor in the history of musical scholarship. He was the first German to follow the example of Burney and Hawkins, by attempting a general history of music. The fact that in the two large volumes he finished he got no further than the middle of the sixteenth century indicates the thoroughness with which he went to work. Forkel was the first person to compile a reference work of musical bibliography. And it was he who first set out to realize the idea of collecting the monuments of the musical past in representative editions. He carefully scored two outstanding collections of Masses of the early sixteenth century; the score was engraved and the first proofs had been corrected when the Napoleonic Wars overtook the publication and the plates were melted down to make bullets.

Forkel, the son of a shoemaker, became one of the leading musicians and theorists of his time. He served as organist, music director, and professor at Göttingen University, which awarded him the honorary degree of doctor of philosophy. He was a successful writer rather than composer. His musical *Almanache* (little annual miscellanies) still make pleasant reading. His piece on the invention of the viola pomposa (No. 364) is an example. Probably his finest piece of writing was the present essay on Bach, the first of its kind and particularly valuable since it contains a considerable amount of information gathered from Carl Philipp Emanuel and Wilhelm Friedemann Bach, and not otherwise preserved. How carefully Forkel used every bit of evidence received from Bach's sons can be seen if one compares the few letters from Carl Philipp Emanuel to him that happen to survive. He obtained much additional material, particularly for his first two chapters, from the Genealogy sent him by Carl Philipp Emanuel (No. 303) and the first part of the

Obituary (No. 306). The reader will observe, however, that he did not always avoid the temptation to read his own views into this material.

Forkel's monograph, published in 1802, is subtitled "For Patriotic Admirers of True Musical Art." Forkel wrote at a time when the tide of nationalism was running high. It was thus natural for him to emphasize this aspect in presenting a new hero to the people of Germany, then divided into many small states and held together only nominally by the dying Holy Roman Empire of the German Nation.

The work was "dedicated most reverently by the author to his Excellency the Freyherr van Swieten." Baron Gottfried van Swieten (1734–1803), born in Leiden, was the son of the personal physician of the empress Maria Theresa. He served for a number of years as imperial ambassador to Frederick the Great (see No. 360). A fervent lover of music, he spurred Carl Philipp Emanuel on to write his Six Symphonies for Strings, of 1773—among his most important works. Mozart arranged oratorios by Handel for performance at the baron's house, and it was there that he and later Beethoven became acquainted with certain works by Bach (cf. pp. 489–90). Haydn's *Creation* and *Seasons* were written to Swieten's translations and arrangements of the English originals. Beethoven dedicated his First Symphony to the baron. In his later years Swieten, as director of the Imperial Library in Vienna, stained his reputation by causing to be removed, for doctrinaire reasons, a considerable number of valuable old books.

Samuel Wesley wrote to Benjamin Jacob, on September 17, 1808, that "Mr. Stephenson the Banker" had translated the biography into English (see p. 496), and Stephenson's translation was advertised for sale in that year. But the response to the announcement of the project was apparently not sufficient. The translation that follows, executed (at least in part) by Augustus Frederic Christopher Kollman, was finally issued in 1820 (see Walter Emery, "The English Translator of Forkel," *Music & Letters* 28 [1947]: 301–2). Kollmann (1756–1829), a native of the duchy of Hanover, was active in London from 1784 on and became one of the first promoters of Bach's music in England. He was not the first to publish works of Bach in England. That distinction belongs to Sir John Hawkins, who included in his *General History of the Science and Practice of Music* (1776) the aria and two variations from the Goldberg set. But Kollmann did publish in his *Essay on Practical Musical Composition* (1799) all the canons given in abbreviated notation in the *Musical Offering,* with indications of their solution; a prelude and fugue from *The Well-Tempered Clavier;* one of Bach's organ sonatas—from the set conspicuously mentioned in the Comparison of Bach and Handel (No. 396); and excerpts from Forkel's biography of Bach in his magazine, the *Quarterly Musical Register* (1812).

Preface

I have for many years had the intention of communicating to the public an account of the Life of John Sebastian Bach, with some information and reflections upon his Genius[1] and Works; because the short essay by C. Ph. Eman. Bach and Mr. Agricola, formerly composer to the Prussian court, which is inserted in the third volume of Mitzler's Musical Library[2] can hardly satisfy the admirers of that great man. I should certainly have executed my purpose long ago had I not been hitherto so much engaged in the composition of the "General History of Music." As Bach more than any other artist has made an era in the history of this art, I resolved to reserve for the last volume of the above work the materials which I had collected for the history of his life. The laudable determination of Messrs. Hoffmeister and Kühnel, music dealers and publishers at Leipzig, to publish a complete and critically correct edition of Sebastian Bach's works induced me to change my intention.

This undertaking is not only of the highest advantage, in every respect, to the art itself, but must contribute more than any other of the kind to the honor of the German name. The works which John Sebastian Bach has left us are an invaluable national patrimony, with which no other nation has anything to be compared. Whoever rescues them from the danger of being disfigured by faulty copies, and being thus gradually consigned to oblivion and destruction, erects to the artist an imperishable monument and deserves well of his country; and everyone to whom the honor of the German name is dear is bound to support such a patriotic undertaking and to promote it to the utmost of his power. I considered it as my duty to remind the public of this obligation, to rouse this noble enthusiasm in the breast of every true German; and this is the reason why these pages appear earlier than they would otherwise have done. I hope also that I shall be able in this manner to address a greater number of my German contemporaries: what I have to say of Bach in my History of Music might perhaps be read by only the small number of persons learned in the art, and yet, the preservation of the memory of this great man (let me be allowed to repeat it) is an object in which not merely the interest of the art but the honor of the nation itself is deeply involved.

1. Here, as in later instances, the word "genius" is used in the old translation to represent *Kunst* ("art") in the German original.
2. See No. 306.

The most efficacious means of preserving in lasting vigor musical works of art is undoubtedly the public execution of them before a numerous audience: by these means a number of great works always has been, and still continues to be, extensively circulated. The public hears them first with pleasure in the concert room, the church, or the theater, remembers the pleasing impression, and purchases them on publication, perhaps without being able to make any use of them. But where, through whom, shall the public hear Bach's works, as the number of persons capable of performing them in a proper manner has always been so extremely limited? The case would have been very different if Bach could have publicly executed them himself in several places; but for this he had neither time nor inclination. Whenever one of his scholars did it, though none of them executed them in the same perfection as their master, the astonishment and admiration of the auditors never failed to be excited by such extraordinary effusions of an art so great and yet so easily to be comprehended. Whoever was at all able then played at least one or some of the pieces over which the scholar of Bach had the most command and which consequently gave the most pleasure. Nobody found these pieces difficult, because they had heard before how they ought to sound.

Before a true relish of great musical compositions can become more general, we must, above all things, have better music masters. The want of good teachers is properly the source of all musical evil. In order to maintain his own credit, the unskillful and himself ill-informed teacher must necessarily give his pupils a bad opinion of good works, because he might otherwise run the risk of being asked by his scholar to play them to him. Thus the pupil is obliged to spend his time, labor, and money on useless jingle and in half a dozen years is perhaps not a step farther advanced in real musical knowledge than he was at the beginning. With better instruction, he would not have wanted half the time, trouble, and money to be put into a way on which he might have safely advanced progressively to greater perfection all his life. Time will show us how much this evil may be checked by the exposing of the works of Bach to sale in all music shops, at least, and by the connoisseurs and admirers of real musical genius joining to extol their merit and to recommend the study of them.

It is certain that if the art is to remain an art and not to be degraded into a mere idle amusement, more use must be made of classical works than has been done for some time past. Bach, as the first classic that ever was, or perhaps ever will be, can incontestably perform the most important services in this respect. A person who has for some time studied his works will readily distinguish mere jingle from real music and will show himself a good and well-informed artist in whatever style he may choose in the sequel. The study of classics who, like Bach, have exhausted the whole extent of the art is besides eminently calculated to preserve us from that mere partial knowledge to which the prevailing taste of the day so easily leads. In a word, it would be no less injurious to musical science to throw aside the classics in our art than it would be prejudicial to good taste in literature to banish the study of the Greeks and Romans from our schools. The spirit of the times, which is directed rather to trifles capable of affording immediate though fleeting enjoyment than to what is great and cannot be attained without some pains and even efforts, has, in some places, really led to a proposal, at least, to banish the Greeks and Romans from our schools, and there can be no doubt but it would be glad to get rid of our musical classics also; for, if we view the matter in its true light, this frivolous spirit must be heartily ashamed of its great poverty, compared with them, and most of all with our Bach, who is rich almost to excess.

How do I wish I were able to describe according to its merit the sublime genius of this first of all artists, whether German or foreign! After the honor of being so great an artist, so pre-eminent above all as he was, there is perhaps no greater than that of being able duly to appreciate so entirely perfect an art and to speak of it with judgment. He who can do the last must have a mind not wholly uncongenial to that of the artist himself and has therefore in some measure the flattering probability in his favor, that he might perhaps have been capable of the first, if similar external relations had led him into the proper career. But I am not so presumptuous as to believe that I could ever attain to such an honor. I am, on the contrary, thoroughly convinced that no language in the world is rich enough to express all that might and should be said of the astonishing extent of such a genius. The more intimately we are acquainted with it, the more does our admiration increase. All our eulogiums, praises, and admiration will always be and remain no more than well-meant prattle. Whoever has had an opportunity of comparing together the works of art of several centuries will not find this declaration exaggerated; he will rather have adopted the opinion that Bach's works cannot be spoken of by him who is fully acquainted with them except with rapture, and some of them even with a kind of sacred awe. We may indeed conceive and explain his management of the internal mechanism of the art; but how he contrived at the same time to inspire into this mechanic art, which he alone has attained in such high perfection, the living spirit which so powerfully speaks to us even in his smallest works will probably be always only felt and wondered at.

I have not chosen to enter upon any comparison of John Sebastian Bach with particular artists. Whoever wishes to see him compared with Handel will find a very just and equitable estimate of their respective merits, drawn up by a man fully competent to the task, in the first number of the 81st volume of the Universal German Library [*Allgemeine Deutsche Bibliothek*], pages 295–303.[3]

For my accounts, as far as they differ from the above-mentioned little essay in Mitzler's Library, I am indebted to the two eldest sons of John Seb. Bach. I was not only personally acquainted with both, but kept up a constant correspondence with them for many years, chiefly with C. Ph. Emanuel.[4] The world knows that they were both great artists; but it perhaps does not know that to the last moment of their lives they never spoke of their father's genius without enthusiasm and reverence. As I had from my early youth felt the same veneration for the genius of their father, it was a frequent theme of discussion with us, both in our conversations and correspondence. This made me by degrees so acquainted with everything relative to John Seb. Bach's life, genius, and works that I may now hope to be able to give the public not only some detailed but also useful information on the subject.

I have, in doing so, no other object whatever than to call the attention of the public to an undertaking the sole aim of which is to raise a worthy monument to German art, to furnish the true Artist with a gallery of the most instructive models, and to open to the friends of the Muse of Music an inexhaustible source of the sublimest enjoyment.

CHAPTER 1

The Bach Family

If ever there was a family in which an extraordinary disposition for the same art seemed to be hereditary, it was certainly the family of Bach; through six successive generations there were scarcely two or three members of it who had not received from nature the gifts of a very distinguished talent for music and who did not make the practice of this art the main occupation of their lives.

The ancestor of this family which has become so remarkable in the history of music was Veit Bach. He was a baker at Pressburg, in Hungary; but, on

3. See No. 396.
4. See Letters from C. P. E. Bach to Forkel, Nos. 393–95.

the breaking out of the religious troubles in the sixteenth century, he was obliged to seek for another place of abode. He saved as much of his property as he could and retired with it to Thuringia, where he hoped to find peace and security. The place in which he settled was called Wechmar, a village near Saxe-Gotha. Here he soon recommenced his trade of a baker; but in his leisure hours, he amused himself with his cittern, which he even took with him into the mill, and played upon it amidst all the noise and clatter of the mill. He communicated this inclination for music to his two sons, they again to their children, till by degrees there arose a very numerous family, all the branches of which were not only musical, but made music their chief business and soon had in their possession most of the offices of cantors, organists, and town musicians in Thuringia.

All these Bachs cannot possibly have been great masters; but in every generation some members, at least, particularly distinguished themselves. Thus already in the first quarter of the seventeenth century three grandsons of their common ancestor were so eminent that the then reigning Count of Schwarzburg-Arnstadt thought it worth while to send them at his own expense to Italy, at that time the great school of music, to perfect themselves. We cannot say how far they may have answered the expectations of their patron, since none of their works have come down to our times. In the fourth generation there were some members of this family who were still more distinguished and several pieces of whose composition have been preserved by the care of John Sebastian Bach. The most remarkable of them were:

(1) JOHN CHRISTOPHER, Court and Town Organist at Eisenach. He was particularly happy in the invention of beautiful melodies and in the expression of his text. In the Archives of the Bachs, as they were called, which C. Ph. Emanuel possessed, in Hamburg, there was among other pieces a Motet of his composition in which he had ventured to make use of the augmented sixth, which in his day was considered as an extremely bold attempt. He was also an uncommon master of full harmony, as is proved by a Motet composed by him for Michaelmas day, to the words *Es erhub sich ein Streit* & c., which has 22 obbligato parts and yet is perfectly pure in respect to the harmony. A second proof of his great skill in harmony is that he is said never to have played on the organ and clavichord with less than five necessary (or obbligato) parts. C. Ph. Emanuel had a particular esteem for him. It is still quite fresh in my remembrance how good-naturedly the old man smiled at me at the most remarkable and hazardous passages when he once gave me the pleasure, in Hamburg, of letting me hear some of those old pieces.

(2) JOHN MICHAEL, Organist and Town Clerk in the bailiwick of Gehren. He was a younger brother of the preceding and, like him, a very excellent

composer. In the Bach Archives, there are some Motets of his, among which is one for a double chorus with eight voices, and several single pieces of Church Music.

(3) JOHN BERNHARD, Chamber Musician and Organist at Eisenach. He is said to have composed remarkably fine Overtures in the French style.

Not only the above-mentioned, but many other able composers of the earlier generations of the family might undoubtedly have obtained much more important musical offices, as well as a more extensive reputation for their ability and a more brilliant fortune, if they had been inclined to leave their native province, Thuringia, and to make themselves known in other countries both in and out of Germany. But we do not find that any one of them ever felt an inclination for such an emigration: temperate by nature and education, they required but little to live, and the inner enjoyment which their art procured them enabled them not only to be content without the gold chains which used at that time to be given by great lords to esteemed artists as especial marks of honor, but also, without the least envy, to see them worn by others, who, perhaps, without those chains would not have been happy.

Besides this happy contentedness, which is indispensable to the cheerful enjoyment of life, the different members of this family had a very great attachment to each other. As it was impossible for them all to live in one place, they resolved at least to see each other once a year and fixed a certain day upon which they had all to appear at an appointed place. Even after the family had become much more numerous and the one and other of the members had been obliged to settle out of Thuringia, in different places of Upper and Lower Saxony and Franconia, they continued their annual meetings, which generally took place at Erfurt, Eisenach, or Arnstadt. Their amusements, during the time of their meeting, were entirely musical. As the company wholly consisted of cantors, organists, and town musicians, who had all to do with the Church, and as it was besides a general custom at the time to begin everything with Religion, the first thing they did, when they were assembled, was to sing a chorale. From this pious commencement they proceeded to drolleries which often made a very great contrast with it. For now they sang popular songs, the contents of which were partly comic and partly naughty, all together and extempore, but in such a manner that the several parts thus extemporized made a kind of harmony together, the words, however, in every part being different. They called this kind of extemporary harmony a *Quodlibet,* and not only laughed heartily at it themselves, but excited an equally hearty and irresistible laughter in everybody that heard them. Some persons are inclined to consider these facetiæ as the beginning of comic operettas in Germany; but such *quodlibets* were usual in Germany at a much earlier period—I possess, myself, a printed collection of them which was published at Vienna in 1542.

Yet the above-mentioned cheerful Thuringians, as well as some of their later descendants who made a more serious and worthy use of their art, would nevertheless not have escaped oblivion, had not, at length, a man arisen among them, whose genius and reputation beamed forth with such splendor that a part of this light was reflected upon them: this man was John Sebastian Bach, the ornament of his family, the pride of his country, and the dearest, most intimate favorite of the musical art.

CHAPTER 2

Bach's Life

John Sebastian Bach was born on the 21st of March, 1685, at Eisenach, where his father, John Ambrosius, was Musician to the Court and to the Town. This J. A. Bach had a twin brother, John Christopher, who was Musician to the Court and Town at Arnstadt, and was so very like him that even their own wives could not distinguish them except by their dress. These twins were perhaps singulars in their kind and the most remarkable ever known. They tenderly loved each other; their voice, disposition, the style of their music, their manner of performance, and everything, in short, was alike in them. If one was ill, the other was so likewise; they died also within a short time of each other. They were a subject of astonishment to all who saw them.

In the year 1695, when John Sebastian was not quite 10 years of age, his father died; he had lost his mother earlier. Being thus left an orphan, he was obliged to have recourse to an elder brother, John Christopher, who was Organist at Ordruff. From him he received the first instructions in playing on the clavier. But his inclination and talent for music must have been already very great at that time, since the pieces which his brother gave him to learn were so soon in his power that he began with much eagerness to look out for some that were more difficult. The most celebrated composers for the clavier in those days were Froberger, Fischer, John Casp. Kerl, Pachelbel, Buxtehude, Bruhns, Böhm, &c. He had observed that his brother had a book in which there were several pieces of the above-mentioned authors, and earnestly begged him to give it to him. But it was constantly denied him. His desire to possess the book was increased by the refusal, so that he at length sought for means to get possession of it secretly. As it was kept in a cupboard which had only a lattice-door and his hands were still small enough to pass through so that he could roll up the book, which was merely stitched in paper, and draw it out, he did not long hesitate to make use of these favorable circumstances. But, for want of a candle, he could only copy it in moonlight nights; and it took six whole months before he could finish his laborious task. At length, when he thought himself safely possessed of the treasure and intended to make good use of it in secret, his brother found it out and took from him, without pity, the copy which had cost him so much pains; and he did not recover it till his brother's death, which took place soon after.

John Sebastian, being thus again left destitute, went, in company of one of his schoolfellows, named Erdmann, afterwards Imperial Russian Resident in Dantzig, to Lüneburg, and was engaged there in the Choir of St. Michael's School as a discantist. His fine treble voice procured him here a good advancement; but he soon lost it and did not immediately acquire another good voice in its stead.

His inclination to play on the clavier and organ was as ardent at this time as in his more early years and impelled him to try to do, to see, and to hear everything which, according to the ideas he then entertained, could contribute to his improvement. With this view he not only went several times, while he was a scholar, from Lüneburg to Hamburg to hear the organist, John Adam Reinken, who was at that time very famous, but sometimes also to Celle in order to get acquainted with the Prince's band, which consisted chiefly of Frenchmen, and with the French taste, which was then a novelty in those parts.

It is not known on what occasion he removed from Lüneburg to Weimar; but it is certain that he became Court Musician there in 1703, when he was just 18 years of age. He exchanged this place, however, in the following [recte: the same] year for that of Organist to the New Church at Arnstadt, probably to be able to follow his inclination for playing on the organ better than he could do at Weimar, where he was engaged to play the violin. Here he began most zealously to make use of the works of the organists at that time celebrated—whichever of them he could procure in his situation—to improve both in composition and the art of playing on the organ; and, to gratify his desire of learning, even made a journey on foot to Lübeck to hear Dieterich Buxtehude, Organist to St. Mary's Church in that city, with whose compositions for the organ he was already acquainted. For almost a quarter of a year he remained a secret hearer[5] of this organist, who was really a man of talent

---

5. Apparently the obsolete expression *behorchen* in the Obituary induced Forkel to use the words *heimlicher Zuhörer,* but the meaning of his source seems to have been to listen *intently,* rather than *secretly.*

and much celebrated in his times, and then returned with an increased stock of knowledge to Arnstadt.

The efforts of his zeal and persevering diligence must have already excited great attention at this time, for he received, in quick succession, several offers of places as organist. Such a place was offered to him in the year 1707, in the Church of St. Blasius at Mühlhausen, and actually entrusted to him. But when, a year after he had entered upon it, he made a journey to Weimar to perform before the reigning Duke, his performance on the organ was so highly approved of that he was offered the place of Court Organist, which he accepted. The extended sphere of action for his art in which he here lived, impelled him to try out everything possible in this art; and this was actually the period during which he not only made himself so able a performer on the organ, but also laid the foundation of his great body of compositions for that instrument. He had still further occasion to improve in his art when his Prince, in 1717, appointed him Concertmeister, in which office he had also to compose and execute pieces of sacred music.

Handel's master, Zachau, Organist and Director of Music at Halle, died about this time; and J. S. Bach, whose reputation was now already high, was invited to succeed him. He, in fact, went to Halle to prove his qualifications by performing a piece as a specimen of his skill. However, for what reason is not known, he did not enter upon the office, but left it to an able scholar of Zachau's, of the name of Kirchhof.

John Sebastian Bach was now 32 years of age; he had made such good use of his time, had played, composed, and studied so much and, by this unremitting zeal and diligence, acquired such a mastery over every part of the art, that he stood like a giant, able to trample all around him into dust. He had long been regarded with admiration and wonder, not only by amateurs, but by judges of the art, when, in the year 1717, Mr. Marchand, formerly much celebrated in France as a performer on the clavier and organ, came to Dresden, where he performed before the King and obtained such approbation that a large salary was offered him if he would engage in His Majesty's service. Marchand's merit chiefly consisted in a very fine and elegant style of performance; but his ideas were empty and feeble, almost in the manner of Couperin, at least as may be judged by his compositions. But J. S. Bach had an equally fine and elegant style and at the same time a copiousness of ideas which might perhaps have made Marchand's head giddy if he had heard it. All this was known to Volumier, at that time Concertmeister in Dresden. He knew the absolute command of the sturdy young German over his thoughts and his instrument, and wished to produce a contest between him and the French artist in order to give his Prince the pleasure of judging of their respective merits by comparing them himself. With the King's approbation, therefore, a message was at once dispatched to J. S. Bach, at Weimar, to invite him to this musical contest. He accepted the invitation and immediately set out on his journey. Upon Bach's arrival in Dresden, Volumier first procured him an opportunity secretly to hear Marchand. Bach was not discouraged, but wrote to the French artist a polite note, formally inviting him to a musical trial of skill; he offered to extemporize upon the spot whatever Marchand should require of him, but requested the same readiness on his part. As Marchand accepted the challenge, the time and place for the contest were fixed, with the King's consent. A large company of both sexes and of high rank assembled in the house of the Marshal, Count Flemming, which was the place appointed for the contest. Bach did not make them wait long for him, but Marchand did not appear. After a long delay, they at last sent to inquire at his lodgings, and the company learned to their great astonishment that Marchand had left Dresden in the morning of that day, without taking leave of anybody. Bach alone therefore had to perform and in doing so he excited the admiration of all who heard him; but Volumier's intention to show, in a sensible and striking manner, the difference between the French and German art was frustrated. Bach received on this occasion praise in abundance, but it is said that he did not receive a present of 100 Louis d'ors which the King had designed for him.

He had not long returned to Weimar when Prince Leopold of Anhalt-Cöthen, a great judge and lover of music, invited him to take the office of Capellmeister. He immediately entered on this office, which he filled nearly six years, but during this time (about 1722) took a journey to Hamburg in order to perform on the organ there. His performance excited universal admiration. The veteran Reinken, then near a hundred years old, heard him with particular pleasure; and, in regard to the Chorale *An Wasserflüssen Babylons* &c., which he varied for almost half an hour in the true organ style, he paid him the compliment of saying: "I thought that this art was dead, but I see that it still lives in you." Reinken himself had some years before worked out that chorale in this manner and had it engraved, as a work on which he set a great value. His praise therefore was the more flattering to Bach.

On the death of Kuhnau, in the year 1723, Bach was appointed Director of Music and Cantor to St. Thomas's School at Leipzig. In this place he remained till his death. Prince Leopold of Anhalt-Cöthen had a great affection for him, and Bach therefore left his service with regret. But the death of the Prince occurring soon after, he saw that Providence had guided him well. Upon this death, which greatly afflicted him, he composed funeral music, with many remarkably fine double choruses, and executed it himself at Cöthen. That, in his present situation, he also received the title of Capellmeister from the Duke of Weissenfels, and, in the year 1736, the title of Court Composer to the King of Poland and Elector of Saxony is by itself of little consequence, only it is to be observed that the last title was caused to be given by circumstances into which Bach had been brought by his office of Cantor of St. Thomas's School.

His second son, Charles Philip Emanuel, entered the service of Frederick the Great in 1740. The reputation of the all-surpassing skill of John Sebastian was at this time so extended that the King often heard it mentioned and praised. This made him curious to hear and meet so great an artist. At first he distantly hinted to the son his wish that his father would one day come to Potsdam. But by degrees he began to ask him directly why his father did not come. The son could not avoid acquainting his father with these expressions of the King's; at first, however, he could not pay any attention to them because he was generally too much overwhelmed with business. But the King's expressions being repeated in several of his son's letters, he at length, in 1747, prepared to take this journey, in company of his eldest son, William Friedemann. At this time the King used to have every evening a private concert, in which he himself generally performed some concertos on the flute. One evening, just as he was getting his flute ready and his musicians were assembled, an officer brought him the written list of the strangers who had arrived. With his flute in his hand, he ran over the list, but immediately turned to the assembled musicians and said, with a kind of agitation: "Gentlemen, old Bach is come." The flute was now laid aside; and old Bach, who had alighted at his son's lodgings, was immediately summoned to the Palace. William Friedemann, who accompanied his father, told me this story, and I must say that I still think with pleasure on the manner in which he related it. At that time it was the fashion to make rather prolix compliments. The first appearance of J. S. Bach before so great a King, who did not even give him time to change his traveling dress for a black cantor's gown, must necessarily be attended with many apologies. I will not here dwell on these apologies, but merely observe that in William Friedemann's mouth they made a formal dialogue between the King and the apologist.

But what is more important than this is that the King gave up his concert for this evening and invited Bach, then already called the Old Bach, to try his fortepianos, made by Silbermann, which stood in several rooms of the Palace.* The musicians went with him from room to room, and Bach was invited everywhere to try them and to play unpremeditated compositions.

*The pianofortes manufactured by Silbermann, of Freyberg, pleased the King so much that he resolved to buy them all up. He collected 15. I hear that they all now stand, unfit for use, in various corners of the Royal Palace. [Forkel's note]

After he had gone on for some time, he asked the King to give him a subject for a fugue in order to execute it immediately without any preparation. The King admired the learned manner in which his subject was thus executed extempore; and, probably to see how far such art could be carried, expressed a wish to hear also a Fugue with six obbligato parts. But as not every subject is fit for such full harmony, Bach chose one himself and immediately executed it to the astonishment of all present in the same magnificent and learned manner as he had done that of the King. His Majesty desired also to hear his performance on the organ. The next day, therefore, Bach was taken to all the organs in Potsdam as he had before been to Silbermann's fortepianos. After his return to Leipzig, he composed the subject which he had received from the King in three and six parts, added several intricate pieces in strict canon on the subject, had it engraved, under the title of *Musicalisches Opfer* [*Musical Offering*], and dedicated it to the inventor.

This was Bach's last journey. The indefatigable diligence with which, particularly in his younger years, he had frequently passed days and nights, without intermission, in the study of his art, had weakened his sight. This weakness continually increased in his latter years till at length it brought on a very painful disorder in the eyes. By the advice of some friends who placed great confidence in the ability of an oculist who had arrived at Leipzig from England, he ventured to submit to an operation, which twice failed. Not only was his sight now wholly lost, but his constitution, which had been hitherto so vigorous, was quite undermined by the use of perhaps noxious medicines in connection with the operation. He continued to decline for full half a year till he expired on the evening of the 30th of July, 1750, in the 66th year of his age. On the morning of the tenth day before his death, he was all at once able to see again and to bear the light. But a few hours afterwards he was seized with an apoplectic fit; this was followed by a high fever, which his enfeebled frame, notwithstanding all possible medical aid, was unable to resist.

Such was the life of this remarkable man. I only add that he was twice married and that he had by his first wife seven and by the second wife thirteen children, namely, eleven sons and nine daughters. All the sons had admirable talents for music; but they were not fully cultivated, except in some of the elder ones.

CHAPTER 3

Bach the Clavier Player

John Sebastian Bach's manner of managing the clavier was admired by all
those who had the good fortune to hear him, and envied by all those who
might themselves claim to be considered as good performers. That this mode
of playing on the clavier, so generally admired and envied, must have been
very different from that in use among Bach's predecessors and contemporaries
may be easily imagined; but hitherto nobody has explained in what this
difference properly consisted.

If we hear the same piece played by ten equally skillful and practiced
performers, it will produce, under the hand of each, a different effect. Each
will draw from the instrument a different kind of tone, and also give to these
tones a greater or less degree of distinctness. Whence can this difference arise,
if otherwise all the ten performers have sufficient readiness and practice?
Merely from the mode of touching the instrument, which, in playing on the
clavier, is the same thing as the pronunciation in speech. In order to make
the delivery perfect in playing as well as in speaking or declaiming, the
greatest distinctness is required in the production of the tones as in the
pronunciation of the words. But this distinctness is susceptible of very various degrees. Even in the lowest degrees we can understand what is played or
said; but it excites no pleasure in the hearer because this degree of distinctness compels him to some exertion of his attention. But attention to
single tones or words ought to be rendered unnecessary that the hearer may
direct it to the ideas and their connection, and for this we require the highest
degree of distinctness in the production of single tones as in the pronunciation of single words.

I have often wondered that C. Ph. Emanuel, in his "Essay on the True
Manner of Playing on the Clavier," did not describe at length this highest
degree of distinctness in the touch of that instrument, as he not only possessed it himself, but because in this consists one of the chief differences by
which the Bachs' mode of playing on the clavier is distinguished from all
others. He says, indeed, in the chapter on the style of performance: "Some
persons play too stickily, as if they had glue between their fingers; their touch
is too long, because they keep the keys down beyond the time. Others have
attempted to avoid this defect and play too short, as if the keys were burning
hot. This is also a fault. The middle path is the best." But he should have
taught and described to us the ways and means of attaining this middle path.

I will endeavor to make the matter plain as far as such things can be made plain without oral instructions.[6]

According to Sebastian Bach's manner of placing the hand on the keys, the five fingers are bent so that their points come into a straight line, and so fit the keys, which lie in a plane surface under them, that no single finger has to be drawn nearer when it is wanted, but every one is ready over the key which it may have to press down. What follows from this manner of holding the hand is:

(1) That no finger must fall upon its key, or (as also often happens) be thrown on it, but only needs to be *placed* upon it with a certain consciousness of the internal power and command over the motion.

(2) The impulse thus given to the keys, or the quantity of pressure, must be maintained in equal strength, and that in such a manner that the finger be not raised perpendicularly from the key, but that it glide off the forepart of the key, by gradually drawing back the tip of the finger towards the palm of the hand.

(3) In the transition from one key to another, this gliding off causes the quantity of force or pressure with which the first tone has been kept up to be transferred with the greatest rapidity to the next finger, so that the two tones are neither disjoined from each other nor blended together.

The touch is, therefore, as C. Ph. Emanuel Bach says, neither too long nor too short, but just what it ought to be.

The advantages of such a position of the hand and of such a touch are very various, not only on the clavichord, but also on the pianoforte and the organ.[7] I will here mention only the most important.

(1) The holding of the fingers bent renders all their motions easy. There can therefore be none of the scrambling, thumping, and stumbling which is so common in persons who play with their fingers stretched out, or not sufficiently bent.

(2) The drawing back of the tips of the fingers and the rapid communication, thereby effected, of the force of one finger to that following it produces the highest degree of clearness in the expression of the single tones, so that every passage performed in this manner sounds brilliant, rolling, and round, as if each tone were a pearl. It does not cost the hearer the least exertion of attention to understand a passage so performed.

(3) By the gliding of the tip of the finger upon the key with an equable

---

6. The following discussion incorporates information gathered from Quantz's *Versuch einer Anleitung die Flöte traversiere zu spielen* as well as from Carl Philipp Emanuel.

7. It should be noted that Forkel, while starting out to give a description of keyboard technique in general, has now chiefly the clavichord in mind. Of the following points, the third refers exclusively to this instrument.

pressure, sufficient time is given to the string to vibrate; the tone, therefore, is not only improved, but also prolonged, and we are thus enabled to play in a singing style and with proper connection, even on an instrument so poor in tone as the clavichord is.

All this together has, besides, the very great advantage that we avoid all waste of strength by useless exertion and by constraint in the motions. In fact, Seb. Bach is said to have played with so easy and small a motion of the fingers that it was hardly perceptible. Only the first joints of the fingers were in motion; the hand retained even in the most difficult passages its rounded form; the fingers rose very little from the keys, hardly more than in a shake [trill], and when one was employed, the other remained quietly in its position. Still less did the other parts of his body take any share in his play, as happens with many whose hand is not light enough.

A person may, however, possess all these advantages, and yet be a very indifferent performer on the clavier, in the same manner as a man may have a very clear and fine pronunciation, and yet be a bad declaimer or orator. To be an able performer, many other qualities are necessary, which Bach likewise possessed in the highest perfection.

The natural difference between the fingers in size as well as strength frequently seduces performers, wherever it can be done, to use only the stronger fingers and neglect the weaker ones. Hence arises not only an inequality in the expression of several successive tones, but even the impossibility of executing certain passages where no choice of fingers can be made. John Sebastian Bach was soon sensible of this; and, to obviate so great a defect, wrote for himself particular pieces, in which all the fingers of both hands must necessarily be employed in the most various positions in order to perform them properly and distinctly. By this exercise he rendered all his fingers, of both hands, equally strong and serviceable, so that he was able to execute not only chords and all running passages, but also single and double shakes with equal ease and delicacy. He was a perfect master even of those passages in which, while some fingers perform a shake, the others, on the same hand, have to continue the melody.

To all this was added the new mode of fingering which he had contrived. Before his time and in his younger years, it was usual to play rather harmony than melody, and not in all the 24 major and minor keys. As the clavichord was still *gebunden,* which means that several keys struck a single string, it could not be perfectly tuned; people played therefore only in those keys which could be tuned with the most purity.[8] Through these circumstances it

8. The explanation is mistaken, but it is true that unequal temperament on keyboard instruments gave way to equal temperament only during Bach's lifetime.

happened that even the greatest performers of that time did not use the thumb till it was absolutely necessary in stretches. Now when Bach began to unite melody and harmony so that even his middle parts did not merely accompany, but had a melody of their own, when he extended the use of the keys, partly by deviating from the ancient modes of church music, which were then very common even in secular music, partly by mixing the diatonic and chromatic scales, and learned to tune his instrument so that it could be played upon in all the 24 keys, he was at the same time obliged to contrive another mode of fingering, better adapted to his new methods, and particularly to use the thumb in a manner different from that hitherto employed.[9] Some persons have pretended that Couperin taught this mode of fingering before him, in his work published in 1716 under the title of *L'Art de toucher le Clavecin*. But, in the first place, Bach was at that time above 30 years old and had long made use of his manner of fingering; and, secondly, Couperin's fingering is still very different from that of Bach, though it has in common with it the more frequent use of the thumb. I say only "the more frequent," for in Bach's method the thumb was made a principal finger, because it is absolutely impossible to do without it in what are called the difficult keys; this, however, is not the case with Couperin, because he neither had such a variety of passages, nor composed and played in such difficult keys as Bach, and consequently had not such urgent occasion for it. We need only compare Bach's fingering, as C. Ph. Emanuel has explained it, with Couperin's directions, and we shall soon find that, with the one, all passages, even the most difficult and the fullest, may be played distinctly and easily, while with the other we can, at the most, get through Couperin's own compositions, and even them with difficulty. Bach was, however, acquainted with Couperin's works and esteemed them, as well as the works of several other French composers for the harpsichord of that period, because a pretty and elegant mode of playing may be learned from them. But on the other hand he considered them as too affected in their frequent use of graces [ornaments], which goes so far that scarcely a note is free from embellishment. The ideas which they contained were, besides, too flimsy for him.

From the easy, unconstrained motion of the fingers, from the beautiful touch, from the clearness and precision in connecting the successive tones, from the advantages of the new mode of fingering, from the equal development and practice of all the fingers of both hands, and, lastly, from the great variety of his figures of melody, which were employed in every piece in a new and uncommon manner, Sebastian Bach at length acquired such a high degree of facility and, we may almost say, unlimited power over his instru-

9. See C. P. E. Bach on keyboard fingering, No. 352.

ment in all the keys that difficulties almost ceased to exist for him. As well in his unpremeditated fantasies as in executing his compositions (in which it is well known that all the fingers of both hands are constantly employed, and have to make motions which are as strange and uncommon as the melodies themselves), he is said to have possessed such certainty that he never missed a note. He had, besides, such an admirable facility in reading and executing the compositions of others (which, indeed, were all easier than his own) that he once said to an acquaintance,[10] while he lived at Weimar, that he really believed he could play everything, without hesitating, at the first sight. He was, however, mistaken; and the friend to whom he had thus expressed his opinion convinced him of it before a week was passed. He invited him one morning to breakfast and laid upon the desk of his instrument, among other pieces, one which at the first glance appeared to be very trifling. Bach came and, according to his custom, went immediately to the instrument, partly to play, partly to look over the music that lay on the desk. While he was perusing them and playing them through, his host went into the next room to prepare breakfast. In a few minutes Bach got to the piece which was destined for his conversion and began to play it. But he had not proceeded far when he came to a passage at which he stopped. He looked at it, began anew, and again stopped at the same passage. "No," he called out to his friend, who was laughing to himself in the next room, and at the same time went away from the instrument, "one cannot play everything at first sight; it is not possible."

He had an equal facility in looking over scores and executing the substance of them at first sight at the keyboard. He even saw so easily through parts laid side by side that he could immediately play them. This he often did when a friend had received a new trio or quartet for stringed instruments and wished to hear how it sounded. He was also able, if a single bass part was laid before him (and often it was a poorly figured one), immediately to play from it a trio or a quartet; nay, he even went so far, when he was in a cheerful humor and in the full consciousness of his powers, as to add extempore to three single parts a fourth part, and thus to make a quartet of a trio. For these purposes he used two clavichords [manuals] and the pedal, or a harpsichord with two sets of keys [keyboards], provided with a pedal.[11]

10. Spitta suggests that this was J. G. Walther.

11. According to Adlung's *Musica Mechanica Organoedi,* pedals (i.e., sounding pedals corresponding to those of the organ) were built either with a separate set of strings or so attached to a clavichord or harpsichord that the same strings were struck by playing with the hands or feet. Such pedals, however, were not frequently met with. Forkel's information, therefore, is probably not quite accurate. On the organ, Bach may often have used two manuals and pedal even for thorough-bass accompaniment, but he can have had only few opportunities for similar treatment of the harpsichord. He possessed one set of pedals, appar-

He liked best to play upon the clavichord; the harpsichord, though certainly susceptible of a very great variety of expression, had not soul enough for him; and the piano was in his lifetime too much in its infancy and still much too coarse to satisfy him.[12] He therefore considered the clavichord as the best instrument for study, and, in general, for private musical entertainment. He found it the most convenient for the expression of his most refined thoughts, and did not believe it possible to produce from any harpsichord or pianoforte such a variety in the gradations of tone as on this instrument, which is, indeed, poor in tone, but on a small scale extremely flexible.

Nobody could install the quill-plectrums of his harpsichord to his satisfaction; he always did it himself. He also tuned both his harpsichord and his clavichord himself, and was so practiced in the operation that it never cost him above a quarter of an hour. But then, when he played from his fancy, all the 24 keys were in his power; he did with them what he pleased. He connected the most remote as easily and as naturally together as the nearest; the hearer believed he had only modulated within the compass of a single key. He knew nothing of harshness in modulation; even his transitions in the chromatic style were as soft and flowing as if he had wholly confined himself to the diatonic scale. His *Chromatic Fantasy,* which is now published, may prove what I here state. All his extempore fantasies are said to have been of a similar description, but frequently even much more free, brilliant, and expressive.

In the execution of his own pieces he generally took the time very brisk, but contrived, besides this briskness, to introduce so much variety in his performance that under his hand every piece was, as it were, like a discourse. When he wished to express strong emotions, he did not do it, as many do, by striking the keys with great force, but by melodical and harmonical figures, that is, by the internal resources of the art. In this he certainly felt very justly. How can it be the expression of violent passion when a person so beats on his instrument that, with all the hammering and rattling, you cannot hear any note distinctly, much less distinguish one from another?

---

ently for use with clavichords (see the remark that follows No. 279), and presumably working on the clavichord principle. But it is unlikely that Bach used these pedals in ensemble music. For the clavichord, as James Grassineau remarks in his *Musical Dictionary* of 1740, "cannot be heard at any considerable distance; hence some call it the dumb Spinet; whence it comes to be particularly used among the nuns, who learn to play, and are unwilling to disturb the dormitory."

12. See, however, Agricola's notes regarding Bach on Silbermann's pianofortes, No. 358d.

CHAPTER 4

Bach the Organist

What we have said above of J. S. Bach's admirable performance on the clavier may also be applied, in general, to his playing on the organ. The clavier and the organ are nearly related to each other, but the style and mode of managing both instruments are as different as their respective purpose. What on the clavichord sounds well, or expresses something, expresses nothing on the organ, and *vice versa.* The best player on the clavier, if he is not duly acquainted with the difference in the purpose and object of the two instruments, and does not know how to keep it constantly in view, will always be a bad performer on the organ, as indeed is usually the case. Hitherto I have met with only two exceptions. The one is John Sebastian himself, and the second his eldest son, William Friedemann. Both were elegant performers on the clavier; but when they came to the organ, no trace of the clavier player was to be perceived. Melody, harmony, motion, &c., all was different, that is, all was adapted to the nature of the instrument and its destination. When I heard Will. Friedemann on the clavier, all was delicate, elegant, and agreeable. When I heard him on the organ, I was seized with reverential awe. There, all was pretty; here, all was grand and solemn. The same was the case with John Sebastian, but both in a much higher degree of perfection. William Friedemann was here, too, but a child to his father, and most frankly concurred himself in this opinion. Even the organ compositions that have been preserved of this extraordinary man are full of the expression of devotion, solemnity, and dignity; but his unpremeditated playing on the organ, where nothing was lost in writing down, but everything came to life directly out of the imagination, is said to have been still more devout, solemn, dignified, and sublime. What, then, is most essential in this art? I will say what I know; much, however, cannot be said, but must be felt.

When we compare Bach's clavier compositions with those for the organ, we perceive that the melody and harmony in the two are of an entirely different kind. Hence we may infer that, to play properly on the organ, the character of the ideas which the organist employs must be of primary import. This character is determined by the nature of the instrument, by the place in which it stands, and, lastly, by the object proposed. The full tone of the organ is, in its nature, not adapted to rapid passages: it requires time to die away in the large and free space of a church. If it is not allowed this time, the tones become confounded, and the performance indistinct and unintelligible. The movements suited to the organ and to the place must therefore be solemnly slow; an exception from this rule may be made, at the most, in the use of single registers as in a trio, &c.

The purpose of the organ to support church singing, and to prepare and maintain devout feelings by preludes and postludes, requires further that the composition and connection of the tones be effected in a different manner from what is practiced out of the church. The common, the trite can never become solemn, can never excite a sublime feeling; it must, therefore, in every respect be banished from the organ. And who was ever more strict in this point than Bach? Even in his secular compositions he disdained everything common, but in his compositions for the organ he kept himself infinitely more distant from it; so that here, it seems to me, he does not appear like a man, but as a true disembodied spirit, who soars above everything mortal.

The means which he employed to attain such a sacred style lay in his management of the old church modes, as they are called, in his open harmony, in the use of the obbligato pedal, and in his manner of using the stops. That the church modes, on account of their difference from our 12 major and 12 minor keys, are peculiarly adapted to strange, uncommon modulations, such as are fit for the Church, may be seen by anyone who will examine the simple four-part Chorales of John Sebastian. But what an effect open harmony produces upon the organ will not be easily imagined by those who have never heard an organ played upon in this manner. By this means, a chorus, as it were, of four or five vocal parts, in their whole natural compass, is transferred to the organ. Let the following chords, in open harmony, be tried, on a clavier (Fig. 1)[13] and then compare how the following passage (Fig. 2), which common organists are used to employ, sounds in comparison, and it will be evident what an effect it must produce when whole pieces are played in such a manner with four or more parts. In this manner, Bach always played the organ; and employed, besides, the obbligato pedal, of the true use of which few organists have any knowledge. He produced with the pedal not only the fundamental notes, or those for which common organists use the little finger of the left hand, but he played a real bass melody with his feet, which was often of such a nature that many a performer would hardly have been able to produce it with his five fingers.

To all this was added the peculiar manner in which he combined the different stops of the organ with each other, or his mode of registration. It was so uncommon that many organ builders and organists were frightened when they saw him draw the stops. They believed that such a combination of

13. The figures are reproduced from the original English edition on pp. 480–82.

stops could never sound well, but were much surprised when they afterwards perceived that the organ sounded best just so, and had now something peculiar and uncommon, which never could be produced by their mode of registration.

This peculiar manner of using the stops was a consequence of his minute knowledge of the construction of the organ and of all the single stops. He had early accustomed himself to give to each and every stop a melody suited to its qualities, and this led him to new combinations which, otherwise, would never have occurred to him. In general, his penetrating mind did not fail to notice anything which had any kind of relation to his art and could be used for the discovery of new artistic advantages. His attention to the effect of big musical compositions in places of varying character; his very practiced ear, by which he could discover the smallest error, in music of the fullest harmony and richest execution; his art of perfectly tuning an instrument, in so easy a manner—all may serve as proofs of the penetration and comprehension of this great man.

When he was at Berlin, in 1747, he was shown the new opera house. Whatever in the construction of it was good or faulty in regard to the effect of music, and what others had only discovered by experience, he perceived at the first sight. He was taken into the great saloon within the building; he went up to the gallery that runs round it, looked at the ceiling, and said, without first investigating any further, that the architect had here introduced an artifice, perhaps without intending it, and without anybody's knowing it. For if a person up there at one corner of the saloon, which was in the form of an oblong parallelogram, whispered a few words against the wall, another, who stood with his face turned to the wall, at the corner diagonally opposite, could hear them distinctly, but nobody else in the whole room, either in the center or in any other part. This effect arose from the direction of the arches in the ceiling, the particular nature of which he discovered at the first look. Such observations could and naturally did lead him to attempt to produce, by the unusual combination of different stops of the organ, effects unknown before and after him.

The union and application of the above-mentioned means to the usual forms of organ pieces produced John Sebastian Bach's great and solemnly sublime execution on the organ, which was peculiarly adapted to the church and filled the hearer with holy awe and admiration. His profound knowledge of harmony, his endeavor to give all the thoughts an uncommon turn and not to let them have the smallest resemblance with the musical ideas usual out of the church, his entire command over his instrument, both with hand and foot, which corresponded with the richest, the most copious, and uninterrupted flow of fancy, his infallible and rapid judgment by which he knew how to choose, among the overflow of ideas which constantly poured in upon him, those only which were adapted to the present object—in a word, his great genius, which comprehended everything and united everything requisite to the perfection of one of the most inexhaustible arts, brought the art of the organ, too, to a degree of perfection which it never attained before his time and will hardly ever attain again. Quanz was of my opinion on this point. "The admirable John Sebastian Bach," says he, "has at length, in modern times, brought the art of the organ to its greatest perfection; it is only to be wished that after his death it may not decline or be wholly lost, on account of the small number of those who still bestow any pains upon it."[14]

When John Seb. Bach seated himself at the organ when there was no divine service, which he was often requested to do by strangers, he used to choose some subject and to execute it in all the various forms of organ composition so that the subject constantly remained his material, even if he had played, without intermission, for two hours or more. First, he used this theme for a prelude and a fugue, with the full organ. Then he showed his art of using the stops for a trio, a quartet, &c., always upon the same subject. Afterwards followed a chorale, the melody of which was playfully surrounded in the most diversified manner by the original subject, in three or four parts. Finally, the conclusion was made by a fugue, with the full organ, in which either another treatment only of the first subject predominated, or one or, according to its nature, two others were mixed with it. This is the art which old Reinken, at Hamburg, considered as being already lost in his time, but which, as he afterwards found, not only lived in John Sebastian Bach, but had attained through him the highest degree of perfection.

Partly the office which John Sebastian filled and partly also the great reputation which he enjoyed for art and knowledge caused him to be often requested to examine young candidates for places as organists and also to give his opinion of new organs. He proceeded, in both cases, with so much conscientiousness and impartiality that he seldom added to the number of his friends by it. The late Danish Capellmeister Scheibe once, in his younger years, submitted to his examination on an occasion when an organist was to be selected for a post, but found his decision so unjust that he afterwards, in his Critical Musician, sought to revenge himself by a violent attack on his former judge. In his examinations of organs he was not more fortunate. He could as little prevail upon himself to praise a bad instrument as a bad organist. He was, therefore, very severe, but always just, in his trials of organs. As he was perfectly acquainted with the construction of the instrument, he could not be in any case deceived. The first thing he did in trying out an organ

14. See No. 350.

was to draw out all the stops and to play with the full organ. He used to say in jest that he must first of all know whether the instrument had good lungs. He then proceeded to examine the single parts. His justice to the organ builders, by the way, went so far that, when he found the work really good and the sum agreed upon too small, so that the builder would evidently have been a loser by his work, he endeavored to induce those who had contracted for it to make a suitable addition, which he, in fact, obtained in several cases.

After the examination was over, especially when the instrument had his approbation, he generally, to amuse himself and those present, showed his skill in performing as above described; and thereby always proved anew that he was really "the prince of all players on the clavier and organ," as the late organist Sorge of Lobenstein once called him in a dedication.[15]

CHAPTER 5

Bach's Harmony

John Sebastian Bach's first attempts at composition were, like all first attempts, defective. Without any instruction to lead him into the way which might gradually have conducted him from step to step, he was obliged, like all those who enter on such a career without a guide, to do at first as well as he could. To run or leap up and down the instrument, to take both hands as full as all the five fingers will allow, and to proceed in this wild manner till they by chance find a resting place are the arts which all beginners have in common with each other. They can therefore be only "finger composers" (or "clavier hussars," as Bach, in his riper years, used to call them); that is, they must let their fingers first play for them what they are to write, instead of writing for the fingers what they shall play. But Bach did not long follow this course. He soon began to feel that the eternal running and leaping led to nothing; that there must be order, connection, and proportion in the thoughts; and that, to attain such objects, some kind of guide was necessary. Vivaldi's Concertos for the violin, which were then just published, served him for such a guide. He so often heard them praised as admirable compositions that he conceived the happy idea of arranging them all for his clavier. He studied the chain of the ideas, their relation to each other, the variations of the modulations, and many other particulars. The change necessary to be

15. See No. 339.

made in the ideas and passages composed for the violin, but not suitable to the clavier, taught him to think musically; so that after his labor was completed, he no longer needed to expect his ideas from his fingers, but could derive them from his own fancy. Thus prepared, he wanted only perseverance and unremitting practice to reach a point where he could not only create himself an ideal of his art, but might also hope, in time, to attain to it. In this practice he was never remiss. He labored so constantly and so assiduously that he frequently even took the nights to his aid. What he had written during the day, he learnt to play in the succeeding night. Yet with all the diligence that he bestowed on his own attempts, he never neglected at this time to study with the greatest attention the works of Frescobaldi, Froberger, Kerl, Pachelbel, Fischer, Strunck, Buxtehude, Reinken, Bruhns, Boehm, and some old French organists, who, according to the fashion of those times, were all great masters of harmony and of the fugue.

Not only the character of all these models, which were mostly designed for the Church, but chiefly his own serious disposition led him principally to follow the grave and sublime style in music. In this kind of music but little can be done with a moderate number of musical terms or phrases. He was soon aware that the stock of musical expressions then in use must be increased before the ideal which he had in his mind could be attained. He considered music entirely as a language, and the composer as a poet, who, in whatever language he may write, must never be without sufficient expressions to represent his feelings. Now since, in his youth, the musical expressions were not sufficiently numerous, at least for his musical poetical genius, and were, besides, not pliable enough, he sought to remedy both deficiencies, chiefly by a management of harmony, which, however adapted to its proper nature and purpose, was yet peculiar to himself alone.

So long as the language of music has only melodious expressions, or only successive connection of musical tones, it is still to be called poor. By the adding of bass notes, by which its relation to the modes and the chords in them becomes rather less obscure, it gains not so much in richness as in precision. A melody accompanied in such a manner, even if not merely bass notes were struck, but, by means of middle parts, even the full chords, was still called by our forefathers, and with justice, homophony. Very different is the case when two melodies are so interwoven with each other that they, as it were, converse together, like two persons of the same rank and equally well informed. There the accompaniment was subordinate, and had only to serve the first or principal part. Here there is no such difference; and this kind of union of two melodies gives occasion to new combinations of tones and consequently to an increase of the store of musical expressions. In proportion as more parts are added and interwoven with each other in the same free and independent manner, the store of musical expressions increases, and finally becomes inexhaustible when different time and the endless variety of rhythms are added. Harmony, therefore, is not to be considered as a mere accompaniment of a simple melody, but a real means of increasing the stock of the expressions of the art, or the riches of musical language. But to be this, it must consist not in mere accompaniment, but in the interweaving of several real melodies, each of which may be, and is, heard sometimes in the upper part, sometimes in the middle, and sometimes below.

In such an interweaving of various melodies which are all so singing that each may, and really does, appear in its turn as the upper part, John Sebastian Bach's harmony consists, in all the works which he composed from about the year 1720, or the 35th year of his age, till his death. In this he excels all the composers in the world (see Kirnberger's *Kunst des reinen Satzes,* p. 157).[16] At least, I have found nothing like it in any of those with whose works I have become acquainted. In his compositions in four parts, you may sometimes even leave out the upper and lower part, and still hear in the two middle parts an intelligible and pleasing music.

But to produce such harmony, in which the single parts must be in the highest degree flexible and yielding towards each other if they are all to have a free and fluent melody, Bach made use of quite peculiar means, which had not been taught in the treatises of musical instruction in those times, but with which his great genius inspired him. These means consisted in the great liberty which he gave to the progress of the parts. He thereby transgressed in appearance, but not in reality, all the long-standing rules which, in his time, were held sacred. For he fulfilled the object of these rules most perfectly, though in an unusual manner, this object being no other than the promotion of pure harmony and melody, or of successive and co-existent euphony. I must explain myself more particularly on this head.

As in single intervals it is easily felt whether the following note must rise or fall, so it is very observable in whole phrases (or in single parts of them, if they are of any extent) to what goal they tend with regard to modulation,[17] i.e., according to their intrinsic meaning. This presentiment of a certain goal may be excited in each part by means of very different intervals. But for every part to achieve a free and flowing melody, it is necessary to have, between the notes which can indicate the above-mentioned goal and those which began the phrase, other notes, which are often very much opposed to the notes of

16. No. 361.

17. The term "modulation" is used here primarily in a sense now obsolete. The old and the new meanings are covered in the following definition from James Grassineau's *Musical Dictionary* (London 1740): "*Modulation,* the art of keeping in or changing the mode or key. Under this term is comprehended the regular progression of several parts, through the sounds that are in the harmony of any particular key, as well as the proceeding naturally and regularly from one key to another."

the other parts, also lying between the two principal points, but which may yet be sounded at the same time with them. This is what is called a passing of tones of the most extensive kind. They proceed all together from one place, separate on the way, but meet punctually again at the end. Nobody has made freer use of this kind of passing tones than Bach, in order thereby to give to all his single parts a perfectly free and flowing melody. Now if his works of this kind are not played with perfect fluency, there sometimes occurs great harshness between the beginning and end of a phrase, and we are at first inclined to accuse him of an exaggeration. But he has exaggerated nothing; for when we have once acquired skill sufficient to perform them according to their true character they sound the more beautiful, and, by their indeed strange but yet natural modulations, new avenues of hearing are opened in us into which no tone ever before penetrated.

However, to say something circumstantial respecting Bach's manner of transgressing the ordinary rules, I observe:

(1) that he made octaves and fifths, when they sounded well; that is, when the cause of their being forbidden no longer existed. Everybody knows that there are cases in which they sound well, and that they must be avoided only when they cause a great emptiness or nakedness of the harmony (or, if someone prefers to call it that, a gap in the harmony). But Bach's octaves and fifths never sounded empty or bad. However, he himself made in this point a great difference. Under certain circumstances he could not even endure covered octaves and fifths between two middle parts, which, otherwise, we at the most attempt to avoid between the two extreme parts; under other circumstances, however, he wrote them down so plainly that they offended every beginner in composition, but afterwards soon justified themselves. Even in the later corrections of his earlier works, he has changed passages which, according to the first reading, were blameless, merely for the sake of greater harmony, so that evident octaves are really met with in them. A remarkable instance of this kind occurs in the first part of his *Well-Tempered Clavier,* in the Fugue in E major, between the fifth and fourth bars from the end. I regret to this hour that in looking through the copy after which the edition of Hoffmeister and Kühnel (now C. F. Peters) is engraved, I have been so weak, merely on account of these octaves, which really improve the harmony, to suffer the ancient reading to stand, which is, indeed, quite according to the rules, but stiff. In the new reading, there is only easy unconstrained melody in all the three parts: which is better?[18]

---

18. Forkel evidently thought that in BWV 854/2 the bass at the beginning of m. 26 should read E instead of D♯; cf. *NBA* V/6.1, Krit. Bericht, p. 340, for Forkel's problematic manuscript source.

(2) Every note raised by an accidental sharp, as well as the *semitonium modi* [leading tone], cannot, according to the rule, be doubled, because the raised note must, from its nature, rise upwards, or ascend. If it is doubled, it must rise doubled and, consequently, make octaves. Bach very often really doubled not only accidental sharp notes of the scale, but also the *semitonia modi,* and yet made no octaves. Such cases are to be found precisely in his very finest works.

(3) It may be considered not as a violation but rather as an extension of the rule that he was of opinion, and proceeded accordingly, that, to a holding fundamental note in the bass, all notes from the entire storehouse of music might be played, no matter to which of the three musical species [diatonic, chromatic, or enharmonic] they belong. This properly pertains to what is called *point d'orgue* [pedal point], which is usually nothing more than a retarded final close. But Bach has made use of it also in the course of his pieces, of which the last jig of what are called his English Suites is, in particular, a remarkable example. At first, this jig does not sound at all well; but gradually it appears more and more beautiful, and that which at first, when imperfectly played, seemed harsh and rough, by degrees begins to be softer and more pleasing till, at length, one is never tired of hearing and playing it.

With the peculiar kind of harmony of which I have been speaking, Bach's modulation, which is no less of a peculiar kind, hangs very closely together. The ideas of harmony and modulation can scarcely be separated, so nearly are they related to each other. And yet they are different. By harmony we must understand the sounding together of the various parts; by modulation, their progression. Modulation may, therefore, take place in a single part; but harmony only in several. I will endeavor to express myself more clearly.

In most composers we find that their modulation, or, if you will, their harmony, advances slowly. In musical pieces to be executed by numerous performers, in large places, as, for example, in churches, where a loud sound can die away but slowly, this arrangement indisputably shows the prudence of a composer who wishes to have his work produce the best possible effect. But in instrumental or chamber music that slow progress is not necessarily a proof of prudence, but far oftener a sign that the composer was not sufficiently rich in ideas. Bach has distinguished all this very well. In his great vocal compositions, he well knew how to repress his fancy, which otherwise overflowed with ideas; but in his instrumental music this reserve was not necessary. As he besides never worked for the crowd, but always had in mind his ideal of perfection, without any view to approbation or the like, he had no reason whatever for giving less than he had and could give, and, in fact, he never did this. Hence, in the modulation of his instrumental works, every advance is a new thought, a constantly progressive life and motion within the circle of the keys chosen and those nearest related to them. Of the harmony which he already has he retains the greatest part; but at every advance he mixes something related to it; and, in this manner, he proceeds to the end of a piece so softly, so gently and gradually, that no leap or harsh transition is to be felt; and yet no bar (I might even say, no part of a bar) is like another. With him, every transition was required to have a connection with the preceding idea and to appear to be a necessary consequence of it. He knew not, or rather he disdained, those sudden sallies by which many composers attempt to surprise their hearers. Even in his chromatics the advances are so soft and tender that we scarcely perceive their distances, though these are often very great: we fancy that he has not deviated a step from his diatonic scale. Thus he knew how to combine everything in the whole extent of the dominion of sound which could by any means be connected together.

CHAPTER 6

Bach's Melody

From the manner in which John Sebastian Bach treated harmony and modulation, his melody necessarily assumed a peculiar form. In the union of several concurrent melodies which are all to be flowing and expressive, no single one can be so prominent as to attract to itself alone the attention of the hearer. This prominency the melodies must, as it were, divide among them; so that sometimes the one, sometimes the other may shine in particular, though its brilliancy seems to be diminished by the equally singing concomitant parts, because the attention of the hearer is shared by them. I say, seems to be diminished; for, in fact, it is not diminished, but rather increased when the hearer has practice enough to survey and to comprehend the whole at once.*

Besides, such a union of many parts obliges the composer to use certain turns in the single melodies to which he is not obliged in homophonic com-

---

*Many persons are of opinion that that melody is the best which everybody can at once understand and sing. This opinion certainly cannot be admitted to pass as a principle: for then, popular airs, which are frequently sung, from South to North, by all classes of people, down to servants and maids, must be the finest and best melodies. I should take the converse of the proposition, and say that the very melody which can be immediately sung by everybody is of the commonest kind. In this form, rather, it might, perhaps, make a valid principle. [Forkel's note]

position. A single part never needs to force itself through, but several must, in their combination, occasionally turn, bend, and yield in a very intricate and delicate manner. This necessity causes uncommon, strange, and entirely new, hitherto unheard-of turns in the melodies, and it is probably one of the causes, at least, why Bach's melodies have so little resemblance with the melodies of other composers, and are so strikingly distinguished from them all. When this strangeness does not degenerate into the unnatural and pompous [*Schwulst*] but is united with fluency and preserves a true singing character, it is an additional merit in him who knows how to produce it, and is properly what is called originality; the only disadvantage of which is that it is not suited to the public in general, but only to the connoisseur well versed in the art.

Not all Bach's melodies, however, are of this description. Though the same originality of thought prevails everywhere, yet the melodies of what are called his free compositions are so open, clear, and intelligible that they, indeed, sound differently from the melodies of other composers, but yet are comprehended by the most unpracticed hearers, and even felt, on account of the spirit that dwells in them. Most of the Preludes in his *Well-Tempered Clavier* as well as most of the pieces in his greater and smaller Suites are of this description.

As his melody has, on the whole, such a stamp of originality, so have also his passages, as they are called, individually; they are so new, so uncommon, and, at the same time, so brilliant and surprising that we do not find the like in any other composer. Examples of this may be found in all his compositions for the clavier; but the most striking are in the Great [Goldberg] Variations, in the First Part of his Practice for the Clavier, in the English Suites, and in the Chromatic Fancy. Here again, all depends on the abundance of the ideas. As all passages are nothing but dismembered chords, their contents must necessarily be richer and more strange, in proportion as the chords are so on which they are founded.

How far Bach's meditation and penetration in the treatment of melody and harmony was carried, how much he was inclined to exhaust all the possibilities of both, appears furthermore from his attempt to contrive a single melody in such a manner that no second singable part could be set against it. At that time it was an established rule that every union of parts must make a whole and exhaust all the notes necessary to the most complete expression of the contents, so that no deficiency should anywhere be sensible by which another part might be rendered possible. Till Bach's time, this rule had been applied only to compositions in two, three, or four parts, and that but very imperfectly. He not only fully satisfied this rule in settings for two, three, and four parts, but attempted also to extend it to a single part. To this attempt we are indebted for six solos for the violin and six others for the violoncello, which are without any accompaniment and which absolutely admit of no second singable part set to them. By particular turns in the melody, he has so combined in a single part all the notes required to make the modulation complete that a second part is neither necessary nor possible.

It is not a quality, but rather a consequence of its qualities, that Bach's melody never grows old. It remains ever fair and young, like Nature, from which it is derived. Everything that Bach took from the prevailing taste of his time (and mixed into his earlier works) is now antiquated; but where, as in his later works, he developed his melodies from the internal sources of the art itself, without any regard to the dictates of fashion, all is as fresh and as new as if it had been produced but yesterday. Very few compositions equally old will be found of which anything similar can be said. Even the works of such ingenious composers as, for instance, Reinhard Kaiser and Handel have become antiquated sooner than might have been expected, and probably than the authors themselves believed. As composers for the public in general, they were obliged to yield to the prevailing taste, and works of this kind last no longer than this taste. But nothing is more inconstant and changeable than every description of popular taste and, in general, whatever is called fashion. Of Handel, it is, however, remarkable that his vocal fugues are not yet anti- quated, whereas but few of his airs probably would be found still to please the ear.

The particular nature of Bach's harmony and melody was also combined with a very extensive and diversified use of rhythm. Hitherto we have spoken only of the internal or logical relation of the harmonical and melodical thoughts; but these thoughts require also an external or rhythmical relation, by which their already great diversity may be rendered not only more diversi- fied, but also more characteristic. The composers of Bach's time had an admirable opportunity to acquire the due and easy management of the vari- ous kinds of rhythm, by the so-called suites, which were then common instead of our sonatas. In these suites there were, between the preludes and the concluding jigs, many French characteristic pieces and dance tunes, in which the rhythm was the most important object. The composers were there- fore obliged to make use of a great variety of time, measure, and rhythm. Bach carried this branch of the art also much farther than any of his predeces- sors or contemporaries. He tried and made use of every kind of meter to diversify, as much as possible, the character of his pieces. He eventually acquired such a facility in this particular that he was able to give even to his fugues, with all the intricate interweaving of their single parts, striking and characteristic rhythmic proportions in a manner as easy and uninterrupted from the beginning to the end as if they were minuets.

In general, the astonishing art of Bach consists in this everywhere equally easy application of the above-mentioned artistic means. Whether the form which he chose was of the easiest or most difficult kind, his treatment of it was always equally easy, equally happy. We never find a trace to indicate that anything had been difficult for him. He always attained the end at which he aimed. All is complete, perfect in itself; no note can be wished by a connoisseur to be otherwise than it is set. I will apply what has been said to some specific forms.

C. Ph. Emanuel, in the Preface to his father's four-part Chorales, which he edited, says the world was accustomed to have from him nothing but masterpieces.[19] This praise was indeed considered by some reviewers as exaggerated; but it is really not exaggerated if it is applied only to those of his works which he composed after the above-mentioned period, that is, in the years of his maturity. In many species of composition, however, others have produced masterpieces which may be placed with honor by the side of his in the same species. Thus, for instance, we have Allemandes, Courantes, &c., by Handel and a few others which are not less beautiful, though less rich, than those of Bach. But in the fugue and all the kinds of counterpoint and canon related to it, he stands quite alone, and so alone that far and wide around him, all is, as it were, desert and void. Never has a fugue been made by any composer which could be compared with one of his. He who is not acquainted with Bach's fugues cannot even form an idea of what a true fugue is and ought to be. In fugues of the ordinary kind, there is nothing but a certain very insignificant and sloppy routine [*Schlendrian*]. They take a theme, give it a companion, transpose both gradually into the keys related to the original one, and make the other parts accompany them in all these transpositions with a kind of thorough-bass chords. This is a fugue; but of what kind? It is very natural that a person acquainted with only such fugues can have no great opinion of the whole species. How much art does it, then, require to make oneself master of such commonplace?

Bach's fugue is of quite another kind. It fulfills all the conditions which we are otherwise accustomed to demand only of more free species of composition. A highly characteristic theme; an uninterrupted principal melody, wholly derived from it and equally characteristic from the beginning to the end; not mere accompaniment in the other parts, but in each of them an independent melody, according with the others, also from the beginning to the end; freedom, lightness, and fluency in the progress of the whole; inexhaustible variety of modulation combined with perfect purity; the exclusion of every arbitrary note not necessarily belonging to the whole; unity and

19. See No. 378.

diversity in the style, rhythm, and meters; and, lastly, a life diffused through the whole, so that it sometimes appears to the performer or hearer as if every single note were animated—these are the properties of Bach's fugue, properties which necessarily excite admiration and astonishment in every judge who knows how much power of mind is required for the production of such works. Must not then such a work, in which all is united that is found separate in other kinds of composition according to their various destinations, deserve especial admiration? I must say still more. All Bach's fugues composed in the years of his maturity have the above-mentioned properties in common; they are all endowed with equally great excellencies, but each in a different manner. Each has its own precisely defined character; and, dependent upon that, its own turns in melody and harmony. When we know and can perform *one*, we really know only *one*, and can perform but *one*; whereas we know and can play whole folios full of fugues by other composers of Bach's times as soon as we have comprehended and rendered familiar to our hand the turns of a single one.

To such properties and excellencies do the arts of counterpoint lead when they are well employed; that is to say, as Bach employed them. Through them he learned to develop, from a given subject, a whole series of resembling yet different melodies, in every kind of taste, and in all figures; through them he learned not merely to begin well, but also to continue, and to end well; through them he acquired such a command of harmony and its infinite transposition that he could invert whole pieces, note by note, in all the parts, without in the least impairing the flow of the melody or the purity of the harmony;[20] through them he learned to make the most intricate canons, in all intervals and all kinds of motion, so light and flowing that nothing is to be perceived of the art employed in them, and they sound entirely like freer compositions; through them, finally, he was enabled to leave to posterity a great number of works of the most various kinds which are all models of art, and will remain so, till the art itself shall be no more.[*]

What has been hitherto said relates chiefly to Bach's compositions for the clavier and the organ. But as the art is divided, according to its application

20. *The Art of Fugue* contains two fugues (BWV 1080/12–13) that are afterward inverted line for line, the second even in triple counterpoint.

*There are persons who are of opinion that Bach perfected harmony only. But if we have the right conception of harmony, according to which it is a means to extend and increase musical expressions, we cannot even imagine it without melody. When it is, moreover, like that of Bach, a multiplied melody, I do not see how we can be of the above opinion. According to my ideas, we might rather say, such or such a composer has perfected melody only, because fine melody may subsist without harmony, but no fine and true harmony without melody. He, therefore, who has perfected harmony, has perfected the whole; the melodist, on the contrary, only a part of the whole. [Forkel's note]

into two main branches, namely, into instrumental and vocal music, and Bach wrote in both, the reader will, perhaps, like to hear a few words respecting his vocal compositions.

It was at Weimar that he first had occasion to employ himself in vocal composition, when he was appointed Concertmeister and, as such, had to provide the church music for the court chapel. The style which he used in his church music was like the style of his organ pieces—devout, solemn, and in every respect what the style of church music should be. He had in this the very just principle not to indulge in the expression of single words, which leads but to mere trifling, but only the expression of the whole.[21] His choruses are throughout full of magnificence and solemnity. Very often he chose a chorale melody for them, and made the other parts surround it in fugal style, as is done in motets.

The same richness of harmony that is found in his other works prevails here also, only adapted to the vocal parts and the instrumental accompaniment chosen. His recitatives are well declaimed and provided with rich basses. In his arias, of which many have the finest and most expressive melody, he appears frequently to have constrained himself, and to have conformed to the ability of his singers and performers, who, notwithstanding, had ceaseless complaints to make of their difficulty. If he had been so happy as to have had none but capable performers of his church music, they would certainly have left impressions of their excellence and, like his other works, be still used and admired. The inexhaustible treasure of art which they contain would certainly have been worthy of longer preservation.

Among many occasional pieces which he composed in Leipzig, I mention only two funeral cantatas: the one of which was performed at Cöthen, at the funeral ceremony of his beloved Prince Leopold; the other in the Pauliner-Kirche at Leipzig, at the funeral sermon upon the death of Christiane Eberhardine, Queen of Poland and Electress of Saxony. The first[22] contains double choruses of uncommon magnificence and of the most affecting expression; the second has indeed only single choruses, but they are so attractive that he who has begun to play one of them through will never quit it till he has finished it. It was composed in October, 1727.

Besides the vocal works here mentioned, Bach composed also a great many motets, chiefly for the choir of St. Thomas's School at Leipzig. This choir always had 50 singers, and sometimes more, for whose musical improvement

21. Forkel, by rewording a sentence from one of Carl Philipp Emanuel's letters (No. 394), overstates the case. Bach did indulge in the expression of single words though, as Carl Philipp Emanuel states, never "at the expense of the sense of the whole."

22. Forkel refers here erroneously to a work by Johann Ludwig Bach of 1724; cf. *BJ* 1983, pp. 115–18.

Bach provided like a father, and gave them so much practice by motets for one, two, or more choruses that they could become at least correct and good choir singers.[23] Among the motets for two choruses, composed for this purpose, there are some which surpass, in magnificence and richness of harmony and melody, and in life and spirit, everything of the kind. But, like everything of Bach's or, rather, like all great and rich works of art, they are difficult to execute and must, besides, be performed by a numerous chorus to produce their full effect.

These are the most important of Bach's vocal compositions. For the smaller kind of art, dedicated to social entertainment, he has done nothing, or certainly not much, notwithstanding he was of so sociable and friendly a disposition. Thus, for instance, he is said never to have composed a song. For this, however, he was not needed. These pleasing little flowers of art will, nonetheless, never become extinct: Nature produces them herself, even without particular pains being bestowed on their cultivation.

CHAPTER 7

Bach the Teacher

There are many good composers and skillful virtuosos, for all instruments, who are not capable of teaching others what they themselves know or can perform. Either they have not combined sufficient attention with the practice by which their natural capacity was developed, or they have been led by good instruction to a certain point on the shortest way, and have left to their teachers the task of considering why anything must be done so or so, and not otherwise. When such performers are well informed, their practice may be very instructive to beginners, but they cannot give instruction in the proper sense of the term. The fatiguing path of self-instruction, on which the learner goes astray a thousand times before he discovers or reaches the goal, is, perhaps, the only one that can produce a perfectly good teacher. The frequent fruitless attempts and errors make him gradually acquainted with the whole domain of art; he discovers every obstacle to his progress, and learns to avoid

---

23. Forkel is thinking of the total number of singers in the St. Thomas School, which, however, had to provide choirs for four churches. Bach himself had to insist that every chorus should contain at least 12 singers, remarking that "it would be still better with . . . 16 persons." See Nos. 144 and 151.

it. This way is, indeed, the longest; but he who has energy in himself will still accomplish it, and, as a reward for his exertions, learn to find his goal by a way which will be the more agreeable. All those who have founded a school of music of their own have attained to it by such fatiguing ways. The new, more pleasing road discovered by them was what distinguished their school from others.

This is the case with the school of Bach. Its founder long wandered about; he had to attain the age of above thirty years, and gradually to increase his powers by constant exertion before he learned how to conquer all difficulties and obstacles. But, on the other hand, he discovered, at the end, perhaps the most beautiful and delightful road that is to be found in the whole domain of the art.

Only he who knows much can teach much. Only he who has become acquainted with dangers, who has himself encountered and overcome them, can properly point them out and successfully teach his followers how to avoid them. Both were united in Bach. His teaching was, therefore, the most instructive, the most proper, and the most secure that ever was known; and all his scholars trod, at least in some one branch of the art, in the footsteps of their great master, though none of them equaled, much less surpassed him.

I will first speak of his instructions in playing. The first thing he did was to teach his scholars his peculiar mode of touching the instrument, of which we have spoken before. For this purpose, he made them practice, for months together, nothing but isolated exercises for all the fingers of both hands, with constant regard to this clear and clean touch. Under some months, none could get excused from these exercises; and, according to his firm opinion, they ought to be continued, at least, for from six to twelve months. But if he found that anyone, after some months of practice, began to lose patience, he was so obliging as to write little connected pieces, in which those exercises were combined together. Of this kind are the six little Preludes for Beginners, and still more the fifteen two-part Inventions. He wrote both down during the hours of teaching and, in doing so, attended only to the momentary want of the scholar. But he afterwards transformed them into beautiful, expressive little works of art. With this exercise of the fingers, either in single passages or in little pieces composed on purpose, was combined the practice of all the ornaments in both hands.

Hereupon he immediately set his scholars to his own greater compositions, which, as he well knew, would give them the best means of exercising their strength. In order to lessen the difficulties, he made use of an excellent method; this was, first to play to them the whole piece, which they were to study, saying, "so it must sound." It can scarcely be imagined how many advantages this method has. If, by the pleasure of hearing such a piece played through at once in its true character, only the zeal and inclination of the scholar were excited, the advantage would be, even then, very great. But, by giving to the scholar, likewise, an idea how the piece ought to sound, and what degree of perfection he has to aim at, the advantage of this method is far greater still. For, without such a means to facilitate the acquisition, the scholar cannot learn either the one or the other, except gradually, as he conquers the mechanical difficulties, and, even then, perhaps, but very imperfectly. Besides, the understanding has now come into play, and, under its direction, the fingers will obey much better than they could without it. In a word, the pupil has an ideal in his mind, which renders the difficulties in the given piece easier to the fingers; and many a young performer on the keyboard who scarcely knows how to make sense of such a piece after years' practice would, perhaps, have learnt it very well in a month if he had only heard it played to him once in its proper connection and with a due degree of perfection.

Bach's method of teaching composition was as sure and excellent as his method of teaching how to play. He did not begin with dry counterpoints that led nowhere, as was done by other teachers of music in his time; still less did he detain his scholars with calculations of the proportions of tones, which, in his opinion, were not for the composer, but for the mere theorist and the instrument-maker. He proceeded at once to the pure thorough bass in four parts, and insisted particularly on the writing out of these parts because thereby the idea of the pure progression of the harmony is rendered the most evident. He then proceeded to chorales. In the exercises, he at first set the basses himself and made the pupils invent only the alto and tenor to them. By degrees, he let them also make the basses. He everywhere insisted not only on the highest degree of purity in the harmony itself, but also on natural connection and flowing melody in all the parts. Every connoisseur knows what models he has himself produced in this kind; his middle parts are often so singable that they might be used as upper parts. He also made his pupils aim at such excellencies in their exercises; and, till they had attained a high degree of perfection in them, he did not think it advisable to let them attempt inventions of their own. Their sense of purity, order, and connection in the parts must first have been sharpened on the inventions of others, and have become in a manner habitual to them, before he thought them capable of giving these qualities to their own inventions.

Besides this, he took it for granted that all his pupils in composition had the ability to think musically. Whoever had not this, received from him the sincere advice not to apply himself to composition. He, therefore, refrained from beginning, as well with his sons as his other pupils, the study of composition till he had seen attempts of theirs in which he thought he could discern this ability, or what is called musical genius. Then, when the above-mentioned preparations in harmony were ended, he took up the doctrine of fugues, and made a beginning with those in two parts, &c. In all these, and other exercises in composition, he rigorously kept his pupils

(1) To compose entirely from the mind, without an instrument. Those who wished to do otherwise, he called, in ridicule, "knights of the keyboard" [Clavier-Ritter];

(2) To pay constant attention to the consistency of each single part, in and for itself, as well as to its relation to the parts connected and concurrent with it. No part, not even a middle part, was allowed to break off before it had entirely said what it had to say. Every note was required to have a connection with the preceding: did any one appear of which it was not apparent whence it came, nor whither it tended, it was instantly banished as suspicious. This high degree of exactness in the management of every single part is precisely what makes Bach's harmony a manifold melody. The confused mixture of the parts, so that a note which belongs to the tenor is thrown into the alto, and the reverse; further, the untimely falling in of several notes in certain harmonies—notes which, as if fallen from the sky, suddenly increase the established number of the parts in a single passage, to vanish in the next following, and in no manner belong to the whole; in short, what Bach is said to have called *mantschen* [daub, to mix notes and parts among each other in disorderly manner]—is not to be found either in himself or in any of his scholars. He considered his parts as if they were persons who conversed together like a select company. If there were three, each could sometimes be silent and listen to the others till it again had something to the purpose to say. But, if in the midst of the most interesting part of the discourse, some uncalled and importunate strange notes suddenly rushed in and attempted to say a word, or even a syllable only, without sense or vocation, Bach looked on this as a great irregularity, and made his pupils comprehend that it was never to be allowed.

With all his strictness in this point, he allowed his pupils, in other respects, great liberties. In the use of the intervals, in the turns of the melody and harmony, he let them dare whatever they would and could, only taking care to admit nothing which could be detrimental to the musical euphony and the perfectly accurate and unequivocal expression of the intrinsic sense, for the sake of which all purity of harmony is sought. As he himself attempted everything possible in this respect, he liked to see his scholars do the same. Other teachers of composition before him, for instance, [Angelo] Berardi, [Antonio Maria] Bononcini, and Fux, did not allow so many liberties. They were afraid that their pupils might thereby get entangled in dangers, but thus evidently prevented them from learning to overcome dangers.

Bach's mode of teaching is, therefore, undoubtedly better and leads the pupil farther. Furthermore, he does not confine himself, in general, as did his predecessors, merely to the purity of writing, but everywhere pays attention to the other requisites of a truly good composition, namely, to unity of character through a whole piece, to diversity of style, to rhythm, melody, &c. Whoever desires to become acquainted with Bach's method of teaching composition in its whole extent finds it sufficiently explained in Kirnberger's "Art of Pure Composition" [*Kunst des reinen Satzes*].

Lastly, as long as his scholars were under his musical direction, he did not allow them to study or become acquainted with any but classical works, in addition to his own compositions. The understanding, by which alone what is really good is apprehended, develops itself later than the feeling; not to mention that even this understanding may be misled and spoiled by being frequently engaged on spurious productions of art. The best method of instructing youth, therefore, is to accustom them to what is good. The right understanding of it follows in time, and can then still further confirm their attachment to none but genuine works of art.

With this admirable method of teaching, all his scholars became distinguished artists, though one more than another, according as they either came sooner into his school, or had in the sequel more opportunity and encouragement further to perfect, and to apply, the instruction they had received from him. His two eldest sons, however, William Friedemann and Ch. Ph. Emanuel, were, indeed, the most distinguished among them; certainly not because he gave them better instruction than his other pupils, but because they had, from their earliest youth, opportunity in their father's house to hear good music, and no other. They were therefore accustomed early, and even before they had received any instruction, to what was most excellent in the art; whereas the others, before they could participate in his instructions, had either heard nothing good, or were already spoiled by common compositions. It is a proof of the goodness of the school, that, notwithstanding these disadvantages, even these scholars of Bach all acquired a noble sense of art, and distinguished themselves in one way or another.*

His oldest scholar was John Caspar Vogler [1695–1765], who received instruction from him already at Arnstadt and Weimar and, even according to his master's testimony, was a very able performer on the organ. He was, first, Organist in Weimar, and, at last, Burgomaster of that city, still

---

*We here speak only of those scholars who made the art their chief occupation. But Bach had, besides these, a great many other scholars. Every dilettante living in his neighborhood desired at least to be able to boast of having enjoyed the instructions of so great and celebrated a man. Many, too, posed as his scholars without ever having been so. [Forkel's note]

retaining his place as Organist. Some chorale preludes for an organ with two manuals and pedal by him were engraved in 1737.

The other scholars of Bach who have attained celebrity were:[24]

(1) Gottfried August Homilius, in Dresden, not only an excellent organist, but also a distinguished composer for the Church.

(2) Christoph Transchel, in Dresden. He was a fine performer on the clavier and a good music master. There are six Polonoises by him for the clavier, in manuscript, which, excepting those of William Friedemann, perhaps surpass all the polonoises in the world.

(3) Johann Gottlieb Goldberg, from Königsberg. He was a very skillful performer on the clavier, but without any particular talent for composition.

(4) Johann Ludwig Krebs, Organist at Altenburg. He was not only a very good organ player, but also a fertile composer of organ, clavier, and church music. He had the opportunity to enjoy Bach's instruction for nine years together [1726–35]. To indicate his excellence, the witty music lovers said in his time that there had been caught only one crab [*Krebs*] in one creek [*Bach*].[25]

(5) Johann Christoph Altnikol, Organist at Naumburg and son-in-law of his master. He is said to have been a very able organist and composer.

(6) Johann Friedrich Agricola, Prussian Court Composer and Director of the Royal Capelle]. He is less known by his compositions than by his knowledge of the theory of music. He translated [Pier Francesco] Tosi's directions for singing from the Italian into German and accompanied the work with very instructive notes.

(7) Johann Gottfried Müthel, in Riga. He was an able clavier player and composer for his instrument. His published duet for two keyboard instruments, as well as his sonatas, which appeared earlier, are proofs of this.

(8) Johann Philipp Kirnberger, Court Musician to the Princess Amalia of Prussia [the sister of Frederick the Great], in Berlin. He was one of the most remarkable of Bach's scholars, full of the most useful zeal and genuine noble sense of the art. Besides the development of Bach's mode of teaching composition, the musical world is indebted to him for the first and only tenable system of harmony, which he has abstracted from his master's practical works. He has done the first in his "Art of Pure Composition" [*Die Kunst des reinen Satzes*], and the second in "The True Principles for the Use of Harmony" [*Die wahren Grundsätze sum Gebrauch der Harmonie*]. He has, besides, been of service to the art by other writings and compositions, as well

24. Given names of Bach's pupils have been added editorially. For further references to these and other pupils of Bach see above, pp. 314–23.

25. According to Reichardt's *Musikalischer Almanach* of 1796, Bach himself was the author of this pun.

as by teaching. The Princess Amalia herself was his pupil.

(9) Johann Christian Kittel, Organist in Erfurt. He is a very solid (though not very ready) organ player. As a composer, he has distinguished himself by several trios for the organ, which are so excellent that his master himself would not have been ashamed of them. He is the only scholar of Bach's now living.

(10) Voigt, in Anspach, and an organist of the name of Schubert were also named to me, by C. Ph. Emanuel, as pupils of his father. But he knew nothing of them, except that they came into his father's house after he had left it.[26]

I have said above that Bach's sons were the most distinguished of his scholars. The eldest, William Friedemann, approached the nearest to his father in the originality of all his thoughts. All his melodies have a different turn from those of other composers, and yet they are not only extremely natural, but, at the same time, uncommonly fine and elegant. When performed with delicacy, as he himself performed them, they cannot fail to enchant every connoisseur. It is only to be regretted that he loved more to play from his fancy, and to seek after musical delicacies only in improvisation, than to write; the number of his beautiful compositions is therefore small.

C. Ph. Emanuel is the next to him. He went soon enough into the great world to remark in time how it is proper to compose for a numerous public. In the clearness and easy intelligence of his melodies, he therefore approaches in some degree the popular style, but is always perfectly free from everything common. Both the eldest sons, by the way, confessed frankly that they had been necessarily obliged to choose a style of their own because they could never have equaled their father in his style.

John Christopher Frederick, Concertmeister at the Court of Bückeburg, imitated Emanuel's manner, but did not equal his brother. According to the testimony of William Friedemann, he was, however, the ablest performer of all the brothers, and the one who played his father's clavier compositions in the most finished manner.

John Christian, called Bach of Milan, and afterward of London, being the youngest son of the second marriage, had not the good fortune to receive instructions from his father. The original spirit of Bach is therefore not to be found in any of his works. He became, however, a popular composer who was universally liked in his time.

---

26. Johann Georg Voigt was, according to Walther, an oboist and flutist at Ansbach. Johann Martin Schubart was, according to Walther, "a miller's son, born 1690, . . . learned clavier playing from Mr. Johann Sebastian Bach and sojourned with the latter continuously from 1707 to 1717; was also, when Bach moved away, accepted in the same year, toward Advent, as Chamber Musician and Court Organist here in Weimar; and died April 2, 1721, of an inflammatory fever."

CHAPTER 8

Bach's Character

Besides Bach's great merit as so accomplished a performer, composer, and teacher of music, he had also the merit of being an excellent father, friend, and citizen. His virtues as a father he showed by his care for the education of his children; and the others by his conscientious performance of his social and civil duties. His acquaintance was agreeable to everybody. Whoever was in any respect a lover of the art, whether a foreigner or a native, could visit his house and be sure of meeting with a friendly reception. These social virtues, united with the great reputation of his art, caused his house to be very seldom without visitors.

As an artist, he was uncommonly modest. Notwithstanding the great superiority which he had over the rest of his profession, and which he could not but feel; notwithstanding the admiration and reverence which were daily shown him as so outstanding an artist, there is no instance of his having ever assumed upon it. When he was sometimes asked how he had contrived to master the art to such a high degree, he generally answered: "I was obliged to be industrious; whoever is equally industrious will succeed equally well." He seemed not to lay any stress on his greater natural talents.

All the opinions he expressed of other artists and their works were friendly and equitable. Many works necessarily appeared to him trifling, as he was almost always employed exclusively on the sublimer branches of the art, yet he never allowed himself to express a harsh opinion, unless it were to one of his scholars, to whom he thought himself obliged to speak pure and strict truth. Still less did he ever suffer himself to be seduced by the consciousness of his strength and superiority to be a musical bravado, as is so frequently the case with performers who think themselves strong, when they believe they have an inferior one to do with. His modesty in this respect went so far that he never spoke voluntarily even of the musical contest which he was to have had with Marchand, though he was not the challenger in this case, but the challenged. The many, sometimes adventurous pranks that are related of him, as, for example, that occasionally, dressed like a poor village schoolmaster, he went into a church and begged the organist to let him play a chorale, in order to enjoy the general astonishment excited in the persons present by his performance, or to hear the organist say he must be either Bach or the devil, &c., are mere fables. He himself would never hear of anything of the sort. Besides, he had too much respect for the art thus to make a plaything of it. An artist like Bach does not throw himself away.

In musical parties where quartets or fuller pieces of instrumental music were performed and he was not otherwise employed, he took pleasure in playing the viola. With this instrument, he was, as it were, in the middle of the harmony, whence he could best hear and enjoy it, on both sides. When an opportunity offered, in such parties, he sometimes also accompanied a trio or other pieces on the harpsichord. If he was in a cheerful mood and knew that the composer of the piece, if he happened to be present, would not take it amiss, he used, as we have said above, to make extempore, either out of the figured bass a new trio, or of three single parts a quartet. These, however, are really the only cases in which he proved to others how strong he was. A certain Hurlebusch of Brunswick, a conceited and arrogant clavier player, once visited him, at Leipzig, not to hear him, but to let himself be heard. Bach received him kindly and politely, listened to his very indifferent performance with patience; and when Hurlebusch, on taking leave, made the eldest sons a present of a printed collection of sonatas, exhorting them to study them diligently (they who had studied very different things), Bach only smiled to himself and did not at all change his friendly behavior to the stranger.

He was fond of hearing the music of other composers. If he heard, in a church, a fugue for a large body of musicians, and one of his two eldest sons happened to stand near him, he always, as soon as he had heard the first entries of the theme, said beforehand what the composer ought to introduce, and what possibly might be introduced. Now, if the composer had performed his work well, what Bach had predicted happened; then he was delighted, and jogged his son to make him observe it. This is a proof that he valued, too, the skill of others.

The composers whom he studied, esteemed, and loved in his youth have been already mentioned. At a more advanced age, when his judgment was fully matured, he had other favorites. He then had a great esteem for the Emperor's first Capellmeister, Fux; for Handel, Caldara, Reinh. Kayser, Hasse, the two Grauns, Telemann, Zelenka, Benda, &c.; and, in general, all the most distinguished musicians at that time living in Dresden and Berlin. He was not personally acquainted with the first four, but with all the rest. In his youth, he had frequent intercourse with Telemann.

He had a very great esteem for Handel, and often wished to be personally acquainted with him. As Handel was also a great performer on the clavier and the organ, many lovers of music at Leipzig and in its neighborhood wished to hear these two great men confronted. But Handel never could find time for such a meeting. He came three times from London to Halle, his native town. On his first visit, about the year 1719, Bach was still at Cöthen, only four German miles from Halle. He was immediately informed of Handel's arrival, and lost not a moment in paying him a visit; but Handel left

Halle the very day of his arrival. At the time of Handel's second visit to Halle, between 1730 and 1740, Bach was at Leipzig, but ill. As soon, however, as he was informed of Handel's arrival at Halle, he immediately sent his eldest son, William Friedemann, thither, with a very polite invitation to visit him at Leipzig. But Handel regretted that he could not come. On Handel's third visit, approximately in 1752 or 1753, Bach was dead. Thus his wish to be personally acquainted with Handel was not fulfilled any more than that of many lovers of music who would have been glad to see and hear him and Handel together.

At the time that Hasse was Capellmeister at Dresden, the orchestra and the opera there were very brilliant and excellent. Bach had had there already in his earlier years many acquaintances, by all of whom he was much honored. Hasse and his wife, the celebrated Faustina, had also come several times to Leipzig and admired his great talents. He was therefore always received in an exceedingly honorable manner at Dresden, and often went thither to hear the opera. He generally took his eldest son with him. He used to say in joke, some days before his departure: "Friedemann, shan't we go again to hear the lovely Dresden ditties?" Innocent as this joke was in itself, I am convinced that Bach would not have uttered it to anybody except this son who, at that time, already knew what is great in art and what is only beautiful and agreeable.

Bach did not make what is called a brilliant success in this world. He had, on the one hand, a lucrative office, but he had, on the other, a great number of children to maintain and to educate from the income of it. He neither had nor sought other resources. He was too much occupied with his business and his art to think of pursuing those ways which, perhaps, for a man like him, especially in his times, would have led to a gold mine. If he had thought fit to travel, he would (as even one of his enemies has said) have drawn upon himself the admiration of the whole world. But he loved a quiet domestic life, constant and uninterrupted occupation with his art, and was, as we have said of his ancestors, a man of few wants.

Moreover, he enjoyed during his life manifold proofs of love and friendship, and of great honor. Prince Leopold of Cöthen, Duke Ernest Augustus of Weimar, and Duke Christian of Weissenfels had a sincere attachment to him, which must have been the more valuable to the great artist as these princes were not mere lovers, but also connoisseurs, of music. At Berlin and Dresden also he was universally respected and honored. If we add the admiration of the connoisseurs and lovers of music who had heard him or were acquainted with his works, we shall easily conceive that a man like Bach, "who sung only for himself and the muses," had received from the hands of fame all that he could wish, and it had more charms for him than the equivocal honors of a ribbon or a gold chain.

It would be hardly worth while to mention that in 1747 he became a member of the Society of the Musical Sciences, founded by Mitzler, did we not owe to this circumstance his admirable chorale *Vom Himmel hoch*, &c. He presented this Chorale to the Society on his admission, and had it afterwards engraved.

C H A P T E R   9

Bach's Works

To be able to produce such accomplished works as Bach has left behind him in various branches, he had necessarily to compose a great deal. He who is not daily employed upon his art, even if he were the greatest genius in the world, will yet never be able to produce a work which can be pronounced by a competent judge to be throughout perfect and complete. Only uninterrupted practice can lead to true mastery. But if we were to consider all the works produced during this practice to be masterpieces, because masterpieces at length proceeded from it, we should greatly err. This is the case even with Bach's works. Though we certainly find in his earlier attempts undeniable evidences of a distinguished genius, yet they contain, at the same time, so much that is useless, so much that is one-sided, extravagant, and tasteless that they are not worth preserving (at least, for the public in general), and, at most, may be interesting to the connoisseur who wishes to make himself more intimately acquainted with the course which such a genius has followed from the commencement of his training.

For the separation of these attempts or youthful exercises from the real masterpieces, Bach has himself given us two means, and we have a third in the art of critical comparison. At the appearance of his first work, he was above 40 years of age. What he himself, at so mature an age, judged worthy of publication has certainly the presumption in its favor that it is good. We may, therefore, consider all the works which he himself had engraved to be especially good.[27]

27. Forkel here makes a salient point neglected in most studies of Bach. It should be added, however, that in selecting works for publication, Bach was necessarily somewhat limited by the prospect of sales for works of any specific category—it was certainly not because he considered his vocal works inferior that he did not undertake to publish any of them.

With respect to those among his compositions which circulate only in manuscript copies, and which are by far the greater number, we must have recourse, in order to know what is worth preserving, partly to critical comparison, partly to the second means which Bach has given us. For, like all really great geniuses, he never laid aside the critical file with which to make his beautiful compositions still more beautiful, and the more beautiful ones perfectly so. Any of his early works that was at all susceptible of improvement, he improved. This desire to improve was extended even to some of his engraved works. Hence, there arose various readings in the older and more recent copies: he himself conceived all these pieces which are found with various readings to be worthy of improvement over their original shape and thought he could make of them really excellent works of art. I reckon under this head the most of what he composed before the year 1725, as shall be mentioned more particularly in the ensuing list. A great many later compositions, but which, for reasons easily understood, are likewise known only in manuscript, bear too evidently about them the stamp of perfection to allow us to doubt whether we shall reckon them among the essays, or among the works of the accomplished master.

Bach's Engraved Works
are the following:[28]

(1) "*Clavierübung*, or Exercises for the Clavier; consisting of Preludes, Allemandes, Courants, Sarabands, Jigs, Minuets, &c., for the amusement of amateurs. Opus I. Published by the Author. 1731"

This first work consists of six Suites, the first of which came out in 1726, and the others followed successively, till they were all engraved together in 1731. This work made in its time a great noise in the musical world. Such excellent compositions for the clavier had never been seen and heard before. Anyone who had learnt to perform well some pieces out of them could make his fortune in the world thereby; and even in our times, a young artist might gain acknowledgment by doing so, they are so brilliant, well-sounding, expressive, and always new. In the new edition, already off the press, they have received the title *Exercises pour le Clavecin.*[29]

(2) "*Clavierübung*, or Exercises for the Clavier; consisting of a Concerto in the Italian taste, and an Overture in the French manner, for a harpsichord

28. More exact translations of Bach's original titles appear in Part II of this volume.

29. Bach used the term *Clavier-Übung* in a general sense, which, of course, allows of no plural; the translation of the word as *Exercices*, which has been used frequently, narrows the meaning down to a specific one, corresponding to *études*, which obviously misrepresents Bach's original intention.

with two rows of keys. Second Part. Published by Christopher Weigel, in Nuremberg."

(3) "*Clavierübung*, or Exercises for the Clavier; consisting of various Preludes, to the Catechismal and other Hymns, for the Organ, composed for the amusement of amateurs, and particularly judges of such works. Third Part. Published by the Author."

Besides the preludes, fugues, and chorale preludes for the organ, which are all masterpieces, this collection contains also four duets for a single clavier, which, as models of duets, admit no third part.

(4) "*Sechs Choräle*, or Six Chorale Melodies of different kinds, to be played on one organ, with two rows of keys and pedal. Zella at the Thuringian Forest. Published by Ioh. G. Schübler."

They are full of dignity and religious expression. In some of them we may see how Bach, in his choice of stops, departed from the usual manner. Thus, for instance, in the second chorale, *Wo soll ich fliehen hin?* he gives to the first keyboard 8-foot tone, to the second 16, and to the pedal 4, for the pedal has to perform the *cantus firmus*.

(5) "*Clavierübung*, or Exercise for the Clavier; consisting of an Air, with several variations, for the Harpsichord, with two rows of keys. Published by Balthasar Schmid at Nuremberg."

This admirable work consists of 30 variations, in which there are canons in all intervals and motions, from the unison to the ninth, with the most easy and flowing melody. There is also a regular four-part fugue and, besides many other extremely brilliant variations for two keyboards, at last, a *quodlibet*, as it is called, which might alone render its author immortal though it is far from being here the best part.[30]

For this model, according to which all variations should be made, though, for reasons easily understood, not a single one has been made after it, we are indebted to Count Kaiserling, formerly Russian Ambassador at the Court of the Elector of Saxony, who frequently resided in Leipzig, and brought with him Goldberg, who has been mentioned above, to have him instructed by Bach in music. The Count was often sickly, and then had sleepless nights. At these times Goldberg, who lived in the house with him, had to pass the night in an adjoining room to play something to him when he could not sleep. The Count once said to Bach that he should like to have some clavier pieces for his Goldberg, which should be of such a soft and somewhat lively character that he might be a little cheered up by them in his sleepless nights. Bach thought he could best fulfill this wish by variations, which, on account

---

30. This number, which contains strains from two German folk songs, may have been written in reminiscence of the quodlibets sung at the gatherings of the Bach family as mentioned by Forkel in his Chapter 1.

of the constant sameness of the fundamental harmony, he had hitherto considered as an ungrateful task. But as at this time all his works were models
of art, these variations also became such under his hand. This is, indeed, the
only model of the kind that he has left us. The Count thereafter called them
nothing but *his* variations. He was never weary of hearing them; and for a
long time, when the sleepless nights came, he used to say: "Dear Goldberg,
do play me one of my variations." Bach was, perhaps, never so well rewarded
for any work as for this: the Count made him a present of a golden goblet,
filled with a hundred Louis d'ors. But their worth as a work of art would not
have been paid if the present had been a thousand times as great. It must be
observed that, in the engraved copies of these variations, there are some
important errata, which the author has carefully corrected in his copy.

(6) "*Einige kanonische Veränderungen.* Some Canonic Variations on the
Christmas Hymn *Vom Himmel hoch da komm ich her*, for the organ, with two
sets of keys and pedal. Published at Nuremberg by Balthasar Schmid."

These are five variations, in which a great amount of canonic artifice is
introduced in the most unconstrained manner.

(7) "*Musicalisches Opfer (Musical Offering)*, dedicated to Frederick II, King
of Prussia."

The theme received from the King, of which we have spoken above (in
Chapter I), appears here, first, as a three-part clavier fugue, under the name
of *Ricercar*, or with the [acrostic] superscription *Regis Iussu Cantio Et Reliqua
Canonica Arte Resoluta* [At the King's command, the song and the remainder
resolved with canonic art]. Secondly, the composer has also made of it a six-
part *Ricercar* for the clavier. Then follow *Thematis regii elaborationes canonicae*
[Canonic elaborations of the Royal theme] of various kinds. Fourthly and
lastly, a Trio for the flute, violin, and bass, upon the same theme, is added.

(8) "*Die Kunst der Fuge*" (that is *The Art of the Fugue*). This admirable work,
unique in its kind, did not appear till after the author's death, in 1752, but
was, for the most part, engraved by one of his sons during his lifetime.
Marpurg, then at the helm of musical writing in Germany, accompanied this
edition with a preface which contains many good and just observations on
the value and use of works of this kind. But this work of Bach's was, nevertheless, too high for the great world; it was forced to withdraw into the small
world inhabited by a few connoisseurs. This small world was soon provided
with copies; the plates lay unused, and were at length sold by the heirs as
old copper.[31] If a work of this kind, by a man of such extraordinary reputation
as Bach, and recommended besides as something extraordinary by a writer
whose opinion on these subjects was considered authoritative, had been pub-

---

31. See No. 376.

lished in any country besides Germany, perhaps ten elegant editions would have been exhausted, out of mere patriotism. In Germany, there was not sold a sufficient number of copies of such a work to pay the cost of the copper plates used in engraving it.

The work consists of variations on a great scale. For the intention of the author was to show clearly what can possibly be done upon a fugue theme. The variations, which are all complete fugues upon the same theme, are here called counterpoints. The last fugue but one has three themes; in the third, the composer reveals his name by *B A C H* [= B♭ACB♮]. This fugue was, however, interrupted by the disorder in the author's eyes, and as the operation did not succeed, was not finished. It is said to have been his intention to take in the last fugue four themes, to invert them in all the four parts, and thus to close his great work. All the various kinds of fugues upon one main theme have, by the way, the common merit that all the parts are of a properly singing character, and none less than the other.

To make up for what is wanting to the last fugue, there was added to the end of the work [in the original edition] the four-part Chorale: *Wenn wir in höchsten Nöthen seyn* &c.[32] Bach dictated it a few days before his death to his son-in-law, Altnikol. Of the art displayed in this Chorale, I will say nothing; it was so familiar to the author that he could exercise it even in his illness. But the expression of pious resignation and devotion in it has always affected me whenever I have played it; so that I can hardly say which I would rather miss—this Chorale, or the end of the last fugue.

(9) Lastly, there were published after Bach's death: "Four-Part Chorale Songs [*Vierstimmige Choralgesänge*], collected by C. Ph. Em. Bach, Berlin and Leipzig, published by Birnstiel, 1765. Part I. Ditto, 1769. Part II." Each part contains 100 chorales, mostly from the author's series of compositions for the church year. At a later period, Kirnberger also edited four collections of such four-part chorales by John Sebastian Bach. These were published by Breitkopf.[33]

The Unpublished Works of Bach

may be divided into compositions for the clavier and organ, with and without accompaniment; compositions for stringed instruments; and for the voice. I will mention them in their natural order.

---

32. "When we are caught in dire distress," BWV 668. It should be noted that in a manuscript variant of this organ chorale BWV 668a Bach had chosen the first line of another stanza for his title: *Vor Deinen Thron tret' ich hiemit* ("Before Thy throne I now appear"); cf. Wolff, pp. 282–94.

33. The story of these editions is revealed in "On the Four-Part Chorales" (pp. 374–84), including Nos. 378–84.

i. Clavier Pieces

(1) Six little Preludes for the use of beginners.

(2) Fifteen two-part *Inventiones*.

A musical subject which was so contrived that, by imitation and transposition of the parts, the whole of a composition might be unfolded from it was
called an invention. The rest was only elaboration, and if one but knew
properly the means of development, did not need to be invented.

These 15 Inventions are of a great use for forming a young clavier player.
The author has taken care that not only one hand may be exercised thereby
as well as the other, but also each finger as well as the rest. They were
composed at Cöthen in 1723, and had at first a long title, which begins:

*Auffrichtige Anleitung, Wormit denen Liebhabern des Clavires...eine deutliche Art
gezeiget wird,...mit zweyen Stimmen reine spielen zu lernen,* &c., which means liter-
ally in English: "A plain introduction, by which the lovers of the clavier are
taught a clear method of playing correctly in two parts, &c." [34]

In several of these inventions some stiff and mean turns in the melody and
also other defects had at first crept in. Bach, who even at a later period found
them fundamentally very useful to his scholars, gradually took from them
whatever did not suit his more refined taste, and at length made them true,
expressive masterpieces, without, however, lessening their use in exercising
the hands and fingers and forming the taste. A careful study of them is the
best preparation for Bach's greater works.

(3) Fifteen three-part *Inventiones*, which are also known by the name of
Sinfonias. They have the same object as the preceding, only they are intended
to lead the scholar still farther.

(4) *"The Well-Tempered Clavier;*[35] or Preludes and Fugues in all the keys,
composed for the use of inquisitive musical youth, as well as for the amusement of those who are already versed in this art. Part I. 1722."

The Second Part of this work, which also contains 24 preludes and 24
fugues in all the keys, was composed at a later period. It consists, from the
beginning to the end, entirely of masterpieces. In the First Part, on the other
hand, there are still some preludes and fugues which bear marks of
the immaturity of early youth and have probably been retained by the author
only to have the number of four-and-twenty complete. But even here the
author corrected, in course of time, whatever was capable of amendment.
Whole passages are either thrown out, or differently turned, so that in the
later copies there are very few pieces left which can still be reproached as

---

34. The complete title is given in No. 92.
35. Complete titles are given in Nos. 90 and 227.

imperfect. Among these few I reckon the fugues in A minor, G major and G minor, C major, F major and F minor, &c. But the rest are all excellent, and some of them in such a degree as not to be inferior to those in the Second Part. Even this Second Part, which was originally the more perfect, received in the course of time great improvements, as may be seen by comparing older and newer copies. In general, both parts of this work contain such a treasure of art as can certainly not be found anywhere but in Germany.

(5) *Chromatic Fantasy and Fugue.* I have taken infinite pains to discover another piece of this kind by Bach, but in vain. This fantasia is unique, and never had its like. I first received it from Brunswick, from Will. Friedemann. A friend of his and mine who liked to write doggerel, wrote on an inserted leaf:

Anbey kommt an	[here, my good man,
Etwas Musik von Sebastian,	Is some music by Sebastian,
Sonst genannt: Fantasia chromatica;	Called otherwise: *Fantasia chromatica,*
Bleibt schön in alle Saecula.	Will last through all the *saecula.*]

It is remarkable that this work, though of such intricate workmanship, makes an impression even on the most unpracticed hearer if it is but performed at all clearly.

(6) A Fantasy (Fig. 3).[36] It is not of the same kind as the preceding, but, like the allegro in a sonata, divided into two parts, and must be performed throughout in the same movement and time. Otherwise it is excellent. In old copies we find a fugue annexed, which, however, cannot belong to it, and is not quite finished (Fig. 4). But it cannot be doubted that at least the first 30 measures are by Seb. Bach, for they contain an extremely bold attempt to make use of diminished and augmented intervals and their inversions in a three-part harmony. None but Bach ever hazarded an attempt like this. What follows the first 30 bars seems to have been added by another hand, for it bears no trace of Sebastian's manner.[37]

(7) Six great Suites, consisting of preludes, Allemandes, courants, sarabands, jigs, &c. They are known by the name of the English Suites because the composer made them for an Englishman of rank (Fig. 5). They have all great worth as works of art; but some single pieces among them, for example, the jigs of the fifth and sixth suite, are to be considered as perfect masterpieces of original harmony and melody (Fig. 6 and 7).

(8) Six little Suites, consisting of Allemandes, courants, &c. (Fig. 8). They

---

36. See the figures, pp. 480–82.

37. Forkel's doubts are ungrounded—the entire fragment BWV 906/2 is an authentic composition by Bach and was meant as a sequel to the Fantasy.

are generally called French Suites because they are written in the French taste. By design, the composer is here less learned than in his other suites, and has mostly used a pleasing, more predominant melody. In particular the fifth suite deserves to be noticed on this account, in which all the pieces are of the smoothest melody; just as in the last jig none are used but consonant intervals, especially sixths and thirds.

These are the most outstanding clavier works of John Sebastian Bach, which may be all considered as classical.

A great number of single suites, toccatas, and fugues which have been preserved besides the above have all much artistic merit in one way or another; but belong, nevertheless, among his youthful attempts. At the most, 10 or 12 single pieces out of this number are worth preservation; some because they may be of great use as exercises for the fingers, for which the author originally designed them; others because they are at least better than similar works of many other composers. As practice for the fingers of both hands, I particularly reckon a Fugue in A minor, in which the composer has truly endeavored, by an uninterrupted succession of running passages, to ensure to both hands equal strength and facility (Fig. 9). For beginners, a little two-part fugue might still be useful, as it is very singing and contains nothing antiquated (Fig. 10).

ii. Pieces for Clavier with the Accompaniment of Other Instruments

(1) Six Sonatas for the clavier with the accompaniment of a violin obbligato. They were composed at Cöthen and may be reckoned among Bach's first masterpieces in this field. They are throughout fugued; there are also a few canons between the clavier and the violin which are extremely singing and full of character. The violin part requires a master. Bach knew the possibilities of that instrument and spared it as little as he did his clavier. The keys in which these six sonatas are composed are the following: B minor, A major, E major, C minor, F minor, and G major.

(2) Many single Sonatas for the harpsichord with accompaniment of violin, flute, viola da gamba, &c., all admirably composed, and so that even in our days most of them would be heard by connoisseurs with pleasure.

(3) Concertos for the harpsichord, with accompaniment of many instruments. Notwithstanding the treasure of art which they contain, they are antiquated as regards their form and their setting in other respects.

(4) Two Concertos for two claviers, with accompaniment of two violins, viola, and violoncello (Fig. 11 and 12). The first is very old, but the second as new as if it had been composed but yesterday. It may be played entirely without the stringed instruments and has then an excellent effect. The last

allegro is a strictly regular and magnificent fugue. This species of composition [that is, for two keyboard instruments] was also first perfected and,
perhaps, even first attempted by Bach. At least, I have not met with more
than a single attempt of another composer which may be older. William
Hieronymus Pachelbel, at Nuremberg, made it in a toccata, as it is called.
But first, Pachelbel was a contemporary of Bach's and may, therefore, have
easily been led by him to this attempt; and, secondly, his attempt is of such
a nature that it can scarcely be taken into account. One instrument merely
repeats what the other has played, without ever playing against it.

Indeed, it seems as if Bach, about this time, desired to attempt everything
that could be done with many and with few parts. As he descended even to
music in one part, in which everything necessary to make it complete
was crowded together, so he now ascended, to combine together as many
instruments as possible, each rich in itself. From his concertos for two keyboard instruments, he proceeded to the union of three, of which kind we also
have

(5) two Concertos, with an accompaniment for four stringed instruments
(Fig. 13 and 14). In these concertos it is remarkable that, besides the harmonical combination and constant concerting of the three principal instruments,
the stringed instruments also carry on among themselves in their own manner. One can hardly conceive the art which is bestowed on this work. If we
reflect, besides, that these works so full of art are at the same time as fine,
characteristic, and expressive as if the composer had had only a simple melody to manage (as is particularly the case with the Concerto in D minor), we
hardly know what to say for admiration.

And yet, this was not enough for Bach. He also made an attempt with

(6) a Concerto for four claviers, accompanied by four stringed instruments
(Fig. 15). I cannot judge of the effect of this concerto as I have never been
able to get together four instruments and four performers for the purpose.
But that it is admirably composed may be seen by the comparison of the
single parts.

iii. Organ Pieces

The pedals are an essential part of the organ: by them alone is it exalted
above all other instruments, for its magnificence, grandeur, and majesty
depend upon them. Without the pedals, this great instrument is no longer
great: it approaches the little positives, which are of no value in the eyes of
competent judges. But the great organ, provided with pedals, must be so
managed that its whole compass is brought into action; in other words, the
composer and the player must require from it all that it can perform. Nobody

has ever done this more than John Sebastian Bach, not merely by his rich harmony and melody, adapted to the instrument, but also by giving to the pedals their own part. He did this even in his earlier compositions. It was, however, only in the course of time that he made himself quite master of this manner of managing the pedals, so that his perfect masterpieces in this field also belong only to the period in which his compositions for the clavier began to be masterpieces. His preceding labors, through which he had to attain this goal, are spread in the world in great numbers. As soon as an artist begins to distinguish himself, everybody is desirous of possessing some specimen of his work. But, before he can entirely complete his career, the curiosity of the public is usually already satisfied, especially if, by uncommon progress toward perfection, he departs too far from their ideas. This seems to have been the case with Bach. Hence it appears that his most perfect works are less diffused than his preparatory labors. But, as the latter can by no means be received into a critical, correct edition of his works, I have noted only those works which merit to be received, as I have done in the preceding articles.

The best organ compositions of John Sebastian Bach are, accordingly, to be divided into three classes, in which are contained:

(1) Grand Preludes and Fugues, with obbligato pedal. Their number cannot be precisely ascertained; but I believe that it does not exceed a dozen. At least, with all my inquiries for many years, at the best sources, I have not been able to collect more than 12, the themes of which I will here set down (Fig. 16). To these I add a very intricately worked-out Passacaglia (Fig. 17), which, however, is rather for two clavichords and pedal than for the organ.[38]

(2) Preludes on the Melodies of several Chorales. Bach began already when he was at Arnstadt to compose such pieces, with variations, under the title of *Partite diverse*. Most of them, however, might be played with the hands alone. But those [preludes] of which I speak here absolutely require the obbligato pedals. The number of them may amount to 100; at least, I myself possess above 70 and know that, here and there, more of them exist. Nothing can be more dignified, sublime, and holy than these Preludes. But they cannot be listed here because they are too numerous. Besides these greater Preludes, there is a great number of shorter and easier ones, which are also spread in manuscript copies only and are designed for young organists.

(3) Six Sonatas, or Trios, for two claviers and obbligato pedals.[39] Bach

38. Bach regularly uses the designation *für zwey Claviere und Pedal* ("For two manuals and pedal") for organ works.

39. Ibid.

composed them for his eldest son, William Friedemann, who, by practicing them, had to prepare himself to become the great performer on the organ that he afterward was. It is impossible to say enough of their beauty. They were composed when the author was in his most mature age and may be considered as his chief work of this description. For the themes of them, see Fig. 18. Several others, which are in the hands of different persons, may also be reckoned fine though they do not equal the first mentioned.

iv. Instrumental Pieces

There are few instruments for which Bach has not composed something. In his time, it was usual to play in the church, during the communion, a concerto or solo upon some instrument. He often wrote such pieces himself and always contrived them so that his performers could, by their means, improve upon their instruments. Most of these pieces, however, are lost.

But, on the other hand, two principal works of another kind have been preserved which, in all probability, richly indemnify us for the loss of the other; namely:

(1) six Solos [three sonatas and three partitas] for the violin, without any accompaniment; and

(2) six Solos [suites] for the Violoncello, likewise without any accompaniment.

For a long series of years, the violin solos were universally considered by the greatest performers on the violin as the best means to make an ambitious student a perfect master of his instrument. The solos for the violoncello are, in this respect, of equal value.

v. Vocal Compositions

(1) Five complete sets of Church Music [cantatas] for all the Sundays and Holidays of the year.

(2) Five compositions of the Passion, one of which is for two choruses.

(3) Many Oratorios, Masses, Magnificats, single *Sanctus;* compositions for birthdays, name days, and funerals; Wedding Cantatas; Serenades; also a few Italian [secular] Cantatas.

(4) Many Motets for one and two choruses.

Most of these works, however, are now dispersed. The annual sets were divided after the author's death between the elder sons, and in such a manner that William Friedemann had the larger share because, in the place which he then filled at Halle, he could make the most use of them. In the sequel, his circumstances obliged him to part, by degrees, with what he had obtained. Of the great vocal compositions, too, nothing has remained together. Only of the Motets for two choruses, there still exist eight or ten; but even those not in the hands of one person, but of several. In the collection of music left by the Princess Amalia of Prussia to the Joachimsthaler Gymnasium, at Berlin, there are, perhaps, more of Bach's vocal compositions together than anywhere else, although these are not many either. I have found there the following:

(1) 21 Church Cantatas. In one of them, upon the text *Schlage doch, gewünschte Stunde* &c. ["Strike, oh strike, desired hour"], the composer has introduced obbligato bells; whence we may conclude, at least, that this cantata was not composed in the period when his taste had been purified.

(2) Two Masses for five voices with accompaniment of many instruments.

(3) A Mass for two choruses. The first chorus is accompanied by stringed instruments and the second by wind instruments.[40]

(4) A Passion for two choruses. The text is by Picander.

(5) A Sanctus for four voices and accompaniment of instruments.

(6) A Motet for four voices [part of a cantata] *Aus tiefer Noth schrey ich zu Dir* &c. ["Out of the depths I cry to Thee"].

(7) A Motet for five voices *Jesu, meine Freude* &c. ["Jesus, my joy"].

(8) Four Motets for eight voices, in two choruses; *viz.*

   (a) *Fürchte dich nicht, ich bin bey dir* &c. ["Be not afraid, I am with thee"].

   (b) *Der Geist hilft unserer Schwachheit auf* &c. ["The spirit helpeth our infirmities"].

   (c) *Komm, Jesu, komm* &c. ["Come, Jesus, come"].

   (d) *Singet dem Herrn ein neues Lied* &c. ["Sing unto the Lord a new song"].

(9) A single Fugue for four voices [part of a cantata] *Nimm was dein ist, und gehe hin* &c. ["Take what thine is and go thy way"].

(10) A Cantata, with recitatives, arias, a duet, and a chorus. This is a peasant cantata.[41]

To this last cantata is prefixed a notice; and to the Mass for two choruses, No. 3, an explanation, written by Kirnberger, of the great art shown in the composition.

---

40. Forkel is referring to BWV Anh. 167, erroneously published as a work by J. S. Bach in 1805 by Breitkopf & Härtel.

41. *Mer han en neue Oberkeet* ("We've got another squire and chief"), BWV 212.

CHAPTER 10

Bach the Reviser of His Own Works

We have several times spoken of the great care with which Bach endeavored all his life long to improve his works. I have had opportunities of comparing together many copies of his principal works, written in different years, and I confess that I have often felt both surprise and delight at the means which he employed to make, little by little, the faulty good, the good better, and the better perfect. Nothing can be more instructive than such comparisons, for a connoisseur as well as for everyone who is eager in the study of his art. It were therefore much to be wished that to the complete edition of Bach's works a small supplementary volume might be added, simply for the purpose of preserving and comparing together the most important and instructive variants from his best works. Why should not this be done with the works of the composer, the poet in tones, as well as with the works of the poet in words?

In Bach's earlier works it very often happened to him, as to other beginners, that he repeated the same idea several times, only in other words; that is to say, the same modulation was repeated, perhaps in a lower, perhaps in the same octave, or with another turn of melody. In his riper years he could not bear such poverty; whatever he found of this description was therefore cut out without hesitation, in however many hands copies of the piece might be, and however many persons might have approved of it. Two of the most remarkable examples of this are the two preludes in C major and C-sharp major, in the First Part of the *Well-Tempered Clavier*. Both are thereby rendered shorter by one half, but are at the same time freed from all useless superfluities.

In other pieces, Bach often said too little. His idea was not fully expressed and wanted various additions. The most remarkable example of this that has occurred to me is the Prelude in D minor, in the Second Part of the *Well-Tempered Clavier*. I possess several different copies of this piece. In the oldest, the first transposition of the theme into the bass is wanting, as are many other passages which were necessary for the complete expression of the thought. In the second, the transposition of the theme into the bass is inserted whenever it occurs in related keys. In the third, several other passages are more fully expressed and better connected together. Lastly, there still remained some turns or figures of the melody which did not seem to correspond with the spirit and style of the whole. These are so amended in the fourth copy that now this prelude is one of the most beautiful and impeccable in the whole *Well-Tempered Clavier*. Many persons enjoyed the piece even in its original form, and thought it less beautiful after the subsequent alteration. Bach, however, did not suffer himself to be misled by this; he continued to correct till he was pleased with it himself.

At the beginning of the last century it was the fashion to overload single principal notes upon instruments with so much running up and down as it has lately become the fashion again to do with vocal music. Bach so far showed his deference for this fashion as to compose some pieces in this style, too. One of them is the Prelude in E minor in the First Part of the *Well-Tempered Clavier*. But he soon returned to Nature and to pure taste, and altered it into the form in which it is now engraved.

Every decade has some forms or turns of melody which are peculiar to it, but which generally grow out of fashion before it expires. A composer who thinks to have his works descend to posterity must take care to avoid them. Bach, too, in his earlier years, struck on this rock. His first compositions for the organ, and his two-part Inventions, in their original form, are full of flourishes in the taste of the times. The compositions for the organ have remained as they were; but the Inventions have been greatly improved. The public will soon have an opportunity to compare them together in their ancient and later form, as the publishers have taken the laudable resolution to suppress the first edition and to deliver to the subscribers an improved one in its stead.

The methods of improvement hitherto mentioned extend, however, only to the external form, to the too much or too little in the expression of a thought in the large. But Bach even more frequently employed, to perfect his works, more refined means which can scarcely be described. Unity of style and character are often achieved by the alteration of a single note against which, in its former situation, the most rigid musical grammarian could not make any objection, but which yet did not entirely satisfy the connoisseur. Even commonplace passages are frequently changed into the most elegant by changing, taking away, or adding a single note. In these cases only the most thoroughly trained feeling and the finest, most polished taste can decide. This fine feeling and polished taste were possessed by Bach in the greatest perfection. He had gradually so improved both that at last no thought could occur to him which, in all its properties and relations, did not accord with the whole as it should and must. His later works, therefore, are all as if they were one cast: so gentle, soft, and even flows the inconceivably rich stream in them of the most diversified ideas blended together. This is the lofty summit of perfection in art which, in the most intimate union of melody and harmony, nobody besides John Sebastian Bach has ever yet attained.

CHAPTER 11

The Spirit of Bach

When an artist has produced a great number of works which are all of the most various kind, which are distinguished from those of all other composers of every age, and have in common the greatest abundance of the most original ideas, and a most lively spirit which appeals to everybody (whether he be a connoisseur or not), there can hardly be room to ask whether such an artist was really a great genius of art or not. The most fertile fancy; the most inexhaustible invention; the most acute and accurate judgment in the just application, to every object, of the rich flow of thoughts issuing from the imagination; the most refined taste, which cannot endure one single arbitrary note, or which does not duly accord with the spirit of the whole; the greatest ability in the suitable use of the most refined and ingenious resources of the art; and lastly, the highest degree of skill in execution—all qualities in which not one, but all the powers of the soul must act in the most intimate union— these must be the characteristics of a real genius, or there are none such; he who cannot find these characteristics in the works of Bach is either not acquainted with them at all or not sufficiently so. He who does not know them cannot possibly have an opinion of them or of the genius of their author; and he who does not know them sufficiently must consider that works of art, in proportion as they are great and perfect, require to be the more diligently studied to discover their real value in its full extent. That butterfly spirit which flutters incessantly from flower to flower, without resting upon any, can do nothing here.

But with all the great and beautiful gifts which Bach received from nature, he would not have become the accomplished artist that he was if he had not learned betimes to avoid many rocks on which so many artists, perhaps as richly endowed with genius, are wont to split. I will communicate to the reader some scattered remarks on this subject, and then conclude this essay with the discussion of some characteristic features of Bach's genius.

The greatest genius, with the most unconquerable propensity to an art, is in its original nature never more than a disposition, or a fruitful soil upon which an art can never properly thrive except it be cultivated with indefatigable pains. Industry, from which all art and science is properly derived, is one of the first and most indispensable conditions thereof. It not only enables genius to make itself master of the mechanical resources of art, but it gradually excites judgment and reflection to take part in all that it produces. But the ease with which genius makes itself master of some mechanical resources of art, as well as its own satisfaction and that of others with the first essays, which are commonly far too early looked upon as successful, frequently seduce it to pass over the first principles of the art, to venture on difficulties before it is fully master of what is more easy, or to fly before its wings are grown. If now such a genius is not led back at this period, either by good advice and instruction or by the attentive study of classic works already existing, in order to recover what it has neglected, it will uselessly lavish its best strength and never attain an elevated rank in art. For it is certain that great progress never can be made, nor the highest possible perfection attained, if the first principles are neglected; that people never learn to overcome difficulties if they have not overcome what is more easy; and, lastly, that no one can ever become great by his own experience unless he has previously profited by the knowledge and experience of others.

Bach did not split on such rocks. His ardent genius was attended by an equally ardent industry, which incessantly impelled him, when he could not yet succeed by his own strength, to seek aid from the models existing in his time. At first, Vivaldi's violin concertos afforded him this assistance; afterward, the works of the best composers for the clavier and the organ of those times became his counselors. But nothing is more able to excite the reflection of a young composer than the arts of counterpoint. Now, as the composers of the last-mentioned works were distinguished fugue writers in their way, who, at least, were mechanically masters of the arts of counterpoint, the diligent study and imitation of them gradually sharpened his understanding, his judgment, and his reflection, so that he soon perceived where he had left deficiencies and had anything to fetch up in order to be then able to make with certainty greater advances in his art.

A second rock upon which many a fine but not sufficiently cultivated genius has split is public applause. Though we would not so far depreciate public applause as the Greek who said to his disciple who had played with applause in the theater: "You have played ill, otherwise the public would not have applauded you"—it is not to be denied that most artists are led astray by it, especially if it is given them too early, that is, before they have acquired sufficient reflection and self-knowledge. The public requires everything to be human, and the true artist ought properly to make everything divine. How, then, should the applause of the multitude and true art exist together? Bach never sought this applause. He thought, like Schiller:

Kannst du nicht allen gefallen durch deine That und dein Kunstwerk,
Mach' es wenigen recht; vielen gefallen ist schlimm.

(If you cannot please all by your art or your work,
Satisfy the few: to please many is bad.)

He labored for himself, like every true genius; he fulfilled his own wish, satisfied his own taste, chose his subjects according to his own opinion, and, lastly, derived the most pleasure form his own approbation. The applause of connoisseurs could not then fail him and, in fact, never did fail him. How else could a real work of art be produced? The artist who endeavors to make his works so as to suit some particular class of amateurs either has no genius, or abuses it. To follow the prevailing taste of the multitude needs, at the most, some dexterity in a very partial manner of treating tones. Artists of this description may be compared to the artisan who must also make his goods so that his customers can make use of them. Bach never submitted to such conditions. He thought the artist could form the public, but that the public could not form the artist. When he was asked by someone, as frequently happened, for a very easy clavier piece, he used to say: "I will see what I can do." In such cases, he usually chose an easy theme, but, in thoroughly working it out, always found so much of importance to say upon it that the piece could not turn out easy after all. If complaints were made that it was still too difficult, he smiled, and said: "Only practice it diligently, it will go very well; you have five just as healthy fingers on each hand as I." Was this caprice? No, it was the real spirit of the art.

This true spirit is what led him to the great and sublime as the highest object of the art. We owe it to this spirit that Bach's works do not merely please and delight, like what is merely agreeable in art, but irresistibly carry us away with them; that they do not merely surprise us for a moment, but produce effects that become stronger the oftener we hear the works, and the better we become acquainted with them; that the boundless treasure of ideas heaped up in them, even when we have a thousand times considered them, still leaves us something new, which excites our admiration, and often our astonishment; lastly, that even he who is no connoisseur, who knows no more than the musical alphabet, can hardly refrain from admiration when they are well played to him and when he opens his ear and heart to them without prejudice.

Nay more: to this genuine spirit of art it is owing that Bach united with his great and lofty style the most refined elegance and the greatest precision in the single parts that compose the great whole, which otherwise are not thought so necessary here as in works the only object of which is the agreeable; that he thought the whole could not be perfect if anything were wanting to the perfect precision of the single parts; and, lastly, that if, notwithstanding the main tendency of his genius to the great and sublime, he sometimes composed and performed something gay and even jocose, his cheerfulness and joking were those of a sage.

It was only through this union of the greatest genius with the most indefatigable study that John Sebastian Bach was able, whichever way he turned, so greatly to extend the bounds of his art that his successors have not even been able to maintain this enlarged domain in its whole extent; and this alone enabled him to produce such numerous and perfect works, all of which are, and ever will remain, true ideals and imperishable models of art.

And this man, the greatest musical poet and the greatest musical orator that ever existed, and probably ever will exist, was a German. Let his country be proud of him; let it be proud, but, at the same time, worthy of him!

NOTE: The figures are reproduced from the English edition (London, 1820)

Fine

PART VII

Bach
in the
Romantic
Era

Bach in the
Romantic Era

The term "Romantic" is used here not in its narrow sense as a descriptor of a musical style period subsequent to so-called Viennese Classicism but rather as a historiographical term with broad literary and cultural implications for the European scene from the later eighteenth century well into and through much of the nineteenth. In fact, the conceptual development of historicism, one of the chief phenomena of Romantic thought, reaches far back into the eighteenth century. Hence in the reception history of Bach's music, "Romantic era" is understood as the formative period as it unfolded relatively soon after Bach's death (documented primarily in Part V of this volume) and proceeded with much verve until the time of the Bach centennial in 1850.

Section Seven of the original *Bach Reader* (1945) was titled "The Rediscovery of Bach," and the first two sentences of the essay "The Story of His Fame" originally read, "Bach and his works have met a strange fate at the hands of posterity. They were fairly well recognized in their day; practically forgotten by the generations following his; rediscovered and revived; and finally accorded an eminence far beyond the recognition they had originally achieved." Bach scholarship of recent decades has found it necessary to turn away from a perception of the evolution of the Bach reception that resembles the metaphorical paradigm of "Death and Resurrection"—the characteristic heading of the pertinent chapter in Albert Schweitzer's *J. S. Bach* (1908). It became necessary to differentiate between two complementary aspects: on the one hand, the beginning of a more broadly based public reception of Bach's music in the early nineteenth century, for which Mendelssohn's 1829 performance of the *St. Matthew Passion* represents a decisive milestone; on the other hand, the uninterrupted reception of a more private kind, largely confined to circles of professional musicians, who regarded Bach's fugues and chorales in particular as a continuing challenge, a source of inspiration, and a yardstick for measuring compositional quality. Thus it seems appropriate to emphasize the strong element of continuity in the story of Bach's fame that bridges Parts V, VI, and VII.

THE STORY OF BACH'S FAME

It began in the later eighteenth century, but throughout the nineteenth and twentieth centuries Bach and his works accorded an eminence far beyond the recognition they had originally achieved. It is a tale of posthumous success unique in the history of music.[1]

In the sense that Bach developed and intensified the forms, principles, and ideas evolved by his predecessors, he was, as the discussion of his inheritance and achievement has shown, a thoroughly progressive figure. However, all his endeavors were determined by the ideals of concerted polyphonic music, ideals that had guided musical development without a break since the early seventeenth century. A new trend in strong opposition to those ideals set in while he was at work. The up-to-date composer again denounced counterpoint, as his forerunners had done at the end of the sixteenth century, and cultivated instead a popular type of melody and an airy elegance of setting. The process of simplification was carried out most significantly in the field of opera. In the music of Pergolesi, who died fourteen years before Bach, the new style first blossomed. On a lower level, the trends of the time are strikingly expressed in the pieces by the composing amateur Domenico Alberti, who gave his name to the stereotype bass patterns of which he made excessive use.

Bach himself took up certain elements of the new style, and particularly in his later years he often attained a transparency and sprightliness that were an astonishing achievement within what always remained a basically contrapuntal style. He also helped his sons become modern musicians without losing the solidity of craftsmanship that was their greatest heritage from him. But he did not abandon any of his concepts, and while he went ahead, steadily and stubbornly, to reach goals that had hardly been dreamed of before, the very basis for the understanding of his art was swept away. Admired by a few connoisseurs, most of whom were his own pupils, he wrote music that became increasingly unpopular. And at his death the Leipzig councilors did not hide their relief at losing a capellmeister who had only too well lived up to the pledges of seriousness and sobriety he had made them a generation ago.

---

1. As in Part I, cross references have been avoided; the reader is invited to trace the implied references particularly to Parts IV and V with the help of the Index.

Bach's work was thus, to some extent, outmoded even before it was completed. *The Art of Fugue,* though recommended by Mattheson and prefaced by Marpurg, had sold only thirty copies by 1756. Nevertheless, it is remarkable that this very work lived on as one of the principal subjects of Marpurg's *Abhandlung von der Fuge* (Berlin, 1753) and, moreover, that by the turn of the century the time was ripe for two new editions of *The Art of Fugue,* one published in Paris (Vogt, 1801) and the other in Zurich (Nägeli, 1802). Eighteen hundred was also the year in which the Leipzig publisher Hoffmeister & Kühnel began the first complete edition of Bach's keyboard works, a project that included their commissioning Forkel to write a companion monograph on the life and works of the composer, the 1802 biography (pp. 415–82). The competing Leipzig firm of Breitkopf & Härtel began in 1802 with a complete edition of the Bach motets, to be followed by other vocal works. Music publishers clearly saw a growing need as well as a promising international market, a situation that had emerged out of three separate developments: first, the increasing and legendary fame of Johann Sebastian Bach, as it was particularly promoted by the success and influence not only of the Bach sons but also of a host of direct and indirect Bach students; second, the prominent featuring of Bach and his music in virtually all the major treatises on music theory and musical composition; third, the remarkably broad manuscript dissemination of Bach's keyboard music (with considerable emphasis on the organ works and *The Well-Tempered Clavier*) and, to a much lesser extent, of his vocal works. Still, the four-part chorales were published twice within a span of twenty years, once in the 1760s (Birnstiel, two volumes) and once in the 1780s (Breitkopf, expanded to four volumes). And then, Franz Joseph Haydn in Vienna was by no means the only owner of a manuscript score of the B Minor Mass.

The name Bach used during the later eighteenth century in Germany meant Carl Philipp Emanuel, and in England it meant Johann Christian. Their creative impact on the contemporaneous scene can scarcely be underestimated, but at the same time their father's influence grew both latently and openly, as well as steadily and strikingly. Indeed, the fresh ingenuity of Haydn, the subtle genius of Mozart, and the aesthetic and technical premises of the art of composition among the musicians of subsequent generations relate in many ways, indirect and direct, to the legacy of Johann Sebastian Bach.

The quotations on the following pages may reveal more about the attitude of their own period than they reveal about Bach. But a biography of Bach is not complete unless it shows, at least in a few bold strokes, how he affected a number of important figures.

Wolfgang Amadeus Mozart

Mozart seems to have been the first to whom the recognition of Bach's qualities was a kind of revelation or even shock, and therefore his relation to Bach—however casual and incomplete it may have been—is clearly different from that of a Marpurg, a Kittel, or even a Forkel, to whom Bach was still known through continuous tradition. During a visit to Leipzig in 1789, Mozart was confronted with some of Bach's vocal works, as an eyewitness, Friedrich Rochlitz recalled:

On the initiative of the late Doles, then Cantor of the St. Thomas School in Leipzig, the choir surprised Mozart with the performance of the double-chorus motet *Singet dem Herrn ein neues Lied,* by Sebastian Bach. Mozart knew this master more by hearsay than by his works, which had become quite rare; at least his motets, which had never been printed, were completely unknown to him. Hardly had the choir sung a few measures when Mozart sat up, startled; a few measures more and he called out "What is this?" And now his whole soul seemed to be in his ears. When the singing was finished he cried out, full of joy "Now, there is something one can learn from!" He was told that this School, in which Sebastian Bach had been Cantor, possessed the complete collection of his motets and preserved them as a sort of sacred relic. "That's the spirit! That's fine!" he cried. "Let's see them!" There was, however, no score of these songs; so he had the parts given to him; and then it was for the silent observer a joy to see how eagerly Mozart sat himself down, with the parts all around him—in both hands, on his knees, and on the chairs next to him—and, forgetting everything else, did not get up again until he had looked through everything of Sebastian Bach's that was there. He requested a copy, valued it very highly, and, if I am not very much mistaken, no one who knows Bach's compositions and Mozart's *Requiem* will fail to recognize, particularly in the great fugue *Christe eleison,* the study, the esteem, and the full comprehension of the spirit of the old contrapuntist achieved by Mozart's versatile and unlimited genius.[2]

In Vienna, Mozart had had opportunity to become acquainted with other works of Bach. In a letter to his father dated April 10, 1782, Mozart reports that every Sunday at noon he goes to Baron van Swieten's house "and there nothing is played but Händl and Bach." Mozart himself arranged for strings five fugues by Johann Sebastian—from *The Well-Tempered Clavier* and *The Art of Fugue*—and one by Wilhelm Friedemann, and composed introductory adagios for four of them. He also ventured to write a prelude and fugue himself, as the first of a projected set of six, to be dedicated to the baron. On April 20, 1782, he dispatched the new compositions to his sister, commenting,

---

2. Rochlitz, "Anekdoten aus Mozarts Leben," *Allgemeine Musikalische Zeitung,* 1 (1798–99): cols. 116–17.

The cause of this fugue's coming into the world is really my dear konstanze. Baron van suiten, to whom I go every Sunday, has let me take all the works of händl and Sebastian Bach home, after I played them through for him. When konstanze heard the fugues she fell quite in love with them. She will hear nothing but fugues, especially (in this field) nothing but Händl and Bach. Now, since she had heard me frequently improvise fugues, she asked me whether I had never written any down, and when I said "No," she gave me a proper scolding for not wanting to write the most intricate and beautiful kind of music, and she did not give up begging me until I wrote her a fugue, and that is how it came about. I have conscientiously written *Andante maestoso* on it, so that at least it will not be played fast— for if a fugue is not played slowly one cannot hear the entrance of the subject distinctly and clearly, and consequently it is of no effect. When I have time and opportunity, I shall make five more, and then offer them to the Baron, who has, as a matter of fact, though in quality a very large store of good music, yet in quantity a very small one.[3]

Ludwig van Beethoven

Approximately a year later (on March 2, 1783), a new genius was announced to the musical world, in a magazine article describing the Bonn Court Capelle, published anonymously but written by Christian Gottlob Neefe:

Louis van Betthoven [*sic*], son of the above-mentioned tenor, a boy of eleven years, who has a talent that promises much. He plays very fluently and powerfully on the clavier, reads very well at sight, and, to say everything in a word, he plays most of *The Well-Tempered Clavier* by Sebastian Bach, which Mr. Neefe has placed in his hands. Anyone who knows this collection of preludes and fugues in all the keys (which one could almost call the *non plus ultra*) will know what that means. . . . Mr. Neefe has also, so far as his other affairs permitted, given him some instruction in thorough bass. Now he is teaching him composition, and to encourage him he has had Nine Variations on a March for clavier by him engraved in Mannheim. This young genius would deserve support so that he might travel. He would certainly become a second Wolfgang Amadeus Mozart if he were to continue as he had begun.[4]

When Beethoven came to Vienna, it was his superb playing of *The Well-Tempered Clavier* that first established his reputation there. Anton Schindler tells how he was drawn into Swieten's circle:

3. Mozart, *Briefe und Aufzeichnungen: Gesamtausgabe,* ed. Wilhelm A. Bauer and Otto Erich Deutsch, vol. 3 (Kassel, 1962), p. 202.

4. Neefe, "Nachricht von der churfürstlich-cöllnischen Hofcapelle zu Bonn, etc.," *Magazin der Musik* (Hamburg), March 30, 1783, pp. 394–95; cf. *Thayer's Life of Beethoven,* rev. and ed. Elliot Forbes (Princeton, 1967), p. 66.

One of his first, and for a long time most influential, acquaintances was the celebrated Van Swieten, formerly physician in ordinary[5] to the Empress Maria Theresa,
a man who could appreciate art and artists according to their real worth. Van Swieten
was, as it were, the cicerone of the newcomer, and attached young Beethoven to his
person and to his house, where indeed the latter soon found himself at home. The
musical treats in Van Swieten's house consisted chiefly of compositions by Handel,
Sebastian Bach, and the greatest masters of Italy up to Palestrina, performed with a
full band; and they were so truly exquisite as to be long remembered by all who had
been so fortunate as to partake of them.

For Beethoven those meetings had this peculiar interest, that he not only gained
an intimate acquaintance with those classics, but also that he was always obliged to
stay longest because the old gentleman had an insatiable appetite for music, so that
the night was often pretty far advanced before he would suffer him to depart; nay,
frequently he would not suffer him to go at all; for, to all that he had heard before,
Beethoven was obliged to add half a dozen Fugues by Bach, "by way of final prayer."
Among the notes addressed by that eminent physician to Beethoven, and carefully
preserved by the latter, one runs thus:

"If you are not prevented next Wednesday, I should be glad to see you here at
half-past eight in the evening, with your nightcap in your pocket."[6]

Throughout his life Beethoven documented his interest in Bach's works.
He asked his publishers—Hoffmeister, Nägeli, Breitkopf—to send him copies of all their Bach publications, trying, in particular, to acquire a copy of
the B Minor Mass. He enthusiastically endorsed Hoffmeister's plan for a
complete edition of Bach's instrumental works.[7] He planned to devote the
proceeds of a publication or a concert to Bach's last surviving daughter,
Regina Susanna, who was spending her declining years in poverty. He called
Bach the father of harmony and exclaimed, "Not *Bach* (brook), but *Meer* (sea)
should be his name." He wrote a humorous canon on B A C H, and for years
he thought of writing an overture on the same theme. But in Beethoven's
mind, the phalanx of musical heroes was led by Mozart and Handel, followed
by Bach. When Johann Andreas Stumpff, a Thuringian harp maker, who
lived in London, visited Beethoven in 1824, Beethoven asked at the mention
of Bach's name, "Why is he dead?" And when Stumpff asserted, "He will
live again," Beethoven skeptically remarked, "Yes, if he is studied, and for
that we have no time." At Beethoven's own death, it was found that he

5. The physician was actually the baron's father.

6. Anton Schindler, *Biographie von Ludwig van Beethoven* (1840; 2nd ed., Münster, 1845),
pp. 25–26. The translation has been taken from *The Life of Beethoven, Edited by Ignace
Moscheles, Esq., Pianist to His Royal Highness Prince Albert* (London, 1841), vol. 1, pp. 39–40.
It should be noted that in the third German edition the text was substantially altered.

7. See Schumann's quotation of Beethoven's endorsement, p. 503.

possessed Bach's motets, *The Well-Tempered Clavier,* three books of the *Clavier-Übung,* the Inventions and Sinfonias, and the Toccata in D Minor.

Carl Czerny

Editions of Bach's clavier works had begun to appear in 1801, when *The Well-Tempered Clavier* was issued simultaneously in Zürich, Bonn, and Leipzig, and soon a modest first attempt at a complete edition of the clavier works was made. This was accompanied by the publication of Forkel's biography, which became one of the great forces within the Bach movement. The vocal works followed slowly. The motets were brought out in 1802–3; the Magnificat and the Ode of Mourning, hardly noticed, in the 1810s. The copies of the first cantata published after Bach's death (1821) became, as Zelter sarcastically remarked, so much wastepaper. A publication of the B Minor Mass was announced in 1818, but it took two publishers to fulfill the promise, and the task was not finished until 1845.

All these editions simply—although not always quite accurately—reproduced Bach's original text. In 1821, however, there appeared an edition of the *Chromatic Fantasy* provided by Friedrich Conrad Griepenkerl with "an indication of its true interpretation as it was handed down from J. S. Bach to W. Friedemann Bach, from him to Forkel, and from Forkel to his pupils." The markings in this edition are modest and fairly sensible, but the very fact that a work by Bach had been released in an "edited" form had wide repercussions. In the 1830s a complete edition of Bach's "piano" music was put on the market, "enriched by the addition of the fingering, where necessary, the proper marks of expression and style, and the exact time of each movement (according to Maelzel's metronome)." The first volume, edited by Carl Czerny, contained *The Well-Tempered Clavier.* Czerny, who had been Beethoven's pupil from 1800 to 1803 and the teacher of Beethoven's nephew Karl from 1816 to 1818, explained, "We have indicated the time and style (1) from a consideration of the unmistakable character of each movement; (2) from a vivid recollection of the manner in which we have heard many of the fugues played by the great Beethoven; and (3) lastly, by profiting from the ideas that we have gained during more than 30 years' patient study of this incomparable work."[8] There is no reason to doubt Czerny's claim that he based his editing on his memory of Beethoven's interpretation. In Beethoven's conception of music, dynamics were of primary importance, and it is altogether likely that he played Bach's works with crescendos and diminuen-

---

8. *Le clavecin bien tempéré par Jean Sebastien Bach,* vol. 1 of *Oeuvres complets* (Leipzig: C. F. Peters [1837]), and the first English reprint, *C. Czerny's New Edition of John Sebastian Bach's "48 Preludes and 48 Fugues" for the Piano Forte, or Organ* (London: R. Cocks, 1838).

dos such as he used in his own. Czerny's edition may reflect in detail the pedantry of the étude writer rather than the spontaneity of a congenial interpreter, but apparently it was Beethoven who had shown the way toward an "effective" presentation of *The Well-Tempered Clavier*—a presentation that must have been a deliberate dramatization.

Friedrich Rochlitz

Among the writers who furthered the cause of Bach in Germany, Friedrich Rochlitz (1769–1842) was, next to Forkel, the most influential. For twenty years, beginning in 1798, Rochlitz edited the newly founded *Allgemeine Musikalische Zeitung* of Leipzig. Gifted, earnest, incorruptible, he fought for the recognition of Beethoven as eagerly as for a deeper and more general understanding of Bach. In the long-winded, leisurely style of his day, he describes how he himself struggled for a grasp of Bach's polyphony. As a student at the St. Thomas School, during the cantorate of Johann Friedrich Doles (Harrer's successor), he had been forced to sing in Bach's motets and, frightened by their difficulty, had been able to view them only from the viewpoint of an anxious participant in their performance. After Mozart's visit, Rochlitz made for himself a collection of works by Bach, but he still felt at a loss before them. When the magazine was entrusted to him, he set out again to conquer these works. He turned to the chorales, then to Handel's simpler polyphony—he later recommended Bach's own little preludes instead—and then to *The Well-Tempered Clavier*. He marked the pieces that appealed to him without particular intellectual effort, and thus, finally, one by one they opened up before him.

Samuel Wesley and Carl Friedrich Horn

Equally insistent but far more eloquent were the endeavors of Samuel Wesley (1766–1837) to introduce Bach into England. A nephew of John Wesley, he was considered one of the most brilliant organists of his time. His own efforts on behalf of Bach had been foreshadowed by Kollmann's, and they were paralleled by those of Carl Friedrich Horn (1762–1830) and Benjamin Jacob (1778–1829).

Horn, who was born in Nordhausen, had studied with Schröter and had come to England in 1782. A protégé of Count von Brühl (who was then serving as Saxon ambassador), he became music master to the queen, succeeding Johann Christian Bach. He edited works by Bach in arrangements for string quartet and for piano (three hands). Jacob served from 1794 to 1825 as organist of Surrey Chapel, which was built octagonally so that "the devil should not occupy any corners." In 1808 he introduced "organ exhibitions" at his chapel. They began at eleven o'clock in the morning, lasted for four hours, and were attended by up to 5,000 persons. Jacob was occasionally joined in performance by Wesley, who also played the violin, or by the violinist Johann Peter Salomon, who had introduced Haydn to the English public. In the programs Bach's works were given a prominent place.

Wesley's letters to Jacob—unfortunately Jacob's answers are not preserved—express most vividly the spirit that carried the Bach movement to success.[9] They are devoted in large part to discussion of the conversion of Dr. Charles Burney (1726–1814). Though Burney had a breadth of knowledge and experience that few of his contemporaries could equal, he held Bach in only moderate esteem. In an article on Bach for Abraham Rees's *Cyclopaedia*[10] (which began to appear in 1802), he restated opinions previously expressed in his *General History of Music* (1789)—opinions that could not help provoking the Bach enthusiasts:

Sebastian Bach is said by Marpurg, in his *Art de la Fugue* [sic] to have been "many great musicians in one, profound in science, fertile in fancy, and in taste easy and natural"; he should rather have said *original and refined,* for to the epithets easy and natural many are unwilling to assent, as this truly great man seems by his works for the organ to have been constantly in search of what was new and difficult, without the least attention to nature and facility.

Wesley's first letter to Jacob, of September 17, 1808, tells how he first made the old doctor, who was still a man of great influence, aware of Bach's true stature:

DEAR SIR,

I am much obliged by your ingenious and circumstantial Detail of your success with *Saint* Sebastian, as you very properly term him, and am rejoiced to find that you are likely to regard his Works with me as a musical Bible unrivaled and inimitable.

I am grieved to witness in my valuable Friend Doctor Burney's Critique (for he is a man whom I equally respect and love), so slight an acquaintance with the great and matchless Genius whom he professes to analyze: and I have however much satisfaction in being able to assure you, *from my own personal experience,* that his present judgment of our Demi-God is of a very different Nature from that at the Time he imprudently, incautiously, and we may add, *ignorantly* pronounced so rash and false a verdict (although a false Verdict is a contradiction in Terms), as that which I this

---

9. *Letters of Samuel Wesley to Mr. Jacobs* [sic], ed. Eliza Wesley, 2nd ed. (London, 1878).
10. The article also describes an alleged meeting between Bach and Handel at Salzburg. The *General History* does not contain this item, but includes an equally false story (No. 399). The article on Carl Philipp Emanuel Bach in the *Cyclopaedia* contains Abel's remarks on the compositional styles of Bach and C. P. E. Bach (No. 368).

Day read for the first Time upon "the greatest Master of Harmony in any Age or Country."

It is now I think nearly a twelvemonth since I wrote to the Doctor respecting my profound admiration (and Adoration if you like it as well) of Sebastian: I stated to him that I had made a Study of his Preludes and Fugues, adding that his compositions had opened to me an entirely new musical World, which was to me at least as surprising as (when a child) I was thunderstruck by the opening of the *Dettingen Te Deum* [by Handel] at the Bristol Cathedral with about an hundred Performers (a great Band in those Days). I went into something like a general Description of what I conceived to be his characteristic Beauties, and particularly specified *Air* as one of the chief and most striking. I have by me the Doctor's reply to my letter, although I cannot at the present moment advert to it, but I fully remember his observing in nearly the following Words: "In order to be consistent with myself with regard to the great Sebastian Bach, before I precisely coincide with you, I must refer to what I have written at various Times and in various Places of my History, Travels, &c., in which I had occasion to mention him; but I shall feel exceedingly gratified in hearing his elaborate and erudite Compositions performed by you (for I never yet *heard* any one of them), and can tell you that I have a very curious and beautiful Copy of *his Fugues,* which was presented to me many years since by his Son Emanuel, and which I shall have much pleasure in showing you."

When I waited on my venerable Friend he had been kind enough to previously lay upon his Music Desk, the MS. in question (together with several other beautiful and superb Works of our immortal Master); but when I came to examine this said rare Present, how much was I surprised to find it so full of *scriptural* Faults, that it was not without some Difficulty I could manage to do justice to one of the Fugues which I had been formerly the most familiar with; and although I did not *boggle,* yet I played with extreme Discomfort. My Friend, however, was extremely delighted, and the very first Part of his Critique expressed his Wonder *how such abstruse harmony* and such perfect and enchanting melody could have been so marvellously united!

What a convincing Proof this is, that his *former* criticism upon our matchless Author was an hasty and improvident Step!

I conceive that the Fact stands thus: When Burney was in Germany, the universal Plaudits and Panegyricks upon the Father of *universal Harmony* were so interesting that it would have been impossible for him to have avoided giving such a Man a Place in his Account of Musical Authors in his *General History:* Nevertheless it appears very evident from the erroneous Sentence he has pronounced therein upon the Comparative Merit of him and Handel that he never could have taken due Pains to make himself Master of the Subject, otherwise his late candid acknowledgment would not have been made, and is proof sufficient that he only wanted *experience* of the *Truth* to make him ready and willing to own it.

I must also tell you another Piece of News;—namely that this imperfect and incorrect volume, this *valuable* and inestimable Gift of Sebastian's dutiful Son, happens to contain only the 24 *first* Preludes and Fugues; all written in the Soprano Clef (to make them more easily understood, I suppose), and the Preludes so miserably mangled and mutilated that had I not met them in such a collection as that of the learned and highly illuminated Doctor Burney, I verily believe that I should have exclaimed, "An Enemy hath done this." I should have at once concluded that such a manuscript could have been made only by him who was determined to disgrace instead of promote the cause of correct Harmony.

Ever since I had the privilege of so great a triumph (for I can call it nought else) over the Doctor's Prejudice, he has evinced the most cordial veneration for our Sacred Musician, and when I told him that I was in Possession of 24 *more* such precious Relicks, he was all aghast in finding that there could be any Productions of such a Nature which he had not seen: this again is another proof of his having hastily judged, and also how remiss the Germans must have been not to have made him better acquainted with the Works of their transcendant Countryman.

I am told by the Rev. Mr. Picart (one of the Canons of Hereford Cathedral) that Seb. B. has written Pieces for *three* Organs, and innumerable others, which are not sent to England purely from the contempt which the Germans entertain of the general state of Music in this Country, and which unfavorable sentiment I am sorry to say has but too much foundation on the Truth.

You see that there are others who have as much cause to apologize for the length of Letters as you, if apology were at all necessary among Friends; but yours which I this Day received has given me so much real satisfaction, as I fully trust that you are determined to defend the cause of Truth and Sebastian (for they are one) against all the frivolous objections of Ignorance, and the transparent Cavils of Envy, that I safely rely upon you as one of my right-hand men against all the prejudiced Handelians. It has been said that Comparisons are odious; but without Comparison, where is Discrimination? and without Discrimination, how are we to attain a just judgment? Let us always weigh fairly as far as human Powers will allow, and endeavor to divest ourselves of the Propensity which leads us either to idolize or execrate whatever we have been unfortunately habituated so to do without previous and due examination.

I feel great gratification in having been *accessory* to your study of Sebastian: I knew that you had only to know him to love and adore him and I sincerely assure you that in meeting so true an Enthusiast in so good a Cause (and depend on it that nothing very good or very great is done without enthusiasm), I experience a warmth of Heart which only enthusiasts know or can value.

That our *Friendship* may long continue, either with or without enthusiasm (tho' I think a spice of it even there no bad thing), believe me, is the very cordial wish of,

Dear Sir, Yours very faithfully,
S. WESLEY

A month later, Wesley speaks of having met Horn, a man "longing to find some spirited enthusiasts like himself to co-operate in bringing the Musical World to Reason and Common Sense, and to extort a Confession of the true State of the Case against the Prepossession, Prejudice, Envy, and Ignorance of all Anti-Bachists." He continues,

We are (in the first place) preparing for the Press an authentic and accurate Life of Sebastian, which Mr. Stephenson the Banker (a most zealous and scientific member of our Fraternity) has translated into English from the German of Forkel, and wherein is a list of *all* the Works of our Apollo.

This we propose to publish by subscription as a preparatory measure to editing the Fugues, and which will naturally cause a Considerable Sensation, not only in the Musical but also in the Literary World. . . .

It appears by the Life of Sebastian, he was not only the greatest Master in the World, but also one of the most worthy and amiable Characters that ever adorned Society. I remember often exclaiming when working at him, "I am sure that none but a *good* man could have written thus"; and you perceive that my conjecture was accurate.

Mr. Horn has a vast quantity of his Compositions that have never seen the light; among the rest, Stupendous Trios for the Organ, which he used to play thus: his right hand played the first part on the Top Row of the Clavier; his left the second Part on the second Row, and he played the Bass *wholly* upon the Pedals. There are Allegro Movements among them, and occasionally very brisk notes in the Bass Part, whence it appears that he was alike dexterous both with hands and feet.

Horn has a further Design than the mere Publication of our 48 Preludes and Fugues; he wishes to extend the Work to a Complete Edition of all his Compositions that are to be found; and if God spare our Health, why should we despair of presenting the world with "all these Treasures of Wisdom and Knowledge"?

He is as indefatigable as yourself, and has written with his own hand whole centuries of Pages which would amaze you. He has not only transcribed all the 48 Preludes and Fugues, but also written them on paper ruled for the purpose, capacious enough to contain an *entire Fugue,* however long, upon two pages only, thus avoiding the Inconvenience of turning over, for which there is hereby no necessity even from the beginning of the Work to the end.

The book (which forms Part VI of this volume) was announced in 1808, but it was not published until 1820. In later letters, Wesley further suggested the foundation of a Bach society (which did not materialize); the publication of the organ trios (which actually took place); and the publication of the Credo from the B Minor Mass on subscription (for which the number of subscribers proved insufficient). The plan of publishing *The Well-Tempered Clavier* was realized in installments beginning in 1810. This edition, which followed the sound principle of suggesting an adequate interpretation by analytical marks rather than dynamic differentiation, was prefaced by an instructive introduction signed by Wesley and Horn, but presumably written by the former:

It seems to be with some stupendous Works of Art, as with those of Nature: the Surprise and Admiration they excite render Praise not only superfluous, but also show it inadequate to the Subject producing them.

Among such Instances we conceive the following Pieces of Harmony to be meritoriously enumerated.

The 48 Preludes and Fugues, the first 12 of which are here presented to the Musical World (in a more correct manner than they have ever yet appeared, even in the Country where they were constructed) have always been regarded by the most scientific among scientific Musicians (the Germans) as matchless Productions.

These introductory Remarks are not designed as a Panegyric upon Compositions which have perpetually delighted the candid Lover of Truth, Science, Taste, and Expression, and even extorted the Approbation of those whose Prejudices had formerly superseded their better Judgment.

Too many there are who illiberally confine their notions of musical Excellence to the Compositions of one Country only (and even still more absurdly to one Composer). As our Acquaintance with the Excellence to be found (more or less) in all Countries becomes more extended, these narrow and ill-founded Prepossessions will necessarily diminish, until we may reasonably hope they will be finally exterminated.

The chief Intention of this prefatory Address is to recommend and explain the most eligible Method of studying and practicing these immortal Exercises, for the Advancement of all who are desirous of forming a perfect and symmetrical Style of Counterpoint, and of manual Execution on the Organ, Piano Forte, or Harpsichord, both which Purposes they will soon be found amply to answer.

Towards a solid and permanent Improvement in musical Composition, we recommend as the best Method, to set the following Fugues in Score. This must be done attentively and carefully, and will not be found a Task of much Difficulty, when it is remembered that the Number of Parts in which every one is composed is previously expressed at the Head of the Page commencing each Fugue, from those in two Parts to those in five; therefore the Student has only to peruse the said Notices (whether of two, three, four, or five Parts) and he will then be able readily to arrange them on ruled Paper, in their proper Number and Order.

Moreover, great Advantage will be hence derived to those desirous of perfecting themselves in the Viola Clef (placed upon the third Line) and consequently the Method proposed will become eminently useful to those Performers who study the Tenor Violin in Instrumental Quartettos; a Species of Music at present much, and most deservedly, cultivated and encouraged among us.

Musical Students whose principal Aim may be only to execute these Pieces on a keyed Instrument are earnestly admonished to begin their Practice upon those which are the least complicated, for Example, the first Prelude (omitting the Fugue following it), the second Prelude with the Fugue, the fifth Prelude and Fugue, the sixth, ninth, and eleventh of both; and by the Time these are mastered, they will be enabled and well qualified to venture upon any remaining among the twelve. We however recommend the third Prelude and Fugue, and the eighth and twelfth, among the last to be attempted, because they are set in Keys less in Use in England than upon the Continent, and therefore are at first puzzling, and require a constant and persevering Application.

The daily Practice of the Diatonic Scale throughout all the Keys, Major & Minor, will also be found a powerful Assistance towards the correct Performance of the more abstruse Passages.

One most essential Advice must be added, that whoever determines upon executing the following Pages with Precision must steadily resolve upon practicing them at first in very slow Time, for since there is not a single Note among them that can be omitted, without a material Injury to their Effect, it is absolutely indispensable thoroughly to understand the Career of the whole Modulation, which will not be possible unless each Bar be studied with that patient Industry which shall secure the true Position of every Finger upon its designed Key. This certainly is attainable by no other Means whatever than practicing at an exceedingly slow Pace, until the Fingers shall have (as it were mechanically) found their exact Places on the Clavier, which by constant careful Habit they surely will, with hardly a Probability of any Failure. And as soon as the Student can play one of the Pieces set in five or six Sharps, or as many Flats, without the Necessity of looking at his Fingers in order to hit the true Distances, he may securely venture to increase the Speed of his March (although only by slow Degrees) and he will gradually arrive at the true Time of performing those Movements which require a brisk Execution.

The present Edition is characterized not only by Clearness and Precision in the Text and the Manner of engraving it, but also by Annotations, explanatory of the several ingenious and surprising Contrivances in the Treatment of the Subject throughout all the Fugues.

The following Marks are employed for the aforesaid Purpose:

Λ points out the Subject in its direct Ratio, or in its natural Order in the Scale of Intervals chosen for it.

V denotes the contrary, and that the Subject is inverted at the Interval where this Mark is applied.

Λ Ʌ Ʌ these show that either the first, second, or third Subject (if so many are employed) are repeated in direct Ratio.

V Ʋ Ʋ denote the contrary, as in the Explanation of the second Mark above.

◻ shows that the Subject is diminished in its Measure, by one Half, or repeated in Intervals as quick again as at first.

⇓ means that the Subject is diminished and inverted at the same Time.

▭ shows that the Subject is augmented in double Ratio, or that it is repeated in Intervals just as slow again as before.

The Utility of these Notices must be obvious to every attentive Observer, and materially enhance the public Estimation of our present Edition; this first Specimen of which, we hope and trust, will be found in all Respects satisfactory to those Lovers of Sublime and Beautiful Music who have honored it with their Names and Support.[11]

S. WESLEY   C. F. HORN

---

11. *S. Wesley and C. F. Horn's New and Correct Edition of the Preludes and Fugues of John Sebastian Bach* (London, 1810–13), introd.

Johann Wolfgang von Goethe and Carl Friedrich Zelter

Among those who were introduced to Bach in the early 1800s was Johann Wolfgang von Goethe (1749–1832). Universality of knowledge being one of his highest goals, he cultivated all the arts, including music, for which he had no creative talent. In December 1818 he spent three weeks at Berka, a modest spa, in order to write the poems for a pageant. Johann Heinrich Friedrich Schütz (1779–1829), inspector of the baths there and an enthusiastic organist who had been a student of Johann Christian Kittel, played daily for Goethe from three to four hours and, at his request, selections from Bach to Beethoven in historical order. Years later, on June 21, 1827, Goethe described his impressions:

Of course, at this juncture, I thought of the worthy organist of Berka; for it was there, when my mind was in a state of perfect composure and free from external distraction, that I first obtained some idea of your grand master. I said to myself, it is as if the eternal harmony were conversing within itself, as it may have done in the bosom of God just before the Creation of the world. So likewise did it move in my inmost soul, and it seemed as if I neither possessed nor needed ears, nor any other sense—least of all, the eyes.[12]

Goethe acknowledged the information and pleasure the inspector had afforded him by the gift of a copy of the chorales and *The Well-Tempered Clavier,* into which he wrote some dedicatory verses.

In his study of music, Goethe realized that he needed expert guidance, and this he evidently hoped to receive from Carl Friedrich Zelter (1758–1832). Zelter, the son of a mason, had started out as a mason himself, but he assiduously studied music and became one of the leading personalities in the musical life of Berlin. He was the conductor of a well-trained chorus, which met at the Royal Academy and was therefore called the Singakademie. Zelter helped to propagate Bach's music, which he ardently admired; in his correspondence with Goethe the name of Bach occurs often enough, although Zelter could not back up his enthusiasm by extended historical knowledge or a particularly deep understanding of Bach's works. Modestly enough, he quotes a remark that he attributes on one occasion to Wilhelm Friedemann and on another to Carl Philipp Emanuel: "Compared with him, we all remain children." He calls Bach "one of God's phenomena, clear, but unfathomable." And yet his reverence did not prevent him from tampering with Bach's works (letter to Goethe, April 8, 1827):

12. F. W. Riemer, ed., *Briefwechsel zwischen Goethe und Zelter,* 6 vols. (Berlin, 1833–34); trans. A. D. Coleridge (1887).

Old Bach, with all his originality, is a son of his country and of his age, and could not escape French influence, especially that of Couperin. One wants to show one's willingness to oblige, and so one writes only for the moment. We can, however, dissociate him from this foreign element; it comes off like thin froth and the shining contents lie immediately beneath. Consequently, I have arranged many of his church compositions, solely for my own pleasure, and my heart tells me that old Bach nods approval, just as the worthy Haydn used to say, "Yes, yes, that was what I wished!"

Felix Mendelssohn Bartholdy

Zelter occasionally performed a motet by Bach with the Berlin Singakademie, and he studied various cantatas with a smaller group in his own house. It was here that Felix Mendelssohn Bartholdy was first introduced to Bach. How the plan to perform the *St. Matthew Passion* was conceived and carried out is told, in the second section of this part, in the words of a participant. Among those who owed their recognition of Bach's greatness to the performance of the *St. Matthew Passion* was Friedrich Wilhelm Hegel (1770–1831). In his lectures on aesthetics—a course Mendelssohn himself had taken— Hegel in later years spoke of Bach's "grand, truly Protestant, robust, and, so to speak, erudite genius which we have only recently learned again to appreciate at its full value."[13]

Immediately after the first performances of the *St. Matthew Passion,* Mendelssohn began the years of travel that took him to England, Italy, and France. On his way to Italy, he visited Goethe. He described the visit in a letter to Zelter, dated Munich, June 22, 1830:

I often had to play for Goethe in the morning. He wanted to have an idea of how music had developed, and therefore asked to hear things by various composers in the order in which they followed one another. He was not anxious to hear Beethoven, but I could not spare him that, since he wished to know "what turn the language of tones had taken" now, and I played him the first movement of the C Minor Symphony, which appealed to him very much. In the Overture by Seb. Bach in D Major, with the trumpets, which I played to him on the piano as well as I could, he had great pleasure. The beginning was so pompous and aristocratic, he said, that one could really see a procession of elegantly dressed people proceeding down a great staircase. I also played him the Inventions and much of *The Well-Tempered Clavier.*

One noon he asked whether I did not want to greet a colleague and go over to the organist's, so that he could let me see and hear the organ in the Town Church. . . . When I was asked to play something, I let loose with the D Minor Toccata by Sebastian, remarking that this was both learned and for the people, that is, for some people. But behold! hardly had I started to play when the superintendent sent his

---

13. Hegel, *Ästhetik* (Berlin, 1838), vol. 3, p. 208. The author having died in 1831, the book was published largely from students' notebooks.

servant to say that the organ playing should stop at once, since it was a weekday and the noise prevented him from studying. Goethe was very much amused at the tale.[14]

In 1835 Mendelssohn accepted the post of conductor of the Gewandhaus Orchestra of Leipzig. Remaining in this position until the year of his death (1847), he worked zealously and successfully for the cause of Bach. In 1840 the *St. Matthew Passion,* under his baton, returned to the Church of St. Thomas, where it had first been presented by Bach.

Robert Schumann

At Leipzig, Mendelssohn was steadily and efficiently seconded by his friend Robert Schumann, an active journalist as well as a musician. To break a lance for young composers, Schumann founded, in 1834, the *Neue Zeitschrift für Musik.* His first published article introduced Chopin; his last, Brahms. He had, at the same time, the greatest esteem for music of the past. "Do not think," he wrote, "that old music is outmoded. Just as a beautiful true word can never be outmoded, so a beautiful piece of true music." He possessed, in particular, a deep comprehension of what he called Bach's "boldly labyrinthine style." Among his works were a keyboard accompaniment to Bach's sonatas for violin alone—Mendelssohn likewise wrote an accompaniment to the Chaconne—and a magnificent set of six Fugues on B A C H for the *Pedalklavier* (a pianoforte with a sounding pedal keyboard), op. 60 (1845). At a time when Bach's stature had not been fully recognized, Schumann, by invoking the name of Bach again and again, helped gain for Bach's work a secure place in the minds of educated musicians.

Schumann's "Maxims for Home and Life" *(Haus-und Lebensregeln)* contain this oft-quoted advice: "Play conscientiously the fugues of good masters, above all those of Johann Sebastian Bach. Let *The Well-Tempered Clavier* be your daily bread. Then you will certainly become a solid musician." What is less widely known is that Schumann fervently advocated the erection of a Bach monument and the preparation of a complete edition of Bach's works. He was deeply disturbed when he found that Bach's grave in Leipzig was not marked; and when Mendelssohn gave an organ concert to raise funds for the memorial slab, Schumann wrote the following review, which gives us an insight into his feeling for this music:

Would that I could record last evening in these pages with golden letters! It was, for a change, a concert for men, a complete whole from beginning to end. Again I thought how we are never at an end with Bach, how he seems to grow more profound

14. Mendelssohn, *Briefe aus den Jahren 1830 bis 1847,* ed. Paul and Carl Mendelssohn Bartholdy, 4th ed. (Leipzig, 1878), pp. 12–13.

the oftener he is heard. Zelter, and afterward Marx, wrote excellent and striking things concerning him; and yet, while we listen, it would seem again as if we could only distantly approach him through the understanding of words. The music itself still serves as the best means to bring his works before our senses and to explain them; and whom can we expect to accomplish this more warmly and faithfully than the artist who accomplished it yesterday?—who has devoted the greatest part of his life to this very master, who was the first to refresh, with the full power of his own enthusiasm, the memory of Bach in Germany, and who now gives the first impulse toward bringing Bach's image nearer the eyes of our contemporaries by an outward image?

A hundred years have passed without anyone else's attempting this; shall, perhaps, another hundred pass before it is realized? It is not our intention to beg for a Bach memorial by means of a formal appeal; those of Mozart and Beethoven are not yet ready, and probably they will still have to wait some time. But the idea that has emanated from here should be taken as a suggestive one, especially in Berlin and Breslau, which cities have lately won particular honor by the performance of works by Bach, and where there must be many people who know what is owed by art itself to Bach; this is, in the small sphere of music, hardly less than what a religion owes to its founder. In the circular announcing the concert, Mendelssohn expresses himself clearly and simply on this subject:

"As yet, no outward symbol testifies to the living memory, in Leipzig, of the greatest artist this city ever possessed. One of his successors [J. A. Hiller] has already been given the honor of a memorial in the vicinity of the St. Thomas School—which should have been bestowed on Bach above all. However, since in these days his spirit and his works are coming to the fore with new strength, and the interest in them can never become extinguished in the hearts of the true friends of music, it is hoped that such an undertaking will meet with sympathy and assistance from the inhabitants of Leipzig," etc., etc.[15]

As might have been expected, the beginning of this undertaking, led by such an artist's hand, was a worthy one, and its success richly supported the purpose. How well Mendelssohn understands the treatment of Bach's royal instrument is generally known; and yesterday he laid before us nothing but precious jewels, in the most glorious variety and gradation, which he only prefaced, as it were, at the beginning, and concluded with a fantasy of his own. After a short introduction, he played a very splendid Fugue in E-flat Major, containing three ideas, one built upon the other; then a Fantasy on the Chorale "Deck Thyself, Beloved Soul," as priceless, deep, and full of soul as any piece of music that ever sprang from a true artist's imagination; then a grandly brilliant Prelude and Fugue in A Minor, both very difficult, even for

15. The monument was dedicated on April 23, 1843. Among those who attended was the last male descendant of Johann Sebastian—Wilhelm Friedrich Ernst Bach (1759–1845), a son of Johann Christoph Friedrich. He had been a pupil of his father and then of his uncle Johann Christian in London. At the height of a successful career, he had held the post of capellmeister to Queen Louise, and later received a life pension, which assured him of an existence free from care.

a master of organ playing. After a pause, these were followed by the Passacaille in C Minor (with 21 variations, intertwined so ingeniously that one can never cease to be amazed) admirably handled in the choice of registers by Mendelssohn; then a Pastorella in F Major, mined from the deepest depths in which such a composition may be found; which was followed by a Toccata in A Minor with a Prelude typical of Bach's sense of humor. Mendelssohn ended with a fantasy of his own, in which, then, he showed himself in the full glory of his artistry; it was based on a chorale (if I am not mistaken, with the text "O Sacred Head, now wounded"), into which he afterward wove the name B A C H and a fugued movement—the entire fantasy was rounded out into such a clear and masterly whole that, if printed, it would appear a finished work of art.

A fine summer evening shone through the church windows; even outside, in the open air, many may have reflected on the wonderful sounds, thinking that there is nothing greater in music than the enjoyment of the twofold mastery displayed when one master expresses the other. Fame and honor to old and to young alike!

A performance by Mendelssohn of the D Minor Clavier Concerto, in 1837, prompted Schumann to ask,

Will it be believed that in the music cabinets of the Berlin Singakademie, to which old Zelter bequeathed his library, at least seven such Concertos and countless additional compositions, in manuscript, are carefully preserved? Few persons know about it, but there they are for sure. Altogether, would it not be a timely and useful undertaking, if the German Nation decided to publish a *complete* collection and edition of *all* the works of Bach? One might think so, and one could use the words of an expert, who speaks about this plan on page 76 of the current volume of the *Neue Zeitschrift,* as a motto. For there you can read:

"That you want to publish Sebastian Bach's works delights my heart, which beats wholly for the great and lofty art of this father of harmony, and I wish soon to see the enterprise in full swing."

Just look it up.[16]

The Bach-Gesellschaft

In 1850 the Bach-Gesellschaft was founded by Moritz Hauptmann, cantor at St. Thomas's and professor at the Leipzig Conservatory; Otto Jahn, professor of classical philology at Leipzig University and author of the first scholarly Mozart biography; Carl Ferdinand Becker, organist at St. Nicholas's, music historian and teacher at the Leipzig Conservatory, and compiler of valuable bibliographical works; and Robert Schumann, music director in

16. Schumann, *Gesammelte Schriften über Musik und Musiker,* 5th ed., ed. Martin Kreisig (Leipzig, 1914); the translation is based in part on that by Fanny Raymond Ritter (1877 and 1881). The concluding quotation is from Beethoven's letter to Hoffmeister of January 15 (?), 1801.

Düsseldorf. It included some of the most famous and influential public figures in the musical life of that time: Siegfried Wilhelm Dehn (curator of the music collection in the Berlin Royal Library), Hermann Härtel (managing director of the music publisher Breitkopf & Härtel in Leipzig), Franz Liszt (court capellmeister in Weimar), Ignaz Moscheles (professor at the Leipzig Conservatory), Johann Theodor Mosewius (music director in Breslau), Louis Spohr (court capellmeister in Kassel), and Carl von Winterfeld (member of the Prussian Academy of Arts and music historian in Berlin). The aim of the society was the publication of Bach's complete works, without editorial additions. Wilhelm Rust (1822–1892), who served as editor-in-chief beginning in 1853 and who himself contributed no fewer than 26 volumes to the ambitious project, set the exemplary philological standards that provided a model for virtually all musicological editions to come. The Bach-Gesellschaft edition—completed in 1900 with the appearance of the forty-sixth volume—established the basis for an immeasurably more comprehensive and thorough study of Bach than had previously been possible.

Hector Berlioz and Friedrich Nietzsche

With the foundation of the Bach-Gesellschaft the battle for Bach was fairly won. Nevertheless, a few dissenting voices were still heard. Hector Berlioz, for one, never conceded the greatness of Bach. When he heard a concerto for three claviers played by Chopin, Liszt, and Hiller, he commented, "It was heart-rending, I assure you, to see three such admirable talents, full of fire, brilliant in youthful vitality, united in a bundle to reproduce this ridiculous and stupid psalmody." And of a performance of another concerto by some Russian artists he remarked, "I do not think they meant to annoy me."[17] Friedrich Nietzsche, too, could not resist referring to Bach in a thoroughly unorthodox way: "In Bach there is too much crude Christianity, or Germanism, crude scholasticism. He stands at the threshold of modern European music, but he is always looking back toward the Middle Ages."[18]

Richard Wagner

What endangered the Bach movement more seriously than dissent was Romantic distortion. The Romanticists, from Weber onward, failed or refused to see Bach in his relations to forebears and contemporaries. Bach was idolized as if he had created music out of chaos, and such notions, given

---

17. Berlioz, quoted in W. J. Turner, *Berlioz* (London, 1934), and J. H. Elliott, *Berlioz* (London and New York, 1938).
18. Nietzsche, *Menschliches, Allzumenschliches* (1878), vol. 2, pt. 2, § 149, in *Nietzsche's Werke* (Leipzig, 1906), vol. 3.

wide currency at one time, have continued to prevail. An effusion of Richard Wagner's (1865) shows how the picture of Bach's background (and so of Bach himself) was twisted:

> Let anyone who wishes to grasp the wonderful individuality, power, and signifi-cance of the German spirit in an incomparably eloquent image but look keenly and thoughtfully at the otherwise almost unexplainably puzzling phenomenon of the musical miracle man Sebastian Bach. He is in himself the history of the German spirit through that horrible century during which the light of the German people was completely extinguished. Look then upon this head, disguised in its absurd French full-bottomed wig, this master—a wretched cantor and organist wandering from one little Thuringian village to another, hardly known even by name, dragging out his existence in miserably paid posts, remaining so unknown that it took a whole century for his works to be retrieved from oblivion; even in music finding an art form already in existence that was externally the perfect picture of its time—dry, stiff, pedantic, like a wig and pigtail portrayed in notes. And now see what a world the inconceivably great Sebastian constructed out of these elements! To these cre-ations I only refer, for it is impossible to characterize their riches, their loftiness and all-comprehending significance by any comparison whatsoever.[19]

Philipp Spitta

Romantic imagination, however, finally gave way to a more scholarly approach. In 1873 and 1880 there appeared Philipp Spitta's *J. S. Bach*—the biography that described, for the first time, the whole scope and import of Bach's work in an objective and historically sound manner. The industry with which Spitta gathered his materials was matched by his deep insight into Bach's personality and works. What becomes more and more remarkable as time goes on is the extent to which he exhausted the material available to him, which represented by far the larger part of what is available today. He was proud, it is true, to be a Romantic, and to a certain extent he could not help seeing Bach through the eyes of his time. But the following summation, taken from an essay of 1879, not part of the biography, shows how much truth he was able to convey even in the expression of his most personal and dated opinion:

> Vocal and instrumental or poetic and pure—these are the poles by whose powers of attraction and repulsion the development of music is kept in a state of flux. When both appear in the same person, his actions must bear witness to the liveliest mutual interpenetration of their influences. A constant passing from one domain to another

19. Wagner, *Was ist deutsch?* (1865–78), in *Gesammelte Schriften und Dichtungen von Richard Wagner* (Leipzig, 1871–83), vol. 10, pp. 51ff.

is a striking element in Bach's artistic character. Now the content of ideas sways the balance toward the poetic side, as in the organ chorale, and creates vocal pieces based on chorales; now the free vocal pieces in the cantatas, Passions, oratorios, and Masses lean far toward the domain of pure music, and seek to float the words on the musical stream. But always these two tendencies combine to form an indissoluble unity. This mixture is what makes it possible to call Bach a Romantic in the highest sense; and this is, finally, the trait of affinity that irresistibly leads the art world of our time toward him and gives us the firmest grounds for hoping that we shall see a far-reaching revival of his works.[20]

What Philipp Spitta well over a century ago had hoped for has long come true. In fact, from the perspective of the late twentieth century, one may well speak of the omnipresence of Bach's music in musical life. The complete works of Bach are almost everywhere and practically at all times available in print, in live performance, and in recorded sound. Yet, no matter in what style they are performed, or from what point of view they are studied, the works of Bach represent a standard of perfection and vitality that is not likely to be lost again: the further we climb in our own musical education, the higher the mountain of Bach's music thrusts its peak into the sky.

THE FIRST EDITION OF THE MASS IN
B MINOR, BWV 232

410. Hans Georg Nägeli's subscription announcement of the first edition of Bach's B Minor Mass (June 1818)
(*NBA* II / 1, Krit. Bericht, p. 215)

ANNOUNCEMENT
of the Greatest Work of Art
of All Times and Nations

The incomparably great Johann Sebastian Bach has now, in our own time, been accorded a degree of recognition that makes it possible to proceed toward the publication of the work that, in content and length alone, but above all in grandeur, style, and wealth of invention, surpasses his works hitherto printed, to the same extent that these, without considering the vicissitudes of taste and the contingency of art forms, surpass those by all other composers. This is a

---

20. Spitta, *Über Johann Sebastian Bach,* Sammlung musikalischer Vorträge, 1 (Leipzig, 1879), p. 58.

Mass in five voices with full orchestra,

of which I bought, some time ago, through the good offices of Music Director Schwenke in Hamburg, the autograph from the estate of his son C. P. E. Bach. A discussion of its contents can here amount to no more than a suggestion. Just a few words! As regards its technique, it contains within its twenty-seven spacious numbers all manners of the art of counterpoint and canon in that degree of perfection always admired in Bach's work. The instrumentation, too, and even the art of interlude are advanced to such an extent as to inspire astonishment. From the point of view of aesthetic judgment, it may suffice to refer to the Credo, praised as "the masterpiece of the Greatest of all harmonists" in Ebeling's "In Praise of Harmony." . . . This Credo (even its first extensive movement on the words *Credo in unum deum*) is truly the most amazing piece of music in existence. The difficult task so often discussed by the judges of art in his day and ours—how the church composer is to deal with the Credo—is here resolved in an ageless paradigm, as the immediate awakening of the powers of faith through the wondrous force of music.

This work, which should not be absent from any collection of sacred music, from the holdings of any choir school, from any library of scores at all—equally important to the organist, performer of fugues, scholar, and composer—should be recommended to the interest of great and affluent patrons, so that through them it might come into the hands of worthy artists and devotees of the art. It would be of the greatest benefit for their artistic knowledge to obtain such an extraordinary treasure, comparable to that of a journey to Rome for the aspiring student of the graphic arts.

The subscription price is 8 Saxon thaler, most reasonable, since in number of leaves this work is the largest of printed scores, exceeding even that for Handel's *Messiah*. Subscription will be valid until New Year's of 1819. The work will then be issued at the Easter Fair. The names of subscribers will be printed in the front of the volume.

Nägeli, a composer, educator, and music publisher in Zurich, had acquired the autograph score of the B Minor Mass in 1805 from the estate of Anna Carolina Bach, C. P. E. Bach's daughter, in Hamburg. The publication of the first edition of the Mass suffered many delays; it finally came out in two parts (Zürich, 1833 and 1845). The poem "Lobgesang auf die Harmonie," by C. D. Ebeling, a close friend of C. P. E. Bach's, originated in conjunction with the Hamburg performance of the Mass in 1786; see No. 367. A few years before Nägeli began to pursue the project of publishing the B Minor Mass, Samuel Wesley in London had considered publishing the Symbolum Nicenum; *see above, p. 496. Several copies of that section of Bach's Mass were circulating in England by the end of the eighteenth century. A letter of February 15, 1816, indicates Wesley's intention thereby "to prove that the great Sebastian Bach could not [only] compose truly Vocal Music. I mean also that the present Work be regarded as a study for Masters in Orchestral Composition."*

Mendelssohn Revives the St. Matthew Passion, BWV 244

Introductory Note

Eduard Devrient (1801–1877), one of the most brilliant members of a family of outstanding actors, started out as an opera singer and later became a highly successful theater director. He was the author of a comprehensive history of German histrionic art. A friend of Mendelssohn's in the latter's Berlin years, Devrient published near the end of his life a book of recollections of Mendelssohn, *Meine Erinnerungen an Felix Mendelssohn-Bartholdy* . . . (Leipzig, 1869). Here the revival of the *St. Matthew Passion* is told by one who had himself played an important part in it and who, in his old age, confessed, "The remembrance that it was I who stubbornly gave the impulse toward this great event is one of the dearest memories of my life." But the story was written so long after the event itself that the narration seems somewhat tinged by Romantic embellishment. The translation below (pp. 19–20, 41–42, and 48–69 of Devrient's book) is based on that by Natalia Macfarren (London, 1869).

When Mendelssohn, at the age of twenty, set out to perform the *St. Matthew Passion*, few of Bach's vocal works were known. The motets had been kept alive at Leipzig, and they were available in a printed score. But the music for voices with instruments was still unpublished (except for a few isolated examples) and practically unknown, as it had been to Forkel, whose biography was still the only book on Bach in existence.

In his ambitious undertaking, Mendelssohn had the help of numerous friends. Zelter had paved the way by the performance of various Bach cantatas. Devrient and Fanny Mendelssohn, like many others, enthusiastically supported the plan. Adolph Bernhard Marx, Mendelssohn's teacher, devoted pages and pages of his *Berliner Allgemeine Musikalische Zeitung* to essays, written in a somewhat overblown style, designed to introduce the public to the extraordinary work, and Friedrich Rellstab, music critic of the *Vossische Zeitung,* followed suit. The performance itself was an immediate success.

The importance of Mendelssohn's deed may occasionally have been over-rated, but unquestionably no other event in the long struggle for a public reevaluation of Bach's works was equally colorful and had such wide repercus-sions. The *St. Matthew Passion* was soon taken up in other cities as well. The B Minor Mass and the *St. John Passion* were introduced into the concert repertoire, and one cantata after another was rescued from oblivion.

411. Excerpt from *My Recollections,* by Eduard Devrient

... Meanwhile [1823] Felix was steadily progressing with his studies and compositions. Not less valuable for his experience than the orches-tral performances (which were repeated from time to time on Sunday mornings) were, in another direction, the Friday practices at Zelter's. At these were assembled a select number of the members of the Singa-kademie who were desirous to know the difficult works of the old mas-ters. Here we used to sing what Zelter called the "bristly pieces" of Sebastian Bach, who was at that time generally considered as an unin-telligible musical arithmetician, with an astonishing facility in writing fugues; only a few of his motets were sung by the Singakademie, and these but seldom.

As Zelter's pupil, I was drawn into the Friday practices at his house soon after my entering the Singakademie (1818). I there met Felix and Fanny [his sister], who both sang alto in the chorus; both had been occasionally called upon to accompany at the piano, but henceforth this task devolved upon Felix alone.

Thus he became acquainted with the musical works that Zelter kept hidden as a mysterious, sacred treasure from the world, which he sup-posed no longer capable of prizing them. Here, too, Felix heard a few pieces from Bach's Passions for the first time, and it became his ardent longing to possess a copy of the great *Passion according to the Gospel of St. Matthew;* this longing was fulfilled by his grandmother on Christ-mas, 1823. It had not been easy to obtain permission from Zelter to transcribe it, for he was a jealous collector; the transcription was under-taken by Eduard Rietz, an excellent young violinist, of a delicate and sensitive organization, who had replaced Henning as violin master to Felix, and in whom the young pupil confided with the full ardor of a first friendship. On Christmas Day, when Therese [Schlesinger, Devrient's wife] and I were invited there, Felix, with a countenance beaming with reverence and joy, showed me the admirably written copy of the sacred masterpiece, which was now to form his favorite study.

The social intercourse at the home of the Mendelssohn family received yet another stimulant when, besides the usual Sunday performances, Felix began, in the winter of 1827, to assemble a small and trusty choir, which met one evening each week, usually on Saturdays, for the practice of rarely heard works. We soon entered upon his revered *St. Matthew Passion*. With this work a new world opened to us, as we grasped it piece by piece. The cursory reading of single numbers during the Friday music meetings at Zelter's could not have had a similar result. That the impersonation of the several characters of the Gospel by different voices formed the pith of the work struck us with deep amazement, the antiquity of this practice in old church music being long forgotten. The dramatic treatment that arose from it; the overwhelming power of the choruses; above all the wondrous declamation of the part of Christ, which was to me a new and revered form of Bible speech, had with every rehearsal increased our astonishment and admiration at the greatness of this work. Not Therese only, but all our singing friends shared these impressions, and Felix had no reason to complain of our lack of zeal. He, in turn, had so identified himself with the work, had conquered its difficulties with such ease, and with such exquisite skill and tact knew how to impart to us his mastery of the material and his vivid perception of its essence, that what had hitherto been deemed a mysterious, cryptic musical language only for the initiated became to us natural and familiar.

I longed more and more ardently to sing the part of Christ in public, and with ever-increasing eagerness we expressed to each other the wish that it might be possible to perform the wonderful work. But all were dismayed, on the other hand, at the insurmountable difficulties, not only in the work itself, with its double orchestra and double chorus, but also in the punctiliousness of the Academy and the reserved, uncooperative attitude of Zelter. Moreover, it was seriously questioned whether the public would take to a work so utterly foreign to this world. In sacred concerts, a short movement by Bach might be accepted now and then as a curiousity enjoyed by only a few connoisseurs, but how would it be to have for an entire evening nothing but Sebastian Bach, whom the public conceived as unmelodious, mathematical, dry, and unintelligible? It seemed a rash undertaking.

Even the parents of Felix, who were nothing loath to see the problem of a revival of the Passion solved by their son, felt doubtful as to the result. Marx hesitated, and the old ladies of the Academy shook their heads. Felix so utterly disbelieved that it could be done that he replied to my entreaties, and those of the more courageous among our friends,

Baur, Schubring, and Kugler, only with jest and irony. He offered to contribute to public performance by playing on a rattle and penny trumpet [*Knarre* and *Waldteufel*, noisemakers used by the children of Berlin on New Year's Eve], painted the different phases through which the undertaking would have to pass in the most ludicrous colors, and especially pictured the temerity it would be for him, without any credentials and insignia of office, to attempt to move Berlin out of its time-honored groove. So hopeless seemed the chance of reviving the Passion that had lain buried for a century, even among its truest worshipers.

I could not let the matter rest. One evening in January 1829, after we had gone through the entire first part, Baur singing the Evangelist and Kugler the principal bass parts, and we had all gone home profoundly impressed, a restless night brought me counsel as to how a performance might be brought about. I waited impatiently for the late winter dawn to break; Therese encouraged me, and so I set out to see Felix.

He was still asleep. I was going away when his brother Paul suggested that it was quite time to wake him; so he commenced the operation. I found on this occasion that Felix had not exaggerated what he told me about his deathlike sleep. Paul took hold of him under the arms and raised him, calling out, "Wake, Felix, it is eight o'clock." He shook him, but it was some time before Felix said, dreamily, "Oh! leave off—I always said so—it is all nonsense!"; but his brother continued to shake him and call out to him until he knew that Felix was roused, when he let him fall back on the pillow. Now Felix opened his eyes wide and, perceiving me, said in his usual pleasant way, "Why, Edeward, where do you come from?" I now told him that I had something to discuss with him. Paul took me to Felix's low-ceilinged workroom, where, on the large white writing table, his breakfast was waiting, while his coffee stood on the stove.

When he came in, I told him to make a hearty good breakfast and not to interrupt me too often. With good humor and even better appetite he went at it, and I now roundly told him that during the night I had determined to have the Passion publicly given, at the Singakademie, and that in the course of the next few months, before his intended journey to England.

He laughed. "And who is going to conduct?"

"You."

"The d——— I am! My contribution is going to be—"

"Leave me alone with your penny trumpets! I am not jesting any more, and have seriously thought the matter through."

"Good heavens, you are growing solemn. Well, let us hear."

My argument was that, all of us having the conviction that the *St. Matthew Passion* was the greatest and most important of German musical works, it was our duty not to rest until we had brought it to life again so that once more it might edify men's spirits. As Felix could make no rejoinder to this, I was free to draw the conclusion: "No living man but you can undertake the performance with convincing success, and on this account you are bound to do it."

"If I were sure I could carry it through, I would."

I now explained that in case he felt he really could not himself succeed in organizing the enterprise, I had hit upon the following solution. He knew that both Zelter and the Singakademie felt obliged to me for my cooperation at all their concerts over a period of almost ten years. Accordingly I should be well entitled to ask a favor in return, and this should be the permission for the use of the room for the concert and the permission for, and recommendation of, the participation of the society in the performance of the Passion.

Felix could not deny that my two requests would not be turned down. I went on to say that if he would not despise me for a partner, with himself as the active member of the firm, the musical credit of the whole transaction, too, would be assured; and, finally, that if we devoted the proceeds to some charitable object, all cavillers would be silenced. So I concluded, saying, "Herewith, then, I offer you this honest partnership, promising to take upon myself all the business cares, and to sing the part of Christ, while you are to conduct the forgotten treasure out into the world again."

Felix still looked thoughtful; then he said, "What pleases me most about the affair is that we are to do this together; that is nice, but believe me, Zelter will never give us his countenance. He, as well as others, has not been able to bring about a performance of the Passion, and therefore he believes it cannot be done."

I had more confidence in Zelter's upright nature and the strong sentiments latent in his rough character, but I was resolved, if the worst should happen, to appeal directly to the officers of the Singakademie, even in the face of Zelter's objection, and to force him to give in. Felix was most reluctant to take such extreme steps, considering them disrespectful; but I persuaded him that they would not be necessary, and thus, after long-drawn-out discussions, he finally agreed not to hold back from the enterprise.

His parents and Fanny approved my plan, which they considered the only one promising success. It pleased them, of course, that Felix, before taking his flight into the world, should accomplish a great and memorable task. The father was still somewhat worried about Zelter's opposition, but I was of good cheer.

Felix, whose attention was now thoroughly occupied by the idea, thought out a clever manner of proceeding so as to avoid exposing himself and the enterprise. The choir rehearsals should be continued in the small hall of the Academy monthly with the members who were in the habit of assembling in his house—without the announcement of any further plan. This group should be slowly increased by members of the Singakademie, according to their inclination and desire (or, perhaps, curiosity). Thus he would gain a reliable nucleus and could, if everything went well, get the mass of singers to follow him; but if the study was not promising, or other obstacles turned up, the matter could be relinquished before the intended performance was even mentioned.

Thus prepared, we set out at once for Zelter's room, on the ground floor of the Academy. At the very door Felix said to me, "If he grows abusive, I shall leave. I cannot squabble with him." "He is sure to be abusive," said I, "but I will take the squabbling in hand myself."

We knocked. A loud, rough voice bid us come in. We found the old giant in a thick cloud of smoke, his long pipe in his mouth, sitting at his old two-manual harpsichord. The quill pen he used in writing was in his hand, a sheet of music paper before him; he wore drab-colored, old-fashioned knee breeches, thick woolen stockings, and embroidered slippers. He raised his head, with its white hair combed back, turned his plain, yet impressive face toward us, and, recognizing us through his spectacles, he said kindly in his broad manner, "Why, how is this? Two such fine young fellows so early in the morning! Now, what gives me the honor? Here, sit down." He led us to a corner of the room and sat down on a plain sofa; we took chairs.

Now I began my well-considered speech about our admiration of Bach's work, which we had first learned to prize in his Friday group and further studied at the Mendelssohns'; that we felt irresistibly impelled to make a trial of the work in public; and that we desired, by his leave, to ask the Academy to cooperate with us.

"Well," he said, slowly putting up his chin, as he generally did when he was particularly emphatic, "if it were only as easy as that! But more is needed than we have to offer nowadays." He enlarged upon the demands and difficulties of the work: the choruses required resources such as existed in the St. Thomas School when Bach himself was cantor there; a double orchestra was needed; the violinists of today were no longer able to treat this music properly. All this had long and often been considered, and if the inherent obstacles could be so easily got over, not one but all four Passions of Bach would have been revived long ago.

He had become excited, rose, put aside his pipe, and began walking about the room. We, too, had risen; Felix pulled me by the sleeve; he thought nothing more could be done.

I replied that we, particularly Felix, considered the difficulties very great indeed, but had the courage not to imagine them insuperable. The Singakademie had become familiar with Bach through Zelter himself, and he had so splendidly schooled the choir that it could cope with any difficulty. Felix had acquired knowledge of the work through him and had received from him the directions for his conducting. I was burning with the desire to sing the part of Christ in public. And we might hope that the same enthusiasm that moved us would take hold of the other participants and make the enterprise a success.

Zelter had become more and more angry. He had thrown in several doubtful and derogatory remarks during my last speech, which caused Felix to pull me again by the sleeve and then draw near to the door. At last the old gentleman broke out, "That one should have the patience to listen to all this! Quite different people have had to give up trying to do this very thing; and here is a pair of greenhorns who think it is all child's play."

This rough sally he fired off with the utmost energy. I could scarcely help laughing. Zelter had the privilege of being as abusive as he pleased: for the sake of Bach we were ready to put up with more than this from our dear old master.

I looked round at Felix, who was at the door holding the handle; he looked somewhat pale and hurt and beckoned me to come away. I motioned to him that we must stay and recommenced my argument. I said that, though young, we were no longer wholly green, since he had entrusted to us many a difficult task; I pleaded that youth was the time to grapple with difficulties, and that it should please him if two of his pupils proposed to attempt the most difficult task he had shown them.

My arguments now began to take visible effect; the crisis was passed. "We only want to see," I continued, "whether the enterprise can be carried through"; only this we asked him to permit and support; if it did not succeed, we could give it up, and that without shame.

"But how do you want to go at it?" he asked, standing still. "You think of nothing. First there are the officers, who must consent—many heads and many minds, including feminine ones, by the way—they are not so easily brought into agreement."

I replied that the officers were well disposed toward me, and the principal ladies, as participants in the practice hours at Mendelssohn's house, were already won over; so I hoped to succeed in getting permission for use of the hall and cooperation from the members.

"Oh yes, the members," Zelter exclaimed, "that is where the real trouble starts. Today ten will come to rehearsal, and tomorrow twenty of them will stay away."

We laughed heartily, with good reason, for we knew now that we had gained our point. Felix explained to the old man that he intended to hold the rehearsals at first in the small room, and discussed the arrangement of the orchestra, which was to be lead by Eduard Rietz. Zelter, who finally had no more practical objections to make, said, "Well, I don't want to cross you—I shall say a good word for you when it is needed. In God's name, go ahead; we shall see what will come of it."

So we left our capital old bear with thankful feelings and as good friends.

"We came through," I said, when we were in the hall. "But listen," replied Felix, "you are really a d—— rascal, an arch-Jesuit." "Anything you like for the honor of God and Sebastian Bach!" and triumphantly, we stepped out into the keen winter air, now that the most important step had been a success.

Now everything went smoothly; the obstacles vanished as ghosts do when you approach them. The principals of the Academy consented without hesitation to all we asked; at our first chorus rehearsal in the small hall twice as many attended as at Mendelssohns', and the number increased on every occasion to such an extent that the copyist could not supply parts quickly enough. After our fifth practice we had to remove to the large concert hall. It should not be forgotten, however, that the many members of the Academy, attracted by the novelty of the undertaking, would, as Zelter had foretold, scarcely have returned had they not been won and fascinated at the very first meeting.

Felix, therefore, did not take up single pieces (for instance, the easy ones) first, but chose an entire section of the composition as the object of study; and so he continued in the first rehearsals. He worked out the choruses right away with inflexible exactness until the full expression was reached, and then he transmitted to the singers a quite complete impression of the special quality of the work. His explanations and directions were clear, concise, full of meaning, and yet given in the manner of unpretentious youth.

Felix and I had several meetings to consider how the work could be shortened for performance. It could not be our purpose to give the work, which was influenced in many points by the taste of the period, in the entirety, but we had to convey the impression of its outstanding value. Most of the arias had to be omitted; of others only the introductions, the so-called symphonies [*Accompagnements*] could be given; even the part taken from the Gospel would have to be shorn of all that was not essential to the recital of the Passion. We often differed, for matters of conscience were involved; but what we finally determined upon seems to have been the right thing, for it has been adopted at most of the performances of the work.

It was now time to invite the solo singers, and we decided to make the rounds together. Felix was child enough to insist on our being dressed exactly alike on the occasion. We wore blue coats, white waistcoats, black neckties, black trousers, and yellow chamois gloves that were then fashionable.* In this Passion uniform we started happily off on our way, after Therese, to whom this was a solemn occasion, had offered us some festival chocolate, which Felix loved. We spoke of the strange chance that just a hundred years had to pass after the last Leipzig performance before this Passion would again see the light. "And to think," said Felix exuberantly, standing still in the middle of the Opern Platz, "that it should be an actor and a Jew who give back to the people the greatest of Christian works."

Felix on other occasions avoided all reference to his Jewish descent; but the striking truth of his observation and his joyful mood carried him away.

"You shall do the talking, and I will do the bowing," said Felix at the first door where we had to call. We had little need of either; the four principal singers of our opera were ready and willing to help us. Their participation in the rehearsals, and the greater completeness the work assumed, gave a fresh impetus to our studies. Musicians and amateurs all thronged to the rehearsals, anxious to understand it better and better. All were amazed, not so much at its architectonic grandeur of structure, but at its abundance of melody, its wealth of expression and

---

*On this occasion I became aware under what strict control the young man of twenty yet stood. His pocket money being run out, I lent him a thaler for the purchase of the gloves. His mother was displeased with me for this, saying, "One ought not to assist young people in poor management." [Devrient's note]

of passion, its peculiar declamation, and the power of its dramatic effects. No one indeed had ever suspected old Bach of all this.

But Felix's share in making these properties of the work felt and its wonderful structure known in full splendor is as memorable as the entire momentous undertaking itself. The ingenuity of comprehension with which he had taken hold of the work and made it his most sacred possession was only half his merit. His ability, energy, perseverance, and clever calculation of the resources at hand made the antiquated masterpiece modern, intelligible, and lifelike once more. Those who did not witness this can scarcely appreciate the magnificent talents and early maturity of this youth of twenty. In his entire life he has accomplished no other achievement of conducting like this, the first and perhaps the most difficult of all.

The authoritative presence of Zelter contributed to the rehearsals. As long as no orchestra took part, Felix had both to accompany and to conduct, a difficult matter with the rapid entrances of choral movements in ever-changing rhythms; here he had to achieve the feat of playing the entire accompaniment with the left hand, while with the right he wielded the baton.

When the orchestra had been added, the piano was placed, across the platform, between the two choirs; for it was then not yet considered decorous for the conductor to turn his back to the audience, which at the opera he had always been permitted to do. By this means, though the first choir was behind Felix, he faced at least the second and the orchestra. This latter consisted mainly of amateurs of the Philharmonic Society; only the leaders of the string instruments and the principal wind players belonged to the Royal orchestra. The wind instruments were placed at the back, above the semicircular platform, and extended toward the small concert room through three open doors. The task of steadying this wavering mass was attended to by Eduard Rietz.

Felix, the novice, was as calm and collected in his difficult post as though he had already conducted a dozen festivals. The quiet and simple way in which, by a look, a movement of the head or hand, he reminded us of the inflections of performance agreed upon, and thus ruled with gentle strength; the quiet confidence with which he would drop his baton in dress rehearsals and performance when longer pieces of steady tempo were well started, with a hardly noticeable nod as if to say, "This will go very well without me," and listen with the radiant countenance that strangely transfigured him when he made music, occasionally glancing toward me, until he anticipated again that it would be necessary to use the baton—in all this he was as great as he was lovable.

We had had many discussions about musical conducting. The continued beating throughout a movement, which must necessarily become mechanical, vexed me, and does so still. Compositions are, as it were, whipped through by this process. It has always appeared to me that the conductor ought to beat time only when the difficulty of certain passages or a possible unsteadiness of the performers renders it necessary. Surely the aim of the conductor should be to make himself forgotten. Felix determined on this occasion to show me how far this could be done, and in the performance of the Passion he succeeded to perfection.

I recall these circumstances with peculiar satisfaction, as of late years the extraordinary gesticulations of conductors have been made a primary attraction in musical performances.

Nothing less than the absolute success of the first resuscitation of Bach's masterpiece, on March 11, 1829, could have initiated the revolutionary influence Bach was to win through the Passion on the music of modern times; and on this account the performance is memorable. The Singakademie achieved in these choral performances its most outstanding accomplishment, and whoever heard the sound of these three to four hundred highly trained amateurs, whoever experienced with what fervent zeal great music could inspire them, will understand that, with perfect leadership, perfection was achieved.

Stümer sang the Evangelist with the most agreeable precision, entirely true to his role of Narrator, and without placing himself, in the expression of feeling in the Second Part, on an equal plane with the dramatic personages who speak for themselves. He also sang the aria "I watch beside my Jesus" [Ich will bei meinem Jesu wachen], which was too high for Bader, who, in his unassuming willingness to help, sang the parts of Peter and Pilate. The ladies, too, achieved the full effect with their moving numbers: Madame Milder, with her ingratiating voice, particularly the accompanied recitative "Thou dearest Savior" [Du lieber Heiland], Miss von Schätzel, with her full-throated tone, the aria "Have mercy, Lord" [Erbarme dich]. The latter was accompanied by Eduard Rietz, with his big and rich violin tone, in appropriate style and expression—an incomparable song of repentance.

So far as I was concerned, I knew that the impression of the entire work depended largely on that created by the presentation of the part of Jesus; here, too, everything is fashioned toward that end. It meant for me the greatest task a singer could be given. What gave me confidence was that the part lay well in my voice, and that I had long studied it with Felix and fully satisfied him. Carried along by the performance as a whole, I could thus sing with my whole soul, and I felt that the thrills of devotion that ran through me at the most impressive passages were also felt by the hearers, who listened in deadly silence.

Never have I felt a holier solemnity vested in a congregation than in the performers and audience that evening.

Our concert made an extraordinary sensation in the educated circles of Berlin. The resuscitation of the popular effect created by a half-forgotten genius was felt to be of epochal import. A second performance was called for, which took place on March 21, and was crowded like the first.* There was yet one more, under Zelter, after Felix's departure, on Good Friday, April 17, in lieu of the usual *Tod Jesu* by Graun.

All the musical world of today knows how the sensation made by these performances caused other towns to make similar attempts; how the other Passions of Bach were taken in hand, especially that according to St. John; how attention was then turned upon the instrumental productions of the old master, how they were published, made into bravura pieces for concert use, etc. The worshipers of Bach, however, must not forget that this new cult of Bach dates from March 11, 1829, and that it was Felix Mendelssohn who gave new vitality to the greatest and most profound of composers.

AN AMERICAN VISITS THE BACH SITES
IN LEIPZIG

Introductory Note

From 1851 to 1853 Lowell Mason (1792–1872), the eminent American organist, conductor, composer, music educator, hymnologist, and church music reformer, undertook an extensive European trip, on which he reports in his *Musical Letters from Abroad.* (New York, 1854; the selections below are on pp. 51–54, 66–69, and 80–83). This published collection includes eleven letters presenting his impressions of Leipzig, its various musical institutions, and their continuing Bach tradition. He draws a lively picture that also includes important information not available in any other sources, as he pays

---

*The proceeds of both concerts went towards founding two sewing schools for poor girls. [Devrient's note]

attention to many details, especially those pertaining to church practices, which German observers would have taken for granted but which struck an American of Presbyterian and Congregational background as worthy of reporting.

412. Three "Letters from Abroad," by Lowell Mason

a. Leipzig, March 1, 1852

The church of St. Thomas is a venerable and antique-looking building, both inside and out. The present edifice dates as far back as 1482. It is upwards of 280 feet long, and 115 feet wide. It has double galleries, as most of the churches seem to have here; besides which there are perhaps twenty or more private boxes or apartments, which I suppose belong to distinguished or wealthy persons. I have seen one of these occupied during a part of the sermon by clergymen, in their officials, several being present. At the altar, at the extreme end of the church, is a figure of the Saviour on the cross; and, during the service, candles are kept burning. Between this and the nave is a reading-desk; and in the nave, perhaps 180 feet from the altar, stands the pulpit. During the devotional services belonging to the officiating minister, or performed by him, he stands at the altar, in front of and facing the cross, and with his back to the people. He does not remain there, however, during the singing exercises, but retires to an adjoining room. The organ loft is in the second gallery. The organ appears large, and shows in its outside front (as nearly as I could estimate) two hundred and thirty pipes. These are not gilded, as with us, but are of the natural color of the metal. The choir for the ordinary service consists of a few boys; perhaps a man or two, though I believe usually only boys. By the ordinary service, I mean that which includes no music except singing of the hymns, or chorales, which is always done by all the people. There is always an introductory motette sung by the choir, without any accompaniment; and when this is sung there is an extra choir, numbering say forty or fifty, and all the parts are represented, boys singing soprano. There is also, every other Sabbath morning, a motette by some of the great composers, performed with full orchestral accompaniments; and for this the number of the choir is still increased. But as soon as the singing is over, the members of the orchestra and choir all leave, with the exception of the boys, retained for the leading of the congregational chorales. There is, in connection with this church, a school where boys are fitted for the University. This school is large, and employs about fifteen teachers. Provision is made for the gratuitous education, and I believe support, of sixty pupils; and these charity pupils are the musical boys whence the choir is sustained. They are regularly taught music, and are required to sing on the Sabbath, on Saturday at $1\frac{1}{2}$ o'clock, and at funerals. On Saturday regularly at the hour mentioned, there is a short service, and the choir commence it by singing one or two motettes, without accompaniment. The same choir, with orchestra, alternate between the St. Thomas and the St. Nicholas Church; and the same motette is sung in one church which was sung in the other the previous Sabbath. I have heard fine pieces performed by the choir, by *Bach*, who was formerly organist here; and they sometimes sing *Palestrina*; motettes by *Mozart*, *Haydn*, and other modern authors, are often done. Yesterday, Sunday, 29th Feb., I was at St. Thomas. There was no motette with orchestra, on account of Lent. The services were as follows; the order is so different from ours, that I have thought it would be interesting to many to have it given in detail. I timed each piece, and give the time which each occupied.

1. Organ	2	minutes.
2. Motette, without accompaniment	9	"
3. Organ	1	"
4. Chorale	4	"
5. Liturgical service	2	"
6. Reading	2	"
7. Organ	$-\frac{1}{2}$	"
8. Chorale	6	"
9. Reading	2	"
10. Organ	$-\frac{1}{2}$	"
11. Chorale	14	"
12. Sermon (about)	35	"
13. Chorale	2	"

The motette (2) may be found, with a free translation of the words, at p. 290, *Cantica Laudis*, "Though all earthly joys should perish"; and this will give some idea of what kind of music is done by the choir *without accompaniment*. The liturgical service (5) was chanted by the minister at the altar, with responses by the choir. The reading (6) was also at the altar, but the minister turned and faced the people. The reading (9) was from the reading desk. Sermon (12) from the pulpit. The ministers all wear a black robe, with a white surplice over it, as well in preaching as in prayer; also a large ruff, say two and a half or three inches wide, round the neck, as is seen in portraits of the Reformers and clergymen of 300 years ago. No fires in the churches, however cold. The service begins punctually at $\frac{1}{2}$ past 8 o'clock in the morning, and it requires something of an effort to be up and ready on the morning of a short and cold winter's day. . . .

b. Leipzig, March 21, 1852

A brief account of a public service, or rather two services, which I attended at the *Nicholaikirche,* on Sunday, may perhaps interest some of your readers; at least they will see it is quite a different thing from "going to meeting" in New England. This fine old church was erected many centuries ago, but it was greatly improved and enlarged in 1513, and again repaired in the inside in 1796. A church record informs us that on the 25th of May, in the afternoon, *Dr. Martin Luther* preached in this house.

The first service commenced at $8\frac{1}{2}$ o'clock in the morning; and as the mornings are short and dark in the winter season, it requires some effort to be punctual. The church is a large one, and the stone walls and uncushioned seats are very cold, yet is there no fire found there, save the burning candles on the altar, which, though they shed some light around, afford no warmth. It is not a Papal, but a Protestant church; the Lutherans use the crucifix, candles, &c., though less than the Romanists. There are two galleries, one rising high above the other, each capable of containing, perhaps, five hundred people; so that the church may accommodate, say three thousand, on its three floors. The organ is large, with three rows of keys, pedals, and fifty-four registers.

The exercises commenced punctually at the hour, by a short prelude, played in fine organ style, but not more than about two minutes long. This was followed by a choir piece, sung without any accompaniment, by a choir of men and boys, and without much effect. The choir had not power sufficient for so large a building. An interlude of a few minutes upon the organ followed, when a *chorale* was sung by the congregation, accompanied with full organ. The congregation was not yet large, but the people were constantly coming in, and it was fast increasing. Still the effect of the general singing was quite animating. This being concluded, the minister began his part of the service, by chanting a short sentence, which was immediately responded to by the choir; and again the minister, and again the response. By this time the church was well filled. From an estimate that I made, I concluded that there could not be less than about twenty-five hundred people present. The organ loft, too, capable of accommodating, perhaps, a hundred, was completely filled with vocal and instrumental performers, including the common orchestral instruments, with trumpets and drums conspicu-

ous. When the slow solemn chant was ended, the organ burst out in a
loud minor voluntary, which continued three or four minutes, during
which time the violins, violoncellos, double basses, and wind instruments tuned. Yet so carefully was this done, that it was hardly perceptible, for the organ was giving out its full progressive chords, so as to
nullify the tuning process, at least upon the ears of the people. Tune
being secured, the choir, with organ and orchestra accompaniment,
sung a motette, or hymn by Beethoven. This had been announced in
the newspapers of Saturday, and was, I suppose, with many an object
of attention. It occupied, perhaps, fifteen minutes, and was very well
done; the drums and trumpets especially doing fine execution in the
great church in the *forte* passages. It closed with a short fugue, in which
the points were distinctly taken up and marked. The choir did not
number more than from thirty to forty persons, and had not sufficient
power for the building; but still the performance was quite effective. I
perceived that while most of the people gave close attention to the
music, others were not so much interested, and one goodly-looking old
man directly in front of me spent the time in reading over his psalm-
book. As soon as the motette was concluded, the members of the
orchestra took up their instruments and left the house, having nothing
to do with the remaining service. And now came the grand singing—
for the great congregation were now together. The organ gave out a
choral, when all the people lifted up the loud chorus of praise. The
whole house was filled with sound. It was sublime, and I found myself
much more moved by this than by the previous choir and orchestra
performance. The hymn (486) was indicated on tablets in different
parts of the house, and every person had his book in his hand. Even the
standers-up in the aisles (for there were hundreds of these) had their
books and joined in the song. The singing was in unison; I could not
tell, being at the opposite side of the house, whether the choir sang the
parts or not; the organ did indeed pour forth full harmony, but even
this was vastly overpowered by the multitude of voices—men's voices,
and women's voices, and children's voices, mingled in one mighty tor-
rent of sound, rolling through the high arches like the rush of many
waters. At the end of each line of the stanza there was an interlude of
a few chords upon the organ, but there was no long interlude at the end
of the stanza, as in the American churches. Indeed the hymn seemed to
flow along from beginning to end, as a whole, and without interrup-
tion. I observed, too, that in the hymn-singing I heard in England,
the interludes between the stanzas were very short, and often omitted
altogether. A very pleasing effect was produced at the close of this and

every choral hymn, thus: as soon as the voices ceased on the last word of the last stanza, every head was inclined forward as in the attitude of prayer, while the organ died away *piano,* in a very short post-lude of perhaps half or three-quarters of a minute, the people retaining their position until the last sound was heard, when they gently resumed an erect posture. After this followed liturgical prayers, read by the clergyman, for a few minutes; and then the chorale was resumed, another stanza or two of the same hymn being sung to the same chorale as before. After this followed the sermon. I did not understand it, but if one might judge by the appearance of the people, it was good, for they all seemed to give close attention for at least three-quarters of an hour.

When the sermon was ended, and a short prayer offered, "Vater unser," the hymn was resumed again, and still another stanza sung to the same tune as before; so that *the same tune was sung three times in the same service.* A closing prayer of a few words, and the great congregation gradually dispersed, amid the loud rolling of the diapasons. . . .

c. Leipzig, March 22, 1852

The "Thomas School" is connected with the Thomas Church; and the choir of the latter is obtained from it. *John Sebastian Bach* was formerly Music Director here; and he has been succeeded by several distinguished men. The present incumbent is *M. Hauptmann,* who is also Professor of Harmony in the Conservatory. The place was procured for him by *Mendelssohn,* with whom it was a favorite object to gather around him men of science, and Hauptmann most deservedly ranks among these. He is now everywhere known as one of the most profound theorists living. He has also published Motets, and other pieces of Church Music, which are held in high estimation by musicians. But there is something more attractive about Hauptmann than either genius or learning; it is amiability. He seems to be filled with kindness, gentleness, and courtesy; and I have met no German, nor indeed any one, in whose presence one is made more perfectly at home, and by whom one is treated with more affability and attention than by him. Although standing at the very head of musical science, he has, as yet, published no work of importance on harmony; he says that he waits for more experience, so that when he publishes a book, *it may be of some value.* A good hint is this to some of us, who write and publish works on the theory of music in the United States, without knowledge and without experience. How often we see verified the old saying (and frequently in musical productions), that "a little knowledge is a dangerous thing." Hauptmann is now, however, engaged in the preparation of a philosophical treatise, which he intends to give to the public in a few years. His health is not firm; he is a diligent student, and bodily infirmity is probably the result of severe and long-continued mental labor. He is very popular, and is, perhaps, equally respected for his knowledge, and beloved for his goodness. He called yesterday, bringing tickets to a musical performance, on the occasion of the dedication of the Music Hall of the School. It is not indeed a new hall, but an old one repaired, painted, and ornamented; it is in the same house where *Bach* lived, and is the very room where *Bach, Hiller* and others labored and conducted musical performances. Hauptmann now occupies the same apartments which were formerly occupied by the great Fuguist. The exercises, with the exception of a short address by one of the pupils, were exclusively musical, as follows:

   I. Prayer. "Kommt, lasset uns anbeten." ....*Hauptmann.*
  II. Motette. "Der Geist hilft unserer Schwachheit." ....*J. S. Bach.*
 III. Four part-songs:—
     1. "O Thaeler weit, o Hoehen." ....*Mendelssohn.*
     2. "O sanfter, suesser Hauch" ....*Mendelssohn.*
        [The above may be found in the "Social Glee Book," and have been
          sung in the Boston Musical Conventions.]
     3. "Waldeinsamkeit." ....*Hauptmann.*
     4. "Ich stand auf Berges Hoehen." ....*Hauptmann.*
  IV. Motette. "Jauchzet dem Herrn." ....*Schicht.*

The singing was by the choir of the school and church, which consisted of about fifty voices; Soprano and Alto by boys. It was entirely without accompaniment. A grand Pianoforte in the room was only used to announce the pitch before each piece. This singing most difficult music without accompaniment is something wholly unknown with us in America. I know full well that there are choirs and Quartet clubs who sing comparatively easy music in public without accompaniment; but even in this, what is often the result? Bach's music is exceedingly difficult. Handel, in comparison to Bach, may be said to be easy; and yet our choirs could but few of them sing Handel and sustain themselves well without instrumental aid. But here is a chorus who stand up and sing Bach's and other most difficult motets, the most difficult vocal music perhaps ever written, by voices alone, with as much certainty as the sure aim of an experienced marksman.

I think I have never before witnessed such devotion to the work as in these singers. Here is indeed entire self-committal. Every one throws all the powers he has, physical and spiritual, into the performance of the music. Every tone is attacked with a conscious certainty of success; no matter how complicated the rhythm, it is given with an energy and truthfulness that a first-rate violinist can hardly excel. The singers seem to have a perfect command of their vocal organs, and are no less certain of results than is the accomplished pianist when he strikes the keys, or the violinist when he draws the bow. There is an entire absence of that sleepiness, drowsiness, inattention, and foolish levity too often witnessed in our choirs. No looking about, or whispering, or laughing, or silliness; but close attention is ever manifested. I wish I had words to point out that consecration to the work, that deep, heartfelt interest which these choir members seem to possess; so that it might be sought for by our American singers. But we cannot obtain it unless we use the appropriate means; education only will do it; musical training, such as we have but little idea of, must go before; and as we plant, so we shall reap in these things. This choir is *drilled* daily; five o'clock is the hour when they come together every day for their lesson, or rather their *training* and *practice.* For so far as I have had opportunity to observe, the *teaching* here consists mostly in *training.* But I must not enlarge. I have never before heard a vocal chorus so prompt, so energetic, and perfect in time and tune, as on this occasion. The place, too, was holy ground, for all the great musicians have visited that saloon; *Bach* lived there as his home, and *Handel,* and *Haydn,* and *Mozart,* and *Beethoven* have been there. A new portrait of Bach (or rather an old one put in perfect order) has been placed at the head of the hall, and opposite to it is a fine bust of [Johann Gottfried] *Schicht,* who, though less known, was a very profound musician, as his works testify. On the whole, I have not attended a more interesting musical performance in Germany.

Money and Living Costs in Bach's Time

MONETARY UNITS

1 pf. (pfennig—copper coin)	= smallest unit
1 gr. (groschen—silver coin)	= 12 pf.
1 old fl. (e.g., No. 279)	= 16 gr.
1 fl. (gulden, florin, *or* guilder—silver coin)	= 21 gr.
1 thlr. *or* rthl. (thaler *or* reichsthaler—silver coin)	= 24 gr. (1 fl. 3 gr.)
1 species thlr. (regional variants, cf. Nos. 28 and 279)	= 32 gr. (1 fl. 11 gr.)
1 dukat (gold coin)	= 66 gr. (2 rthl. 18 gr.)
1 dukat (adjusted parity)	= 72 gr. (3 rthl.)
1 louis d'or (gold coin)	= 5 rthl.

COST OF LIVING

Fundamental socioeconomic changes and inflation make it very difficult to compare the value and purchasing power of eighteenth-century currency with that of today's money. The conversion into a modern decimal currency system is meant to provide merely a general sense of proportions:

1 pfennig	= $ .25	1 thaler	= $ 72.00
1 groschen	= $ 3.00	1 dukat	= $198.00
1 gulden	= $ 63.00	1 dukat (adj.)	= $216.00
1 dukat	= $198.00	1 louis d'or	= $360.00

1. Selected cost-of-living figures for early eighteenth-century Leipzig* (in 1721 the thaler replaced the guilder as the standard currency denomination in Electoral Saxony):

*SOURCE: M. J. Elias, *Umriss einer Geschichte der Preise und Löhne in Deutschland vom ausgehenden Mittelalter bis zum Beginn des neunzehnten Jahrhunderts,* vol. 2 (Leiden: Sijthoff, 1940).

Household goods

5 pf.	[$1.25]	1 quart [*Kanne*] of milk (1725)
6 pf.	[$1.50]	1 quart of beer (1699)
3 gr. 2 pf.	[$9.50]	1 quart of ordinary wine
6 gr.	[$18.00]	1 quart of better wine
3 gr. 3 pf.	[$9.75]	1 set of 15 [*Mandel*] eggs (1762) [1 egg = $.65]
4 gr. 9 pf.	[$14.25]	1 tub [4 quarts = *Fass*] of butter (1710)
1 gr. 2 pf.	[$3.50]	1 pound of veal (1699)
1 gr. 3 pf.	[$3.75]	1 pound of beef (1699) or ham (1697)
21 gr. 6 pf.	[$64.50]	1 bushel [Saxon *Scheffel* = c. 103 liters] of grain (rye)
10 gr.	[$2.50]	1 pound of wax candles (1726)
20 gr. 8 pf.	[$62.00]	1 ream [*Ries* = 480 sheets] of ordinary paper (1725)
1 thlr. 2 gr. 5 pf.	[$79.25]	1 ream of fine paper (1717)

Wages

6 pf.	[$1.50]	a maid's (female child) daily pay (1700)
1 gr. 6 pf.	[$4.50]	a maid's (female adult) daily pay (1699)
6 gr.	[$18.00]	a gravedigger's pay per grave (1700–8)
7 gr.; 8 gr.	[$21.00; 24.00]	a carpenter's daily pay: 7 gr. / winter; 8 gr. / summer (1725)
50 rthl.	[$3,600.00]	annual income of a barber (1722–29)
175 rthl.	[$12,600.00]	annual salary of a pastor (1722–29)

2. Selected examples drawn from Bach documents:

Salaries, honoraria, fees

400 rthl.	[$28,800]	Bach's annual salary—without benefits—as capellmeister in Cöthen, 1717 (No. 70)
300 rthl.	[$21,600]	Anna Magdalena Bach's annual salary as Cöthen court singer, 1722 (No. 87)
100 rthl.	[$7,200]	Bach's annual fee for private study with him, including room and board, 1712 (No. 312)
50 rthl.	[$3,600]	Bach's honorarium for a congratulatory cantata, 1736, 1738 (Nos. 172, 201)
22 rthl.	[$1,584]	Bach's (variable) organ examination fee, 1746 (*BD* II, no. 548; see also Nos. 73 and 158)

12 rthl.	[$864]	Bach's (variable) honorarium for a guest performance (church music), 1713, 1717 (Nos. 47, 63; see also No. 116)
6 rthl.	[$432]	Bach's fee for a keyboard lesson to a nobleman (No. 250)
1 rthl.	[$72]	cantor's fee for weddings and funerals in Leipzig (*Ordnung der Schule zu St. Thomae,* Leipzig 1723)
16 gr.	[$48]	travel expenses; per diem for meals [*Kostgeld*], 1713 (No. 44)

Publications

1 rthl.	[$72]	*Musical Offering,* 1747 = 3 typeset, 26 engraved pages (No. 248)
2 rthl.	[$144]	*Clavier-Übung,* Part I, 1731 = 37 engraved pages (*BD* II, no. 506); J. D. Heinichen, *Der General-Baß in der Composition,* 1728 = 994 typeset pages (No. 140)
3 rthl.	[$216]	*Clavier-Übung,* Part III, 1739 = 78 engraved pages (No. 333); *The Art of Fugue,* 1751 = 2 typeset, 67 pages (No. 282)

Musical instruments

115 rthl.	[$8,280]	fortepiano (No. 262)
50 / 80 rthl.	[$3,600/5,760]	harpsichord (No. 279)
21 rthl.	[$1,512]	lute (No. 279)
8 rthl.	[$576]	violin, made by Jacobus Stainer (No. 279)
3 rthl.	[$216]	spinet (No. 279)
2 rthl.	[$144]	ordinary violin (No. 279)
1 rthl. 8 gr.	[$96]	harpsichord rental, 1 month (No. 249)
8 rthl. 3 gr. 6 pf.	[$586.50]	Bach's (variable) semi-annual fee for maintenance of instruments belonging to St. Nicholas Church, 1728 (*BD* II, no. 161; see also Nos. 37 and 110)

Bibliography

Introductory Note

The principal source material on Bach is collected and published in *Bach-Dokumente* (*BD*), which contains the original—usually German—versions of most of the documents included in this volume. Other important sources appear in the pages of the *Bach-Jahrbuch* (*BJ*). Full citations for these works may be found on p. xiv, together with full citations for the *Bach-Werke-Verzeichnis* (*BWV*) and the *Neue Bach-Ausgabe* (*NBA*). Other books and articles from which one or more documents and references were drawn for this volume are listed below.

Adlung, Jakob. *Musica mechanica organoedi,* ed. J. L. Albrecht, Berlin 1768; reprint, 1961.

Bitter, Carl Hermann. *Johann Sebastian Bach.* 2nd ed. 4 vols. Berlin, 1881.

Clark, Stephen L., ed. *The Letters of C. P. E. Bach.* Oxford, 1997.

David, Werner. *Johann Sebastian Bachs Orgeln.* Berlin 1951.

Devrient, Eduard. *Meine Erinnerungen an Felix Mendelssohn-Bartholdy. . . .* Leipzig, 1869; English trans. by Natalia Macfarren, London, 1869.

Forkel, Johann Nikolaus. *Ueber Johann Sebastian Bachs Leben, Kunst und Kunstwerke.* Leipzig, 1802; facs. ed., Frankfurt, 1950; English trans., London, 1820.

Freyse, Conrad, ed. *Eisenacher Dokumente um Sebastian Bach.* Leipzig, 1933.

Gerber, Christian G. *Geschichte der Kirchen-Ceremonien in Sachsen.* Leipzig, 1732.

Gerber, Ernst Ludwig. *Historisch-Biographisches Lexikon der Tonkünstler.* Leipzig, 1790–92; reprint, 1977.

Glöckner, Andreas. "Neue Spuren zu Bachs Weimarer Passion." *Leipziger Beiträge zur Bach-Forschung* 1 (1995): 35.

Hilgenfeldt, Carl Ludwig. *Johann Sebastian Bach's Leben, Wirken und Werke: ein Beitrag zur Kunstgeschichte des achtzehnten Jahrhunderts.* Leipzig, 1850; reprint, 1965.

Hopkins, Edward John. *The Organ.* London, 1855.

Kirnberger, Johann Philipp. *Die Kunst des reinen Satzes in der Musik.* Berlin, 1774–79; reprint, 1968.

Kittel, Johann Christian. *Der angehende praktische Organist.* Erfurt, 1808.

Kock, Hermann. *Genealogisches Lexikon der Familie Bach.* Gotha, 1995.

Krautwurst, Franz. "Anmerkungen zu den Augsburger Bach-Dokumenten." *Festschrift Martin Ruhnke zum 65. Geburtstag.* Neuhausen-Stuttgart, 1986: 176–84.

Küster, Konrad. *Der junge Bach.* Stuttgart, 1996.

Kunzen, Friedrich Ludwig Aemilius, and Johann Friedrich Reichardt. *Studien für Tonkünstler und Musikfreunde.* Berlin, 1793.

Leaver, Robin A. *Bach's Theological Library: A Critical Bibliography.* Neuhausen-Stuttgart, 1983.

Mason, Lowell. *Musical Letters from Abroad.* New York, 1854.

Niedt, Friedrich Erhardt. *Musicalische Handleitung.* 2nd ed. Hamburg, 1721; reprint, 1977.

Odrich, Evelin, and Peter Wollny, eds. *Die Briefkonzepte des Johann Elias Bach.* Leipziger Beiträge zur Bach-Forschung, 3 (1998).

Reichardt, Johann Friedrich. *Musikalischer Almanach.* Berlin, 1796.

Scheibe, Johann Adolph. *Critischer Musikus.* 2nd ed. Leipzig, 1745; reprint 1970.

Smend, Friedrich. *Bach in Köthen.* Berlin, 1951. English trans. by John Page, edited and annotated by Stephen Daw. St. Louis, 1985.

Spitta, Philipp. *Johann Sebastian Bach,* 2 vols. Leipzig 1783–1880; English trans. by C. Bell and J. A. Fuller Maitland. London, 1884–85; later reprints.

Stauffer, George B., ed. *The Forkel-Hoffmeister & Kühnel Correspondence: A Document of the Early 19th-Century Bach Revival.* Trans. and annotated by Arthur Mendel. New York, 1990.

Szeskus, Reinhard. "Bach und die Leipziger Universitätsmusik," *Alte Musik als ästhetische Gegenwart: Bach, Händel, Schütz.* Congress Report Stuttgart 1985. 2 vols., ed. D. Berke and D. Hanemann. Kassel, 1987. Vol. 1, pp. 405–12.

Terry, Charles S. *Bach: A Biography.* London, 1928; rev. ed., 1933.

Trautmann, Christoph. "Unregistriertes Dokument belegt Graf Wrbna als österreichischen Bach-Schüler." Bachfest der Neuen Bachgesellschaft, [Graz,] May 24–29, 1983. [Program Book]: 58.

Wenke, Wolfgang. "Die Orgel Johann Sebastian Bachs in Arnstadt." *Der junge Bach in Arnstadt* (Arnstadt: Stadtmuseum, n.d. [1995]).

Wolff, Christoph. *Bach: Essays on His Life and Music.* Cambridge, Mass., 1991; 3rd ed., 1996.

Wustmann, Gustav. *Quellen zur Geschichte Leipzigs,* vol. 1. Leipzig 1889: 193–456 [Riemer chronicle].

Index

Note: References in the index are to page numbers, not item numbers. *Italic* numbers in parentheses are those assigned to Bach family members in the genealogical table (item no. 303, pp. 283–94); **bold** numbers indicate that the reference is to the writing of the referenced individual; ***bold italic*** numbers indicate a facsimile.

Lübeck

Hamburg

Bremen

Lüneburg

Elbe R.

Place
Bach

B R A

Celle

Hannover

Havel

Bückeburg

Brunswick

Magdeburg

Weser R.

Zerbst

Cöthen

Göttingen

Sangerhausen

Halle

Sondershausen

Leipzig

Cassel

Unstrut R.

Mühlhausen

Weissenfels
Naumburg

Eisenach

Gotha

Erfurt

Weimar

Zeitz

Altenbu

Wechmar
Ohrdruf

Dornheim

Jena

Gera

Ronneburg

Werra R.

Arnstadt

T H U R I N G I

Suhl

Gehren

Rudolstadt

Meiningen

Saale R.

Schleitz

Weisse Elster R.

Coburg

Frankfurt

Schweinfurt

Main R.

0   100 km

Rhine R.

0   60 miles

Nuremberg

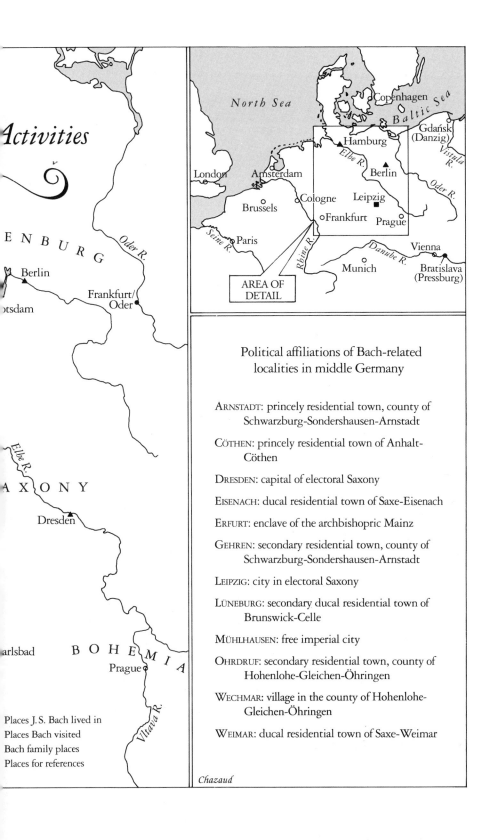

Activities

North Sea
Copenhagen
Baltic Sea
Gdańsk (Danzig)
Hamburg
Vistula R.
Berlin
London
Amsterdam
Oder R.
Cologne
Leipzig
Brussels
Frankfurt
Prague
Seine R.
Paris
Rhine R.
Danube R.
Vienna
Munich
Bratislava (Pressburg)

AREA OF
DETAIL

ENBURG
Oder R.
Berlin
Frankfurt/ Oder
otsdam

Elbe R.
AXONY
Dresden

arlsbad
BOHEMIA
Prague
Vltava R.

Places J. S. Bach lived in
Places Bach visited
Bach family places
Places for references

Political affiliations of Bach-related
localities in middle Germany

ARNSTADT: princely residential town, county of
Schwarzburg-Sondershausen-Arnstadt

CÖTHEN: princely residential town of Anhalt-
Cöthen

DRESDEN: capital of electoral Saxony

EISENACH: ducal residential town of Saxe-Eisenach

ERFURT: enclave of the archbishopric Mainz

GEHREN: secondary residential town, county of
Schwarzburg-Sondershausen-Arnstadt

LEIPZIG: city in electoral Saxony

LÜNEBURG: secondary ducal residential town of
Brunswick-Celle

MÜHLHAUSEN: free imperial city

OHRDRUF: secondary residential town, county of
Hohenlohe-Gleichen-Öhringen

WECHMAR: village in the county of Hohenlohe-
Gleichen-Öhringen

WEIMAR: ducal residential town of Saxe-Weimar

Chazaud